PERGAMON GENERAL PSYCHOLOGY SERIES
EDITORS
Arnold P. Goldstein, *Syracuse University*
Leonard Krasner, *SUNY at Stony Brook*

Special Education
Research and Trends

edited by

Richard J. Morris, *The University of Arizona*
Burton Blatt, *Syracuse University*

PERGAMON PRESS
New York Oxford Beijing Frankfurt
São Paulo Sydney Tokyo Toronto

Pergamon Press Offices:

U.S.A.   Pergamon Press, Maxwell House, Fairview Park,
                               Elmsford, New York 10523, U.S.A.

U.K.   Pergamon Press, Headington Hill Hall,
                               Oxford OX3 0BW, England

PEOPLE'S REPUBLIC   Pergamon Press, Qianmen Hotel, Beijing,
OF CHINA   People's Republic of China

FEDERAL REPUBLIC   Pergamon Press, Hammerweg 6,
OF GERMANY   D-6242 Kronberg, Federal Republic of Germany

BRAZIL   Pergamon Editora, Rua Eça de Queiros, 346,
                               CEP 04011, São Paulo, Brazil

AUSTRALIA   Pergamon Press (Aust.) Pty., P.O. Box 544,
                               Potts Point, NSW 2011, Australia

JAPAN   Pergamon Press, 8th Floor, Matsuoka Central Building,
                               1-7-1 Nishishinjuku, Shinjuku-ku, Tokyo 160, Japan

CANADA   Pergamon Press Canada, Suite 104, 150 Consumers Road,
                               Willowdale, Ontario M2J 1P9, Canada

---

First printing 1986

Library of Congress Cataloging in Publication Data

Special education.

(Pergamon general psychology series; 137)
Includes index.
1. Special education literature. I. Morris, Richard J.
II. Blatt, Burton, 1927-   . III. Series.
LC3969.S7 1986   371.9   86-5098
ISBN 0-08-032816-4
ISBN 0-08-032815-6 (pbk.)

Printed in the United States of America

PERGAMON INTERNATIONAL LIBRARY
of Science, Technology, Engineering and Social Studies

The 1000-volume original paperback library in aid of education,
industrial training and the enjoyment of leisure

Publisher: Robert Maxwell, M.C.

Special Education
(PGPS – 137)

THE PERGAMON TEXTBOOK
INSPECTION COPY SERVICE

An inspection copy of any book published in the Pergamon International Library
will gladly be sent to academic staff without obligation for their consideration for
course adoption or recommendation. Copies may be retained for a period of 60 days
from receipt and returned if not suitable. When a particular title is adopted or
recommended for adoption for class use and the recommendation results in a sale
of 12 or more copies the inspection copy may be retained with our compliments.
The Publishers will be pleased to receive suggestions for revised editions and new
titles to be published in this important international Library.

Book

Pergamon Titles of Related Interest

Becker/Greenberg EDUCATIONAL REHABILITATION OF THE HANDICAPPED IN THE GERMAN DEMOCRATIC REPUBLIC AND IN THE UNITED STATES OF AMERICA: An Overview

Cartledge/Milburn TEACHING SOCIAL SKILLS TO CHILDREN: Innovative Approaches, Second Edition

Plas SYSTEMS PSYCHOLOGY IN THE SCHOOLS

Wielkiewicz BEHAVIOR MANAGEMENT IN THE SCHOOLS: Principles and Procedures

Wang/Reynolds/Walberg HANDBOOK OF SPECIAL EDUCATION: Research and Practice

Related Journals
(Free sample copies available upon request)

ANALYSIS AND INTERVENTION IN DEVELOPMENTAL DISABILITIES
APPLIED RESEARCH IN MENTAL RETARDATION
CHILD ABUSE AND NEGLECT
JOURNAL OF SCHOOL PSYCHOLOGY

This book is dedicated to the memory of Burton Blatt (1927–1985). Few contemporary writers have had the impact on special education that Burton Blatt has had. He taught us the meaning of honesty, of courage, and of dedication and self-sacrifice. His words, his deeds, and his impact on special education will be felt for a very long time.

CONTENTS

CONTENTS

ACKNOWLEDGMENTS

Work on this book was supported by a number of individuals. First, we would like to express our appreciation to the contributors to the book. Their understanding and patience through the various stages of the production of this book has been wonderful. Second, we would like to thank Jerry Frank at Pergamon Press and Arnold P. Goldstein, Ph.D., Pergamon General Psychology series editor, for their support in the preparation of the manuscript. In addition, we would like to express our appreciation to Alice Schoenberger for her secretarial assistance.

After the untimely death of Burton Blatt, other individuals were very helpful in the preparation of the manuscript. First, appreciation is due to Rebecca A. McReynolds, Ph.D., for her assistance in orchestrating the final phases of manuscript preparation and Richard Green for his editorial assistance. Most of all, special thanks are due to Vinnie Morris and Ethel Blatt for their understanding and support throughout the various preparatory phases of this book.

1 INTRODUCTION AND OVERVIEW OF SPECIAL EDUCATION RESEARCH

Richard J. Morris
Burton Blatt

Research literature in the field of special education has grown at an exponential rate during the past 15–20 years, and society has spent millions of dollars supporting research in this area. There is good reason for our society to spend all of this money on research in special education. After all, history—especially the history of scientific research in the medical and physical sciences—has taught us that research can produce the means, for example, to improve the overall quality of our lives, help us live longer, conquer life-threatening diseases, permit us to fly into space, find new planets and track enormous comets, and use laser technology for delicate surgery. So, research efforts have had a very positive impact on society.

What has the field of special education gained from the millions of dollars that society has spent on research and from the millions of person-hours that have been spent conducting this research and analyzing the findings? Some people would say we have learned a great deal. Others would say we have learned a fair amount, but only the most severe critic would say we have learned nothing.

Examine, for the moment, the research on mental retardation. In the more than 185 years

that we have been studying mental retardation, we have not only learned a great deal about this condition, but our research has also positively changed the quality of life for persons who are mentally retarded. Research findings and related scholarly writings have, for example, led to the following: blood screening for phenylketonuria (PKU; Guthrie, 1961, 1984), the deinstitutionalization and normalization movements (e.g., Blatt, 1968; Blatt & Kaplan, 1966; Nirje, 1969; Wolfensberger, 1969, 1972), developmental theories (e.g., Bijou, 1966; Kounin, 1941; Zigler, 1961, 1969), behavior modification approaches (e.g., Lovaas, 1981; Watson, 1973; Williams, 1959; Wolf, Risley, & Mees, 1964), labeling theory (e.g., Edgerton, 1967; Edgerton & Bercovici, 1976), and curriculum development (e.g., Goldstein, 1969, 1974)—to name just a few of the many notable developments over the last few decades.

Examine, too, the decades of research on learning disabilities, including the thousands of hours spent by those teachers and students who participated in this research. Many scholars would say we have made substantial progress in this area in terms of our understanding of learning disabilities and in curriculum development, others have suggested that progress has been hampered by our inability to agree on what constitutes "learning disability". As Kirk (1984) has stated:

> Originally we conceived of a child with a learning disability as one who had a major psychological or neurological impediment to the learning of reading, spelling, writing, or arithmetic. These are relatively rare cases, probably only one or two percent of school children. Today, however, the term *learning disability* applies to nearly every kind of learning problem a child may encounter. (p. 48)

Definitional problems notwithstanding, it is clear, however, that progress has been made over the past 2 decades in research in some areas, for example, in the area of effective instruction with children having learning problems (e.g., Bereiter & Engelmann, 1966; Engelmann, 1969; Engelmann & Carnine, 1982; Hallahan, Lloyd, Kosiewicz, Kauffman, & Graves, 1979; Hallahan, Lloyd, Kauffman, & Loper, 1983; Haring & Hauck, 1969; Ramp & Rhine, 1983).

Also, examine the research literature on the education of emotionally disturbed children. Again, many observers would say we have learned a great deal, while others would take the position that very little progress has been made. However, few can deny, the impact that, for example, behavior modification research has had on the education of these children (e.g., Goldstein, Sprafkin, Gershaw, & Klein, 1980; Kauffman, 1981; Kazdin, 1977, 1980) or the contribution of ecological models to the education of these children (e.g., Apter, 1981; Hobbs, 1966; Morse, 1984; Rhodes & Tracy, 1972). Questions regarding the definition of this handicapping condition are still prevalent and have not been fully answered, and curriculum issues still exist. But this does not mean that research progress in this area has not taken place.

Although we know that progress has been made over the years in research in special education, we do not necessarily know how much of this progress has been incorporated into the daily educational practices of professional special educators. One wonders, for example, how much of what is published in the research literature is viewed by practitioners as little more than an academic or scholarly exercise on the part of the researcher and not actually relevant to the classroom setting (Blatt, 1981). Further, one wonders how many practitioners, during their training, were never taught how to read research articles and develop an appreciation for research. If teachers are not taught about research, can we really then expect them to read and utilize the research literature in order to derive new techniques and practices? Perhaps teachers, as part of their preservice training, should be taught to be researchers. They certainly could contribute a tremendous amount to the advancement of knowledge in research in special education. We need to build on the research work that already has been done, and practitioners and researchers have to work together to advance our understanding of handicapping conditions.

As the subsequent chapters in this book will demonstrate, there has been some exciting and innovative research conducted in special education over the past several years—research that has both direct usability for professional special educators as well as long-term implications for the advancement of knowledge in the field. The 11 general topics addressed in this book represent some of the most frequent special education areas that come to the attention of professionals in the field. Seven of the chapters deal specifically with particular handicapping conditions, while the remaining four chapters address topics that cut across many of these handicapping conditions, namely, assessment issues, behavior modification approaches, the sociology of special education, and special education research in perspective. Each of the 11 chapters has been written by individuals who have extensive experience with their respective content area, as well as a thorough knowledge of the research literature on the topic. They have been encouraged to sample widely from various sources in the research literature, and to present what they consider to be some of the major trends as well as the status of research on the topic being reviewed.

In Chapter 2, James Ysseldyke presents an

overview of assessment-based decision making in special education. After reviewing the history on the assessment of students, Ysseldyke then discusses the various uses of assessment in special education. He points out that although assessment has many uses, its primary use is for classification and placement to determine eligibility for special services. He also reviews the kinds of research strategies that have been used in assessment practices and critically examines research findings in this area. Reflecting on more than a decade of his research, as well as that of others, Ysseldyke takes the position that classification in special education is not reliable and that many students are incorrectly labeled as having a handicapping condition. Ysseldyke provides recommendations regarding future directions for assessment research and suggests that future research in the field should concentrate on the development of measurement technologies to assist educators in making placement decisions that are individually based rather than based on an individual's performance relative to a normative group. Research should also focus on decision-making policy and the development of decision-making methods. This chapter will surely raise many questions for the reader about our current assessment-based decision-making practices regarding the placement of students in special education.

Chapter 3, by Diane Bricker, reviews the research literature on early intervention programs. She discusses the rationale underlying the purpose of early intervention with exceptional children — the basic presumption is that early learning provides a foundation for later development. A review of the history of research on the early intervention strategy is also presented, suggesting that such interventions should address broad ecological considerations if its effects are to be maintained. Bricker also describes contemporary early intervention research programs for Down syndrome and other biologically impaired children, as well as programs for children who are medically or environmentally at risk for developing a handicapping condition. Although methodological difficulties are present in these research programs, causing the data to be interpreted with some caution, Bricker maintains that, on the whole, preschool intervention programs produce positive results for exceptional children. She questions, however, the suitability of the data on the acquisition of instructional skills by parents, careprovider–child interaction, and quality of life changes for the families having a young handicapped child. Bricker also reviews areas of study needing further resolution, as well as intervention variables in need of further clarification. Methodological concerns that limit the applicability of research data are also described, as are issues regarding service delivery systems, curriculum, and evaluation strategies. This well-written chapter will surely prove to be informative about the current state-of-the-art in early childhood intervention programs.

Chapter 4, on behavior modification with exceptional children, is written by Richard J. Morris and Rebecca A. McReynolds. The authors note that there have been many changes over the past 20 years in the settings in which such intervention takes place — with the most notable change being in the application of behavior modification procedures in the classroom and other school-related settings. Morris and McReynolds present an overview of the behavioral research that has been conducted with exceptional children on modifying a variety of behaviors that are present either in a classroom setting, residential treatment center, or in the home. Specifically, the research literature on the modification of 20 frequently cited target behaviors is critically reviewed. Future directions for research on behavior modification with handicapped children is also discussed, as is a brief overview of the ethical issues associated with the use of behavior modification approaches. The authors also provide summary information on the most frequently used behavioral approaches with the various target behaviors that have been reviewed.

Chapter 5 is written by Lou Brown, Betsey Shiraga, Alison Ford, Jan Nisbet, Pat Van-Deventer, Mark Sweet, Jennifer York, and Ruth Loomis, who discuss those factors associated with educating severely handicapped persons for vocational functioning. The authors differentiate sheltered from nonsheltered work environments and simulated work from meaningful work, and describe the costs, efficiency, and quality of life features associated with nonsheltered work settings. Brown et al. describe in detail their elaborate nonsheltered training program and how it evolved from evaluating the results of earlier training programs. The authors use direct instruction in their training that is specifically oriented to teaching the skills and attitudes needed by people functioning in nonsheltered work sites. As the authors state, "This chapter is a mixture of philosophy, ideology, empiricism, pragmatism, frustration, and hope" (p. 186). What they reveal in their research program, however, is that severely handicapped individuals can be taught to perform meaningful work in a non-sheltered setting. Brown et al. present a tremendous amount of data and information on the importance of directing our efforts to working with these people in nonsheltered environments and teaching them how to perform meaningful work. Their work is without question very compelling.

The education of the gifted is the subject of Chapter 6 by C. June Maker. She reviews some of the significant trends in the education of gifted students and discusses the various attempts to define *giftedness* as well as the place of giftedness in our society. Maker also reviews the methods used and rationales employed to assess persons for giftedness and presents programs and curricula developed for gifted students. She discusses the research that has been conducted on the relative use of models for enrichment, resource teacher, special class, and so forth, and concludes that the resource model is the most popular approach, but that comparison research has not yet been performed on the relative effectiveness of these different models. Maker also reviews efforts to develop a curriculum for gifted students that matches conceptions of what giftedness is and includes a model she developed. Last, the author addresses the issues of gifted handicapped students and underachieving gifted students. Maker's chapter clearly reflects her extensive knowledge of the research and practice concerning the education of gifted students.

The next chapter, Chapter 7 by Deborah Smith and Suzanne Robinson, is on educating learning disabled students. Their discussion focuses on the development of instructional methods and materials for these students, especially those areas concerned with academic and social skills. Focusing on environmental variables, Smith and Robinson argue that instructional methods should be matched to student learning patterns. The chapter reviews educational approaches of direct and daily measurement, staged learning, findings from information processing research, and research on teaching tactics. The authors indicate, for example, that research on information processing has led to the recognition that metacognitive strategies (such as the intent to learn) should be incorporated into a teaching strategy rather than the teacher relying on a student's self-initiative of facilitative behaviors. Smith and Robinson also offer views on such current issues as the definition of *learning disability*, making the delivery of services more cost effective, and achieving greater precision in research. The authors also examine areas for future research — areas that will increase the validity of future research findings, increase the listening and problem-solving skills of students, and expand services for learning disabilities beyond the primary grades to older students. Their chapter is articulate and filled with a great deal of information.

Chapter 8, by James M. Kauffman, examines how special education deals with children having behavior disorders or emotional disturbances. Kauffman describes the characteristics of children with behavior disorders and reviews the early and current research issues in the field. In comparing these issues, Kauffman notes that many of the issues are the same: namely, definition, terminology, and prevalence. Current issues in classification are also discussed, noting that the major classificatory system is based on the psychiatric diagnostic system although other systems, like those based on factor analysis, are also utilized. Issues related to educational programming for children with behavior disorders are also critically reviewed. Kauffman notes that a great deal of research has been conducted over the years on the educational programming of these children and that this research has led to a diversity of intervention strategies and techniques for handling behavior problems in these children. Kauffman concludes his chapter by stating that special education for children with behavior disorders is currently at a crossroads. For example, major questions regarding definition and terminology need to be resolved, and teachers of children with behavior disorders will be needed in larger numbers to meet the present and future educational needs of these children. More rigorous program evaluation is also needed. Kauffman's chapter is well written and provocative and it covers every aspect of educating children with behavior disorders.

In Chapter 9, Katharine G. Butler examines research and practice in language education — drawing on research in psycholinguistics, cognitive psychology, sociology, and other related fields. Butler first reviews the historical features of the rise of communication disorders as a field of study. She also covers the relations of language deficits to autism, mental retardation, hearing impairment, visual impairment, learning disorders, and multiple handicapping conditions. Butler indicates, too, that assessment practices are beginning to move from the clinic to the classroom, where teachers are being used as observers, and reliance on the criterion-referenced tests is increasing. In addition, using newer models of assessment, Butler points out that the following patterns of language difficulty are being discovered: inefficient processing, difficulties in organizing a narrative, and limited semantic knowledge. The chapter also reviews the shift in emphasis from the works of Chomsky and Piaget to information processing models, offering more fine-grained analyses. Butler further reviews research in such areas as phonology, syntax, semantics, and pragmatics. The chapter ends with a discussion of future issues for researchers and practitioners. This excellent and well organized chapter covers a topic on which many special educators are not well informed.

Chapter 10 is written by Ivan S. Terzieff and Shirin D. Antia and covers children with sensory impairments. Since the loss of vision or hearing can seriously affect contact with one's environment, the research related to the impact of these losses is discussed as it pertains to the following three areas: communication, cognitive development, and psychosocial development. Terzieff and Antia report, for example, delays in the syntactic, semantic, and pragmatic aspects of communication as a result of hearing impairment but that such delays have not been as definitive in those persons experiencing visual impairment. The authors, however, comment on the paucity of research on the pragmatic aspects of communication. They further report that, in the cognitive domain, hearing and visually impaired children experience early developmental lags of 2 to 6 years, catching up at later stages of development. Research is also reported that concerns the relationship between such delays and linguistic competency, while commentary is made concerning the need for more research on the relationship between cognitive delays and academic achievement and on the effects of intervention programs. The authors also review the research on the psychosocial development of these children. The chapter ends with a discussion of adaptive technology and the need for research and development in this area. The chapter is quite thorough in its coverage and provides an outstanding overview of research in this area.

Chapter 11, by Robert Bogdan, offers a sociological perspective on the practices in special education. Bogdan reviews some of the assumptions of the field and provides an interesting view concerning the concept of handicap as a social construction rather than a personal difficulty. Basic to the thrust of this chapter are concepts from symbolic interaction theory, where phenomena are examined from the perspective of the subject rather than that of the researcher. Such a conceptualization provides different meanings to such terms as *label* and *handicap*. Bogdan applies symbolic interaction theory to a variety of concerns in special education, including the concept of disability and prevalence rates. The conceptualization is also extended to moral understanding of what society values, such as intelligence and beauty, and the impact of this on the special treatment of some people. Finally, Bogdan applies symbolic interaction theory to a research strategy in which a person's subjective life history becomes the data base for understanding the person's disability. Bogdan has presented a thoroughly thought-provoking chapter that challenges our typical thinking regarding handicapping conditions.

The last chapter, Chapter 12 by Kathryn A. Blake and Charlotte L. Williams, addresses the whole area of research in special education. The authors point out that although personal experience and a knowledge of normative standards are useful in guiding decision making with regard to the delivery of special education services, research data add to the power of this decision making. The authors provide a view of the types of and methods used in research in special education and discuss some of the problems that hamper such research. After citing some examples of sound research in the field, Blake and Williams indicate that what is needed is a means of assimilating the plethora of existing research. The chapter then turns to the problem of identifying, limiting and studying areas for future research. Blake and Williams raise some very good points regarding research in the field and certainly encourage the reader to conduct more research.

As the reader can discern from this overview, the chapters contain detailed discussions of various aspects of research in special education and are written by those who are experts in their particular area of research. The information contained in these chapters is compelling and provides the reader with an extensive review of the state of the art of research in the field of special education.

REFERENCES

Apter, S. (1981). *Troubled children/troubled systems*. New York: Pergamon Press.

Bereiter, C., & Engelmann, S. (1966). *Teaching disadvantaged children in the preschool*. Englewood Cliffs, NJ: Prentice-Hall.

Bijou, S. W. (1966). A functional analysis of retarded development. *International Review of Research in Mental Retardation, 1*, 1–19.

Blatt, B. (1968). The dark side of the mirror. *Mental Retardation, 6*, 42–44.

Blatt, B. (1981). *In and out of mental retardation: Essays on educability, disability, and human policy*. Baltimore, MD: University Park Press.

Blatt, B., & Kaplan, F. (1966). *Christmas in purgatory: A photographic essay on mental retardation*. Boston: Allyn & Bacon.

Edgerton, R. B. (1967). *The cloak of competence: Stigma in the lives of the mentally retarded*. Berkeley, CA: University of California Press.

Edgerton, R. B., & Bercovici, S. (1976). The cloak of competence—years later. *American Journal of Mental Deficiency, 80*, 485–497.

Englemann, S. (1969). *Preventing failure in the primary grades*. Chicago: Science Research Associates.

Engelmann, S., & Carnine, D. (1982). *Theory of instruction: Principles and applications*. New York: Irvington.

Goldstein, A. P., Sprafkin, R. P., Gershaw, N. J., & Klein, P. (1980). *Skillstreaming the adolescent*. Champaign, IL: Research Press.

Goldstein, H. (1969). Construction of a social learning curriculum. *Focus on Exceptional Children, 3*, 1–10.

Goldstein, H. (1974). *The Social Learning Curriculum, Level I*. Columbus, OH: Charles E. Merrill, Inc.

Guthrie, R. (1961). Blood screening for phenylketonuria. *Journal of the American Medical Association, 178*, 863.

Guthrie, R. (1984). Explorations in prevention. In B. Blatt & R. J. Morris (Eds.), *Perspectives in special education: Personal orientations* (pp. 157–172). Glenview, IL: Scott, Foresman and Company.

Hallahan, D. P., Lloyd, J., Kosiewicz, M. M., Kauffman, J. M., & Graves, A. W. (1979). Self-monitoring of attention as a treatment for learning disabled boy's off task behavior. *Learning Disability Quarterly, 2*, 24–32.

Hallahan, D. P., Lloyd, J. W., Kauffman, J. M., & Loper, A. B. (1983). Academic problems. In R. J. Morris & T. R. Kratochwill (Eds.), *The practice of child therapy* (pp. 113–141). New York: Pergamon Press.

Haring, N. G., & Hauck, M. (1969). Improved learning conditions in the establishment of reading skills with disabled readers. *Exceptional Children, 35*, 341–351.

Hobbs, N. (1966). Helping disturbed children: Psychological and ecological strategies. *American Psychologist, 21*, 1105–1115.

Kauffman, J. M. (1981). *Characteristics of children's behavior disorders*. Columbus, OH: Charles E. Merrill.

Kazdin, A. E. (1977). *The token economy: A review and evaluation*. New York: Plenum.

Kazdin, A. E. (1980). *Behavior modification in applied settings* (Rev. ed.). Homewood, IL: Dorsey Press.

Kirk, S. A. (1984). Introspection and prophecy. In B. Blatt & R. J. Morris (Eds.), *Perspectives in special education: Personal orientations*. Glenview, IL: Scott, Foresman & Co.

Kounin, J. (1941). Experimental studies on rigidity: I. The measurement of rigidity in normal and feebleminded persons. *Character and Personality*, *9*, 251–272.

Lovaas, O. I., Freitag, L., Nelson, K., & Whalen, C. (1969). The establishment of imitation and its use for the development of complex behavior in schizophrenic children. *Behaviour Research and Therapy*, *5*, 171–181.

Lovaas, O. I. (1981). *Teaching developmentally disabled children: The ME book.* Baltimore: University Park Press.

Morse, W. C. (1984). Personal perspective. In B. Blatt & R. J. Morris (Eds.), *Perspectives in special education: Personal orientations* (pp. 101–125). Glenview, IL: Scott, Foresman and Company.

Nirje, B. (1969). The normalization principle and its human management implications. In R. B. Kugel & W. Wolfensberger (Eds.), *Changing patterns in residential services for the mentally retarded* (pp. 179–195). Washington, DC: President's Committee on Mental Retardation.

Ramp, E. A., & Rhine, W. R. (1983). Behavior Analysis Model. In W. R. Rhine (Ed.), *Making schools more effective: New directions from Follow Through* (pp. 75–95). New York: Academic Press.

Rhodes, W. C., & Tracy, M. L. (1972). *A study of child variance* (Vol. 2). Ann Arbor, MI: University of Michigan Press.

Watson, L. S. (1973). *Child behavior modification: A manual for teachers.* New York: Pergamon Press.

Williams, C. D. (1959). The elimination of tantrum behaviors by extinction procedures. *Journal of Abnormal and Social Psychology*, *59*, 269.

Wolf, M. M., Risley, T. R., & Mees, H. (1964). Application of operant conditioning procedures to the behavior problems of an autistic child. *Behaviour Research and Therapy*, *1*, 305–332.

Wolfensberger, W. (1969). The origin and nature of our institutional models. In R. Kugel & W. Wolfensberger (Eds.), *Changing patterns in residential services for the mentally retarded* (pp. 59–171). Washington, DC: President's Committee on Mental Retardation.

Wolfensberger, W. (1972). *The principle of normalization in human services.* Toronto, Canada: National Institute on Mental Retardation.

Zigler, E. (1961). Social deprivation and rigidity in the performance of feebleminded children. *Journal of Abnormal and Social Psychology*, *62*, 413–421.

Zigler, E. (1969). Developmental versus difference theories of mental retardation and the problem of motivation. *American Journal of Mental Deficiency*, *73*, 536–556.

2 THE USE OF ASSESSMENT INFORMATION TO MAKE DECISIONS ABOUT STUDENTS

James E. Ysseldyke

Measurement and assessment have been integral parts of special education since tests were first developed and used. Today, few decisions are made about students without first gathering data on the students and their performance in school. Yet, assessment is often misunderstood. Specifically, it is too often equated with testing. Assessment is the process of collecting data for the purpose of making decisions about individuals. In educational settings, many different kinds of psychoeducational decisions are made. Klein, Fenstermacher and Aiken (1971) described five kinds of decisions that are made using assessment data: problem selection, program selection, program operationalization, program improvement, and program certification decisions. Thorndike and Hagen (1977) delineated five kinds of decisions that are made using assessment data: instructional, curricular (program evaluation), selection, placement or classification, and personal. They observe, however, that:

> Measurement procedures do not make decisions; *people* make decisions. Measurement procedures can at most provide information on *some* of the factors that are relevant to a decision. (p. 3)

Salvia and Ysseldyke (1981) described six kinds of decisions that are made using assessment data: referral, screening, classification or placement, intervention planning, and pupil and program evaluation decisions. Since much of this chapter is organized according to the different kinds of decisions described by Salvia and Ysseldyke, it is necessary first to describe these more specifically.

Referral simply refers to a decision on the part of a referring agent (usually a parent or teacher) that a student exhibits sufficient difficulty to warrant evaluation by one or more diagnostic specialists (school psychologist, counselor, speech pathologist, etc.). Referral means different things in different settings. Usually, it means the completion of forms to formally refer a student to the attention of a diagnostic team. Often referral is more informal; teachers simply talk with diagnostic specialists about problems they are having with a student.

Screening is an activity that usually consists of administering group tests to groups of individuals to identify those who differ sufficiently from the norm to warrant further assessment and consideration for special education placement. *Classification or placement* is a relatively formal activity in which school personnel must do three things: they must identify the extent to which an individual is handicapped, they must specify the nature of the handicap, and they must identify the least restrictive environment in which to educate the student.

When school personnel attempt to use assessment data to plan instructional interventions (*intervention planning*) they must do two things. They must decide what particular content is to be used in instructing the student. They must also decide what specific methods or techniques will be used in instructing the student.

Assessment data are collected for the purpose of making two kinds of evaluation decisions: *pupil evaluation decisions* and *program evaluation decisions*. Parents, teachers, and students have a right and a need to know the extent to which the child is making progress in the particular instructional program in which he or she is enrolled. Assessment data are regularly collected to evaluate pupil progress. They are also collected to evaluate the effectiveness of particular instructional programs. This latter use is evidenced when a school district uses tests to evaluate pupil gains in specific instructional programs.

Many different kinds of data are collected in the assessment and decision-making process. Most often, we think of the administration of either norm-referenced or criterion-referenced tests. Yet, school personnel also gather data by means of observing pupils, by interviewing parents or others who regularly observe the student, by searching records, and by gathering medical, social, or adaptive behavior histories.

In this chapter, I focus on the state of the art in assessment and decision making in special education. I review the history of efforts to use assessment data to make decisions about students and then review the kinds of research strategies that have been used to try to learn more about and improve assessment and decision-making practices. I describe some of the

significant findings that have been derived from research on decision making and also describe the major shortcomings of those research efforts. I describe specific problems and issues in conducting research on assessment and decision making and describe future directions for research and practice.

HISTORICAL PERSPECTIVE

Assessment data are used to make decisions about individuals. Most often school personnel engage in assessment because students fail to profit from academic activities. They use the tests to try to prevent failure in school by identifying those likely to experience academic and social difficulties. They also administer tests to help plan remedial or compensatory interventions for students who have academic and behavior problems.

There always have been large numbers of students who failed to profit from the experiences they were given in schools. Those students were not always assessed. Prior to the early 1900s, the educational system responded to failure by excluding students from school. Students who, because they were handicapped or for some other reason, did not make significant progress in school were simply excluded from school. Exclusion was the remedy of choice in response to failure — until the courts in compulsory education statutes ruled such action illegal. By 1908, every state had enacted compulsory education laws. Schools were forced to come up with alternatives to exclusion, one of which was to assign pupils to special classes.

Following World War I, with advances made in the development of tests used in the military, testing activities began to play a major role in education. Intelligence tests were used to assign students to different ability groups and to predict the extent to which students would be successful in school.* Special education classes for retarded and disturbed individuals were established, made possible by the fact that tests (so it was thought) could be used to

---

*This practice continued in Washington, D.C., for example, until 1967, when in a famous court case (Hobson *v.* Hansen) tracking based on pupil performance on intelligence tests was ruled unconstitutional.

identify individuals who should be assigned to such classes. Elaborate classification or categorization schemes were developed and tests became the tools used to classify and place students. As even more students failed to profit from schooling, who could not be identified as having mental or emotional disabilities, new alternatives were created to enable the students to be removed from special classes. Students were placed in Title I classes for the disadvantaged, in classes for learning disabled students, and in vocational education programs. Tests were often used for the purpose of deciding what to call students and where to place them.

Having found standardized tests useful for making classification decisions, educators attempted to use tests for planning instructional interventions for students (Ysseldyke & Algozzine, 1979). And, they used the same tests. Under the fancy terminology *differential diagnosis* or *diagnostic-prescriptive teaching*, educators tried to use tests to make decisions about what kinds of students to assign to what kinds of instructional programs (Arter & Jenkins, 1979; Bateman, 1967).

Throughout the history of the use of standardized tests in the process of decision making, tests (especially, though not exclusively, intelligence tests) and testing practices have been criticized. I believe the controversy has centered on or derived from two concerns. First, tests are used to differentiate among individuals in making selection or classification decisions. Industry selects employees on the basis of aptitude, performance, personality, or interest test scores, and unsuccessful applicants for jobs have been quick to criticize the tests used in the selection process. In school, individuals often are assigned to different educational settings, tracks, or experiences based on intelligence or achievement test performance. Those who are assigned to "lower" placements are quick to be critical of the use of tests in the placement process. In both instances, tests are viewed as tools that are used to make selection decisions that may significantly limit an individual's life opportunities.

The second source of criticism is in the use of tests in a diagnostic process. As Sarason and Doris (1979) observe, "diagnosis is a pathology oriented process activated by someone who thinks something is wrong with somebody else" (p. 39). When people are assessed because somebody thinks something is wrong with them, they are often quick to be critical of the assessment process and the tests used in that process.

In special education, largely in response to the concern that tests may be used to limit students' life opportunities, we have seen repeated calls for moratoria on testing activities (e.g., Black Caucus, 1974). We have also witnessed repeated concern about classification and labeling (Dunn, 1968; Mercer, 1974). Dunn (1968, pp. 11–12) was critical of then-current practices of labeling as *mentally retarded* significant numbers of disadvantaged students and slow-learning students. He stated that:

> Existing diagnostic procedures should be replaced by expecting special educators, in large measure, to be responsible for their own diagnostic teaching and their clinical teaching. In this regard, it is suggested that we do away with many existing disability labels and the present practice of grouping children homogeneously by these labels into special classes. Instead, we should try keeping slow learning children more in the mainstream of education, with special educators serving as diagnostic, clinical, remedial, resource room, itinerant and/or team teachers, consultants, and developers of instructional materials and prescriptions for effective teaching.
>
> The accomplishment of the above *modus operandi* will require a revolution in much of special education. A moratorium needs to be placed on the proliferation (if not continuance) of self-contained special classes which enroll primarily the ethnically and/or economically disadvantaged children we have been labeling educable mentally retarded. Such pupils should be left in (or returned to) the regular elementary grades until we are "tooled up" to do something better for them.

Mercer (1974, p. 132) reported the results of a 12-year study of the practice of classifying students mentally retarded in Riverside, California. She concluded her report with several recommendations:

We believe that psychological assessment procedures have become a civil rights issue because present assessment and educational practices violate at least five rights of children: (a) their right to be evaluated within a culturally appropriate normative framework; (b) their right to be assessed as multi-dimensional, many faceted human beings; (c) their right to be fully educated; (d) their right to be free of stigmatizing labels; and (e) their right to cultural identity and respect.

The criticisms of special education and especially of self-contained special classes have nearly always been accompanied by criticism of the tests and assessment activities used to assign students to special classes. Note that both Dunn and Mercer, in criticizing special classes for mentally retarded students, call specific attention to the tests and diagnostic activities used to assign students to special classes. That kind of early concern led to inclusion of specific mandates on testing and assessment in Public Law 94-142. Thus, the law specifies that tests must be selected and administered in such a way as to be nondiscriminatory. In the due process provisions of PL 94-142, parents are given the right to challenge the schools' assessment of their child.

RESEARCH STRATEGIES

For any kind of psychological or educational problem that investigators choose to study, research on assessment and decision making has involved three kinds of methodologies: illustrative, comparative, and predictive (Ysseldyke & Algozzine, 1982). Investigators described the state of the art, they described differences among students or among assessment practices, and they tried to predict relations among variables or to predict outcomes that result from experimental manipulations of variables. In the following section, I briefly describe the kinds of research strategies used to investigate the psychoeducational assessment and decision-making process. The section is organized on the basis of the kinds of decisions made.

Referral

While some investigators have written about the referral process, few have conducted other than illustrative research on the process. They have conducted a considerable number of descriptive or illustrative studies focusing on the kinds of students referred or the problems for which students are referred. Early investigations of referral consisted of counting referred students by sex, race, reason for referral, and so on (Nicholson, 1967; Ysseldyke, 1968). Investigators attempted to get a handle on the kinds of students referred by searching referral forms and counting the frequency of referral for specific reasons (e.g., academic problems, behavior problems, etc.).

Some research on referral has used a survey format including artificial or bogus case studies. Teachers were given descriptions of student behaviors and asked whether or not they would refer the student for evaluation. Other studies have used a survey format in which teachers were asked to complete sets of questions on the kinds of students they would refer or were asked at the time of referral why they referred students for evaluation.

Classification

While much research has been done on classification, it is important to recognize that much of the writing about classification has been simply that — writing *about* classification. People have developed classification systems and debated the relative merits and limitations of those systems. Special educators have a considerable propensity to build models, whether of cognitive functioning, information processing, or whatnot. In most instances, the models, including classification systems or models, are developed in the absence of empirical evidence for their efficacy (Ysseldyke, 1973).

Special educators have expended considerable research efforts describing the kinds of students in different categories. Long lists of characteristics of specific kinds of students have been developed from such research efforts. In nearly any introductory text, characteristics of specific categories of students are listed and described. Teachers in training are required to learn the lists of characteristics "and the beat goes on."

Much of the research on classification has been comparative in nature. Educators have compared categorized students to "normal" students on everything from the chemical content of their hair (Rimland & Larson, 1983) to the scores they earned on specific tests (Ysseldyke, 1983). Such comparisons are conducted in an effort to refine the categorical systems, to help us differentiate handicapped from normal students.

Not only have categorized students been compared to "normal" ones, they have been compared to one another. Many investigations in special education simply compare specific kinds of handicapped students to one another, usually on psychometric measures. Such comparisons are designed to help us learn how to differentiate better among, for example, emotionally disturbed, learning disabled, and mentally retarded students.

Research on classification has sometimes consisted of or led to the development of new formulas or systems for classifying students (Cone & Wilson, 1981; Hammill, Larsen, Leigh, & McNutt, 1981; Keogh, 1983; McLoughlin & Netick, 1983). We witness today an ever increasing effort to make the diagnostic process more sophisticated, through employment of neuropsychological assessment and mile-long regression equations (Algozzine & Ysseldyke, 1983).

At least one other research strategy has been used to study the ways in which assessment data are used to make classification and placement decisions. Investigators observed the team decision-making process in operation or developed computer simulations of the individual or team decision-making process and, using such strategies, attempted to document what people do.

Intervention Planning and Evaluation

Since placement is often considered an intervention, much of the research on intervention has been restricted to developing better ways to classify and place. In addition, investigators have described the kinds of interventions used with specific kinds of students.

Research comparing the effectiveness of alternative kinds of interventions with specific kinds of students or of the same intervention with different kinds of students typically has been completed using a gain score methodology. Students are given tests before and after intervention; their performance is contrasted.

Considerable predictive research has been completed on intervention planning and effectiveness (Ysseldyke, 1973; Ysseldyke & Mirkin, 1982), much of which has consisted of correlational research. Abilities have been correlated with one another and with achievement. Achievement has been correlated in alternative settings. Early correlational research led to investigations designed to identify aptitude-treatment interactions. As investigators sought to formalize differential diagnosis-prescriptive teaching (Arter & Jenkins, 1979) or diagnostic-prescriptive teaching (Ysseldyke & Salvia, 1974), they increasingly used aptitude-treatment interaction research in efforts to document interactions (Ysseldyke & Salvia, 1980). These efforts, then, led to the development of cookbooks, some of which are computerized, to be used in prescribing differential treatments for students demonstrating different profiles of abilities.

Program Evaluation

A variety of methodologies are available for use in evaluating the effectiveness of specific kinds of curricular interventions for exceptional students. Yet, the most widely used strategies consist of using gain scores on tests as indices of the extent to which programs are effective. In some instances, investigators simply presumed that students have specific kinds of deficits, developed interventions designed to ameliorate or alleviate the deficiencies, and looked at pupil gain in the instructional program as an index of program effectiveness.

In other instances, investigators pretested students who demonstrated observed differences, assigned deficient students to treatments, then looked at the extent to which the students profitted from the program. Gain-score analyses are most often used to investigate program effectiveness.

Recently, research on program evaluation has used a variety of methods derived from applied behavior analysis. The methods are used based on the premise that there is no way to decide ahead of time how best to teach a student and that changes in instruction should be made contingent on pupil performance.

RESEARCH FINDINGS

In this section of this chapter, I review what I believe are major research findings regarding the use of assessment information to make psychoeducational decisions. The review of major findings is limited and simply cannot be exhaustive. Therefore, I focus on the findings of research conducted by myself and others at the University of Minnesota Institute for Research on Learning Disabilities. Major generalizations from that research effort are summarized in a paper by Ysseldyke, Thurlow, Graden, Wesson, Algozzine, and Deno (1983). The following review is organized on the basis of the kinds of decisions made.

Referral Decisions

Teachers regularly refer students for psychoeducational evaluation, and the act of referral is what initiates the assessment process. The referral process has been studied in many different ways, often in an effort to gain a better understanding of the kinds of students referred and the determinants of referral. Reasons stated for referral have been examined relative to the referral source, grade level, sex, and size of school system (Gilbert, 1957; Gregory, 1977; Lietz & Gregory, 1978; Nicholson, 1967; Rice, 1963; Robbins, Mercer & Meyers, 1967; Ysseldyke, 1968). Most studies report sex differences in referral; a larger proportion of boys than girls are referred; however, contradictory findings remain. Although Gilbert (1957) and Nicholson (1967) cited "academic difficulties" as the most frequent reason

for referral, Robbins et al. (1967) reported that "behavior problems" constituted the most frequent referral concern. The most frequent reason for referral remained consistent across grades in some investigations (Gilbert, 1957; Gregory, 1977), while others found that reason for referral varied as a function of grade placement in school (Nicholson, 1967; Rice, 1963; Robbins et al., 1967). Two recent investigations (Davis, 1978; Gregory, 1977) found that a rank order of reasons for referral differed according to sex; girls most often were referred for academic reasons, boys for behavioral or adjustment problems.

Several investigators have looked at the reasons teachers refer students. It has been shown that referral, triggered by someone thinking something is wrong with someone else, may be as much a function of teachers' perceptions of pupil behaviors and characteristics as it is of the pupils' actual behaviors and characteristics (Kornblau & Keogh, 1980). It is clear that teachers' perceptions are intimately related to expectancies held for a student's performance and that ultimately perceptions and expectancies influence teachers' interactions with students (Brophy & Good, 1970; Dusek, 1975; Kornblau & Keogh, 1980).

Ysseldyke, Christenson, Pianta, Thurlow, and Algozzine (1982) report the results of a series of investigations designed to address (a) rate of referral, (b) reasons for referral, (c) characteristics of students referred for evaluation, (d) teachers' attributions for student problems, (e) teacher-initiated prereferral interventions, (f) desired outcomes for referral, and (g) institutional constraints and external pressures that influence the referral process. Algozzine, Christenson and Ysseldyke (1982) reported that nationally 3–6% of the school-age population is referred every year for psychoeducational evaluation. They reported that of those referred, 92% are tested; of those tested 73% are declared eligible for and placed in some kind of special education program. Clearly, very large numbers of students are referred each year, and referral most often results in being declared eligible for services. We witness today a rapid increase in the n·· bers of students being declared eligible fc *cial* education services each year. Few students leave special education services for a regular classroom; hence, we observe a very rapid increase in the numbers of students receiving special education services each year.

Although students are referred for multiple reasons, the most common reasons are academic and behavior problems. Yet, the reasons teachers state for referring students are general, subjective, and lack a consistent pattern (Ysseldyke, Christenson, Pianta, & Algozzine, 1983). More than twice as many boys as girls are currently referred for psychoeducational evaluation. Over half of referred students are rated poor or very poor relative to their classmates on speed of learning, motivation, maturity, and judgment.

What do teachers believe causes students to suffer academic and behavior difficulties? In a 1979 survey conducted by the National Education Association (1979), 81% of regular classroom teachers attributed students' academic and behavior problems to home and family difficulties; 14% said the problems experienced by students were due to internal student dysfunctions, deficits, disabilities, or disorders. Only 1% of the teachers attributed students' problems to inadequate or inappropriate prior instruction; 4% said the problems were due to the ways in which schools are organized.

We asked regular classroom teachers to state their beliefs about the causes of students' academic and behavior problems. Teachers were asked at the time they actually referred a student for evaluation. The majority of teachers attributed students' difficulties to either home and family problems (35.6%) or to within-student disorders (61.7%). Only 2% of the teachers attributed student problems to inadequate instruction, while 1% attributed problems to the way in which the school was organized. The findings were interpreted as having significant implications for both training and practice. While we believe that many students have home and family problems and many have internal deficits or disorders, the problems are as often due to inadequate, inappropriate, or incomplete instruction.

What interventions do teachers try before they refer students for psychoeducational evaluation? When we asked teachers who referred students for evaluation to tell us the interventions they had tried, they listed an average of three interventions. Yet, the interventions teachers listed were nonsystematic ("I changed her book," "I moved him to a different seat") and few teachers collected data on the effectiveness of their interventions (Ysseldyke, Pianta, Christenson, Wang & Algozzine, 1983).

What, then, do teachers hope to gain from referring students for evaluation? We asked teachers this specific question at the time they referred students (Ysseldyke, Christenson, Pianta, & Algozzine, 1983). Teachers told us they desired placement, or placement-related activities, significantly more often than educational suggestions. Teachers' desired outcomes did not differ for students referred primarily for learning or behavior reasons. Regardless of the teacher's primary referral concern, teachers wanted students either tested or placed. There are two alternative suggestions for this finding. It may well be that teachers are stating very precisely when they refer students that they have exhausted their instructional possibilities for the student and want the student out. It may also be that this is the outcome that teachers have learned to expect. When we talk to teachers, they tell us that diagnostic personnel make placement decisions and that if the decision is not to place, they do not get instructional suggestions.

What institutional constraints and external pressures influence decisions to refer students for psychoeducational evaluation? We anticipated that teachers would be influenced in their decisions most by pressures from external agencies, including both community service agencies (like community mental health centers) and advocacy groups (like the National Association for Retarded Citizens or the Association for Children and Adults with Learning Disabilities). I was surprised by the findings of an investigation in which we asked teachers to identify those factors that influenced their decisions to refer students (Christenson, Ysseldyke, & Algozzine, 1982). Teachers decisions to refer students are influenced most by the extent to which the recipient of the referral reinforced them for referring the student, by their opinions and attitudes about the quality of special education services in their buildings or districts, and by the hassle (amount of paperwork associated with the process). Referrals are most likely when teachers have a high regard for the quality of special education services, when psychologists or others who receive referrals reinforce teachers for referring students, and when it is relatively easy to refer students.

Who do teachers refer for psychoeducational evaluation? They refer students who bother *them.* We used a case study format to demonstrate that teachers take varying degrees of action with students as a function of the extent to which the student demonstrates behaviors that bother them. Different behaviors bother different kinds of teachers, and it is difficult to predict which children will get referred without knowing the teachers, the kinds of behaviors that bother the teachers, and the extent to which the student demonstrates those behaviors (Algozzine, Ysseldyke, & Christenson, 1983).

Referral is clearly the most important decision in the referral to placement process. It sets in motion a search for pathology that most often results in finding pathology. While it might be reasonable to conclude that teachers are incredibly accurate in their decisions to refer students, and thus we get the high "hit rate," data I present later support the contention that the rival hypothesis—classification of normal students as handicapped—is more plausible.

Placement/Classification Decisions

A massive classification system governs the current delivery of special education services. This was not always the case; the current system evolved rather than being developed en masse. It evolved in response to a problem: significant numbers of students were failing to profit from the educational experiences they received in regular classrooms (Ysseldyke & Algozzine, 1982, 1984). Initially, educators simply excluded from school students who did not make sufficient academic progress. Early compulsory education laws made such practices illegal. The first special education services (at least by that name) were offered in separate schools, like the American Asylum for the Education and Instruction of the Deaf (1817). Blindness and deafness were the first recognized handicapping conditions. Only later did educators recognize and create classes for physically handicapped, mentally retarded, speech and language impaired, emotionally disturbed, and learning disabled students.

Each of the special education categories was created when it was recognized that there was a group of students who failed, who did not meet the criteria for those categories then in existence, and who had certain behaviors in common. For example, the category "specific learning disabilities" was created in the early 1960s to provide services to students who failed academically, who were not handicapped according to then-existent criteria for then-existent categories (e.g., mentally retarded, blind), and who were thought to have certain disorders in common. The term was chosen because parents did not want the students called other things (e.g., brain-injured, slow learner, dyslexic, aphasic).

Consider carefully the current practice in classifying students handicapped. It is through being called handicapped that students become entitled to special services and benefits in school. Tests are the usual vehicles for obtaining the data that are used in classifying students.

Educators and related services personnel have long debated the merits and limitations of classification and the practice of assessing students to classify them. Early research on classification practices was directed toward finding the best test or battery of tests for classifying students. More recently, researchers have focused their attention on classification *practices* and procedures, looking specifically at how people go through the practice. Until very recently, attention has been focused on how to classify better. Very recent research addresses the question, why classify?

It is not at all clear that research on classification has had an impact on classification practices. Special education classification practices are a mixture of politics, economics, social values, and education. As social values or attitudes change, classification practices change. This was most evident when, in 1973, the American Association on Mental Deficiency revised the criteria for being called *mentally retarded*. The association changed the intellectual standard for retardation from one to two standard deviations below the mean. The change was not made because researchers had suddenly learned more about mental retardation. Rather, the change was made in response to social and political concerns. Too many minority and disadvantaged students were being labeled *mentally retarded*; and this label was thought to stigmatize them and limit their life opportunities. With one stroke of the pen, large numbers of students previously considered mentally retarded were declared normal. Today, increasing numbers of students are being classified learning disabled. There are considerable efforts to modify the definition of learning disabilities and to rewrite the criteria for eligibility for LD services (Hammill et al., 1981). Have we suddenly learned so much more about learning disabilities that it is time to change criteria? No. Rather, it is getting increasingly more expensive to provide special services to larger and larger numbers of students. In tough economic times, the system cannot bear massive spending efforts. The move to change criteria is a move to limit the numbers of students considered eligible for services and thereby to save money.

It is not my purpose here to review in detail the significantly large body of research on classification practices. Entire volumes have been written on the topic (cf. Hobbs, 1975, volumes 1 and 2). Rather, I will highlight aspects of my own and others' research on classification practices. That research has been of two kinds: studies of the outcomes of classification, and studies of the process by which school personnel classify students.

The Outcomes of Classification

We engage in classification practices to differentiate individuals into distinct groups or categories. So, the first test of the system ought to ask, To what extent can we split students into the neat, distinct categories we have created? Several investigators have been conducting research relevant to this question.

Ysseldyke, Algozzine, Shinn and McGue (1982) conducted a psychometric comparison of low achieving students and students labeled *learning disabled*. They compared the performance of the students on 49 separate measures of cognitive, perceptual-motor, personality, and academic functioning. They reported no reliable psychometric differences between the two groups of students; on the average, there was a 96% overlap in the scores students earned on tests. Discriminant function analysis revealed that no scores or combination of scores differentiated between the groups. They concluded that there is currently no defensible system for differentiating between LD and low achieving students.

Shepard and Smith (1981) described the characteristics of students identified as LD in Colorado. They found that fewer than half of their sample of 800 students exhibited behaviors, characteristics, or test scores consistent with criteria for being called *learning disabled* in Colorado.

Ysseldyke, Algozzine, and Epps (1983) report the results of an application of current LD criteria to groups of normal, low achieving, and learning disabled students. Using 17 sets of operational criteria for the definition of learning disabilities, they demonstrated that 85% of normal third, fifth, and twelfth grade students could be labeled LD. Further, 4% of LD students did not meet any of the criteria for being called *LD*.

Algozzine and Ysseldyke (1981) report the results of a computer simulated investigation of the extent to which decision makers are declaring normal students handicapped. They provided more than 200 decision makers with test data entirely indicative of normal performance. Fifty-one percent of the decision makers declared the normal student handicapped.

Perlmutter and Parus (1983) describe the results of an investigation of assessment practices in 14 school districts. They report little uniformity in test selection, extent of testing, and cutoff scores on tests used in classification of students.

Given that we cannot reliably differentiate handicapped from nonhandicapped students on a psychometric basis, a second question arises, What if we rely on clinical judgment? In spite of the fact that clinical judgment has been repeatedly shown to be imprecise (Potter, 1982), decision makers argue that, given sets of scores indicative of pupils' performances on tests, they can differentiate categories. Epps, McGue, and Ysseldyke (1982) and Epps, Ysseldyke, and McGue (in press) report the results of two investigations of clinical judgment in making classification decisions. They sampled groups of teachers, school psychologists, and "naive judges." The latter were undergraduate students who never had more than one course in education or psychology. Using federal criteria and school-identification, the investigators demonstrated about a 55% hit rate for professionals, and a 75% hit rate for naive judges. Given profiles of pupil performance on tests, professionals were able to differentiate students with slightly more than chance accuracy, although not as well as untrained people.

Current classification procedures do not result in accurate classifications. Clearly, large numbers of nonhandicapped students are now being classified handicapped. I suppose the reverse may also be true, that large numbers of handicapped students are being considered normal and remain in regular classes where they fail to profit from their educational experiences.

The Process of Classification

In 1978, as part of the research program at the University of Minnesota Institute for Research on Learning Disabilities, I set out to observe and videotape special education placement team meetings. I wanted to study the ways in which assessment data are used to make decisions about students. I had incredible difficulty finding placement team meetings.

Instead, I found meetings to get ready for meetings to get ready for meetings. I found that placement decisions were seldom made at team meetings, though they were often *conveyed* to parents at team meetings. Rather, decisions were made ahead of time.

When I tried to ascertain primary responsibility for decisions, school personnel were quick to deny responsibility. When asked, Who made the decision? school personnel were quick to abdicate responsibility. Most claimed school psychologists were primary in making decisions. School psychologists claimed they had little power in the decision-making process. I raised questions about the extent to which placement teams actually make decisions about students.

What is the composition of placement teams? Poland, Thurlow, Ysseldyke, and Mirkin (1982) reported that when placement decisions were made, those most often in attendance at meetings were parents, school administrators, special education teachers, school psychologists, and regular education teachers. Yoshida, Fenton, Maxwell, and Kaufman (1978) reported that regular education teachers are the least satisfied (of the five groups) with the team decision-making process. Ysseldyke, Algozzine, and Allen (1981) reported that although regular education teachers attend team meetings, they participate very little in the meetings.

While parents attend most special education placement team meetings, their participation in the meetings is very limited (Ysseldyke, Algozzine & Thurlow, 1980). On the average, parents participate less than 1 minute in team meetings, and their participation is characteristically confirmatory; they simply answer "yes" or "no" to team statements like "Do you also observe this behavior at home?"

Although parents participate very little in team meetings, their perceptions of the process are very positive. When asked for their impressions, parents typically say they are very pleased that school personnel would take the time to sit down with them and discuss their child's educational progress.

Rostollan (1980) reported that teams spend about twice as much time discussing academic data as discussing behavioral data. Ysseldyke, Algozzine, Rostollan, and Shinn (1981) reported the distribution of time spent discussing various domains of assessment data at team meetings. Of that time devoted to discussion of assessment, the majority of the time was spent discussing pupil performance in the classroom or on achievement tests (66%). Yet, less than half of the meeting time was devoted to discussion of pupil performance. The remainder of the time was taken up in discussion of matters not clearly relevant to the decision to be made.

Clearly, the kinds of data used most often to make decisions about students are test data. Thurlow and Ysseldyke (1979) and Ysseldyke, Algozzine, Regan, Potter, Richey, and Thurlow (1980) reported the tests used most often by decision makers. Tests used most often in making placement decisions were the Wechsler Intelligence Scale for Children — Revised, the Bender Visual-Motor Gestalt Test, and an individually administered achievement test (usually the Peabody Individual Achievement Test or the Wide Range Achievement Test). Though team members use a very large number of tests in making decisions, it has been demonstrated that decisions do not change as a function of the numbers of devices used (Algozzine, Ysseldyke, & Hill, 1982).

How technically adequate are the tests used to make decisions about students? Ysseldyke, Algozzine, Regan and Potter (1980) reported the results of a study of the technical adequacy of tests used by professionals in making decisions about students. They looked at the extent to which the tests used had adequate norms, were reliable, and valid. They concluded that while exceptions could surely be shown, for the most part professionals used technically inadequate tests in gathering data for making decisions about students.

Ysseldyke, Algozzine, Richey, and Graden (1982) videotaped special education placement team meetings for the purpose of examining the extent to which school personnel actually *use* test data in making decisions about students. They demonstrated that while large amounts of data are collected, the data are not used in decision making. Rather, decision makers make decisions primarily to appease teachers who are having difficulty dealing with students in class.

Instructional Interventions Decisions

School personnel long have attempted to plan specific instructional interventions based on the ways in which pupils performed on tests. Today, state and federal laws and guidelines require development of individualized educational programs for all handicapped students, individualized educational programs that contain instructional objectives derived from or based on pupil performance on tests. These current efforts clearly have their roots in the observations of early experimental psychologists and early educators that different individuals learned differently (Estes, 1970). Early research in experimental psychology showing significant differences in learning rates and learning processes has led to considerable efforts to reify, identify, and train processes or abilities (cf., Mann, 1981).

In educational settings, efforts to link assessment to instruction have led to development of numerous diagnostic-prescriptive models (Bannatyne, 1969; Bateman, 1967; Cartwright, Cartwright & Ysseldyke, 1973; Farrald & Schamber, 1973; Frostig, 1967a, 1967b; Hammill, 1972; Harris & Roswell, 1953; Kirk & McCarthy, 1961; Wedell, 1970; Ysseldyke & Sabatino, 1973). The efforts have also led to methodologies for differential interpretation of student performance on tests (Massey, Sattler, & Andres, 1978; Sattler, 1965; Valett, 1964), and to the development of diagnostic-prescriptive "cookbooks" (Blanco, 1972; Ferinden, Jacobson, & Kovalinsky, 1969). Efforts to plan instructional interventions based on pupil performance on tests has led to considerable debate on the efficacy of specific procedures (American Academy of Pediatrics, 1972; Bersoff, 1973; Eaves & McLaughlin, 1977; Ewing & Brecht, 1977; Hammill, 1972; Hammill, Goodman & Wiederholt, 1974; Hammill & Larsen, 1974, 1978; Keogh, 1974; Larsen, 1976; Larsen, Rogers & Sowell, 1976; Lund,

Foster, & McCall-Perez, 1978; Mann, 1970, 1971a, 1971b; Mann & Phillips, 1967; McCarthy, 1976; Minskoff, 1975; Newcomer, 1977; Smead, 1977; Waugh, 1975; Wiseman, 1970; Ysseldyke, 1973; Ysseldyke & Salvia, 1974).

Ysseldyke and Salvia (1974) identified two fundamentally different approaches to diagnostic-prescriptive teaching, differing in assumptions about the learner and about how assessment data ought to be used to plan interventions. The first approach, called *ability training*, is characterized by the assumption that inadequate academic performance is primarily caused by within-student deficits, disorders, dysfunctions, or disabilities. The deficits are to be identified and remediated before the student proceeds with instruction. Special education researchers have spent considerable effort attempting to develop diagnostic–prescriptive programs to train visual processes (Bernetta, 1962; Coleman, 1968; Dilbard, Houghton, & Thomas, 1972; Ewalt, 1962; Getman, 1962, 1966a, 1966b, 1972; Greenspan, 1973; Kane, 1972; Sloat, 1971; Swanson, 1972; and Swartwout, 1972), psycholinguistic processes (Kirk & Kirk, 1971; Kirk, McCarthy, & Kirk, 1968; Minskoff, Wiseman, & Minskoff, 1972), perceptual-motor processes (Arena, 1969; Barsch, 1965, 1967, 1968; Dunsing & Kephart, 1965; Frostig, 1967a, 1967b, 1972; Frosting & Horne, 1964; Johnson & Myklebust, 1967; Kephart, 1960, 1964, 1971; Roach & Kephart, 1966), sensory integration (Ayres, 1972), and body rhythm and balance (Rice, 1962).

The second approach, labeled by Ysseldyke and Salvia (1974) as *task analysis*, is one in which academic problems are viewed as most often caused by environmental factors, including inadequate prior instruction. In this approach, abilities are largely disregarded. Emphasis is on assessment of skill development strengths and weaknesses, task analysis of specific skills, and teaching specific skills. Many different diagnostic-prescriptive models have been devised based on a skills-training approach. These are variously called *directive teaching* (Stephens, 1976), *direct instruction*, Carnine & Silbert, 1979; Engelmann & Carnine, 1982), *DISTAR* (Becker & Engelmann, 1969), *data-based instruction* (Deno, 1973; Fox, Egner, Paolucci, Perelman & McKenzie, 1973), *data-based program modification* (Deno & Mirkin, 1977), *exceptional teaching* (White & Haring, 1976), *individual instruction* (Peter, 1972), *precision teaching* (Lindsley, 1964, 1971), and *responsive teaching* (Hall & Copeland, 1971). All of the models are similar: they advocate adherence to systematic, sequential, intensive, individualized, and/or small group instruction on skills directly related to the academic and social requirements of the school program (Ysseldyke & Mirkin, 1982). Assessment within such approaches is both direct and continuous. For example, Bijou and Grimm (1972) state that:

> Diagnosis involves arriving at a set of decisions . . . for designing an academic program that will meet a child's specific academic and social needs. The initial set of decisions is considered tentative and changing through the period of instruction as new findings are revealed. (pp. 23–24)

Reviews of research on diagnostic–prescriptive teaching (Arter & Jenkins, 1979; Ysseldyke, 1973; Ysseldyke & Mirkin, 1982; Ysseldyke & Salvia, 1974) have reached similar conclusions. To date, there is considerably more empirical support for diagnostic prescriptive practices based on a skill training model than for those based on an ability training model.

Several recent investigations have described current practice in the use of assessment information to plan instructional interventions. Thurlow and Ysseldyke (1979) reported the results of a survey of federally funded child service demonstration centers in learning disabilities. They reported that most centers relied on results of pupil performance on norm-referenced ability and achievement tests in efforts to plan instructional programs for students. Poland, Thurlow, Ysseldyke, and Mirkin (1982) surveyed directors of special education on current practices in using assessment information to plan instructional interventions. They reported that instructional decisions were most often made by teams of educators and psychologists, but were again primarily based on pupil performance on tests. Mirkin and Potter (1982) reported that teachers plan instructional interventions based primarily on testimonial evidence and their own experience. Thurlow and Ysseldyke (1982) asked teachers the kinds of information most often found useful in planning instruction. Teachers reported that test information was most useful.

Clearly, most often instruction programs are planned based on the ways in which pupils perform on tests, most often ability tests. The approach to diagnostic–prescriptive teaching most often used is one based on ability training. Yet, there is a considerable lack of empirical evidence to support ability training efforts.

Evaluation Decisions

Assessment data are used for the purpose of evaluating individual pupil progress and/or the efficacy of alternative instructional programs. In general, we want to know how things are going, whether the student is progressing commensurate with our expectations, and whether the kinds of instructional programs we use are any good. Evaluation is a legally mandated activity, at least for handicapped students; it is specified in Public Law 94-142 that school personnel will engage in ongoing evaluation of the effectiveness of the instructional programs they plan for individual students.

For years, researchers evaluated instructional efficacy by looking at pupil performance on standardized tests. More recently, three kinds of approaches have been used: standardized tests, criterion-referenced or objective-referenced tests, and curriculum-based assessment.

The use of standardized tests to evaluate the efficacy of alternative interventions has repeatedly been shown to be a technically inadequate venture (Cronbach & Furby, 1970; Ysseldyke, 1973). Such approaches are summative in nature; they tell us, in a post-mortem sense, the extent to which our actions with the students made any difference.

Recently, practice has shifted away from summative evaluation to formative evaluation, evaluating the effectiveness of interventions while they are being implemented. The shift has taken place on both logical and empirical

bases. Logically, it is argued that it makes more sense to evaluate pupil progress while there is still time to modify the student's instructional program. Empirical support for the shift has come from research demonstrating the methodological problems in summative evaluation and the limited usefulness of summative findings. It has also come from advances in the technology of formative evaluation.

Investigators contrasted the relative merits of formative and summative evaluation. Results of their investigations supports the contention that formative evaluation is superior to summative evaluation in influencing pupil outcomes (Bohannon, 1975; Deno & Mirkin, 1977; Liberty, 1972, 1975; White & Liberty, 1974). Yet, in practice, teachers rely most often on informal observation of pupil progress toward instructional objectives (Fuchs, Fuchs, & Warren, 1982), and their informal observations are highly inaccurate (Fuchs et al., 1982).

Teachers who use direct, repeated measures of pupil progress toward instructional objectives have been shown to be more successful in moving students to accomplishment of those objectives. The more often teachers measure, the better the success rate for students (Mirkin, Deno, Tindal, & Kuehnle, 1980).

In nearly every recent investigation where alternative methods of evaluating instructional outcomes have been contrasted, approaches using frequent, direct measures have proved superior. Teachers can be trained to employ such procedures, and the procedures are not as time-consuming as might be thought (King, Wesson, & Deno, 1982). Still, though, informal observation is the most often used method for ongoing evaluation of pupil progress. Assignment of grades is the most often used formative evaluation technology.

MIS-STARTS AND MISDIRECTIONS

Educators, psychologists, and researchers have spent a considerable amount of time, effort, and money in attempts to improve the assessment and decision-making process. I argue, however, that much of that effort has been misdirected.

Emphasis on Within-Student Disorders

There is no argument about the fact that large numbers of students fail to profit to the extent thought possible from their educational experiences. There is no argument about whether or not those students need assistance to meet the objectives of schooling. There is, of course, considerable argument about the goals of schooling for students who are struggling and about precisely who should receive education services.

As efforts have been made to gain clarification about these matters, researchers have focused on delineation of the nature of the difficulties experienced by students. Over and over again, we see reported descriptions of specific kinds of handicapped students, comparisons of handicapped students to normal students, and comparisons of categorically grouped students. These approaches probably derived from research in medical settings, where knowledge of symptoms sometimes leads to treatments that relieve adverse symptoms. Yet, the research on students and their characteristics has led to disappointingly few specific implications for instructional intervention.

I have repeatedly argued that the only legitimate purpose for assessment is to improve treatments or interventions for students. I believe this is especially so since 1975, when a zero-demission era was ushered in as part of Public Law 94-142. It used to be the case that we could exclude students from school. It was important to predict the extent to which students would be successful in school, for we could "weed out" those who stood little chance of making it. Now, the prediction orientation makes little sense; we need to engage in measurement technologies that are "integral parts of instruction designed to make a *difference* in the lives of children and not just a prediction about their lives" (Reynolds, 1975b, p. 15).

Few researchers are heeding the cogent advice of Cromwell, Blashfield, and Strauss (1975). They told us that the only valid assessment-intervention paradigm was one in which assessment led directly to interventions with known outcomes. So, not only has the considerable research effort to delineate pupil weaknesses *been* a misdirection; it continues *to be* a misdirection of research efforts.

Students fail to profit *in an environment*: the school curriculum. Research efforts, then, that recognize the interactive nature of failure show considerably more promise for improving the state of affairs than do those that concentrate on delineation of pupil characteristics or weaknesses. In this sense, the approach to assessment recommended by Englemann, Granzin, and Severson (1979) is one that looks like it will produce more payoff than competing efforts. Englemann et al. (1979) argue that we should begin assessment efforts with *instructional diagnosis*.

The Search for Aptitude–Treatment Interactions

Research efforts designed to uncover or demonstrate links between pupil characteristics, traits, or behaviors and the effectiveness of specific instructional approaches have been grossly oversimplified. Ever since experimental psychologists and teachers observed considerable differences in the ways in which individuals learn, researchers have been trying to demonstrate aptitude–treatment interactions. The numerous efforts to link instructional intervention to assessment results have been disappointing (Bracht, 1970; Ysseldyke, 1973, 1977, 1978, 1979). We have oversimplified the process.

The effectiveness of any instructional intervention is always the result of at least five factors in complex interaction: the characteristics of the student, the nature of the intervention, the characteristics of the teacher, the setting, and the particular kind of behavior change one is trying to bring about. Researchers have focused their efforts on documentation of pupil aptitude — nature of intervention interactions. The efforts are too limited, yet attempts to demonstrate five-way interactions would be foolhardy.

I think the implication for research and practice is clear. We should concentrate research efforts on development of measurement technologies that will enable us to make better decisions for *individual* students. Attempts to figure out a priori the most appropriate treatment for specific kinds or types of students has been a dead-end effort. It will continue to be one. In practice, we should concentrate more intensively on designing instruction for individuals on the basis of information derived from their progress in specific kinds of interventions (Ysseldyke & Regan, 1980).

Attempts to Reify Unworkable Concepts

Many concepts in special education are proving increasingly unworkable. Nowhere is this more evident than in our attempts to reify the "conditions" we decided were evidenced by individuals who failed in school. Early on, educators decided that large numbers of students failed in school because they were mentally retarded, emotionally disturbed, learning disabled, etc. Researchers have been trying to prove the case ever since.

Research efforts that concentrate on better ways to describe special education conditions or to develop more sophisticated measurement technologies for categorizing students are misdirected. The more difficulty we have in reifying unworkable concepts, the more effort we put into developing more sophisticated ways of doing an unworkable thing (Algozzine & Ysseldyke, 1983).

We need a new set of concepts to guide the delivery of special education services. Our current ones are unworkable. We need a dramatic shift in efforts away from improving categorization to improving instruction (Ysseldyke & Algozzine, 1983).

Research on Handicapped Students

Volumes have been written on research findings on specific kinds or types of handicapped students. I must question the extent to which *any* of that research has validity. To the extent that the findings of research on classification are accurate and generalizable, then research

on classified students has in fact been conducted on unknown groups of students.

DIRECTIONS FOR FUTURE RESEARCH

Assessment data are used to make decisions about students. Or are they? I believe that the research I have touched on in this chapter shows quite clearly that while practitioners gather considerable data for purposes of making decisions about individuals, the data are not often used. I would argue, and have argued elsewhere, that many social, political, and economic factors have more influence than data on the decisions we make. I have argued that special education and the conditions that comprise it are, in fact, whatever society wants them to be, needs them to be, or will pay for. This has major implications for research.

I believe it is time to shift research efforts from discipline research, research designed to add to the knowledge base in a discipline, to policy research, research designed to lead to action. We need to document not only the ways in which social, political and economic factors influence the decision-making process, but also the social, political and economic implications of alternative decision-making approaches.

We should not, however, simply restrict our research efforts to the area of policy. We must facilitate efforts to develop new decision-making methodologies. Such efforts are now under way, labeled *direct instruction*, *direct* and *frequent measurement*, *curriculum-based assessment*, and so forth. They focus on formative evaluation of pupil performance. I do not believe we can and should continue current research efforts to improve categorical practices. The practices and the concepts accompanying them are simply unworkable and will not long be tolerated.

REFERENCES

Algozzine, B., Christenson, S., & Ysseldyke, J. E. (1982). Probabilities associated with the referral to placement process. *Teacher Education and Special Education*, 5, 19–23.

Algozzine, B., & Ysseldyke, J. E. (1981). Special education services for normal students: Better safe than sorry? *Exceptional Children, 48*, 238–243.

Algozzine, B., & Ysseldyke, J. E. (1983). Learning disabilities as a subset of school failure: The over-sophistication of a concept. *Exceptional Children. 50*, 242–246.

Algozzine, B., Ysseldyke, J. E., & Christenson, S. (1983). The influence of teachers' tolerance for specific kinds of behavior on their ratings of a third grade student. *Alberta Journal of Education, 29*, 89–97.

Algozzine, B., Ysseldyke, J. E., & Hill, C. (1982). Psychoeducational decision making as a function of the number of devices administered. *Psychology in the Schools, 19*, 328–334.

American Academy of Pediatrics. (1972). The eye and learning abilities. *Sightsaving Review, 41*.

Arena, J. J. (1969). *Teaching through sensory-motor experiences.* San Rafael, CA: Academic Therapy Publications.

Arter, J. A., & Jenkins, J. R. (1979). Differential diagnosis-prescriptive teaching: A critical appraisal. *Review of Educational Research, 49*, 517–555.

Ayres, A. J. (1972). Improving academic scores through sensory integration. *Journal of Learning Disabilities, 5*, 336–343.

Bannatyne, A. (1969). Diagnosing learning disabilities and writing remedial prescriptions. *Journal of Learning Disabilities, 1*, 242–249.

Barsch, R. H. (1965). *A movigenic curriculum.* Madison, WI: Bureau for Handicapped Children.

Barsch, R. H. (1967). *Achieving perceptual-motor efficiency.* Seattle, WA: Special Child Publications.

Barsch, R. H. (1968). *Enriching perception and cognition.* Seattle, WA: Special Child Publications.

Bateman, B. (1967). Three approaches to diagnosis and educational planning for children with learning disabilities. *Academic Therapy Quarterly, 3*, 11–16.

Becker, W., & Engelmann, S. (1969). *DISTAR.* Chicago, IL: Scott-Foresman.

Bernetta, Sister Mary. (1962). Visual readiness and developmental visual perception for reading. *Journal of Developmental Reading, 5*, 82–86.

Bersoff, D. (1973). Silk purses into sows' ears: The decline of psychological testing and a suggestion for its redemption. *American Psychologist, 28*, 892–899.

Bijou, S. W., & Grimm, J. A. (1972, October). *Behavioral diagnosis and assessment in teaching young handicapped children.* Washington, DC: Bureau of Education for the Handicapped.

Black Caucus. (1974). Position paper at National Planning Conference on Nondiscriminatory Assessment of Handicapped Children. Lexington, KY: Coordinating Office for Regional Resource Centers.

Blanco, R. F. (1972). *Prescriptions for children with learning and adjustment problems.* Springfield, IL: Charles C Thomas, 1972.

Bohannon, R. (1975). *Direct and daily measurement procedures in the identification and treatment of reading behaviors of children in special education.* Unpublished doctoral dissertation, University of Washington, Seattle.

Bracht, G. (1970). Experimental factors related to aptitude–treatment interactions. *Review of Educational Research, 40*, 627–645.

Brophy, J. E., & Good, T. L. (1970). Teachers' communication of differential expectations for children's classroom performance. *Journal of Educational Psychology, 61*, 365–374.

Carnine, D., & Silbert, J. (1979). *Direct instruction reading.* Columbus, OH: Charles E. Merrill.

Cartwright, G. P., Cartwright, C. A., & Ysseldyke, J. E. (1973). Two decision models: Identification and diagnostic teaching of handicapped children in the regular classroom. *Psychology in the Schools, 10*, 4–11.

Christenson, S., Ysseldyke, J. E., & Algozzine, B. (1982). Institutional and external pressures influencing referral decisions. *Psychology in the Schools, 19*, 341–345.

Coleman, H. M. (1968). Visual perception and reading dysfunction. *Journal of Learning Disabilities, 1*, 116–123.

Cone, T. E., & Wilson, L. R. (1981). Quantifying a severe discrepancy: A critical analysis. *Learning Disability Quarterly, 4*, 359–371.

Cromwell, R., Blashfield, R., & Strauss, J. S. (1975). Criteria for classification. In N. Hobbs (Ed.), *Issues in the Classification of Children* (Vol. 1). San Francisco: Jossey-Bass.

Cronbach, L. J., & Furby, L. (1970). How should we measure "change" — or should we? *Psychological Bulletin, 74*, 68–80.

Davis, W. E. (1978). A comparison of teacher referral and pupil self-referral measures relative to perceived school adjustment. *Psychology in the Schools, 15*, 22–26.

Deno, S. (1973). The Seward University Project: A cooperative effort to improve school services and university training. In E. Deno (Ed.), *Instructional alternatives for exceptional children.* Reston, VA: Council for Exceptional Children.

Deno, S., & Mirkin, P. (1977). *Data-based program modification: A manual.* Reston, VA: Council for Exceptional Children.

Dilbard, J. D., Houghton, D. W., & Thomas, D. G. (1972). The effects of optometric care on educable mentally retarded children. *Journal of Optometric Vision Therapy, 3*, 35–57.

Dunn, L. M. (1968). Special education for the mildly retarded — Is much of it justifiable? *Exceptional Children, 35*, 5–22.

Dunsing, J. D., & Kephart, N. C. (1965). Motor

generalizations in space and time. In J. Hellmuth (Ed.), *Learning Disorders*, Vol. 1. Seattle, WA: Special Child Publications.

Dusek, J. B. (1975). Do teachers bias children's learning? *Review of Educational Research, 45,* 661–684.

Eaves, R. C., & McLoughlin, P. (1977). A system's approach for the assessment of the child and his environment: Getting back to basics. *Journal of Special Education, 11,* 99–111.

Engelmann, S., & Carnine, D. (1982). *Theory of instruction.* Chicago: Scott, Foresman & Co.

Engelmann, S., Granzin, A., & Severson, H. (1979). Diagnosing instruction. *Journal of Special Education, 13,* 355–365.

Epps, S., McGue, M., & Ysseldyke, J. E. (1982). Inter-judge agreement in classifying students as learning disabled. *Psychology in the Schools, 19,* 209–220.

Epps, S., Ysseldyke, J. E., & McGue, M. (in press). Differentiating LD and non-LD students: I know one when I see one. *Learning Disability Quarterly.*

Estes, W. K. (1970). *Learning theory and mental development.* New York: Academic Press.

Ewalt, H. W. (1962). Visual performance and its relationship to reading achievement. *Journal of the American Optometric Association, 33,* 828–829.

Ewing, N., & Brecht, R. (1977). Diagnostic/prescriptive instruction: A reconsideration of some issues. *Journal of Special Education, 11,* 323–328.

Farrald, R. R., & Schamber, G. (1973). *A diagnostic and prescriptive technique: Handbook 1: A mainstream approach to identification, assessment and amelioration of learning disabilities.* Sioux Falls, SD: ADAPT Press, Inc.

Ferinden, W. E., Jacobson, S., & Kovalinsky, T. (1969). *Educational interpretation of the Wechsler Intelligence Scale for Children (WISC).* Linden, NJ: Remediation Associates.

Fox, W. L., Egner, A. N., Paolucci, P. F., Perelman, P. F., & McKenzie, H. S. (1973). An introduction to a regular classroom approach to special education. In E. Deno (Ed.), *Instructional alternatives for exceptional children.* Reston, VA: Council for Exceptional Children.

Frostig, M. (1967a). *The relationship of diagnosis to remediation in learning problems.* San Francisco: Rosenburg Foundation.

Frostig, M. (1967b). Testing as a basis for educational therapy. *Journal of Special Education, 2,* 15–34.

Frostig, M. (1972). Visual perception, integrative functioning and academic learning. *Journal of Learning Disabilities, 5,* 1–15.

Frostig, M., & Horne, D. (1964). *The Frostig program for development of visual perception.* Chicago: Follett.

Fuchs, L. S., Fuchs, D., & Warren, L. M. (1982). *Special education practice in evaluating student progress toward goals* (Research Report No. 81). Min-

neapolis: University of Minnesota Institute for Research on Learning Disabilities.

Getman, G. N. (1962). Pre-school perceptual skills: An aid to first grade achievement. *Optometric Weekly, 53,* 1749–1753.

Getman, G. N. (1966a). *How to develop your child's intelligence* (6th ed.). Luverne, MN: Announcer Press.

Getman, G. N. (1966b). The visuomotor complex in the acquisition of learning skills. In J. Hellman (Ed.), *Learning Disabilities* (Vol. 2). Seattle: Special Child Publications.

Getman, G. N. (1972). The mileposts to maturity. *Optometric Weekly, 63,* 321–331.

Gilbert, G. M. (1957). A survey of referral problems in metropolitan child guidance centers. *Journal of Clinical Psychology, 13,* 38–41.

Greenspan, S. B. (1973). The pediatric optometrist as a coordinator of multidisciplinary care. *Journal of the American Optometric Association, 44,* 149–151.

Gregory, M. K. (1977). Sex bias in referrals. *Journal of School Psychology, 15,* 5–8.

Hall, R. V., & Copeland, R. E. (1971, April). *The responsive teaching model: A first step in shaping school personnel as behavioral modification specialists.* Paper presented at the Third Banff International Conference on Behavior Modification.

Hammill, D. (1972). Training of visual perceptual processes. *Journal of Learning Disabilities, 5,* 39–46.

Hammill, D., Goodman, L., & Wiederholt, J. L. (1974). Visual-motor processes: Can we train them? *The Reading Teacher, 27,* 469–478.

Hammill, D. D., & Larsen, S. C. (1974). The effectiveness of psycholinguistic training. *Exceptional Children, 41,* 5–14.

Hammill, D. D., & Larsen, S. C. (1978). The effectiveness of psycholinguistic training: A reaffirmation of position. *Exceptional Children, 44,* 402–417.

Hammill, D. D., Larsen, S. C., Leigh, J., & McNutt, G. (1981). A new definition of learning disabilities. *Learning Disability Quarterly, 4,* 336–342.

Harris, A. J., & Roswell, F. G. (1953). Clinical diagnosis of reading disability. *Journal of Psychology, 36,* 323–340.

Hobbs, N. (Ed.). (1975). *Issues in the classification of children.* San Francisco: Jossey Bass.

Johnson, D. J., & Myklebust, H. R. (1967). *Learning disabilities: Educational principles and practices.* New York: Grune & Stratton.

Kane, M. (1972). Summary report: Experimental program-transitional first grade. *Journal of Optometric Vision Therapy, 3,* 23–29.

Keogh, B. K. (1974). Optometric vision training programs for children with learning disabilities: Review of issues and research. *Journal of Learning Disabilities, 7,* 36–48.

Keogh, B. K. (1983). Classification, compliance,

and confusion. *Annual Review of Learning Disabilities*, *1*, 22.

Kephart, N. C. (1960). *The slow learner in the classroom*. Columbus, OH: Charles E. Merrill.

Kephart, N. C. (1964). Perceptual motor aspects of learning disabilities. *Exceptional Children*, *31*(4), 201–206.

Kephart, N. C. (1971). *The slow learner in the classroom*. Columbus, OH: Charles E. Merrill.

King, R., Wesson, C., & Deno, S. (1982). *Direct and frequent measurement of student performance: Does it take too much time?* (Research Report No. 67). Minneapolis: University of Minnesota Institute for Research on Learning Disabilities.

Kirk, S. A., & Kirk, W. D. (1971). *Psycholinguistic learning disabilities: Diagnosis and remediation*. Urbana, IL: University of Illinois Press.

Kirk, S. A., & McCarthy, J. J. (1961). *The ITPA: An approach to differential diagnosis*. Urbana, IL: University of Illinois Press.

Kirk, S. A., McCarthy, J., & Kirk, W. D. (1968). *Illinois Test of Psycholinguistic Abilities* (rev. ed.). Urbana, IL: University of Illinois Press.

Klein, S., Fenstermacher, G., & Aiken, M. C. (1971). The center's changing evaluation model. *Evaluation Comment*, *2*, 9–12.

Kornblau, B. W., & Keogh, B. K. (1980). Teachers' perceptions and educational decisions. *New directions for exceptional children*, *1*, 87–101.

Larsen, S. C. (1976). Response to James McCarthy. *Journal of Learning Disabilities*, *9*, 334–337.

Larsen, S. C., Rogers, D., & Sowell, V. (1976). The use of selected perceptual tests in differentiating between normal and learning disabled children. *Journal of Learning Disabilities*, *9*, 85–90.

Liberty, K. A. (1972). *Data decisions rules*. Unpublished working paper #20, Regional Resources Center, University of Oregon, Eugene.

Liberty, K. A. (1975). *Decide for progress: Dynamic aims and data decisions*. Seattle: Experimental Education Unit, Child Development and Mental Retardation Center, University of Washington.

Lietz, J. J., & Gregory, M. K. (1978). Pupil race and sex determinants of office and exceptional education referrals. *Educational Research Quarterly*, *32*, 61–66.

Lindsley, O. R. (1964). Direct measurement and prothesis of retarded behavior. *Journal of Education*, *147*, 62–81.

Lindsley, O. R. (1971). Precision teaching in perspective: An interview with Ogden R. Lindsley. *Teaching Exceptional Children*, *3*(3), 114–119.

Lund, K. A., Foster, G. E., & McCall-Perez, F. C. (1978). The effectiveness of psycholinguistic training: A reevaluation. *Exceptional Children*, *44*, 310–319.

Mann, L. (1970). Are we fractionating too much? *Academic Therapy*, *5*, 85–91.

Mann, L. (1971a). Perceptual training revisited: The training of nothing at all. *Rehabilitation Literature*, *32*, 322–335.

Mann, L. (1971b). Psychometric phrenology and the new faculty psychology: The case against ability assessment and training. *Journal of Special Education*, *5*, 3–14.

Mann, L. (1981). *On the trial of process*. New York: Grune & Stratton.

Mann, L. M., & Phillips, W. A. (1967). Fractional practices in special education: A critique. *Exceptional Children*, *33*, 311–317.

Massey, J. O., Sattler, J. M., & Andres, J. R. (1978). *WISC-R scoring criteria*. Palo Alto, CA: Consulting Psychologists Press.

McCarthy, J. J. (1976). A reaction. *Journal of Learning Disabilities*, *9*, 332–334.

McLoughlin, J. A., & Netick, A. (1983). Defining learning disabilities: A new and cooperative direction. *Annual Review of Learning Disabilities*, *1*, 18–20.

Mercer, J. R. (1974). *Labeling the mentally retarded*. Berkeley, CA: University of California Press.

Minskoff, E. (1975). Research on psycholinguistic training: Critique and guidelines. *Exceptional Children*, *42*, 136–144.

Minskoff, E., Wiseman, D. E., & Minskoff, J. G. (1972). *The MWM program for developing language abilities*. Ridgewood, NJ: Educational Performance Associates.

Mirkin, P. K., Deno, S. L., Tindal, J., & Kuehnle, K. (1980). *Formative evaluation: Continued development of data utilization systems* (Research Report No. 23). Minneapolis: University of Minnesota Institute for Research on Learning Disabilities.

Mirkin, P. K., & Potter, M. L. (1982). *A survey of program planning and implementation practices of LD teachers* (Research Report No. 80). Minneapolis: University of Minnesota Institute for Research on Learning Disabilities.

National Education Association. (1979). Teacher opinion poll. *Today's Education*, *68*, 10.

Newcomer, P. L. (1977). Special education services for the "mildly handicapped": Beyond a diagnostic and remedial model. *Journal of Special Education*, *11*, 153–165.

Nicholson, C. A. (1967). A survey of referral problems in 59 Ohio school districts. *Journal of School Psychology*, *4*, 280–286.

Perlmutter, B. F., & Parus, M. V. (1983). Identifying children with learning disabilities: A comparison of diagnostic procedures across school districts. *Learning Disability Quarterly*, *6*, 321–329.

Peter, L. J. *Individual instruction*. (1972). New York: McGraw Hill.

Poland, S. F., Thurlow, M. L., Ysseldyke, J. E., & Mirkin, P. K. (1982). Current psychoeducational assessment and decision-making practices as reported by directors of special education. *Journal of School Psychology*, *20*, 171–179.

Potter, P. (1982). *Application of a decision theory model to eligibility and classification decisions in special education* (Research Report No. 85). Minneapolis: University of Minnesota Institute for Research on Learning Disabilities.

Reynolds, M. C. (1975a). More process than is due. *Theory Into Practice, 14*, 61–68.

Reynolds, M. C. (1975). Trends in special education: Implications for measurement. In W. Hively and M. C. Reynolds (Eds.), *Domain-referenced testing in special education.* Minneapolis, MN: University of Minnesota.

Rice, A. (1962). Rhythmic training and board balancing prepares a child for formal learning. *Nation's Schools, 6*, 72.

Rice, J. P. (1963). Types of problems referred to a central guidance agency at different grade levels. *Personnel and Guidance Journal, 32*, 52–55.

Rimland, B., & Larson, G. E. (1983). Hair mineral analysis and behavior: An analysis of 51 studies. *Annual Review of Learning Disabilities, 1*, 88–96.

Roach, E. G., & Kephart, N. C. (1966). *The Purdue Perceptual Motor Survey.* Columbus, OH: Charles E. Merrill.

Robbins, B., Mercer, J., & Meyers, C. E. (1967). The school as a selecting-labeling system. *Journal of School Psychology, 5*, 270–279.

Rostollan, D. (1980). Domains of data discussed at special education team meetings. In J. E. Ysseldyke, B. Algozzine, & M. L. Thurlow (Eds.), *A naturalistic investigation of special education team meetings* (Research Report #40). Minneapolis: University of Minnesota Institute for Research on Learning Disabilities.

Salvia, J., & Ysseldyke, J. E. (1981). *Assessment in special and remedial education.* Boston: Houghton-Mifflin.

Sarason, S., & Doris, J. (1979). *Educational handicap, public policy, and social history.* New York: Free Press.

Sattler, J. M. (1965). Analysis of functions of the 1960 Stanford-Binet Intelligence Scale, Form L-M. *Journal of Clinical Psychology, 21*, 173–179.

Shepard, L., & Smith, M. L. (1981). *Evaluation of the identifications of perceptual-communicative disorders in Colorado.* Final Report. Boulder: Laboratory of Educational Research, University of Colorado.

Sloat, R. S. (1971). Optometry: What is it worth to education? *Optometric Weekly, 62*, 40–51.

Smead, V. S. (1977). Ability training and task analysis in diagnostic/prescriptive teaching. *Journal of Special Education, 11*, 113–125.

Stephens, T. M. (1976). *Directive teaching of children with learning and behavioral handicaps* (2nd ed.). Columbus, OH: Charles E. Merrill.

Swanson, W. L. (1972). Optometric vision therapy—How successful is it in the treatment of learning disorders? *Journal of Learning Disabilities, 5*, 37–42.

Swartwout, S. (1972). Visual abilities and academic success. *Optometric Weekly, 63*, 1229–1234.

Thorndike, R., & Hagen, E. (1977). *Measurement and evaluation in psychology and education.* New York: Wiley.

Thurlow, M. L., & Ysseldyke, J. E. (1979). Current assessment and decision-making practices in model programs for the learning disabled. *Learning Disability Quarterly, 2*, 15–24.

Thurlow, M., & Ysseldyke, J. E. (1982). Instructional planning: Information collected by school psychologists v. information considered useful by teachers. *Journal of School Psychology, 20*, 3–10.

Valett, R. E. (1964). A clinical profile for the Stanford-Binet. *Journal of School Psychology, 2*, 49–54.

Waugh, R. P. (1975). ITPA: Ballast or bonanza for the school psychologists. *Journal of School Psychology, 13*, 201–208.

Wedell, K. (1970). Diagnosing learning difficulties: A sequential strategy. *Journal of Learning Disabilities, 3*, 311–317.

White, O. R., & Haring, N. G. (1976). *Exceptional teaching.* Columbus, OH: Charles E. Merrill.

White, O. R., & Liberty, K. (1974). *Evaluating the educational process.* Working paper, University of Washington Experimental Education Unit.

Wiseman, D. E. (1970). Remedial education: Global or learning-disability approach? *Academic Therapy, 5*, 165–175.

Yoshida, R. K., Fenton, K. S., Maxwell, J. P., & Kaufman, M. J. (1978). Group decision making in the planning team process: Myth or reality. *Journal of School Psychology, 16*, 237–244.

Ysseldyke, J. E. (1968). *A critical analysis of representative public school psychoeducational referral forms.* Unpublished masters thesis. University of Illinois, Urbana.

Ysseldyke, J. E. (1973). Diagnostic-prescriptive teaching: The search for aptitude-treatment interactions. In L. Mann & D. A. Sabatino (Eds.), *The first review of special education.* New York: Grune & Stratton.

Ysseldyke, J. E. (1977). Aptitude-treatment interaction research with first grade children. *Contemporary Educational Psychology, 2*, 1–9.

Ysseldyke, J. E. (1978). Remediation of ability deficits in adolescents: Some major questions. In L. Mann, L. Goodman, & J. L. Wiederholt (Eds.), *The learning disabled adolescent.* Boston: Houghton-Mifflin.

Ysseldyke, J. E. (1979). Issues in psychoeducational assessment. In G. D. Phye & D. J. Reschly, *School psychology: Perspectives and issues.* New York: Academic Press.

Ysseldyke, J. E. (1983). Current practices in making psychoeducational decisions about learning disabled students. *Annual Review of Learning Disabilities, 1*, 31–38.

Ysseldyke, J. E., & Algozzine, B. (1979). Perspectives on assessment of learning disabled students. *Learning Disability Quarterly, 2*(4), 3–13.

Ysseldyke, J. E., & Algozzine, B. (1982). *Critical issues in special and remedial education.* Boston: Houghton-Mifflin.

Ysseldyke, J. E., & Algozzine, B. (1983). LD or not-LD: That's not the question! *Journal of Learning Disabilities, 16,* 29–31.

Ysseldyke, J. E., & Algozzine, B. (1984). *Introduction to special education.* Boston: Houghton-Mifflin.

Ysseldyke, J. E., Algozzine, B., & Allen, D. (1981). Regular education teacher participation in special education team decision making. *Elementary School Journal,* 160–165.

Ysseldyke, J. E., Algozzine, B., & Epps, S. (1983). A logical and empirical analysis of current practice in classifying students handicapped. *Exceptional Children, 50,* 160–166.

Ysseldyke, J. E., Algozzine, B., Regan, R., & Potter, M. (1980). Technical adequacy of tests used by professionals in simulated decision making. *Psychology in the Schools, 17,* 202–209.

Ysseldyke, J. E., Algozzine, B., Regan, R. R., Potter, P., Richey, L., & Thurlow, M. L. (1980). *Psychoeducational assessment and decision-making: A computer-simulated investigation* (Research Report No. 32). Minneapolis: University of Minnesota Institute for Research on Learning Disabilities.

Ysseldyke, J. E., Algozzine, B., Richey, L. S., & Graden, J. (1982). Declaring students eligible for learning disability services: Why bother with the data? *Learning Disability Quarterly, 5,* 37–44.

Ysseldyke, J. E., Algozzine, B., Rostollan, D., & Shinn, M. (1981). A content analysis of the data presented at special education placement team meetings. *Journal of Clinical Psychology, 37,* 655–662.

Ysseldyke, J. E., Algozzine, B., Shinn, M., & McGue, M. (1982). Similarities and differences between low achievers and students labeled learning disabled. *Journal of Special Education, 16,* 73–85.

Ysseldyke, J. E., Algozzine, B., & Thurlow, M. L. (1980). *A naturalistic investigation of special education team meetings* (Research Report No. 40). Minneapolis: University of Minnesota Institute for Research on Learning Disabilities.

Ysseldyke, J. E., Christenson, S., Pianta, B., & Algozzine, B. (1983). An analysis of teachers' reasons and desired outcomes for students referred for psychoeducational evaluation. *Journal of Psychoeducational Assessment, 1,* 73–83.

Ysseldyke, J. E., Christenson, S., Pianta, B., Thurlow, M. L., & Algozzine, B. (1982). *An analysis of current practices in referring students for psychoeducational evaluation: Implications for change* (Research Report No. 91). Minneapolis: University of Minnesota Institute for Research on Learning Disabilities.

Ysseldyke, J. E., & Mirkin, P. K. (1982). The use of assessment information to plan instructional interventions. In C. Reynolds & T. Gutkin (Eds.), *The handbook of school psychology.* New York: Wiley.

Ysseldyke, J. E., Pianta, B., Christenson, S., Wang, J., & Algozzine, B. (1983). An analysis of pre-referral interventions. *Psychology in the Schools, 20,* 184–190.

Ysseldyke, J. E., & Regan, R. (1980). Nondiscriminatory assessment: A formative model. *Exceptional Children, 46,* 465–466.

Ysseldyke, J. E., & Sabatino, D. (1973). Toward validation of the diagnostic-prescriptive model. *Academic Therapy, 8,* 415–422.

Ysseldyke, J. E., & Salvia, J. A., (1974). Diagnostic-prescriptive teaching: Two models. *Exceptional Children, 41,* 181–186.

Ysseldyke, J. E., & Salvia, J. A. (1980). Methodological considerations in aptitude-treatment interaction research with intact groups. *Diagnostique, 6,* 3–9.

Ysseldyke, J. E., Thurlow, M. L., Graden, J., Wesson, C., Algozzine, B., & Deno, S. (1983). Generalizations from five years of research on assessment and decision making. *Exceptional Education Quarterly, 4,* 75–94.

3 AN ANALYSIS OF EARLY INTERVENTION PROGRAMS: ATTENDANT ISSUES AND FUTURE DIRECTIONS

Diane D. Bricker

Many interventionists hold that the value of early intervention is obvious and has been demonstrated (Hayden & McGinness, 1977); critics, even those predisposed philosophically towards the benefits of early intervention, argue that the efficacy of early intervention efforts still awaits objective verification (Clarke & Clarke, 1976; Gibson & Fields, 1984). In all probability, however, the supporters are too easily convinced of the value and the critics too harsh in their judgement, given current knowledge and resources available for studying program impact.

In addition to the polarization of views about the benefit of early intervention, the field has been crippled by imprecise language. Claims and criticisms tend to be articulated in broad pronouncements that elicit defensive reactions rather than assist in clarifying issues, positions, and evaluation outcomes. For example, statements by Jensen (1969) indicating that compensatory education has been tried and apparently failed led to vigorous counter attacks. Although some responses are carefully reasoned and valuable (e.g., Zigler & Cascione, 1977), other counter arguments lack logic and precision.

The complex array of variables affecting the development of young children requires a compilation of evidence that will enhance our understanding of biological growth factors and the determination of salient environmental variables that may significantly affect developmental outcomes. Understanding the genetic–environment interplay can be compared to weaving a tapestry in which threads emanating from a variety of sources are woven into a pattern. The pattern is influenced by the quality of thread and the weaver's ability to create the conceptualized design. So with children, the outcome is determined by the quality of genetic/biological constitution and by salient environmental determinants (Sameroff & Chandler, 1975).

The purpose of this chapter is to reflect on the state of the art of early intervention while simultaneously recognizing the complexity and multiplicity of variables affecting the young child. The goal is to analyze outcome data from early intervention programs in terms of the programs' impact on enrolled children and their families. This analysis provides a context for examining major issues that require resolution if the field is to make continued progress toward providing more effective intervention programs for at-risk and handicapped infants and children. Specifically, this chapter will present a brief discussion of the historical antecedents of contemporary early intervention efforts. An analysis of selected programs and data on their impact is provided, followed by a discussion of issues that require attention. Finally, projections for the future will be discussed in the context of the contemporary issues set forth.

Although the primary focus of this chapter is to examine early intervention programs designed for the biologically impaired infant and child, selected programs for infants classified as at-risk, for either medical or environmental reasons, will be included for two reasons. First, some of the better controlled investigations have been conducted with at-risk populations. The larger number of children assigned to this category and the more typical behavioral patterns exhibited by the at-risk population permit the use of standard psychometric tools, better controlled designs, and more traditional analysis. In addition, better controlled follow-up studies have been conducted with at-risk populations. Second, there is evidence that if treatment or intervention is not available, many at-risk infants eventually become classified as handicapped children requiring special services (Gottlieb, 1978; Hunt, 1980; Scott & Masi, 1979). For example, a number of investigators (e.g., Heber & Garber, 1975; Ramey & Campbell, 1979) report the test performances of their nonintervention, control subjects from poverty, rural, or metropolitan areas warrant labels of mild to moderate retardation.

THE ARGUMENT FOR EARLY INTERVENTION

Certainly since the introduction of J. Hunt's book, *Intelligence and Experience* (1961), contemporary psychologists and educators have come to acknowledge the importance of the environment on the development of the human organism. For a number of years, many investigators placed such emphasis on environmental variables that the genetic component was over-

looked or, at least, undervalued. Fortunately, the work of investigators such as Sameroff and Chandler (1975) has rekindled interest in the organism-environment interaction. Acknowledgement of genetic limitations with the acceptance that the organism's potential for development can be reduced or enhanced by environmental variables appears the preferred position at present, and this position generates a number of potent theoretical arguments to support early intervention (Sameroff, 1982).

A basic argument for early intervention based on the interactional premise suggests that early learning lays the foundation for subsequent development of more complex behavior (Bricker, Seibert, & Casuso, 1980). Piaget's (1970) theory of early development supports such a position in that he believed that the systematic interaction of early responses with the environment produces increasingly more complex behavior. An underlying assumption of this position is that without the early simple response forms a child does not have the building blocks from which to evolve more complex understanding or knowledge of his or her world. Without systematic early intervention, many handicapped children may not acquire even simple sensorimotor behavior albeit more complex response forms.

This argument in no way suggests the primacy of early experience or a continuing overpowering effect on subsequent development. Rather, in agreement with Clarke and Clarke (1976), early experiences are seen as one segment in the life of the developing organism, and their importance determined, in part, by the child's constitution and subsequent environmental experiences.

A second argument for early intervention concerns the need to provide proper support systems for families and children to inhibit the development of secondary or associated disabilities (Hayden & McGinness, 1977). Many handicapped infants and children are inclined, without proper environmental feedback, to develop a variety of undesirable behaviors (Baumeister & Forehand, 1973; Risley & Wolf, 1966). Such behaviors are not inevitable accompaniments to a handicapping condition but rather result from inappropriate handling. A second aspect of this problem is the apparently irreversible nature of some disabilities, if steps are not taken to correct them during the formative years. For example, without proper exercising and positioning the child with severe spasticity may develop permanent contractures. A hearing impaired child may not learn to use his or her residual hearing unless trained to do so early in life (Horton, 1976). Children with major disabilities may never function completely within the normal range across a number of behavioral domains, but there are data to suggest that such disabled children can be assisted in becoming more adaptive and independent (Bricker, Bailey, & Bruder, 1984; Simeonsson, Cooper, & Scheiner, 1982).

The final argument for early intervention centers on the needs of families who have a handicapped child and appear to undergo considerable stress (Gallagher, Beckman, & Cross, 1983; Roos, 1978). Early intervention may be a valuable resource for parents and siblings in three areas. First, programs can assist families in adjusting to the handicapped infant or child. Second, programs can assist caregivers in acquiring the necessary skills to effectively handle the child at home. Third, programs can assist families in obtaining support such as counseling, social services (e.g., food stamps), appropriate medical assistance, or child care. Without such essential support for families, the probability of alienation from the child is increased with the result that neither child nor family members make or maintain an adequate adjustment to each other. Early intervention programs may be pivotal for many families in the evolution of an acceptable relationship with their handicapped member. Such acceptance should lead to maintaining the handicapped individual in the community and obviate institutionalization.

HISTORICAL BACKGROUND

The crux of examining whether or not early intervention has an effect on handicapped children and their families lies largely in determining what changes can be expected from environmental manipulations. With the organically or structurally impaired child (e.g., the child with Down syndrome, cerebral palsy, hydrocephalus), little can be done to actually change the organism's structural integrity. Manipulation of the nervous, muscular, or skeletal system through drugs or surgical procedures is limited. Consequently, one is left with the option of arranging the environment to assist the disabled infant in acquiring or compensating for the missing behaviors. Compensation can occur by (a) providing some prosthetic device to enable the infant or child to better cope with environmental demands; (b) providing an educational/therapeutic program that will assist the infant or child acquire missing responses or learn substitute responses; or (c) both. From the educational perspective, programs can be designed to assist the handicapped individual learn skills, concepts, or behaviors by presenting the material to be learned in a more systematic manner.

Two investigations conducted before the 1960s offered promise for handicapped children through manipulation of the environment and/or instructional programs: the classic but serendipitous investigation conducted by Skeels and his colleagues (Skeels, 1966) and the pioneer work of Kirk (1958).

According to Kirk (1977), impetus for the landmark Skeels study came from the unprecedented commitment of two "hopelessly" retarded infants to an institution for older retarded persons. A year after their institutionalization, Skeels stumbled upon two active alert 3-year-olds residing in the institution. Upon inquiry, Skeels learned that these children were the "hopelessly" retarded infants. This unexpected outcome led to the design of an experimental investigation. The longitudinal study conducted by Skeels and his colleagues on two groups of infants, in differential environments, produced remarkable findings. Initially, both groups of infants lived in an orphanage and were found to be comparable and generally functioning in the retarded or low normal range at first testing. Thirteen of these infants were placed in an institution for the retarded as "house guests" of a group of retarded females and the ward staff. These 13 children came to constitute the experimental group who, because of marked improvement, were adopted and left the institution. The contrast group was composed of children who remained wards of the state and resided in an institution. The initial differences reported between the experimental and contrast groups were subject to violent attack by Goodenough and her colleagues (cf., Goodenough & Maurer, 1940/1961). These critics were inclined to defend the relative constancy of the IQ and asserted "that the differential patterns of gains and losses upon retest shown by children whose initial IQs fell at the extremes of the distribution is a statistical rather than an educational phenomenon" (Goodenough & Maurer, 1940/1961). In spite of such attacks, Skeels and his coworkers continued to track the progress of the experimental and contrast groups. In a 30-year follow-up study, Skeels (1966) reported that:

> All 13 children in the experimental group were self supporting and none was a ward of an institution, public or private. In the contrast group of 12 children, one had died in adolescence following continued residence in a state institution for the mentally retarded, and four were still wards of institutions, one in a mental hospital, and the other three in institutions for the mentally retarded. In education, the disparity between the two groups was striking. The contrast group completed a median of less than the third grade. The experimental group completed a median of the 12th grade. (p. 55)

As indicated, this investigation has been criticized on methodological and statistical grounds, as well as concerns about the attribution of the difference between groups solely to the children's early experiences. Both Clarke and Clarke (1976) and Ramey and Baker-Ward (1982) point out that the differences are more likely "related to continuing life long environmental changes rather than to early experience alone" (Ramey & Baker-Ward, 1982, p. 277). This conclusion seems warranted, but it does seem pertinent to emphasize that an important part of the experimental children's lives was their early environment and experiences.

A predecessor of current early intervention programs for handicapped children was an investigation conducted some 25 years ago by Kirk (1958). Kirk's intent was to assess the effect of early intervention on a group of retarded preschoolers. The investigation included 81 mentally retarded preschool children aged 3–6 years with IQs that ranged from 45–80. The subjects were from four different groups: a community experimental group in which the children attended a community based preschool program; community contrast group of children who attended no preschool program; an institutional experimental group of children who attended an institutional preschool program; and an institutional contrast group of children who attended no preschool program. Upon completion of the preschool program, the experimental subjects in both the community and institutional preschool groups out-performed the contrast subjects (the differences were greater for the institutionalized subjects). A follow-up after the first year of elementary school found that the initial differences between contrast and experimental community subjects tend to "wash out" either through an acceleration in the contrast subjects and/or limited change in experimental subjects. Nonetheless, Kirk interpreted the findings of his study to be positive:

> The evidence presented indicates that, with reference to mental development, either (a) the deprivation of the children in this experiment displaced their inherent rate of growth one level downward and school experience restored it later, or (b) the first diagnosis represents the inherent rate of growth, and the school experience displaced this rate of growth one level upward. (Kirk, 1958, p. 213)

However, Clarke and Clarke (1977) suggest a somewhat different interpretation or emphasis. The Clarkes argued that the Kirk results, reflecting a gradual fading of differences between the experimental and contrast subjects over time, correctly anticipated the outcomes for the Headstart programs initiated in this country in the 1960s. That is, the provision of preschool education for children residing at a poverty level is doomed to failure without associated attention to the child's larger ecological context and without continued intervention beyond the preschool years. This conclusion was suggested earlier by Blatt and Garfunkel (1969), based on the analyses of their data from a well controlled preschool intervention study with children from low-income homes. A group of 59 preschool-age children were randomly assigned to experimental and nonexperimental groups. The experimental group attended a structured intervention program while the non-experimental group did not. Extensive evaluation of the children's performances found that

> disadvantaged children are influenced more by the home setting than by the external manipulation of their school environment. In light of what we believe to have been the face validity of an enriched preschool program, the inability of this program to produce measurable differences between experimental and nonexperimental children causes us to suggest that it is not enough to provide preschool disadvantaged children with an enriched educational opportunity. (Blatt & Garfunkel, 1969, p. 119-120)

This conclusion has been echoed more recently by Bronfenbrenner (1975).

Many of the investigations that provided the historical roots for contemporary intervention efforts can be criticized on methodological grounds, which may render them scientifically questionable. However, their impact on the development of social policy and their influence on intervention programs developed during the 1970s has been significant.

CONTEMPORARY PROGRAMS

There have been major developments in early intervention programs since the early 1970s and these have been directed toward two populations: biologically impaired children and children at-risk for medical or environmental reasons. The distinction between these two populations is important. The biologically impaired child has clear evidence of some significant structural or behavioral deficit or deficiency, usually identifiable early in life. This group includes children with genetic abnormalities (e.g., Down syndrome), metabolic

disorders (e.g., phenylketonuria), neurological disorders (e.g., cerebral palsy) and sensory impairments. The children classified as at-risk for medical and/or environmental reasons include those who were born premature or suffered some medical difficulty early in life (e.g., respiratory distress syndrome), have caregivers with questionable competency (e.g., teenage mothers), or come from an abusive/neglecting environment. It is well for the reader to acknowledge the distinctions between these populations in terms of etiology, homogeneity, incidence, prognosis, and the possible need for different approaches to intervention.

The contemporary intervention programs reviewed in this chapter were included only if they met the following criteria: (a) objective outcome data were presented; (b) the results were published in generally accessible sources (e.g., journals or books rather than inhouse reports); and (c) the intervention efforts used formalized approaches with more than one child. It is important to note that the review of the intervention efforts focused on children medically and environmentally at risk includes only representative studies and is not comprehensive.

Programs for Children with Down Syndrome

The biologically impaired population receiving considerable attention from intervention researchers is the children with Down syndrome. This population holds appeal because the majority of these children: (a) are identifiable at birth; (b) have a common genetic aberration (trisomy 21); and (c) constitute the largest population with a specific genetic abnormality (Hayden & Beck, 1982). These commonalities have led to the conclusion that Down syndrome individuals are a homogenous population, consequently treatment effects on individuals or subgroups have been largely ignored. This tendency probably has masked a wide range of variability in this population (LaVeck & Brehm, 1978). Data on the Down syndrome infant has indicated ranges in intellectual impairment from mild to severe

(Bricker & Carlson, 1982; Bricker & Sheehan, 1981), interactional differences (Cicchetti & Sroufe, 1976) and differences in motor development and tone (Harris, 1981). In addition, many of these youngsters have heart defects, hearing impairments, and other serious difficulties that interfere with development. Such defects and population variability affect the outcome of treatment; however, as we shall see, intervention researchers appear to have given little attention to these important variables.

Early in the 1970s, Alice Hayden and her colleagues began a project that produced a decade of information and material on the child with Down syndrome (Dmitriev, 1979; Hayden & Dmitriev, 1975; Hayden & Haring, 1976; Hayden & Haring, 1977). In 1977, Hayden and Haring reported program impact data on three groups of Down syndrome children: those involved in the Model Preschool Project ($N = 53$); those who formerly attended the program but were now in public schools ($N = 13$); and those who did not participate in the early intervention project ($N = 28$). Demographics for the three groups were similar; however, the age ranges for the three groups differed: model preschool group ranged from 20–78 months of age (median 42 months); graduates ranged from 72–118 months of age (median 96 months); and nonparticipants 70–162 months of age (median 118 months). Unfortunately, the analysis of outcome data is difficult to interpret because of the age discrepancies in the three groups. When comparing the performances on the Down Syndrome Performance Inventory of model program children with nonparticipating children matched for age using a cross-sectional analysis, it appears that the model program children initially functioned higher and maintained this advantage. Further analysis, in which comparisons were made on rates of development, appear to indicate that the rate declines for the model program children and increases for the nonparticipating children. A final analysis conducted between performance level and rates of progress are interpreted by Hayden and Haring to indicate the value of early intervention. Alter-

native interpretations of these analyses are less favorable. First, the rates of growth reported for the model population often exceed those of a normal population, which renders the Down Syndrome Performance Inventory suspect. Second, the most interpretable data indicate, as the authors themselves note, "that the model preschool program is not changing the basic developmental patterns of its children, but simply maintains the same developmental patterns at a higher overall rate" (p. 134). It seems plausible that a selection factor was operating. That is, more concerned caregivers sought early programming for their child—and this early advantage was maintained over time. Whether the model program was instrumental in creating and maintaining such differences is unanswerable with the available data.

An investigation conducted by Ludlow and Allen (1979) reflects a similar phenomena. In this study, the progress of three groups of children with Down syndrome was compared over a 10-year period. Group A ($N = 72$) was composed of children living at home who attended at least two years of preschool before their fifth birthday and whose parents received counseling. Group B ($N = 79$) was composed of children living at home who had no preschool experience and whose families received no counseling. Group C ($N = 33$) was composed of children with Down syndrome placed in a residential placement before their second birthday. Using the Griffiths Scale, the children's development was compared from birth to 10 years. Testing the children at the same age was not possible and thus interpretation of scores was required. A rapid decline in development for all groups during the first three years was reported. For Group A, development continued to decline slightly until age 10. For Group B, development declined until age 5 and then stabilized until age 10. For Group C, the initial sharp decline was modified but the downward trend occurred at age 10. Although the shapes of the curves for the groups are similar, Group A scored approximately 10 IQ points higher initially and maintained this superiority over Group B until approximately age 8. The mean difference in Group C's performance dropped from 10 IQ points initially to approximately 23 IQ points by age 10 when compared with Group A. Similar though less dramatic differences are reported on the Stanford-Binet. A measure of personal-social development and speech development found Group A functioning significantly better than Groups B and C. Perhaps the most significant finding reported was that the percentage of Group A children attending public schools at ages 5 and 10 was much higher than for Group B children.

These optimistic outcomes should be tempered by several factors. First, the initial superior performance of Group A (in the range of 10+ IQ points) strongly suggests these children may have come from a more concerned, responsive home environment. Ludlow and Allen suggest this may not be so because no selection was made in terms of family/children included in the early intervention and counseling. Second, Groups A, B, and C "showed remarkable homogeneity on the variables examined (e.g., social class, parent education, etc.)." The investigators explain the early difference as the probable effect of the early programming and counseling. Nonetheless, although the program did not discriminate or select, the parents themselves may have. Another potential contaminant recognized again by the investigators was the possibility of biased testing in that the investigators did a significant portion of the assessments.

Addressing the same issue, the effects of early training on children with Down syndrome, Aronson and Fallstrom (1977) conducted a less global, better controlled investigation. Sixteen children with Down syndrome, ranging in age from 21–69 months, living in a small residential home, were matched for CA and sex and divided into training and no-training groups. Although the investigators were unable to match individual children for MA, the mean MAs for each group was 20.6 months. All children participated in a preschool program, and the training group received an additional 15 minutes to 1 hour of specialized training twice a week for 18 months. The children were tested every 6 months during this period plus were given a follow-up test 12 months after training was completed. The Griffiths Scale revealed an average increase in MA of 10.5 months for the trained group and 3.5 months for the controls, a reliable difference. The follow-up found no statistically significant differences between groups; however, this comparison was marred because one pair was not included, due to the death of a child, and eight of the children had moved to other institutions. Determining the effect of subject attribution is impossible, but nonetheless, when comparing the performances of the remaining matched pairs, the child receiving the training out-performed the control in six out of seven pairs.

Clunies-Ross (1979) assessed the impact of a structured intervention program on three groups of infants with Down syndrome. The groups were composed of children from successive yearly intakes into the program (in 1976, $N = 16$, mean CA = 16.2 months; in 1977, $N = 13$, mean CA = 15.5 months; in 1978, $N = 7$, mean CA = 11.2 months). In addition to the structured classroom program for the infants, parents were required to attend a 10-week course focused on child development and management. The children were assessed at 4-month intervals using the Early Intervention Development Profile (Rogers, D'Eugenio, Brown, Donovan, & Lynch, 1977); other measures were used periodically. Data were reported for 6 test points for the 1976 group, 4 test points for the 1977 group, and 2 test points for the 1978 group. A review of these data indicate steady progress for each group in similar increments over test periods. The 1978 group, for which training was begun earliest, shows the highest developmental index (DI). To attempt to illuminate this finding Clunies-Ross (1979) performed a second analysis. Eight children from each successive enrollment year with at least four completed test periods were assigned to a birth–11-month, 12–23-month, or over-24-month group, depending upon their age at enrollment. The performances of the eight children in each of these age groups was then compared. This comparison revealed the DI of the youngest group was initially highest. Perhaps the most important aspect of these data are the consistent reports of accelerating development, which, as the investigator notes, is in direct conflict with much of the previous reported data on the child with Down syndrome. This is of particular interest because of confirmed diagnosis of trisomy 21 in all but one of the subjects, who was a translocation.

Hanson (1976, 1977) conducted an intervention program similar to that of Clunies-Ross. The intervention was structured, directed towards building specific skills, and parents were included as an integral part of the program; however, the Hanson project delivered services in the home. The interventionist also kept systematic data on the infant's acquisition of developmental milestones. The data were then compared with developmental data on normal infants and home-reared infants with Down syndrome not enrolled in early intervention programs. "These comparisons show that, in general, infants in the intervention program achieved developmental milestones at a slightly later age than the norms (i.e., normal infants) but consistently earlier than the Down syndrome infants not involved in an intervention program" (Hanson & Schwarz, 1978). The differences reported for the intervention infants and the nonintervention infants with Down syndrome are quite dramatic. In some areas for example, a mean difference of 10 months when 50% of the intervention infants could drink unassisted from a cup and a mean difference of 7 months for independent walking was reported. In other areas, differences were minimal. Direct comparisons between investigations conducted in different settings must be made carefully. The use of differential criteria for attainment of the milestone behaviors could significantly shift the outcomes.

Two recent intervention studies of infants with Down syndrome have yielded less optimistic outcomes. Piper and Pless (1980) recruited 37 infants with Down syndrome under the age of 24 months. Twenty-one infants were assigned to the experimental group, while the remaining 16 infants composed the control group. Assignment to groups was made on the basis of referral dates. The experimental infants received center-based biweekly, 1 hour

therapy sessions. Stimulation activities were demonstrated to the parents. At the initiation of the intervention program the Griffith Mental Development Scales and the Home Observation for Measurement of the Environment Inventory (Caldwell, 1978) were administered and were administered again, 6 months later, at the program's termination. A discriminant analysis found the experimental and control groups to be reliably different only on one subscale of the Home Inventory. Change scores from pre- to posttest were not significantly different for the experimental and control groups; however, although mean developmental quotients declined for both groups over the 6 month period, the control group declined less. Piper and Pless acknowledged that this investigation has some limitation. For example, the experimental and control subjects were assessed at different times of the year, which may have produced a bias. In addition, the length of intervention, its intensity, and its location may have affected the outcome. Finally, Piper and Pless were not able to determine the frequency or fidelity with which the parents conducted the prescribed therapy. This investigation has a number of problems; for example, as noted by Bricker, Carlson, and Schwarz (1981), an infant may have received as little as 12 hours of training during a 6 month period. Furthermore, the concordance between the intervention and the chosen outcome measure seems questionable. In the Clunies-Ross (1979) and Hanson (1977) investigations, the length of intervention was considerably longer, the content more comprehensive, and the measurement instruments more relevant to the focus of training. Finally, Piper and Pless did not specify the genetic pedigrees for their infants with Down syndrome, which may have had an influence on the outcomes.

A more focused intervention project was conducted and reported by Harris (1981) in which 20 infants with Down syndrome, ranging in age from 2.7–21.5 months, were provided neurodevelopmental therapy. The Bayley Scale of Infant Development (Bayley, 1969) and the Peabody Developmental Motor Scales (Folio & DuBose, 1974) were administered before and after treatment. Based on the initial assessment, individual neurodevelopment treatment plans were developed for each infant. Equivalent groups of infants were formed then randomly assigned to a treatment or no-treatment group. Forty-minute therapy sessions were conducted three times per week in the infant's home (except for one child) for a period of 9 weeks. The no-treatment infants were enrolled in early intervention programs. A t-test comparison found no differences between groups on the Bayley and the Peabody Gross Motor Scale. There was, however, a statistically reliable difference between groups on the attainment of the treatment objectives. At first glance, these findings might seem inconsistent but probably are not, because treatment was focused on specific objectives and only a few items on the Bayley or Peabody tests reflected the treatment emphasis.

An extensive report on an early intervention program has been provided by Kysela and his colleagues (Kysela, Hillyard, McDonald, & Ahlster-Taylor, 1981). This program had a home-based component that provided educational services for 22 infants who had a mean age of 13.5 months at the initiation of the program. Nineteen of these infants had Down syndrome. The center-based component served eight toddlers with Down syndrome, whose mean age was 28.4 months upon entry into the program. Parents involved in the home-based component were required to complete a formal training program, followed by a home specialist visiting the families weekly or biweekly. The toddlers attended a half-day session 4 or 5 days per week. The investigators provided a detailed description of the conceptual and programmatic aspects of the program.

Results for the home-trained infants and center-based toddlers are reported in terms of progress in the expressive and receptive language program (a primary training target for all infants). These data are difficult to summarize; however Kysela et al. (1981) suggest the results indicate the children "acquire complex language skills with a rapid rate of learning and very few errors" (p. 370).

A second form of evaluation included administering the Bayley Scales of Infant Development, the Stanford-Binet (for older children), and the Reynell Developmental Language Scales (Reynell, 1969). These measures were administered three times over the first 14 months of the project with test intervals of approximately 6–9 months. The children's scores on these instruments were converted to developmental ratios because many of the children scored below the available test norms. The mental ages and developmental ratios increased for both the home and center groups across the three test period, however the changes were statistically significant for only the home group between Test 1 and 2. The overall test trend for the center group approached significance ($p. < 10$). Results from the Reynell Language Scales were reported separately for the expressive and comprehension sections. On the expressive section, the home group showed no significant change over test periods while a significant effect was found for the center group. However, the expressive ratios for the home children were initially significantly higher and no decline in these ratios occurred, while the center group showed a gain in expressive ratios over the three test periods. In the area of comprehension, both groups showed reliable changes from the first test to later tests. Again the comprehension ratios for the home group exceeded those of the center group. On the whole these data indicate that the program had a positive effect on the participating children even though as the investigators note, controls were unavailable for comparison purposes.

In 1968, Rynders and Horrobin (1975, 1980) initiated a "family-center" early intervention project for infants with Down syndrome. From the point of referral until 30 months of age, the infant received instruction conducted in the infant's home, with daily, structured play sessions. Upon reaching 30 months of age, the child was enrolled in a preschool program. This program focussed on concept utilization and communication by the child. At age 5 years, the children moved into a public school program.

To assess the impact of the program, Rynders and Horrobin (1980) created a distal control group. Eighteen control and 17 experimental children, all were trisomy 21, were matched on several demographic and physical variables. Comparisons were made at 60 months, using the Boehm Test of Basic Concepts, an experimental language sampling instrument, the Stanford-Binet, and an adapted version of the Bruininks-Oseretsky Motor Test. Interestingly, these investigators report no differences between the control and experimental subjects on the language measure and the Boehm test, but reliable differences were found favoring the experimental subjects on the Binet and Bruininks-Oseretsky test. These findings were somewhat unexpected because the focus of the experimental program had been on concept formation and communication. The measure chosen to sample these areas did not reflect superiority of performance by the experimental subjects. Rather the experimental subjects out-performed the controls on the more global measures of intelligence and motor behavior.

This investigation is one of the better controlled investigations of early intervention. Although random assignment of control and experimental subjects was not possible, an effort was made to recruit a group of distal controls who looked similar to the intervention subjects on a number of important variables. Importantly, these infants did not perform differently on the Bayley Scales at 12 months of age but did diverge on an IQ measure at 60 months. Similar results were reported by Connolly, Morgan, Russell, and Richardson (1980), who compared two groups of children with Down syndrome matched on CA and parental education. The group participating in an early intervention program out-performed the nonintervention group on measures of IQ and SQ.

Programs for Biologically Impaired Non-Down Syndrome Children

Shifting from intervention projects focused exclusively on the child with Down syndrome, a sizeable descriptive literature is available. Most of these reports tend to be descriptive and provide little material for objective evaluation of program impact. However, a few studies are available that provide limited, if not totally satisfactory, objective information aspects of the program's impact.

In 1975, an early intervention program was begun at the University of Miami (Bricker & Dow, 1980). The focus of this program was on the severely and profoundly handicapped child from birth to 5 years of age. During the 3 years of this program, 50 children met the criteria for inclusion in the evaluation analysis. Of these 50 children, 35 were classified as severely/profoundly retarded, 13 moderately retarded, and 2 mild or not retarded (but having severe motor disabilities). These children attended a daily, full day, center based program. The program was structured to assist each child in acquiring critical skills in the areas of motor, communication, social, self-help, and cognitive development. Daily or weekly probe data were gathered on individual children's progress toward specific objectives. For an overall assessment of the program's impact, the Uniform Performance Assessment System (White, Edgar, & Haring, 1978) was administered. A correlated t-test comparison of pretest and posttest performance indicated a significant improvement ($p < 001$) for each of the four developmental domains and for the overall score in terms of the percent of items passed.

Given the serious problems of this population, these findings were encouraging even though adequate controls were lacking. In addition, upon graduation from this program, 88% of these children were placed in the public school, at a time before P.L. 94-142 was systematically enforced.

Bricker (1981) and Bricker and Sheehan (1981) reported findings from a project at the University of Oregon. During Years 2 and 3 of the project, the Bayley Scales of Infant Development were administered to 18 (mean CA = 20 months) and 17 (mean CA = 15.7 months) infants, respectively, in the fall and again in the spring. Because a number of children scored below 50, index comparisons were not possible, therefore mental age and psychomotor age were used. The analysis revealed a reliable difference from pretest to posttest for the entire groups as well as for subgroup analyses of infants classified as mild, moderately, and severely handicapped (with the exception of two subgroups). The McCarthy Scales of Children's Abilities (McCarthy, 1972) was used with children whose CA exceeded 30 months. Twenty-four children (mean CA = 46.8 months) were included in the Year 2 analysis, while 32 children (mean CA = 45.9 months) were included in the Year 3 analysis. The pre–post comparison using the General Cognitive Index and mental age were significantly different. In addition, the subgroup analyses for Years 2 and 3 were significant except on the GCI for mild and moderate groups and MA for severe groups for Year 3. Two criterion-referenced instruments were used: the Uniform Performance Assessment System (White et al., 1978) and the Student Progress Record (Oregon State Mental Health, 1977). All pre–post comparisons using these two measures for Years 2 and 3 were significant.

This investigation can be criticized because it lacked adequate controls; however, the uniformity of results across years and across instruments suggests the reported change was a real phenomenon. Whether such change would have occurred without the benefit of an early intervention program seems remote but must remain a plausible possibility.

A project described by Rosen-Morris and Sitkei (1981) is similar in many ways to the Bricker and Dow (1980) investigation, in that a highly structured classroom program was developed for severely handicapped infants and young children. Subjects in the Rosen-Morris project ranged in age from 18 months to 6 years. Approximately 50% of the children had cerebral palsy while the remainder had a combination of sensory impairments, Down syndrome, and epilepsy. Three measures were used to assess program impact: the Bayley Scales of Infant Development, the Student Progress Record, and the Preschool Attainment Record. Testing was done in the fall, then 9 months later. Bayley mental and motor age equivalency scores are reported on 11 children. A t-test on the raw score indicated a reliable change. Thirty students were included in the pre–post analysis of the Student Progress

Record and Preschool Attainment Record. The results indicated a significant change on both measures. Given the nature of the target population (i.e., severely handicapped), the uniformly positive outcomes are encouraging; however, qualification of these results are necessary. First, the investigators indicated the need to adapt presentation of the Bayley items. Although this undoubtedly was necessary, it is unclear how such modifications affected the results. Also, the t-test appears to have been computed on the raw scores rather than the age equivalencies. Finally, although the differences were reported as significant, the actual change in scores or age equivalencies are minimal. This small percentage change was true for the Bricker and Dow (1980) investigation as well. A relevant question then becomes how much change is necessary for the effect to be considered educationally significant?

The Portage Project (Shearer & Shearer, 1976) was similar to the Bricker (1981) project but with some important differences. Perhaps the most salient difference was the delivery of educational services in the home rather than in a center. A home teacher visited participating families for 1.5 hours per week. An individual program was developed and the teacher instructed the parents in its implementation. Child progress was monitored through the use of activity charts and progress reports that parents completed weekly. Unfortunately, general evaluation results were only summarized. Shearer and Shearer (1976) report data from the Cattell Infant Test and the Stanford-Binet indicated that, "The average child in the Project gained 15 months in an 8 month period, as measured by these pre–post assessment tools." A second analysis entailed a comparison between a group of children enrolled in the Portage Project and a group of randomly selected children from a program for low-income children. The Binet, Cattell, Alpern-Boll Developmental Profile and the Gesell Developmental Schedules were administered before and after to both groups. "A multiple analysis of covariance was used to control for IQ, practice effect, and age." Portage project children were reported to have made significantly greater gains in mental age, IQ, language, academic and socialization skills. In another article, Shearer and Shearer (1972) reported significant mean IQ gains on the Binet and Alpern-Boll Tests when "children served as their own control." The lack of specificity in terms of the reported results make evaluation difficult. The number of children for whom the evaluation data are presented is not specified nor is the time interval for test administration. The nature of the analysis is described in only the most global fashion. However, Revill and Blunden (1979) also reported positive outcomes when employing the Portage model with a diverse group of 19 handicapped children and their families. The subjects served as their own control and the intervention began after a 2-month baseline period. Although outcomes were variable, the children showed more progress on the Griffith scale following intervention.

Soboloff (1981) reported a project in which 50 cerebral-palsied children seen in a clinic from 1952–1965, but not enrolled in any early intervention program, were compared with 50 cerebral-palsied children seen between 1965–1978 and enrolled in an early intervention program. No systematic attempt was made to match these two groups, instead individuals with complete clinic records were included in the comparison. Records of the 100 children were evaluated independently by an orthopedic surgeon, a physical therapist, a nursery school teacher, and a speech therapist. A number of comparisons were made. First, the percentage of children having some form of corrective surgery was examined and the results indicated that, in the group who had early intervention, 19% had surgery while only 9% of the nonintervention group had surgery. Second, the records indicated that the early intervention group developed mobility and ambulation earlier. Comparison of family reactions also favored the early intervention group. Finally, the number of individuals from the two groups functioning in normal social settings (mainstreamed) were not different. These findings led Soboloff (1981) to conclude, "In the present study there was no question that early stimulation was effective" (p. 265). How-

ever, this conclusion warrants caution for several reasons. A number of significant changes in treatment variables could have occurred between the period of time from which the two samples were drawn. In addition, the type of cerebral palsy in the two groups differed. Finally, the study was confounded by age, in that therapy was begun for the early intervention group considerably earlier than for the comparison groups. This difference alone could have accounted for the discrepancies reported between the groups. Nonetheless, this investigation is one of the few attempts to evaluate the impact of early intervention on a population of motorically impaired children.

Preschool programs for sensory impaired children can be found in most public schools and yet objective documentation of program impact is limited. Simmons-Martin (1981) reported outcome data on 44 deaf children who entered an early intervention program at an average age of 26 months. The Scales of Early Communication Skills were used to evaluate child progress. The children were given the measure twice a year and all children were tested over a $2\frac{1}{2}$ year span receiving five separate communication skill ratings. Simmons-Martin reported that across these five ratings the children's performance reliably improved. Unfortunately, one has no way to link this change directly to program impact rather than maturation or other environmental variables.

Horton (1976) described two projects developed at the Mama Lere Home that also focused on hearing impaired children. In the first study, she reported on three groups of children who were compared on a language competence measure while in the second grade. Group 1 included six hearing impaired children and their parents who had participated in the Mama Lere Home intervention program and were fitted with a hearing aid before age 3. The five hearing impaired children included in Group 2 had not participated in the Mama Lere Home program, but had hearing aids fitted after age 3 and their parents received no formal instruction. Group 3 included six hearing second grade children. The results indicated language competence for Group 1 was similar to that for Group 3 while the performance of Group 2 was significantly different from Groups 1 and 3. Although the severity of hearing loss for Groups 1 and 2 was similar, other differences make the cautious interpretation of these results necessary. First, no mention is made of possible selection factors that may have been operable in the composition of Groups 1 and 2. Further, how Groups 1 and 2 children were selected for inclusion in the comparison was not explained.

The second study described by Horton (1976) entailed comparing the mean percentile ranks on the Metropolitan Achievement Test of six hearing impaired children who attended the Mama Lere program with 53 normal-hearing second grade children. There was a difference in the mean percentile ranks for math scores of approximately 25 points favoring the normal hearing children; however, the mean percentile ranks for reading skills "were virtually equivalent" for the two populations.

A longitudinal study of ten blind infants provides limited comparative data on this population (Fraiberg, 1975). The intervention focused on providing support and guidance for parents as well as techniques for assisting the infant in acquiring adaptive behavior. Homes were visited twice per month and narrative records kept on the infant's progress. These records of behavioral progress were compared with norms reported in a previous study of 66 blind infants on select items in which the criteria used to determine successful acquisition were similar (Adelson & Fraiberg, 1975). On these items, which represent important bench marks (e.g., sits, stands, walks), the early intervention group reached criteria ahead of the comparison group. For early occurring responses, a difference of 2 months was reported but this difference increased over time until a 7–13 month difference separated the groups. As the investigators noted, such a comparison must be carefully qualified; however, the differences in the acquisition of later motor skills were so dramatic as to strongly suggest a program impact.

Programs for At-Risk Children

For reasons discussed earlier, better controlled intervention studies have been conducted on populations of at-risk children than on the biological impaired children. Four of these programs have been selected for discussion. Each program was chosen because it represented a specific population (e.g., premature, low-income), was a well-controlled study, and offered a different perspective on the effects of early intervention.

Scarr-Salapatek and Williams (1973) randomly assigned 30 premature (mean gestation 32 weeks), low-birth weight infants (1300–1800 grams) born to young black mothers from poverty circumstances to an experimental ($N = 16$) and control group ($N = 15$). The experimental infants were placed in a special nursery and were provided designed stimulation activities (mobiles in the isolettes, extra handling). The controls received standard care for low-birth weight infants. After discharge, a visitor made weekly visits to the homes of the experimental infants. Systematic input on handling and stimulation were provided to the mother. A follow-up at 1 year tested 9 control (4 children were lost and 2 families refused to bring the infant in for testing) and 15 experimental subjects with the Cattell Infant Intelligence Scale. The results indicated the experimental group's performance was near normal levels and significantly different from the control infants. The random assignment and independent assessment leave little doubt, as the authors conclude, that this early intervention program produced a significant advantage in the behavioral functioning of the participating infants. An obvious concern with this investigation is the attrition in the control group.

The Scarr-Salapatek and Williams (1973) investigation confounded the variables of poverty and low-birth weight. An investigation by Leib, Benfield and Guidubaldi (1980) compared a special neonatal treatment using a population of preterm infants from white middle class homes. Twenty-eight preterm infants (mean gestation age = 32 weeks) were assigned to a control or experimental group. No significant differences were found between the groups prior to treatment. Treatment consisted of placing a mobile in the isolette, tactile/kinesthetic stimulation during feedings, and auditory stimulation (playing a music box). The control group received standard nursery care. The Brazelton scales were administered prior to treatment and prior to discharge. The experimental infants performed significantly better on items reflecting interactive processes but were not different from the controls on motor and organizational processes. In addition, no significant differences in weight gain were found between groups. At 6 months, the Bayley Scales of Infant Development were administered. The treated infants' developmental status on the mental and motor scale was significantly higher than the untreated infants.

A sizeable number of early intervention programs for infants or children from low-income families have been reported in the literature (e.g., Fowler, 1975; Gray, Ramsey, & Klaus, 1981; Karnes, Schwedel, Lewis, Ratts, & Esry, 1981; Heber & Garber, 1975; Madden, Levenstein, & Levenstein, 1976). A number of excellent reviews of these programs exist (Bronfenbrenner, 1974; Beller, 1979) and thus only one representative program will be discussed here.

Perhaps the most thoroughly researched project on the effects of early intervention on infants from poverty circumstances has been conducted by Ramey and his colleagues (Ramey & Campbell, 1979; Ramey, Farran, & Campbell, 1979). Four yearly cohorts of 121 biological normal infants from low-income homes were randomly assigned to experimental or control groups. The experimental children attended a day-care program with a comprehensive curriculum. Attendance in the program began by 3 months of age and the infants attended full-time, 5 days per week, 50 weeks per year. The Bayley Scales were used until the infants were 18 months old, then the Stanford-Binet, McCarthy Scales, and Wechsler Preschool Scale were used from 24–60 months. The major goal of this project "has been the prevention of a decline in intellectual development in the experimental group of high-risk children" (Ramey & Campbell, 1979, p. 14). At 12 months, no differences between groups was found on the Bayley, but from then on significant differences in the range of 10–15 IQ points have been reported between control and experimental groups. These investigators also report differences in language development and social confidence in favor of the experimental children (Ramey, MacPhee, & Yeates, 1983).

Hunt (1980) provides a fascinating description of an early intervention project conducted in an orphanage in Tehran. For ethical reasons, this project had no simultaneous controls but rather looked at the effect of social and environmental changes by noting the ages the infants acquired selected behaviors. The foundling infants were studied in groups or "waves" for successive years. The first wave ($N = 150$) received the usual institutional care and were tested routinely until age three. The second and third waves ($N = 10$) received "human enrichment," in which the infant–caregiver ratio was reduced and the staff responded to the infants as they deemed appropriate. The fourth wave ($N = 20$) replicated the second wave but was implemented with more care. Wave five ($N = 11$) received human enrichment but the staff was trained to deliver systematic intervention. Testing with the Uzgiris–Hunt Scales (1975) indicated that each successive intervention subsequent to wave two hastened development of the infants with wave five intervention producing the greatest effect. Hunt also noted qualitative differences in language and social-responsiveness in favor of wave five infants.

Follow-up of Contemporary Programs

Evaluation of long-term effects of early intervention programs with handicapped children are limited. There are probably two explanations. First, the conduct of longitudinal research is difficult and costly. Second, if one accepts the perspective that the developing child is affected at each stage in life and that hundreds of variables intercede between childhood and later life, there might be little reason to expect an early advantage to be maintained over time.

Descriptions of follow-up studies by Field, Dempsey, and Shuman; Sigman, Cohen and Forsythe; Hunt; and Caputo, Goldstein and Taub contained in an edited volume by Friedman and Sigman (1981) provide a rich source of longitudinal data on sick, premature, and low-birth weight children. Sameroff (1981) has summarized the findings of these four investigations. First, by entry into school, many at-risk children have developed problems. Second, "The single most potent factor influencing developmental outcome turns out to be the cultural environment of the child, as expressed in socioeconomic status and parental educational level" (Sameroff, 1981, p. 342). This latter finding provides powerful support for early intervention efforts to (a) reinforce families already providing an enriching environment for the infant and (b) assist parents who provide unsatisfactory physical and social environments in acquiring more facilitative strategies.

Apart from the Skeels (1966) report, the most impressive contemporary longitudinal study of children is the consortium effort directed by Irving Lazar. "In 1976, 12 investigators who had independently designed and implemented infant and preschool programs in the 1960s, pooled their original data and conducted a collaborative follow-up of the original subjects" (Lazar, Darlington, Murray, Royce, & Snipper, 1982). This collaborative effort which included the work of Beller, the Deutschs, Gordon, Gray, Karnes, Levenstein, Miller, Palmer, Weikart, Woolman, and Zigler (Lazar et al., 1982) permitted assessment of program effects across a number of projects and follow-up of a substantial group of children through high school. The population enrolled in these 12 projects were infants and young children from low-income homes. The individual projects varied in philosophy and approach; however, enough similarity existed to

pool their results. A recent monograph (Lazar et al., 1982) describes the procedures, analysis and results in detail. The most salient outcome was that significantly fewer children who participated in an early intervention program were assigned to special education classes and fewer were retained in a grade than the control children. No significant differences between experimental and control children on measures of achievement and intelligence were found.

Two notable investigations initiated in the late 1960s and early 1970s also focused on children from low-income families and produced outcome data that supplement the consortium finding. Long-term differences in IQ and other academic/achievement measures in favor of the experimental groups were reported (Garber & Heber, 1977; Heber & Garber, 1975; Ramey & Campbell, 1979).

A follow-up conducted by Moore, Fredericks and Baldwin (1981) focused on 9, 10, and 11 year old moderately to severely handicapped children enrolled in trainable mentally retarded public school classes. This group of children differed in that some ($N = 68$) had no preschool experience, some ($N = 35$) had 1 year and some ($N = 48$) had 2 years of preschool experience. A statewide assessment instrument, the Student Progress Record, was used to compare performances in language, academics, self-help, and motor skills of these three groups of children. The results indicated that those children enrolled in preschools for 2 years performed significantly better on the language, academic, self-help, and motor scales. The performance of the group with 1 year preschool experience was not reliably different from the group with no experience. Such results must be considered tentative because this was a retrospective investigation with all the problems inherent in such an approach. Furthermore, a selection factor may have been operating in that concerned families may be more apt to seek a preschool placement for their handicapped child; thus, the differences may stem not so much from the preschool experience but the family's handling of the child.

The Bureau for the Education of the Handicapped (now Office of Special Education Programs) issued a contract to the Battelle Institute to collect follow-up data on a sample of Handicapped Children's Early Education Programs (Stock, Wnek, Newborg, Gabel, Spurgeon, & Ray, 1976). Thirty-two Handicapped Children's Early Education Programs (HCEEP) were selected to participate in this investigation with a total of 160 handicapped children. Using a developmental instrument, Children's Early Education Developmental Inventory, pre- and posttest performance of the selected children indicated that these programs had a positive impact on the children above what could be expected through maturation. In addition, 82.7% of the parents surveyed reported their child's participation in the project as very successful while 11% indicated somewhat successful (Stock et al., 1976). The Battelle study also examined school placement of 95 graduates from HCEEP. Ninety percent of these children were in special education placements with the remaining 10% in regular education programs. Finally, on cognitive and social skills measures, teachers rated HCEEP graduates more advanced than similarly handicapped peers who had no HCEEP experience.

This investigation can be seen as a parallel endeavor to the Lazar et al. (1982) consortium project except the focus was biologically impaired children. Two major differences exist however. First, the HCEEP did not have control groups for comparison. Second, this follow-up study covered the age range of 5–8 years and thus provided no information on these children's progress and adjustment during adolescence and the early adult years. Even with these constraints the outcomes reported by this independent research agency must be seen as encouraging.

In addition to the Battelle study, a few other investigators have reported information on enrolled children upon entry into the public schools; for example, Zeitlin (1981) and Weiss (1981). Nonetheless, an analysis of such limited information does not invite drawing conclusions.

PROGRAM IMPACT ON FAMILIES

The evaluation conducted on early intervention programs has been primarily focused on addressing child outcome variables. Attempts to examine program impact on other social agents in the child's life have been sparse (Clarke-Stewart, 1981), largely because programs have lacked the necessary resources and tools to conduct such research. The program impact information that has been collected on families can be conveniently categorized into three areas: (a) acquisition of instructional skills by parents; (b) interaction between the caregiver and child; and (c) quality of life changes in the families.

Acquisition of Instructional Skills

One of the most rigorous research investigations on the effects of training parents as interventionists was conducted by Baker and his colleagues (Baker & Heifetz, 1976; Baker, Heifetz, & Murphy, 1980). One hundred sixty families with mentally retarded children between the ages of 3 and 14 participated in this study. The parents were divided into four groups, each having a different training format. A fifth group received delayed training and served as a control. The parents were assessed on a Behavioral Vignettes Test (Baker & Heifetz, 1976) before and after training. The training focus of each group was to assist parents in the acquisition of behavior modification techniques. Four different approaches were used: (a) training manual; (b) training manual and biweekly phone calls; (c) training manual and group meetings; and (d) training manuals, group meetings, and home visits. All methods required the parents to teach specific skills to their children. The training lasted approximately 20 weeks and was completed by 87% of the families. All the mothers involved in training demonstrated a significant improvement on the Behavioral Vignettes Test when compared to control mothers (Baker & Heifetz,

1976). The results for the fathers were related to the type of training they received. The children of trained parents improved significantly in skill acquisition over the control group, suggesting that the child change was directly related to the parent acquisition of behavioral teaching skills.

Sixteen children with Down syndrome were matched on chronological age and mental age and divided into a treatment and control group in a study conducted by Bidder, Bryant, and Gray (1975). Mothers in the treatment group received 12 training sessions on behavior modification techniques during a 6 month period. Following training a significant difference was found in favor of the treatment group on the language and performance scale of the Griffiths and positive trends on the loco-motor and eye-hand scales.

A small number of investigations employing few subjects using single subject analyses report that parents have successfully learned to use specific intervention procedures such as task analysis (Filler & Kasari, 1981), shaping techniques (Adubato, Adams, & Budd, 1981), reinforcement strategies (Petrie, Kratochwill, Bergan, & Nicholson, 1981), and use of more appropriate antecedents (Chelsedine & McConkey, 1979). Each of these investigations reports that parents acquired the targeted behavioral teaching strategy and found that parents were able to employ the acquired skills to effectively instruct their disabled child.

Interactional Change

The Verbal Interactional Project was one of the first early intervention projects to focus on interactional change (Levenstein, 1970; Madden et al., 1976). The goal of the project was to improve low-income mothers' verbal interaction style with their high-risk child. The home visitor brought a toy or book and modeled verbal stimulation techniques. After a year, the experimental mothers demonstrated significantly greater use of these techniques than 31 control parents who received nine home visits with toys but no verbal modeling. The experimental children also had a signifi-

cant increase in Binet IQ scores when compared to the controls.

The Carolina Abecedarian Project has reported that participation in this intervention program enhanced the mother-infant relationship in a population of rural poverty black families (Ramey et al., 1983). Likewise, the Milwaukee Project found that the mildly retarded urban poor mothers involved in their project changed the manner in which they interacted with their children by becoming more responsive and verbal (Garber & Heber, 1977). Similarly, Johnson (1975) described a project involving 200 Mexican-American families living in poverty. After the second year of intervention the experimental mothers, when compared with a nonintervention control group, were found to be significantly warmer, less intrusive, and used more play materials with their infants. The experimental children also scored significantly higher than the control children on the Stanford-Binet.

Gordon and Kogan (1975) intervened with mothers of cerebral palsied children to change interactional patterns. After baseline interactional patterns were determined, parents were divided into an intervention group and a delayed intervention group. The delayed group received training 8 weeks after the first group. The intervention included an interview discussing specific behavioral strategies and an interaction session between parent and child. After the intervention period, both groups of mothers improved their interactional style and significantly more positive behaviors were displayed by both mothers and children. This study was replicated by Tyler and Kogan (1977), and again the intervention was found to significantly reduce negative interactions between mothers and their children.

Christophersen and Sykes (1979) reported a study using three parent-child dyads. The preschool-age children were moderately retarded. A parent-child interactional code was used to measure the effectiveness of intervention. The parents were trained to reward appropriate behavior, and to use time out or a verbal reprimand for inappropriate behaviors. All subjects showed (a) an increase in positive parent-child interactions; (b) a decrease in negative interactions for two subjects; (c) a decrease in parent nonattending; and (d) increase in child compliance.

The few investigations focused on affecting the interactional dimensions of the parent–child relationships conducted with handicapped and environmentally at-risk children taken in tandem with studies conducted on at-risk infants (Minde, Shosenberg, Marton, Thompson, Ripley, & Burns, 1980; Bromwich & Parmelee, 1979; Field, Widmayer, Stringer, & Ignaloff, 1980) have produced encouraging outcomes. Projects designed to enhance positive dimensions of parent–child relationship seems feasible and effective.

Quality of Life Changes

A comprehensive evaluation of the effects of early intervention on families was undertaken by Rescorla and Zigler (1981). Originally, 18 children from low-income families age birth to 3 years participated in this study. Parents of the children were visited in the home twice a month for the first year of the project and monthly thereafter. The focus of the visit was the parents' social and economic needs. These parents were also given free medical care and day care was provided. Child progress was assessed at periodic intervals for the experimental and matched comparison group. An evaluation of the program found that 12 of the 17 mothers in the experimental group sought further education during the program and 8 of these mothers continued their education. There was a decline in the number of experimental parents seeking welfare. An analysis of the 5 year follow-up data indicated a significant difference favoring the experimental group on socioeconomic status, number of children (fewer), employment, and general quality of life. The children in the experimental group also had significantly higher scores on the Peabody Picture Vocabulary Test than control children.

The Milwaukee Project collected data on quality of life changes in participating families (Heber & Garber, 1975). There were more mothers from the experimental group who were employed and, of those who were working, there was an average difference of nearly $40 for weekly salary in favor of the experimental mothers. A significantly greater portion of experimental mothers were literate. Ramey and his colleagues (Ramey et al., 1983) also reported educational and employment changes in project parents. Though the groups were educationally equivalent at the time of the child's birth, the experimental mothers had acquired significantly more formal education by the time their children were 54 months old. As might be expected, more of the experimental mothers held semiskilled or skilled jobs than the control mothers.

Field (1981) compared the effects of two intervention approaches with teenage mothers and their preterm infants. The mothers and infants of the control group were assessed every 4 months for a year while the intervention groups participated in either a home visit program for a year or a center based nursery program for 6 months. The intervention groups received the same type of informational input; however the center-participating mothers served as paid staff members in the nursery program and, as such, were expected to care for other infants besides their own. Post intervention results indicated the infants attending the center based program performed better on growth and developmental measures and these mothers found employment more frequently than the mothers in the other groups. The incidence of repeat pregnancy was also lower among the center mothers.

The Carolina Abecedarian Project, the Milwaukee Project, and the project reported by Field (1981) report favorable attitude changes in participating parents. However, two studies reporting attitude changes in parents of handicapped children are conflicting. Hetherington, Suttill, Holmlund, and Frey (1979) measured the attitudes of 60 parents of severely developmentally delayed children (mean age = 5.6 years). Thirty of these parents participated in an intervention project. After 2 years of intervention, participating parents had more "negative attitudes" towards the severely handicapped child than either before intervention or the control group. The authors suggest the lack of progress by the children during intervention may have caused discouragement in the parents. On the other hand, Spiker (1982) reported that 32 mothers of children with Down syndrome were positive about their experiences when participating in intervention programs.

Summary

The initial portion of this chapter presented a review of a variety of early intervention programs designed to eliminate or attentuate deficits in groups of handicapped children or keep deficits from occurring in groups of medically or environmentally at-risk children and to effect families in a positive manner. Although objective data on program impact was provided, the majority of these studies have serious methodological or design flaws that may lead critics to question the validity of such data in evaluating program effectiveness. Rather than to belittle past efforts at program evaluation, a more serviceable perspective is to use these investigations to provide guidance for developing a template for change. The analyses of available program evaluation data is an ideal base from which to develop future guidelines for investigators interested in documenting program impact.

The remainder of this chapter addresses issues arising from the previous program analysis. These issues require some form of resolution *if* progress is to be made in objectifying program impact on handicapped children and their families.

ISSUES

The issues addressed in this section can be conveniently divided into three broad classes: philosophical dilemmas, influential variables, and limitation of intervention research.

Philosophical Dilemmas

The topics of longevity of program impact, expectancies for child progress, and curricular approaches are discussed under the rubric of philosophical dilemmas. My reading of the literature surrounding these issues has yielded little objective information from which to draw conclusions. Rather, exchanges about these important topics remain in the realm of theory and conjecture. This state of affairs exists, in part, because the issues of longevity of program impact, expectancies and curricular approaches are complex. Limited technology and resources for the conduct of intervention research provides serious barriers to unraveling these dilemmas.

Longevity of Program Impact

A serious criticism of early intervention efforts is that the effects produced on enrolled children tend to disappear or "wash out" over time (Clarke & Clarke, 1977). The investment of resources in early intervention programs are questioned when initial reported superiority of the experimental subjects is not maintained over time. Taken at face value such criticism would seem valid; however, at least two factors need consideration.

Years ago, I remember Sue Gray saying that early intervention is not an inoculation against future educational practice, and she recently reaffirmed this position (Gray et al., 1982). Yet it seems that critics expect early gains made by children to be maintained regardless of the child's future circumstances. Ample evidence indicates that without subsequent proper environmental arrangements, acquired behavior will not necessarily be maintained and/or new responses may not be developed as expected. The literature is replete with examples in which children have acquired behavior that does not generalize to other settings or is not maintained. Does this mean that the intervention should never have occurred? Or, rather does it suggest that additional attention should be given to subsequent environments to assure the generalization and maintenance of learned skills? Research from longitudinal intervention programs suggests that, by continuing systematic educational intervention, gains made during the preschool period can be maintained into the elementary years (Heber & Garber,

1975; Horton, 1976; Ramey et al., 1983; Weiss, 1981).

A second dilemma that arises when studying the longevity of effect is the notion of continuity. The controversy surrounding continuity of behavior has long been a favorite topic of developmental specialists (see, for example, Kagan, Kearsley, & Zelazo, 1978). Some theorists argue that human behavior is continuous. That is, earlier behavior provides the foundation for subsequent development and that clear regularities in growth and development are apparent for individuals over time (Lewis & Starr, 1979). Others argue that there is little evidence of continuity for the human organism as indicated by such factors as the poor predictive power of an infant's performance on a standardized test for later development (McCall, 1979).

The relationship between behavioral continuity and early intervention is important. If early behavioral repertoires are directly linked to future motor and conceptual development, logic would argue for the importance of early experience for the child's subsequent development. If, however, behavior is discontinuous, then early experience may be of less importance to the child's future, as Clarke & Clarke suggested (1976). The continuity dilemma hinges, in part, on the length of time one would expect to be able to predict behavioral continuity. Further, it would seem that some amount of the predictability is predicated on the relative continuity of the individual's environment. Even those strongly committed to the continuity position recognize that dramatic changes in an environment would tend to produce significant changes in a child's behavior.

The continuity issue will no doubt remain a controversy for many years; however, for present purposes a reasonable resolution might be to accept the notion of contiguous continuity. That is, that current behavioral repertoires provide the foundation for the development of the next succeeding stage which, in turn, directly effects the next subsequent stage or level of development. The developmental curves presented in Figure 3.1 illustrate the notion of contiguous continuity.

Curve A represents a normal growth curve in which there is a direct correspondence between mental age and chronological age. The dotted lines indicate the expected convergencies between these two variables. Such a curve permits accurate predictions from adjacent periods (e.g., age 1 to 2 years) as well as nonadjacent periods (e.g., age 2 to 12 years). Curve B illustrates growth that began as expected then gradually tapers off. Reasonable predictions can be made to adjacent periods (e.g., age 1 to 2 or 6 to 7 years) but predicting across several periods would not be accurate (e.g., from age 2 to 6 or age 3 to 12 years). Curve B might represent the growth reported for many children with Down syndrome in which their behavior moves further from the norm as they grow older (see Ludlow & Allen, 1979). The knowledge that prediction diminishes over time especially for young children is certainly not new (see for example Lewis & Starr, 1979); however, little apparent thought has been given to the relationship between longevity of program impact and the diminishing

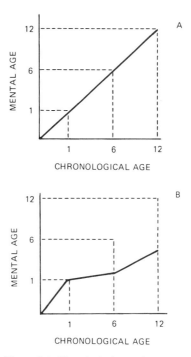

Figure 3.1. Hypothetical growth curves.

capability to predict later development from earlier performance. That is, disappointment, or worse, is voiced when children do not maintain initial headstarts without adequate recognition of the variables that may affect and change their growth over time.

Whether behavior acquired earlier in the child's life is reflected much later is a moot point for now. What is obvious is the immediate impact of the child's current behavioral repertoire on the acquisition of subsequent new response forms. Perhaps the more reasonable hope should be to demonstrate successive impact over time rather than attempting to predict much later behavior based on the preschool years. It seems rather remarkable that investigations have been able to report long term effects such as those described by Lazar et al. (1982). These outcomes suggest the importance of attempting to study the environments of children to determine what aspects have maintained the original gain and/or what changes have occurred to reduce or dilute the initial experimental and control differences. The collection of such information will no doubt reflect the interactive nature of development as has been proposed by a number of theorists (Lewis & Rosenblum, 1974; Piaget, 1970; Sameroff & Chandler, 1975; Uzgiris, 1981). Development is systematically shaped by the "transactions" between the organism and the environment. An intricate web of reciprocal transactions leads to the transformation of the child's behavioral repertoire. Unless the child's biology and environment remain relatively constant, one would be correct to predict variable outcomes for individual children. When investigations report that experimental groups maintain their superiority over time, one might speculate that the early intervention has affected not only the child, but influenced other important environmental factors as well.

What then is a reasonable expectation for the longevity of program impact? A simple answer seems unlikely. Rather, longevity of program impact is most likely determined by a number of variables. The length, quality, and content of an early intervention effort will doubtless affect the longevity of the impact. The Early Training Project developed by Gray and Klaus (Gray et al., 1982) documented the change of the experimental and control children enrolled in this project over a period of 18 years in tandem with attempting to examine changes in the environments of the children and their families. The outcomes of this investigation accurately reflect the issues raised in the preceding discussion. That is, one cannot reasonably hope to evaluate the long term impact of early intervention efforts in a vacuum. Rather, the subsequent environments experienced by the children and their families must be seen as the mediator of subsequent development and responsible, in part, for subsequent outcomes. Early intervention programs cannot protect at-risk or handicapped children from the future. Such programs may be able to enhance the child's development but these enhancements are surely not automatically retained. Rather, the child's progress will depend upon his or her current repertoire and the transactions that occur with subsequent environment.

The Expectancy: Normal Behavior?

Another philosophical issue facing early interventionists and those concerned with the enterprise is the selection of outcome goals. Said another way, what is or should be the expectancies for children participating in early intervention programs? An immediate response is often to mention the paramount need for individualization of goals and objectives for children; thus requiring expectancies to be personalized as well. However, expectancies seem to acquire an added dimension when examining general program impact. For groups of children expectancies appear to drift towards normalcy. Readers may disagree that the expectation of normal functioning is a goal of early intervention programs focused on handicapped children. Nevertheless, the majority of early intervention programs reviewed earlier employed measures that were standardized on normal children. Although such measures may be useful (Ramey, Campbell, & Wasik, 1982), their deployment suggests an implicit comparison to normal behavior. Establishing a target of normal functioning may be at times appropriate and sensible and may become troublesome only when programs that fail to reach that goal are devalued exclusively because of such comparisons.

Although decisions about program effectiveness tend to be made on whether the intervention produced differences found to be statistically significant, a corollary step is to establish the educational significance or worth of such differences. For example, Clunies-Ross (1979) reported that the infants with Down syndrome who were enrolled earlier in an intervention program made the greater progress. The next question to ponder is the significance of such progress. Does an increase in IQ render the quality of the child's or families' life better? I would venture to predict that if a program changed the enrolled children's IQ scores from 40 to 60, a less enthusiastic response by reviewers would be expected than if the IQ scores shifted from 70 to 90. The latter gain suggests the children are functioning within normal limits while the gain from 40 to 60 does not. I do not believe that investigators, practitioners, and consumers consciously make such distinctions but I strongly suspect that an unarticulated hope or expectancy for the handicapped child is for functioning within the realm of normalcy. When programs fall short of this expectancy, their worth may be questioned (Ferry, 1981; Gibson & Fields, 1984; Piper & Pless, 1980).

Given current technology and knowledge, programs often assist handicapped children in making only modest gains (Bricker & Dow, 1980; Hanson & Schwarz, 1978; Ludlow & Allen, 1979), giving rise to the question of whether the resource investment was "worth" the gain. Society appears to have agreed that assisting the handicapped individual to gain more independence is an acceptable goal toward which resources should be expended (e.g., P.L. 94-142). If so, then it seems important to tease from this commitment the often accompanying expectancy that intervention will render the child normal. Expectancies

need to be tempered with the reality that less dramatic outcomes for impaired children are the rule rather than the exception. Although the goal of normal functioning may not be within reach of many children, this does not mean that efforts to assist the handicapped child should be diluted or reduced. Rather, expectancies should be changed to accept consistent progress towards independent and satisfactory functioning even if there is no associated evidence of change on more traditional standardized measures. Such changes in expectancy require that other reliable and valid indices of child progress be developed; a problem addressed in a later section of this chapter.

Curricular Approaches

The historical roots of early intervention programs for biologically impaired infants and children lie in programs designed for older persons that employed the principles derived from the experimental analysis of behavior. Much of the early work was focused on devising educational programs for seriously handicapped children residing in institutions (Bricker & Bricker, 1975).

The nature of residential populations often required rigorous application of behavior modification techniques in order to gain control over the child's behavior before any attempt could be made to introduce an educational program addressed to the acquisition of new skills. The work and technology derived from focusing on such deviant populations was then transferred to programs for children who were younger and living at home (Bricker & Carlson, 1981). The application of the operant technology was found effective — that is, we were able to control the children's behavior and assist them in acquiring a variety of skills. The importance of this work should not be underestimated; however, researchers with more cognitive orientations began wondering about the utility and/or generalizability of the skills being taught to children under such rigorously controlled and structured regimes. These regimes minimized flexibility and adaptability in that children were reinforced for careful adherence to the adult imposed structure. Flights of fancy, initiation of novel behavior, and variations in specified routines were not encouraged and were often openly discouraged. The technology was used to teach specific responses rather than employed to assist the child in developing generative strategies that led to problem solving and independence. The problem was, of course, not in the behavioral technology but rather the manner in which interventionists applied it.

In large measure Piaget, his American interpreters, and some psycholinguists (see for example the volume edited by Schiefelbusch & Lloyd, 1974) provided the impetus for early interventionists to reconsider the impact of their intervention efforts with handicapped infants and children. These theorists and investigators argued that rather than individual skill acquisition, the educational enterprise might be aided by adopting a theoretical framework that would guide the nature and content of early intervention curricular efforts. The initial efforts in undertaking such a process were perhaps predictable in that many interventionists, as behavioral engineers, operationalized early sensorimotor and communicative behavior into a set of independent skills to be acquired response-by-response under structured conditions. Again, the child was viewed as a passive receptacle, who contributed little to the training enterprise even though Piaget (1970) had argued for the need, as had Dewey, for active involvement by the child in discovering the nature of the physical and social environment.

Contemporary views held by interventionists are further moderating or changing curricular approaches. Recently proposed changes are often formulated as a dichotomy that pits the behaviorist against the developmentalist. This dichotomy is unfortunate and does not accurately represent the nature of the disagreement between various curricular approaches (Brinker & Bricker, 1980). The polarization of behavioral and developmental positions has not assisted in clarifying issues. What, then, are the nature of the differences between programs that follow carefully specified arrangements of specific antecedents–responses–consequences versus programs that rely more on freely occurring events and arrangements of the environment to provide the necessary antecedents for instruction? The former programs usually can be identified by their carefully structured lesson plan format in which the interventionist's behavior as well as the child's response is specified. Often it is assumed that programs that do not follow carefully specified sequences are less objective and precise. This, of course, is not necessarily accurate. The objectivity and precision of an instructional program is determined by its implementation. In addition, it is assumed by many that less direct instructional approaches do not employ behavioral teaching principles. Again this is not accurate. All intervention programs use behavioral technology, it is the manner and precision of implementation that is at issue.

Controversy about the implementation of behavioral technology touches several areas that affect curricular approaches and emphasis, such as, child versus adult imposed activities; motivational strategies; generalization procedures; instructional content; and functionality of educational targets.

In curricular approaches where the daily lesson plans are predetermined, the child has little opportunity to affect the content of the daily lesson plans. Rather, the lesson has been specified previously. Other approaches may specify the goals and objectives for the child but leave the implementation to be decided, in part, by events occurring in the environment and the interests of the child. For example, a training goal might be to assist the child in using more agent–action–object phrases and, rather than employ a specific drill on a set number of predetermined phrases, the interventionist uses opportunities that arise during the day to target this activity. Looking at a book chosen by the child might provide the interventionist many opportunities to teach agent–action–object sequences. Using such an approach requires careful attention to the daily activities to assure that each child is receiving adequate training on selected objectives. Often it is difficult to monitor the training given to each objective and successful employment of such a system requires systematic collection of data on the child's progress toward specific objectives. It should be emphasized that programs that employ the use of a specific lesson plan format can use other times of the day to allow the child to select activities and/or enhance generalization of specific responses as done in the Early Education Project (Kysela et al., 1981). The reverse is also true, programs that generally do not employ specific lessons can use planned instruction when and if desirable (e.g., Bricker, 1981). Unfortunately, it seems that program staff tend to adopt one curricula strategy to the exclusion of others.

Another difference found in curricular approaches is in the administration of consequent events. Some programs focus on reinforcement of the desired response using some form of tangible feedback. Often this feedback is in the form of verbal comments, such as, good boy, that's right, you did that well, and so on. If tasks are primarily selected by the adult, one may assume that motivation for children may be a more consistent problem and, therefore, the need for the use of artificial contingencies. In programs where the child has more freedom to determine the activities in which the training exercises will be embedded, reinforcement is often inherent in the activity (Mahoney & Weller, 1980). For example, searching for a desired toy promotes the concept of object permanence and finding the toy provides the reinforcement and subsequent motivation for further searches. It is probably not necessary or useful to tell the child, "Good looking" when the child discovers the toy. Pouring juice into a cup provides practice in wrist rotation and self-help skills and getting to drink the juice may be reward enough to continue to practice the behavior. Conversely, turning uninteresting objects to practice wrist rotation may require the delivery of some form of verbal praise to keep the child engaged in the training activity. All of us engage in activities and responses that are maintained through artificial contingencies but much of our behavior is determined by other motivators. If movement towards independence is a major objective,

might not some curricular approaches be developing in children an undue reliance on artificial or nonfunctional consequences?

Another dimension along which curricula differ is their approach to generalization. Some approaches place an emphasis on first establishing an antecedent-response relationship that is specific and discrete. Once this single-cue–single-response association is developed, the next step becomes generalization of the response to other appropriate exemplars of the class or antecedent events. In such approaches, establishing control over the child's behavior may inadvertently reduce the child's chance for generalization or development of a generative problem solving strategy. By use of careful programming, sources of unsystematic variation are reduced and the child acquires a response as predetermined. Such procedures eliminate or greatly reduce the infusion of variablity in the acquisition of new skills and concepts that might significantly enhance generalization of the action or concept. Of course, some individuals are so impaired that the acquisition of simple contingencies is a reasonable expectation; however, for most handicapped children the future is far more optimistic and thus the need to rethink approaches to assist children in acquiring concepts and responses that lead to dynamic and generative repertoires.

Recently, some significant changes in the content focus of early intervention curricula has occurred; however, historically the emphasis has been on acquiring self-help, motor, and "academic" type skills (Kirk & Johnson, 1951). The presumption is that growth in these areas would be the most facilitative for the child in successive placements. An examination of both curricular and measurement tools used by programs suggests the importance placed on preacademic skills. Indeed, the instructional format followed by many programs emphasizes an academic focus. That is, little children are required to sit in small groups around tables and work on selected schoollike activities. Activities such as "free play" are viewed as fillers between training activities rather than as educational opportunities.

In spite of Piaget's declarations on the importance of play for the young child, it has taken some relatively recent research to convince many early interventionists of its importance (Chance, 1979). A growing body of work suggests that play is the work of little children and it is during these periods that children acquire a number of important behaviors such as appropriate role playing, interactional skills, and how to successfully engage the physical environment. Play allows the young child the freedom to explore, vary, and rearrange without undue curtailment from the environment.

Another area of curricular neglect has been social–communicative or pragmatic development. As we have argued elsewhere (Bricker & Carlson, 1981; Bricker & Schiefelbusch, 1984), early social–communicative exchanges between the child and his or her social environment may serve as an important foundation for the conceptual and more advanced pragmatic structure of later language usage. The importance of acquiring nonacademic, social, and communicative skills to be successful both in school and later in life is obvious, and programs need to give consideration to the inclusion of these areas and activities.

The final curricular issue to be discussed is the usefulness, or functionality of selected training objectives for the young child. This issue has been a concern for investigators and teachers working with populations of severely handicapped persons. To use Brown's terminology, "the criteria of ultimate functioning" (Brown, Nietupski, & Hamre-Nietupski, 1976) should be employed when selecting training objectives for the severely handicapped individual. This perspective does not appear to have been adopted by interventionists working with handicapped preschool children. It is unclear whether early interventionists have not given the issue proper attention or whether a conscious decision is made that the functionality of a response is of less concern because most children served in early intervention programs are not severely handicapped. For whatever reason, ignoring the usefulness of training objectives should no longer be tolerated. The

applicability and usefulness of learned responses underlies, I believe, other issues of child versus adult imposed activities, motivation, generalization and content. If the responses selected for teaching are functional for the child—that is, functional in the sense that they lead to greater independence and adaptability—then acquiring such responses may be largely child directed and reinforcing. Children appear to strive to master behavior and information that offers means for greater control over their environment. The functionality of the response should determine, in large measure, the content of the intervention program. For example, teaching the child to use a pincer grasp can be done in a variety of activities. Most often programmers appear to choose having the child pick up small pegs and place them in containers. This might be the activity of choice, if for some reason, this response/activity is functional for the child. On the other hand, practicing the pincer grasp while picking up Cheerios, raisins, small beads for stringing, turn on light switches, and so on may be more functional for the child in the sense such responses produce a practical and desirable outcome which more likely enhances the child's independence and adaptability.

Summary

This section has discussed some of the major dilemmas currently needing resolution by early interventionists. In particular, problems associated with documenting long term program impact, establishing reasonable expectancies and selecting appropriate curricular approaches were posed. In conjunction with describing the dilemmas, arguments suggesting strategies that might prove productive were made.

Influential Variables

In the early intervention enterprise, a number of important variables need to be considered when attempting to describe and/or evaluate programs. All too often, these variables appear not to receive proper attention in terms of their potential impact on children and families. Programs tend to be described in generic terms that obscure differences (Clarke-Stewart, 1981). The purpose of this section of the chapter is to discuss selected variables that need further explication if more precision is to become possible in evaluating the effects of early intervention programs.

Program Description

A familiar and legitimate criticism of early intervention is the nature of the program descriptions found in the literature. Rarely does one find explicit descriptions of the approach that was used with the children and their families. The reader may be informed that a Piagetian approach has been adopted and the focus of training is on the development of cognitive behavior. Clarification of how such an approach was implemented in a particular program may not be provided. Even programs that do offer more extensive descriptions of their intervention procedures and content generally do not monitor the fidelity of the treatment plan. And, it is the rare study that has systematically compared approaches, such as done by Hunt (1980). In fairness to early intervention programs, resources are often unavailable for the conduct of such systematic comparison. Further, in the development of new programs, several years may be required to develop a system that appears worthy of extensive description and evaluation. Unfortunately, there are hurdles to solving this problem. One of the most influential early intervention program networks in the United States is the Handicapped Children's Early Education Program (DeWeerd & Cole, 1976). These programs are funded for 36 months and, at the end of this period, are encouraged to seek local and/or state support for their continuation. Program development is an arduous process that takes time, and most programs have just begun to smooth out the organization, content, and procedural problems by the end of 3 years, when the resource that would provide support for the detailed description of the project is terminated. Continuation of projects with local and state monies generally means that the budget is primarily directed towards the delivery of service to eligible children and their families. Few resources are available to write program descriptions and to undertake comprehensive evaluation efforts.

More detailed descriptions of program components and the fidelity with which these components are implemented will be necessary if program impacts are to be delineated beyond global indices. Interventionists must begin to design methods for assessing adherence to program guidelines and specification. Collecting data on the fidelity with which parents and interventionists implement instructional content will aid in clarifying the impact of procedures and programs on children. Without such documentation investigators are unable to determine how often and with what precision a procedure has been used, thus leaving in question whether the intervention strategy was implemented in any reasonable manner and confounding the interpretation of the studies' results.

Parents

Another variable of interest to programs is parent involvement and/or education. Contemporary program descriptions emphasize parent involvement (see for example: Bricker et al., 1984; Clarke-Stewart, 1981). These descriptions suggest an array of mechanisms for the inclusion of parents from programs that rely on parents to deliver the services to their child (Barna, Bidder, Gray, Clements, & Gardner, 1980) to programs that include parents in the classroom (Bricker, Bruder, & Bailey, 1982) to programs that focus on mother–child interaction (Bromwich & Parmelee, 1979) to programs in which parents serve as assessors/ evaluators (Field, Dempsey, Hallock, & Shuman, 1978). Some programs focus on assisting parents to acquire specific skills that may make them better teachers of their children (Filler & Kasari, 1981). Others are more interested in improving the caregiver–child interaction

(Field, 1981), while others are interested in assisting parents in even broader areas of education and employment (Ramey et al., 1983). Some programs provide written manuals for parents (Baker & Heifetz, 1976), others depend on home visitors (Levenstein, 1970). Some programs provide both services (Bricker, 1981), while others offer complete day care (Ramey et al., 1983). While all these variations can be seen as positive, they introduce serious problems when attempting to describe and evaluate the impact of parents or, in the larger sense, family involvement. Again, the variation and lack of resources to allow systematic comparison, such as that carried out by Baker and his colleagues, renders this situation somewhat bleak in terms of making progress toward a more scientific delineation of what type of parent involvement and education is effective. No doubt the resolution of this issue must take into account the individuality of participating parents, their goals and expectancies for their child and themselves; the resources, both psychological and physical, available to families; the child; and the approach's ability to affect parents.

Child

Another dimension or influential variable to be reckoned with is the at-risk or disabled infant or child. The prediction for satisfactory parent involvement/progress appears independent of the magnitude of the child's disability. That is, no direct relationship between parental adjustment or progress and the severity of the child's problem seems apparent (Bricker & Casuso, 1979; Bricker & Dow, 1980). The parents' ability to cope and/or adjust to a handicapped child is dependent upon many factors. This reality further emphasizes the need for more accurate program descriptions and evaluation.

Clearly, more attention must be given to describing the child's genetics (if this is an issue), the handicapping condition, as well as the behavioral repertoire that currently exists. More careful delineation of subject populations is necessary before generalized statements can

be made about program impact. In addition, work should begin on attempting to measure the impact of the child on the family A number of measures are being explored and this work should be encouraged.

Environment

As a young researcher, I remember discussions with my colleagues in which we agreed that, in particular, mentally retarded children were living proof that typical environmental arrangements and feedback had not succeeded. More recent findings call into question that conclusion and suggest that biologically handicapped and, in many instances, at-risk children experience different child–caregiver transactions than those of nonhandicapped children (Bakeman & Brown, 1980). These differences may begin before the mother has left the delivery table if she learns or suspects the infant is handicapped or damaged (Klaus & Kennell, 1976). Early disruptions may become magnified over time and child–caregiver interactions may become distorted and nonreinforcing (Denenberg & Thoman, 1976; Lewis, 1978; Massie, 1980).

A number of investigators have reported differences in verbal interactional patterns between caregivers and children when the child is at-risk or handicapped. For example, Jones reported that the verbal exchanges of infants with Down syndrome ($N = 6$) with their mothers were less synchronized and less reciprocal than those of a matched group of nonhandicapped infants (Jones, 1977, 1980). Similar findings have been reported by Buckhalt, Rutherford, and Goldberg (1978), Gutmann and Rondal (1979), and Peterson and Sherrod (1982).

The results from the work of Emde, Katz and Thorp (1978), Cicchetti and Sroufe (1976) and Fraiberg (1975) suggest the onset of smiling and laughter in handicapped infants is significantly delayed, the intensity of the affective response is muted, and the latency between onset of the eliciting stimuli and response is longer than for nonhandicapped infants. The total effect on the infant's social environment is most likely to be negative unless caregivers are aware of the problem and can compensate accordingly.

No one may be surprised by the findings that differences have been found between handicapped and nonhandicapped children, but two aspects of these differences bear mention. First, the source of the difference is not restricted to behaviors generally classified under the rubric of intelligence, but differences also pervade the child's social–interactive repertoire. Second, the source of the difference does not necessarily lie in the handicapped child but rather results from the child's interaction with his or her social and physical environment (Walker, 1982).

Staff

The professional staff is responsible for the shape and flavor of a program's content. The way in which the staff conducts the program is influenced by at least two important variables: the quality of their training and the fidelity with which they adhere to established program goals and objectives. No doubt other factors could be specified as well, but these two seem of overriding importance.

Many early intervention programs are operated by staff members who have had minimal formal training in the area of early childhood/ special education. Often teachers "left over" because student enrollment has decreased in other areas are reassigned to the early intervention program. Although this may be a political reality, the underlying assumption that a teacher who worked effectively with fourth grade learning disabled children can work effectively with handicapped preschoolers is unwarranted. Although there may be an overlap in the educational strategies employed, there are obvious differences. Working effectively with infants and little children would seem somewhat dependent upon understanding the process and content of early childhood. What is the appropriate instructional content and the sequence of that content? What teaching techniques are effective? What type of data collection and measurement strategies are suited to the population? What of managing parent involvement and parent education? What available literature suggests ideas and methods that have been shown to be effective with populations of young disabled children? What are the new and important directions being explored? One does not often hear of an electrical engineer being assigned to design a bridge nor an industrial psychologist to conduct clinical intervention with psychotic individuals; it is perhaps no more reasonable to expect teachers of elementary children to be able to effectively cope with younger children without additional training.

As with many teacher preparation programs, early childhood/special education programs often lack clarity of description and offer little objective evaluation of their products (e.g., teachers). Nonetheless, progress is being made. The reduction of support at the federal level promotes moves to improve accountability. That is, those proposed projects that have more detail and clarity in the presentation of the training program, accompanied with appropriate evaluation mechanisms, are more likely to receive support and be implemented. The systematic deployment of programs described in greater detail and better evaluated will generate further information on how to improve the personnel preparation efforts currently underway. Thus it seems progress hinges on a three phase process:

1. The recognition of early childhood/special education as a legitimate and independent area in which to develop expertise.
2. The development of more carefully specified programs that delineate the content of instruction and manner in which the content is implemented.
3. The use of more sophisticated evaluation techniques to determine the effectiveness of the designed personnel preparation programs.

Summary

To enhance efforts to determine the impact of early intervention programs, increased attention to more complete descriptions of program components appears essential. More precise indices of program content, target populations, and environmental interactions will move the field forward to better understand treatment–trait interaction and, thus, be better able to match intervention to child and family needs.

Limitations of Intervention Research

Ferry (1981) reflects the frustration surrounding the evaluation of early intervention efforts when she states, "the field is hampered by enormous methodologic problems." These problems have been discussed in detail elsewhere and shall only be highlighted here (see for example, Bricker & Sheehan, 1981; Stedman, 1977). The problems or dilemmas focus on populations, measures, designs, analyses, the relationship between dependent and independent variables, and resources, as well as the major difficulty inherent in intervention research.

The population parameters of the biologically impaired infant/child pose an evaluation dilemma for three reasons (Garwood, 1982). First, in comparison with normal and at-risk children, there are fewer handicapped children; second, the handicapped population is more heterogeneous; and third, they often have specific impairments that interfere with normal response patterns. These realities create significant problems when employing more traditional evaluation methodology, which requires the use of standardized tests, controls, and random assignment to groups.

A second dilemma is the availability of appropriate measures. There are large numbers of assessment instruments for infants and preschool children (Cross & Johnston, 1977), but the majority of these instruments were developed for use with nonhandicapped children. Although many of these instruments were designed to assist in the identification and diagnosis of early childhood problems, developers rarely intended that these measures be employed to assess program impact and/or to provide the content for the development of

appropriate education programs for handicapped infants and young children. Indeed, the more child performance differs from normal development, the less applicable and useful are measures that were standardized on nonhandicapped children. Use of norm-referenced measures is often inappropriate because documentation of progress requires strategies that are comprehensive, yet are responsive to relatively small changes in child behavior, a characteristic not present in many standardized instruments.

Limitations of norm-referenced tests have led to the development of criterion-referenced and "homemade" measures. Unfortunately, these instruments tend to have two deficiencies. First, they are not widely used and therefore adequate subject pools cannot be generated to permit the development of expectancies, or norms, for items. Second, these instruments are not used with sufficient numbers of subjects to collect reliability and validity data necessary to establish the psychometric properties of the measures. Interventionists face the dilemma of choosing a standardized measure that may be inappropriate for the population or a measure with questionable validity and reliability.

The use of traditional or even quasi-experimental research designs are often impossible for interventionists to implement. Due to small heterogeneous groups and ethical considerations, random or matched assignment to control groups are often not options (Bricker, Sheehan, & Littman, 1981). The use of comparison or contrast groups is fraught with difficulties as well (Bricker & Sheehan, 1981). Most often the intervention researcher is forced to adopt pre-post or retrospective comparisons (Simeonsson et al., 1982), which are open to familiar and legitimate criticism.

Given the inability to assemble adequate samples and controls, many traditional statistical procedures have limited applicability (Sheehan & Keogh, 1982). In addition, Lewis and Wehren (1982) provide an insightful discussion on what they call the tyranny of central tendency when applied to non-normally distributed populations. They argue that the sole presentation of the central tendency score often masks quite differential effects on subgroups within a population. Unfortunately, alternative strategies that may be appropriate, such as single subject approaches, are limited in other ways. A primary problem of the single subject approach is whether its findings can be generalized to (a) other subjects; (b) use with other behavior change agents; and/or (c) other settings (Hersen & Barlow, 1977). A reported intervention effort may have been successful with one child — for example, getting Dicky to wear his glasses (Wolf, Risley, & Mees, 1964) — but there is no indication of the potential usefulness of that particular technique or content with other children. Without systematic replication of a procedure/content, the external validity of the approach remains in question. Thus, the intervention researcher is faced with the dilemma of applying designs and analyses that are inappropriate for the population and lack generalizability, or using research procedures that lack scientific rigor.

Another dilemma faced in intervention research is the match between the dependent and independent variables. The dependent measures should reflect the program's emphasis; however, often there is a mismatch between program emphasis and the content of the measure selected to assess the impact of the intervention. Should a program that focuses on enhancing caregiver–child interactions and social–communicative behavior use a measure of general cognitive functioning to assess program impact? Choosing a measure that is not congruent with program emphasis may yield misleading outcomes and yet the lack of appropriate measures often forces such choices.

A final dilemma faced by the intervention researcher is the problem of resource allocation. After introducing the numerous problems that researchers must face when attempting to conduct intervention research, Baer (1981) concluded that there are neither adequate resources nor individuals able to make the commitment to conduct completely scientifically defensible intervention research. Many programs do not have the financial resources necessary to conduct systematic reliability checks on data collection procedures or additional independent personnel to conduct pre- and posttest sessions. Following children who have exited from programs takes a considerable financial and human resource commitment if the follow-up data are to be scientifically defensible (see, for example, Gray et al., 1982).

In presenting the constraints facing the intervention researcher, Baer (1981) offers a simple illustration of the number of systematic comparisons necessary to validate the components of an early intervention program. This example leads to the inescapable conclusion that to fund and execute such research ventures is "extraordinarily unlikely." Rather as Baer concludes, intervention research will likely continue as confounded experiments which cannot be realistically or usefully held to the template of controlled laboratory research.

Summary

Problems facing the intervention researcher have been highlighted. The purpose has been to focus attention on the need to evolve toward an acceptable compromise between scientific rigor and what can be accomplished practically. Without rapprochement between factions demanding control and factions recognizing pragmatic realities, the litany of weaknesses found in intervention research efforts will continue to be gracefully deflected by the interventionist's shield of ethics. Progress hinges on both sides' willingness to compromise current attitudes and positions.

THE FUTURE

Any field undergoing growth and change is confronted with problems created by the expansion. The field of early intervention must face problems within as well as external to the enterprise. A number of important issues concerning the quality of services delivered to children and their families require study and formation of solutions, but these solutions need to be developed with an appreciation for the larger ecological context of which they are a part. Pieces of the educational enterprise cannot be usefully viewed apart from the larger political, social, and economic contexts in which they reside. To overlook these contexts may mean that solutions derived to manage internal problems will not be effective because of limitations imposed by the larger context. Just as it is a mistake to view a handicapped child in isolation from the family, so is it a mistake to view early intervention programs apart from the larger educational system and, in turn, that system apart from its political niche in society.

Service Delivery

The position articulated above suggests a bias towards the movement of early intervention programs into the domain of public education — a view not shared by everyone. However a number of sound reasons exist for expanding public school systems to accommodate preschool education for the handicapped child:

1. The public schools are the only social-political institutions suitably equipped to assimilate educational programs for young children.
2. Waste is inevitable if parallel educational systems were to be developed for infants and preschool children.
3. One system should enhance the continuity of delivering services in a more normalized setting.

If the majority of consumers and professionals accept the need for early intervention for handicapped and at-risk children either on philosophical or empirical grounds, then attention should be given to how these programs can be effectively integrated into established public school programs with the intelligent sharing of facilities, administration, and other resources. The current crazy-quilt pattern of program support, location, administration, and so on dramatically reflects the need for leadership at the federal and state levels. An organizational framework within the rubric of public education will lead to the most sensible system of service delivery for handicapped children and their families (Hobbs, 1975).

Personnel Preparation

With the growth of early intervention programs comes the associated need for appropriately trained personnel. Again program developers must consider the larger context as an integral part of the philosophy and training of early intervention personnel. Critical to personnel preparation programs are the decisions concerning the service delivery system chosen for early intervention programs. Current requirements for teachers vary across and within states. Many states do not offer a credential in early childhood/special education. If public schools assume the responsibility for preschool programs, then associated certification will have a significant impact on teacher training programs.

In preparation for the day when an organized system of service delivery for early intervention programs becomes a reality, teacher training programs need to begin planning for that eventuality. Work should begin on locating and developing appropriate practicum sites. Programs of studies that reflect the current knowledge base should be designed and faculties must begin to adjust their thinking about where early childhood/special education fits into the broader area of special education and general education.

It seems unlikely or inadvisable that all institutions of higher education initiate personnel preparation programs for early childhood/special education. Rather, considered decisions about which institutions should expand or shift their program offerings should be made at the state level. With adequate planning and support from federal and state governments, a network of teacher training programs should be established to produce an adequate number of qualified interventionists to meet the future needs of handicapped children and their families.

Parents

Although progress has been made in changing attitudes about roles for parents, the goals of parents as diagnosticians, assessors, and inter-venors specified by Brooks-Gunn and Lewis (1979) are not being met in most programs. Careful questioning of program staff generally reveals that only about 20–40% of the parents are genuinely involved (e.g., consistently work with their child, attend meetings, spend time with staff on a regular basis). For many pro-grams, reports of parent involvement means little more than infrequent attendance at meet-ings and verbal assurances to staff that train-ing regimes are being implemented at home. In addition, although objective data are lack-ing, it seems likely that those parents who are actively involved represent a biased sample of better educated, middle income families. Those families who may require the most help may be those most reluctant to become active participants with their child or other aspects of the program.

Multiple causes exist for the lack of mean-ingful parent involvement; for example, staff attitudes, parent/family problems apart from the child, economic conditions (e.g., both par-ents are employed). The goal is not to allocate blame or responsibility, but rather to recognize for many families efforts at involvement have been unsuccessful.

Just as most of us are discovering there are many ways to work effectively with handi-capped children; we must face the reality that parents have the same need for individualiza-tion. Successful programs are more likely those that attempt systematic assessment of family need and then attempt to assist the family in meeting those needs even if the parental goals do not match the goals set by the professional intervention team.

Curricular Focus

A move has already begun to shift the curric-ular focus from preacademics to include behav-iors of a more social and functional nature. Ideally, this pendulum swing will not eliminate the systematic use of behavioral technology. The behavioral technology that evolved from the experimental analysis of behavior is the most effective instructional strategy current-ly available. A shift in curriculum emphasis should not mean elimination of the systematic arrangement of antecedent events, operation-alization of responses, delivering consequences appropriately, and use of teaching/shaping strategies. If anything, behavioral technology becomes more essential when the content and format are less controlled by the adult. Ar-rangement of antecedent events needs to be woven into the daily activities experienced by the young child and consequences made inher-ent in the activities whenever possible. Such approaches require care and thought in man-aging the environment, operationalizing the response in more detail, and understanding how to integrate consequences into the selected activity. The collection of data to monitor child behavior change with these approaches is con-siderably more difficult.

The preceding description does not preclude the need for working with children on selected targets in a contrived setting. Systematic drill on using the pincer grasp, labeling objects, pulling objects with strings, and rolling balls may be necessary, *but* the use of such formats should be tempered by following the child's lead when possible and working towards mea-sured independence and problem solving abil-ities rather than on isolated skill sequences.

Evaluation Strategies

Without more sensitive, ecologically valid eval-uation strategies, documentation of program impact will remain a challenge rather than a reality. Most contributors to the field recognize this problem and efforts are underway to de-velop alternatives. Although recent work in the area of measurement is encouraging, the enor-mous effort to develop evaluation alternatives suggests an interim of several years before satisfactory solutions become widely available.

During this interim, the most useful solution may be to use a combination of assessment tools. The pairing of standardized measures, which have known psychometric properties, with experimental instruments, which are more program relevant, may simultaneously yield valuable information about the target population and about the new instrument.

In particular, work is needed on instruments that: (a) provide information from which to develop individual intervention programs; and (b) assess aspects of programs previously ignored. Interventionists need tools that are practical to administer and yield precise data on the child's behavioral repertoire. The nature of these data should be such that relevant long-term goals, short-term objectives, and specific intervention programs can be formulated (Bricker & Littman, 1982). Further, the tool, when used periodically, should provide systematic feedback on the child's progress toward the selected training targets.

There is also a need to assess other program features, tools are needed to examine program effectiveness with parents, which may range from support, counseling, education, to parent–child interactions. Cost analyses are woefully lacking and thus knowledge about cost-effective parameters of programs are limited. Lack of evaluation efforts in these areas may be related to the complexity of developing adequate tools to assess these critical variables. Nonetheless we must move ahead, for only through exploration can alternative evaluation strategies be developed.

SUMMARY

The intent of this chapter was to provide a brief historical perspective for a discussion of contemporary early intervention programs that have produced interpretable data on enrolled children and their families. Emerging from this review were a number of salient issues that require resolution, or at least understanding, if the field is to progress toward delivering more effective educational services to handicapped and at-risk children. The problem is, after all, to assist the children in developing a repertoire of adaptive and success-producing behaviors that will work in subsequent environments. Failing to do that, a corollary goal is to maximize the child's progress, to whatever degree possible, and the family's adjustment to its

handicapped member. Determining the extent to which programs have met these goals still largely eludes the intervention researcher because of available methodology and resources. Thus, criticism of evaluation efforts, although legitimate, should be tempered with an understanding of the limitations facing the field.

Striking a balance between agitating for needed change and recognizing unavoidable barriers is difficult. This chapter has tried to present a program analysis in the light of what can be changed and what will remain for the future. Whether this balance or judgements are accurate awaits progress forthcoming in the decade of the 1980s.

REFERENCES

Adelson, E., & Fraiberg, S. (1975). Gross motor development in infants blind from birth. In B. Friedlander, G. Sterritt, & G. Kirk (Eds.), *Exceptional infant: Assessment and intervention, Vol. 3*. New York: Brunner/Mazel.

Adubato, S., Adams, M., & Budd, K. (1981). Teaching a parent to train a spouse in child management techniques. *Journal of Applied Behavior Analysis*, *14*, 193–205.

Aronson, M., & Fallstrom, K. (1977). Immediate and long-term effects of developmental training in children with Down's syndrome. *Developmental Medicine and Child Neurology*, *19*, 489–494.

Baer, D. (1981). The nature of intervention research. In R. Schiefelbusch & D. Bricker (Eds.), *Early language: Acquisition and intervention*. Baltimore: University Park Press.

Bakeman, R., & Brown, J. (1980). Early interaction: Consequences for social and mental development at three years. *Child Development*, *51*, 437–447.

Baker, B., & Heifetz, L. (1976). The Read Project: Teaching manuals for parents of retarded children. In T. Tjossem (Eds.), *Intervention strategies for high risk infants and young children*. Baltimore: University Park Press, 1976.

Baker, B., Heifetz, L., & Murphy, D. (1980). Behavioral training for parents of mentally retarded children: One year follow-up. *American Journal of Mental Deficiency*, *85*, 31–38.

Barna, S., Bidder, R., Gray, O., Clements, J., & Gardner, S. (1980). The progress of developmentally delayed preschool children in a home-training scheme. *Child: Care, Health and Development*, *6*, 157–164.

Baumeister, A., & Forehand, R. (1973). Stereotyped acts. In N. Ellis (Ed.), *International review of research in mental retardation* (Vol. 6). New York: Academic Press.

Bayley, N. (1969). *Bayley Scales of Infant Development.* New York: The Psychological Corporation.

Beller, E. (1979). Early intervention programs. In J. Osofsky (Ed.), *Handbook of infant development.* New York: Wiley.

Bidder, R., Bryant, G., & Gray, O. (1975) Benefits to Down's syndrome children through training their mothers. *Archives of Disease in Childhood, 50,* 383–386.

Blatt, B., & Garfunkel, F. (1969). *The educability of intelligence.* Washington, DC: The Council for Exceptional Children.

Bricker, D. (1981, January). A handicapped children's early education program: Rationale, program description and impact. Final report for the Division of Innovation and Development, Office of Special Education.

Bricker, D., Bailey, E., & Bruder, M. (1984). The efficacy of early intervention and the handicapped infant: A wise or wasted resource? *Advances in Developmental and Behavioral Pediatrics* (Vol. 5). Greenwich, CT: JAI Press.

Bricker, D., Bruder, M., & Bailey, E. (1982). Developmental integration of preschool children. *Analysis and Intervention in Developmental Disabilities, 2,* 207–222.

Bricker, D., & Carlson, L. (1981). Issues in early language intervention. In R. Schiefelbusch & D. Bricker (Eds.), *Early language: Acquisition and intervention.* Baltimore: University Park Press.

Bricker, D., & Carlson, L. (1982). The relationship of object and prelinguistic social-communicative schemes to the acquisition of early linguistic skills in developmentally delayed infants. In G. Edgar, N. Haring, J. Jenkins, & C. Pious (Eds.), *Mentally handicapped children.* Baltimore: University Park Press.

Bricker, D., Carlson, L., & Schwarz, R. (1981). A discussion of early intervention for infants with Down's syndrome. *Pediatrics, 67,* 45–46.

Bricker, D., & Casuso, V. (1979). Family involvement: A critical component of early intervention. *Exceptional Children, 46,* 108–116.

Bricker, D., & Dow, M. (1980). Early intervention with the young severely handicapped child. *Journal of the Association for the Severely Handicapped, 5,* 130–142.

Bricker, D., & Littman, D. (1982). Intervention and evaluation: The inseparable mix. *Topics in Early Childhood Special Education, 1,* 23–33.

Bricker, D., & Schiefelbusch, R. (1984). Infants at risk. In L. McCormick & R. Schiefelbusch (Eds.), *Early language intervention: An introduction.* Columbus, OH: Charles E. Merrill.

Bricker, D., Seibert, J., & Casuso, V. (1980). Early intervention. In J. Hogg & P. Mittler (Eds.), *Advances in mental handicap research.* London: Wiley.

Bricker, D., & Sheehan, R. (1981). Effectiveness of an early intervention program as indexed by child change. *Journal of the Division for Early Childhood, 4,* 11–27.

Bricker, D., Sheehan, R., & Littman, D. (1981). *Early intervention: A plan for evaluating program impact.* Seattle: WESTAR Publication.

Bricker, W., & Bricker, D. (1975). Mental retardation and complex human behavior. In J. Kauffman & J Payne (Eds.), *Mental retardation.* Columbus, OH: Charles E. Merrill.

Brinker, R., & Bricker, D. (1980). Teaching a first language: Building complex structures from simpler components. In J. Hogg & P. Mittler (Eds.), *Advances in mental handicap research.* London: Wiley.

Bromwich, R., & Parmelee, A. (1979). An intervention program for pre-term infants. In T. Field, A. Sostek, S. Goldberg, & H. Shuman (Eds.), *Infants born at risk.* Jamaica, NY: Spectrum Publications.

Bronfenbrenner, U. (1974). *Is early intervention effective? A report on longitudinal evaluations of preschool programs.* (Vol. II) (DHEW Publication No. OHD 75-25). Washington, DC: U.S. Department of Health, Education, and Welfare.

Bronfenbrenner, U. (1975). Is early intervention effective? In B. Friedlander, G. Sterritt, & G. Kirk (Eds.), *Exceptional infant: Assessment and intervention, Vol. 3.* New York: Brunner/Mazel.

Brooks-Gunn, J., & Lewis, M. (1979, June). Parents of handicapped infants: Their role in identification, assessment, and intervention. Paper presented at the Ira Gordon Memorial Conference, Chapel Hill.

Brown, L., Nietupski, J., & Hamre-Nietupski, S. (1976). Criterion of ultimate functioning. In *Hey, don't forget about me! Education's investment in the severely, profoundly and multiply handicapped.* Reston, VA: Council for Exceptional Children.

Buckhalt, J., Rutherford, R., & Goldberg, K. (1978). Verbal and nonverbal interaction of mothers with their Down's syndrome and nonretarded infants. *American Journal of Mental Deficiency, 82,* 337–343.

Caldwell, B. (1978). *Home observation for measurement of the environment.* Syracuse, NY: Syracuse University Press.

Chance, P. (1979). *Learning through play.* New York: Gardner Press.

Cheseldine, S., & McConkey, R. (1979). Parental speech to young Down's syndrome children: An intervention study. *American Journal of Mental Deficiency, 83,* 612–620.

Christophersen, E., & Sykes, B. (1979). An intensive, home based family training program for developmentally delayed children. In L. Hamerlynck (Ed.), *Behavioral systems for the developmentally disabled: (I) School and family environments.* New York: Brunner/Mazel.

Cicchetti, D., & Sroufe, A. (1976). The relationship between affective and cognitive development in Down's syndrome infants. *Child Development*, *47*, 920–929.

Clarke, A., & Clarke, A. (1976). *Early experience: Myth and evidence*. New York: The Free Press.

Clarke A., & Clarke, A. (1977). Prospects for prevention and amelioration of mental retardation: A guest editorial. *American Journal of Mental Deficiency*, *81*, 523–533.

Clarke-Stewart, K. (1981). Parent education in the 1970's, *Educational Evaluation and Policy Analysis*, *3*, 47–58.

Clunies-Ross, G. (1979). Accelerating the development of Down's syndrome infants and young children. *The Journal of Special Education*, *13*, 169–177.

Connolly, B., Morgan, S., Russell, F., & Richardson, B. (1980). Early intervention with Down syndrome children. *Physical Therapy*, *60*, 1405–1408.

Cross, L., & Johnston, S. (1977). A bibliography of instruments. In L. Cross & K. Goin (Eds.), *Identifying handicapped children: A guide to casefinding, screening, diagnosis, assessment, and evaluation*. New York: Walker Publishing Co.

Denenberg, V., & Thoman, E. (1976). From animal to infant research. In T. Tjossem (Ed.), *Intervention strategies for high risk infants and young children*. Baltimore: University Park Press.

DeWeerd, J., & Cole, A. (1976). Handicapped children's early education program. *Exceptional Children*, *43*, 155–157.

Dmitriev, V. (1979). Infant learning program for Down's syndrome. In B. Darby & M. May (Eds.), *Infant assessment: Issues and applications*. Seattle, WA: WESTAR Publication.

Emde, R., Katz, E., & Thorpe, J. (1978). Emotional expression in infancy: II. Early deviations in Down's syndrome. In M. Lewis & L. Rosenblum (Eds.), *The development of affect*. New York: Plenum Press.

Ferry, P. (1981). On growing new neurons: Are early intervention programs effective? *Pediatrics*, *67*, 38–41.

Field, T. (1981). Intervention for high-risk infants and their parents. *Educational Evaluation and Policy Analysis*, *3*, 69–78.

Field, T., Dempsey, J., Hallock, N., & Shuman, H. (1978). The mother's assessment of the behavior of her infant. *Infant Behavior and Development*, *1*, 156–167.

Field, T., Widmayer, S., Stringer, S., & Ignaloff, E. (1980). Teenage, lowerclass black mothers and their preterm infants: An intervention and developmental follow up. *Child Development*, *51*, 426–436.

Filler, J., & Kasari, C. (1981). Acquisition, maintenance and generalization of parent-taught skills with two severely handicapped infants. *The Journal of the Association for the Severely Handicapped*, *6*, 30–38.

Folio, R., & DuBose, R. (1974). *Peabody developmental motor scales*. IMRID Behavioral Science Monograph, No. 25. Nashville, TN: Peabody College.

Fowler, W. (1975). A developmental learning approach to infant care in a group setting. In B. Friedlander, G. Sterritt, & G. Kirk (Eds.), *Exceptional infant: Assessment and intervention, Vol. 3*. New York: Brunner/Mazel.

Fraiberg, S. (1975). Intervention in infancy: A program for blind infants. In B. Friedlander, G. Sterritt, & G. Kirk (Eds.), *Exceptional infant: Assessment and intervention, Vol. 3*. New York: Brunner/Mazel.

Friedman, S., & Sigman, M. (Eds.). (1981). *Pre-term birth and psychological development*. New York: Academic Press.

Gallagher, J., Beckman, P., & Cross, A. (1983). Families of handicapped children: Sources of stress and its amelioration. *Exceptional Children*, *50*, 10–19.

Garber, H., & Heber, R. (1977). The Milwaukee project. In P. Mittler (Ed.), *Research to practice in mental retardation, Vol. 3, Care and intervention*. Baltimore: University Park Press.

Garwood, G. (1982). Early childhood intervention: Is it time to change outcome variables? *Topics in Early Childhood Special Education*, *1*, ix–xi.

Gibson, D. & Fields, D. (1984). Early stimulation programs for Down's syndrome: An effectiveness inventory. *Advances in Developmental and Behavioral Pediatrics* (Vol. V). Greenwich, CT: JAI Press.

Goodenough, F., & Maurer, K. (1961). The relative potency of the nursery school and the statistical laboratory in boosting the IQ. In J. Jenkins & D. Paterson (Eds.), *Studies in individual differences*. New York: Appleton-Century-Crofts. (Originally published in 1940.)

Gordon, N., & Kogan, K. (1975). A mother instruction program: Behavior changes with and without therapeutic intervention. *Child psychiatry and Human Development*, *6*, 89–105.

Gottlieb, M. (1978). Exceptional children intervention programs: From conception to cradle. *Allied Health and Behavioral Sciences*, *1*, 31–46.

Gray, S., Ramsey, B., & Klaus, R. (1982). *From 3 to 20: The early training project*. Baltimore: University Park Press.

Gutmann, A., & Rondal, J. (1979). Verbal operants in mothers' speech to nonretarded and Down's syndrome children matched for linguistic level. *American Journal of Mental Deficiency*, *83*, 446–452.

Hanson, M. (1976). Evaluation of training procedures used in a parent-implemented intervention program for Down's syndrome infants. AAESPH Review, *1*, 36–52.

Hanson, M. (1977). *Teaching your Down's syndrome infant: A guide for parents*. Baltimore: University Park Press.

Hanson, M., & Schwarz, R. (1978). Results of a longitudinal intervention program for Down's syndrome infants and their families. *Education and Training of the Mentally Retarded, 13*, 403–407.

Harris, S. (1981). Effects of neurodevelopmental therapy on motor performance of infants with Down's syndrome. *Developmental Medicine and Child Neurology, 23*, 477–483.

Hayden, A., & Beck, G. (1982). The epidemiology of high-risk and handicapped infants. In C. Ramey & P. Trohanis (Eds.), *Finding and educating high-risk and handicapped infants*. Baltimore: University Park Press.

Hayden, A., & Dmitriev, V. (1975). The multidisciplinary preschool program for Down's syndrome children at the University of Washington model pre-school center. In B. Friedlander, G. Sterritt, & G. Kirk (Eds.), *Exceptional infant: Assessment and intervention, Vol. 3*. New York: Brunner/Mazel.

Hayden, A., & Haring, N. (1976). Programs for Down's syndrome children at the University of Washington. In T. Tjossem (Ed.), *Intervention strategies for high-risk infants and young children*. Baltimore: University Park Press.

Hayden, A., & Haring, N. (1977). The acceleration and maintenance of developmental gains in Down's syndrome school-age children. In P. Mittler (Ed.), *Research to practice in mental retardation. Vol. I: Care and intervention*. Baltimore: University Park Press.

Hayden, A., & McGinness, G. (1977). Bases for early intervention. In E. Sontag, J. Smith, & N. Certo (Eds.), *Educational programming for the severely and profoundly handicapped*. Reston, VA: Council for Exceptional Children.

Heber, R., & Garber, H. (1975). The Milwaukee Project: A study of the use of family intervention to prevent cultural-familial mental retardation. In B. Friedlander, G. Sterritt, & G. Kirk (Eds.), *Exceptional infant: Assessment and intervention, Vol. 3*. New York: Brunner/Mazel.

Hersen, M., & Barlow D. (1977). *Single case experimental designs*. New York: Pergamon.

Hetherington, R., Suttill, J., Holmlund, C., & Frey, D. (1979). Evaluation of a regional resource center of multiply handicapped retarded children. *American Journal of Mental Deficiency, 83*, 367–379.

Hobbs, N. *The futures of children*. (1975). San Francisco: Jossey-Bass.

Horton, K. (1976). Early intervention for hearing-impaired infants and young children. In T. Tjossem (Ed.), *Intervention strategies for high risk infants and young children*. Baltimore: University Park Press.

Hunt, J. (1961). *Intelligence and experience*. New York: Ronald Press.

Hunt, J. (1980). Implications of plasticity and hierarchical achievements for the assessment of development and risk of mental retardation. In D. Sawin, R. Hawkins, L. Walker, & D. Penticuff (Eds.), *Exceptional infant. Psychosocial risks in infant-environment transactions, Vol. 4*. New York: Brunner/Mazel.

Jensen, A. (1969). A theory of primary and secondary familial mental retardation. In N. Ellis (Ed.), *International review of research in mental retardation* (Vol. 4). New York: Academic Press.

Johnson, D. (1975). The development of a program for parent-child education among Mexican-Americans in Texas. In B. Friedlander, G. Sterritt, & G. Kirk (Eds.), *Exceptional infant: Assessment and intervention, Vol. 3*. New York: Brunner/Mazel.

Jones, O. (1977). Mother-child communication with prelinguistic Down's syndrome and normal infants. In H. Schaffer (Ed.), *Studies in mother-infant interaction*. New York: Academic Press.

Jones, O. (1980). Prelinguistic communication skills in Down's syndrome and normal infants. In T. Field (Ed.), *High-risk infants and children*. New York: Academic Press.

Kagan, J., Kearsley, R., & Zelazo, P. (1978). *Infancy: It's place in human development*. Cambridge, MA: Harvard University Press.

Karnes, M., Schwedel, A., Lewis, G., Ratts, D., & Esry, D. (1981). Impact of early programming for the handicapped: A follow-up study into the elementary school. *Journal of the Division for Early Childhood, 4*, 62–79.

Kirk, S. *Early education of the mentally retarded*. (1958). Urbana: University of Illinois Press.

Kirk, S. (1977). General and historical rationale for early education of the handicapped. In N. Ellis & L. Cross (Eds.), *Planning programs for early education of the handicapped*. New York: Walker & Co.

Kirk, S., & Johnson, G. (1951). *Educating the retarded child*. Cambridge, MA: Houghlin-Mifflin.

Klaus, M., & Kennell, J. (1976). *Maternal–infant bonding*. St. Louis: Mosby Co.

Kysela, G., Hillyard, A., McDonald, L., & Ahlster-Taylor, J. (1981). Early intervention, design and evaluation. In R. Schiefelbusch & D. Bricker (Eds.), *Early language: Acquisition and intervention*. Baltimore: University Park Press.

LaVeck, B., & Brehm, S. (1978). Individual variability among children with Down's syndrome. *Mental Retardation, 16*, 135–137.

Lazar, I., Darlington, R., Murray, H., Royce, J., & Snipper, A. (1982). Lasting effects of early education: A report from the consortium for longitudinal studies. *Monographs of the Society for Research in Child Development, 47*, serial no. 195.

Leib, S., Benfield, G., & Guidubaldi, J. (1980).

Effects of early intervention and stimulation on the preterm infant. *Pediatrics, 66,* 83–90.

Levenstein, P. (1970). Cognitive growth in preschoolers through verbal interaction with mothers. *American Journal of Orthopsychiatry, 40,* 426–432.

Lewis, M. (1978). The infant and its caregiver: The role of contingency. *Allied Health and Behavioral Sciences Journal, 1,* 469–492.

Lewis, M., & Rosenblum, L. (1974). *The effect of the infant on the caregiver.* New York: Wiley.

Lewis, M., & Starr, M. (1979). Developmental continuity. In J. Osofsky (Ed.), *Handbook of infant development.* New York: Wiley & Sons.

Lewis, M., & Wehren, A. (1982). The central tendency in study of the handicapped child. In D. Bricker (Ed.), *Intervention with at-risk and handicapped infants.* Baltimore: University Park Press.

Ludlow, J., & Allen, L. (1979). The effect of early intervention and preschool stimulus on the development of the Down's syndrome child. *Journal of Mental Deficiency Research, 23,* 29–44.

Madden, J., Levenstein, P., & Levenstein, S. (1976). Longitudinal IQ outcomes of the mother-child home program. *Child Development, 47,* 1015–1025.

Mahoney, G., & Weller, E. (1980). An ecological approach to language intervention. In D. Bricker (Ed.), *A resource book on language intervention with children.* San Francisco: Jossey-Bass.

Massie, H. (1980). Pathological interactions in infancy. In T. Field (Ed.), *High-risk infants and children.* New York: Academic Press.

McCall, R. (1979). The development of intellectual functioning in infancy and the prediction of later IQ. In J. Osofsky (Ed.), *Handbook of infant development.* New York: Wiley.

McCarthy, D. (1972). *McCarthy scales of children's abilities.* New York: Psychological Corporation.

Minde, K., Shosenberg, N., Marton, P., Thompson, J., Ripley, J., & Burns, S. (1980). Self help groups in a premature nursery—A controlled evaluation. *The Journal of Pediatrics, 96,* 933–940.

Moore, M., Fredericks, H., & Baldwin, V. (1981). The long-range effects of early childhood education on a trainable mentally retarded population. *Journal of the Division for Early Childhood, 4,* 93–110.

Oregon State Mental Health Division. (1977). *The student progress record,* Salem, OR: Author.

Petersen, G., & Sherrod, K. (1982). Relationship of maternal language to language development and language delay of children. *American Journal of Mental Deficiency, 86,* 391–398.

Petrie, P., Kratochwill, T., Bergan, J., & Nicholson, G. (1981). Teaching parents to teach their children: Applications in the pediatric setting. *Journal of Pediatric Psychology, 6,* 275–292.

Piaget, J. (1970). Piaget's theory. In P. Mussen (Ed.), *Carmichael's manual of child psychology* (Vol. I). New York: Wiley.

Piper, M., & Pless, I. (1980). Early intervention for infants with Down's syndrome: A controlled trial. *Pediatrics, 65,* 463–468.

Ramey, C., & Baker-Ward, L. (1982). Psychosocial retardation and the early experience paradigm. In D. Bricker (Ed.), *Intervention with at-risk and handicapped infants.* Baltimore: University Park Press.

Ramey, C., & Campbell, F. (1979). Supplemental preschool education for disadvantaged children. *School Review, 82,* 171–189.

Ramey, C., Campbell, F., & Wasik, B. (1982). Use of standardized tests to evaluate early childhood special education programs. *Topics in Early Childhood Special Education, 1,* 51–60.

Ramey, C., Farran, D., & Campbell, F. (1979). Early intervention: From research to practice. In B. Darby & M. May, *Infant assessment: Issues and applications.* Seattle: WESTAR.

Ramey, C., MacPhee, D., & Yeates, K. (1983). Preventing developmental retardation: A general systems model. In L. Bond & J. Joffe (Eds.), *Facilitating infant and early childhood development.* Hanover, NH: University Press of New England.

Rescorla, L., & Zigler, E. (1981). The Yale child welfare research program: Implications for social policy. *Education Evaluation and Policy Analysis, 3,* 5–14.

Revill, S., & Blunden, R. (1979). A home training service for preschool developmentally handicapped children. *Behaviour Research and Therapy, 17,* 207–214.

Reynell, J. (1969). *Reynell developmental language scales.* Windsor, England: N.F.E.R. Publishing Co. Ltd.

Risley, T., & Wolf, M. (1966). Experimental manipulation of autistic behaviors and generalization in the home. In R. Ulrich, T. Stachnik, & J. Mabry (Eds.), *Control of human behavior, Vol. 1.* Glenview, IL: Scott, Foresman & Co.

Rogers, S., D'Eugenio, D., Brown, S., Donovan, C., & Lynch, E. (1977). *Early intervention developmental profile.* Ann Arbor: University of Michigan Press.

Roos, P. (1978). Parents of mentally retarded children—Misunderstood and mistreated. In A. Turnbull & H. Turnbull (Eds.), *Parents speak out.* Columbus, OH: Charles E. Merrill.

Rosen-Morris, D., & Sitkei, E. (1981). Strategies for teaching severely/profoundly handicapped infants and young children. *Journal of the Division for Early Childhood, 4,* 79–93.

Rynders, J., & Horrobin, M. (1975). Project Edge: The University of Minnesota's communication stimulation program for Down's syndrome infants. In B. Friedlander, G. Sterritt, & G. Kirk (Eds.), *Exceptional infant: Assessment and intervention, Vol. 3.* New York: Brunner/Mazel.

Rynders, J., & Horrobin, M. (1980). Educational provisions for young children with Down's syndrome. In J. Gottlieb (Ed.), *Educating mentally retarded persons in the mainstream.* Baltimore: University Park Press.

Sameroff, A. (1981). Longitudinal studies of preterm infants: A review of chapters 17–20. In S. Friedman & M. Sigman (Eds.), *Preterm birth and psychological development.* New York: Academic Press.

Sameroff, A. (1982). The environmental context of developmental disabilities. In D. Bricker (Ed.), *Intervention with at-risk and handicapped infants: From research to application.* Baltimore: University Park Press.

Sameroff, A., & Chandler, M. (1975). Reproductive risk and the continuum of caretaking casualty. In F. Horowitz, M. Hetherington, S. Scarr-Salapatek, & G. Siegel (Eds.), *Review of child development research* (Vol. 4). Chicago: University of Chicago Press.

Scarr-Salapatek, S., & Williams, M. (1973). The effects of early stimulation on low-birth-weight infants. *Child Development, 44,* 94–101.

Schiefelbusch, R., & Lloyd, L. (Eds.) (1974). *Language perspectives: Acquisition, retardation and intervention.* Baltimore: University Park Press.

Scott, K., & Masi, W. (1979). The outcome from the utility of registers of risk. In T. Field, A. Sostek, S. Goldberg, & H. Shuman (Eds.), *Infants born at risk.* Jamaica, NY: Spectrum Publications.

Shearer, D., & Shearer, M. (1976). The Portage Project: A model for early childhood intervention. In T. Tjossem (Ed.), *Intervention strategies for high risk infants and young children.* Baltimore: University Park Press.

Shearer, M. & Shearer, D. (1972). The Portage Project: A model for early childhood education. *Exceptional Children, 39,* 210–217.

Sheehan, R., & Keogh, B. (1982). Design and analysis in the evaluation of early childhood special education programs. *Topics in Early Childhood Special Education, 1,* 81–88.

Simeonsson, R., Cooper, D., & Scheiner, A. (1982). A review and analysis of the effectiveness of early intervention programs. *Pediatrics, 69,* 635–641.

Simmons-Martin, A. (1981). Efficacy report: Early education project. *Journal of the Division for Early Childhood, 4,* 5–10.

Skeels, H. (1966). Adult status of children with contrasting early life experiences. *Monographs of the Society for Research in Child Development, 31* (3, Serial No. 105).

Soboloff, H. (1981). Early intervention — Fact or fiction? *Developmental Medicine and Child Neurology, 23,* 261–266.

Spiker, D. (1982). Parent involvement in early intervention activities with their young children with Down's syndrome. *Education and Training of the Mentally Retarded, 17,* 24–29.

Stedman, D. (1977). Important considerations in the review and evaluation of educational intervention programs. In P. Mittler (Ed.), *Research to practice in mental retardation: Care and intervention* (Vol 1). Baltimore: University Park Press.

Stock, J., Wnek, L., Newborg, E., Gabel, J., Spurgeon, M., & Ray, H. (1976). *Evaluation of handicapped children's early education program (HCEEP).* Final report to Bureau of Education for the Handicapped, U.S. Office of Education. Columbus, OH: Battelle.

Tyler, N., & Kogan, K. (1977). Reduction of stress between mothers and their handicapped children. *The American Journal of Occupational Therapy, 31,* 151–155.

Uzgiris, I. (1981). Experience in the social context. In R. Schiefelbusch & D. Bricker (Eds.), *Early language: Acquisition and intervention.* Baltimore: University Park Press.

Uzgiris, I., & Hunt, J. McV. (1975). *Assessment in infancy: Ordinal scales of psychological development.* Urbana: University of Illinois Press.

Walker, J. (1982). Social interaction of handicapped infants. In D. Bricker (Ed.), *Intervention with at-risk and handicapped infants.* Baltimore: University Park Press.

Weiss, R. (1981). INREAL intervention for language handicapped and bilingual children. *Journal of the Division for Early Childhood, 4,* 40–51.

White, O., Edgar, E., & Haring, N. (1978). *Uniform performance assessment system.* College of Education, Experimental Education Unit, Child Development and Mental Retardation Center, University of Washington, Seattle.

Wolf, M., Risley, T., & Mees, H. (1964). Application of operant conditioning procedures to the behavior problems of an autistic child. *Behavior Research and Therapy, 1,* 305–312.

Zeitlin, S. (1981). Learning through coping: An effective preschool program. *Journal of the Division for Early Childhood, 4,* 53–61.

Zigler, E., & Cascione, R. (1977). Head Start has little to do with mental retardation: A reply to Clarke and Clarke. *American Journal of Mental Deficiency, 82,* 246–249.

4 BEHAVIOR MODIFICATION WITH SPECIAL NEEDS CHILDREN: A REVIEW*

Richard J. Morris
Rebecca A. McReynolds

In recent years, the educational programs and intervention procedures that are utilized in special education settings have gone through many changes. Most noteworthy has been the tremendous increase in the application of behavior modification procedures with children who have special needs or exceptional children (see, for example, Hallahan & Kauffman, 1981; Lahey, 1979; Matson & Andrasik, 1983; Matson & McCartney, 1981; Morris, 1976, 1978, 1985; O'Leary & O'Leary, 1977; Repp, 1983; Ross, 1976; Ross & Ross, 1982; Snell, 1983; Whitman, Scibak, & Reid, 1983). Twenty years ago, few published studies specifically investigated the use of behavior modification procedures with exceptional children within a classroom, and few preservice special education programs offered courses or practice on behavior modification procedures and/or classroom. Within a 5–10 year period (1965–1975), however, numerous research articles, books, and journals focused on the successful use of behavior modification procedures in classroom settings, residential environments, and in the child's home. It was reported, and supported with data, that these procedures could be used not only by skilled researchers but by parents, teachers, and teacher aides (e.g., Ashem & Poser, 1973; Becker, 1971; Morris, 1976; O'Leary & O'Leary, 1971, 1977; Tharp & Wetzel, 1969).

Since the early to mid-1970s, so much has been written about the relative effectiveness of behavior modification procedures that few special educators would discount its utility—although some might question the ethical and legal aspects of using these procedures (e.g., Braun, 1975; Cunningham, 1984; Friedman, 1977; Martin, 1975; Morris, 1985; Morris & Brown, 1983; Vargas, 1975; Wexler, 1973). In fact, as one can see from Table 4.1, a wide array of behaviors have been modified—both in and out of the classroom—using behavioral procedures.

The present chapter presents an overview of some of the research that has been conducted with special needs children on modifying a variety of behaviors that are present either in a classroom, residential treatment center, or in the home. To aid in the organization of this chapter, we have divided it into sections with each section reviewing the relevant behavior modification research on a particular target behavior.

*Portions of this chapter are based on Morris, R. J. (1978). Treating mentally retarded children: A prescriptive approach. In A. P. Goldstein (Ed.). (1978). *Prescriptions for child mental health and education*. New York: Pergamon.

TABLE 4.1. SELECTED CHILDREN'S BEHAVIORS TREATED
USING BEHAVIOR MODIFICATION PROCEDURES

Behaviors Strengthened	Behaviors Developed	Behaviors Reduced
Assertiveness	Arm/leg movement	Bowel movement in pants
Attending to educational tasks/teacher	Color discrimination	Classroom disruption
Completion of educational tasks	Cooperative play	Climbing
Eating solid foods	Copying/tracing pictures	Constipation
Gross/fine motor skills	Echoing sounds	Crawling
Instruction/command following	Eye contact	Destroying objects
Math skills	Imitation (motoric and verbal)	Fears/phobias
Memory for spoken words	Independent dressing/undressing	Fecal smearing
Performing educational tasks	Independent walking	Fire setting
Personal hygiene skills	Letter discrimination	Gestures with fingers
Playing with toys	Making change	Hair pulling
Question answering/asking	Manual communication/use	Headbanging
Reading	of signs	Hitting others
Sitting	Name discrimination	Hyperactivity
Social interaction	Naming objects	Loud vocal utterances
Speech articulation	Pedestrian skills	Mutism/selective mutism
Spontaneous speech	Reading	Overeating
Talking to others	Self-feeding	Pinching, biting, kicking
Toileting	Shoe tying	others
Use of eating utensils	Size discrimination	Refusing to eat
Use of orthopedic devices for walking	Smiling	Rocking
Use of particular arm/leg	Speech	Self-hitting/scratching
Vocational/prevocational skills	Toilet training	Self-stimulation
Walking unaided	Tooth brushing	Stealing/grabbing food
Writing skills	Tricycle/bike riding	Stuttering/stammering
	Using telephone	Tantrums, crying
	Washing face/hands	Throwing objects
	Word discrimination	Thumbsucking
		Tics
		Urinating in bed/
		urinating in pants
		Vomiting
		Yelling, screaming, hand-
		slapping

EYE CONTACT

Eye contact appears to be a necessary prerequisite for the establishment of most cognitive and social behaviors in severely handicapped children. Without eye contact, many mentally handicapped and autistic children have difficulty responding to instructions, learning to imitate, developing communication and self-help skills, learning various academic tasks and/or vocational skills, or interacting socially with other people. In fact, Bandura (1969) states that one of the necessary components of a contiguity-mediational theory of imitation learning is the presence of attentional processes.

Using a reversal design, McConnell (1967) reported a case study concerning the effects of social reinforcement on the development of eye contact in a $5\frac{1}{2}$-year-old autistic and retarded child. Specifically, contingent social reinforcement was used each time the child spontaneously looked at the therapist in an unstructured situation. McConnell found that under these conditions the child's eye contact level increased substantially above his baseline performance, but the frequency of eye contacts decreased to approximately baseline level when social reinforcement was made noncontingent on eye contact; however, when contingent social praise was reinstituted, the boy's level of eye contact returned to its previous level. Similar findings regarding the development of eye contact have been reported by Ney (1973), who worked with a 5-year-old autistic child, and by Brooks, Morrow, and Gray (1967/68), working with a 19-year-old autistic and deaf girl.

Although only one subject was used in each of these studies, the findings suggest that spontaneous eye contact can be effectively increased by using contingent reinforcement. On the other hand, Morris (1977) and Morris and O'Neill (1975) investigated the development of eye contact within an instruction-following framework. They found that eye contact could be effectively taught to severely and profoundly retarded children in response to the instruction, "(Child's name), look at me," provided reinforcement is made contingent on the child's eye contact response. Moreover, they reported that this response was maintained at follow-up assessment. Unfortunately, no setting generalization data were reported.

An alternative intervention for strengthening eye contact in retarded and autistic children has been reported by Foxx (1977). The three subjects in this study only occasionally responded to edible and social reinforcers and were at times noncompliant. During the treatment phase, if the child did not respond to the instruction "Look at me" within 5 seconds, functional movement training (FMT) (Foxx & Azrin, 1973b) was introduced. This procedure involved the trainer manually guiding the child's head in the desired direction and remaining there for 15 seconds. The FMT procedure lasted from 2–5 minutes. Following treatment, a substantial increase in all three children's eye contact was observed compared to using instructions and positive reinforcement alone. Foxx (1977) cautioned, however, that FMT should be used only as a last resort when positive reinforcement interventions have proved ineffective.

MOTORIC IMITATION

It has been suggested that children increase their fund of knowledge, repertoire of behaviors, and develop strong emotional responses to specific situations by observing others under certain conditions, then imitating the observed behaviors (e.g., Bandura, 1969). However, the observer requires more than simple exposure to a model, if there is to be imitation. The observer must also possess the ability to attend to the various cues provided by the model and the capacity to develop "internal mediating events" (e.g., a self-instruction like "Do as she/he does") before successful imitative skills can be learned (Bandura, 1969, 1977).

Since many mentally handicapped and autistic children have a very limited symbolic representational system and a rather circumscribed behavioral repertoire, it is understandable that their level of imitativeness is not very high. Some investigators have shown that the presentation of the behavior to be imitated coupled with continuous contingent tangible and social reinforcement is sufficient to develop motoric imitation in nonimitative retarded children. For example, Metz (1965) and Garcia, Baer, and Firestone (1971) did not provide instructions to the children in their study but provided continuous tangible reinforcement, paired with social reinforcement, when the children imitated the modeled behaviors. A different approach was taken by Lovaas, Freitag, Nelson, and Whalen (1967) who investigated whether autistic and schizophrenic children could be taught increasingly more complex behaviors. Using 60 behavior tasks, ranging from simple to complex, Lovaas et al. found that within 4 months all subjects had learned all 60 tasks. Edible reinforcement was provided contingent on correct imitations, along with prompting and fading. These investigators also found that subjects' speed of mastery of new tasks increased as the number of tasks they learned increased.

A number of studies have demonstrated that motoric imitation can be developed in severely retarded children by using a combination of instructions to imitate and contingent reinforcement for correct imitative responding. For example, Baer, Peterson, and Sherman (1967) report the successful induction of imitation in three, 9–12-year-old severely retarded, nonverbal children, who exhibited no imitative tendencies prior to the study. Preceding each modeled behavior, the experimenter instructed the child to "Do this" and then modeled a simple response, such as raising arms or clapping hands. Using a shaping and fading procedure, the experimenter provided the child with edible and social reinforcement for increasingly closer approximations to the modeled behavior. When a child did not approximate the modeled behavior, a prompting procedure was initiated and gradually faded out as the child learned to imitate that particular behavior. Training sessions were conducted three to five times per week, once or twice per day. Using this method, Baer et al. (1967) were able to demonstrate that these children could imitate as many as 130 different responses.

O'Neill and Morris (1979) studied the relative contribution of instruction and reinforcement on the strengthening of motoric imitation in nonimitative, severely retarded children. Using a variation of the Baer et al. (1967) method, these experimenters first modeled the particular behavior to the imitated, with or without instructions. If the child did not respond within 10 seconds, a prompting procedure was used. A correct imitative response resulted in immediate edible and social reinforcement. The results of this experiment, which ran over a 6-month period, indicated that subjects who received contingent reinforcement plus instructions and contingent reinforcement only increased their level of imitative responding. Little improvement, however, was evident in either the instructions only condition, the noncontingent reinforcement plus instructions condition, the noncontingent reinforcement only condition, or in the no-treatment control condition. These findings are consistent with those reported by Bry and Nawas (1972), who compared instructions plus reinforcement to instructions only and found that reinforcement was necessary to establish

imitation learning in severely and profoundly retarded children. O'Neill and Morris (1979) also found, as did Striefel and Phelan (1972), that when contingent reinforcement was withdrawn and only verbal instructions were presented, subjects' imitative behavior decreased. This finding suggested that the reinforcement procedure was controlling the behavior of the subjects. No assessment of setting generalization or follow-up, however, was reported by either O'Neill and Morris (1979) or Striefel and Phelan (1972).

The relative importance of instructions to subjects and contingent reinforcement in the establishment of imitation learning has been repeatedly addressed in the research literature. Martin (1971), for example, showed that when reinforcement was delivered noncontingently on a child's response, the type of instruction (e.g., "Do this" or "Don't do this") affected the level of imitative responding; however, when reinforcement was combined with either positive or negative instructions following a correctly imitated response, the type of instruction did not influence subjects' level of responding. Thus, type of instruction, per se, does have an influence on imitative behavior, but when the type of instruction is combined with reinforcement or when reinforcement is presented alone, reinforcement rather than instruction seems to be necessary to establish imitative responding.

A large body of research has also accumulated on generalized imitation learning first observed in retarded children by Baer et al. (1967; see also, Bandura & Barab, 1971; Martin, 1971; Steinman, 1970a, 1970b; Suckerman & Morris, 1974). *Generalized imitation learning* refers to the learning by imitative subjects of responses that were never previously reinforced or modeled for these subjects. Essentially, this research has shown that children tend to imitate a model's new behaviors following an initial demonstration of these responses by the model without being reinforced for this imitative responding. For example, Baer et al. (1967) discovered that as long as children were reinforced for some of their previous imitative responding, they would imitate new behaviors even though these new behaviors were not reinforced. The investigators interpreted this to mean that the children were being reinforced not necessarily for imitating specific responses but for learning the instruction "Do as the experimenter does." Thus, subjects may have imitated nonreinforced responses because of their inability to discriminate between "to-be-reinforced" and "not-to-be-reinforced" behavior (Gewirtz & Stingle, 1968).

Contradictory findings (e.g., Steinman, 1970a, 1970b; Suckerman & Morris, 1974) have led to a second explanation in terms of the social demand factors associated with the instructions "Do this," the social environment, and the characteristics of the model; all of which have been assumed to contribute to subjects' generalized imitative behavior. For whatever reason, it seems clear that once children have learned to imitate at an appreciable level, new behaviors can be introduced without reinforcing the child for modeling these specific behaviors. Some reinforcement, however, of the previous imitative responses appears to be necessary.

With regard to generalization or transfer of training to new conditions, most of the research in the area of generalized imitation learning has been conducted in laboratory settings with few tests reported for transfer of training to the natural environment.

Commentary

One problem with the procedures discussed in this section is that often behaviors acquired by handicapped children in a one-to-one teaching situation do not generalize or transfer to a larger group situation, such as the classroom. For example, Koegel and Rincover (1974) found that when autistic children were individually taught motoric and verbal imitation skills, each individual child's performance of these behaviors was greatly reduced when tested with only one additional child (i.e., in a group of two). It was also shown that in a classroom of eight autistic children, performance of these behaviors deteriorated even

further and no new learning occurred after a period of 4 weeks.

Given these results, Koegel and Rincover (1974) developed a procedure to facilitate transfer of autistic students' learning to a classroom. This procedure involved initially teaching the children in one-to-one sessions and gradually thinning the reinforcement schedule from CRF to FR:2. When each child individually met the criterion of 80% appropriate responding for one reinforcer, two children were placed together with one teacher and two aides, who alternately reinforced children's correct responses. When these children met the 80% criterion, the reinforcement schedule was further thinned to FR:4 and two additional trained children were introduced to the group. These procedures continued until all children were responding correctly in a group of eight. These investigators also found that the children continued to learn new behaviors when one teacher instructed the entire group.

COOPERATIVE PLAY AND SOCIAL INTERACTIONAL SKILLS

Of the multitude of social behaviors taught to handicapped children, one that seems to be a prerequisite to learning more complex social skills is the establishment of cooperative and interactional play. In addition to the numerous studies that have been concerned with strengthening cooperative play in "typical" children (e.g., Azrin & Lindsley, 1956; Hart, Reynolds, Baer, Brawley, & Harris, 1968), a number of studies have concentrated on enhancing this behavior in handicapped children.

Whitman, Mercurio, and Caponigri (1970), for example, trained two nonverbal retarded children in cooperative play skills. These investigators reinforced the children for rolling a ball and passing a block to each other. Physical guidance and modeling were also necessary in order for the children to perform the skills under the trainer's verbal cues. Generalization was achieved by gradually phasing two other peers into the ball-rolling. In another controlled experiment using ball-rolling, Morris and Dolker (1974) studied the effectiveness of three approaches in strengthening cooperative play skills: (a) a high–low dyad play condition, in which a high-interacting retarded peer was paired with a low-interacting child in a play session; (b) a low–low dyad play condition, in which two low-interacting children were paired together; and (c) an experimenter-shaping condition, where the experimenter shaped ball-rolling in a low-interacting retarded child. Results showed that both the high–low condition and the shaping procedure produced the greatest amount of cooperative play. No appreciable increase was shown in the play behavior of children in the low–low condition or in the no-treatment control condition. Morris and Dolker (1974) also present data showing that these results were maintained at a 3-week follow-up evaluation.

Imitation proved to be an effective procedure for teaching other social play skills to retarded children, as is supported in a study by Paloutzian, Hasazi, Striefel, and Edgar (1971). After training 10 severely and profoundly retarded children in generalized imitation skills, these investigators instructed particular children to imitate a response of another child. Social praise and edible reinforcers were provided for correct imitations. Results showed that the level of social interaction increased over those of the control children, suggesting that retarded children can imitate the play behaviors of other children.

While it is recognized that the typical child acquires many social skills in the context of playing with toys with other children, it is apparent that children having severe behavior disorders often lack such social skills and do not always use toys appropriately. For example, Romanczyk, Diament, Goren, Trunell, and Harris (1975) attempted to teach appropriate play skills to a group of children diagnosed as having neurological impairments, childhood schizophrenia, or autism in order to strengthen their social interaction skills. After establishing a baseline, food and social reinforcement were introduced for isolate play, defined as the manipulation of a toy with which no other child was playing. The next phase involved

presenting reinforcement for social play, while isolate play was ignored. Because the children in this study rarely engaged in socially interactive play, a passive shaping procedure was implemented. This procedure consisted of simply placing one child next to another who was playing with a toy, so that both children's hands were touching the toy. No verbal cues were given or reinforcement dispensed during passive shaping. The results showed that contingent reinforcement and passive shaping produced increases in isolate and social play; however, following a reversal period, both target behaviors decreased to their previous baseline levels.

Romanczyk et al. (1975) undertook a second study in order to determine how their procedure might be modified to produce greater resistance to the extinction of social play skills. Four older, equally handicapped children participated in this study. These experimenters essentially replicated their previous study except that the passive shaping procedure was gradually withdrawn. Their findings indicated that the gradual withdrawal of passive shaping led to the maintenance of social play, which stabilized at twice the level that was recorded during baseline.

More recently, Ollendick, Shapiro, and Barrett (1982) examined the vicarious effects of one child seeing another child receive direct reinforcement for appropriate play with a toy. Subjects in this study were 14 children in a hospital program for emotionally disturbed and mentally retarded children. During the intervention phase, the children were placed in pairs and direct social reinforcement for appropriate block play was delivered to a one target child within each pair. Results showed that the children who received direct reinforcement exhibited higher levels of appropriate play than children who observed their peers being reinforced. Thus, it was shown that observing another child receive reinforcement appeared to initially facilitate children's play behavior but eventually led to overall decrements in children's appropriate play.

In terms of teaching children to be in close proximity to other children, Redd (1969) examined the effects of different reinforcement schedules on one mentally retarded child's physical contact with another. Within each training session, Redd varied the type of reinforcement schedule over the 30-minute period. The results showed playing with a toy while in physical contact with another child increased over sessions and that subjects learned to emit play responses when in the presence of an adult who provided contingent, rather than noncontingent, reinforcement. Wiesen, Hartley, Richardson, and Roske (1967) investigated the effects of reinforcement on the physical proximity of one child to another. In this study, each target child was paired with another child with whom she or he had no contact at baseline. A conditioned generosity response was used, where if child A gave an M & M to child B, then the experimenter would give child A an M & M. At other times, child B was treated by the experimenter in the same way as child A. When all children had learned to give each other candy, the experimenter thinned the reinforcement schedule from a continuous to a variable interval reinforcement schedule. Wiesen et al. (1967) found that the amount of time that the children were within 3 feet of one another increased following this procedure.

Another social skill that has been strengthened in retarded children is smiling. Hopkins (1968) initially recorded the frequency of discrete smiles exhibited during short walks with two retarded boys. He then reinforced each child with candy each time the child smiled within 5 seconds of any initiation of conversation by the trainer. Hopkins found that only one child's frequency of smiling increased under the reinforcement contingency; however, when the second child was instructed to smile and then reinforced for smiling, his smile responses also increased.

Nelson, Gibson, and Cutting (1973) attempted to strengthen a mildly retarded boy's appropriate smiling responses and appropriate statements and questions using a combination of techniques that included videotaped modeling, instructions, and social reinforcement. A modified multiple baseline design was employed, with the training procedures presented sequentially across the three target behaviors. Results showed that all three target behaviors increased following training. Although the study's design does not allow for a differential assessment of the relative effectiveness of the three training procedures, these investigators suggest that a combination of the three training techniques would be the most powerful treatment package. At a $3\frac{1}{2}$ month follow-up assessment, it was reported that the subject's appropriate statements had decreased but that smiling responses and appropriate questions had increased in the classroom. In a similar study, Cooke and Apolloni (1976) sought to increase smiling, sharing, positive physical contact, and verbal compliments in a group of seven learning disabled students who exhibited low rates of appropriate social behaviors in school. Four of the children received training using a teaching package composed of instructions, modeling, and trainer-delivered social reinforcement. Immediately following each training session, the three remaining children were brought to the experimental setting to determine the effects of integrating trained and nontrained peers. Cooke and Apolloni found that the training package served to increase the frequency of target behaviors in all four experimental subjects. Generalization was demonstrated across nontrained target behaviors as well as across nontrained subjects who were integrated with trained subjects.

Two studies have concentrated on strengthening interpersonal language in retarded children. For example, Whitman, Barrish, and Collins (1972) implemented a token reinforcement system in order to increase interpersonal language in four moderately retarded adolescents. Two of the subjects were instructed that they would earn tokens, which could later be exchanged for candy, for talking to each other during a game. Following training, it was shown that both trained and nontrained subjects' use of interpersonal language increased markedly.

Strain and associates (e.g., Strain, 1977; Strain & Timm, 1974; Strain, Shores, & Timm, 1977) conducted a number of studies aimed at strengthening the social interaction skills of children who are socially withdrawn. For example, Strain and Timm (1974) worked to increase a preschool child's social interaction skills in a classroom for behaviorally disordered children. Verbal praise and physical contact were presented contingent on any positive contact between her and any other child. During the baseline period, the target child's frequency of social contacts was essentially zero. The first intervention consisted of reinforcing the target child's peers for initiating and responding to any contacts with her and resulted in an increase in her frequency of social interactions. In a second intervention, adult attention was presented directly to the target child whenever she initiated or responded to a peer contact. This intervention produced an increase in the target child's frequency of social contacts, with most of her interactions being initiated by the child herself. Each time that contingent adult attention was withdrawn, however, the child's target behaviors returned to near baseline levels. These investigators suggest that perhaps longer periods of intervention, in which reinforcement is continuous initially, then intermittent, and gradually faded altogether, might maintain appropriate peer social interactions.

Strain, Shores, and Timm (1977) subsequently demonstrated the utility of peers as confederates of the therapist for increasing the social interaction skills of withdrawn children. Six behaviorally handicapped boys enrolled in a private treatment center served as subjects in this study. Two other preschool boys served as "therapists" and were instructed to initiate social play with the target children. Following this intervention, the positive social behavior of all target children increased dramatically. They responded to their peers' invitations and initiated play on their own. Because this study was conducted in a laboratory, no information about the intervention's effectiveness outside the experimental setting was available. Strain (1977) subsequently addressed this issue in a replication of the Strain et al. (1977) study. Here, the subjects' social behaviors were recorded in the classroom during free play periods. Results from this study showed that two of the children's increased social responding generalized across settings. In both studies, it was shown that differences were apparent in the degree to which individual children responded to the intervention. Specifically, children who exhibited the lowest frequency of positive social behaviors during the baseline period responded least to the peer-initiated interactions.

READING

Reading is defined by Risko (1981) as a process for obtaining meaning from print. Many special education students have specific reading problems, and a vast number of different reading approaches and instructional programs are available. From an applied behavior analysis perspective, reading consists of a set of independent skills, such as word recognition, word analysis, and comprehension, and each is viewed as a behavior to be learned (Lahey & McNees, 1974). Staats and his colleagues were one of the first researchers to conceptualize reading as an operant behavior and to systematically apply operant learning principles to improve children's reading skills (e.g., Staats & Butterfield, 1965; Staats, Minke, Finley, Wolf, & Brooks, 1964). From this perspective, reading may be construed as a sequence involving presentation of a stimulus (the word printed on a page) and emission of a verbal response (the child says the word out loud). If, following a correct response, the teacher says "Good," and the child's correct responses are shown to increase in frequency, then the teacher's praise is functioning as a positive reinforcer.

An operant conditioning conceptualization of reading would dictate the use of reinforcement contingencies in order to improve students' reading skills. Folk and Campbell (1978), for example, applied reinforcement procedures to teach functional reading skills that included sight words and phonetic and word attack skills to three trainable mentally handicapped students who had no reading skills. Using primary reinforcers, subjects were taught to correctly recognize names, read phrases and sentences, match phrases with objects, and use specific words in sentences. Correct use of word attack and phonetic analysis skills were also reinforced. At the end of the study, all subjects showed improvement in their sight word vocabulary and phonetic skills. In addition, two subjects were able to read from a pre-primer.

Modeling has often been used to strengthen students' reading skills. Through the use of modeling, teachers are able to capitalize on the strength of observational learning (Bandura, 1969) to initially present specific reading skills to students. For example, Pany and Jenkins (1978) provide a clear example of the use of modeling to teach word meaning to academically deficient students. In this study, the teacher told students correct synonyms for words and then required them to practice giving the synonyms. Results showed that students' performance on various measures of word definition knowledge improved significantly. Smith (1979) also reported that demonstrating correct oral reading performance prior to students' participation in oral reading exercises had a significant influence on their rate and accuracy of oral reading.

Two studies have employed a combination of reinforcement and modeling to teach reading to trainable mentally handicapped students. In one study, Brown et al. (1972) trained two subjects to first identify and associate common objects with their printed word names and subsequently to associate certain adjective and noun phrases. These investigators used edible reinforcers along with experimenter modeling correct responses. At baseline, neither subject was able to recognize any words. Following training, both subjects learned to associate specific objects with the correct word names as well as recognize certain adjective-noun phrases. Brown, Huppler, Pierce, York, and Sontag (1974) followed a seven-step program to teach trainable mentally handicapped students to read action verbs. The program was implemented with three students and consisted of the following steps: (a) a baseline period, (b) teaching subjects to engage in specific actions following verbal cues, (c) teaching subjects to

verbally label action pictures, with modeling of correct responses and tangible and social reinforcement for correct imitation, (d) discrimination learning, (e) verbal labeling of word cards, with the experimenter initially modeling the correct labels, (f) associating action words with action pictures, and (g) associating action word cards with specific performed actions. All subjects were trained together and progressed successfully throughout all steps of the program. The most difficult step appeared to be learning to label word cards correctly.

Self-instruction and self-control techniques have also been successful in improving handicapped students' reading comprehension (see, for example, Hallahan, Lloyd, Kauffman, & Loper, 1983; Malamuth, 1979). For example, Knapczyk and Livingston (1974) showed that prompting mildly retarded students to ask questions on reading tasks produced increased accuracy in answering reading comprehension questions; however, Lloyd, Kneedler, and Cameron (1982) did not find that requiring learning disabled students to verbalize a strategy for reading unfamiliar words would increase their reading accuracy.

Schwartz (1977) conducted a well-controlled study investigating the effectiveness of using college student tutors as contingency managers in a program to develop reading skills in seventh grade students who read below grade level. Four different control conditions were used to evaluate the individual tutoring program. The tutoring program lasted for a 10-week period, with students meeting with a tutor for one hour per week. The tutoring program consisted of using praise and ignoring for students' positive and negative statements, respectively, regarding reading as well as the establishment of a reading contract with students. Students were tested on the Gates-MacGintie Reading Test prior to the tutoring program, immediately following the program, and 6 months later. Results showed that compared to pretest the experimental subjects' rate of growth in reading had accelerated three times the expected rate of average students and four times their own previous growth rate. In contrast, control subjects improved only 1.4

times the average expected rate of growth and only twice their own previous rate.

In an innovative study using token reinforcement, Kirby, Holborn, and Bushby (1981) examined the use of a modified bingo game to teach sight words to a small group of children who were placed in a resource classroom because of reading problems. Bingo playing cards were constructed by dividing cards into equal squares and typing various words within each square. Essentially, the game was identical to regular bingo, except that words, instead of numbers, were called out. A child who had the word that was called out on his or her card, placed a plastic chip over the word. A child who met the criterion for bingo (i.e., all words in a horizontal or diagonal row covered) called out "Bingo!" The winner of every bingo game was awarded a star next to his or her name on a chart. At the end of each work period, subjects were allowed to exchange their stars for back-up reinforcers of their choice. A variation of a multiple baseline across three different sets of words was used in this study, with the addition of social reinforcement for correct reading of one word. A 6-month follow-up revealed that experimental subjects' growth in reading continued to accelerate compared to control subjects and even exceeded the average expected growth. Although the tutoring program was clearly effective and superior to the other approaches included in the study, Schwartz points out that providing poor readers with special attention of any form is also generally beneficial.

Manipulating consequences of students' reading behaviors are also sometimes necessary in order to improve performance. For example, Lovitt and Hansen (1976) instituted an intervention for improving reading performance that involved combining reinforcement with correction consequences. Students were initially assigned to reading texts appropriate to their skill levels. A contingent skipping and drilling procedure was introduced next, in which students read assigned materials and answered comprehension questions on these materials. A student whose answers were at or above a pre-set criterion level was allowed to

skip a specific portion of the text and the subsequent assignment was derived from a later portion of it. If the criterion was not reached, however, the student was required to practice skills specifically related to the unmet criteria. This intervention was employed over the course of an entire school year and was found to result in substantial improvements in students' oral reading and reading comprehension.

SPELLING

Spelling can be a difficult academic area, particularly for handicapped students, because standard English contains as many exceptions as there are rules. Smith (1981) suggests that students having difficulty with spelling may require more concentrated efforts in this area rather than a different approach to spelling instruction.

There seem to be two general approaches to spelling remediation. One involves simply adapting the traditional instructional approach, while the other requires the development of specialized instructional sequences for particular students' difficulties (Smith, 1981). A number of studies have incorporated reinforcement procedures to improve students' spelling performance. For example, Sidman (1979) employed both group and individual free time contingencies to improve spelling test scores and found that accuracy increased more during the group contingency. In an often cited study, Lovitt, Guppy, and Blattner (1969) provided free time activities contingent on mastering weekly spelling word lists to a 100% accuracy criterion. These researchers found that substantial increases in spelling performance followed this intervention.

In contrast to the intervention just discussed, other studies have shown that for some handicapped students modifying the traditional approach to teaching spelling is not sufficient. An unusual intervention procedure is reported by Kauffman, Hallahan, Haas, Brame, and Boren (1978), who used modeling combined with contingent imitation of students' spelling errors. During the imitation phases, the teacher told students which words were spelled incorrectly, copied the incorrectly spelled words, showed them the correct spelling, then demonstrated the correct spelling. These procedures resulted in marked improvements in students' spelling performance. Stowitschek and Jobes (1977) applied modeling, drill, and contingent praise in order to help students deficient in spelling skills to earn and retain new words. For each student, the following steps were followed by the teacher during spelling instruction. First, the teacher said the word out loud and used it in a sentence. Next, she spelled the word out loud and showed the student the word written on a card. Then she spelled the word again while pointing to each letter and, finally, the student spelled the word out loud and wrote it on the blackboard. Spelling acquisition and retention were shown to improve appreciably.

Matson and associates conducted two well-designed studies to compare the effects of positive reinforcement combined with practice along with positive practice for improving handicapped students' spelling performance. In one study, Ollendick, Matson, Esveldt-Dawson and Shapiro (1980) conducted two experiments with children who were hospitalized for extreme aggressive behavior and failure to learn in school. An alternating treatments design was used to compare the two treatments (positive practice alone and reinforcement plus positive practice) with a no-remediation control procedure for each word spelled incorrectly. Positive practice intervention consisted of having the child listen to the misspelled word pronounced by the teacher, pronounce the word correctly, say each letter of the word out loud, and write the misspelled word correctly. Reinforcement consisted of verbal praise plus a "star" for each word spelled correctly. Results showed that both subjects' spelling improved under both treatment conditions and that positive practice plus reinforcement resulted in more rapid learning and 100% spelling accuracy. In the second experiment reported by Ollendick et al. (1980), the effect of positive practice plus reinforcement was compared to a traditional spelling instruction approach plus reinforcement and to reinforcement alone in increasing students' spelling accuracy. Matson, Esveldt-Dawson, and Kazdin (1982) investigated using positive practice overcorrection alone and in combination with positive reinforcement to improve spelling accuracy of mildly retarded children with behavior disorders. This study's design and method was very similar to that reported by Ollendick et al. Consistent with previous findings, the results of this study showed that positive practice overcorrection plus reinforcement was superior to overcorrection alone in increasing students' spelling accuracy.

MATH

Although an often undervalued area of instruction, basic mathematics skills are necessary for independent functioning in daily life. Experts in the area of mathematics have questioned both the content and sequence of the standard mathematics curriculum for normal as well as handicapped students (Smith, 1981). For example, Chandler (1978) emphasizes the importance of handicapped people acquiring basic arithmetic skills and maintains that fourth grade level numeration, computation, measurement, and problem solving skills are vital for maintaining employment. For these reasons, a number of different classroom behavioral interventions have been applied to strengthen handicapped students' math skills.

It has been shown, for example, that changing both the antecedents and consequences of children's responses on math tasks is successful in improving their respective performance. For example, Lovitt and Curtiss (1968) found that when children verbalized math problems (e.g., "Six plus two equals what?") prior to computing the answers the accuracy of their answers improved substantially. Parsons (1972) discovered that if children who often performed incorrect math operations were required to circle and correctly name the operation sign (e.g., + or −) before writing their answer, a higher percentage of correct responses were made. Coleman (1970) reports a case study in which a trainable mentally handicapped child was taught to count objects by using tangible and social reinforcement.

Ayllon, Garber, and Pisor (1976) attempted to improve three mildly retarded students' math computation accuracy through token reinforcement and systematic manipulation of time limits. Students were awarded marbles that could be exchanged for certain privileges contingent on each math problem completed correctly within a specific time period. The time limits for completion of all math problems varied from 5–20 minutes. Results showed that an abrupt change in time limits (e.g., from 20 minutes to 5 minutes) led to a marked decrease in the accuracy of students' math problems, while a series of graduated temporal shifts increased the math accuracy rate for all students. McCarty, Griffin, Apolloni, and Shores (1977) applied a group contingency reinforcement program to increase arithmetic problem completion in four behaviorally disordered adolescents in a psychiatric hospital. Under a cumulative condition, students earned five cents for every multiplication problem computed correctly. During a mixed contingency phase, students were required to complete at least three problems correctly in order to receive a reward. Students' rates of problem completion and rates of antecedent peer-teaching verbalizations increased when group-oriented contingencies were in effect. Thus, it is suggested that the use of a group-oriented contingency program may stimulate peer-teaching in the classroom.

Modeling can also be an effective technique for teaching academic tasks to handicapped students. For example, Smith and Lovitt (1975) employed modeling to help students acquire computational arithmetic skills, such as borrowing and carrying. It was shown that demonstration each day of how to solve particular math problems led to mastery of these skills within several school days. Smith (1981) maintains, however, that the use of modeling as an instructional strategy for a group of students is sometimes equivocal due to the varying entry

skill levels of the stud‹
that the teacher be a
skill levels and grou
Given the uniqu‹
capped children, it is ...
searchers are continually investigating new approaches to instruction and to strengthening school-related behaviors. One area that has received increasing attention over the last several years is the use of self-control as a method for changing the classroom behaviors and academic performance of handicapped people (e.g., Hallahan et al., 1983; Shapiro & Klein, 1980). One type of self-management technique that has been successful in improving students' math skills is self-instruction training. This procedure was developed and based on the theories and laboratory research on language development by Luria (1961) and Vygotsky (1962). Self-instruction training involves teaching the child to ask himself or herself questions about the task, give himself or herself instructions about performing the task, and provide self-reinforcement and corrective feedback. Training typically follows a sequence of activities beginning with the teacher modeling the task with overt self-instructions, the student imitating the teacher's self-instructions and task behavior, gradual fading of the teacher's prompts, and finally, the student performing the task with covert self-talk (Meichenbaum & Goodman, 1971).

Two studies that have used self-instruction training with mentally handicapped students are by Burgio, Whitman, and Johnson (1980) and Johnston, Whitman and Johnson (1980). For example, Burgio et al. (1980) developed a self-instruction training program that included a generalization component to increase academic and attending skills of mildly and moderately retarded children. Arithmetic and printing were used during training, while a phonics task was used to assess generalization. Self-instruction training consisted of the following types of self-statements: asking and answering questions, giving directions, self-reinforcement, self-cues to ignore distractions, and coping statements for task failure. Modng and prompting were used to teach students to instruct themselves. Results revealed that students who received self-instruction training exhibited less off-task behavior and a high rate of self-instruction statements in the training and classroom settings compared to a control student. Self-instruction subjects also extensively used self-statements on generalized tasks.

In another study, Johnston et al. (1980) attempted to teach addition and subtraction regrouping skills to three mildly retarded children using self-instruction training procedures. Self-instructions consisted of questions about the nature and demands of each math problem, answers regarding the specific steps required for successfully completing each problem, self-controlling statements to help the student focus his or her attention and "slow down" his or her responding, coping self-statements for handling errors and frustration, and self-reinforcement. Food and social reinforcement was initially provided for correct self-instruction and was gradually faded when self-instructions were learned. Results showed that self-instruction training was an effective technique for teaching addition and subtraction skills to mildly retarded children. It was observed that while self-instruction improved students' accuracy, a decrease in rate of responding was also noted. Thus, as the children engaged in self-instruction, they completed fewer math problems. Johnston et al. suggest that an increase in response rate might follow more long-term use of self-instructions to improve academic skills.

Self-instruction training was also used by Cullinan, Lloyd and Epstein (1981) to teach multiplication facts to students. Their design for teaching a strategy included (a) the development of the instructional procedure that is nearly foolproof and contains simple steps that can be learned quickly and (b) the actual implementation of the program. Although the research literature on self-instruction training for learning mathematics and other academic skills is limited, the current research findings seem to indicate that this method is a potentially viable procedure for increasing a student's knowledge base in school as well as his or her overall academic performance.

HANDWRITING

Prior to learning to write, children must have acquired some specific skills. For example, Miller and Schneider (1970) have identified a number of skills that are prerequisite to freehand printing: the ability to hold a pencil correctly, draw straight and curved lines at various angles, draw freehand lines, and draw different shapes with lines crossing and joining specific points. LeBrun and Van de Craen (1975) maintain that spatial orientation and directional sense are also important precursors to the establishment of handwriting skills. When instruction in manuscript writing is initiated, Fauke, Burnett, Powers, and Sulzer-Azaroff (1973) suggest several general guidelines that should be followed. They state that students should first be able to orally identify letters using the correct letter names, then be able to trace letters using their index finger, followed by a magic marker, and then a pencil. Once students are able to trace the letters, they should next copy letters from a model provided by the teacher. Finally, they should be required to print letters without a model.

One difficulty with writing often experienced by many handicapped students is the occurrence of reversals (letters and/or numerals that are written backwards), letters substituted for similar letters, or mirror image words (Hallahan et al, 1983). Handwriting reversals have been decreased by using a combination of correction and reinforcement techniques. Essentially, the intervention consists of the teacher providing reinforcement to the student contingent on the correct writing of the target letter, numeral, or word and requiring the student to correctly rewrite an incorrectly written target item. Stromer (1977) remediated several learning disabled students' letter and number reversals through modeling and providing corrective feedback. Smith and Lovitt (1973) report a case study in which a learning disabled boy's b and d reversals were reduced by showing him a teacher error and providing him with instructions to write the correct letter.

With regard to cursive writing, Trap, Milner-Davis, Joseph, and Cooper (1978) suggest that instruction should include the components of modeling, copying, feedback, rewriting of errors, and reinforcement. In their study, students were required to write letters following teacher modeling of the correct letter formation. The teacher then provided corrective feedback, a redemonstration of incorrect letters, and required students to rewrite incorrect letters. Reinforcement was given contingent on correct letter production.

Although the use of writing as a primary communication mode decreases throughout the school years, there are a number of writing skills that handicapped people should possess if they are to become independent adults (Smith, 1981). Little research is available, however, to guide one in selecting a particular instructional strategy for strengthening the mechanical, composition, and creative writing skills of handicapped students. Van Houten, Morrison, Jarvis, and McDonald (1974), for example, attempted to improve the quality of writing in a remedial fifth grade classroom. Students were given a topic to write about and were awarded points for improvement in number of words written, number of different words used, number of new words used. During reinforcement phases, both the frequency of the target areas and the quality (e.g., mechanical aspects, vocabulary, development of ideas) of students' compositions improved.

Ballard and Glynn (1975) implemented a self-management intervention that included self-assessment and self-scoring components in order to improve third grade students' story writing skills. Target areas for improvement were number of sentences, number of different action words, and number of different descriptive words. These investigators found that free-time reinforcement contingent on each target area resulted in improved story writing. When students graded their own compositions, story writing also improved, as evaluated by objective raters.

Kosiewicz, Hallah (1982) report a case tional training (Me 1971) combined wit dure (identifying one's own errors on ... ous day's assignment) to improve a learning disabled elementary student's copying of written work. Both procedures were effective in reducing the student's errors, but since no comparison was made between these self-instructional procedures and teacher-managed interventions (e.g., teacher correction, differential reinforcement), it is not possible to suggest which procedure was more effective.

MEALTIME SKILLS

One of the first areas to which behavior modification procedures were applied with mentally retarded and physically handicapped persons was self-help skills. The systematic use of behavioral procedures for training mealtime skills first began in the early 1960s (e.g., Morris, 1978). Subsequently, a considerable amount of research was conducted demonstrating that various training strategies based on operant learning principles were successful in teaching various self-help skills, including mealtime skills, to handicapped persons. In normal human development, self-feeding is one of the first self-help behaviors to be learned. Some mentally retarded children, however, only occasionally feed themselves, others never feed themselves, and still others possess a number of appropriate feeding skills but prefer to use their hands for eating. Thus, it is important to teach mealtime skills to handicapped children, for without these skills they may exert only a limited degree of independence in their environments (Reid, 1983).

Independent self-feeding has been considered one of the easiest self-help skills to teach to mentally retarded children, provided that the necessary motor skills (i.e., arm and hand movements to bring food to the mouth, as well as the ability to chew and swallow) are present. Watson (1967) points out that self-feeding is relatively easy to teach because of the in-rent reinforcer being used and because the shaping and chaining procedures used in training are typically straightforward and easy to implement.

Much of the research on teaching self-feeding skills to mentally retarded children has utilized shaping plus prompting strategies (e.g., Groves & Carroccio, 1971; Miller, Patton & Herton, 1971; O'Brien, Bugle, & Azrin 1972). Typically, these procedures first involve having the trainer initially physically guide the child's hand through the feeding sequence, with the physical guidance then being gradually reduced as the child begins to show progress. Although many of the studies discussed in this section were conducted with retarded children in institutional settings, it appears that these behavioral procedures can be adapted easily for teaching mealtime skills in school.

Bensberg, Colwell, and Cassel (1965) published one of the first studies concerned with using behavioral techniques to teach self-feeding to retarded children. This skill was first broken into its component parts, then both shaping and prompting procedures, as well as special prosthetic eating utensils were used to teach the simplest skill components first. At the end of the study, experimental subjects' self-feeding skills were approaching an independent level. Berkowitz, Sherry, and Davis (1971) also used a shaping and prompting procedure to teach self-feeding to a group of 14 profoundly retarded children who had never fed themselves prior to the study. A seven-step shaping program was employed, with the experimenter gradually fading out the use of physical prompts. A child who grabbed food was immediately removed from the dining area and allowed to return after all the other children had completed their meals. The child who grabbed food a second time was again removed from the area and missed the remainder of the meal. Results showed that one group of children took 2–21 days of training at each of three meals to learn to feed themselves independently. A second group, containing some disruptive children, took 13–60 days to be completely trained. At a 23-month follow-up

evaluation, all children continued to be self-feeding, and 10 children had retained this skill after a 41-month follow-up period.

Two studies have shown that once a child has reliably learned the skill of self-feeding, specific components to maintain the use of this skill must be implemented. For example, after Whitney and Bernard (1966) established self-feeding in their subject, the child was placed on an extinction schedule for 7 days, removing all prompts for independent eating as well as time out and reprimands for inappropriate behaviors. As a result, the child's self-feeding decreased to the point that she did not feed herself at all but increased when the training procedures were reinstated. O'Brien et al. (1973) also showed that once a child was taught to self-feed using a combination of manual guidance, interruption, and extinction procedures, correct feeding responses diminished to zero following withdrawal of these procedures. Thus, not only must retarded children be trained to feed themselves, but continued motivation must be provided to maintain self-feeding skills.

Azrin and Armstrong (1973) developed an intensive program for teaching self-feeding skills to mentally retarded persons. This program was designed as a quick and effective intervention for use with people having severe feeding deficits. Numerous procedures were combined in this program, which include "mini-meals" (brief meals served hourly throughout each day), manual graduated guidance, separate training procedures for each feeding utensil, physical interruption and overcorrection for inappropriate mealtime behaviors, and initially the use of a 2:1 trainer-to-trainee ratio. Specific maintenance components (e.g., no manual guidance but continued use of overcorrection) were also built into the program. Results indicated that the intensive training procedures were far superior to more traditional approaches in terms of overall amount of improvement in self-feeding and drinking skills. A 28-week follow-up assessment revealed that these improvements were maintained.

Several recent trends are apparent in the

research on mealtime skills with mentally re-tarded persons. In general, much of the previous research in this area focused on teaching the rudimentary skills necessary for independent feeding, such as eating with a spoon. More recently, researchers have become concerned with expanding the type of mealtime skills taught as well as developing independent mealtime skills in public dining places. These trends are reflected in a rapidly growing body of research that has been labeled "community survival skills" (Reid, 1983). For instance, Nelson, Cone, and Hanson (1976) taught a group of 24 retarded children to correctly use a knife, fork, and spoon by visual physical guidance and praise for correct utensil use. Van den Pol et al. (1981) used a classroom-based instructional program to teach restaurant skills to mentally retarded teenagers and adults. Modeling and role playing in conjunction with photo slides of a restaurant and a simulated ordering counter were used to teach such skills as ordering, playing, and eating. Results showed that subjects' performance improved and generalized to novel settings.

DRESSING AND UNDRESSING

A problem frequently encountered by classroom teachers and parents is the inability of many mentally retarded and other developmentally delayed persons to dress and undress themselves. Dressing and undressing skills are important to handicapped persons in much the same way as are independent mealtime skills. Teaching these individuals to dress and undress themselves independently not only saves teachers and others an appreciable amount of time but provides these handicapped persons greater control over their living environments and increases their self-esteem, confidence, and sense of independence. Reid (1983) maintains that teaching mentally retarded persons to dress independently and socially appropriately probably enhances the effect their appearance has on other people. While the impact appro-

priate dress has on handicapped persons' social interactions has not been specifically addressed experimentally, it is assumed that clothing (i.e., style, neatness, appropriateness) appreciably affects handicapped individual's interpersonal interactions (Newton, 1976). Thus, it seems important to examine both specific methods for teaching self-dressing and undressing skills to handicapped persons as well as skills related to dressing in accordance with social customs.

A number of training programs and curricula have been developed for teaching self-dressing and undressing skills to handicapped individuals (e.g., Lovaas, 1981; Morris, 1976, 1985; Snell, 1983). Some of the skills that have been successfully taught include putting on and removing shirt, pants, dress, sweater, coat, socks, shoes, underpants, and undershirt; tying shoes, buttoning, unbuttoning, and zipping (Colwell, Richards, McCarver, & Ellis, 1973; Karen & Maxwell, 1967; Morris, 1985; Reid, 1983). Most of these programs incorporate the systematic use of instructions, shaping, prompting, and if necessary, modeling and/or graduate manual guidance. Physical guidance is then gradually faded, while target dressing or undressing behaviors are reinforced. Watson and Uzzell (1980) provide a good description of a training model for teaching dressing skills to mentally retarded and other developmentally delayed persons.

Minge and Ball (1967) taught six severely and profoundly retarded girls to dress and undress themselves. Skills taught included putting on and taking off pants, dresses, and shoes. In order to maintain the children's interest and motivation level, their breakfast and lunch were made contingent on their performance in the training sessions. The results showed that compared to no-treatment, matched control subjects, the experimental group's independent dressing skills improved following training. Similar findings were reported by Martin, Kehoe, Bird, Jensen, and Darbyshire (1971). These investigators successfully taught a number of dressing skills, including putting on a sweater, lacing and tying shoes, putting on a bra, socks, underpants, and undershirt to a group of severely retarded girls using a combination of reinforcement, prompting, manual guidance, and brief time out for incorrect responses.

As with the research on self-feeding skills, several recent trends in the research on self-dressing are apparent. For example, recent studies have focused on teaching a wider variety and more advanced set of self-dressing skills and have examined various experimental uses. For example, early research in this area targeted a relatively limited and simple set of dressing skills, such as putting on and taking off a shirt and pants (Minge & Ball, 1967), whereas later studies included these basic skills plus more complex ones, such as tying shoes and buttoning (Adelstein-Bernstein & Sandow, 1978; Martin et al., 1971). While Karen and Maxwell (1967) report that the use of reinforcement and modeling were successful in teaching buttoning to a retarded boy, a later study conducted by Kramer and Whitehurst (1981) evaluated specific button design features in terms of their effect on teaching buttoning skills to mentally retarded preschool children. These investigators found that both size and position of buttons on the garment were related to the speed and ease of children's learning to button.

The second trend in the recent research on dressing skills has been a focus more on community living skills related to dressing in accordance with social customs and care and preparation of clothing items. For instance, Nutter and Reid (1978) successfully taught a group of severely and profoundly retarded women to select color coordinated clothing items based on popular fashion using a combination of behavioral procedures, including modeling, instructions, practice, feedback, and praise. Follow-up data indicated that these results were maintained 7–14 weeks following training. Cronin and Cuvo (1979) first task analyzed three mending skills: sewing hems, buttons, and seams. These investigators then taught five trainable mentally retarded adolescents these three mending skills using instructions, modeling, physical guidance, information feedback, and reinforcement. A 1-

and 2-week follow-up evaluation indicated that these skills were maintained.

GROOMING AND PERSONAL HYGIENE SKILLS

The statement made earlier by Reid (1983) concerning the teaching of dressing skills to handicapped persons is entirely applicable to the areas of grooming and personal hygiene. That is, the personal hygiene skills of handicapped persons may further enhance the effect of their appearance on other people. In addition, teaching children these skills will increase their self-confidence and help them to function independently.

Although most of the research literature in the area of self-help skills has concentrated on self-feeding and self-dressing skills, a few studies have been published on developing personal hygiene and grooming skills in handicapped persons. With regard to personal hygiene skills, Abramson and Wunderlich (1972) report a series of multiple case studies in which a group of severely retarded adolescents were taught toothbrushing skills. Subjects were taught to correctly select their own toothbrush, apply toothpaste, and brush their teeth according to a three-stage training procedure that employed tangible, social, and token reinforcers for correct responding, trainer modeling, and physical prompts. Following training, subjects were rated higher on a checklist designed to assess appropriate toothbrushing skills than prior to the training program.

Horner and Keilitz (1975) taught a group of mildly and moderately retarded adolescents to brush their teeth. Subjects first watched videotapes describing the task-analyzed components of toothbrushing and showing staff members and other teenagers brushing their teeth. Using a multiple baseline design, subjects were exposed to four treatment conditions: (a) no assistance with toothbrushing, (b) verbal instructions, (c) demonstration plus verbal instructions, and (d) physical guidance plus verbal instructions. One group of subjects also received token reinforcers plus social praise for correct responses, while a second group received only praise. Horner and Keilitz found that subjects' toothbrushing skills improved dramatically compared to their individual baseline performance levels. Improvement was evident for subjects in both the praise-alone and tokens plus praise conditions. In another study, Bouter and Smeets (1979) attempted to teach toothbrushing skills to moderately retarded persons using five types of assistance techniques: (a) no help, (b) instructional guidance alone, (c) instructional guidance plus demonstration, (d) instruction plus partial physical guidance, and (e) instruction plus total physical guidance. In addition, experimenter feedback was sequentially reduced from verbal praise plus explicit head nodding to explicit head nodding only to inconspicuous nodding, and finally to no feedback. Results were consistent with the findings of Horner and Keilitz (1975) and showed that all but one subject acquired all toothbrushing skill steps. These findings also indicate, however, that differences in training efficacy were apparent both within and across the various assistance techniques used. For instance, instructional guidance with or without demonstration was almost 100% effective overall for teaching all subjects the entire toothbrushing skills sequence. When one examines individual skill steps, such as the three actual toothbrushing steps, these same assistance techniques were shown to be 70% effective for three subjects. At follow-up, all subjects were shown to maintain toothbrushing skills over a period of 8–17 days.

Other personal hygiene skills that have been taught to mentally retarded children are washing and drying hands, showering, and for adolescent females, menstrual care. Treffry, Martin, Smaels, and Watson (1970) task-analyzed the skill of hand washing and drying into a 12-step shaping program. Tangible and social reinforcers, along with prompting, were used to teach each of the steps to a group of 11 severely retarded girls. As each girl mastered a particular step, the physical prompts were gradually faded out. Any demonstration of resistance resulted in a firm verbal reprimand

and a short time out period. Severe disruptive behavior (e.g., throwing soap) was consequated by a slap on the subject's hands. By the ninth week of training, Treffry et al. found that 71% of the subjects were able to wash and dry their hands without assistance, compared to only 16% during baseline. Thompson and Faibish (1970) used modeling demonstration and filmstrips to teach moderately retarded adolescents various personal hygiene skills. In this study, boys were taught washing and showering while girls were taught washing and menstrual care. Ratings by teachers and parents following training showed significant improvement in subjects' personal hygiene skills, with demonstration plus filmstrips procedures group slightly better than the group who received only demonstrations.

Zifferblatt, Burton, Homer, and White (1977) investigated generalization of training effects for several different target behaviors that included wiping and washing one's hands after using the toilet. Subjects were 12 children diagnosed as autistic, and the study took place at both school and at home. One group of children were reinforced with tokens at school for wiping themselves, with generalization data recorded for hand washing. At home, this group earned tokens for washing their hands, while generalization data were collected for wiping themselves. For a second group of children, these procedures were reversed. Results showed that the treatment was effective in improving both target behaviors. In addition, generalization across settings occurred for each of these behaviors.

TOILET SKILLS

The most exasperating, difficult, and yet most desired behavior that teachers, parents and other careproviders try to develop in handicapped children is the appropriate use of the toilet. The inability to remain clean and dry is unacceptable for placement in the community, except for very young children. As a result, the older child or teenager who has not acquired toileting skills may be severely restricted in

his or her environmental interactions (McCartney & Holden, 1981). In addition, toileting
skills are often prerequisite for developing
more advanced skills (Baumeister & Klosowski, 1965).

The literature on teaching toilet skills reveals
that, prior to the 1960s, few systematic studies were published about attempts to improve
the appropriate use of the toilet by handicapped persons. It was presumed that these
individuals were unable to learn proper toilet
skills; however, with the introduction of behavior modification principles for solving applied
human problems, many innovative programs
developed in the early 1960s for teaching toileting skills to handicapped persons. For example, since 1963 numerous studies have been
published concerned with training appropriate
toileting skills to mentally retarded children.
The majority of these studies have involved the
use of contingent reinforcement for appropriate elimination (e.g., Azrin & Foxx, 1971;
Baumeister & Klosowski, 1965; Hundziak,
Maurer, & Watson, 1965; Mahoney, Van
Wagenen, & Meyerson, 1971). In many of
these studies, the child is immediately presented with praise, edible reinforcers, or both,
following appropriate eliminations. The use of
this procedure, however, is sometimes complicated by the fact that a child's voiding responses are not always readily discernible. For
this reason, electronic signaling devices were
developed by researchers (e.g., Azrin & Foxx,
1971; Mahoney et al., 1971) to assist teachers
and others to determine when a child was dry
or wet. The electronic device was placed on the
child's underpants and a signal was activated
by the slightest elimination. Some devices
(e.g., Azrin, & Foxx, 1971) were also attached
to inserts in the toilet bowl so careproviders
would know when a child was using the toilet
appropriately.

Many of the early studies focused only on
modifying accidental defecations and/or urinations, with little emphasis on establishing fully
independent toileting skills. In one of the first
studies, Baumeister and Klosowski (1965) attempted to establish a toilet training program
for 11 severely retarded adolescent boys. Stimulus conditions were held constant by confining subjects to a prescribed area of their
residence with an adjacent toilet. Therapy
aides first charted the time that each subject
urinated or defecated. Following this pattern
analysis, aides then reinforced a subject each
time he eliminated in the toilet or engaged in
behaviors in the bathroom area associated with
appropriate use of the toilet (e.g., pulling down
pants). After accidents, subjects remained in
their wet clothing for at least 45 minutes. The
results showed that subjects' toilet skills improved. Specifically, compared to the baseline period, 58% of all urinations and 63% of
all defecations took place in the toilet, with one
subject becoming fully independent in his
toileting. However, when the subjects were
allowed out of the program, their toileting skills
greatly decreased — although many of the adolescents retained parts of the behavior chain
associated with the use of the toilet. For example, some subjects were observed to walk into
the bathroom and defecate in their pants, while
others took off their clothes correctly and eliminated in the dayroom. Generalization of these
results to other populations is limited as the
subject sample was a select group from the
lowest functioning individuals in an institution.
In addition, it was shown that slight changes
in stimulus conditions led to a decrease in
appropriate responses, which suggests that if
training is expected to transfer to other settings, it should probably occur in a more normal environment.

Another early toilet training study by Hundziak, Maurer, and Watson (1965) compared an
operant conditioning approach to a conventional training and a no-treatment control condition. Twenty-six severely retarded boys were
included in the study. Whenever a subject in
the operant conditioning condition urinated or
defecated in the toilet, a light went on, a tone
sounded, and candy was provided to the child
from a large dispenser. Each subject in this
group was placed on the toilet at least every 2
hours. Subjects in the conventional training
group were taken to the bathroom several
times a day and were given praise for successes
in the toilet and scolded for accidents. It was

shown that the operant training approach led to increased appropriate urinations and defecations and that the no-treatment control group showed an increase in appropriate urinations. No appreciable changes for the conventional training group were found. Unlike the findings from the Baumeister and Klosowski (1965) study, the performance of the children in the operant group were also found to generalize from the training setting to each boy's residence. Similar findings using operant conditioning procedures were also reported by Waye and Melnry (1973), who toilet trained a 15-year-old blind, profoundly retarded boy, and by Connally and McGoldrick (1976), who worked with nine severely retarded children.

In another study, Ando (1970) developed an operant conditioning program to toilet train a group of five profoundly retarded children, who also exhibited behaviors characteristic of autism. Baseline data were initially collected on the time of occurrence and frequency of urinations in the toilet after being prompted, in the toilet without any prompts, and in places other than the toilet. During training, the children were taken to the toilet every 2 hours or whenever they indicated a need to urinate. Initially, social and edible reinforcers were presented immediately after a child eliminated in the toilet. As the training program progressed, however, reinforcement was made contingent on self-initiated toilet use. Following accidents, aversive procedures, such as spanking, scolding, or time-out, were administered. Results showed that two of the five children were observed to self-initiate for 60% of the occasions that they urinated. The remaining children showed little or no improvement in toileting skills even after as long as 12 months of exposure to the training procedure. While these findings are not very encouraging nor as dramatic as the previous or other studies (e.g., Azrin & Foxx, 1971), Ando (1970) points out that some children's toileting behavior may not have come under control of the reinforcement contingencies because they were unresponsive to any of the reinforcers that were used.

A number of investigators also focused on developing the complete chain of behaviors associated with a person being totally independent in his or her use of the toilet. These behaviors include indicating the need to use the toilet, approaching the toilet at the appropriate time, removing and replacing clothing, washing and drying hands, and so forth. In an attempt to deal with this chain of behaviors, Singh (1976) trained a $4\frac{1}{2}$-year-old severely retarded epileptic boy to use the toilet in his classroom. The child was reminded to go to the toilet at those times when he was most likely to eliminate. The teacher then used as little prompting and guidance as possible to encourage the child to walk to the toilet, lower his pants and underwear, sit on the toilet, wipe himself, pull up his underwear and pants, and wash and dry his hands. If elimination did not occur immediately, the child remained on the toilet for 5–10 minutes and then completed the chain of appropriate toileting behaviors. Edibles and social reinforcement were given for the correct performance of each step in the chain. Once the child was able to use the toilet himself without manual guidance, he was required to indicate his need to eliminate by pulling the teacher toward the bathroom. When the child did this consistently, he was simply instructed to go to the bathroom every half hour. Finally, all instructions and manual guidance were terminated, and rewards were faded as each component in the chain of behaviors was successfully performed. Training lasted 14 days, and at the end of the training, no accidents were observed. A 10-week posttraining phase was also instituted following the formal training period. Here, the child was checked before meals and snacks and praised for being dry. If an accident occurred, the child was required to change his clothes and practice the entire chain of toileting behaviors. During this phase, the child had only one accident.

Van Wagenen, Meyerson, Kerr, and Mahoney (1969) used a different approach to teach toileting skills to eight profoundly retarded children. Subjects wore a moisture-sensitive set of underpants that produced an audible tone alarm whenever a small amount of urine was emitted onto the underpants.

When the tone sounded, the trainer quickly approached the child and yelled, "No," escorted the child to the bathroom and used manual guidance to prompt the child to remove his or her clothes. The child was next encouraged to continue voiding and prompted to replace his or her clothes. Finally, the child was reinforced for voiding in the toilet. It was shown that all children were trained to be fully independent in urinating in the toilet. Follow-up periods ranged from 3 weeks to 7 months and showed that the program's effectiveness was maintained. In a later study, Mahoney et al. (1971) used a similar training procedure except that prior to having the child actually urinate in the toilet, she or he was trained to approach the toilet and remove his or her underpants in response to a particular auditory signal that was later produced by the underpants alarm. Subjects were three normal and five severely and profoundly retarded children. Training lasted from 17–48 hours, in which time four of the five retarded subjects achieved fully independent toileting skills. Follow-up data, 6 months later, showed that the relative effectiveness of the program was maintained. The most comprehensive toilet training package to date was developed by Azrin and Foxx (1971). These investigators toilet trained nine incontinent severely and profoundly retarded adults by first equipping them with a pants alarm and then confining them in the toilet area for 8 hours per day. A toilet seat alarm was also installed so that all eliminations would be detected immediately by the trainer. To increase the frequency of urinating, subjects were given as much liquid as they were able to consume. Every half hour, subjects were instructed to sit on the toilet for 20 minutes and were given liquid and social reinforcers for appropriate eliminations. Each subject was also reinforced with liquids, edibles, and praise every 5 minutes for maintaining dry pants. When an inappropriate elimination occurred, cleanliness training was instituted—consisting of a verbal reprimand and requiring the subject to shower, change clothes, wash out and hang up the soiled clothes, as well as mop and clean the soiled area. This procedure was fol-

lowed by a 1-hour time-out from reinforcement period. The results showed that the number of accidents decreased after 4–6 days of training from a baseline level of approximately two accidents per day to one every fourth day. Azrin and Foxx's training procedure also produced a decrease in incontinence in 90% of their subjects. A maintenance program was also established with each subject in their residential setting. The results of this intervention showed that 100% of the subjects remained continent within the following 5 months. Successful results using this method, or adaptations of this procedure, have also been reported by other researchers (e.g., Luiselli, Reisman, Heifen, & Pemberton, 1979; Song, Song, & Grant, 1977; Trott, 1977).

Sadler and Merkert (1977) compared an updated Azrin and Foxx procedure (i.e., Foxx & Azrin, 1973c) to a scheduling group—where the children were taken to the toilet four times daily—and to a no-treatment control group. The participants in the study were 14 profoundly retarded children who had never previously been exposed to a toilet training program. During the first phase of the study, subjects received one of the three training conditions for 4 months. Phase II lasted 2 months and consisted of exposing all of the scheduling group and half of the no-training subjects to the Foxx and Azrin procedure. All remaining subjects continued in their original treatment groups. The results showed that during Phase I the number of toileting accidents in the Foxx and Azrin group decreased by 90%, while the number of accidents in the scheduling group decreased by 40%, and the number of toileting accidents in the no-treatment control group did not change. During Phase II, it was shown that those children who continued in the Foxx and Azrin program further reduced their frequency of toileting accidents. Children who had been switched from the scheduling group to the Foxx and Azrin condition exceeded an 80% reduction in the number of accidents. Finally, those children who previously received no training showed a 75% decrease in toileting accidents using the Foxx and Azrin procedure. In addition to evaluating the efficacy of different training methods, Sadler and Merkert (1977) addressed the issue of cost effectiveness of training. They suggested that although the Foxx and Azrin (1973) training program was certainly more effective than the scheduling approach, it involved significantly more staff time (i.e., an average of 35 staff hours per child than did the scheduling group). In another study, Smith (1979) also reports that although a modified Foxx and Azrin (1973c) approach was found to reduce toileting accidents by 95%, and an individual timing procedure decreased accidents by 80%, a group training approach (similar to the "scheduling condition" described by Sadler & Merkert, 1977) was found to reduce accidents by 45–50% and required only one-half the staff time in comparison to the other two intervention approaches. Unfortunately, no long term follow-up data were reported on the relative effectiveness of these three toilet training procedures.

In spite of the amount of staff time required to implement the Azrin and Foxx procedure, it does appear to be an effective procedure and the results seem to be maintained over a long period of time. When the necessary staff time is not available to implement the procedure, then it appears that a procedure using scheduling plus reinforcement for successful voiding would be an effective alternative method.

PREVOCATIONAL AND VOCATIONAL TRAINING SKILLS

A recent major focus of special education and rehabilitation has been the placement of handicapped individuals in the community; a trend largely fostered by adherents of the principle of normalization (Wolfensberger, 1972). In order to be successfully integrated into the community, however, handicapped persons need adequate prevocational training to provide them community-relevant vocational skills.

One area of research on prevocational training has focused on increasing the job finding skills and employability of handicapped persons. For example, Kelly, Wildman, and Berler (1980) successfully taught job interview skills to a group of mildly mentally retarded adolescents using instructions, modeling, and behavioral rehearsals. It was shown that the skills taught (e.g., providing positive information to the interviewer regarding previous work, asking job-related questions, and expressing interest in the prospective position) increased following training and generalized to an in vivo interview in a restaurant. Hall, Sheldon-Wildgen, and Sherman (1980) also attempted to teach job interview and application skills to a group of mildly and moderately retarded adolescents and adults. These investigators used a combination of procedures that included instructions, providing rationales, modeling, role playing, and constructive feedback. The results indicated that all subjects improved their performance of these skills following training.

Clark, Boyd, and MacRae (1975) developed a classroom program to teach mildly retarded adolescents how to provide the biographical information frequently requested on job application forms. These investigators employed a variety of procedures that included praise, token reinforcement, and a standard correction procedure. The subjects progressed through the program at their own pace. Training consisted of initially copying biographical information from the teacher's model, which was gradually faded until subjects were filling out job application forms. Results showed that following training subjects exhibited an average of 92% correct responses for writing their telephone numbers on three regular job application forms, compared to an average of 27% correct responses on the pretest. In addition, subjects averaged 86% accuracy on generalization application forms, compared to a 20% accuracy level prior to training.

Most of the literature in the area of vocational skills training has been directed toward training and managing work behavior in sheltered workshops. In these settings, behavioral techniques have been successfully applied to people with a wide range of handicaps and for a variety of target behaviors, including teaching new tasks and changing the rate of task performance, as well as other work-related and job survival behaviors. Two studies demonstrated that mentally retarded adolescents and adults are able to learn to make the visual discriminations necessary to assemble bicycle brakes. For example, Gold and Barclay (1973a) examined the effects of verbal labels on acquisition and retention of a bicycle brake assembly task using 16 moderately and severely retarded subjects. One group of subjects received specific verbal cues regarding the task, while a second group of subjects were simply instructed to "Try another way." It was shown that specific verbal cues were more effective than general cues. In a subsequent study, Gold and Barclay (1973b) attempted to train 16 adolescents and adults to sort bolts of four different lengths, an easy-to-hard discrimination task. Subjects were assigned to either an "easy" or "hard" group and were provided individual instruction in sorting the bolts. The "easy" group learned the task when initially required to sort $1\frac{1}{2}$ inch and $\frac{3}{4}$ inch bolts, followed by 1 inch and $\frac{3}{4}$ inch, and 1 inch and $\frac{7}{8}$ inch. The "hard" group did not learn to correctly sort the 1 inch and $\frac{7}{8}$ inch bolts until they were taught to discriminate between $1\frac{1}{2}$ and $\frac{3}{4}$ inch bolts.

Several studies in the area of vocational skill training attempted to increase attending to task by using reinforcement techniques. For example, Jackson (1979) found that differentially reinforcing a mentally retarded client's attending to task resulted in a substantial increase in the rate at which the clients cut chain links. The reinforcement procedure consisted of a component for visual feedback via a light that served to cue the client that he had earned his reinforcer. A study by Rusch (1970) also suggests a relationship between attending to task and task production. Subjects were six mentally retarded males, who were randomly assigned to one of two groups. One group was reinforced for speed of task completion, while the second group was reinforced for amount of time attending to task. The task consisted of a 15-step sequence for cleaning and wiping tables in a restaurant. The results indicated that when subjects did not attend to task, they did not complete their work. Reinforcing speed of task completion led to speedier completion of work as well as improved attending to task. Mithaung (1978) also reported a case in which a reinforcement procedure was used with a 20-year-old severely handicapped man to increase time on task. The procedure consisted of instituting time-out following inappropriate laughing and providing edible and liquid reinforcers for attending to task. This program resulted in a decrease in the rate of laughing and an increase in time spent on task.

Previous research in vocational skills training has been primarily concerned with the acquisition of specific job skills and the improvement of skill performance. The majority of the studies in the literature have demonstrated that handicapped persons can acquire a variety of vocational skills, including tasks requiring long skill sequences previously considered too complex for them to learn. Much of this research has employed task analysis to break down the skill to be learned into its discrete components and then sequencing the components in a fashion that is appropriate for completing the particular task (Gold, 1972). For example, mentally retarded persons have been trained to perform skills such as assembly of cable harnesses (Hunter & Bellamy, 1976) and saw chains (O'Neill & Bellamy, 1978).

The vocational training literature has also begun to examine ways that may facilitate the entry of handicapped persons into nonsheltered work settings and competitive jobs. For example, some studies have addressed the acquisition and performance of particular service occupations on the part of handicapped persons. For example, Cuvo, Leaf, and Borakove (1978) successfully taught six moderately retarded adolescents to clean a restroom using a task analysis of 181 response components. In addition, it was shown that the skills acquired generalized to a nontraining setting and were maintained in this later setting without additional programming. Bricker and Campbell (1981) trained 17 mildly and moderately retarded persons to work at McDonald's Restaurants. Trainees were initially given training in sheltered workshop cafeterias followed by exposure to McDonald's training films as well as field trips to various company restaurants. Results showed that all but three subjects remained employed after a 12- and 24-month follow-up period. Subjects were able to perform a variety of jobs at the restaurant, including lobby cleaning and grounds maintenance, as well as food preparation.

SELF-STIMULATORY BEHAVIOR

Self-stimulatory behavior (such as, ritualistic and/or stereotyped repetitive spinning of objects, flapping of arms or fingers, and rhythmic rocking) is a frequently observed behavioral excess exhibited primarily by mentally retarded, autistic, or schizophrenic children (Ross, 1981). Wehman and McLaughlin (1979) found that self-stimulatory behavior was second only to noncompliance as the most frequently identified behavior problem by teachers of handicapped students. In fact, this behavior is often included in some of the descriptions of the identifying characteristics of autism (Rimland, 1964). Foxx and Azrin (1973b) suggest that developmentally disabled persons perform self-stimulatory behaviors because they have failed to learn other more appropriate adaptive behaviors; self-stimulation therefore evolves into a dominant behavior pattern, with adaptive behaviors seldom occurring.

There is some research evidence to suggest that increasing adaptive behaviors by differential reinforcement of other behaviors (DRO) decreases self-stimulatory behaviors in retarded and autistic children. For example, in an early study Mulhern and Baumeister (1969) found that rocking could be reduced by reinforcing children for not moving for short periods of time. Similarly, Flavell (1973) showed that reinforcing playing with toys reduced self-stimulatory behaviors in three retarded children; as toy play increased, self-stimulation decreased. Hollis (1976) also successfully reduced body rocking in five retarded children by reinforcing play with a tetherball. Other researchers have also reported the successful use of DRO procedures for reducing self-stimulatory behav-

iors (e.g., Denny, 1980; Repp, Deitz, & Deitz, 1976; Repp, Deitz, & Speir, 1974). In contrast, Harris and Wolchik (1979) were only able to produce a marginal reduction in hand-patting by an autistic child using a DRO procedure. In addition, these investigators found no effect in two other children, and an increase in self-stimulatory behavior in a fourth child.

In another study, Single, Dawson, and Manning (1981) examined the effects of a differential reinforcement of low rates of responding (DRL) procedure on three profoundly retarded adolescents who exhibited high rates of finger movements, repetitive body movements, rocking, or mouthing of body parts and objects. Results showed that the introduction of DRL immediately decreased subjects' self-stimulatory behaviors and produced an increase in their rates of appropriate social behaviors.

Some investigators (e.g., Foxx & Azrin, 1973b) maintain that punishment, or the occurrence of annoying or noxious consequences immediately following the behavior(s) to be reduced, should be used to treat self-stimulatory behavior. This notion is based on the findings of some of the studies that positive reinforcement interventions were only marginally successful—presumably, because the reinforcement procedure failed to increase adaptive behavior. This is exemplified in a study by Risley (1968), in which a continuous powerful reinforcement contingency failed to increase adaptive behavior in an autistic child who exhibited self-stimulatory climbing and head weaving. The implementation of a punishment procedure reduced these behaviors and led Risley (1968) to conclude that the elimination of self-stimulation may be a prerequisite for the acquisition of adaptive behavior.

Punishment in its mildest form was employed by Murphy, Nunes, and Hutchings-Ruprecht (1977) to reduce hyperventilation and mouthing in two profoundly retarded adolescents. Treatment took place in the classroom and consisted of the teacher delivering continuous vibratory stimulation when subjects did not exhibit self-stimulatory behavior and contingently withdrawing vibratory stimulation when self-stimulatory behavior occurred. Results showed that self-stimulation was greatly reduced in the treatment setting as well as across settings. In another mild punishment study, Greene, Joats, and Hornick (1970) applied music distortion contingent on body rocking. They found that this procedure completely eliminated self-stimulatory behavior. Koegel, Firestone, Kramme, and Dunlap (1974), on the other hand, successfully decreased a variety of self-stimulatory behaviors (including handwaving and handflapping) using a more intrusive punishment procedure with two autistic children. A verbal reprimand ("No!") and a quick slap or restraint of the relevant body part were presented following the target behavior(s). Koegel et al. (1974) found that these procedures reduced self-stimulation and increased children's spontaneous play.

Mayhew and Harris (1978) found that the use of a punishment procedure resulted in producing several negative side effects. In this study, subjects were two profoundly retarded adolescents who engaged in high frequency self-stimulatory behavior. Punishment (consisting of the experimenter shouting, "No!" followed by a hard slap on the subject's hand) was presented contingent on each occurrence of self-stimulation. The results showed that although self-stimulatory behavior was reduced, both adolescents exhibited behaviors that might be characterized as negative side effects of the procedure. Specifically, aggressive behavior increased in one subject, while the second subject displayed a decrease in social behavior. These side effects are consistent with those listed by Morris (1985) as potential, unwanted outcomes of the use of physical punishment with handicapped children.

Another frequently used procedure is overcorrection. Developed by Foxx and Azrin (1973b), overcorrection requires the target child to perform adaptive behaviors as a consequence of engaging in undesirable behaviors. Foxx and Azrin (1973b) applied overcorrection to the treatment of several different self-stimulatory behaviors exhibited by four 7- and 8-year-old profoundly retarded children. For two of the children, mouthing of objects was eliminated by the use of overcorrection, which consisted of saying "No" in a firm voice, brushing the child's mouth with a toothbrush and an oral antiseptic, and wiping the child's lips with a washcloth. This overcorrection was demonstrated to be more effective than reinforcement for nonmouthing or painting the child's hand with a distasteful solution for both children.

Foxx and Azrin (1973b) also attempted to decrease head weaving by using the following overcorrection procedure: the trainer restrained the child's head, instructing her to hold it in one of three positions, up, down, or straight ahead for 15 seconds, and randomly changing these positions for a 5-minute period, providing as little manual guidance as necessary to get the child to perform these behaviors. This procedure eliminated the child's head weaving within 10 days. Foxx and Azrin (1973) designed a similar overcorrection procedure to decrease handclapping, which involved manually guiding the child's hands through five different positions. Handclapping was reduced to zero by the third day of treatment.

The publication of Foxx and Azrin's (1973) study stimulated much interest by researchers in the use of overcorrection to decrease self-stimulatory behavior and a number of studies on this topic followed (see, for example, Feretti & Cavalier, 1983 and Ollendick & Matson, 1978 for reviews on this topic). For example, Epstein, Doke, Sajwaj, Sorrell, and Rimmer (1974) used an overcorrection procedure with two profoundly disturbed children who exhibited self-stimulatory hand and foot movements. Their results parallel those of Foxx and Azrin (1973) and suggest some additional effects of overcorrection. These researchers found that when the overcorrection procedure for inappropriate hand movements was made contingent on self-stimulatory foot movements, these latter behaviors were also reduced. Doke and Epstein (1975) further investigated the effects of oral overcorrection to reduce hand- and objects-mouthing. They found that the response contingent application of a strong mouthwash was effective in decreasing the mouthing behaviors as well as other inappropriate behaviors that did not involve the mouth.

Coleman, Whitman, and Johnson (1979) examined the effects of overcorrection and a DRO procedure in reducing self-stimulatory behavior and increasing appropriate use of toys in a 17-year-old profoundly retarded boy. Treatment consisted of praise and edible reinforcers for appropriate toy play, manual physical guidance and verbal prompts to teach the subject how to use a particular toy, and the hand overcorrection procedure outlined by Foxx and Azrin (1973b). Results indicated that self-stimulatory behavior was reduced and that appropriate play behavior increased following treatment. These changes, however, were not observed to generalize outside of the treatment situation, for example, to the subject's residence.

Because a number of studies had reported various side effects associated with using overcorrection (e.g., Doke & Epstein, 1975; Epstein et al., 1974), Wells, Forehand, Hickey, and Green (1977) conducted a study to investigate this aspect of overcorrection. Subjects were two severely retarded 10-year-old fraternal twins who engaged in a variety of self-stimulatory behaviors, such as flipping toys in front of their eyes, mouthing objects and body parts, hand and finger flapping, body rocking, and masturbation. The purpose of the overcorrection procedure was to engage the boys in appropriate toy play each time they exhibited one of the target behaviors and involved a verbal command to stop the behavior followed by manual guidance in appropriate toy play. It was shown that the frequency of self-stimulatory behavior in both boys reduced abruptly upon the introduction of overcorrection. For one of the boys, as the percentage of time spent in appropriate toy play increased, his self-stimulatory behavior decreased. In contrast, the other twin did not spontaneously engage in toy play, even though his self-stimulatory behavior was markedly reduced, and playing failed to increase even when appropriate play was explicitly reinforced. These findings led Wells et al. to conclude that for some children overcorrection may be sufficient to teach the appropriate behaviors practiced during the manual guidance component

of the procedure. However, other children may require a high frequency of positive reinforcement to acquire incompatible adaptive behaviors. Other investigators have noted that when overcorrection has been used to decrease a specific self-stimulatory behavior, other appropriate behaviors of this same class have increased (e.g., Doke & Epstein, 1975; Epstein et al., 1974; Harris & Wolchik, 1979). Positive side effects of overcorrection have been reported by Ollendick, Matson, and Martin (1978), who noted that when overcorrection was used to decrease self-stimulatory behavior in the classroom, the teacher reported an increase in students' learning and attending.

Other researchers studied the effects of physical restraint on the reduction of self-stimulatory behavior. For example, Azrin and Wesolowski (1980) reprimanded students for engaging in self-stimulatory behavior by saying "No, don't . . ." and guiding their hands to their laps or table tops for 2 minutes. Intensive individual training in adaptive behaviors was also provided to students outside of the classroom. As soon as students were able to go 30 consecutive minutes without self-stimulation, they advanced to a special class where they received praise and snacks as reinforcers for adaptive behaviors. Gradually, the time of interruption was reduced until the teacher simply provided the verbal cue, "No, don't . . ." and required students to momentarily place their hands on the table or on their laps. Within the special class, self-stimulatory behavior was reduced from approximately $1\frac{1}{2}$ times per hour to zero after twelve classes. When students returned to their original class, the reinforcement and interruption procedures were implemented. In this class, self-stimulatory behavior was virtually eliminated by the eleventh class session. Cinciripini, Epstein, and Kotanchik (1980) also used an interruption and restraint procedure to reduce self-stimulatory behavior in a 7-year-old child with cerebral palsy. When the child engaged in self-stimulatory behavior, the teacher held his hands to his side for 3–5 seconds while giving the verbal cue, "No, don't do that." Praise and edible reinforcers were provided when the child used his hands appropriately, and teacher attention was withdrawn for off-task behavior. The restraint and DRO procedures were associated with significant decreases in self-stimulatory behavior and increases in on-task behavior. A 1-year follow-up evaluation indicated that these changes were maintained.

Shapiro, Barrett, and Ollendick (1980) attempted to compare the relative efficacy of physical restraint and positive practice overcorrection in reducing stereotypic mouthing and face patting in three mentally retarded and severely disturbed children. Physical restraint consisted of a verbal warning followed by manual restraint of the child's hands on the table for 30 seconds. Positive practice overcorrection involved a verbal warning and manual guidance of the child's hands to appropriately use the task materials. Both procedures were shown to be equally effective in reducing self-stimulatory behavior for all subjects. In an extension of this study, Ollendick, Shapiro, and Barrett (1981) again compared the effects of physical restraint and positive practice overcorrection with a no-treatment control condition. Subjects for this study were three mentally retarded, emotionally disturbed children who exhibited a high frequency of self-stimulatory hand movements. Treatment was the same as that used by Shapiro et al. (1980) with the inclusion of a no-treatment control phase. Both active treatments were shown to be effective in reducing the target behaviors when compared to no treatment. In addition, these findings suggest that the treatment procedures were differentially effective for different children, an issue that previous research failed to address.

Barrett, Matson, and Shapiro (1981) compared a DRO and punishment procedure for reducing two mentally retarded and behaviorally disturbed children's self-stimulatory behaviors. The DRO procedure consisted of providing primary reinforcers contingent on the absence of the target behaviors. Punishment for mouthing behavior consisted of the contingent use of a visual screening procedure. As a consequence for tongue protusion, a wooden tongue depressor was lightly placed against the child's tongue. For both children,

it was shown that the punishment procedures were more effective in reducing self-stimulatory behavior than DRO or no treatment. These results were maintained at a 6-month follow-up evaluation.

ATTENTION DEFICIT DISORDER

Attention Deficit Disorder (ADD) is a problem frequently encountered by special education teachers in classrooms. Children who are labeled *ADD with hyperactivity* exhibit difficulties in the following areas: inattention, impulsivity, and hyperactivity; children labeled *ADD without hyperactivity* typically exhibit difficulties in the areas of inattention and impulsivity (American Psychiatric Association, 1980). Both groups of children have also been described as consistently violating rule-governed behavior (Barkley, 1983). Those children who are typically labeled *hyperactive* in school have the diagnosis ADD with hyperactivity. These children have difficulty remaining seated in their chairs, completing assignments, and cause frequent classroom disruptions. Hyperactive children are more likely to display specific learning disabilities, which only further compound their already difficult classroom behavior problems. After years of failure, both academically and in terms of behavior, such children are likely to be referred to special education classes for learning disabled, emotionally disturbed, or behavior disordered children (Barkley, 1981).

Stimulant drugs, such as methylphenidate (Ritalin), pemoline (Cylert), and d-amphetamine (Dexedrine) are often prescribed for, and have been shown to be effective in reducing the behavior of, children diagnosed as having ADD (for reviews, see Barkley, 1981, 1983; Cantwell, 1978; Conners & Werry, 1979; O'Leary, 1980; Ross & Ross, 1982). These drugs primarily serve to increase children's attention span and decrease their impulsivity. Children who are placed on stimulants generally tend to exhibit improvements in their play, social conduct, and compliance to rules and directions. However, in spite of these changes, stimulant medication produces little improvement in the academic achievement or performance of these children (e.g., Barkley, 1981; Ross & Ross, 1982). A number of studies (e.g., Ayllon, Layman, & Kandel, 1975; Christensen, 1975; O'Leary & Pelham, 1978; Wolraich, Drummond, Salomon, O'Brien, & Sivage, 1978) have shown that classroom behavior modification procedures are just as effective as stimulant medication in reducing hyperactive behavior and are more effective in improving academic performance than medication. At least one study (Pelham, Schnedler, Bologna, & Contreras, 1980), however, has suggested that a combination of stimulants and behavior modification may be more effective than either treatment alone in the short term management of hyperactive children in the classroom. Finally, some writers (e.g., Sroufe, 1975) point out that various ethical and social issues are associated with the use of stimulant drugs to treat ADD children.

Patterson (1965) and Patterson, Jones, Whittier, and Wright (1965) reported the earliest studies using behavior modification procedures to decrease hyperactive behaviors in the classroom. Specifically, they found that the use of contingent social and tangible reinforcement was effective in increasing attending and decreasing hyperactivity in the classroom. Similarly, Walker and Buckley (1968) found that awarding points contingent on task-oriented and attending behavior immediately increased attending and decreased inattention in a 9-year-old hyperactive boy. Doubros and Daniels (1966) reinforced children with tokens for not engaging in hyperactive behaviors for specified periods of time. The results showed that the frequency of hyperactive behaviors decreased and this decrease was maintained during an extinction period and at a 3-week follow-up evaluation. Twardosz and Sajwaj (1972) showed that prompting and DRO increased sitting in a hyperactive retarded boy and had other desirable effects, including increasing toy play and proximity to other children.

Many of these early studies focused on teaching children behaviors incompatible with their hyperactive behavior, such as sitting still and paying attention in the classroom. While these studies proved to be successful in increasing such behaviors, this approach did not ensure that children completed more assignments or learned more academic skills (Winett & Wickler, 1972). Thus, later researchers, who chose academic productivity and accuracy as the targets of their interventions, found that not only did these target behaviors improve but children also spent more time sitting in their seats and paying attention to tasks. For example, Ayllon, Layman, and Kandel (1975) compared a classroom token reinforcement system with stimulant medication in reducing hyperactive behavior and improving the academic performance of three hyperactive children. Using a multiple baseline design across two class periods, the teacher reinforced each child with tokens for correct responses in reading and math. Results showed that reinforcement of academic performance both reduced the children's hyperactive behaviors and improved their performance in reading and math — in contrast with the children's lack of academic progress when only the medication was being administered. Robinson, Newby, and Ganzell (1981) implemented a token reinforcement program with a class of underachieving, hyperactive third graders. Tokens were awarded contingent on completion of reading assignments and vocabulary performance as measured by standardized mastery level tests. Results showed that the class completed nine times as many tasks under the token system than when it was not in effect and that the rate of completion of vocabulary mastery tests increased with the implementation of this system. In addition, the frequency of disruptive behaviors decreased substantially, as subjectively observed by the classroom teacher.

Barkley (1983) maintains that praise and attention simply are not sufficient to increase and maintain appropriate classroom behavior and academic performance in ADD children with hyperactivity. These children require more frequent and more powerful reward programs than "normal" children in order to perform equally as well. Thus, as the research reviewed so far suggests, highly structured reinforcement programs such as token reinforcement programs have proved to be quite effective in reducing hyperactive behaviors and in increasing academic performance in the classroom. For example, Rosenbaum, O'Leary, and Jacob (1975) compared the effectiveness of group and individual token reinforcement systems with a group of elementary school hyperactive children. Target behaviors were chosen for individual children and included in-seat behavior and completion of assignments. The results showed that both individual and group token reinforcement systems were associated with significant reductions in hyperactivity, as measured by a teacher rating scale. In addition, these positive effects were maintained at a 4-week follow-up evaluation. O'Leary, Pelham, Rosenbaum, and Price (1976) describe a teacher-managed, home-based reward program that was used for increasing academic and prosocial behaviors in a group of nine hyperactive children. This intervention consisted of the classroom teacher specifying goals for each child and sending a daily report card to parents on their child's progress. Parents were then responsible for rewarding the child for his or her behavior for that day. At the end of the 10-week treatment period, children who had been exposed to the behavioral intervention were rated by their teachers as significantly less hyperactive than children in a no-treatment control group.

A number of studies have investigated the efficacy of various self-control procedures for reducing the impulsivity and overactivity that are characteristic of ADD children with hyperactivity. For example, Palkes, Stewart, and Kahana (1968) and Palkes, Stewart, and Freedman (1971) used Meichenbaum's (1977) self-instructional training procedure to teach hyperactive children to verbalize directions prior to attempting or responding to a task. In both studies, it was shown that children increased their overall performance and reduced their number of errors on pretest and posttest measures of impulsivity. Neither study, however, looked for generalization to other tasks or situations, an issue that was later addressed by Meichenbaum and Goodman (1971). These investigators also used verbal self-instruction to reduce impulsive responding in learning disabled, hyperactive children. Although a significant improvement in performance on various psychometric measures was shown, these procedures failed to affect the children's classroom behavior.

Using a multiple baseline across subjects design, Bornstein and Quevillon (1976) investigated the effectiveness of self-instructional training in modifying overactive, impulsive preschool children. These researchers used a single, 2-hour massed self-instructional training session to teach children a more reflective response style. In contrast to previous studies, the results showed that children's on-task behavior observed in the classroom increased following training, and follow-up indicated that these effects were maintained over a 3-month period. A replication of this study with older hyperactive children by Friedling and O'Leary (1979), however, failed to demonstrate generalization to the classroom.

Self-monitoring interventions have also been implemented to reduce the overactivity and attentional problems that are characteristic of ADD children. For example, Hallahan, Lloyd, Kneedler, and Marshall (1982) compared the effectiveness of self- versus teacher-assessment of on-task behavior for a learning disabled boy who had severe attentional problems. The procedure consisted of a tone sounding intermittently on an audiotape recorder in the classroom. During the self-assessment phase, the boy was instructed to ask himself, "Was I paying attention?" when he heard the tone and to record his answer on a recording sheet at his desk. During the teacher-assessment phase, identical procedures were in effect except that the teacher judged whether the child was paying attention and indicated what he should record. It was shown that both of these procedures increased on-task behavior but that the self-assessment procedure was significantly more effective than the teacher-assessment procedure. Both procedures also were effective in increasing the number of math problems computed correctly. Follow-up indicated that these results were maintained even when the self-recording procedure was withdrawn. Schulman, Suran, Stevens, and Kupst (1979) used a combination of auditory feedback from a biomotometer (an electronic device that measures activity level and provides auditory feedback) and material reinforcement to reduce the activity level of nine emotionally disturbed, hyperactive children in the classroom. Children were instructed to try to slow down when they heard beeps from the biomotometer and that, to earn a reward, they should try to get as few beeps as possible. The results showed that all children reduced their activity level during the contingent reinforcement-auditory feedback phase; however, this reduction failed to generalize once these procedures were withdrawn. In addition, no evidence was presented concerning the intervention's effect on the children's academic performance and skills.

Barkley, Copeland, and Sivage (1980) established an experimental classroom that involved training in various self-control procedures for six hyperactive boys. During group activities, the teacher modeled methods of problem-solving and self-instruction that could be used to solve various academic and social problems. Each boy was then required to role play a situation, incorporating the behaviors previously modeled by the teacher, and received token reinforcers for his performance. During individual seatwork, children were trained to self-evaluate and self-administer tokens for appropriate on-task behavior. It was shown that following the implementation of the self-control procedures, most of the boys' on-task behavior exceeded 90% level. The data for a comparison group of six hyperactive matched control children, who remained in their regular classrooms, showed that they continued to exhibit low rates of on-task behavior and engage in high rates of disruptive behavior. For the experimental subjects, there was no generalization of treatment effects from the experimental classroom to the subjects' regular classroom during the study.

The effect of behavior modification procedures on the reduction of the problematic classroom behaviors of ADD children appears to be well established. The issue at present seems to be whether the modified behaviors can be maintained over time and whether they can generalize to settings other than the particular classroom in which they were changed.

ENURESIS AND ENCOPRESIS

A problem common to many handicapped children is their inability to control their bodily functions in a socially acceptable manner. Enuresis is defined as a disorder in which an involuntary discharge of urine occurs while the child is sleeping (nocturnal) and/or during the day (diurnal) beyond the age at which children usually gain bladder control and no organic or urologic pathology is responsible for such discharge (Doleys, 1977; Siegel, 1983). A wide variety of treatment approaches have been applied to decrease enuresis in children, including behavioral approaches, which have received the most systematic attention.

The most effective and most frequently used behavioral procedure for reducing enuresis is the bell-and-pad or urine alarm procedure first developed by Mowrer and Mowrer (1938) to assist children in learning nocturnal bladder control. In the bell-and-pad procedure, the child sleeps on a special pad constructed of two foil outersheets separated by an absorbent paper connected to a buzzer. When the child urinates, a bell or buzzer is activated. The noise awakens the child when his or her bladder is full and, after a number of pairings, the child learns to wake up to the cues for the need to urinate. This procedure usually takes 4–8 weeks to be effective.

Sloop and Kennedy (1973) used the bell-and-pad procedure to treat a group of enuretic retarded persons. The participants in the study slept in a special treatment cottage until they remained dry for 14 successive nights. When a buzzer sounded, indicating urination, subjects were awakened and taken to the bathroom. Subjects in a control group slept in their regular cottages and were taken to the bathroom twice per night. It was shown that following treatment significantly more subjects in the experimental group achieved the dryness criterion than control subjects. Unfortunately, follow-up indicated that less than half of those subjects considered successes relapsed. It should be noted that generalization of these results to children or adolescents is questionable, as the subjects' ages were not specified.

A second method of treating enuresis in children is described by Kimmel and Kimmel (1970). Their bladder retention training procedure involves teaching the child to increase his or her bladder capacity through a day-time shaping program. Essentially, the child is taught to voluntarily delay urination for increased periods of time starting when bladder tension is sufficiently strong to stimulate urination. With this procedure, it is assumed that increased bladder control during the child's waking hours will generalize to nighttime urine retention.

Singh, Phillips, and Fischer (1976) report the successful treatment of a 13-year-old enuretic girl using a modification of Kimmel and Kimmel's (1970) procedure. Bladder retention training was initiated during the day for 7 months. The nighttime training procedure involved initially having the subject set her alarm to ring 2 hours after she went to bed, at which time she would get up and use the toilet. After having 7 consecutive dry nights, she was to set the alarm to ring 90 minutes after going to bed. The time interval was gradually reduced, contingent on dry nights, to 30 minutes, which was the amount of time the girl was able to sustain bladder tension before urinating during the day. This procedure was reported to be effective in controlling enuresis. An 8-month follow-up evaluation indicated that no instances of bedwetting had occurred at the subject's home or when she was at camp.

Azrin, Sneed, and Foxx (1974) developed a "dry-bed training" procedure that used a combination of procedures, including a bell-and-pad apparatus, retention control training, hourly wakenings, positive practice for using the toilet, punishment for wetting, and positive reinforcement for correct use of the toilet at night. Smith (1981) modified the dry-bed training procedure to use with five severely and profoundly retarded enuretics. An enuresis alarm was placed in each subject's bed and

when it sounded the subject was awakened, firmly reprimanded, and required to "feel his or her nasty bed." The child was placed on the toilet and then assisted with changing the bed. In the morning, if the children were dry, they were praised and reinforced with various tangible, edible, and activity rewards. Spontaneous use of the toilet during the night was also reinforced. It was shown that all subjects succeeded in staying dry, with training periods ranging 18–92 weeks. Follow-up indicated that three of the subjects remained dry at night over a 2-year period, one for 18 months, and one for 9 months. Training was also shown to generalize to the subjects' homes.

Encopresis is defined as the voluntary or involuntary elimination of feces in a socially unacceptable place or that results in soiled clothing (Siegel, 1983). This elimination disorder generally occurs beyond the age of 3 or 4 years and in the absence of any organic pathology (Wright, 1973). As with enuresis, a number of behavioral approaches have been employed to treat encopresis in children. These procedures have included both positive reinforcement and punishment, used either alone and in combination, to establish appropriate defecation.

Neale (1963) used physiological and operant reinforcement procedures to treat four encopretic boys on an in-patient psychiatric unit. The physiological procedures consisted of a physical exam and the use of bulk laxatives. The reinforcement program involved taking the child to the toilet four times daily, rewarding him for bowel movements on the toilet, ignoring both soiled and clean pants, instructing the child to use the bathroom when he experienced the sensation of rectal fullness, and rewarding him for doing so. These procedures were shown to be rapidly successful for three of the four subjects. Young and Goldsmith (1972) describe the implementation of a simple behavioral program for an 8-year-old boy who had been encopretic for approximately 1 year. This program, which took place in a day treatment center, involved reinforcing the child with a small toy car at the end of each day if his clothing remained unsoiled and if he had defecated at least once in the toilet. The results showed that within 3 weeks the child no longer soiled and was having an average of one bowel movement a day. Approximately 1 month following the beginning of treatment, the child no longer required the toy reinforcer for appropriate defecation. These results were also shown to generalize to the child's home.

Ayllon, Simon, and Wildman (1975) instituted a token reinforcement system with a 7-year-old boy who chronically soiled both at home and in school. The program consisted of awarding a star to the child for each day that he did not soil. Each week with no occurrences of soiling earned him a special outing with the therapist. Soiling was completely eliminated after 4 weeks, at which point the token reinforcement program was gradually faded out. Following this phase of treatment, the child's mother continued to praise him for remaining free from soiling, and special trips for him were provided on an informal basis. An 11-month follow-up evaluation indicated no further instances of soiling.

Freiden and Van Handel (1970) report the use of a punishment procedure for treating an encopretic child in school. Each time the child soiled at school, he was required to wash his clothing in cold water using a soap that caused a mild skin irritation. In addition, the time he lost from class attendance was made up by remaining after school. Within 5 months, this program eliminated the child's soiling both at school and at home. No recurrence of soiling was reported at a 6-month follow-up evaluation.

A combination of reinforcement and punishment procedures were used successfully by Gelber and Meyer (1965) to eliminate soiling in a 13-year-old boy who had been encopretic since birth. Treatment was conducted in a hospital, where staff checked the child's pants four times per day. For each instance of "clean pants," he earned one-half hour of free time on the hospital grounds. For soiling, 15 minutes were deducted from previously earned free time. The positive reinforcement program involved awarding the child an additional half hour of free time off the ward for each appropriate defecation in the toilet. Treatment was

reported to be effective after 9 weeks. Once soiling had been significantly reduced, random pants checks were conducted and gradually faded out. At a 6-month follow-up evaluation, only two soiling incidents had occurred, and these were the result of the child not having access to a bathroom when he indicated the need to defecate.

Doleys and Arnold (1975) report a case study in which a multicomponent program was used for the treatment of encopresis. The subject was an 8-year-old trainable mentally retarded boy. Following 1 day of intensive training to shape sitting on the toilet at home and at school, the boy's parents were instructed to check his pants on a regular basis and to reinforce him for having clean, dry pants. The time interval between pants checks was gradually lengthened throughout the program. In addition, token reinforcement was used for successful defecations in the toilet. Following each soiling incident, the child was exposed to "full cleanliness training," based on a procedure described by Foxx and Azrin (1973c). The results showed that following treatment an immediate decrease in soiling and an increase in appropriate toileting occurred. Full bowel control was established by the 16th week of treatment. At a 10-week follow-up evaluation, only two soiling incidents had occurred. Doleys and Arnold emphasize that it is necessary to continue intermittent reinforcement along with aversive consequences for soiling after training has ended. After 24 weeks, the child continued to soil once a week because his mother discontinued the "full cleanliness training" procedure and his teacher no longer required him to sit on the toilet at school.

AGGRESSIVE BEHAVIOR

The management of aggressive, acting-out students in the classroom presents a formidable problem for teachers and other school personnel (Walker, 1979). Such students obviously disrupt the normal classroom routine but more importantly pose a potential danger to the teacher, other students in the classroom, and themselves. These behaviors may be so severe in some handicapped students that they must be constantly watched by staff or be physically restrained throughout the school day. As a result, the total amount of time that the teacher is able to devote to instruction and training is limited. Some of the specific behaviors often identified as aggressive include hitting, spitting, biting, kicking, pulling hair, choking, punching, shoving others, and throwing furniture.

A vast body of research has demonstrated that behavior modification procedures are quite effective for managing aggressive behavior in the classroom. Some of the behavioral procedures that have been employed to reduce aggressive behaviors include extinction, differential reinforcement, individual and group token reinforcement systems, relaxation, modeling/behavioral rehearsal, time out, and overcorrection. Of these procedures, many writers (e.g., Martin, 1975; Morris, 1985; Repp & Brulle, 1981) recommend that professionals first use positive behavior modification methods before proceeding to the punishment procedures.

Forehand (1973), for example, reports a case study in which an extinction procedure was used to completely eliminate spitting in a young boy labeled mentally retarded, emotionally disturbed, and immature. During the baseline period, the child's classroom teacher and aides generally used reprimands and required him to clean the area where he spit; following the baseline period, the staff completely ignored his spitting. This intervention led to an immediate reduction in the boy's spitting, which was maintained at zero level through the end of the school year. Using a multiple baseline across behaviors design, Rotatori, Switzky, Green and Fox (1980) applied extinction plus verbal reinforcement for task completion and on-task behavior in order to decrease hitting, tearing, and throwing objects by a severely retarded teenage girl. This intervention proved effective in eliminating these aggressive behaviors and increasing the percentage of time she spent on task-oriented behaviors. Frankel, Moss, Schofield, and Simmons (1976) used a DRO procedure with a 6-year-old profoundly retarded girl who frequently engaged in pinch-

ing, biting, hair-pulling, and head banging. Praise and edible reinforcers were provided to the child for periods as short as 5 seconds for the absence of aggressive behaviors and compliance to directions. This program led to an immediate reduction in aggressive behaviors and a steady decrease in head banging. The intervals between reinforcer presentation were gradually increased until the entire program was eliminated 16 days later, with no recurrence of the problem behaviors.

Token reinforcement systems have been used with a variety of behavioral procedures to modify aggressive behaviors in the classroom. Such systems represent a powerful reinforcement technique because they can incorporate a variety of back-up reinforcers as well as other procedures, such as group contingencies, peer- and self-administered reinforcement, and punishment. In an experimental classroom setting, Mattos, Mattson, Walker, and Buckley (1968) instituted a token reinforcement system to modify two groups of students who engaged in physical and verbal abuse, and were hyperactive, defiant, and distractable. Points earned for appropriate academic and social behaviors were redeemed for free time or tangible rewards. Treatment consisted of a combination of individual and group reinforcement for appropriate behaviors, ignoring minor disruptions, and time out or school suspension for major disruptions. The result showed that individual token reinforcement with no consequences for disruptions produced a low percentage of task-oriented behaviors in the classroom. The combination of treatment components produced the largest percentage of task-oriented behaviors. Working in a preschool classroom for severely retarded children, Perline and Levinsky (1968) established a token reinforcement program combined with response cost and time out in order to modify aggressive behaviors. Tokens were awarded to students contingent on behaviors incompatible with aggression and were removed following each occurrence of aggressive behavior. Time out consisted of physical restraint and was instituted for half the students. Following treatment, aggressive behaviors decreased overall, with no differences evident between students who only received token reinforcement and students who received token reinforcement plus time out.

Budd, Liebowitz, Riner, Mindell, and Goldfarb (1981) implemented a home-based reinforcement system to decrease negative statements, wandering out-of-area, and aggressive behaviors among kindergarten children in a class for students with behavior problems. Children were awarded tokens, praise, and feedback for the absence of disruptive behaviors in the classroom and later exchanged their tokens for privileges at home. For one group of students, all target behaviors were reduced at school when the contingencies were instituted. For a second group of students, the use of tokens with no back-up reinforcers did not affect out-of-area behavior, while the home reinforcement program resulted in reducing aggressions and negative statements at school. For a third group of students, a combination of school- and home-based contingencies was necessary to reduce all target behaviors at school.

Several studies compared the effectiveness of token reinforcement systems with other behavioral techniques for reducing aggression in the classroom. For example, Axelrod (1973) compared the efficacy of individual and group response cost systems for modifying aggressive behaviors in two classrooms of mildly retarded students. During the group contingency phase, the entire class forfeited tokens contingent on individual students' behavior. Under the individual contingency, the teacher subtracted tokens from individual students contingent on their individual behaviors. Results showed that both systems were equally effective in reducing aggressive behaviors in both classrooms. Kaufman and O'Leary (1972) compared the effects of token reinforcement, response cost, and self-evaluations in modifying several categories of disruptive behavior, including aggression, in a psychiatric hospital school reading program for adolescents. Following the baseline period, some students received tokens for following class rules while other students were initially given a specific number of tokens that were removed when they broke class rules. Following this intervention, an attempt was made to transfer responsibility for evaluation of student behavior from the teacher to the students. Overall, results indicated that both the token reinforcement and response cost systems decreased disruptive and aggressive behaviors and that the self-evaluation procedures maintained these behaviors at low levels. In addition, students' performances in reading improved.

In an exploratory study, Graziano and Kean (1968) examined the utility of teaching muscle relaxation to children in order to inhibit the high excitement responses that generally preceded aggressive outbursts. Subjects were four autistic children who exhibited a variety of maladaptive behaviors, including generalized excitement followed by frequent violent and destructive tantrums. Treatment consisted of muscle relaxation training along with social reinforcement for approximations to a relaxed state and responses to verbal cues to relax. After 7 months of treatment, excitement responses were shown to decrease during training sessions and during other periods of the day. A 3-month follow-up showed that excitement responses and aggressive outbursts were extinguished. Robin, Schneider, and Dolnick (1976) developed the "turtle technique" in order to modify impulsive and aggressive behaviors exhibited by two classes of emotionally disturbed students. First, students were taught to emit the "turtle response" (i.e., to pull their arms and legs close to their body, place their heads down on their desks, and imagine they were turtles in shells) whenever they perceived a potentially aggressive interchange or felt angry or frustrated. Teacher cues and reinforcement also followed correct turtle responses. Next, instruction in muscle relaxation was provided while practicing the turtle response. The final phase incorporated role playing and discussions of alternative coping responses to problem situations, while teacher cues and reinforcement were gradually faded. Following treatment, students' aggressive behaviors observed in the classroom decreased significantly across time.

Several studies have employed reinforcement, modeling, and behavioral rehearsal techniques to develop appropriate alternative responses to behaving aggressively in conflict situations. For example, Goodwin and Mahoney (1975) attempted to modify aggressive behavior in three hyperactive, impulsive boys using behavioral modeling, coping self-verbalizations, coaching, and rehearsal. Following participation in a verbal taunting game, subjects viewed a videotape of a young boy who modeled coping self-statements and calm responses to other children's verbal assaults. The experimenter then discussed the model's coping behaviors, and subjects practiced these behaviors. Following observation of the modeling tape, subjects' coping responses did not change. However, with the addition of experimenter coaching and behavioral rehearsal, subjects' coping responses increased and were maintained at a 1-week follow-up.

Bornstein, Bellack, and Hersen (1980) employed social skills training with four aggressive child psychiatric in-patients. During training, the therapist modeled each skill within the context of a role play situation. Each child then role played a situation and was given feedback and praise regarding his or her performance. Target behaviors, which included eye contact, tone of voice, requests, facial expression, and assertiveness, were treated one at a time to mastery, with booster training provided as necessary. Appropriate responding increased and was maintained for up to 6 months when assessed in a role-play situation. However, naturalistic observations showed little improvement for two of the children. Fleming and Fleming (1982) attempted to use structured learning training (Goldstein, 1973), a training package that combines modeling, role playing, social reinforcement, and transfer training, to teach appropriate assertive responses to passive and aggressive, mildly retarded children. It was shown that children who received training evidenced greater learning of assertiveness skills on questions and answer measures than children in the attention control groups. Learning, however, did not transfer to in vivo situations.

Time out and overcorrection are the two primary aversive behavior modification procedures that have been used to reduce aggressive behavior in the classroom. A considerable amount of research has accumulated on the use of time out from positive reinforcement while fewer studies are available on using overcorrection in the classroom. For example, Sachs (1973) used seclusionary time out to modify a 10-year-old hyperactive boy's hitting, throwing, and other inappropriate classroom behaviors. Following each behavior that disrupted the class, damaged classroom property, or injured others, the child was placed in a time out room for 5 minutes. With the introduction of the time out program, the child's inappropriate classroom behaviors decreased and attentive behaviors increased. Drabman and Spitalnik (1973) sought to determine the efficacy of seclusionary time out in controlling disruptive classroom behavior in a state child psychiatric residential center. Subjects were six children who frequently displayed aggressive and out-of-seat behaviors. Children were placed in a time out room for 10 minutes contingent on these behaviors. Results revealed that the frequencies of aggressiveness and time out-of-seat were significantly less during the time out phase than during the baseline period.

Several research investigations have attempted to identify factors that influence the effectiveness of time out in reducing aggressive behavior in the classroom. For example, Solnick, Rincover, and Peterson (1977) examined whether the opportunity to engage in a high probability behavior, such as self-stimulation, during time out was associated with increasing the frequency of tantrums exhibited by a 6-year-old autistic girl. The initial time out intervention involved the teacher removing herself from the child immediately following each tantrum. The second intervention involved physical restraint of some part of the child's body that she did not use for self-stimulation. Finally, the teacher restrained the subject's self-stimulatory behavior following each tantrum. The child also received social and edible reinforcers for correct task responses. It was shown that during time out periods and when allowed to engage in self-stimulation, the frequency of tantrums increased. When self-stimulation was restrained, the child's tantrums were reduced to zero, thus, demonstrating that the opportunity to engage in self-stimulatory behavior served as a reinforcer during the time out program. Solnick et al. suggest that teachers using time out programs should monitor the student's behavior during time out so that she or he does not engage in a preferred behavior.

Frankel et al. (1976) present a case demonstrating that several types of aggressive behavior were maintained by escape and avoidance contingencies time out procedures provided for a 6-year-old profoundly retarded girl. Two time out procedures were sequentially instituted to reduce biting, pinching, hair-pulling, and head-banging. Exclusionary time out was first applied to the aggressive behaviors, while head-banging was ignored. Seclusionary time out was subsequently made contingent on the aggressive behaviors. Finally, a DRO program was implemented for the absence of the target behaviors and for compliance to instructions. Following the first time out intervention, aggressive behaviors increased while head-banging decreased. The second time out intervention was discontinued because the child spent an entire day in seclusion time out. The DRO program led to an immediate reduction in aggressive behaviors and a steady decrease in head-banging. Thus, time out becomes ineffective if the student uses it as a means of escape from the classroom.

Several studies investigated the effects of various time out schedules on reducing aggressive behavior in the classroom. For example, Jackson and Calhoun (1977) found that a variable ratio of four schedule (VR4) of time out was more effective than a VR8 schedule in reducing inappropriate verbalizations of a 10-year-old retarded child. In addition, it was shown that the child's appropriate social behaviors increased slightly with the time out intervention, nontarget disruptive behaviors were reduced most with the VR4 schedule, and tantrums were not consistently affected by either time out schedule. Calhoun and Matherne (1975) compared the effectiveness of two fixed ratio (FR) and a continuous (CRF) schedule of

time out on the hitting, kicking, spitting, and throwing by a 7-year-old retarded girl. The results revealed that the FR5 schedule produced no effect on the child's aggressive behaviors, while the FR12 and CRF schedules resulted in a significant decrease in the target behaviors, with the CRF schedule most effective. A 5-week follow-up evaluation indicated that low levels of aggressive behaviors were maintained following removal of the time out contingencies.

Clark, Rowbury, Baer, and Baer (1973) conducted two experiments on the use of time out with an 8-year-old child in a special preschool classroom for problem children. Experiment 1 examined the effect of a continuous 3-minute time out period across three aggressive behaviors: chokes and armwraps, other attacks toward people, and attacks toward materials. The child was initially placed in a time out room following each instance of chokes and armwraps. Eight days later, time out was made contingent on all aggressive behaviors. The results of this intervention showed that the rates of all three target behaviors were immediately reduced with the application of time out. Experiment 2 sequentially presented four schedules of time out (VR4, VR8, VR3, and differential punishment) on high rates of disruptive behaviors. Results from this experiment revealed that the VR3 time out schedule produced the lowest rates of disruptive behaviors, while the VR8 schedule produced a substantial increase in rates of disruptive behaviors. Thus, it was shown that high rates of aggressive behaviors can be just as effectively maintained by intermittent time out schedules as with continuous schedules.

With regard to the duration of time out, Kendall, Nay, and Jeffers (1975) compared the effects of a 5-minute time out with a 30-minute time out on reducing physical and verbal aggressive, noncompliance, and out-of-area wandering by adolescent delinquents. Time out, consisting of a chair enclosed by an opaque curtain, was instituted following the establishment of rules. No significant differences were detected between specific treatment conditions. However, trends toward a reduction in verbal aggression and out-of-area wandering were apparent during the initial 5-minute time out phase, along with an initial suppression then gradual increase in physical aggression. Both verbal and physical aggressions increased when the 30-minute time out period was introduced and became even more elevated with the second 5-minute time out period. Freeman, Somerset, and Ritvo (1976) employed three durations of time out to modify aggressive behaviors and screaming in an autistic child. When either target behavior occurred, the child was secluded for 3 minutes, 1 hour, or 15 minutes. Time out for 3 minutes initially produced a small decrement in screaming and aggressions. Time out for 1 hour initially appeared to be effective; however, after 3 days, the child began falling asleep while in time out. With the 15-minute time out period, the subject's disruptive behaviors were reduced to one incident per day.

Pendergrass (1971) examined the effects of both duration and schedule of time out by using isolationary time out to control aggressive hitting by 5-year-old brain damaged girl. Time out for either 5 or 20 minutes was administered according to continuous or intermittent schedules following each hitting incident. Results showed that the frequency of hitting did not change under intermittent schedules of 5- and 20-minute time out periods. When a continuous schedule of 5-minute time out periods was applied, hitting decreased immediately. Subsequent application of a continuous schedule of 20-minute time out periods reduced the frequency of hitting even further. However, the child developed various side effects, including wetting, trembling, and crouching, which occurred prior to each time out period. Thus, the method of applying time out appears to be more important than duration in reducing aggressive behavior.

At least one study used an innovative time out procedure that does not involve total exclusion of an aggressive child from the classroom. Foxx and Shapiro (1978) examined the effectiveness and practicality of using a time out ribbon in a classroom of disruptive, aggressive, severely and profoundly retarded children. Each child was required to wear a ribbon that signified access to reinforcement. When a child misbehaved, the ribbon was removed for 3 minutes and all reinforcement and participation in class activities were terminated. Reinforcement was again available when the ribbon was returned. Results revealed that reinforcement for only wearing the ribbon and for the absence of target behaviors produced little effect on children's target behaviors. When the time out procedure was combined with reinforcement, disruptive and aggressive behaviors decreased substantially. Follow-up indicated that these behavioral changes were maintained. In addition, teachers rated the procedures as practical and less aversive than seclusionary time out.

Although initially applied to the modification of extremely aggressive institutionalized people (e.g., Foxx & Azrin, 1972; Webster & Azrin, 1973), several studies have investigated the use of positive practice overcorrection and restitutional overcorrection to modify aggressive behavior in the classroom. For example, Clements and Dewey (1979) combined positive practice overcorrection with functional movement training (Foxx & Azrin, 1973b) to modify the object-breaking, hand-biting, and eye-poking in an 11-year-old severely retarded boy. The overcorrection procedure for eye-poking and hand-biting required the child to thoroughly cleanse and dry his eye or hand then engage in a brief period of functional movement training. For object-breaking, the child was required to repair the damaged object as well as straighten other toys in the classroom. A brief period of functional movement training then followed this procedure. Results showed that the sequential application of the overcorrection treatment across the three target behaviors produced rapid and enduring suppression of these behaviors. A 6-month follow-up evaluation revealed that the effects of treatment were maintained and had generalized to another classroom. Similar findings regarding the use of overcorrection have also been reported by Polvinale and Lutzker (1980) and Shapiro (1979).

In two experiments, Luce, Delquardri, and Hall (1980) attempted to determine the effects of contingent exercise, an alternative to overcorrection, on aggressive behavior and to compare contingent exercise with DRO. Contingent exercise requires the child to repeatedly engage in a simple exercise task, such as standing up and sitting down, immediately following a verbal or physical aggression. The first experiment applied contingent exercise alone in order to decrease hitting in a young developmentally delayed boy who also exhibited autistic behaviors. Contingent exercise involved standing up and sitting down, with verbal and physical prompts that were gradually faded. With the introduction of this procedure, hitting was rapidly reduced. Two months following treatment, only three hitting incidents had occurred, and an 18-month follow-up evaluation revealed that hitting was completely extinguished. A second experiment compared contingent exercise with DRO in reducing aggressive comments and physically aggressive behaviors exhibited by a moderately retarded boy with autistic behaviors. Contingent exercise and DRO were applied sequentially across verbally and physically aggressive behaviors. During DRO phases, a point system was instituted, with points awarded for the absence of fighting and for talking nicely. Results showed that following contingent exercise, all target behaviors were greatly reduced compared to baseline. Although the DRO procedure produced an initial decrease in the target aggressive behaviors, the mean frequencies of these behaviors under contingent exercise was less than under periods of DRO. A 6-week follow-up evaluation showed that these reductions were maintained. Luce et al. point out the advantages of contingent exercise over other forms of overcorrection: the exercise trials are very short, i.e., less than 30 seconds, and require little manual guidance training. Thus, the child quickly returns to the learning environment where appropriate behaviors may be reinforced.

SELF-INJURIOUS BEHAVIOR

An appreciable number of children who are labeled *mentally retarded*, *autistic*, or *psychotic* have been found to engage in self-injurious behavior (SIB) at one time or another. This behav-

ior may take various forms: head banging, arm banging, hair pulling, face beating, hitting or gouging one's eyes, biting parts of one's body, or repeated intense scratching that creates deep open wounds (Morris, 1978; Ross, 1981). These behaviors are often of such magnitude as to cause permanent blindness, concussions, large infected lesions, the loss of a finger, or even the child's life. School personnel often feel so inadequate about dealing with this problem that they place the child in restraints (e.g., a helmet, boxing gloves or mittens, or arm/elbow splints) in order to prevent any further self-injury.

Investigators are faced with a number of difficulties when attempting to conduct research in SIB. To begin with, SIB is most prevalent in severely and profoundly retarded, as well as autistic, persons, who also tend to have a high incidence of organic dysfunction, a long history of SIB, and difficulties in communication. Since the relative number of children who engage in SIB is small, the research available on treatment is often based largely on studies of single cases or a small number of dissimilar children. Because children who are labeled mentally retarded or autistic represent quite heterogeneous groups, a trainable mentally handicapped child is not the same as a profoundly retarded child who requires a large amount of maintenance care and an autistic child who has no language is quite different from one who possesses some language.

In addition, SIB occurs in a variety of topographies and ranges in intensity from mild face slapping to violent head banging. Thus, to speak of treating SIB as if the categories of these behaviors were clearly delineated is an overgeneralization.

A large number of hypotheses regarding the etiology of SIB have been proposed (e.g., Baumeister, 1978; Carr, 1977). Viewing SIB as a learned operant is valuable from both a research and a practical standpoint. This perspective offers testable hypotheses, variables that are accessible and manipulatable, and a body of treatment procedures that permit some degree of optimism. One hypothesis suggests that SIB is maintained by positive social reinforcement from adult attention that this behavior elicits (e.g., Lovaas, Freitag, Gold, & Kassorla, 1965). Another hypothesis proposes that SIB is maintained by negative reinforcement, or that it allows the child to terminate or avoid an aversive stimulus (e.g., Carr, Newsom, & Binkoff, 1976; Weeks & Gaylord-Ross, 1981). A variety of intervention procedures based on both of these hypotheses have been applied in an effort to reduce SIB.

One frequently used behavioral intervention for the reduction of SIB is the differential reinforcement of other behaviors (DRO) and/or behaviors incompatible (DRI) with SIB. Peterson and Peterson (1968) reinforced a child with edible and social reinforcers for not engaging in SIB for a 3–5-second period. When SIB did occur, the child's food was removed and the experimenter turned away from the child. When the child stopped the SIB for 10 seconds, the experimenter turned back and reinforced the child. These procedures were later discontinued and replaced with instructing the child to walk across the room and sit on a chair after each SIB. The results showed that the frequency of SIB decreased appreciably. Weiher and Harman (1975) used a DRO procedure called omission training to reduce the SIB exhibited by a 14-year-old severely retarded adolescent. The procedure consisted of reinforcing the young man for 3-second periods in which no head banging occurred. With this method head banging was reduced to almost zero. In addition, although no specific procedures were included for strengthening alternative behaviors, it was observed that the subject began to exhibit such socially desirable behaviors as smiling, laughing, and vocalizing. Repp and Deitz (1974) used a DRO procedure to eliminate severe face scratching and nose picking by a 10-year-old severely retarded girl. The SIB was so intense that she was regularly required to wear elbow splints that prevented her from reaching her face. The procedure consisted of reinforcing the girl with M & M candies for increasingly longer periods of time without the elbow splints during which no SIB occurred. When the girl attempted to hurt herself, the teacher said, "No" and pulled her hand down to her side. The DRO interval was gradually increased from 1 second to 2 hours,

and the girl was phased into an activity room where other teachers and students were present. Within 7 days after the DRO procedure was implemented, the rate of SIB was reduced to zero, and it was maintained at that level, or close to it, for the remainder of the study. Similarly, Ragain and Anson (1976) found that self-injurious scratching and head banging by a 12-year-old severely retarded girl was reduced using a DRO schedule of edible reinforcers.

Some researchers maintain that explicit plans for establishing alternative, incompatible responses must be included in any treatment program aimed at eliminating SIB. For example, Favell, McGimsey, and Jones (1978) found that when an 8-year-old retarded boy could earn brief periods of being restrained on his bed, contingent on engaging in string play, activities with no SIB, that SIB was decreased. Saposnek and Watson (1974) report the successful treatment of a 10-year-old diagnosed as profoundly retarded and autistic who engaged in severe head slapping. Treatment involved having the therapist hold the boy on his lap in a horizontal position and encouraging him to hit the therapist's hand instead of himself. This procedure continued until the boy became relaxed. Following this intervention, the child was given edible and social reinforcement during skill training activities and play with toys. It was found that the child soon began hitting the therapist's hand instead of his own head and, at the end of the study, when the SIB was virtually eliminated, he was observed to playfully and lightly slap various adults' hands or the armrests of furniture. Tarpley and Schroeder (1979) compared the effectiveness of DRO and DRI (differential reinforcement of incompatible behavior) procedures in reducing the face and mouth jabbing of an 8-year-old profoundly retarded boy. It was shown that DRI suppressed the SIB more than the DRO procedure. In addition, the degree of prompting (i.e., manual vs. verbal) of incompatible behaviors necessary varied according to subject. For a compliant child, verbal prompts were sufficient for DRI to be effective.

Withdrawal of positive reinforcement in the form of extinction, or ignoring, has also been used to control SIB in handicapped children. Though this form of treatment is effective, it often poses great risks since the child may seriously injure himself or herself during the intervention. In addition, the initial withdrawal of the attention, physical contact, and so forth, may lead to an increase in the SIB before a decrease occurs. Because studies with animals have shown that the rate of extinction depends on their conditioning history, it may be reasonable to assume that the longer the history of SIB, the longer it would take to extinguish the behavior. Theoretically, extinction should work if, in the past, the child has been rewarded for engaging in SIB; however, it has not always been proven to be effective (e.g., Corte, Wolf, & Locke, 1971).

Tate and Baroff (1966) showed that the frequency of SIB exhibited by a psychotic child was reduced when the therapist withdrew his or her hands and ignored the child each time he hit himself during a week. Rubin, Griswald, Smith, and DeLeonardo (1972) also found that a 6-year-old retarded girl's SIB and crying could be eliminated if the experimenter left the room immediately after the SIB. Lucero, Fireman, Spoering, and Fehrenbacher (1976) compared the effects of food withdrawal and withdrawal of attention on the SIBs of three profoundly retarded adolescents. It was shown that food withdrawal alone and the removal of both food and adult attention together were more effective in reducing SIB than the withdrawal of attention alone.

Another type of treatment, which has been much more effective than extinction in reducing SIB, is time out from reinforcement. Duker (1975) used seclusion time out for 10 minutes combined with a DRI program to reduce a profoundly retarded adolescent's head banging and head hitting. Although a temporary increase was observed in such behaviors as elbow hitting, vomiting, and self biting when the program was initiated, these behaviors disappeared and staff noted an overall general improvement in the girl's behavior.

Another time out technique, facial screening, has also shown some promise in the reduction of children's SIB. This technique involves briefly covering the child's face with a nonabra-sive cloth bib or some other opaque material as a visual screen contingent on SIB. Lutzker (1978) examined the effectiveness of facial screening for reducing SIB in three special education classrooms. The subject was a 20-year-old retarded man who engaged in head slapping and head hitting. Following each instance of SIB, the procedure involved saying "No," immediately placing a large, terry cloth bib over the subject's face and head, and holding it loosely behind his head until the SIB had stopped for 3 seconds. The results showed that facial screening was effective in reducing SIB in all three classrooms. Barmann and Vitali (1982) used facial screening to reduce trichotillomania (repetitive hair pulling) in three developmentally disabled children. Two of the three children pulled out their hair so severely that they caused multiple bald spots, inflamed areas on the scalp, and serious scalp tissue damage. Following each occurrence of hair pulling, the child was told, "No, hands down," and a large terry cloth bib was placed over his or her face for 5 seconds. They received verbal praise for not pulling their hair. For two of the children, hair pulling was completely eliminated with the facial screening intervention, and for the third child, her SIB was reduced by more than 65% from baseline level. Over a 7-month follow-up period, the treatment gains were maintained for all subjects.

Harris and Romanczyk (1976) used an overcorrection procedure to treat the SIB of a moderately retarded 8-year-old boy. Each time the boy exhibited head- and/or chin-banging behavior, the trainer guided his head up and down, left and right, with this cycle being repeated every 5 seconds for a 5 minute period. Following this, a cycle of guiding his arms to side, in front, over head, and back to side was implemented. It was found that after 3 weeks of training the child's SIB had decreased substantially, though this reduction did not generalize to his home. When the program was instituted at home, however, the frequency of SIB in this setting dropped rapidly. A 9-month follow-up evaluation revealed that the child's SIB remained at or near zero and that his appropriate behavior had increased. DeCatanzaro and Baldwin (1978) used an arm exercise overcorrection procedure combined with DRO to reduce head hitting with fists exhibited by two profoundly retarded children. The arm exercise procedure consisted of repeated up and down arm movements contingent on SIB, while DRO involved providing social reinforcement and physical contact for every 30 seconds without SIB. For both children, head hitting was reduced substantially as a result of the overcorrection procedure. It was impossible to implement DRO alone for one child because his baseline rate of SIB was extremely high. At a 2-month follow-up evaluation, head hitting was maintained at a near zero level for both children.

A combination of procedures that included overcorrection were reemployed by Azrin, Gottlieb, Hughart, Wesolowski, and Rahn (1975) to reduce self-injurious behaviors in a group of mentally retarded persons, who varied in age up to 22 years old. These procedures, called *educative procedures*, included required relaxation, hand control, and hand-awareness training. Required relaxation involves having the person lie in bed with his or her arms lowered for 10 minutes following an SIB. Hand-control consists of various arm and hand movements that are incompatible with the SIB. Hand-awareness training was instituted on a daily basis in order to provide feedback and positive reinforcement for keeping hands away from the head or other body part(s) that was the target of the SIB. Azrin et al. report rapid success with all 11 subjects in this study. On the first day of treatment, there was an average reduction of SIB of approximately 90% and by the seventh day, this reduction was 96%. Three months following treatment, SIB was less than 99% of its baseline rate, although overcorrection appears to be an effective treatment for SIB.

Measel and Alfieri (1976) assessed the effects of combining DRO with overcorrection to reduce head slapping and head banging in two profoundly retarded adolescents. For both subjects, it was shown that, used alone, DRO had little effect on SIB. However, the addition of overcorrection reduced both subjects' SIBs. Wesolowski and Zawlocki (1982) examined the

differential effects of DRO, auditory time out, response interruption, and overcorrection in eliminating the self-injurious eye-gouging by two profoundly retarded, identical twin girls. Auditory time out consisted of placing earmuffs over the child's ears for 2 minutes following each SIB, while response interruption involved yelling "No!" and briefly holding each child's hands down on her lap. Auditory time out combined with DRO was shown to be most effective in reducing SIB for both children and maintained this behavior at zero for 2 months. Approximately 1 year after this initial study, however, eye-gouging was again observed in both subjects. This time an overcorrection procedure combined with DRO was shown to be effective in eliminating the SIB and maintaining it at zero up to 1 year later. Thus, DRO combined with auditory time out or overcorrection were both more effective than response interruption and auditory time out alone in reducing the SIB.

Because of the intensity with which some children engage in SIB, along with the serious and sometimes permanent physical damage that often results, adults who work with these children are likely to try to protect them from injuring themselves or prevent the behavior. Some interventions that have been applied include physical restraint of their arms or feet to a bed or chair, using arm splints, straitjackets, helmets, or psychotropic medications. It is apparent that these interventions do, in fact, prevent the SIB as long as they are being used, but once the restraints are removed or the medication is discontinued, the child again will exhibit the SIB. In addition, while in restraint or on medication, the child has little opportunity to learn any other applicable behaviors. In addition, Favell et al. (1978) have noted that prolonged physical restraint may become reinforcing for the child who engages in SIB, with the immediate attention of adults rushing in to put on the restraints and stop the SIB serving as the reinforcing consequence.

Nevertheless, brief contingent physical restraints have been successful in suppressing head banging (Hamilton, Stephens & Allen,

1967) and pica (Bucher, Reykdal, & Albin, 1976). Parrish, Aguerrevere, Dorsey, and Iwata (1980) evaluated the use of a physical restraint in reducing the SIB exhibited by a 17-year-old profoundly retarded adolescent, who also had visual and hearing impairments. The target behavior was head hitting and the restraint apparatus consisted of a foam-padded helmet with a protective plastic face shield. The results showed that when the subject wore the helmet his rate of SIB was quite low compared to the baseline level. Thus, it is suggested that the suppressive effects of protective equipment may help to effect rapid and substantial reductions in SIB, though the specific contingencies responsible for such reductions are unclear.

Sometimes, there are instances where none of the treatment alternatives discussed thus far have been found to be effective in reducing SIB. In such cases, a punishment procedure involving the response contingent application of pain may be the method of last resort. Punishment is a highly controversial procedure that raises both ethical and moral issues. Responsible therapists who have used physical punishment to treat SIB attempt to address these issues and point out that the use of punishment is typically the least objectionable of two undesirable alternatives, where the choice was between the possibility of a child's permanent injury or even death and the teacher's or therapist's use of punishment.

Punishment in the form of electric shock has been shown to be a highly effective procedure for suppressing SIB when it is presented immediately following each instance of such behavior (Lovaas, Freitag, Gold, & Kassorla, 1965; Lovaas, Schaeffer, & Simmons, 1965; Lovaas & Simmons, 1969; Risley, 1968; Tate & Baroff, 1966). Each of these studies also used, in addition to the punishment intervention, a positive reinforcement procedure to teach and strengthen constructive and desirable behaviors as alternatives to the SIB. In fact, it is unlikely that SIB would be eliminated with punishment unless there were naturally reinforced alternative adaptive behaviors in the child's environment as well.

Corte et al. (1971) compared three procedures for reducing the SIBs of four profoundly retarded adolescents who engaged in face slapping, face banging, face scratching, hair pulling, and finger biting. Contingent edible reinforcement and extinction proved to be ineffective for two of the subjects. Only when response-contingent electric shock was applied did the SIB of all four subjects rapidly decrease. Ball, Sibbach, Jones, Steele, and Frazier (1975) used an accelerometer-activated shock device that was wired into a jacket to reduce a 7-year-old mildly retarded girl's SIB. Rapid movement of the girl's arm associated with SIB resulted in generating a shock impulse to her triceps. This punishment device resulted in terminating the child's SIB. After 2 months, a verbal reprimand along with swats were effective in reducing the behavior, and after 8 months, the jacket was no longer necessary for controlling the behavior.

Romanczyk and Goren (1975) describe in a detailed case report a treatment program involving the use of contingent electric shock to reduce severe scratching and head banging in a $6\frac{1}{2}$-year-old autistic boy. The initial phase of the program took place at the boy's home, with the intervention consisting of delivering a painful shock to his forearm contingent on any SIB. This intervention resulted in a dramatic decrease in the target behaviors relative to baseline level. The second phase was conducted in a clinic, where the punishment procedure was combined with teaching socially adaptive behaviors. Again, the boy's SIB decreased in both frequency and intensity, with all restraints being removed. The third treatment phase was implemented in the child's school. For 2 months, his SIB was totally suppressed both at home and in school, and he was making progress in learning speech, self-help, academic, and social skills. However, after this 2-month period, the SIBs previously under control began to escalate. Romanczyk and Goren (1975) hypothesized that intermittent punishment combined with the use of physical restraints and the parents' excitement may have been responsible for the reoccurrence of the boy's SIB. During the last treatment phase, the boy was placed in an institution. In this setting, he was able to attend school in only partial restraints. Approximately 1 year later, the rate of his SIBs were usually less than 5 per hour, compared to 5400 per hour prior to treatment, and never intense enough to cause bleeding or injury.

Other types of punishment procedures have also been shown to be effective in reducing children's SIB (e.g., Altman, Haavik, & Cook, 1978; Dorsey, Iwata, Ong, & McSween, 1980; Morrison, 1972; Tanner & Zeiler, 1975). For example, Morrison (1972) found that a mild punishment procedure consisting of a light tap on the head followed by "No" was effective in reducing an 8-year-old mentally retarded child's head banging. Tanner and Zeiler (1975) and Altman, Haavik, and Cook (1978) employed aromatic ammonia as the punishing stimulus to reduce several different SIBs in mentally retarded children and adolescents. In both studies, it was shown that when an ammonia capsule was broken and crushed underneath subjects' noses contingent on SIB that the SIB was rapidly reduced. Follow-up data presented by Tanner and Zeiler (1975) suggest that this treatment remained effective for at least 3 weeks. However, it has been suggested by Whitman et al. (1983) that the use of aromatic ammonia capsules be carefully monitored due to their potential negative side effects.

DISRUPTIVE BEHAVIOR

A wide variety of behavior modification procedures has been successfully used to manage disruptive behavior by handicapped students in the special education classroom (e.g., Lahey, 1979; O'Leary & O'Leary, 1977). These procedures have included positive and negative reinforcement, extinction, token reinforcement, response cost, time out, self-management procedures, positive practice, and overcorrection.

Teacher attention, in the form of smiles, praise, and physical proximity, contingent on desirable behaviors combined with extinction, or ignoring, of undesirable behaviors have

been shown to be effective in reducing disruptive classroom behaviors (Zimmerman & Zimmerman, 1962). In an early study, Hall et al. (1971) present the results of a series of single case experiments in which teachers systematically gave praise, attention, and other forms of reinforcement and ignoring in order to reduce talking out and arguing in a classroom for mildy retarded students. Follow-up data for one case showed that the low levels of disruptive behaviors were maintained over a 6-week period. One important aspect of these studies is that the teachers served as the program designers, observers, and behavior change agents.

Several types of differential reinforcement procedures have been used to reduce handicapped students' disruptive classroom behaviors. For example, Deitz, Repp, and Deitz (1976) present several case studies in which programs involving DRO and DRI were effective in decreasing a variety of disruptive behaviors, including talking and yelling out and being out-of-seat. The subjects in the Deitz et al. (1976) report were all mildly retarded students. As another example, Russo, Cataldo, and Cushing (1981), showed that the reinforcement of compliance to adult requests was effective in decreasing the noncompliance of three children with behavior disorders. In addition, untreated disruptive behaviors, such as crying, were reduced as the children's compliancy increased.

Luiselli, Colozzi, Heifen, and Pollow (1980) evaluated the effects of a DRI procedure for reducing the inappropriate verbalizations and out-of-seat behavior exhibited by a moderately retarded boy and an autistic girl, respectively. Both children received praise and edible reinforcements for not engaging in the target disruptive behaviors for gradually lengthened time intervals. The results showed that these inappropriate behaviors decreased substantially following the DRI intervention. No generalization to other settings, however, was observed. Another type of differential reinforcement procedure, differential reinforcement of low rates (DRL), has also been successful in reducing disruptive classroom behavior (Deitz et al., 1976). Deitz and Repp (1973) demonstrated that a DRL procedure was effective in reducing moderately retarded students talking out in the classroom. Essentially, students were awarded free playtime and edible reinforcers if they exhibited fewer target behaviors than a specified criterion within a certain period of time.

Repp, Barton, and Brulle (1983) compared the relative effectiveness of two methods of DRO in reducing the disruptive behaviors of three mildly retarded students and one moderately retarded student. A momentary DRO schedule consisted of providing reinforcement if the student was not engaged in the target behavior at the end of a time interval, while whole-interval DRO involved reinforcement contingent on the absence of target behavior throughout the entire time interval. Overall, the results showed that the whole-interval DRO procedure was more effective in decreasing disruptive behaviors. The results also suggest that the momentary DRO procedure may be effective in maintaining previously suppressed levels of inappropriate responding.

Several studies have suggested that the use of contingent social disapproval and verbal reprimands are effective in reducing mildly disruptive behaviors. In one study, Jones and Miller (1974) trained teachers of behaviorally disordered students to dispense negative attention in the form of verbal or physical disapproval, contingent on students' disruptive behaviors, which included interrupting, talking without permission, out-of-seat, and throwing objects. Teachers were also instructed to apply differential reinforcement contingent on students' appropriate classroom behaviors. Following these interventions, it was shown that disruptive behaviors in target classrooms were reduced to levels that were comparable to comparison classrooms. Schultz, Wellman, Renzaglia, and Karan (1978) employed verbal reprimands in an effort to reduce a severely retarded adolescent's inappropriate social behaviors (e.g., body rocking and bizarre vocalizations). Results showed that firm reprimands for each occurrence of the target behaviors were effective in decreasing the disruptive vocalizations and behaviors.

The efficacy of token reinforcement systems for modifying disruptive classroom behaviors is well documented in the literature (e.g., Graziano & Mooney, 1984; O'Leary & O'Leary, 1977). In fact, some of the earliest studies on the use of token reinforcement in the classroom were conducted in special education classes. O'Leary and Becker (1967) implemented a token reinforcement system in order to modify a variety of disruptive behaviors exhibited by a class of emotionally disturbed students. Tokens were awarded for following class rules and were exchanged for a number of back-up reinforcers, such as candy, comics, or other small prizes. Students' disruptive behaviors were reduced significantly from baseline to treatment. In addition, by the end of the study, students were able to tolerate a 4-day delay in exchanging their tokens without exhibiting increased rates of disruptiveness. Using a multiple baseline design, Ayllon, Layman, and Burke (1972) implemented a token reinforcement system in a classroom for highly disruptive, mildly retarded boys. By providing differential reinforcement for academic performance in reading and math, it was shown that not only did students' performance in reading and math improve, but the percentage of classroom disruptive behaviors was reduced substantially. Token reinforcement systems have also been shown to be effective in controlling disruptive behaviors in combinations with other types of intervention, such as response cost (Iwata & Bailey, 1974), group contingencies (Axelrod, 1973; Sulzbacher & Houser, 1969), and time out (Baker, Stanish, & Fraser, 1972). In addition, at least one study has shown token reinforcement contingencies to be superior to psychotropic medication in reducing the bizarre and disruptive behaviors in mildly retarded persons (Sanford & Nettelbeck, 1982).

The use of self-management or self-control techniques to change various problem behaviors in the classroom is becoming increasingly common (e.g., Graziano & Mooney, 1984; Hallahan et al., 1983; Rosenbaum & Drabman, 1979; Shapiro & Klein, 1980). It has only been relatively recently, however, that the use of these procedures with mentally retarded children has been reported in the research literature (Shapiro & Klein, 1980).

Drabman, Spitalnik, and O'Leary (1973) conducted one of the first studies using self-management procedures to reduce the disruptive behaviors of a group of emotionally disturbed students in a classroom. In essence, students were taught to evaluate their own behaviors within the context of a token reinforcement system. In a replication and extension of this study, Turkewitz, O'Leary, and Ironsmith (1975) attempted to demonstrate the efficacy of self-management procedures in generalizing and maintaining positive behavioral changes in a "transitional adjustment" class. A token reinforcement program was instituted. In this program points and back-up reinforcers were contingent upon accurate self-ratings, matching teacher ratings faded until the students completely controlled point distribution, and finally back-up reinforcers were faded. It was shown that the reduction in disruptive behavior was maintained following the withdrawal of all back-up reinforcers; however, the students' appropriate social behaviors did not generalize from the special class setting to the regular classrooms. In a study modeled after that of Drabman et al. (1973), Robertson, Simon, Pachman, and Drabman (1979) examined the use of self-management procedures in a classroom of mildly and moderately mentally retarded students who were described as highly disruptive. Following the implementation of a token reinforcement system, students were trained to rate their own behavior and were rewarded for matching the teacher's ratings of their behavior. During the next series of phases, the matching requirements, as well as the use of points, were gradually faded. The results showed that the levels of disruptive behavior were substantially reduced and were maintained even when the procedures were gradually faded. In addition, these positive behavioral changes generalized to a time period when the procedures were not in effect.

Rhode, Morgan, and Young (1983) investigated the use of self-management procedures in facilitating generalization of students' ap-

propriate classroom behaviors from a special education class (resource room) to a regular classroom. Subjects were six behaviorally handicapped students who exhibited high rates of disruptive behavior such as noncompliance, inappropriate talking, and wandering out-of-seat. During the first phase, a token reinforcement system was implemented in the resource room and students were taught to evaluate themselves. Back-up reinforcers were gradually faded, so that students' appropriate classroom behaviors were maintained with only minimal external reinforcement. During the second phase, generalization and maintenance conditions were introduced and consisted of students' using the self-evaluation procedures in their regular classrooms, further fading of back-up reinforcers, and fading of self-evaluations. The results revealed that students' appropriate behaviors transferred to their regular classrooms and were maintained at high levels once the self-evaluation program was extended to these settings. All components of the self-evaluation program were completely faded for four of the six students, while two students required a modification of the original intervention in order to maintain their behavior gains in the regular classroom.

Shapiro and his associates evaluated the relative effectiveness of self-management procedures in classrooms for mentally retarded, behaviorally disturbed students. In the first study, Shapiro and Klein (1980) instituted a teacher-managed token reinforcement system to increase on-task behaviors. Next, students were taught self-assessment, or to determine whether their behavior was on-task at specific times. Following this phase, training was provided in self-reinforcement, in which students were taught to reward themselves for accurate self-assessment. The results showed that the initial token reinforcement program substantially increased students' on-task behavior. High levels of on-task behavior were then maintained across all phases of self-management and at follow-up. Shapiro, McGonigle, and Ollendick (1981) replicated the Shapiro and Klein (1980) study to some degree. Using a similar population of subjects, Shapiro et al.

(1981) compared self-assessment and self-re-inforcement in a token reinforcement system. Initially, a classroom token system was implemented similar to that used in Shapiro and Klein (1980). A brief phase was next introduced in which the teacher verbally instructed and modeled the self-management procedures at the beginning of class each day. Following this phase, training in self-assessment and self-reinforcement was conducted. It was shown that the self-management procedures were able to maintain the high levels of on-task behavior previously established with the teacher-managed token reinforcement system. In addition, it was found that instruction only in self-management was insufficient to maintain students' on-task behavior.

Though more often applied to the management of aggressive behavior, time out from reinforcement has also been shown to be effective in controlling various disruptive behaviors in special education groups. For example, Lahey, McNees, and McNees (1973) used a seclusionary time out program in an effort to reduce a mildly retarded boy's frequency of obscene vocalizations and extremely disruptive facial twitches. The time out intervention consisted of placing the boy in a time out room for 5 minutes immediately following each disruptive behavior. With the introduction of the time out program, the boy's rate of disruptive behaviors was markedly reduced. However, during a reversal condition, the boy's behaviors returned to their baseline levels.

Time out does not necessarily mean totally secluding or excluding a student from the ongoing class activity or from students. For example, Huguenin and Mulick (1981) applied a nonexclusionary time out procedure in order to reduce the disruptive behaviors of a 19-year-old severely retarded man. The intervention consisted of having the subject wear a large, loose ribbon around his neck as long as he behaved appropriately. Whenever he was wearing the ribbon, he received edible and social reinforcement according to a DRO:10 minute schedule. If he engaged in one of the target behaviors, the ribbon was removed, and the subject was placed in "nonexclusionary time out" for 5 minutes; i.e., he was required to remain in his seat without any materials, attention, or any form of reinforcement. At the end of this period, the ribbon was returned to him. The results showed that the rate of the target behaviors declined immediately in three different settings following this intervention. Ford and Veltri-Ford (1980) examined the use of time out from auditory reinforcement (music) for reducing the inappropriate verbal/vocal behaviors and out-of-seat behaviors exhibited by two moderately retarded children. Essentially, a short time out from music followed each incident of disruptive behavior. Once the disruptive behavior terminated, the music was reinstated. It was shown that response contingent time out from auditory reinforcement was effective in reducing both children's disruptive behaviors.

Positive practice and overcorrection procedures have also been suggested as alternatives for controlling disruptive behaviors in special populations. Azrin and Powers (1975) employed a positive practice procedure with six extremely disruptive boys who were in a special class for emotionally disturbed students. The target behaviors were talking or leaving one's seat without permission. The intervention involved having the student practice the correct procedure for asking permission to talk or leave one's seat for a 5-minute period. A fading process was implemented so that the duration of positive practice was gradually reduced until the student only was required to repeat the rule she or he had broken. With the institution of positive practice, class disruptions were substantially reduced. Immediate positive practice was shown to be more effective than warnings, reminders, a loss recess contingency, and a delayed positive practice condition in reducing students' disruptive behaviors.

Some studies have focused on the various parameters and side effects of positive practice and overcorrection procedures. For example, Carey and Bucher (1983) compared the effects of long (3 minutes) and short (30 seconds) durations of positive practice on reducing off-task behavior with a group of moderately and severely retarded children. Immediately following any instance of off-task behavior, the children were required to perform an object-placement task for either 30 seconds or 3 minutes. It was shown that both durations of positive practice were equally effective in rapidly reducing off-task behavior. However, over time it was shown that less time was required for positive practice when short durations were in effect and that negative side effects (e.g., aggressive and disruptive behaviors) occurred primarily during long durations of positive practice. These results led Carey and Bucher (1983) to conclude that using short durations of positive practice can reduce the time required for treatment as well as eliminate any negative side effects that might result from using this procedure. Epstein et al. (1974) investigated whether positive practice overcorrection designed for one inappropriate behavior would produce similar effects on another topographically different, untreated problem behavior. Using two children diagnosed as schizophrenic, a hand overcorrection and foot overcorrection procedure was applied sequentially for inappropriate hand and foot movements. The results showed that for both children when the hand overcorrection procedure was applied to inappropriate hand movements, inappropriate foot movements also decreased. Thus, it was concluded that an overcorrection procedure that is effective for one response class may be used to weaken a topographically different behavior. For at least one subject, both desirable and undesirable effects were noted.

A few reports are available on the use of punishment for reducing disruptive behaviors. For example, Doleys, Wells, Hobbs, Roberts, and Cartelli (1976) found that a social punishment procedure (i.e., loud verbal reprimand, physical hold, and glaring) was superior to time out and positive practice in reducing the noncompliant behaviors of four mentally retarded and autistic children. However, as with other aversive procedures, both positive and negative side effects were associated with the use of social punishment. Singh, Winton, and Dawson (1982) employed a 1-minute facial screening procedure to control a 20-year-old

profoundly retarded woman's excessive, frequent screaming across three different settings. At a 6-month follow-up evaluation, it was observed that she screamed less than twice a month.

FEARS AND PHOBIAS

Although there is a fair amount of literature on the treatment of fears and phobias in "normal" children (e.g., Graziano, De Giovanni, & Garcia, 1979; Morris & Kratochwill, 1983, 1985; Morris, Kratochwill, & Dodson, in press), relatively little research has been published on methods of reducing fear in handicapped people (e.g., Boyd, 1980; Kandel, Ayllon, & Rosenbaum, 1977; Luiselli, 1978; Morris & McReynolds, 1986; Runyan, Stevens, & Reeves, 1985).

Guarnaccia and Weiss (1974) and Runyan et al. (1985) maintain that because mentally retarded persons often have not been exposed to new situations and/or have lived highly regimented lives, they tend to avoid and are fearful of unfamiliar stimuli. Also, Bijou (1966) noted that the fear that precipitates avoidance behavior can and frequently does interfere with the ability of mentally retarded persons to adequately adapt to their environment.

In spite of the pioneering work on the treatment of fears and phobias by Mary Cover Jones in 1924 and Joseph Wolpe in the 1950s, and in spite of the hundreds of articles on various fear reduction methods that have been published since the 1920s, there has been little systematic research on treating fears in handicapped children. Ince (1976) treated a 12-year-old boy who became fearful and reluctant to go to school as a result of developing epileptic seizures. Treatment consisted of systematic desensitization for school anxiety along with cue-controlled relaxation to reduce the child's seizures. Following the 3-month treatment, the child's frequency of seizures and reluctance to go to school were greatly reduced. At a 6- and 9-month follow-up evaluations, both the school and the child's parents reported observing no seizures in the child.

Utilizing a somewhat different procedure,

Boyd (1980) adapted the emotive imagery procedure developed by Lazarus and Abramovitz (1962) to treat a 16-year-old "school phobic" boy who was mildly retarded. After 2 weeks of treatment, the boy was able to remain at school for a full day and, in fact, completed the school year with no recurrence of the school phobia. He did, however, miss a few days occasionally.

In another study, which adapted systematic desensitization treatment to a mentally retarded boy, Morris and McReynolds (1986) used a contact desensitization procedure to reduce the severe clinical fear of dogs in a 6-year-old boy. The child was led through a series of hierarchy steps that included approach of the dog, petting, walking, brushing, feeding, and stroking the dog. Each step involved modeling by the therapist followed by the child being encouraged to perform the steps with physical guidance by the therapist if necessary. The results showed that contact desensitization was effective in reducing the child's fear and that treatment effects generalized to other dogs of various sizes and colors and in different settings. Social validation ratings from the boy's teacher and his parents confirmed that he was very much improved as a result of treatment.

Another method that has been used to reduce children's fears and phobias is flooding, which unlike systematic desensitization, requires the child to imagine a very fearful and threatening scene. In addition, this scene is presented to the child for a prolonged period of time without previously training the child to relax. The purpose of this procedure is for the child to imagine such an extremely frightening experience that it will actually result in reducing the child's fear rather than heightening it. Like the desensitization therapies, only a very small number of studies using this method with handicapped children have been published. For example, Kandel et al., (1977) used a modified flooding method, called in vivo flooding, with two children who exhibited extreme social withdrawal. One child, a 4-year-old, was diagnosed as having minimal brain disorder (MBD) with hyperactivity and emotional problems and the other child, an 8-year-old, was diagnosed as autistic and MBD. The treatment

procedure showed that both children could learn to interact with and respond to other people following treatment in their natural school environment.

A second type of flooding treatment, developed by Stampfl (1961), is implosive therapy, which is based on an extinction model. In this procedure, the therapist represents or symbolically reproduces the feared object or situation to which the anxiety response has been conditioned without presenting the concomitant reinforcement that maintains this response (Stampfl & Levis, 1967).

Just as in the case of flooding, presently there is limited empirical support for the use of implosive therapy to reduce fears and phobias in handicapped, as well as nonhandicapped, children. For example, Ollendick and Gruen (1972) applied implosive therapy to treat an 8-year-old boy whose phobia of bodily injury brought him sleepless nights, hives, and asthmatic bronchitis. After only two therapy sessions, the child's number of sleepless nights were reduced to approximately two per week. At a 6-month follow-up evaluation, no recurrence of the hives or bronchitis was reported, and the boy had not experienced any sleepless nights for 2 consecutive months.

Another frequently cited behavioral method of fear reduction, which has been systematically used to treat children and adults, is contingency management. Contingency management procedures emphasize the importance of the causal relationship between stimuli (i.e., feared objects or situations) and behavior (i.e., approach behaviors), and the procedures include positive reinforcement, shaping, and stimulus fading. Although few controlled studies have been published that support the efficacy of these procedures with handicapped children, these methods, like the others described, have been reported to be successful with nonhandicapped children. For example, Patterson (1965), used playing with a doll plus candy and social reinforcers to reduce the "school phobia" of a 7-year-old boy with a severe articulation disorder and low reading skills. Treatment consisted of reinforcing the child during play for making fearless verbal statements and not being afraid to separate from his mother. By the ninth treatment session, a visiting teacher began assisting the child with reading and eventually accompanied him to school. The teacher's presence in the classroom was then gradually faded, and the child began attending school full-time. At a 3-month follow-up, the school reported that the child's general adjustment had dramatically improved and there was no further evidence of his fearfulness.

In another study, Luiselli (1977) combined reinforcement with a time-out procedure to reduce a severely mentally retarded adolescent's toilet phobia. Although previously completely toilet trained, the subject began to avoid the bathroom, plugging his ears and hyperventilating whenever the toilet was mentioned to him. Following a baseline period, he was awarded token reinforcers and praise for appropriately using the toilet and was reinforced for approaching the toilet. The reinforcement schedule was gradually changed to an increasingly intermittent schedule. The subject was also encouraged to record his use of the toilet. A 40-minute exclusion time out procedure was instituted whenever an accident occurred. Results indicated that his frequency of wetting per week dropped appreciably over time, to only two to three accidents a week by the end of treatment. At the 4-month follow-up session, one incident was recorded, while the 6-month and 1-year follow-up evaluations revealed no incidents during the period.

Luiselli (1978) also used a contingency management procedure with a 7-year-old boy, labeled autistic, who was afraid to ride a school bus. Using a graduated exposure/shaping procedure, the child was initially familiarized with the bus by sitting in the parked bus with his mother. His mother also reinforced him for this behavior. Next, the mother and therapist gradually removed themselves from the bus. The child was then reinforced for riding to school on the bus with his mother and the therapist, which was followed by rides with only the therapist, and finally alone. This program took 7 days and, 1 year later, the boy continued to ride the bus alone.

Adaptations of Bandura's (1969) modeling procedure have also been used to reduce fear in handicapped persons. Furthermore, Matson (1981) reports one of the few studies treating fears in mentally retarded children using participant modeling. Subjects were three 8- to 10-year-old moderately retarded children who had long-standing fears of adult strangers. In this study, each child's mother served as the therapist. Treatment involved having the mother model an appropriate greeting for an adult then verbally and physically prompt the child to practice the behavior, with a tangible reinforcer provided each time the child made a correct greeting. The child also practiced this behavior in the presence of a stranger. Following treatment, it was shown that all subjects' fearful behaviors decreased and were maintained at a 6-month follow-up evaluation.

Several studies have successfully used a combination of behavioral procedures, or a treatment package, to reduce handicapped children's fears and phobias. For example, Obler and Terwilliger (1970) worked with a group of neurologically impaired children who were extremely fearful of dogs and using a public bus. The treatment approach combined in vivo systematic desensitization with social reinforcement for approaching the feared object and therapist modeling. Following treatment, all but 1 of the 15 fearful children were rated by their parents as improved, while only 2 children in an untreated control group showed improvement.

SUMMARY AND CONCLUSIONS

As is very apparent from this overview of the clinical and educational research literature on behavior modification with children and adolescents who have special needs, there has been an exponential growth in the amount of research that has been published over the past 15 years. What has emerged from this research is the well-documented view that many behavioral procedures now have sufficient empirical support to merit their use in a wide variety of educational, clinical, and other settings, with a wide variety of target behaviors, and with children having many different handicapping conditions. In Table 4.2, we have summarized the types of behavioral procedures used with each of the 20 target behavior categories that we have reviewed in this chapter.

As can be seen in this table, by far the most frequently used procedure is positive reinforcement and its variants (i.e., shaping, chaining, DRO, DRI, DRL, group reinforcement, token economy programs). These reinforcement procedures account for 50% of all the procedures used to modify the 20 target behavior categories listed.

The literature on behavior modification with handicapped children has also revealed that there is now sufficient information available — based on replicated research findings — to allow us to develop prescriptions regarding the modification of several behaviors exhibited by these children and adolescents. For example, Morris (1985) has listed 18 specific prescriptions and 4 general prescriptions for changing various self-help and social behaviors in exceptional children. Hallahan et al. (1983) discuss behavioral procedures for working with children having academic problems, and Barkley (1981, 1983) describes behavioral programs for treating hyperactive children. Methods for developing language in handicapped children have been described by Harris (1975) and Lovaas (1977) to name just a few researchers, while programs for children having communication disorders have been discussed by Mahoney and Carpenter (1983; see also Chapter 9 by Butler). Finally, behaviorally based programs and prescriptions for the modification of various behaviors in mentally retarded children and adolescents have been presented in several articles and books by Matson and his colleagues (e.g., Matson, 1983; Matson & Andrasik, 1983; Matson & McCartney, 1981; Matson & Mulick, 1983).

Although more than 1000 studies have been published over the last 25–30 years that support the relative effectiveness of behavior modification procedures with handicapped children, a large majority of these studies have failed to provide setting generalization data regarding

treatment outcome and/or data on the relative contribution of therapist/behavior modifier, client, and setting variables on the outcome of the behavior modification treatment. In addition, few comparison outcome studies have been published that permit us to determine which procedure(s) is best (under which conditions) for the modification of which particular target behavior(s). Until this information is available, the findings reported in this chapter must be viewed with caution.

In spite of this cautionary note, it is clear that our knowledge base regarding the application of behavior modification procedures with special needs children has increased tremendously since the early work in the later 1950s and early 1960s (e.g., Bijou & Orlando, 1961; Ferster & DeMeyer, 1961; Zimmer & Zimmerman, 1962). The most prominent changes have been in the expansion of use of these procedures from the development of rudimentary self-help and social skills and language acquisition in mentally retarded and autistic children to the modification of the classroom behaviors and the reading, math, and handwriting skills of children and adolescents having varying handicapping conditions. Changes can also be seen from the use of behavioral interventions to change children's behaviors on a one-to-one basis in a laboratory or clinic to the development and application of procedures to change the behavior of children within a classroom. Finally, changes can be seen away from the use of procedures that follow the strict tenets of operant conditioning and experimental analysis of behavior (e.g., Skinner, 1938, 1953) and toward the use of cognitively-based behavioral procedures (e.g., Hallahan et al., 1983; Meichenbaum & Gerest, 1980; Shapiro & Klein, 1980) and intervention strategies based on social learning theory (e.g., Bandura, 1969, 1977).

One area, however, that has not been addressed very often in the research literature is the ethical and legal issues associated with the use of behavior modification procedures with handicapped children. Since a number of articles, chapters and books (e.g., Braun, 1975; Kazdin, 1980; Martin, 1975; May, Risley,

TABLE 4.2. BEHAVIOR MODIFICATION PROCEDURES USED TO CHANGE VARIOUS
BEHAVIORS IN SPECIAL NEEDS STUDENTS

Behavior	Procedure*	Behavior	Procedure*
Eye Contact	Positive Reinforcement	Fears and Phobias	Implosive Therapy
	Shaping	(continued)	Positive Reinforcement
	Functional Movement		Shaping
	Training		Time Out
Motoric Imitation	Positive Reinforcement		Modeling
	Shaping	Prevocational and	Positive Reinforcement
	Modeling	Vocational	Modeling
Cooperative Play;	Positive Reinforcement	Training Skills	Behavioral Rehearsal
Interactional	Shaping		Corrective Feedback
Skills	Modeling	Self-Stimulation	DRO
Reading	Positive Reinforcement		DRL
	Modeling		Physical Punishment
	Token Reinforcement		Overcorrection
	Program		Contingent Physical
	Self-Control		Restraint
Spelling	Positive Reinforcement	Attention Deficit	Positive Reinforcement
	Modeling	Disorder	DRO
	Positive Reinforcement		Token Economy
	Overcorrection		Procedures
Math	Positive Reinforcement		Self-Control
	Self-Control	Enuresis	Bell and Pad/Urine
	Token Economy Program		Alarm
	Modeling		Bladder Retention
Handwriting	Positive Reinforcement		Training
	Modeling		Positive Reinforcement
	Corrective Feedback	Encopresis	Positive Reinforcement
	Self-Control		Physical Punishment
Mealtime Skills	Positive Reinforcement		Response Cost
	Shaping	Aggression	Extinction
	Chaining		Token Economy
	Time Out		Program
	Overcorrection		DRO
	Modeling		Positive Reinforcement
	Behavioral Rehearsal		Group Reinforcement
Dressing and	Positive Reinforcement		Modeling
Undressing Skills	Shaping		Overcorrection
	Chaining		Time Out
Grooming and	Positive Reinforcement		Response Cost
Personal	Shaping		Self-Monitoring
Hygiene Skills	Chaining		Relaxation Training
	Modeling	Self-Injurious	DRO
Toilet Skills	Positive Reinforcement	Behavior	DRI
	Shaping		Time Out
	Chaining		Extinction
	Pants Alarm		Positive Reinforcement
	Overcorrection		Overcorrection
Fears and Phobias	Contact		Required Relaxation
	Desensitization		Contingent Physical
	Systematic		Restraint
	Desensitization		Physical Punishment
	In Vivo	Classroom	Positive Reinforcement
	Desensitization	Disruption	Extinction
	Emotive Imagery		Token Economy
	Flooding		Program
	In Vivo Flooding		Response Cost
			Time Out
			Self-Control
			Overcorrection
			Punishment

*Note: Many of the procedures listed in this column have been used both separately and in combination with other types of interventions to change the particular target behavior. See chapter for details.

Twardosz, Bijou, & Wexler, 1975; Morris, 1985; Morris & Brown, 1983; Roos, 1974, 1977) have already critically discussed this topic, we will not review this area in detail. Suffice it to say, at this point, that it is our belief that reinforcement programs, as well as programs that are the least intrusive and restrictive for students, should first be tried before a teacher or other professional utilizes behavior reduction programs such as time out, overcorrection, response cost, punishment, and so forth. By providing the children and adolescents with the least restrictive and intrusive program, as well as a reinforcement-based procedure, we are providing them with the opportunity to change under minimally restrictive conditions. As we mentioned earlier, since few comparison outcome studies have been published in which the same set of procedures is compared across handicapping conditions using the same target behavior, we are not in a strong position to advance the position that intrusive and restrictive behavior reduction programs should be used before reinforcement procedures. As a general rule, therefore, it is our position that teachers and/or other behavior modifiers should document with data (and graphic representations of these data) that reinforcement and/or other more positive behavioral procedures (i.e., self-control, modeling, relaxation training, contingency contracting, etc.) have been ineffective in controlling a particular target behavior before proceeding to the use of the more restrictive and intrusive behavior reduction programs. Behavior modifiers may even wish to establish a peer monitoring system like those discussed by May et al. (1975) and Morris, Barber, Hoschouer, Karrels, and Bijou (1979), where independent committees advise the behavior modifier and his or her agency or school of the appropriateness and technical feasibility of a proposed behavioral intervention.

These cautionary moves are needed we believe, because behavior modification procedures have been found to be very effective in changing the behaviors of handicapped children and adolescents and because these procedures emphasize the control of behavior. As such, they can also be misused and abused—

the fruits of any scientific research can be used for a multitude of purposes. Thus, to protect those children who are being exposed to these behavioral programs, we believe that a peer monitoring or quality assurance system should be established to advise behavior modifiers regarding the use of various programs and/or whether they meet the restrictive and intrusive criteria, as well as the criterion of being reinforcement based and/or involving the use of positive behavioral procedures.

It is clear that behavior modification procedures work well with children having special needs, and that these methods will continue to be a viable part of the special education service delivery system for years to come.

REFERENCES

Abramson, E. E., & Wunderlich, R. A. (1972). Dental hygiene training for retardates: An application of behavioral techniques. *Mental Retardation, 10,* 6–8.

Adelstein-Bernstein, N., & Sandow, L. (1978). Teaching buttoning to severely profoundly retarded multihandicapped children. *Education and Training of the Mentally Retarded, 5,* 178–183.

Altman, K., Haavik, S., & Cook, J. W. (1978). Punishment of self-injurious behavior in natural settings using contingent aromatic ammonia. *Behavior Research and Therapy, 16,* 85–96.

American Psychiatric Association (1980). *Diagnostic and statistical manual of mental disorders* (3rd ed.). Washington, DC: Author.

Ando, H. (1977). Training autistic children to urinate in the toilet through operant conditioning techniques. *Journal of Autism and Childhood Schizophrenia, 7,* 151–163.

Ashem, B. A., & Poser, E. G. (Eds.). (1973). *Adaptive learning: Behavior modification with children.* New York: Pergamon.

Axelrod, S. (1973). Comparison of individual and group contingencies in two special classes. *Behavior Therapy, 4,* 83–90.

Ayllon, T., Garber, S., & Pisor, K. (1976). Reducing time limits: A means to increase behavior of retardates. *Journal of Applied Behavior Analysis, 9,* 247–252.

Ayllon, T., Layman, D., & Burke, S. (1972). Disruptive behavior and reinforcement of academic performance. *The Psychological Record, 22,* 315–323.

Ayllon, T., Layman, D., & Kandel, H. J. (1975). A behavioral-educational alternative to drug control of hyperactive children. *Journal of Applied Behavior Analysis, 8,* 137–146.

Ayllon, T. A., Simon, S. J., & Wildman, R. A. (1975). Instructions and reinforcement in the elimination of encopresis: A case study. *Journal of Behavior Therapy and Experimental Psychiatry, 6,* 235–238.

Ayllon, T., Smith, D., & Rogers, M. (1970). Behavioral management of school phobia. *Journal of Behavior Therapy and Experimental Psychiatry, 1,* 125–138.

Azrin, H. H., & Armstrong, P. M. (1973). The "mini-meal"—A method for teaching eating skills to the profoundly retarded. *Mental Retardation, 11,* 9–13.

Azrin, N. H., & Foxx, R. M. (1971). A rapid method of toilet training the instutionalized retarded. *Journal of Applied Behavior Analysis, 4,* 89–99.

Azrin, N. H., Gottlieb, L., Hughart, L., Wesolowski, M. D., and Rahn, T. (1975). Eliminating self-injurious behavior by educative procedures. *Behavior Research and Therapy, 13,* 101–111.

Azrin, N. H., & Lindsley, O. R. (1956). The reinforcement of cooperation between children. *Journal of Abnormal and Social Psychology, 52,* 498–505.

Azrin, N. H., & Powers, M. A. (1975). Eliminating classroom disturbances of emotionally disturbed children by positive practice procedures. *Behavior Therapy, 6,* 525–534.

Azrin, N. H., Sneed, T. J., & Foxx, R. M. (1974). Dry-bed: Rapid elimination of childhood enuresis. *Behavior Research and Therapy, 12,* 147–156.

Azrin, N. H., & Wesolowski, M. D. (1980). A reinforcement plus interruption method of eliminating behavioral stereotype of profoundly retarded persons. *Behavior Research and Therapy, 18,* 113–120.

Baer, D. M., Peterson, R. F., & Sherman, J. A. (1967). The development of imitation by reinforcing behavioral similarity to a model. *Journal of the Experimental Analysis of Behavior, 10,* 405–416.

Baker, T. G., Stanish, B., & Fraser, B. (1972). Comparative effects of a token economy in nursery school. *Mental Retardation, 10,* 16–19.

Ball, T., Sibbach, L., Jones, R., Steele, B., & Frazier, L. (1975). An accelerometer-activated device to control assaultive and self-destructive behavior in retardates. *Journal of Behavior Therapy and Experimental Psychiatry, 6,* 223–238.

Ballard, K. D., & Glynn, T. (1975). Behavioral self-management in story writing with elementary school children. *Journal of Applied Behavior Analysis, 8,* 387–398.

Bandura, A. (1969). *Principles of behavior modification.* New York: Holt, Rinehart, & Winston.

Bandura, A. (1977). *Social learning theory.* Englewood Cliffs, NJ: Prentice-Hall.

Bandura, A., & Barab, P. G. (1971). Conditions governing nonreinforced imitation. *Developmental Psychology, 5,* 244–255.

Barkley, R. A. (1981). *Hyperactive children: A handbook for diagnosis and treatment.* New York: The Guilford Press.

Barkley, R. A. (1983). Hyperactivity. In R. J. Morris & T. R. Kratochwill (Eds.), *The practice of child therapy.* New York: Pergamon.

Barkley, R. A., Copeland, A., & Sivage, C. A. (1980). A self-control classroom for hyperactive children. *Journal of Autism and Developmental Disorders, 10,* 75–89.

Barmann, B. C., & Vitali, D. L. (1982). Facial screening to eliminate trichotillomania in developmentally disabled persons. *Behavior Therapy, 13,* 735–742.

Barrett, R. P., Matson, J. L., & Shapiro, E. S. (1981). A comparison of punishment and DRO procedures for treating stereotypic behavior of mentally retarded children. *Applied Research in Mental Retardation, 2,* 247–256.

Baumeister, A. A. (1978). Origins and control of stereotyped movements. In C. E. Meyers (Ed.), *Quality of life in severely and profoundly mentally retarded people: Research foundations for improvement.* Washington, DC: American Association of Mental Deficiency Monograph, No. 3.

Baumeister, A. A., & Klosowski, R. (1965). An attempt to group toilet train severely retarded patients. *Mental Retardation, 3,* 24–26.

Becker, W. C. (1971). *Parents are teachers.* Champaign, IL: Research Press.

Bensberg, G. J., Colwell, C. N., & Cassel, R. H. (1965). Teaching the profoundly retarded self-help activities by behavior shaping techniques. *American Journal of Mental Deficiency, 69,* 674–679.

Berkowitz, S., Sherry, P., & Davis, B. (1971). Teaching self-feeding skills to profound retardates using reinforcement and fading procedures. *Behavior Therapy, 2,* 62–67.

Bijou, S. W., & Orlando, R. (1961). Rapid development of multiple-schedule performances with retarded children. *Journal of Experimental Analysis of Behavior, 4,* 7–16.

Bijou, S. W. (1966). A functional analysis of retarded development. In N. R. Ellis (Ed.), *International review of research in mental retardation.* New York: Academic Press.

Bornstein, D. H., & Quevillon, R. P. (1976). The effects of a self-instructional package on overactive preschool boys. *Journal of Applied Behavior Analysis, 9,* 179–188.

Bornstein, M., Bellack, A. S., & Hersen, M. (1980). Social skills training for highly aggressive children. *Behavior Modification, 4,* 173–186.

Bouter, H. P., & Smeets, P. M. (1979). Teaching toothbrushing behavior in severely retarded adults: Systematic reduction of feedback and duration training. *International Journal of Rehabilitation Research, 2,* 62–69.

Boyd, L. T. (1980). Emotive imagery in the behavioral management of adolescent school phobia: A case approach. *School Psychology Digest*, *9*, 186–189.

Braun, S. H. (1975). Ethical issues in behavior modification. *Behavior Therapy*, *6*, 51–62.

Bricker, M., & Campbell, K. (1981). Fast food employment of moderately and mildly mentally retarded adults: The McDonald's Project. *Mental Retardation*, *19*, 113–116.

Brooks, B., Morrow, J., & Gray, W. (1967/68). Reduction of autistic gaze aversion of reinforcement of visual attention responses. *Journal of Special Education*, *2*(3), 307–309.

Brown, L., Huppler, B., Pierce, L., York, B., & Sontag, E. (1974). Teaching trainable level students to read unconjugated action verbs. *Journal of Special Education*, *8*, 51–56.

Brown, L., Jones, S., Troccolo, E., Heiser, C., Bellamy, T., & Sontag, E. (1972). Teaching functional reading to young trainable students: Toward longitudinal objectives. *Journal of Special Education*, *6*, 237–246.

Bry, P. M., & Nawas, M. M. (1972). Is reinforcement necessary for the development of a generalized imitation operant in severely and profoundly retarded children. *American Journal of Mental Deficiency*, *12*, 35–50.

Bucher, B., Reykdal, B., & Albin, J. (1976). Brief physical restraint to control pica. *Journal of Behavior Therapy and Experimental Psychiatry*, *1*, 137–140.

Budd, K. S., Leibowitz, J. M., Riner, L. S., Mindell, C., & Goldfarb, A. L. (1981). Homebased treatment of severe disruptive behaviors: A reinforcement package for preschool and kindergarten children. *Behavior Modification*, *5*, 273–298.

Burgio, L. D., Whitman, T. L., & Johnson, M. R. (1980). A self-instructional package for increasing attending behavior in educable mentally retarded children. *Journal of Applied Behavior Analysis*, *13*, 443–460.

Calhoun, K. S., & Matherne, P. (1975). The effects of varying schedule of time out on aggressive behavior of a retarded girl. *Journal of Behavior Therapy and Experimental Psychiatry*, *6*, 139–143.

Cantwell, D. P. (1980). Drugs and medical intervention. In H. Rie & E. Rie (Eds.), *Handbook of minimal brain dysfunctions*. New York: Wiley.

Carey, R. G., & Bucher, B. (1983). Positive practice overcorrection: The effects of duration of positive practice on acquisition and response reduction. *Journal of Applied Behavior Analysis*, *16*, 101–109.

Carr, E. G. (1977). The motivation of self-injurious behavior. *Psychological Bulletin*, *84*, 800–816.

Carr, E. C., Newsom, C. D., & Binkhoff, J. A. (1976). Stimulus control of self-destructive behavior in a psychotic child. *Journal of Abnormal Child Psychology*, *4*, 139–153.

Chandler, H. N. (1978). Confusion compounded: A teacher tries to use research results to teach math. *Journal of Learning Disabilities*, *11*, 361–369.

Christensen, D. E. (1975). Effects of combining methylphenidate and a classroom token system in modifying hyperactive behavior. *American Journal of Mental Deficiency*, *80*, 266–276.

Cinciripini, P. M., Epstein, L. H., & Kotanchik, N. L. (1980). Behavioral intervention for self-stimulatory, attending, and seizure behavior in a cerebral palsied child. *Journal of Behavior Therapy and Experimental Psychiatry*, *11*, 313–316.

Clark, H. B., Boyd, S. B., & MacRae, J. W. (1975). A classroom program teaching disadvantaged youth to write biographic information. *Journal of Applied Behavior Analysis*, *8*, 67–75.

Clark, H. B., Rowbury, T., Baer, A. M., & Baer, D. M. (1973). Time out as a punishing stimulus in continuous and intermittent schedules. *Journal of Applied Behavior Analysis*, *6*, 443–455.

Clements, J., & Dewey, M. (1979). The effects of overcorrection: A case study. *Behavior Research and Therapy*, *17*, 515–518.

Coleman, R. (1970). A pilot demonstration of the utility of reinforcement techniques in trainable programs. *Education and Training of the Mentally Retarded*, *5*, 68–70.

Coleman, R. S., Whitman, T. L., & Johnson, M. R. (1979). Suppression of self-stimulatory behavior of a profoundly retarded boy across staff and settings: An assessment of situational generalization. *Behavior Therapy*, *10*, 266–280.

Colwell, C., Richards, E., McCarver, R., & Ellis, N. (1973). Evaluation of self-help habit training of the profoundly retarded. *Mental Retardation*, *11*, 14–18.

Connally, J., & McGoldrick, M. (1976). Behavior modification toilet training procedure in a special care unit. *Child Care, Health, and Development*, *2*, 267–272.

Conners, C. K., & Werry, J. S. (1979). Pharmacotherapy. In H. Quay & J. S. Werry (Eds.), *Psychopathological disorders of childhood* (2nd ed.). New York: Wiley.

Cooke, T. P., & Apolloni, T. (1976). Developing positive social-emotional behaviors: A study of training and generalization effects. *Journal of Applied Behavior Analysis*, *9*, 68–78.

Corte, H. E., Wolf, M. M., & Locke, B. J. (1971). A comparison of procedures for eliminating self-injurious behavior of retarded adolescent. *Journal of Applied Behavior Analysis*, *4*, 201–213.

Cronin, K. A., & Cuvo, A. J. (1979). Teaching mending skills to mentally retarded adolescents. *Journal of Applied Behavior Analysis*, *12*, 401–406.

Cullinan, D., Lloyd, J. W., & Epstein, M. H. (1981). Strategy training: A structured approach to arithmetic instruction. *Exceptional Education Quarterly*, *2*, 41–49.

Cunningham, S. (1984, May). Pennhurst ruling limits federal role. *APA Monitor*, *15*, 14.

Cuvo, A. J., Lelaf, R. B., & Borakove, L. S. (1978). Teaching anitorial skills to the mentally retarded. Acquisition, generalization, and maintenance. *Journal of Applied Behavior Analysis*, *11*, 345–355.

DeCatanzaro, D. A., & Baldwin, G. (1978). Effective treatment of self-injurious behavior through a forced arm exercise. *American Journal of Mental Deficiency*, *82*, 433–439.

Denny, M. (1980). Reducing self-stimulatory behavior of mentally retarded persons by alternative positive practice. *American Journal of Mental Deficiency*, *84*, 610–615.

Deitz, S. M., & Repp, A. C. (1973). Decreasing classroom misbehavior through the use of DRL schedules of reinforcement. *Journal of Applied Behavior Analysis*, *6*, 457–463.

Deitz, S. M., Repp, A. C., & Deitz, D. E. (1976). Reducing inappropriate classroom behavior of retarded students through three procedures of differential reinforcement. *Journal of Mental Deficiency Research*, *20*, 155–170.

Doke, L. A., & Epstein, L. H. (1975). Oral overcorrection: Side effects and extended applications. *Journal of Experimental Child Psychology*, *20*, 469–511.

Doleys, D. M. (1977). Behavioral treatment of nocturnal enuresis in children: A review of the recent literature. *Psychological Bulletin*, *84*, 30–54.

Doleys, D. M., Wells, K. C., Hobbs, S. A., Roberts, M. W., & Cartelli, L. M. (1976). The effects of social punishment on noncompliance: A comparison with time out and positive practice. *Journal of Applied Behavior Analysis*, *9*, 471–482.

Doleys, N. M., & Arnold, S. (1975). Treatment of childhood encopresis: Full cleanliness training. *Mental Retardation*, *13*, 14–16.

Dorsey, M. F., Iwata, B. A., Ong, P., & McSween, T. E. (1980). Treatment of self-injurious behavior using a water mist: Initial response suppression and generalization. *Journal of Applied Behavior Analysis*, *13*, 343–353.

Doubros, S. G., & Daniels, G. J. (1966). An experimental approach to the reduction of overactive behavior. *Behavior Research and Therapy*, *4*, 251–258.

Drabman, R., & Spitalnik, R. (1973). Social isolation as a punishment procedure: A controlled study. *Journal of Experimental Child Psychology*, *16*, 236–249.

Drabman, R. S., Spitalnik, R., & O'Leary, R. D. (1973). Teaching self-control to disruptive children. *Journal of Abnormal Psychology*, *82*, 10–16.

Duker, P. (1975). Intra-subject controlled time-out (social isolation) in the modification of self-injurious behavior. *Journal of Mental Deficiency Research*, *19*, 107–112.

Epstein, L. H., Doke, L. A., Sajwaj, T. E., Sorrell, S., & Rimmer, B. (1974). Generality and side effects of overcorrection. *Journal of Applied Behavior Analysis*, *7*, 385–390.

Esveldt-Dawson, K., Wisner, K. L., Unis, A. S., Matson, J. L., & Kazdin, A. E. (1982). Treatment of phobias in a hospitalized child. *Journal of Behavior Therapy and Experimental Psychiatry*, *13*, 77–82.

Fauke, J., Burnett, J., Powers, M. A., & Sulzer-Azaroff, B. (1973). Improvement of handwriting and letter recognition skills: A behavior modification procedure. *Journal of Learning Disabilities*, *6*, 296–300.

Favell, J. E., McGimsey, J. F., & Jones, M. L. (1978). The use of physical restraint in the treatment of self-injury and as positive reinforcement. *Journal of Applied Behavior Analysis*, *11*, 225–241.

Ferretti, R. P., & Cavalier, A. R. (1983). A critical assessment of overcorrection procedures with mentally retarded persons. In J. L. Matson & F. Andrasik (Eds.), *Treatment issues and innovations in mental retardation*. New York: Plenum.

Ferster, C. B., & DeMeyer, M. K. (1961). The development of performances in autistic children in an automatically controlled environment. *Journal of Chronic Disabilities*, *13*, 312–345.

Flavell, J. (1973). Reduction of stereotypes by reinforcement of toy play. *Mental Retardation*, *11*, 21–23.

Fleming, E. R., & Fleming, D. C. (1982). Social skill training for educable mentally retarded children. *Education and Training of the Mentally Retarded*, *17*, 44–50.

Folk, M. C., & Campbell, J. (1978). Teaching functional reading skills to the TMR. *Education and Training of the Mentally Retarded*, *13*, 322–326.

Ford, J. E., & Veltri-Ford, A. (1980). Effects of time out from auditory reinforcement on two problem behaviors. *Mental Retardation*, *18*, 299–304.

Forehand, R. (1973). Teacher recording of a deviant behavior: A stimulus for behavior change. *Journal of Behavior Therapy and Experimental Psychiatry*, *4*, 39–40.

Foxx, R. M. (1977). Attention training: The use of overcorrection avoidance to increase the eye contact of autistic and retarded children. *Journal of Applied Behavior Analysis*, *10*, 489–499.

Foxx, R. M., & Azrin, N. H. (1972). Restitution: A method of eliminating aggressive-disruptive behavior of retarded and brain-damaged patients. *Behavior Research and Therapy*, *10*, 15–27.

Foxx, R. M., & Azrin, N. H. (1973a). Dry pants: A rapid method of toilet training children. *Behavior Research and Therapy*, *11*, 435–442.

Foxx, R. M., & Azrin, N. H. (1973b). The elimination of autistic self-stimulatory behavior by overcorrection. *Journal of Applied Behavior Analysis*, *6*, 1–14.

Foxx, R. M., & Azrin, N. H. (1973c). *Toilet training the retarded: A rapid program for day and nighttime independent toileting.* Champaign, IL: Research Press.

Foxx, R. M., & Shapiro, S. T. (1978). The time out ribbon: A nonexclusionary time-out procedure. *Journal of Applied Behavior Analysis, 11,* 125–136.

Frankel, F., Moss, D., Schofield, S., & Simmons, J. O. (1976). Case study: Use of differential reinforcement to suppress self-injurious and aggressive behavior. *Psychological Reports, 39,* 843–849.

Freeman, B. J., Somerset, T., & Ritvo, E. R. (1976). Effect of duration of time out in suppressing disruptive behavior of a severely autistic child. *Psychological Reports, 38,* 124–126.

Freiden, W., & Van Handel, D. (1970). Elimination of soiling in an elementary school child through application of aversive techniques. *Journal of School Psychology, 8,* 267–269.

Friedling, C., & O'Leary, S. G. (1979). Effects of self-instructional training on second- and third-grade hyperactive children: A failure to replicate. *Journal of Applied Behavior Analysis, 12,* 211–219.

Friedman, P. (1977). Human and legal rights of mentally retarded persons. *International Journal of Mental Health, 6,* 50–72.

Garcia, E., Baer, D. M., & Firestone, I. (1971). The development of generalized imitation within topographically determined boundaries. *Journal of Applied Behavior Analysis, 4,* 101–112.

Gelber, H., & Meyer, V. (1965). Behavior therapy and encopresis: The complexities involved in treatment. *Behavior Research and Therapy, 2,* 227–231.

Gewirtz, J. L., & Stingle, K. D. (1968). The learning of generalized imitation as the basis of identification. *Psychological Bulletin, 75,* 374–397.

Gold, M. (1972). Stimulus factors in skill training of the retarded on a complex assembly task: Acquisition, transfer, and retention. *American Journal of Mental Deficiency, 76,* 517–526.

Gold, M., & Barclay, C. R. (1973a). *The effects of verbal labels on the acquisition and retention of a complex assembly task.* Urbana: Children's Research Center, University of Illinois.

Gold, M., & Barclay, C. R. (1973b). The learning of difficult visual discrimination by the moderately and severely retarded. *Mental Retardation, 111,* 9–11.

Goldstein, A. P. (1973). *Structured learning theory.* New York: Academic Press.

Goodwin, S. E., & Mahoney, M. J. (1975). Modification of aggression through modeling: An experimental probe. *Journal of Behavior Therapy and Experimental Psychiatry, 6,* 200–202.

Graziano, A. M., De Giovanni, I. S., & Garcia, K. (1979). Behavioral treatments of children's fears: A review. *Psychological Bulletin, 86,* 804–830.

Graziano, A. M., & Kean, J. E. (1968). Pro-grammed relaxation and reciprocal inhibition with psychotic children. *Behavior Research and Therapy, 6,* 433–437.

Graziano, A. M., & Mooney, K. C. (1984). *Children and behavior therapy.* New York: Aldine.

Greene, R. J., Joats, D. L., & Hornick, A. J. (1970). Music distortion: A new technique for behavior modification. *Psychological Record, 20,* 107–109.

Groves, I. D., & Carroccio, D. F. (1971). A self-feeding program for the severely and profoundly retarded. *Mental Retardation, 9,* 10–12.

Guarnaccia, V. J., & Weiss, R. L. (1974). Factor structure of fears in the mentally retarded. *Journal Clinical Psychology, 30,* 540–544.

Hall, C., Sheldon-Wildgen, J., & Sherman, J. (1980). Teaching job interview skills to retarded clients. *Journal of Applied Behavior Analysis, 13,* 433–442.

Hall, R. V., Fox, R., Willard, D., Goldsmith, L., Emerson, M., Owen, M., Davis, F., & Porcia, E. (1971). The teacher as observer and experimenter in the modification of disputing and talking-out behaviors. *Journal of Applied Behavior Analysis, 4,* 141–149.

Hallahan, D. P., & Kauffman, J. M. (1981). *Exceptional children.* Englewood Cliffs, NJ: Prentice-Hall.

Hallahan, D. P., Lloyd, J. W., Kauffman, J. M., & Loper, A. B. (1983). Academic problems. In R. J. Morris & T. R. Kratochwill (Eds.), *The practice of child therapy.* New York: Pergamon.

Hallahan, D. P., Lloyd, J. W., Kneedler, R. D., & Marshall, K. J. (1982). A comparison of the effects of self versus teacher-assessment of on-task behavior. *Behavior Therapy, 13,* 715–723.

Hamilton, H., Stephens, L., & Allen, P. (1967). Controlling aggressive and destructive behavior in severely retarded institutionalized residents. *American Journal of Mental Deficiency, 71,* 852–856.

Harris, S. B. (1975). Teaching language to nonverbal children — with emphasis on problems of generalization. *Psychological Bulletin, 82,* 565–580.

Harris, S. L., & Romanczyk, R. G. (1976). Treating self-injurious behavior of a retarded child by overcorrection. *Behavior Therapy, 7,* 235–239.

Harris, S. L., & Wolchik, S. A. (1979). Suppression of self-stimulation: Three alternative strategies. *Journal of Applied Behavior Analysis, 12,* 185–198.

Hart, B. M., Reynolds, N. J., Baer, D. M., Brawley, E. R., & Harris, F. R. (1968). Effect of contingent and noncontingent social reinforcement on the cooperative play of a preschool child. *Journal of Applied Behavior Analysis, 1,* 73–76.

Hollis, J. H. (1976). Steady and transition states: Effects of alternative activity on body-rocking in retarded children. *Psychological Reports, 39,* 91–104.

Hopkins, B. (1968). Effects of candy and social

reinforcement, instructions, and reinforcement schedule learning on the modification and maintenance of smiling. *Journal of Applied Behavior Analysis*, *1*, 121–129.

Horner, R. D., & Keilitz, I. (1975). Training mentally retarded adolescents to brush their teeth. *Journal of Applied Behavior Analysis*, *8*, 301–309.

Huguenin, N. H., & Mulick, J. A. (1981). Nonexclusionary time out: Maintenance of appropriate behavior across settings. *Applied Research in Mental Retardation*, *2*, 55–67.

Hundziak, M., Maurer, R., & Watson, L. (1965). Operant conditioning in toilet training of severely mentally retarded boys. *American Journal of Mental Deficiency*, *70*, 120–124.

Hunter, J., & Bellamy, T. (1976). Cable harness construction for severely retarded adults: A demonstration of a training technique. *AAESPH Review*, *1*, 2–13.

Ince, L. P. (1976). The use of relaxation training and a conditioned stimulus in the elimination of epileptic seizures in a child: A case study. *Journal of Behavior Therapy and Experimental Psychiatry*, *7*, 39–42.

Iwata, B. A. & Bailey, J. S. (1974). Reward versus cost token systems: An analysis of the effects of students and teachers. *Journal of Applied Behavior Analysis*, *7*, 567–576.

Jackson, G. M. (1979). The use of visual orientation feedback to facilitate attention and task performance. *Mental Retardation*, *17*, 281–284.

Jackson, J. K., & Calhoun, J. S. (1977). Effects of two variable-ratio schedules of time out: Changes in target and nontarget behaviors. *Journal of Behavior Therapy and Experimental Psychiatry*, *8*, 195–199.

Johnston, M. B., Whitman, T. L., & Johnson, M. (1980). Teaching addition and subtraction to mentally retarded children: A self-motivational program. *Applied Research in Mental Retardation*, *1*, 141–160.

Jones, F. H., & Miller, W. H. (1974). The effective use of negative attention for reducing group disruption in special elementary school classrooms. *The Psychological Record*, *24*, 435–448.

Jones, M. C. (1924). A laboratory study of fear: The case of Peter. *Pedagogical Seminary*, *31*, 308–315.

Kandel, H. J., Ayllon, T., & Rosenbaum, M. S. (1977). Flooding or systematic exposure in the treatment of extreme social withdrawal in children. *Journal of Behavior Therapy and Experimental Psychiatry*, *8*, 75–81.

Karen, R., & Maxwell, S. (1967). Strengthening self-help behavior in the retardate. *American Journal of Mental Deficiency*, *71*, 546–550.

Kauffman, J. M., Hallahan, D. P., Haas, K., Brame, T., & Boren, R. (1978). Imitating children's errors to improve their spelling performance. *Journal of Learning Disabilities*, *11*, 217–222.

Kaufman, K. F., & O'Leary, K. D. (1972). Reward, cost, and self-evaluation procedures for disruptive adolescents in a psychiatric hospital school. *Journal of Applied Behavior Analysis*, *5*, 293–309.

Kazdin, A. E. (1980). *Behavior modification in applied settings* (Rev. ed.). Homewood, IL: Dorsey Press.

Kelly, J. A., Wildman, B. G., & Berler, E. S. (1980). Small group behavioral training to improve the job interview skills repertoire of mildly retarded adolescents. *Journal of Applied Behavior Analysis*, *13*, 461–471.

Kendall, P. C., Nay, W. R., & Jeffers, J. (1975). Time out duration and contrast effects: A systematic evaluation of a successive treatments design. *Behavior Therapy*, *6*, 609–615.

Kimmel, H. D. & Kimmel, E. (1970). An instrumental conditioning method for the treatment of enuresis. *Journal of Behavior Therapy and Experimental Psychiatry*, *1*, 121–123.

Kirby, K. C., Holborn, S. W., & Bushby, H. T. (1981). Word game bingo: A behavioral treatment package for improving textual responding to sight words. *Journal of Applied Behavior Analysis*, *14*, 317–326.

Knanpczyk, D. R., & Livingston, G. (1974). The effects of prompting question-asking upon on-task behavior and reading comprehension. *Journal of Applied Behavior Analysis*, *7*, 115–121.

Koegel, R. L., Firestone, P. B., Kramme, K. W., & Dunlap, G. (1974). Increasing spontaneous play by suppressing self-stimulation in autistic children. *Journal of Applied Behavior Analysis*, *7*, 521–528.

Koegel, R. L., & Rincover, A. (1974). Treatment of psychotic children in a classroom environment: Learning in a large group. *Journal of Applied Behavior Analysis*, *7*, 45–59.

Kosiewicz, M. M., Hallahan, D. P., Lloyd, J., & Graves, A. W. (1982). Effects of self-instruction and self-correction procedures on handwriting performance. *Learning Disability Quarterly*, *5*, 71–78.

Lahey, B. B. (Ed.). (1979). *Behavior therapy with hyperactive and learning disabled children*. New York: Oxford University Press.

Lahey, B. B., & McNees, M. P. (1975). Letter discrimination errors in kindergarten through third grades: Assessment and operant training. *Journal of Special Education*, *9*, 191–199.

Lahey, B. B., McNees, M. P., & McNees, M. C. (1973). Control of an obscene "verbal tic" through time out in an elementary school classroom. *Journal of Applied Behavior Analysis*, *6*, 101–104.

Lazarus, A. A., & Abramovitz, A. (1962). The use of emotive imagery in the treatment of children's phobias. *Journal of Mental Science*, *108*, 191–195.

LeBrun, Y., & Van de Craen, P. (1975). Developmental writing disorders and their prevention. *Journal of Special Education*, *9*, 201–207.

Lloyd, J. W., Kneedler, R. D., & Cameron, N. (1982). Effects of verbal self-guidance on word reading accuracy. *Reading Improvement*, *19*, 84–89.

Lovaas, O. I. (1977). *The autistic child: Language development through behavior modification.* New York: Irvington.

Lovaas, O. I. (1981). *Teaching developmentally disabled children: The me book.* Baltimore: University Park Press.

Lovaas, O. I., Freitag, G., Gold, V. J., & Kassorla, I. C. (1965). Experimental studies in childhood schizophrenia: Analysis of self-destructive behavior. *Journal of Experimental Child Psychology*, *2*, 67–84.

Lovaas, O. I., Freitag, G., Nelson, J., & Whalen, C. (1967). The establishment of imitation and its use of the development of complex behavior in schizophrenic children. *Behavior Research and Therapy*, *5*, 171–182.

Lovaas, O. I., Schaeffer, B., & Simmons, J. O. (1965). Building social behavior in autistic children by use of electric shock. *Journal of Experimental Research in Personality*, *1*, 99–109.

Lovaas, O. I., & Simmons, J. O. (1969). Manipulation of self-destruction in three retarded children. *Journal of Applied Behavior Analysis*, *2*, 143–157.

Lovitt, T. C., & Curtiss, K. A. (1968). Effects of manipulating an antecedent event on mathematics response rate. *Journal of Applied Behavior Analysis*, *1*, 329–333.

Lovitt, T. C., Guppy, T. E., & Blattner, J. E. (1969). The use of a free-time contingency with fourth graders to increase spelling accuracy. *Behavior Research and Therapy*, *7*, 151–156.

Lovitt, T. C., & Hansen, C. L. (1976). The use of contingent skipping and drilling to improve oral reading and comprehension. *Journal of Learning Disabilities*, *9*, 481–487.

Luce, S. C., Delquadri, J., & Hall, R. V. (1980). Contingent exercise: A mild but powerful procedure for suppressing inappropriate verbal and aggressive behavior. *Journal of Applied Behavior Analysis*, *13*, 583–594.

Lucero, W. J., Fireman, J., Spoering, J., & Fehrenbacher, J. (1976). Comparison of three procedures in reducing self-injurious behavior. *American Journal of Mental Deficiency*, *80*, 548–554.

Luiselli, J. E. (1977). Case report: An attendant-administered contingency management program for the treatment of a toileting phobia. *Journal of Mental Deficiency Research*, *21*, 283–288.

Luiselli, J. E. (1978). Treatment of an autistic child's fear of riding a school bus through exposure and reinforcement. *Journal of Behavior Therapy and Experimental Psychiatry*, *9*, 169–172.

Luiselli, J. K., Colozzi, G. A., Heifen, C. S., & Pollow, R. S. (1980). Differential reinforcement of incompatible behavior (DRI) interacting classroom management problems of developmentally disabled children. *Psychological Record*, *30*, 261–270.

Luiselli, J. K., Reisman, J., Heifen, C. S., & Pemberton, B. W. (1970). Toilet training in the classroom: An adaptation of Azrin and Foxx's rapid toilet training procedure. *Behavioral Engineering*, *5*, 89–93.

Luria, A. R. (1961). *The role of speech in the regulation of normal and abnormal behaviors.* New York: Liveright.

Mahoney, G. & Carpenter, L. I. (1983). Communication disorders. In R. J. Morris & T. R. Kratochwill (Eds.), *The practice of child therapy.* New York: Pergamon.

Mahoney, K., Van Wagenen, R., & Myerson, L. (1971). Toilet training of normal and retarded children. *Journal of Applied Behavior Analysis*, *4*, 173–181.

Malamuth, Z. N. (1979). Self-management training for children with reading problems: Effects on reading performance and sustained attention. *Cognitive Therapy and Research*, *3*, 279–289.

Martin, G. (1975). Brief time-outs as consequences for errors during training programs with autistic and retarded children: A questionable procedure. *Psychological Record*, *25*, 71–89.

Martin, G., Kehoe, B., Bird, E., Jensen, V., & Darbyshire, M. (1971). Operant conditioning in dressing behavior. *Mental Retardation*, *9*, 27–31.

Martin, J. A. (1971). The control of imitative and nonimitative behaviors in severely retarded children through generalized instruction following. *Journal of Experimental Child Psychology*, *11*, 390–400.

Martin, R. (1975). *Legal challenges to behavior modification: Trends in schools, corrections, and mental health.* Champaign, IL: Research Press.

Masters, J. C. (1981). Assessment and treatment of clinical fears in mentally retarded children. *Journal of Applied Behavior Analysis*, *42*, 385–397.

Matson, J. L. (1981). Assessment and treatment of clinical fears in mentally retarded children. *Journal of Applied Behavior Analysis*, *14*, 287–294.

Matson, J. L., & Andrasik, F. (Eds.). (1983). *Treatment issues and innovations in mental retardation.* New York: Plenum.

Matson, J. L., Esveldt-Dawson, K., & Kazdin, A. E. (1982). Treatment of spelling deficits in mentally retarded children. *Mental Retardation*, *20*, 76–81.

Matson, J. L., & McCartney, J. R. (Eds.). (1981). *Handbook of behavior modification with the mentally retarded.* New York: Plenum.

Matson, J. L., & Mulick, J. A. (Eds.). (1983). *Handbook of mental retardation.* New York: Pergamon.

Mattos, R. L., Mattson, R. H., Walker, H. M., & Buckley, N. K. (1968). Reinforcement and aversive control in the modification of behavior. *Academic Therapy*, 5, 37–52.

May, J. G., Risley, T. R., Twardosz, S., Friedman, P., Bijou, S. W., & Wexler, D. (1975). Guidelines for the use of behavioral procedures in state programs for retarded persons. *M. R. Research*, 1, 1–17.

Mayhew, G. L., & Harris, F. C. (1978). Some negative side effects of a punishment procedure for stereotyped behavior. *Journal of Behavior Therapy and Experimental Psychiatry*, 9, 245–251.

McCartney, J. R., & Holden, J. C. (1981). Toilet training for the mentally retarded. In J. L. Matson & J. R. McCartney (Eds.), *Handbook of behavior modification with the mentally retarded*. New York: Plenum Press.

McCarty, T., Griffin, S., Apolloni, T., & Shores, R. E. (1977). Increased peer-teaching with group-oriented contingencies for arithmetic performance in behavior-disordered adolescents. *Journal of Applied Behavior Analysis*, 10, 313.

McConnell, O. L. (1967). Control of eye contact in an autistic child. *Journal of Child Psychology and Psychiatry*, 8, 249–255.

McReynolds, L. V. (1970). Reinforcement procedures for establishing and maintaining echoic speech by a nonverbal child. In F. L. Girardeau & J. E. Spradlin (Eds.), *ASHA Monographs*, No. 14, 60–66.

Measel, C. J., & Alfieri, P. A. (1976). Treatment of self-injurious behavior by a combination of reinforcement for incompatible behavior and overcorrection. *American Journal of Mental Deficiency*, 81, 147–153.

Meichenbaum, D. H. (1977). *Cognitive-behavior modification: An integrative approach*. New York: Plenum.

Meichenbaum, D. H., & Gerest, M. (1980). Cognitive behavior modification: An integration of cognitive and behavioral methods. In F. H. Kanfer & A. P. Goldstein (Eds.), *Helping people change* (2nd ed.). New York: Pergamon.

Meichenbaum, D. H., & Goodman, J. (1971). Training impulsive children to talk to themselves: A means of developing self-control. *Journal of Abnormal Psychology*, 77, 115–126.

Metz, J. R. (1965). Conditioning generalized imitation in autistic children. *Journal of Experimental Child Psychology*, 2, 389–399.

Miller, H., Patton, M., & Herton, K. (1971). Behavior modification in a profoundly retarded child: A case report. *Behavior Therapy*, 2, 442–447.

Miller, L. K., & Schneider, R. (1970). The use of a token system in Project Head Start. *Journal of Applied Behavior Analysis*, 3, 191–197.

Minge, M., & Ball, T. (1967). Teaching of self-help skills to profoundly retarded patients. *American Journal of Mental Deficiency*, 71, 864–868.

Mithaug, D. E. (1978). Case studies in the management of inappropriate behaviors during prevocational training. *AAESPH Review*, 3, 132–144.

Morris, R. J. (1976). *Behavior modification with children: A systematic guide*. Boston: Little, Brown.

Morris, R. J. (1977). A program for establishing eye contact in severely and profoundly retarded children. *Rehabilitation Psychology*, 20, 236–240.

Morris, R. J. (1978). Treating mentally retarded children: A prescriptive approach. In A. P. Goldstein (Ed.), *Prescriptions for child mental health and education*. New York: Pergamon.

Morris, R. J. (1985). *Behavior modification with exceptional children: Principles and practices*. Glenview, IL: Scott, Foresman & Co.

Morris, R. J., Barber, R. S., Hoschouer, R. H., Kanels, K. V., & Bijou, S. (1979). A working model for monitoring intervention programs in residential treatment settings: The peer review ethics committee. *Rehabilitation Psychology*, 26, 155–166.

Morris, R.J., & Brown, D. K. (1983). Legal and ethical issues in behavior modification with mentally retarded persons. In J. L. Matson & F. Andrasik (Eds.), *Treatment issues and innovations in mental retardardation*. New York: Plenum.

Morris, R. J., & Dolker, M. (1974). Developing cooperative play in socially withdrawn retarded children. *Mental Retardation*, 12, 24–27.

Morris, R. J., & Kratochwill, T. R. (1983). *Treating children's fears and phobias: A behavioral approach*. New York: Pergamon.

Morris, R. J., & Kratochwill, T. R. (1985). Behavioral treatment of children's fears and phobias: A review. *School Psychology Review*, 14, 84–93.

Morris, R. J., Kratochwill, T. R., & Dodson, C. L. (in press). Fears and phobias in adolescence: A behavioral perspective. In R. L. Feldman & A. Stiffman (Eds.), *Advances in adolescent mental health*. Greenwich, CT: JAI Press.

Morris, R. J., & McReynolds, R. A. (1986). *Reduction of a clinical dog phobia in a mentally retarded child through contact desensitization: A case study*. Unpublished paper, The University of Arizona.

Morris, R. J., & O'Neill, J. H. (1975). Developing eye contact in severely and profoundly retarded youth. *Mental Retardation*, 13, 42–43.

Morrison, D. (1972). Issues in the application of reinforcement theory in the treatment of a child's self-injurious behavior. *Psychotherapy: Theory, Research, and Practice*, 9, 40–45.

Mowrer, O. H., & Mowrer, W. M. (1938). Enuresis: A method for its study and treatment. *American Journal of Orthopsychiatry*, 8, 436–459.

Mulhern, T., & Baumeister, A. A. (1969). An experimental attempt to reduce stereotypy by reinforcement procedures. *American Journal of Mental Deficiency*, *74*, 69–74.

Murphy, R. J., Nunes, D. L., & Hutchings-Ruprecht, M. (1977). Reduction of stereotyped behavior in profoundly retarded individuals. *American Journal of Mental Deficiency*, *82*, 238–245.

Myers, J. J., & Deibert, A. N. (1971). Reduction of self-abusive behavior in a blind child by using a feeding response. *Journal of Behavior Therapy and Experimental Psychiatry*, *2*, 141–144.

Neale, D. (1963). Behavior therapy and encopresis in children. *Behavior Research and Therapy*, *1*, 139–149.

Neisworth, J. T., Madle, R. A., & Goeke, K. E. (1975). "Errorless" elimination of separation anxiety: A case study. *Journal of Behavior Therapy and Experimental Psychiatry*, *6*, 79–82.

Nelson, G. L., Cone, J. D., & Hanson, C. R. (1976). Training correct utensil use in retarded children: Modeling vs. physical guidance. *American Journal of Mental Deficiency*, *80*, 114–122.

Nelson, R., Gibson, F., & Cutting, S. (1973). Videotaped modeling: The development of three appropriate social responses in a mildly retarded child. *Mental Retardation*, *11*, 24–28.

Newton, A. (1976). Clothing: A positive part of the rehabilitation process. *Journal of Rehabilitation*, *43*, 18–22.

Ney, P. G. (1973). Effect of contingent and noncontingent reinforcement on the behavior of an autistic child. *Journal of Autism and Childhood Schizophrenia*, *3*, 115–127.

Nutter, D., & Reid, D. (1978). Teaching retarded women a clothing selection skill using community norms. *Journal of Applied Behavior Analysis*, *11*, 475–487.

Obler, M., & Terwilliger, R. F. (1970). Pilot study of the effectiveness of systematic desensitization with neurologically impaired children with phobic disorders. *Journal of Consulting and Clinical Psychology*, *34*, 314–318.

O'Brien, F., Bugle, C., & Azrin, N. H. (1972). Training and maintaining a retarded child's proper eating. *Journal of Applied Behavior Analysis*, *5*, 389–399.

O'Leary, K. D. (1980). Pills or skills for hyperactive children. *Journal of Applied Behavior Analysis*, *1*, 191–204.

O'Leary, K. D., & Becker, W. C. (1967). Behavior modification of an adjustment class: A token reinforcement program. *Exceptional Children*, *33*, 637–642.

O'Leary, K. D., & O'Leary, S. G. (Eds.). (1971). *Classroom management*. New York: Pergamon.

O'Leary, K. D., & O'Leary, S. G. (Eds.). (1977). *Classroom management*. (2nd ed.). New York: Pergamon.

O'Leary, K. D., Pelham, W. E., Rosenbaum, A., & Price, G. H. (1976). Behavioral treatment of hyperkinetic children: An experimental evaluation of its usefulness. *Clinical Pediatrics*, *15*, 510–515.

O'Leary, S. G., & Pelham, W. E. (1978). Behavior therapy and withdrawal of stimulant medication with hyperactive children. *Pediatrics*, *61*, 211–217.

Ollendick, T. H. (1979). Behavioral treatment of anorexia nervosa: A five year study. *Behavior Modification*, *3*, 124–135.

Ollendick, T. H., & Gruen, G. E. (1972). Treatment of bodily injury phobia with implosive therapy. *Journal of Consulting and Clinical Psychology*, *38*, 389–393.

Ollendick, T. H., & Matson, J. L. (1978). Overcorrection: An overview. *Behavior Therapy*, *9*, 830–842.

Ollendick, T. H., Matson, J. L., Esveldt-Dawson, K., & Shapiro. E. S. (1980). Increasing spelling achievement: An analysis of treatment procedures utilizing an alternating treatments design. *Journal of Applied Behavior Analysis*, *13*, 645–654.

Ollendick, T. H., Matson, J. L., & Martin, J. E. (1978). Effectiveness of hand overcorrection for topographically similar and dissimilar self-stimulatory behavior. *Journal of Experimental Child Psychology*, *25*, 396–403.

Ollendick, T. H., Shapiro, E. S., & Barrett, R. P. (1981). Reducing stereotypic behaviors: An analysis of treatment procedures utilizing an alternative treatments design. *Behavior Therapy*, *12*, 570–577.

Ollendick, T. H., Shapiro, E. S., & Barrett, R. P. (1982). Effects of vicarious reinforcement in normal and severely handicapped children. *Journal of Consulting and Clinical Psychology*, *50*, 63–70.

O'Neill, C. T., & Bellamy, G. T. (1978). Evaluation of a procedure for teaching saw chain assembly to a severely retarded woman. *Mental Retardation*, *16*, 37–41.

O'Neill, J. H., & Morris, R. J. (1979). The development of imitation in nonimitative severely retarded children: Contribution of reinforcement and instruction. *Rehabilitation Psychology*, *26*, 79–89.

Palkes, H., Stewart, M., & Freedman, J. (1971). Improvement in maze performance of hyperactive boys as a function of verbal training procedures. *Journal of Special Education*, *5*, 337–342.

Palkes, H., Stewart, M., & Kahana, B. (1968). Porteus maze performance of hyperactive boys after training in self-directed verbal commands.

Paloutzian, R., Hasazi, J., Streifel, J., & Edgar, C. L. (1971). Promotion of positive social interactions in severely retarded young children. *American Journal of Mental Deficiency*, *75*, 519–524.

Pany, D., & Jenkins, J. R. (1978). Learning word

meanings: A comparison of instructional procedures. *Learning Disability Quarterly, 1*, 21–32.

Parrish, J. M., Aguerrevere, L., Dorsey, M. F., & Iwata, B. A. (1980). The effects of protective equipment on self-injurious behavior. *The Behavior Therapist, 3*, 28–29.

Parsons, J. A. (1972). The reciprocal modification of arithmetic behavior and program development. In C. Semb (Ed.), *Behavior analysis and education—1972.* Lawrence: University of Kansas.

Patterson, G. R. (1964). An application of conditioning techniques to the control of the hyperactive child. In L. P. Ullmann & L. Krasner (Eds.), *Case studies in behavior modification.* New York: Holt, Rinehart, & Winston.

Patterson, G. R. (1965). A learning theory approach to the treatment of the school phobic child. In L. P. Ullmann & L. Krasner (Eds.), *Case studies in behavior modification.* New York: Holt, Rinehart, & Winston.

Patterson, G. R., Jones, R., Whittier, J., & Wright, M. A. (1965). A behavior modification technique for the hyperactive child. *Behavior Research and Therapy, 2*, 217–226.

Pelham, W. E., Schnedler, R. W., Bologna, N. C., & Contreras, J. A. (1980). Behavioral and stimulant treatment of hyperactive children: A therapy study with methylphenidate probes in a within-subject design. *Journal of Applied Behavior Analysis, 13*, 221–236.

Pendergrass, V. E. (1971). Effects of length of time out from positive reinforcement and schedule of application in suppression of aggressive behavior. *Psychological Record, 21*, 75–80.

Perline, I. H., & Levinsky, D. (1968). Controlling maladaptive classroom behavior in the severely retarded. *American Journal of Mental Deficiency, 73*, 74–78.

Peterson, R., & Peterson, L. (1968). The use of positive reinforcement in the control of self-destructive behavior in a retarded boy. *Journal of Experimental Child Psychology, 6*, 351–368.

Phillips, D., & Wolpe, S. (1982). Multiple behavioral techniques in severe separation anxiety of a 12 year old. *Journal of Behavior Therapy and Experimental Psychiatry, 12*, 329–332.

Polvinale, R. A., & Lutzker, J. R. (1980). Elimination of assaultive and inappropriate sexual behavior by reinforcement and social restitution. *Mental Retardation, 18*, 27–30.

Ragain, R., & Anson, J. E. (1976). The control of self-mutilating behavior with positive reinforcement. *Mental Retardation, 14*, 22–25.

Redd, W. (1969). Effects of mixed reinforcement contingencies on adults' control of children's behavior. *Journal of Applied Behavior Analysis, 2*, 249–254.

Reid, D. H. (1983). Trends and issues in behavioral research on training, feeding and dressing skills. In J. Matson & I. Andrasik (Eds.), *Treatment issues and innovations in mental retardation.* New York: Plenum.

Repp, A. C. (1983). *Teaching the mentally retarded.* Englewood Cliffs, NJ: Prentice-Hall.

Repp, A. C., Barton, L. E., & Brulle, A. R. (1983). A comparison of two procedures for programming the differential reinforcement of other behaviors. *Journal of Applied Behavior Analysis, 16*, 435–445.

Repp, A. C., & Brulle, A. R. (1981). Reducing aggressive behavior of mentally retarded persons. In J. L. Matson & J. R. McCartney (Eds.), *Handbook of behavior modification with the mentally retarded.* New York: Plenum.

Repp, A. C., & Deitz, S. M. (1974). Reducing aggressive and self-injurious behavior of institutionalized children through reinforcement of other behaviors. *Journal of Applied Behavior Analysis, 7*, 313–325.

Repp, A., Deitz, S., & Deitz, D. (1976). Reducing inappropriate behaviors in classrooms and in individual sessions through DRO schedules of reinforcement. *Mental Retardation, 14*(1), 11–15.

Repp, A. C., Deitz, S. M., & Speir, N. C. (1974). Reducing stereotypic responding of retarded persons by the differential reinforcement of other behavior. *American Journal of Mental Deficiency, 79*, 279–284.

Rhode, G., Morgan, D. P., & Young, K. R. (1983). Generalization and maintenance of treatment gains of behaviorally handicapped students from resource rooms to regular classrooms using self-evaluation procedures. *Journal of Applied Behavior Analysis, 16*, 171–188.

Rimland, B. (1964). *Infantile autism.* New York: Appleton-Century-Crofts.

Risko, V. J. (1981). Reading. In D. D. Smith, *Teaching the learning disabled.* Englewood Cliffs, NJ: Prentice-Hall.

Risley, T. R. (1968). The effects and side effects of punishing autistic behaviors of a deviant child. *Journal of Applied Behavior Analysis, 1*, 21–34.

Robertson, S. J., Simon, S. J., Pachman, J. S., & Drabman, R. J. (1979). Self-control and generalization procedures in a classroom of disruptive retarded students. *Child Behavior Therapy, 1*, 347–362.

Robin, A., Schneider, M., & Dolnick, M. (1976). The turtle techniques: An extended case study of self-control in the classroom. *Psychology in the Schools, 13*, 449–453.

Robinson, P. W., Newby, T. J., & Ganzell, S. L. (1981). A token system for a class of underachieving hyperactive children. *Journal of Applied Behavior Analysis, 14*, 307–315.

Romanczyk, R. G., Diament, C., Goren, E. R. Trunell, G., & Harris, S. L. (1975). Increasing isolate and social play in severely disturbed children: Intervention and postintervention effectiveness. *Journal of Autism and Childhood Schizophrenia*, *5*, 57–70.

Romanczyk, R. G., & Goren, E. (1975). The problem of clinical control. *Journal of Consulting and Clinical Psychology*, *43*, 730–739.

Roos, P. (1974). Human rights and behavior modification. *Mental Retardation*, *12*, 3–6.

Roos, P. (1977). Issues and implication of establishing guidelines for the use of behavior modification. *Journal of Applied Behavior Analysis*, *10*, 531–540.

Rosenbaum, A., O'Leary, K. D., & Jacob. R. G. (1975). Behavioral intervention with hyperactive children: Group consequences as a supplement to individual contingencies. *Behavior Therapy*, *6*, 315–323.

Rosenbaum, M. S., & Drabman, R. S. (1979). Self-control training in the classroom: A review and critique. *Journal of Applied Behavior Analysis*, *12*, 467–485.

Ross, A. O. (1976). *Psychological aspects of learning disabilities and reading disorders*. New York: McGraw-Hill, Inc.

Ross, A. O. (1981). *Child behavior therapy*. New York: Wiley.

Ross, D., & Ross, S. (1982). *Hyperactivity*. New York: Wiley.

Ross, D. M., Ross, S. A., & Evans, T. A. (1971). The modification of extreme social withdrawal by modeling with guided participation. *Journal of Behavior Therapy and Experimental Psychiatry*, *2*, 273–279.

Rotatori, A. F., Switzky, H., Green, H., & Fox, R. (1980). Teachers as agents of behavioral change for severely retarded students. *Psychological Reports*, *47*, 1215–1220.

Rubin, G., Griswald, K., Smith, I., & DeLeonardo, C. (1972). A case study in the remediation of severe self-destructive behavior in a six year old mentally retarded girl. *Journal of Clinical Psychology*, *28*, 424–426.

Runyan, M. C., Stevens, D. H., & Reeves, R. (1985). Reduction of avoidance behavior of institutionalized mentally retarded adults through contact desensitization. *American Journal of Mental Deficiency*, *90*, 222–225.

Rusch, F. R. (1970). A functional analysis of the relationship between attending and producing in a vocational training program. *Journal of Special Education*, *13*, 399–411.

Russo, D. C., Cataldo, M. F., & Cushing, P. J. (1981). Compliance training and behavioral covariation in the treatment of multiple behavior problems. *Journal of Applied Behavior Analysis*, *14*, 209–222.

Sachs, D. A. (1973). The efficacy of time out procedures in a variety of behavior problems. *Journal of Behavior Therapy and Experimental Psychiatry*, *4*, 237–242.

Sadler, W., & Merkert, F. (1977). Evaluating the Foxx and Azrin toilet training procedure for retarded children in a day training center. *Behavior Therapy*, *8*, 499–500.

Sanford, D., & Nettelbeck, T. (1982). Medication and reinforcement within a token programme for disturbed mentally retarded residents. *Applied Research in Mental Retardation*, *3*, 21–36.

Saposnek, D. T., & Watson, L. D. (1974). The elimination of the self-destructive behavior of a psychotic child: A case study. *Behavior Therapy*, *5*, 79–89.

Schulman, J. L., Suran, B. C., Stevens, T. M., & Kupst, M. J. (1979). Instructions, feedback, and reinforcement in reducing activity levels in the classroom. *Journal of Applied Behavior Analysis*, *12*, 441–447.

Schultz, R., Wellman, P., Rezaglia, A., & Karan, O. (1978). Efficacy of contingent social disapproval on inappropriate verbalizations of two severely retarded males. *Behavior Therapy*, *9*, 657–662.

Schwartz, G. J. (1977). College students and contingency managers for adolescents in a program to develop reading skills. *Journal of Applied Behavior Analysis*, *10*, 645–655.

Shapiro, E. (1979). Restitution and positive practice overcorrection in reducing aggressive-disruptive behavior: A long-term follow-up. *Journal of Behavior Therapy and Experimental Psychiatry*, *10*, 131–134.

Shapiro, E. S., Barrett, R. P., & Ollendick, T. H. (1980). A comparison of physical restraint and positive practice overcorrection in treating stereotypic behavior. *Behavior Therapy*, *11*, 227–233.

Shapiro, E. S., & Klein, R. D. (1980). Self-management of classroom behavior with retarded/disturbed children. *Behavior Modification*, *4*, 83–97.

Shapiro, E. S., McGonigle, J. J., & Ollendick, T. H. (1981). An analysis of self-assessment and self-reinforcement in a self-managed token economy with mentally retarded children. *Applied Research in Mental Retardation*, *1*, 227–240.

Sidman, M. T. (1979). The effects of group free time and contingency and individual free time contingency on spelling performance. *The Directive Teacher*, *1*, 4–5.

Siegel, L. J. (1983). Psychosomatic and psychophysiological disorders. In R. J. Morris & T. R. Kratochwill (Eds.), *The practice of child therapy*. New York: Pergamon.

Singh, N. (1976). Toilet training a severely retarded nonverbal child. *Australian Journal of Mental Retardation*, *4*, 15–18.

Singh, N. N., Dawson, M. J., & Manning, P. (1981). Effects of spaced responding DRL on the stereotyped behavior of profoundly retarded persons. *Journal of Applied Behavior Analysis, 14,* 521–526.

Singh, N. N., Winton, A. S., & Dawson, M. J. (1982). Suppression of antisocial behavior by facial screening using multiple baseline and alternating treatments designs. *Behavior Therapy, 13,* 511–520.

Singh, R., Phillips, D., & Fischer, S. C. (1976). The treatment of enuresis by progressively earlier waking. *Journal of Behavior Therapy and Experimental Psychiatry, 7,* 277–278.

Skinner, B. F. (1938). *The behavior of organisms.* New York: Appleton-Century-Crofts.

Skinner, B. F. (1953). *Science and human behavior.* New York: MacMillan.

Sloop, E. W., & Kennedy, W. A. (1973). Institutionalized retarded nocturnal enuretics treated by a conditioning technique. *American Journal of Mental Deficiency, 77,* 717–721.

Smith, D. D. (1979). The improvement of children's oral reading rate through the use of teacher modeling. *Journal of Learning Disabilities, 12,* 172–175.

Smith, D. D. (1981). *Teaching the learning disabled.* Englewood Cliffs, NJ: Prentice-Hall.

Smith, D. D., Lovitt, T. C. (1973). The educational diagnosis and remediation of written b and d reversal problems: A case study. *Journal of Learning Disabilities, 6,* 356–363.

Smith, D. D., & Lovitt, T. C. (1975). The use of modeling techniques to influence the acquisition of computational arithmetic skills in learning-disabled children. In E. Ramp & C. Semb (Eds.), *Behavior analysis: Areas of research and application.* Englewood Cliffs, NJ: Prentice-Hall.

Smith, L. J. (1981). Training severely and profoundly mentally handicapped nocturnal enuretics. *Behavior Research and Therapy, 19,* 67–74.

Smith, P. D. (1979). A comparison of different methods of toilet training the mentally handicapped. *Behavior Research and Therapy, 17,* 33–43.

Smith, R. F., & Sharpe, T. M. (1970). Treatment of a school phobia with implosive therapy. *Journal of Consulting and Clinical Psychology, 35,* 239–243.

Snell, M. E. (Ed.). (1983). *Systematic instruction of the moderately and severely handicapped* (2nd ed.). Columbus, OH: Charles E. Merrill.

Solnick, J. V., Rincover, A., & Peterson, C. R. (1977). Some determinants of the reinforcing and punishing effects of time out. *Journal of Applied Behavior Analysis, 10,* 415–424.

Song, A. Y., Song, R. H., & Grant, P. A. (1976). Toilet training in school and its transfer in the living unit. *Journal of Behavior Therapy and Experimental Psychiatry, 7,* 281–284.

Sroufe, A. (1975). Drug treatment of children with behavior problems. In F. Horowitz (Ed.), *Review of child development research* (Vol. 4). Chicago: University of Chicago Press.

Staats, A. W., & Butterfield, W. J. (1965). Treatment of nonreading in a culturally deprived juvenile delinquent: An application of reinforcement principles. *Child Development, 36,* 925–942.

Staats, A. W., Minke, K. A., Finley, J. R., Wolf, M. M., & Brooks, L. D. (1964). A reinforcer system and experimental procedure for the laboratory study of reading acquisition. *Child Development, 35,* 209–231.

Stampfl, T. G. (1961). Implosive therapy: A learning theory derived psychodynamic therapeutic technique. Paper presented at the University of Illinois.

Stampfl, T. G., & Levis, D. J. (1967). Essentials of implosive therapy: A learning-based-psychodynamic behavioral therapy. *Journal of Abnormal Psychology, 72,* 496–503.

Steinman, W. M. (1970a). Generalized imitation and the discriminating hypothesis. *Journal of Experimental Child Psychology, 10,* 79–99.

Steinman, W. M. (1970b). The social control of generalized imitation. *Journal of Applied Behavior Analysis, 3,* 159–167.

Stowitschek, C. E., & Jobes, N. K. (1977). Getting the bugs out of spelling—or an alternative to the spelling bee. *Teaching Exceptional Children, 9,* 74–76.

Strain, P. S. (1977). An experimental analysis of peer social limitations on the behavior of withdrawn preschool children: Some training and generalization effects. *Journal of Abnormal Child Psychology, 5,* 445–455.

Strain, P. S., Shores, R. E., & Simm, M. A. (1977). Effects of peer social initiation on the behavior of withdrawn preschool children. *Journal of Applied Behavior Analysis, 10,* 289–298.

Strain, P. S., & Timm, M. A. (1974). An experimental analysis of social interaction between a behaviorally disordered preschool child and her classroom peers. *Journal of Applied Behavior Analysis, 7,* 583–590.

Striefel, J., & Phelan, J. (1972). Use of reinforcement of behavioral similarity to establish imitative behavior in young mentally retarded children. *American Journal of Mental Deficiency, 77*(2), 239–241.

Stromer, R. (1977). Remediating academic deficiencies in learning disabled children. *Exceptional Children, 43,* 432–440.

Suckerman, K. R., & Morris, R. J. (1974). Effects of social demands on generalized imitation learning in retarded children. *Journal of Abnormal Child Psychology, 2,* 313–322.

Sulzbachev, S., & Houser, J. (1969). A tactic to eliminate disruptive behaviors in the classroom: Group contingent consequences. *American Journal of Mental Deficiency, 73,* 88–90.

Tanner, B. A., & Zeiler, M. (1975). Punishment of self-injurious behavior using aromatic ammonia as the aversive stimulus. *Journal of Applied Behavior Analysis*, *8*, 53–57.

Tarpley, H. D., & Schroeder, S. R. (1979). Comparison of DRO and DRI on rate of suppression of self-injurious behavior. *American Journal of Mental Deficiency*, *84*, 188–194.

Tate, B., & Baroff, G. (1966). Aversive control of self-injurious behavior in a psychotic boy. *Behavior Research and Therapy*, *4*, 281–287.

Tharp, R. G., & Wetzel, R. J. (1969). *Behavior modification in the natural environment*. New York: Academic Press.

Thompson, M. M., & Faibish, G. M. (1970). The use of filmstrips in teaching personal hygiene to the moderately retarded adolescent. *Education and Training of the Mentally Retarded*, *5*, 113–118.

Trap, J. J., Milner-Davis, P., Joseph, S., & Cooper, J. O. (1978). The effects of feedback and consequences on traditional cursive letter formation. *Journal of Applied Behavior Analysis*, *11*, 381–393.

Treffry, D., Martin, G., Smaels, J., & Watson, C. (1970). Operant conditioning of grooming behavior of severely retarded girls. *Mental Retardation*, *8*, 29–33.

Trott, M. (1977). Application of Foxx and Azrin's toilet method for the retarded in a school programme. *Education and Training of the Mentally Retarded*, *12*, 336–338.

Turkewitz, H., O'Leary, K. D., & Ironsmith, M. (1975). Generalization and maintenance of appropriate behavior through self-control. *Journal of Consulting and Clinical Psychology*, *43*, 577–583.

Twardosz, S., & Sajwaj, T. (1972). Multiple effects of a procedure to increase sitting in a hyperactive, retarded boy. *Journal of Applied Behavior Analysis*, *5*, 73–78.

Van den Pol, R. A., Iwata, B. A., Ivancic, M. T., Page, T. J., Neef, N. A., & Whitley, F. P. (1981). Teaching the handicapped to eat in public places: Acquisition, generalization, and maintenance of restaurant skills. *Journal of Applied Behavior Analysis*, *14*, 61–69.

Van Houten, R., Morrison, E., Jarvis, R., & McDonald, M. (1974). The effects of explicit timing and feedback on compositional response rate in elementary school children. *Journal of Applied Behavior Analysis*, *7*, 547–555.

Van Wagenen, R., Meyerson, L., Kerr, N., & Mahoney, K. (1969). Field trials of a new procedure for toilet training. *Journal of Experimental Child Psychology*, *8*, 147–150.

Vargas, E. A. (1975). Rights. A behavioristic analysis. *Behaviorism*, *3*, 178–190.

Vygotsky, C. (1962). *Thought and language*. New York: Wiley.

Walker, H. M. (1979). *The acting-out child: Coping with classroom disruption*. Boston: Allyn & Bacon, Inc.

Walker, H. M., & Buckley, N. K. (1968). The use

of positive reinforcement in conditioning attending behavior. *Journal of Applied Behavior Analysis*, *1*, 245–252.

Watson, L. S. (1967). Application of operant conditioning techniques to institutionalized severely and profoundly retarded children. *Mental Retardation Abstract*, *4*, 1–18.

Watson, L. S., & Uzzell, R. (1980). Teaching self-help skills to the mentally retarded. In J. L. Matson & J. R. McCartney (Eds.), *Handbook of behavior modification with the mentally retarded*. New York: Plenum.

Waye, M., & Melnry, W. (1973). Toilet training of a blind retarded boy by operant conditioning. *Journal of Behavior Therapy and Experimental Psychiatry*, *4*, 267–268.

Webster, D. R., & Azrin, N. H. (1973). Required relaxation: A method of inhibiting agitative-disruptive behavior of retarded. *Behavior Research and Therapy*, *11*, 67–68.

Weeks, M., & Gaylord-Ross, R. (1981). Task difficulty and aberrant behavior in severely handicapped students. *Journal of Applied Behavior Analysis*, *14*, 449–463.

Wehman, P., & McLaughlin, P. J. (1979). Teachers' perceptions of behavior problems with severely and profoundly handicapped students. *Mental Retardation*, *17*, 20–21.

Weiher, R., & Harman, R. (1975). The use of omission training to reduce self-injurious behavior in a retarded child. *Behavior Therapy*, *6*, 261–268.

Wells, K. C., Forehand, R., Hickey, K., & Green, K. D. (1977). Effects of a procedure derived from the overcorrection principle on manipulated behaviors. *Journal of Applied Behavior Analysis*, *10*, 679–687.

Wesolowski, M. D., & Zawlocki, R. J. (1982). The differential effects of procedures to eliminate an injurious self-stimulatory behavior (digito-ocular sign) in blind retarded twins. *Behavior Therapy*, *13*, 334–345.

Wexler, D. (1973). Tokens and taboo: Behavior modification, token economies, and the law. *California Law Review*, *61*, 81–109.

Whitman, T. L., Barrish, T., & Collins, C. (1972). Development of interpersonal language responses in two moderately retarded children. *Mental Retardation*, *10*, 40–45.

Whitman, T., Mercurio, J., & Caponigri, V. (1970). Development of social responses in two severely retarded children. *Journal of Applied Behavior Analysis*, *3*, 133–138.

Whitman, T. L., Scibak, J., & Reid, D. H. (1983). *Behavior modification with the severely and profoundly retarded: Treatment and research*. New York: Academic Press.

Whitney, L., & Bernard, K. (1966). Implications of operant learning theory for nursing care of the retarded child. *Mental Retardation*, *4*, 26–29.

Wiesen, A., Hartley, G., Richardson, C., & Roske, A. (1967). The retarded child as a reinforcing agent. *Journal of Experimental Child Psychology, 4,* 109–113.

Winett, R. A., & Winkler, R. C. (1972). Current behavior modification in the classroom: Be still, be quiet, be docile. *Journal of Applied Behavior Analysis, 5,* 449–504.

Wolraich, M. L., Drummond, T., Salomon, M. K., O'Brien, M. L., & Sivage, C. (1978). Effects of methylphenidate alone and in combination with behavior modification procedures on the behavior and academic performance of hyperactive children. *Journal of Abnormal Child Psychology, 6,* 149–161.

Wolfensberger, W. (1972). *The principle of normalization in human services.* Washington, DC: National Institute on Mental Retardation.

Wright, L. (1973). Handling the encopretic child. *Professional Psychology, 4,* 137–144.

Young, I. L., & Goldsmith, A. L. (1972). Treatment of encopresis in a day treatment program. *Psychotherapy: Theory, Research, and Practice, 9,* 231–235.

Yule, W., Sacks, B., & Hersov, L. (1974). Successful flooding treatment of a noise phobia in an 11 year old. *Journal of Behavior Therapy and Experimental Psychiatry, 5,* 209–211.

Zifferblatt, S. M., Burton, S. D., Homer, R., & White, T. (1977). Establishing generalization effects among autistic children. *Journal of Autism and Childhood Schizophrenia, 7,* 337–347.

Zimmerman, E. H., & Zimmerman, J. (1962). The alteration of behavior in a special classroom situation. *Journal of the Experimental Analysis of Behavior, 5,* 59–60.

5 TEACHING SEVERELY HANDICAPPED STUDENTS TO PERFORM MEANINGFUL WORK IN NONSHELTERED VOCATIONAL ENVIRONMENTS*

Lou Brown
Betsy Shiraga
Alison Ford
Jan Nisbet
Pat VanDeventer
Mark Sweet
Jennifer York
Ruth Loomis

The contents of this chapter are predicated on three major biases that represent substantial departures from traditional conceptualizations and practices. First, the overwhelming majority of severely handicapped persons** are capable of performing meaningful work in nonsheltered vocational environments. Second, nonsheltered vocational environments are inherently less restrictive, more conducive to the performance of meaningful work, more educationally and developmentally defensible, and more cost efficient than sheltered vocational environments. Third, public schools and adult service agencies can and must operate in such ways as to maximize the probability that severely handicapped persons function in nonsheltered vocational environments from early adolescence throughout adulthood.

---

*This chapter is dedicated to Marc Gold, 1939–1982, who spent a substantial portion of his remarkably productive life demonstrating that severely handicapped persons could reach heights never dreamed of by most of us. His ideas, his inspiration, and his personal force are clearly imbedded in the hopes expressed here. If disabled persons are helped in any way as a result of this effort, it will be but another small tribute to this wonderful man.

**The label *severely handicapped* refers to approximately the lowest intellectually functioning 1% of the school age population. This 1% range includes students who also have been ascribed such labels as *psychotic, autistic, moderately/severely/profoundly retarded, trainable level retarded, physically handicapped, multihandicapped*, and *deaf/blind*. Certainly, a student can be ascribed one or more of the labels delineated immediately above and still not be referred to as severely handicapped for purposes here, as he or she may not be currently functioning intellectually within the lowest 1% of a particular age.

INTRODUCTION

If 100 of the most ingenious, creative, intelligent, competent, efficient, and productive people in the world were placed in one room, many fascinating outcomes would be realized and many wonderful emotional and intellectual experiences would be had, but only for a short time. Soon, all would realize that there are events to be experienced and options to be explored, but not in that room. Most, if not all, would then choose to go elsewhere.

In the past, it was believed that severely intellectually disabled persons should function in large multipurpose especially designed environments. As a result, virtually every state in our nation operates "institutions for the retarded." This great service delivery model experiment has now been judged as a tragic, costly, and inhumane failure by almost all. The institutionalization era has passed and noninstitutionalization and deinstitutionalization policies and practices now proliferate.

For decades it was assumed that if severely intellectually disabled persons were to benefit from educational services, they must attend "handicapped schools." Many, however, have now concluded that segregated schools are ideologically unsound, educationally counterproductive, and ridiculously cost inefficient. Each year more and more severely handicapped students attend age appropriate regular schools that are close to their homes.

When nonhandicapped persons complete high school or college, they have a reasonable array of environments in which they can choose to work. Indeed, it would be considered blatantly unconstitutional to require a person to work only in a particular place because his or her I.Q. score is 110. In contrast, a severely handicapped adult rarely works in a particular environment because he or she chooses to be there, because it is designed specifically for his or her unique vocational skills and interests, or because it allows him or her to be most productive. The general rule is that if you have an I.Q. score of less than 55, or the label *severely handicapped*, you must function in a segregated

(i.e., handicapped only) day program or stay at home (Bellamy, Sowers, & Bourbeau, 1983; Gold & Pomerantz, 1978). Consequently, almost all severely handicapped adults are denied access to competitive enterprise, and the relatively high cost of lifelong sheltered maintenance has generated many pervasive negative attitudes and actions.

Of the many theses offered to justify sheltered vocational environments, five seem particularly relevant:

- Severely handicapped persons can function best or only in sheltered environments;
- Sheltered facilities will always be needed because of parental and societal expectations, severe medical and behavioral problems, the absence of acceptable alternatives, and the need for back-up environments for nonsheltered failures;
- Most people do not want to see or be near severely handicapped adults who are functioning vocationally in nonsheltered environments;
- Millions of tax dollars have been spent on special facilities and taxpayers will be irate if they are not used; and
- If sheltered facilities are closed, many nonhandicapped persons will lose their jobs.

Unfortunately, these and similar theses are usually converted into policies and actions that waste money, limit habilitation, deny opportunities, and impede or prevent the development of better alternatives.

No room, ward, center, or workshop can allow the reasonable vocational habilitation of more than but a few severely handicapped persons at one time. Thus, no longer can the placement of large numbers of severely handicapped persons in one environment be tolerated. If individually meaningful vocational habilitation is to be even approximated, many environments must be explored and complementary matches must be generated between the demands of an environment and the unique characteristics of an individual.

The primary purpose of this chapter is to address factors public school systems can contribute to the vocational habilitation of severely handicapped students. The a priori assumption is that sufficient data are available to support the contention that sheltered vocational environments are inherently restrictive, cost inefficient, nonproductive, and thus not nearly as tenable as other realizable options. Therefore, public school programs oriented toward the less dangerous outcome of preparing for functioning in nonsheltered vocational environments at graduation must be designed and implemented (Donnellan, 1984).

A FUNCTIONAL DEFINITION OF MEANINGFUL WORK

Some argue that there will always be a proportion of our citizenry who, for intellectual, behavioral, physical, or other reasons, are not capable of working, either because they cannot learn to perform work skills or because they have life sustaining needs that transcend working. Perhaps this is so. However, in the past, when it was assumed that those assigned to certain levels, groups, or categories could not work, unfortunate errors were made in far too many individual instances. Thus, because of an overexclusion mentality, many capable persons were denied access to meaningful and productive jobs.

It has been repeatedly demonstrated that many severely handicapped persons can be taught to perform a wide variety of work skills once considered beyond their capabilities. The skills necessary to assemble television rectifier units (Huddle, 1967), to operate drill presses (Crosson, 1969), to assemble 24-piece bicycle brakes (Gold, 1972, 1974), and to assemble cam switch actuators (Bellamy, Peterson, & Close, 1975) are but a few examples. More recently, curricular strategies involving ecological inventories, discrepancy analyses, and individualized adaptations have been utilized to engender the skills necessary for severely handicapped adults to function as chambermaids, buspersons, clerical workers, and custodians (Pumpian et al., 1980).

Fortunately, it is now realized that in most instances it is extremely precarious to predict who can and who cannot learn to perform meaningful work; that determining who is capable of learning to work requires the individualized and systematic application of a variety of affirmative ideological, conceptual, and empirical processes; and that, if the performance of meaningful work is established as a major longitudinal educational priority, many severely handicapped students can become substantially more productive than their predecessors. Thus, if we are to make an error, it should be on the side of *over* rather than *under* inclusion in meaningful vocational training programs.

Meaningful work refers to a series of actions that, if not performed by a severely handicapped person, must be performed by a nonhandicapped person for money. Assume that a severely handicapped student is asked to put a nut on a bolt, assemble a bicycle brake, assemble an electronic circuit board, package and unpackage pink fuzz, sort colored pipe cleaners, and make piles of popsicle sticks, but does not. If it is now necessary to pay a nonhandicapped person to perform those actions, by definition they can be considered meaningful work. If not, they can be called *simulated work tasks, prerequisite work skills, work attitude builders, artificial work, putting a nut on a bolt*, etc., but by definition they cannot be called *meaningful work.*

Meaningful work is usually performed in two kinds of environments: *sheltered* and *nonsheltered.* Sheltered vocational environments are those in which most or all workers are handicapped, for example, sheltered workshops and activity centers. Nonsheltered vocational environments are those in which almost all workers are nonhandicapped. For a vocational environment to be considered nonsheltered, the number of severely handicapped persons should be a reasonable approximation of the number of severely handicapped persons in the general population, for example, approximately 1%. Justifiable exceptions to this definition of a nonsheltered vocational environment might include a small business that employs seven or eight people, two of whom are severely handicapped.

THE 1971–1978 FOLLOW-UP STUDY

Madison Metropolitan School District and University of Wisconsin personnel examined the life spaces of 53 severely handicapped students who graduated from 1971–1978 (Van-Deventer et al., 1981) and determined that:

- Of the 53 graduates, only 1 worked in a nonsheltered vocational environment. Of the 52 others, 49 functioned in sheltered workshops and activity centers and 3 had no employment or were on day programs, though 1 was on a waiting list to be reinstated at a sheltered workshop (see Table 5.1).
- Almost all those who functioned in sheltered vocational environments were grossly underachieving socially, vocationally, and economically; and
- Almost all of those who functioned in sheltered vocational environments were taught many skills as part of their school programs that they were not allowed, encouraged, or required to perform. Using public buses, communicating with nonhandicapped persons, making purchases in community stores,

and acting appropriately during work breaks were but a few examples.

Unfortunately, the VanDeventer et al. (1981) findings are not dramatically informative to those who have been close observers of the life spaces of severely handicapped adults, in that most are maintained in cost inefficient and relatively nonproductive sheltered environments (Greenleigh Associates, Inc., 1975; U.S. Department of Labor, 1977, 1979; Whitehead, 1979b).

THE NATURAL PROPORTION

After too many years of underachievement and wasted lives and dollars, it is abundantly clear that handicapped only environments—including institutions for the retarded, segregated schools, sheltered workshops, and activity centers—are particularly inappropriate for severely intellectually handicapped persons. Why, after investing millions of dollars, after usurping the talents of some of the brightest and most dedicated people in a variety of professional disciplines, and after undergoing decades of revisions, have these homogeneous service delivery models failed? Rational and empirical responses to such an enormously complex question are no doubt legion. The response emphasized here is that homogeneous

TABLE 5.1. FIFTY-THREE SEVERELY HANDICAPPED GRADUATES OF THE MADISON METROPOLITAN SCHOOL DISTRICT FROM 1971–1978 AND WHERE THEY FUNCTIONED DURING THE WORK DAY AS OF DECEMBER 1981

Year	Number of Graduates	Home	Sheltered Environment	Nonsheltered Environment
1971	2	0	2	0
1972	5	0	5	0
1973	7	0	7	0
1974	8	1	7	0
1975	9	1	8	0
1976	10	1	9	0
1977	10	0	9	1
1978	2	0	2	0
Totals	53	3	49	1

services grossly violate the natural proportion and thus were and are de facto doomed to fail. The *natural proportion* refers to the definitional fact that approximately 1% of our population at any chronological age can be referred to as severely intellectually handicapped (Brown et al., 1983). Further, environments that substantially violate the natural proportion, for example, environments in which more than 1% of the population consists of severely handicapped persons, are inherently dangerous. However well intentioned, well funded, and well staffed these environments may be, too many of those who are supposed to benefit are actually prevented from achieving anywhere near the levels realizable in environments that are naturally proportioned.

THE RESTRICTIVE NATURE OF SHELTERED VOCATIONAL ENVIRONMENTS

Sheltered environments are not the most habilitative, the least restrictive, the most cost-efficient, or the most individually tenable work places for most, if not all, severely handicapped adults. Further, given reasonable preparatory experiences, work in a nonsheltered environment is a practical and realizable alternative. There are many reasons why sheltered vocational environments are considered less acceptable than nonsheltered ones:

- Economic survival activities transcend external placement efforts;
- Work related skills are rarely required or developed;
- Instruction is not emphasized;
- The performance of nonmeaningful work is often required;
- Work and play are often fused;
- Opportunities to benefit from interaction with nonhandicapped workers are not available;
- Few meaningful reasons to achieve are operative;
- Deviant actions are tolerated; and
- Waiting lists, rejections, exclusions, and reduced schedules abound.

Economic Survival Activities Transcend External Placement Efforts

Activities related to the economic survival of a sheltered environment often conflict with the placement of workers elsewhere (Lynch, 1979; Wehman, Hill, & Koehler, 1979; Wehman & McLaughlin, 1980; Whitehead, 1979a). For example, in order to maintain a sheltered environment:

- Staff members are assigned to supervise production rather than to secure work in nonsheltered environments;
- Workers are asked to perform jobs even though they may not be representative of the types of jobs available in nonsheltered environments;
- Workers remain because the facility is dependent upon their productivity to generate operating income; and
- As staff members must spend most of their working hours in sheltered environments they become increasingly "out-of-touch" with the work and work related requirements of nonsheltered environments.

Consequently, arbitrary and often capricious prerequisites are often set for access into training programs that have a nonsheltered orientation (Gold, 1973; Stodden, Casale, & Schwartz, 1977). Furthermore, the work performed is often limited to "sit down" assembly and packaging tasks in order to minimize the equipment and personnel costs that might be incurred if a greater variety of jobs was available (Pomerantz & Marholin, 1977; U.S. Department of Labor, 1977, 1979). While many sheltered environment personnel proclaim the intention of preparing clients to function in nonsheltered environments, less than 12% of all who are placed in sheltered facilities ever move to nonsheltered environments and severely handicapped persons represent only a small fraction of that 12% (Greenleigh Associates, Inc., 1975; Shiraga, 1983; U.S. Department of Labor, 1977). If a severely handicapped adult is moved from a sheltered workshop, it is almost always to an activity center or to some other less demanding sheltered environment (VanDeventer et al., 1981).

Work Related Skills Are Rarely Required or Developed

A normal daily work routine usually involves the utilization of more than just work skills. Getting to and from the work place, maintaining an acceptable appearance, socializing with nonhandicapped coworkers, communicating food preferences in a cafeteria or at a nearby restaurant, and refraining from bothering others are but a few examples. Most severely handicapped workers do not fail in nonsheltered environments primarily because of production capabilities. Failure is usually the result of less than acceptable social/attitudinal skills, transportation skills, etc. (Greenspan & Shoultz, 1981; Rusch, Weithers, Menchetti, & Schutz, 1980; Sowers, Thompson, & Connis, 1979; Wehman, 1981), or what Martin, Flexer, and Newbery (1979) have referred to as the lack of a work ethic.

> We continued to find that "our" clients, as well as other clients in workshops, continued to be poor workers. In spite of good job skill training, time on task training and some tangential skill training, such as money handling and money counting, we were plagued with the persistent observation that "these clients don't know what work is all about — they don't know what they are doing here." (p. 137)

In sum, severely handicapped workers in sheltered environments are rarely provided opportunities to perform, develop, or build upon important work related skills in meaningful contexts.

Instruction Is Not Emphasized

The higher the proportion of severely handicapped persons in an environment, the greater the tendency to segregate, to create "levels," and to make decisions about a group rather than about an individual. For example, a common practice of persons who operate environments with a high proportion of disabled persons is to evaluate an individual and then based on some predetermined criteria place her in a homogeneous *level* or group (Brolin, 1982; Madison Opportunity Center, Inc., 1981). Unfortunately, the criteria used to determine placement are often arbitrary and unrelated to nonsheltered functioning. The person who functions acceptably in an assigned level or group remains. The person who does not is then placed in a less demanding level or group and eventually might be referred to a nonwork activity or a prework group. Rarely is individualized, direct, systematic, and longitudinal instruction provided that is designed to maximize the probability of functioning in reasonable accordance with capability (Gold, 1973; Nisbet, 1983; Sowers et al., 1979; Whitehead, 1979b). Tragically, without this much needed instruction, severely handicapped adults are much less productive than they would be otherwise.

Parenthetically, it is extremely dangerous to attach the prefix *pre* to any phenomenon associated with a severely handicapped person. Prevocational, precommunity, preacademic, and prereading usually mean that a severely handicapped person will never work or live in the community or will never read, write, and compute meaningfully. Parsimoniously, *pre* means *never*.

The Performance of Nonmeaningful Work Is Often Required

Persons familiar with sheltered workshops often report "dry periods" or intervals during which there is not enough meaningful work to occupy all workers (Greenleigh Associates, Inc., 1975; U.S. Department of Labor, 1979; Whitehead, 1979b). It is during these periods that one often observes the performance of "busy work" (Lynch & Gerber, 1977). Folding and unfolding boxes, stuffing and then unstuffing envelopes are but two examples. When meaningful work becomes scarce, the lowest functioning workers in the environment are usually the first to be required to perform nonmeaningful work (Bellamy et al., 1983). Further, the absence of meaningful work often results in free time. Severely handicapped persons are notorious for using free time to practice or develop self-stimulatory, counter-productive, and socially inappropriate skills. Obviously, severely handicapped persons must function in environments that do not require the performance of nonmeaningful work or allow large intervals of free time.

Work and Play Are Often Fused

Many sheltered work environments have incorporated preacademic, domestic living, and recreation/leisure activities into their services (Bellamy, Sheehan, Horner, & Boles, 1980). Unfortunately, adults are often interrupted from their production schedules to receive such services. For example, instead of providing recreation/leisure instruction during breaks, lunch periods, evenings, and on weekends, adults are often taken to a bowling class from 9:00 to 9:50 A.M. and to ceramics class from 2:00 to 3:00 P.M. The predictable negative effects on achievement motivation, on the probability of functioning in nonsheltered environments, and on developing an understanding of the nature of real work, are obvious.

Opportunities to Benefit from Interactions with Nonhandicapped Workers Are Not Available

Severely handicapped persons have demonstrated that they can secure information from observing those functioning in their presence (Baumgart, 1981; Egel, Richman, & Koegel, 1981; Guralnick, 1981; Voeltz, 1980b; Wehman, 1981). The absence of nonhandicapped models in sheltered environments renders it virtually impossible to gain much needed information imitatively. Further, handicapped only environments do not allow severely handicapped workers opportunities to learn to respond to the social cues and correction procedures utilized by nonhandicapped persons in the nonsheltered world of work (Falvey, Brown,

Lyon, Baumgart & Schroeder, 1980; Rusch & Menchetti, 1981). Concomitantly, nonhandicapped persons functioning in nonsheltered environments are not provided opportunities to learn to work with, to socialize with, and to supervise severely handicapped workers.

Few Meaningful Reasons to Achieve Are Operative

Severely handicapped persons typically do not perform under the incentive systems that are apparently effective for most nonhandicapped persons. For example, rarely do severely handicapped persons view work as a means of acquiring the funds necessary to pay for a car, buy a boat, save for retirement, or meet rent or mortgage payments. Nevertheless, they need subjectively meaningful reasons to perform at reasonable criteria over long periods of time. Under what conditions do severely handicapped adults perform efficiently and consistently? Several seem reasonable:

- When others in the environment are working productively;
- When coworkers and supervisors communicate respect and appreciation for the work performed;
- When less than acceptable performance is corrected clearly and consistently; and
- When direct instruction that fosters the gradual expansion and accumulation of work skills and attitudes is available.

Unfortunately, these conditions are rarely, if ever, present in sheltered environments (Pomeranz & Marholin, 1977).

Deviant Actions Are Tolerated

When severely handicapped persons are congregated, performance usually becomes increasingly discrepant from that of nonsheltered peers (Bijou, 1966; Wolfensberger, 1980). For example, assume that eight severely handicapped adults were seated around a table putting plastic knives, forks, and spoons into plastic bags for use at fast food restaurants. One person might say the same word over and over. A second person might interrupt her work routine consistently by looking at her fingers for 25–35 seconds at a time; a third person might pick his nose and eat that picked; a fourth person might . . . and so forth. When most of the people at the table are behaving deviantly, it is extremely difficult, if not impossible, for a supervisor to provide all the interventions necessary for acceptable functioning. Unfortunately, many deviant actions must then be tolerated, ignored, unnoticed, or given euphemistic labels (Wehman & Hill, 1982). The probability of learning to function acceptably in nonsheltered environments is minimized with each passing day.

Waiting Lists, Rejections, Exclusions, and Reduced Schedules Abound

Many parents are told that because their young children will be severely handicapped throughout their lives, they will need to attend handicapped only schools until age 21 and a sheltered workshop or another such day program that serves only handicapped persons throughout life. For many parents, this life plan represents a state of relief in that they can feel comfortable that cradle to grave places and services will be available. However, parents and professionals must now address several hard facts. First, sheltered work environments are quite expensive. Many communities are putting limits on expenditures and thus on the number of persons who can attend (Bellamy et al., 1983). As rapidly increasing numbers of such environments have waiting lists, those who anticipated that their children would be maintained in a sheltered environment now must find alternatives. The usual alternative is staying at home. This, of course, results in tremendous economic, social, and employment pressures. Second, most sheltered environments reserve the right to try persons out and then judge them unacceptable or acceptable. Parents of children labeled *autistic* are well aware of the difficulties of trying to induce an adult environment to accommodate to the needs of their children

before they are rejected. Third, in some places persons who must function in wheelchairs, who are not toilet trained, or who have pronounced social and communication difficulties are excluded. Fourth, in an attempt to reduce expenses, many sheltered work environments are offering reduced schedules or services. Some places have proposed a reduction in the number of days per week that individuals can attend from 5 to 3. Where would those individuals function the remaining 4 days of the week? Quite likely, they would be confined to their homes.

Waiting lists, rejections, exclusions, and reduced schedules place educators and parents in extremely precarious positions. It is a questionable strategy to lead parents to believe that their severely handicapped child will function in a sheltered work environment when, in fact, such an environment might be unavailable. Concomitantly, it is unfair to provide an education without even attempting to provide the training and experiences necessary for functioning in nonsheltered environments. Clearly, it is more responsible to provide the preparatory experiences necessary for nonsheltered functioning and to live with less if absolutely necessary. The severely handicapped worker who cannot function in a nonsheltered environment can move to a more sheltered environment more readily because fewer skills are needed. On the other hand, the inverse is not tenable. Training and placement in sheltered work environments systematically minimize the probability of effective functioning in nonsheltered environments (Moss, 1979; Shiraga, 1983; U.S. Department of Labor, 1977).

In view of the information presented above, at least the following questions seem in order:

- How much longer should school systems prepare their severely handicapped students to function in sheltered vocational environments when data are available that can be interpreted as supporting the notion that such environments are inherently restrictive and cost ineffective?
- Can educational curricula be designed and implemented to prepare severely handi-

TABLE 5.2. FIFTY SEVERELY HANDICAPPED GRADUATES OF
THE MADISON METROPOLITAN SCHOOL DISTRICT
FROM 1979–1983 AND WHERE THEY FUNCTIONED
DURING THE WORK DAY AS OF AUGUST 1983

Year	Number of Graduates	Home	Sheltered Environment	Nonsheltered Environment
1979	5	1	3	1
1980	9	1	2	6
1981	13	0	3	10
1982	11	0	1	10
1983	12	2	1	9
Totals	50	4	10	36

capped students to function acceptably in a wide variety of nonsheltered vocational environments?

- Can school personnel, adult service agencies, and parents/guardians develop cooperative arrangements in order to facilitate habilitative and efficient transitions from school to postschool nonsheltered vocational environments?

The responses offered here are that public schools should no longer prepare severely handicapped students to function in sheltered vocational environments; that longitudinal and comprehensive educational curricula that prepare for functioning effectively in a wide variety of nonsheltered vocational environments can and must be generated; and that personnel representing such disciplines as education, and physical, occupational, and communication therapy, along with members of the business community, adult service providers, and parents/guardians must design and implement a variety of strategies that can be used to transition, i.e., to move, a severely handicapped

person from school to habilitative postschool nonsheltered vocational environments (Brown et al., 1981).

THE 1979–1983 FOLLOW-UP STUDY

Shiraga (1983) examined the postschool employment of 50 severely handicapped persons who were residents of Dane County and graduated from the Madison Metropolitan School District in 1979–1983. Her findings were remarkably different than those of VanDeventer et al. (1981), who examined the 1971–1978 graduates.* As of August 1983,

- Of the 50 graduates, 36 functioned in nonsheltered vocational environments, 10 functioned in sheltered environments, and 4 stayed at home all day (see Table 5.2);
- Those who functioned in nonsheltered environments maintained and expanded upon the meaningful work and work related skills acquired during their school years. In addi-

*Madison is located in Dane County, Wisconsin. In addition to serving severely handicapped city residents, the Madison Metropolitan School District also serves a number of severely handicapped students who are residents of Dane County but not the city of Madison. The 50 severely handicapped graduates from 1979–1983 reported here included 3 students who were residents of Dane County but not Madison at the time of graduation. The school district also serves a number of severely handicapped students who live at Central Wisconsin Center for the Developmentally Disabled, a state operated "institution." However, as only a few who reside there are from Madison or Dane County, they remain the responsibility of the state of Wisconsin after age 21. Tragically, because the adult service agencies in Dane County are only authorized to serve Dane County residents, most spend their adulthood on the wards of the institution. Four of the 1979–1983 graduates lived at Central Wisconsin Center and were also residents of Dane County. These 4 individuals were included in the 50 graduates examined.

tion, numerous opportunities for interactions with nonhandicapped persons were available within their work environments; and

- The 34 graduates who functioned in nonsheltered environments prior to graduation were still in those or other nonsheltered environments.

The number of graduates who functioned in nonsheltered vocational environments from 1971–1983 is communicated graphically in Figure 5.1. During 1971–1983, there was a significant shift in placement of severely handicapped graduates from sheltered to nonsheltered environments. During 1971–1976, not one graduate worked in a nonsheltered vocational environment. However, 29 out of 36, or 81%, of the 1981–1983 graduates worked in nonsheltered vocational environments. Although the reasons for these pronounced shifts are numerous, complex, and interactive, five appear to be of particular relevance:

- The earlier graduates received their educational and related services primarily in a segregated school. The more recent graduates attended regular public schools;
- In the mid-1970s a number of significant changes were initiated in the vocational training of severely handicapped students

in the Madison Metropolitan School District. Specifically, students started to receive direct instruction designed to prepare them to function in nonsheltered vocational environments as adults;

- Vocational services were designed to assist handicapped adults to function in nonsheltered vocational environments;
- A variety of work-pay relationships were developed that allowed the performance of meaningful work in nonsheltered environments; and
- Transition strategies were designed and implemented to improve communication and coordination between school and postschool service personnel.

Table 5.3 presents more specific information pertaining to each of the 50, 1979–1983 graduates and their vocational environments as of August 1983. The following paragraphs summarize some of the information in Table 5.3.

THE ENHANCING NATURE OF NONSHELTERED VOCATIONAL ENVIRONMENTS

Those addressing the vocational needs of severely handicapped students are in a dilemma. It is known that most severely handicapped

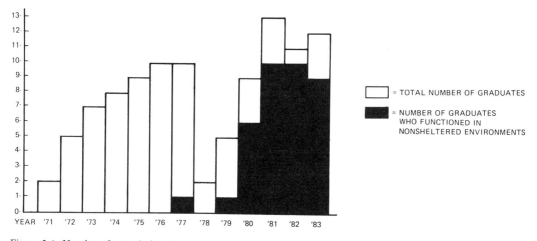

Figure 5.1. Number of severely handicapped graduates of the Madison Metropolitan School District, 1971–1983, who functioned in nonsheltered environments compared to the total number of graduates. (Note: Totals for the 1971–1978 graduates were obtained from VanDeventer et al., 1981, and totals for the 1979–1983 graduates were obtained from Shiraga, 1983.)

adults function in sheltered environments, but it is apparent that those environments are inherently restrictive. Two major options seem reasonable. First, attempts can be made to improve the nature of sheltered environments (Bellamy, Horner, & Inman, 1979; Redkey, 1979; Whitehead, 1979b). Second, attempts can be made to arrange for nonsheltered functioning. While the negative characteristics ascribed to shelters could also be operative anywhere, nonsheltered environments by nature offer severely handicapped workers many more opportunities to function adaptively and productively. Thus, the second is offered as the option of choice. Some, but certainly not all, of the more enhancing characteristics of nonsheltered environments would include:

- Job rotation is more feasible
- A continuous flow of meaningful work is available;
- There are more opportunities to acquire and perform work related skills;
- Transportation services are less costly and more normal;
- The nature of the supervision available is more acceptable;
- Access to health services can be available, if necessary; and
- The social climate is more conducive to success and personal growth.

Job Rotation Is More Feasible

Many people assume that the more intellectually handicapped a person is, the more appropriate that person is for work that is performed repetitively. Thus, it is often recommended that severely handicapped persons be required to perform exactly the same job in exactly the same place over long periods of time. Such is the case in many sheltered vocational environments (Greenleigh Associates, Inc., 1975; U.S. Department of Labor, 1979). This assumption is rarely valid. In fact, nonhandicapped persons seem to be much more capable of performing the same job year after year than severely handicapped persons; perhaps this is because they must work to fulfill major respon-

sibilities: mortgage payments, dental bills, car payments, and so forth. Thus, it is important that the vocational environment of a severely handicapped person contain opportunities to engage in a variety of different, meaningful work tasks daily or weekly. This variety is often available in nonsheltered vocational environments. Pete, a 22-year-old severely handicapped graduate of the Madison Metropolitan School District, works afternoons in a large university office building. He spends the first half of the afternoon collecting outgoing mail from individual offices on four floors within the building. The second half of the afternoon is spent on a variety of general clerical tasks, such as collating paper, labeling and stuffing envelopes, inserting cards into diploma covers, and validating student identification cards. In the judgment of all concerned, this diversity of work tasks has played a major role in maintaining his interest in his job over several years.

A Continuous Flow of Meaningful Work Is Available

Given free time, many severely handicapped persons engage in obtrusive, self-stimulatory, maladaptive, or otherwise counterproductive actions. In addition, it is extremely important that severely handicapped persons realize that the work they do has value and is respected by nonhandicapped persons. Thus, their vocational environments must have a continuous flow of meaningful work. Conversely, environments must be avoided that tolerate blocks of time during which work is not available or that allow the performance of nonmeaningful work. Sheltered environments, of course, are notorious for offering large blocks of time during which meaningful work is unavailable (Greenleigh Associates, Inc., 1975).

There Are More Opportunities to Acquire and Perform Work Related Skills

It is generally more enhancing to function in work environments that allow and require the performance of a variety of work related skills.

SPECIAL EDUCATION

TABLE 5.3. VOCATIONAL FUNCTIONING OF THE 50 SEVERELY HANDICAPPED GRADUATES

A	B	C		D		E	F
				Persons in Environment			
Graduate (G) Year and IQ Score (IQ)	Primary Disabilities	Environment		D1 — Handicapped Workers	D2 — Nonhandicapped Workers and Others	Activities	Days/ Week
		C1 — Sheltered	C2 — Nonsheltered				
G1, 1979 IQ = 42	Moderate MR	MARC[5]		116	0	Making ceramic items	5
G2, 1979 IQ = 53	Moderate MR	MOC		190	0	Packaging drapery hooks	5
G3, 1979 IQ = 46	Moderate MR	MOC		190	0	Packaging drapery hooks	5
G4, 1979 IQ = 48	Moderate MR	Home of biological parent		Not applicable (NA)	N/A	N/A	N/A
G5, 1979 IQ = no record	Moderate MR, Unintelligible speech		Rocky Rococo's Pizza (Store #1)	1	53	Cleaning the restaurant, busing tables, and washing dishes	5
			WHA Radio Station	4	55	Preparing a variety of material for mailing	3
G6, 1980 IQ = no record	Moderate MR, nonambulatory		WI Department of Natural Resources	1	45	Collating, labeling and sorting mail	5
G7, 1980 IQ = 47	Moderate MR		National Promotions	1	5	Silk screening and packaging T-shirts and other items	5
			Washington Host Restaurant	1	75	Busing tables	5

A brief glossary is included on page 164.
Level of supervision:
  1. Supervision totally provided by the employer and/or other nonhandicapped coworkers in the work environment;
  2. On site supervision provided bimonthly;
  3. On site supervision provided once per week;

OF THE MADISON METROPOLITAN SCHOOL DISTRICT FROM 1979–1983 AS OF AUGUST 1983

G	H	I		J	K	L	M
		Supervision					
Hours/ Day	Type and Amount of Payment	I1 — Source	I2 — Level	Time on Job	Previous Job(s) and Reason(s) For Leaving	Transportation	Domestic Environment
6	Piece rate, $17/month	MARC	7	6/79–8/83, 50 months		Provided by MARC	Group home
6	Piece rate, $41/month	MOC	7	6/79–8/83, 50 months		Provided by MOC	Group home
6	Piece rate, $42/month	MOC	7	6/79–8/83, 50 months		Provided by MOC	Group home
N/A	N/A	N/A	N/A	N/A		N/A	Natural home
2	$3.35/hour $144/month	VEA	3	6/82–8/83, 14 months	MARC-6/79–6/82, 36 months. Group home parents dissatisfied with sheltered placement. Referred to VEA for nonsheltered placement	Public bus	Group home
$2\frac{1}{2}$	Disability benefits	VEA	5				
$3\frac{1}{2}$	Disability benefits	Employer Only	1	1/81–8/83, 31 months	University of WI Hospital and Clinics-1/80–1/81, 12 months. Moved to challenging work by VEA supervisor	Public elderly and handicapped service	Foster home
3	$3.35/hour, $216/month	VEA	2	12/82–8/83 8 months		Public bus	Natural home
$2\frac{1}{2}$	$3.35/hour, $180/month	VEA	2	10/79–8/83 46 months			

continued

4. On site supervision provided twice per week;
5. On site supervision provided a minimum of once per day;
6. On site supervision provided the entire time that graduate is in the environment; and
7. Supervision totally provided by persons that are employed specifically for this purpose.

TABLE 5.3. continued

A	B	C		D		E	F
				Persons in Environment			
Graduate (G) Year and IQ Score (IQ)	Primary Disabilities	Environment		D1 Handicapped Workers	D2 Nonhandicapped Workers and Others	Activities	Days/ Week
		C1 Sheltered	C2 Nonsheltered				
G8, 1980 IQ = 28	Severe MR	Pathways		26	0	Learning self-help and leisure skills	5
G9, 1980 IQ = 37	Severe MR		Oakwood Nursing Home	1	35	Washing dishes and cleaning kitchen and storeroom	5
G10, 1980 IQ = 25	Severe MR, Unintelligible speech	MARC		116	0	Learning self-help and leisure skills	5
G11, 1980 IQ = Reported within the severe range	Severe MR, Unintelligible speech		Rocky Rococo's Pizza (Store #2)	2	40	Cleaning the restaurant	
			St. Mary's Hospital Pharmacy	2	150	Labeling hospital supplies	
G12, 1980 IQ = Reported to be untestable	Severe MR, Nonambulatory	Home of biological grandparent		N/A	N/A	N/A	N/A
G13, 1980 IQ = Reported within the the severe range	Severe MR, Visually impaired		University of of WI Extension Conference Center-Registrar's Dept.	4	80	Preparing a variety of material for mailing and assembling information notebooks	5
			WHA Radio Station	4	55	Preparing a variety of material for mailing	3

A brief glossary is included on page 00.
Level of supervision:
   1. Supervision totally provided by the employer and/or other nonhandicapped coworkers in the work environment;
   2. On site supervision provided bimonthly;
   3. On site supervision provided once per week;

TABLE 5.3. continued

G	H	I		J	K	L	M
		Supervision					
Hours/ Day	Type and Amount of Payment	I1 — Source	I2 — Level	Time on Job	Previous Job(s) and Reason(s) For Leaving	Transportation	Domestic Environment
6	None	Pathways	7	9/80–8/83 35 months		Provided by Pathways	Natural home
6	$2.50/hour, $323/month	Employer Only	1	1/80–8/83, 43 months		Public bus	Foster home
6	None	MARC	7	6/80–8/83 38 months		Provided by MARC	Group home
2	$1.90/hour, $98/month	VEA	3	6/80–8/83, 38 months		Public bus	Group home
$2\frac{1}{2}$	Disability benefits	VEA	3	2/83–8/83 6 months	University of WI Hospital and Clinics-2/80–1/83, 35 months. Job being performed was phased out.		
N/A	N/A	N/A	N/A	N/A	Pathways-10/80– 7/81, 9 months. Terminated due to behavior problems	N/A	Grandparent's home
3	Disability benefits	VEA	6	6/82–8/83, 14 months	MARC-6/80–6/82, 24 months. Group home parents dissatisfied with sheltered placement. Referred to VEA for nonsheltered placement.	Public elderly and handicapped service	Group home
$2\frac{1}{2}$	Disability benefits	VEA	6	6/82–8/83, 14 months			

continued

4. On site supervision provided twice per week;
5. On site supervision provided a minimum of once per day;
6. On site supervision provided the entire time that graduate is in the environment; and
7. Supervision totally provided by persons that are employed specifically for this purpose.

TABLE 5.3. continued

A	B	C		D		E	F
		Environment		Persons in Environment			
Graduate (G) Year and IQ Score (IQ)	Primary Disabilities	C1 — Sheltered	C2 — Nonsheltered	D1 — Handicapped Workers	D2 — Nonhandicapped Workers and Others	Activities	Days/ Week
G14, 1980 IQ = 42	Moderate MR, Unintelligible speech		University of WI Hospital and Clinics Decontamination Dept.	2	200	Disposing waste materials	5
			Forest Products Research Laboratory	1	40	Cleaning conference rooms and maintaining grounds	5
G15, 1981 IQ = 31	Severe MR, Unintelligible speech		Burger King Restaurant	1	100	Busing tables, washing dishes, and filling condiments	5
G16, 1981 IQ = 25	Severe MR, Nonverbal		Madison General Hospital- Central Supply Dept. and Pharmacy	4	175	Folding laundry and labeling, opening and packaging pharmaceuticals	5
G17, 1981 IQ = no record	Severe MR, Unintelligible speech	Pathways		26	0	Learning self-help and leisure skills	5
G18, 1981 IQ = 54	Moderate MR		Madison Fire Station #1	1	40		3

A brief glossary is included on page 164.
Level of Supervision:
 1. Supervision totally provided by the employer and/or other nonhandicapped coworkers in the work environment;
 2. On site supervision provided bimonthly;
 3. On site supervision provided once per week;

TABLE 5.3. continued

G	H	I		J	K	L	M
		Supervision					
		I1	I2				
	Type and	—	—		Previous Job(s)		
Hours/	Amount of			Time on	and Reason(s)		Domestic
Day	Payment	Source	Level	Job	For Leaving	Transportation	Environment
4	$3.80/hour, $327/month	VEA	2	1/80–8/83, 43 months		Public bus	Natural home
3	Disability benefits	Employer Only	1	5/80–8/83 39 months			
$2\frac{1}{2}$	$2.00/hour, $110/month	VEA	3	10/80–8/83, 34 months		Public bus	Natural home
6	Disability benefits	VEA	5	6/81–8/83, 26 months		Public elderly and handi-capped service	Group home
6	None		Path-ways	8/82–8/83, 12 months	MARC-6/81–8/82, 14 months. Term-inated due to be-havior problems	Provided by Pathways	Foster home
5	Disability benefits	VEA	6	5/83–8/83, 3 months	Washington Host Restaurant-10/80–12/81, 14 months. Fired for poor quality work and poor work attitude Bittersweet Res-taurant-12/81–7/82, 7 months. Fired for stealing University of WI Hospital and Clinics-9/82–3/83, 6 months. Fired for poor quality work and poor work attitude	Public bus	Group home

continued

4. On site supervision provided twice per week;
5. On site supervision provided a minimum of once per day;
6. On site supervision provided the entire time that graduate is in the environment; and
7. Supervision totally provided by persons that are employed specifically for this purpose.

TABLE 5.3. continued

A	B	C		D		E	F
		Environment		Persons in Environment			
Graduate (G) Year and IQ Score (IQ)	Primary Disabilities	C1 — Sheltered	C2 — Nonsheltered	D1 — Handicapped Workers	D2 — Nonhandicapped Workers and Others	Activities	Days/ Week
G19, 1981 IQ = 38	Severe MR, Nonverbal Hearing impaired		Madison General Hospital- Pharmacy	4	175	Sorting pharmacy orders by room number and un- packing and label- ing phar- maceuti- cals	5
			Madison Civic Center	3	50	Preparing a variety of mate- rial for mailing and dis- tributing programs at events	2
G20, 1981 IQ = 41	Moderate MR		Rocky Rococo's Pizza (Store #3)	1	45	Cleaning the res- taurant and mak- ing pizza	5
G21, 1981 IQ = 41	Moderate MR		Inn on the Park Hotel	2	35	Cleaning hotel rooms	5
			Madison Civic Center	3	50	Preparing a variety of mate- rial for mailing and dis- tributing programs at events	2
G22, 1981 IQ = 34	Severe MR Seizure disorder		University of WI Ex- tension Conference Center- Registrar's Dept.	4	80	Preparing a vareity of mate- rial for mailing and assembl- ing infor- mation notebooks	5

A brief glossary is included on page 164.
Level of Supervision:
  1. Supervision totally provided by the employer and/or other nonhandicapped coworkers in the work environment;
  2. On site supervision provided bimonthly;
  3. On site supervision provided once per week;

TABLE 5.3. continued

G	H	I		J	K	L	M
		Supervision					
		I1	I2				
Hours/ Day	Type and Amount of Payment	Source	Level	Time on Job	Previous Job(s) and Reason(s) For Leaving	Transportation	Domestic Environment
3	Disability benefits	VEA	5	1/81–8/83, 31 months		Public bus	Natural home
2	Disability benefits	VEA	3	1/81–8/83, 31 months			
$2\frac{1}{2}$	$3.35/hour $180/month	VEA	4	2/83–8/83, 6 months	The Treehouse Restaurant-9/80–1/83, 28 months. Fired for poor quality work.	Public bus	Natural home
4	$1.70/room, (3 rooms), $110/month	VEA	4	9/80–8/83, 35 months		Public bus	Foster home
2	Disability benefits	VEA	3	10/80–8/83, 34 months			
3	Disability benefits	VEA	6	6/82–8/83, 14 months	Madison General Hospital 1/81–6/82, 18 months. Moved to a job that was better suited to capabilities by VEA supervisor	Public elderly and handi-capped service	Natural home

continued

continued

4. On site supervision provided twice per week;
5. On site supervision provided a minimum of once per day;
6. On site supervision provided the entire time that graduate is in the environment; and
7. Supervision totally provided by persons that are employed specifically for this purpose.

TABLE 5.3. continued

A	B	C		D		E	F
		Environment		Persons in Environment			
Graduate (G) Year and IQ Score (IQ)	Primary Disabilities	C1 — Sheltered	C2 — Nonsheltered	D1 — Handicapped Workers	D2 — Nonhandicapped Workers and Others	Activities	Days/ Week
G23, 1981 IQ = 40	Severe MR, Autism		Madison General Hospital-Pharmacy	4	175	Labeling, opening, and packaging pharmaceuticals	5
G24, 1981 IQ = 45	Moderate MR, Seizure Disorder		Rocky Rococo's Pizza (Store #2)	2	40	Cleaning the restaurant	6
			St. Mary's Hospital-Pharmacy	2	150	Labeling hospital supplies	3
G25, 1981 IQ = 45	Moderate MR		Rocky Rococo's Pizza (Store #4)	2	130	Cleaning the restaurant, busing tables, and washing dishes	5
			Madison Civic Center	3	50	Preparing a variety of material for mailing and distributing programs at events	2
G26, 1981 IQ = Reported within the severe range	Severe MR	CWC Workshop Program		40	0	Assembling drapery pulleys	5
G27, 1981 IQ = 55	Mild MR, Nonambulatory, Blind	MOC		190	0	Assembling drapery pulleys	5

A brief glossary is included on page 164.
Level of Supervision:
  1. Supervision totally provided by the employer and/or other nonhandicapped coworkers in the work environment;
  2. On site supervision provided bimonthly;
  3. On site supervision provided once per week;

TABLE 5.3. continued

G	H	I		J	K	L	M
		Supervision					
Hours/ Day	Type and Amount of Payment	I1 — Source	I2 — Level	Time on Job	Previous Job(s) and Reason(s) For Leaving	Transportation	Domestic Environment
6	Disability benefits	VEA	6	6/81–8/83, 26 months		Public elderly and handi-capped service	Natural home
2	$1.90/hour, $98/month	VEA	3	2/78–8/83, 66 months		Public bus	Supervised apartment
$2\frac{1}{2}$	Disability benefits	VEA	3	2/83–8/83, 6 months	University of WI Hospital and Clinics-2/80–1/83, 35 months. Job being performed was phased out.		
3	$3.35/hour, $216/month	Goodwill	3	9/82–8/83, 11 months	Howard Johnson's Hotel 9/78–8/82, 47 months. Fired for stealing	Public bus	Orchard Hill
2	Disability benefits	VEA	3	10/80–8/83, 34 months			
6	None	CWC	7	6/81–8/83, 26 months		Provided by CWC	CWC
6	Piece Rate, $9/month	MOC	7	1/82–83, 19 months		Provided by MOC	Group home

continued

4. On site supervision provided twice per week;
5. On site supervision provided a minimum of once per day;
6. On site supervision provided the entire time that graduate is in the environment; and
7. Supervision totally provided by persons that are employed specifically for this purpose.

TABLE 5.3. continued

A	B	C		D		E	F
		Environment		Persons in Environment			
				D1	D2		
Graduate (G) Year and IQ Score (IQ)	Primary Disabilities	C1 Sheltered	C2 Nonsheltered	Handicapped Workers	Nonhandicapped Workers and Others	Activities	Days/ Week
G 28, 1982 IQ = 48	Moderate MR, Blind		University of WI Extension Conference Center-Registrar's Dept.	4	80	Preparing a variety of material for mailing and assembling information notebooks	5
			Peterson Office Building-Payroll Dept.	3	150	Preparing a variety of material for mailing, collating materials and disposing of old forms	5
G 29, 1982 IQ = 42	Moderate MR		Madison General Hospital-Pharmacy	4	175	Sorting pharmacy orders by room and operating Xerox machine	5
G 30, 1982 IQ = Reported with the severe range	Severe MR, Nonverbal		University of WI Extension Conference Center-Food Service Dept.	1	80	Setting tables and preparing food	5
			Peterson Office Building-Payroll Dept.	3	150	Preparing a variety of material for mailing and stamping and alphabetizing forms	5

A brief glossary is included on page 164.
Level of Supervision:
   1. Supervision totally provided by the employer and/or other nonhandicapped coworkers in the work environment;
   2. On site supervision provided bimonthly;
   3. On site supervision provided once per week;

TABLE 5.3. continued

G	H	I		J	K	L	M
		Supervision					
		I1	I2				
Hours/ Day	Type and Amount of Payment	Source	Level	Time on Job	Previous Job(s) and Reason(s) For Leaving	Transportation	Domestic Environment
3	Disability benefits	VEA	6	6/82–8/83 14 months		Public elderly and handi- capped service	Foster home
$2\frac{1}{2}$	Disability benefits	VEA	6	3/82–8/83 17 months			
6	Disability benefits	VEA	5	6/82–8/83, 14 months		Public bus	Group home
3	Disability benefits	VEA	6	6/82–8/83 14 months		Public elderly and handi- capped service	Group home
$2\frac{1}{2}$	Disability benefits	VEA	6	3/82–8/83, 17 months			

continued

4. On site supervision provided twice per week;
5. On site supervision provided a minimum of once per day;
6. On site supervision provided the entire time that graduate is in the environment; and
7. Supervision totally provided by persons that are employed specifically for this purpose.

TABLE 5.3. continued

A	B	C		D		E	F
				Persons in Environment			
Graduate (G) Year and IQ Score (IQ)	Primary Disabilities	Environment		D1	D2	Activities	Days/ Week
		C1 Sheltered	C2 Nonsheltered	Handicapped Workers	Nonhandicapped Workers and Others		
G31, 1981 IQ = 50	Moderate MR		Inn on the Park Hotel	2	35	Cleaning hotel rooms	5
			Wisconsin State Capitol	3	50	Collating senate and assembly bills and preparing a variety of material for mailing	1
G32, 1982 IQ = 43	Moderate MR		The Flamingo Restaurant	1	10	Cleaning the restaurant	3
			Peterson Office Building- Mail Room and Registrar's Dept.	1	150	Picking up and sorting mail, preparing diplomas, preparing a variety of material for mailing, and stamping forms	5
G33, 1982 IQ = Reported within the severe range	Severe MR, Cerebral palsy, Non-ambulatory, Nonverbal		WHA Radio Station	4	55	Preparing a variety of material for mailing	2
G34, 1982 IQ = 33	Severe MR, Deaf, Nonverbal		University of WI Engineering Extension	4	85	Preparing a variety of material for mailing, compiling information brochures, and xeroxing	5

A brief glossary is included on page 00.
Level of Supervision:
  1. Supervision totally provided by the employer and/or other nonhandicapped coworkers in the work environment;
  2. On site supervision provided bimonthly;
  3. On site supervision provided once per week;

TABLE 5.3. continued

G	H	I1	I2	J	K	L	M
		Supervision					
Hours/ Day	Type and Amount of Payment	I1 — Source	I2 — Level	Time on Job	Previous Job(s) and Reason(s) For Leaving	Transportation	Domestic Environment
6	$1.70/ room, (5 rooms), $183/month	VEA	3	9/81–8/83, 24 months		Public bus	Group house
3	Disability benefits	VEA	3	3/83–8/83 5 months			
3	$3.35/hour $130/month	VEA	4	9/81–8/83, 23 months		Public bus	Group home
$2\frac{1}{2}$	Disability benefits	VEA	5	1/81–8/83, 19 months			
$2\frac{1}{2}$	Disability benefits	VEA	6	6/82–8/83, 14 months		Private specialized transportation service	CWC
3	Disability benefits	VEA	6	10/82–8/83 10 months		Public elderly and handi- capped service	Foster home

continued

4. On site supervision provided twice per week;
5. On site supervision provided a minimum of once per day;
6. On site supervision provided the entire time that graduate is in the environment; and
7. Supervision totally provided by persons that are employed specifically for this purpose.

TABLE 5.3. continued

A	B	C		D		E	F
				Persons in Environment			
Graduate (G) Year and IQ Score (IQ)	Primary Disabilities	Environment		D1 — Handicapped Workers	D2 — Nonhandicapped Workers and Others	Activities	Days/ Week
		C1 — Sheltered	C2 — Nonsheltered				
G35, 1982 IQ = 62	Mild MR, Cerebral palsy, Nonambulatory		Group Health Cooperative	4	65	Preparing information packets	2
			University of WI Engineering Extension	4	85	Preparing a variety of material for mailing and compiling information brochures	3
G36, 1982 IQ = 37	Severe MR, Cerebral palsy, Deaf, Nonverbal		University of WI Extension Conference Center-Registrar's Dept.	4	80	Preparing a variety of material for mailing and assembling information notebooks	2
			Camp Randall Memorial Sports Center	1	150	Checking identification cards and distributing towels	3
G37, 1982 IQ = 32	Severe MR, Cerebral palsy, Non-ambulatory		Group Health Cooperative	2	65	Preparing information packets	2
			University of WI Engineering Extension	4	85	Preparing a variety of material for mailing and compiling information brochures	3

A brief glossary is included on page 164.
Level of Supervision:
   1. Supervision totally provided by the employer and/or other nonhandicapped coworkers in the work environment;
   2. On site supervision provided bimonthly;
   3. On site supervision provided once per week;

TABLE 5.3. continued

G	H	I		J	K	L	M
		Supervision					
		I1	I2				
Hours/ Day	Type and Amount of Payment	Source	Level	Time on Job	Previous Job(s) and Reason(s) For Leaving	Transportation	Domestic Environment
3	Disability benefits	VEA	5	1/82–8/83, 19 months		Public elderly and handi-capped service	Supervised apartment
3	Disability benefits	VEA	5	10/82–8/83, 10 months			
3	Disability benefits	VEA	5	6/82–8/83, 14 months		Public bus	Group home
3	Disability benefits	VEA	3	11/82–8/83, 9 months			
3	Disability benefits	VEA	5	1/82–8/83, 19 months		Private specialized transportation service	Foster home
3	Disability benefits	VEA	5	10/82–8/83, 10 months			

continued

4. On site supervision provided twice per week;
5. On site supervision provided a minimum of once per day;
6. On site supervision provided the entire time that graduate is in the environment; and
7. Supervision totally provided by persons that are employed specifically for this purpose.

TABLE 5.3. continued

A	B	C		D		E	F
				Persons in Environment			
Graduate (G) Year and IQ Score (IQ)	Primary Disabilities	Environment		D1 — Handicapped Workers	D2 — Nonhandicapped Workers and Others	Activities	Days/ Week
		C1 — Sheltered	C2 — Nonsheltered				
G38, 1982 IQ = Reported within the severe range	Severe MR, Hearing impaired, Visually impaired	Pathways		26	0	Learning self-care and leisure skills	5
G39, 1983 IQ = 35	Severe MR, Seizure disorder		American Automobile Association	3	85	Preparing a variety of material for mailing and stamping forms	5
			Madison Fire Station #1-Administrative Offices	2	45	Cleaning entrance bathrooms, and halls	5
G40, 1983 IQ = 20	Profound MR, Nonverbal		American Automobile Association	3	85	Preparing a variety of material for mailing and stamping forms	5
			Madison Fire Station #1-Administrative Offices	2	45	Cleaning entrance bathrooms and halls	5
G41, 1983 IQ = Reported within the profound range	Profound MR, Cerebral Palsy, Nonambulatory, Nonverbal, Seizure disorder	Home of biological parent		N/A	N/A	N/A	N/A
G42, 1983 IQ = 45	Moderate MR		Rocky Rococo's Pizza (Store #4)	2	130	Cleaning restaurant	5
			Capitol Center Foods Grocery Store	1	110	Cleaning storeroom and straightening and stocking shelves	5

A brief glossary is included on page 164.
Level of Supervision:
   1. Supervision totally provided by the employer and/or other nonhandicapped coworkers in the work environment;
   2. On site supervision provided bimonthly;
   3. On site supervision provided once per week;

TABLE 5.3. continued

G	H	I		J	K	L	M
		Supervision					
		I1	I2				
		—	—				
Hours/ Day	Type and Amount of Payment	Source	Level	Time on Job	Previous Job(s) and Reason(s) For Leaving	Transportation	Domestic Environment
6	None	Pathways	7	7/82–8/83, 13 months		Provided by Pathways	CWC
$3\frac{1}{2}$	Disability benefits	VEA	6	2/83–8/83, 6 months		Public bus	Group home
2	Disability benefits	VEA	6	5/83–8/83, 3 months			
$3\frac{1}{2}$	Disability benefits	VEA	6	5/83–8/83, 3 months		Public elderly and handicapped service	Group home
2	Disability benefits	VEA	6	5/83–8/83, 3 months			
N/A	N/A	N/A		N/A		N/A	Natural home
$2\frac{1}{2}$	$3.35/hour $180/month	Goodwill	3	3/83–8/83, 5 months		Public bus	Natural home
$2\frac{1}{2}$	$3.35/hour, $180/month	VEA	3	1/83–8/83, 7 months			

continued

4. On site supervision provided twice per week;
5. On site supervision provided a minimum of once per day;
6. On site supervision provided the entire time that graduate is in the environment; and
7. Supervision totally provided by persons that are employed specifically for this purpose.

TABLE 5.3. continued

A	B	C		D		E	F
				Persons in Environment			
Graduate (G) Year and IQ Score (IQ)	Primary Disabilities	Environment		D1 — Handicapped Workers	D2 — Nonhandicapped Workers and Others	Activities	Days/ Week
		C1 — Sheltered	C2 — Nonsheltered				
G43, 1983 IQ = 35	Severe MR, Muscular dystrophy		American Automobile Association	3	85	Preparing a variety of material for mailing, stamping and retrieving membership numbers from computer terminal	5
			Madison Fire Station #1-Station House	2	30	Washing vehicles	5
G44, 1983 IQ = 34	Severe MR, Hearing impaired		Rocky Rococo's Pizza (Store #5)	1	40	Cleaning restaurant	5
			Langdon Area Grocery Collective	2	45	Cleaning store and packaging food items	2
			Wisconsin State Capitol	3	50	Collating senate and assembly bills and preparing a variety of material for mailing	1
G45, 1983 IQ = Reported within the severe range	Severe MR, Nonverbal	Pathways		26	0	Learning self-help and leisure skills	5

A brief glossary is included on page 164.
Level of Supervision:
   1. Supervision totally provided by the employer and/or other nonhandicapped coworkers in the work environment;
   2. On site supervision provided bimonthly;
   3. On site supervision provided once per week;

TABLE 5.3. continued

G	H	I		J	K	L	M
		Supervision					
		I1 —	I2 —		Previous Job(s)		
Hours/	Type and Amount of			Time on	and Reason(s)		Domestic
Day	Payment	Source	Level	Job	For Leaving	Transportation	Environment
$3\frac{1}{2}$	Disability benefits	VEA	6	2/83–8/83, 6 months		Public bus	Foster home
2	Disability benefits	VEA	6	2/83–8/83, 6 months			
$1\frac{1}{2}$	$3.35/hour, $108/month	Goodwill	3	1/83–8/83, 7 months		Public bus	Orchard Hill
$2\frac{1}{2}$	Disability benefits	Goodwill	3	1/83–8/83, 7 months			
3	Disability benefits	VEA	3	3/83–8/83, 5 months			
6	None	Pathways	7	6/83–8/83, 2 months		Provided by Pathways	CWC

continued

4. On site supervision provided twice per week;
5. On site supervision provided a minimum of once per day;
6. On site supervision provided the entire time that graduate is in the environment; and
7. Supervision totally provided by persons that are employed specifically for this purpose.

TABLE 5.3. continued

A	B	C		D		E	F
		Environment		Persons in Environment			
Graduate (G) Year and IQ Score (IQ)	Primary Disabilities	C1 — Sheltered	C2 — Nonsheltered	D1 — Handicapped Workers	D2 — Nonhandicapped Workers and Others	Activities	Days/ Week
G46, 1983 IQ = 36	Severe MR		Veteran's Administration Hospital Pharmacy	1	175	Labeling and packaging pharmaceuticals, preparing a variety of material for mailing, and stocking shelves	5
			Langdon Area Grocery Collective	2	45	Stocking shelves and packaging food items	2
			Wisconsin State Capitol	3	50	Collating senate and assembly bills and preparing a variety of material for mailing	1
G47, 1983 IQ = 42	Moderate MR		University of WI Engineering Extension	4	85	Preparing a variety of material for mailing and compiling information brochures	5
			Madison Fire Station #1-Station House	2	30	Washing vehicles	5

A brief glossary is included on page 164.
Level of Supervision:
  1. Supervision totally provided by the employer and/or other nonhandicapped coworkers in the work environment;
  2. On site supervision provided bimonthly;
  3. On site supervision provided once per week;

TABLE 5.3. continued

G	H	I		J	K	L	M
		Supervision					
		I1 — Source	I2 — Level				
Hours/ Day	Type and Amount of Payment	Source	Level	Time on Job	Previous Job(s) and Reason(s) For Leaving	Transportation	Domestic Environment
$3\frac{1}{2}$	Disability benefits	VEA	3	9/81–8/83, 23 months		Public bus	Supervised apartment
$2\frac{1}{2}$	Disability benefits	Goodwill	3	10/82–8/83, 10 months			
3	Disability benefits	VEA	3	3/83–8/83, 5 months			
3	Disability benefits	VEA	6	7/83–8/83, 1 month		Public bus	Group home
2	Disability benefits	VEA	6	2/83–8/83, 6 months			

continued

4. On site supervision provided twice per week;
5. On site supervision provided a minimum of once per day;
6. On site supervision provided the entire time that graduate is in the environment; and
7. Supervision totally provided by persons that are employed specifically for this purpose.

TABLE 5.3. continued

A	B	C		D		E	F
		Environment		Persons in Environment			
Graduate (G) Year and IQ Score (IQ)	Primary Disabilities	C1 — Sheltered	C2 — Nonsheltered	D1 — Handicapped Workers	D2 — Nonhandicapped Workers and Others	Activities	Days/ Week
G48, 1983 IQ = 30	Severe MR		University of WI Extension Conference Center-Registrar's Dept.	4	80	Preparing a variety of materials for mailing and assembling information notebooks	5
			WHA Radio Station	4	55	Preparing a variety of material for mailing	3
G49, 1983 IQ = 42	Moderate MR		University of WI Hospital and Clinics-Materials Redistribution Dept.	2	200	Preparing surgical instruments for sterilization	5
			McArdle Cancer Research Laboratory	1	50	Cleaning and storing laboratory glassware	5
G50, 1981 IQ = 34	Severe MR, Visually impaired	Home of biological parent		N/A	N/A	N/A	N/A

A brief glossary is included below.
Level of Supervision:
1. Supervision totally provided by the employer and/or other nonhandicapped coworkers in the work environment;
2. On site supervision provided bimonthly;
3. On site supervision provided once per week;
4. On site supervision provided twice per week;
5. On site supervision provided a minimum of once per day;
6. On site supervision provided the entire time that graduate is in the environment; and
7. Supervision totally provided by persons that are employed specifically for this purpose.

GLOSSARY:

MARC — The Madison Area Association for Retarded Citizens Work Activity Center is a work activity center in Madison, Wisconsin, operated by the Madison Area Association for Retarded Citizens that serves approximately 116 developmentally disabled adults.

MOC — Madison Opportunity Center is a sheltered workshop in Madison, Wisconsin, that serves approximately 270 handicapped adults.

VEA — Vocational Education Alternatives, Inc. is an agency in Madison, Wisconsin, designed to assist disabled adults to function in nonsheltered vocational environments. At any given time it serves approximately 200 handicapped adults.

TABLE 5.3. continued

G	H	I		J	K	L	M
		Supervision					
		I1 — Source	I2 — Level				
Hours/ Day	Type and Amount of Payment			Time on Job	Previous Job(s) and Reason(s) For Leaving	Transportation	Domestic Environment
3	Disability benefits	VEA	6	7/83–8/83, 1 month		Public elderly and handi- capped service	Foster home
$2\frac{1}{2}$	Disability benefits	VEA	6	4/83–8/83, 4 months			
$3\frac{1}{2}$	Disability benefits	VEA	3	9/80–8/83, 35 months		Public bus	Natural home
2	$2.00/hour, $86/month	Goodwill	3	10/81–8/83, 22 months			
N/A	N/A	N/A	N/A	N/A		N/A	N/A

CWC — Central Wisconsin Center for the Developmentally Disabled is a state institution located in Madison, Wisconsin, that houses approximately 700 developmentally disabled citizens.

Orchard Hill is a residential facility in Madison, Wisconsin, that serves 96 retarded adults. It consists of eight cottages and a general purpose building. Twelve residents live in each cottage and are supervised by resident houseparents.

Pathways is an activity center in Madison, Wisconsin that serves approximately 25 developmentally disabled adults.

Goodwill Industries is an agency in Madison, Wisconsin, that provides vocational services to approximately 110 handicapped adults; approximately 20% of whom receive these services in nonsheltered environments.

Notes. The most recent I.Q. scores that were available in school records of 30 of the 36 graduates who functioned in nonsheltered vocational environments ranged from 20–62 and averaged 39.5. Of the remaining 6, the records of 4 did not contain specific I.Q. scores but did include judgments that intellectual functioning was within the "severe range" and 2 whose records had been destroyed at a parent's request (Column A). The most recent I.Q. scores that were available in school records of 6 of the 10 graduates who functioned in sheltered vocational environments ranged from 25–55 and averaged 41.5. Of the remaining 4, the records of 3 did not contain a specific I.Q. score but did include judgments that intellectual functioning was within the "severe

continued

range" and 1 whose records had been destroyed at a parent's request (Column A). Of the 4 graduates who stayed at home, 2 were assigned I.Q. scores of 48 and 34 respectively, 1 had records that did not contain a specific I.Q. score but did include judgments that intellectual functioning was within the "profound range," and 1 was reported to be untestable (Column A).

Of the 36 graduates who functioned in nonsheltered environments, 1 was labeled *mildly retarded*, 16 were labeled *moderately retarded*, 18 were labeled *severely retarded*, and 1 was labeled *profoundly retarded*. In addition, 7 were nonverbal, 4 had speech that was unintelligible, 4 were nonambulatory, 4 had cerebral palsy, 1 was visually impaired, 1 was blind, 2 were auditorily impaired, 2 were deaf, 3 had seizure disorders, and 1 was labeled *autistic* (Column B).

Of the 10 graduates who functioned in sheltered environments, 1 was labeled *mildly retarded*, 3 were labeled *moderately retarded*, and 6 were labeled *severely retarded*. In addition, 1 was nonverbal, 2 had speech that was unintelligible, 1 was nonambulatory, 1 was blind, and 1 was both auditorily and visually impaired (Column C). Of the 50 graduates, 36 functioned in 35 different nonsheltered vocational environments, 10 functioned in 4 sheltered environments and 4 stayed at home all day (Columns C1 and C2). Please note that some graduates functioned in more than one nonsheltered environment.

The 35 nonsheltered vocational environments were in reasonable accordance with the natural proportion, whereas all 4 of the nonsheltered environments grossly violated the natural proportion (Columns D1 and D2). The numbers of handicapped and nonhandicapped persons in each vocational environment are presented in Columns D1 and D2, respectively. Column D2 does not include persons who were employed for the specific purpose of providing services to the handicapped individuals, but does include persons such as customers, students, or visitors.

Greater varieties and amounts of meaningful work were being performed by those functioning in nonsheltered vocational environments than by those functioning in sheltered environments (Column E).

All graduates who functioned in sheltered environments were occupied 5 days a week for an average of 6 hours per day. This time was the total number of hours present in the environment and included time spent engaging in nonvocational activities such as basic skill building and leisure time classes. All but 2 of the 36 graduates who functioned in nonsheltered environments were also occupied 5 days a week. These graduates worked an average of 4.4 hours per day. This time included *only* the number of hours spent performing meaningful work. It did not include time spent for lunch or any nonvocational activities that may have been incorporated into their day. For example, drinking coffee with a friend or going to the library after work or, for those who functioned in two different vocational environments, transportation between the two environments (Columns F and G).

The 36 graduates who functioned in nonsheltered environments received wages within a wide range of payment, these will be examined more fully later (in Table 5.4). Seven received subminimum wage, 8 received the typical wage of a nonhandicapped person performing the same work at the same standards, and 21 received indirect pay in the form of noncontingent disability benefits. Included in the 15 who received direct payment in the form of subminimum or typical wages were 10 who also received indirect payment. Of the 10 graduates who functioned in sheltered environments, 4 were paid on a piece rate basis and 6, because they did not perform meaningful work, did not receive payment. The average monthly wage of those who received direct payment in nonsheltered environments was *$191.00*. The average monthly wage of those who received direct payment in sheltered environments was *$27.00* (Column H).

The 10 graduates who functioned in sheltered environments were supervised by facility staff only. In addition to that provided by the staff of Vocational Education Alternatives, Inc. and Goodwill Industries, much of the supervision of those who functioned in nonsheltered environments was provided by their employers and/or nonhandicapped coworkers (Columns 11 and 12).

The 10 graduates who functioned in sheltered environments had been in those or other sheltered environments since they graduated. Indeed, of the 61 graduates placed in sheltered environments since 1971, only 2 had been replaced to nonsheltered environments. This replacement seems to have resulted from the urgings of group home parents rather than from sheltered facility staff. Of the 34 graduates who functioned in nonsheltered environments prior to graduation, 27 were successfully working in the same environments in which they functioned at graduation; 2 had moved to more demanding nonsheltered environments, 2 were placed in a different nonsheltered environments when their original jobs were phased out; and 3 had been fired. Of the 3 who had been fired, 2 were replaced in other nonsheltered environments of approximately the same level of difficulty and 1 was placed in a nonsheltered environment where more external supervision could be provided. None of the 34 had been moved from nonsheltered to sheltered environments (Columns J and K).

The 10 graduates who functioned in sheltered environments were provided handicapped only transportation services by the facilities. Of the 36 graduates who functioned in nonsheltered environments, 23 utilized the public bus system, 11 utilized the public transportation system designed to meet the needs of elderly and handicapped persons, and 2 were transported by a private specialized transportation service for disabled and elderly persons (Column L).

Of the 10 graduates who functioned in sheltered environments, 5 lived in group homes, 1 lived in his natural home, 1 lived in a foster home, and 3 lived at Central Wisconsin Center, a state operated institution for the developmentally disabled. Of the 36 who functioned in nonsheltered environments, 13 lived in group homes, 9 lived in their natural homes, 8 lived in foster homes, 1 lived at Central Wisconsin Center, an institution, 2 lived at Orchard Hill, a residential facility that serves 96 retarded adults, and 3 lived in supervised apartments (Column M).

Severely handicapped persons working in nonsheltered environments can learn to use vending machines, stores, parks, and recreation facilities as natural components of their work day. Jan, a 24-year-old severely handicapped individual, works each morning as a housekeeper at a downtown hotel and each afternoon as a clerical worker at the Madison Civic Center. During her lunch hour she utilizes a variety of general community and recreation environments such as stores, restaurants, and the public library, all of which are located within a short walking distance of her two jobs. Because use of these environments has been incorporated into the overall routine of her work day, she has been able to develop and maintain a variety of life enhancing, work related skills.

Transportation Services Are Less Costly and More Normal

Direct nonsheltered vocational instruction starts in the Madison Metropolitan School District upon entering middle school at age 11 or 12. Whenever possible, public transportation is used from school to work and back, although the cars of school personnel are used occasionally. At these young ages, environments can be selected for training purposes with minimal regard to the transportation issues that will be salient upon graduation. As chronological age increases, however, issues associated with travel to and from the work place assume increasing importance. At approximately age 18, vocational training sites that students can travel to and from when they graduate are sought and environments that are difficult to reach are avoided. That is, as some students can learn to ride specific public buses to and from designated environments, vocational sites on public bus lines are selected. As others need various kinds of more specialized transportation services, vocational environments accessible to those kinds of services are chosen. Shopping centers and hospitals are often preferred vocational sites because they are on the routes of specialized handicapped and elderly transportation services. For those who cannot use public buses or specialized handicapped and elderly transportation systems, subsidized car pools with nonhandicapped workers are becoming increasingly feasible. Several years ago many nonhandicapped workers would not have considered having a severely handicapped person in their car pool. However, after dramatic changes in attitudes as a function of direct experiences in school (Brown et al., 1983; Voeltz, 1980a) and work places (Pumpian, 1981), heterogeneous car pools are becoming socially realistic and economical transportation options.

Most sheltered vocational environments purchase or contract for a bus or buses to transport only handicapped workers to and from their homes (Sowers et al., 1979). This expenditure includes the salary and benefits of one or more drivers, bus maintenance, fuel, insurance, etc. Few of these expenses are incurred when severely handicapped adults work in nonsheltered environments because they utilize transportation alternatives that are much less costly.

The Nature of the Supervision Available Is More Acceptable

External supervision refers to that provided by persons who are paid specifically for the purpose of providing that service. Clearly, severely handicapped persons will need the direct supervision of adult service professionals throughout their lives. However, the kinds and degrees of professional supervision needed vary across environments and persons. Some individuals in some environments need daily external supervision while others can function quite well with much less. John, a 24-year-old severely handicapped graduate of the Madison Metropolitan School District, has worked as a busperson at a restaurant for almost 4 years. On a daily basis, he functions quite well and his adult service agency supervisor merely maintains bimonthly contact with his employer. However, from time to time he has difficulties with grooming and social skills. When these difficulties arise, the external supervisor visits him at work and at home on a more frequent basis, to intervene directly with all concerned until the problems are corrected. Conversely, Donna, 24 years old and labeled *autistic*, works in the pharmacy of a hospital. When left alone for even short periods of time, she will stray from her work place and stimulate herself in socially obtrusive ways. Because of these persistent difficulties and the degree of sophistication needed to manage them, an external supervisor provides continuous daily monitoring at her work.

Internal supervision refers to that provided by nonhandicapped coworkers in nonsheltered vocational environments. If the only supervision available is external in nature, many logistical and economic strains are placed upon adult service agencies. Nonsheltered vocational environments, however, often offer reasonable probabilities that, after acclimation and training, nonhandicapped workers will assume individually appropriate and significant supervisory responsibilities. Karen was trained to perform meaningful work in a cancer research laboratory by public school teachers as a part of her educational program. During her final two school years she attended high school in the mornings and worked at the laboratory for $2.00 per hour for a total of 10 hours per week in the afternoons. Almost all supervision was provided by the nonhandicapped workers who also worked in the laboratory. External supervision was offered only as needed.

Access to Health Services Can Be Available, If Necessary

Some severely handicapped students function in continuous states of biological distress. Brittle bones, seizures, and chronic infections are but a few examples. For these individuals, nonsheltered environments must be relatively safe, contain large numbers of reasonably informed and healthy nonhandicapped persons, and have reasonable temporal and geographic access to appropriate health facilities and personnel. David, 24 years old, has a long history of severe and frequent grand mal seizures. Thus, his teachers prepared him to work in the central supply department of a local hospital, where he is always in the presence of many nonhandicapped workers and has immediate access to health facilities and personnel. He has had several major seizures and his nonhandicapped coworkers have become both accustomed to and adept at dealing with them constructively.

The Social Climate Is More Conducive to Success and Personal Growth

However difficult to define, one of the most important attributes of a nonsheltered voca-

tional environment for a severely handicapped person is its social climate. It is extremely important that severely handicapped persons have opportunities to develop friendships with others who have handicapped conditions *as well as with those who do not.* In addition, it is very important that they be surrounded by coworkers who model appropriate social and work behaviors, who can provide common sense intervention and assistance when difficulties arise, and who can provide protection in cases of actual or potential harm. These conditions, while not feasible in sheltered environments, are typical in most nonsheltered environments.

FIVE RELATIONSHIPS BETWEEN MEANINGFUL WORK AND PAY

Perhaps in the near future, most severely handicapped persons will perform meaningful work in nonsheltered environments for 40 hours per week and will receive payment that is substantially above the minimum wage. Unfortunately, at this time, such circumstances seem relatively rare. Nevertheless, economically and ideologically feasible strategies to provide reasonable recompense for meaningful work must be designed and implemented. Five types of relationships between meaningful work and direct and indirect pay are outlined in Table 5.4. Each will be discussed briefly. *Direct pay* refers to the contingent receipt of money for the performance of meaningful work. *Indirect pay* refers to the noncontingent relationship between the receipt of tax dollars in the form of disability benefits and the performance of meaningful work.

Type A refers to the conditions under which a severely handicapped student performs meaningful work, but does not receive pay because the person is in a training program. For example, it was arranged that two severely handicapped students would be taught to perform meaningful work such as unpackaging supplies, cleaning plumbing materials, and cleaning up around the shop and storage room at the Blied Plumbing Company of Madison, Wisconsin. If the owner had been asked at

TABLE 5.4. FIVE RELATIONSHIPS BETWEEN MEANINGFUL
WORK AND DIRECT AND INDIRECT PAY

Type of Relationship	Reason	Nonsheltered Environment
A — No Pay	Training	Blied Plumbing Co.
B — Subminimum Wage	Substandard Performance	McArdle Cancer Research Laboratory
C — Typical Wage	Standard Performance	Washington Host Restaurant
D — Indirect Pay (Noncontingent Disability Benefits)	Substandard Performance	Madison General Hospital — Pharmacy
E — Direct Pay *and* Indirect Pay	To Avoid Benefit Loss and/or a Sheltered Environment	University of Wisconsin Hospital and Clinics (direct pay) and Forest Products Research Laboratory (indirect pay)

the onset to pay these untrained students, he would not have agreed to the arrangement. In an effort to initiate a relationship, it was agreed that school personnel would teach the performance of meaningful work at no cost to the company in exchange for the use of the nonsheltered training environment. Obviously, the company realizes economic gains in that if the students did not perform the work, nonhandicapped persons would be paid to do so.

Type B refers to the conditions under which a severely handicapped person performs meaningful work and is paid a subminimum wage. The reason for a subminimum wage is the level of competence manifested, that is, a student is unable to perform work skills in accordance with the minimal standards expected of a minimum wage employee. Karen works at the McArdle Cancer Research Laboratory on the campus of the University of Wisconsin for 10 hours per week at $2.00 per hour. Most of the work she performs consists of sterilizing and putting away laboratory glassware. If she could perform these skills in accordance with the quantity and quality standards expected of nondisabled workers, she would be paid a minimum wage. Until she can, based on her present level of production, it has been determined by those directly involved and approved by the Wisconsin Department of Industry, Labor, and Human Relations that $2.00 per hour is fair remuneration.

Type C refers to the conditions under which a severely handicapped person performs mean-

ingful work for the same wages as nondisabled workers. Clearly, many severely handicapped individuals are able to perform in accordance with the standards expected of nondisabled workers who perform the same functions. Jim works as a busperson for $2\frac{1}{2}$ hours per day at the Washington Host Restaurant and receives $3.35 per hour, plus 10% of the tips the waiters and waitresses receive that utilize his busing services. This is the same arrangement available to nondisabled buspersons in this restaurant.

Type D refers to the conditions under which a severely handicapped person performs meaningful work but receives only indirect payment such as Supplemental Security Income benefits. The basic reason is that while a worker is not sufficiently competent to be paid directly by an employer, she is receiving medical insurance, general living allowances, and other tangible economic benefits because she is disabled. Rather than describing such work as "volunteering" or as a "day program," it seems more accurate and enhancing to refer to it as meaningful work in exchange for the disability benefits received from taxpayers, even though the benefits are not contingently related. Donna is 24 years old, has autism, and is severely intellectually handicapped. She works in the pharmacy of Madison General Hospital where she unpackages supplies and labels and sorts a variety of pharmaceuticals. If she did not perform this work, nondisabled workers would be paid to do so. Donna, however, requires continuous external supervision and cannot perform at criteria that would allow hospital officials to pay her directly. She could stay at home or function in a much more costly and restrictive sheltered environment and essentially do nothing for the benefits she receives from taxpayers. However, performing meaningful work in a hospital is a more productive, cost efficient, and personally satisfying option.

Type E refers to the conditions under which a severely handicapped person receives direct payment for meaningful work performed in one environment and indirect payment for meaningful work performed in another, during the same work day or week. There are basically two reasons for this relationship. First, there are those who can earn enough money to disqualify them for disability benefits but not enough money to cover all of their daily living needs and medical expenses. Rather than disqualifying them from these needed benefits, refusing them work at all, or forcing them to work in an unnecessarily restrictive sheltered environment, a reasonable alternative seems to be that of arranging part time work for direct payment and part time work for indirect payment. Second, some persons can perform meaningful work in nonsheltered environments but are either not needed 8 hours per day or have difficulty functioning effectively in one place for more than 3 or 4 hours. By arranging for them to work half a day in one place for direct pay and the other half in another place for indirect pay, placement in a sheltered workshop can be avoided.

Certainly, these work–pay relationships are not the only possibilities. No doubt, as knowledge and experience accrue and as disability benefit eligibility criteria evolve, more varied and innovative relationships will be realized. Additionally, however distasteful, it must be acknowledged that severely handicapped persons work for many reasons but money is typically not one of them. If at all possible, quality of life must transcend money. Many of us will agree to earn less if we like our job, the place in which we work, the people with whom we work, and if we sense that what we do is appreciated. Further, exploitation refers to tak-

ing something and giving little, if anything, in return. Most taxpayers will better understand both the need for and the spirit of disability payments if they sense that the recipients are at least trying to give something in return.

Finally, given the present state of the American economy (i.e., economic recession and high unemployment) and the strength of organized labor, it is often asked, how can it be expected that severely handicapped adults be employed in nonsheltered environments. The response offered here is twofold. First, the jobs that the majority of severely handicapped persons can be taught to perform are primarily nonunion, low wage, and part time in nature. Most severely handicapped persons receive economic subsidies in the form of medical insurance and food, shelter, and clothing allowances that are not available to nonhandicapped persons; therefore, they can afford to work in such jobs over long periods of time. Consequently, while many of these jobs are not financially viable for nonhandicapped persons, they offer meaningful and enhancing employment opportunities for severely handicapped workers. Second, since it is extremely doubtful at this time that many severely handicapped adults can secure high paying and high status union jobs, it seems reasonable to arrange for severely handicapped persons to function in environments in which organized labor will interfere minimally, if at all. Small family businesses such as restaurants and independent groceries, and small franchises such as pizza stores and motels are but a few examples of workplaces that may not have unions or that have unions which might not impede the vocational functioning of severely handicapped persons.

THE RELATIVE COST OF SHELTERED AND NONSHELTERED VOCATIONAL ENVIRONMENTS

The notion that everyone should contribute to the enterprise of the nation is a cultural expectation clearly imbedded in the fabric of American society. Indeed, the person who does not work, is on welfare, is in need of extended unemployment compensation, or does not visibly contribute in some way, is not nearly as valued, as respected, as absorbed as those who do. Americans have been remarkably understanding of the need to expend tax dollars in ways that support the realization of the dream that as many as possible contribute to the enterprise of our country. If those who work, produce, contribute, and pay taxes are valued and respected, and those who do not are not, how do severely handicapped adults fare? Generally, not well. Most would agree that if a severely handicapped person absolutely cannot contribute to the enterprise of a community, so be it. Still, our obligation is to provide a decent and humane quality of life. However, the preferred cultural option is to contribute.

What would happen if, as a nation, we chose not to assume financial or programmatic responsibilities for severely disabled adults? While a few parents would have both the inclination and the financial resources to pay others directly to provide services to their children, the overwhelming majority could not afford to hire others to meet comprehensive direct service needs, and could not stay at home for financial, cultural, or personal reasons.

Fortunately, over the past few decades, taxpayers have assumed more of the responsibility for providing a variety of direct services to severely handicapped persons, and providing no public services to severely handicapped adults is not an option. However, taxpayers do have a right to require services that are fair and reasonable for all concerned. The position offered here is that when the vocational habilitation of severely handicapped adults is addressed, the most cost efficient and the highest quality services can be provided in nonsheltered as opposed to sheltered environments.

In sum, for severely handicapped adults to have no option but to stay at home with their parents is untenable; to place such persons in institutions is dangerous, antihabilitative, and ridiculously costly; and to utilize sheltered workshops and activity centers is developmentally unsound, unnecessary, and too cost inefficient. Preparing for work in nonsheltered vocational environments requires less money, makes better use of the money expended, and allows for a more reasonable quality of life. If the statements just delineated can be ascribed even minimal credence, at least the following must be demonstrated:

- That it is *less costly* for severely handicapped adults to work in nonsheltered as opposed to sheltered environments;
- That taxpayers realize a *greater return for their investment* when severely handicapped adults perform meaningful work in nonsheltered environments; and
- That the *quality of life* for all concerned is better when functioning in nonsheltered environments is realized.

Cost

The cost per person in most sheltered vocational environments has been reported to range from $3738 to over $5000 per year (Hill & Wehman, 1983; Sowers et al., 1979). At this time, it is difficult to compare the costs of providing vocational services to severely handicapped adults in sheltered as opposed to nonsheltered environments because of the unavailability of data on precisely matched groups. However, there are rudimentary data that can be reasonably interpreted as suggestive that significant savings can be realized when severely handicapped persons are prepared to function in nonsheltered environments.

As of January 1983, the average cost to the Dane County Unified Services Board of maintaining a severely handicapped graduate of the Madison Metropolitan School District in a sheltered environment in Madison, Wisconsin, was approximately $5251 per year. The average cost of maintaining a graduate in a nonsheltered environment was approximately $1681 per year (F. Genter, Personal Communication, September 7, 1983). However, those who functioned in sheltered and nonsheltered environments spent an average of 6.0 and 4.4 hours per day in their work places respectively (Shiraga, 1983). If adjusted for this difference in time, the annual cost per person to the Dane County Unified Services Board for non-sheltered functioning would be $2303.

Upon examination of this information two questions seem obvious. First, why is it so costly to maintain one severely handicapped adult in a sheltered environment? Sheltered environments costs also bear the financial responsibility for group transportation to and from the facility, heat, the purchase of supplies and materials, the salaries of clerical personnel, insurance, and equipment (U.S. Department of Labor, 1977). In nonsheltered environments, those responsible for training and supervision are not paying for light, equipment, supplies, heat, rent, and so forth, at the work place. Almost all of the $1681 per year is devoted to the salary and fringe benefits of the direct supervisor, a relatively small amount of overhead, and in some cases transportation to and from work.

Second, are those in sheltered environments less intellectually, and/or physically, capable than those who function in nonsheltered environments? While precisely controlled studies are not available, the follow-up studies of the severely handicapped graduates of the Madison Metropolitan School District conducted by VanDeventer et al. (1981) and Shiraga (1983) indicate a negative answer. In fact, when the 49 graduates in the 1981 follow-up study who worked in sheltered environments were compared with the 36 graduates in the 1983 follow-up study who worked in nonsheltered environments, *more of the graduates in nonsheltered environments* were nonverbal, nonambulatory, visually or auditorily impaired, deaf, blind, cerebral palsied, and were referred to as within the severe as opposed to the moderate range of mental retardation.

It should be noted and emphasized that without a longitudinal public school training program oriented toward functioning in nonsheltered environments, it is extremely doubtful that these cost figures would hold across settings. That is, if a severely handicapped person spent the first 20 years of her life on a ward of the local institution and, upon reaching age 21, an adult service agency was asked to teach all the work and work related skills necessary for functioning in a nonsheltered environment, increases in the amount of training time and money needed would be mandatory. This does not mean that sheltered vocational environments should then be considered acceptable options for such persons. Given adequate training and supervision, the costs necessary to train and maintain them in nonsheltered environments should progressively decrease until they approximate the annual costs of persons who had access to nonsheltered vocational training from an early age.

Cost Efficiency

Cost efficiency refers to the returns, economic and otherwise, realized from a financial investment. Cost efficiency can be determined by evaluating the relative cost of programmatic outcomes or by considering the relative productivity of individuals. Preparing for work in nonsheltered environments offers a greater return on invested tax dollars than training for work in sheltered environments for at least two reasons. First, given the relatively high annual cost of operating sheltered vocational programs and the few severely handicapped persons who progress to more productive environments (U.S. Department of Labor, 1977, 1979; Whitehead, 1979b), these high costs must be viewed as life long. Second, severely handicapped adults in sheltered work environments often spend substantial proportions of time performing nonmeaningful work (Greenleigh Associates, Inc., 1975). The cost of producing this nonmeaningful work is substantial in that supervisors still have to be paid, transportation and overhead costs still have to be met, and so forth. Severely handicapped persons in nonsheltered vocational environments rarely, if ever, perform nonmeaningful work.

When analyzing the actual and projected costs and benefits of nonsheltered versus sheltered vocational programs, Schneider, Rusch, Henderson, and Geske (1981) found that at the end of the 10th year, an individual in nonsheltered employment could be expected to have earned $16,153 more than the cumulative cost of training, placement, and follow-up services. If that same individual had been employed in a typical sheltered setting, the earnings would never exceed the training costs, and the cumulative cost over 10 years would be $50,276. Likewise, Hill and Wehman (1983) analyzed the costs incurred and the tax monies saved through the implementation of a nonsheltered job training and placement program for 90 moderately and severely handicapped workers and found that, over a 4 year period, the total direct financial benefit to taxpayers was $90,376.

Before leaving the topic of cost efficiency, it should be noted parenthetically that public schools have a responsibility to produce severely handicapped graduates who contribute to the enterprise of a community. Assume that the costs of progressing through two public school systems are approximately the same. Assume further that the graduates of School System *A* function in nonsheltered vocational environments at the average maintenance cost of $2000 per year per person; that the graduates of School System *B* function in sheltered vocational environments at the average maintenance cost of $5000 per year per person; and that productivity and earned income were constant across graduates. As the costs of training and dollars earned were approximately the same, but the costs of maintenance in adulthood were substantially higher for graduates of School System *B*, School System *A* is more cost efficient than School System *B* on the dimensions addressed.

Quality of Life

The phrase *quality of life* refers to the nature of the social and emotional characteristics of sheltered and nonsheltered vocational environments. The quality of life possible in an environment limited to those handicapped is substantially different from that which can be realized in an environment that is in accordance with the natural proportion. Van-Deventer et al. (1981) interpreted their data as suggestive that the graduates of the Madison Metropolitan School District who functioned in sheltered vocational environments led unduly restrictive lives. That is, they interacted with too few nondisabled people, the number of environments in which they functioned per week was depressingly small, and the skills they were required to perform or to learn were remarkably few.

The situation for graduates who functioned in nonsheltered vocational environments was quite different (Shiraga, 1983). Specifically, they functioned in substantially more environments per week, they interacted consistently and intensively with a much wider variety of nondisabled persons; and they were required to learn and perform substantially more skills per day. Additionally, the social environments available in most nonsheltered vocational environments are more enhancing than those available in sheltered environments. Assume that a person has autism and severe difficulties refraining from overt and disruptive self-stimulation, communicating meaningfully, and establishing social and emotional relationships with others. Should she spend 40 hours per week with other autistic and severely handicapped persons with similar difficulties or with a wide variety of nondisabled persons? Clearly, her life will be more rich and varied if she functions in the presence of many nondisabled persons.

In sum, severely handicapped adults who work in nonsheltered environments have a greater probability of experiencing a more enhanced quality of life than their developmental twins in sheltered environments in that there are experiences that can be realized in nonsheltered environments that cannot be realized in sheltered environments. Some of these include:

- Interactions with nondisabled persons;
- The rich array of sounds and sights offered in the real world;
- Friendships with nondisabled persons that extend beyond the work time and space;
- Feelings of self-worth when a severely disabled person understands that his work is valuable and that if he did not do it, nondisabled persons would have to;

- The respect offered by parents/guardians and nondisabled coworkers when one makes a contribution in a nonsheltered environment;
- The sense of accomplishment associated with being allowed to take calculated risks and overcome initial obstacles and failure; and
- The pride that comes from being in a position to help nondisabled persons.

AT WHAT AGE SHOULD DIRECT INSTRUCTION IN NONSHELTERED VOCATIONAL ENVIRONMENTS BEGIN?

Indirect vocational instruction refers to teaching those skills and attitudes not actually required in a real work environment; or teaching skills and attitudes that are required, but teaching them in some place other than a real work environment. Most would agree that indirect vocational instruction should start shortly after birth. That is, from an early age all children should be taught to complete tasks, to seek pride in what they do, to assume responsibility for the results of their actions, to overcome obstacles in order to reach goals, to cooperate with others, and that to struggle to achieve is an honored cultural endeavor. It is generally presumed that these cherished general skills and attitudes can be converted readily to the specifics needed for success in actual vocational environments. Unfortunately, this presumption of transferability is untenable when severely handicapped students are of concern.

Direct vocational instruction refers to teaching the actual skills and attitudes needed to function in a particular nonsheltered vocational environment in that actual environment. The direct vocational instruction of severely handicapped students should begin, unless medically contraindicated, no later than age 11 for at least the following reasons.

First, people are labeled *severely intellectually handicapped* because of such learning and performance difficulties as the length of time and relatively large number of instructional trials needed to bring them to a meaningful level of performance, severe problems retaining learn-

ing, and severe difficulties transferring training from one person, environment, material, or language cue to another (Brown et al., 1983).

Second, few adult vocational service systems for severely handicapped adults are sufficiently instructional in nature (Gold, 1973; Nisbet, 1983; VanDeventer et al., 1981; Whitehead, 1979b). Thus, if a severely handicapped adult is to acquire the skills and attitudes needed for nonsheltered functioning, it is extremely important that those skills and attitudes be acquired prior to graduation.

Third, most severely handicapped adults who fail to survive in nonsheltered vocational environments do so because of attitudinal and social problems, not because they lack specific vocational skills (Gold, 1973; Greenspan, & Shoultz, 1981; Martin et al., 1979; Rusch et al., 1980; Sowers et al., 1979; Wehman, 1981). Many years and experiences are needed to develop these extremely important attitudes and social behaviors. Obviously, it is much easier to develop positive work attitudes in young children than to change the negative attitudes of adults.

Obviously, individual decisions about the instructional needs of each student must be made. However, several general rules seem tenable.

- Direct vocational instruction should start no later than age 11;
- At least a half-day, or 3 hours, per week should be spent receiving instruction in actual vocational environments by age 11;
- The amount of time spent in actual vocational environments should increase with age;
- No student should spend more than 2 years in a particular work environment prior to graduation;
- Over a 10 year period, each student should be given intensive, individualized, and sustained instruction in *at least* five different nonsheltered work environments and *at least* four different types of meaningful work; e.g., food service, clerical, janitorial, and industrial;

- At about age 17 or 18, those responsible for the development of an individual should start making tangible projections and decisions about the actual jobs that the individual can hold at graduation; and
- From approximately ages 19–21, a comprehensive school to postschool transition plan should be designed and implemented. (Brown et al., 1981)

CHARACTERISTICS OF THE NONSHELTERED VOCATIONAL PREPARATION PROGRAM OFFERED BY THE MADISON METROPOLITAN SCHOOL DISTRICT

The vocational preparation program operated by the Madison Metropolitan School District is enormously diverse, complex, and dependent upon a wide variety of idiophenomena. Nevertheless, from 1969–1983, this program seemed to pass through at least four major, discernible phases. We say *seemed* because these phases overlap, are cumulative in nature, and exceptions can certainly be cited.

Phase I

During the late 1960s and early 1970s, the school district and associated University of Wisconsin personnel assumed that severely handicapped students could not or would not function in nonsheltered vocational environments and arranged its services accordingly. The result was quite predictable: almost all graduates lacked the skills and attitudes necessary for nonsheltered functioning. Specifically, from 1971–1978, 53 severely handicapped students completed their public education in the Madison Metropolitan School District. According to VanDeventer et al. (1981), only 1 graduate worked in a nonsheltered vocational environment, as a part-time dishwasher in a luncheonette; 3 graduates spent almost their entire lives at home with their parents; and the remaining 49 graduates spent their days in activity centers or sheltered workshops (see Table 5.1). Additionally, almost all were labeled *high functioning trainable level retarded* as, during much of this time, most students with more severe disabilities were excluded or rejected from the school system.

Phase II

II-A

Several parents, who in the early 1970s were very happy to have a public school system that served their children, became relatively disenchanted with the services then offered. That is, after observing the development of their children for 5, 6, or 7 years, they started to ask such questions as, Is this the best that can be done? Are we teaching the things that really need to be learned? and Where does this all lead? The typical responses to such appropriate and penetrating questions were that sheltered vocational environments were the only or the best environments available upon graduation and, thus, school personnel should attempt to teach the skills and attitudes needed to succeed in those environments. Stated another way, Why should school personnel spend valuable instructional resources teaching the skills and attitudes required for nonsheltered functioning when it is known that after graduation their students will be confined to sheltered vocational environments?

II-B

While school personnel maintained the concepts described in Phase II-A, those providing services to severely disabled adults utilized a slightly different conceptual system. Parents of severely disabled adults started to ask adult service providers why their children could not work in nonsheltered environments. The parents were told, The public school system has not taught your child the skills and attitudes necessary to function efficiently in nonsheltered environments, It is too late now, and Even if we wanted to, we do not have the staff or the resources to provide the instruction and supervision necessary for training, placement, and maintenance in a nonsheltered environment.

Phase III

About 1976, more and more parents and professionals began to study, understand, and scrutinize the self-fulfilling prophecy, the circular reasoning, and the negative tracking that was so powerfully controlling almost everyone at the time.

III-A

A small number of public school and university personnel started hypothesizing that even though it was highly likely that these students would ultimately function in sheltered workshops or activity centers, they should at least be given a chance to demonstrate that they could actually perform in nonsheltered environments. Accordingly, components of the curriculum and mode of service delivery were modified to provide limited, but nevertheless significant, direct and systematic instruction in nonschool settings, including nonsheltered vocational environments.

III-B

While public school personnel were teaching a small number of students to function in nonsheltered vocational environments as a component of their public school programs, some adult service agency personnel and parents started to arrange for a few disabled adults to learn how to work in nonsheltered environments.

Phase IV

During Phases I, II, and III there was little, if any, communication between parents of severely handicapped students and parents of severely handicapped adults or between public school personnel and those who would provide direct services upon graduation. In 1980, public school personnel established cooperative working relationships with Vocational Education Alternatives, Inc., an agency that provided nonsheltered services to a wide variety of disabled adults in the Madison area. At this writing, approximately 20% of those served by this agency are severely handicapped. Thus, for the first time, a mechanism for coordinating school and postschool training and monitoring functions was established. This cooperative relationship between sending and receiving agencies and parents has played a significant role in the rather dramatic shift from sheltered to nonsheltered functioning. When the 50 severely handicapped students of Madison and Dane County who graduated from 1979–1983 were studied, 36 worked in nonsheltered environments, 10 worked in sheltered environments, and 4 remained at home (see Table 5.2; Shiraga, 1983).

SERVICE DELIVERY MODEL

In an effort to communicate how one school system attempts to provide reasonable vocational instruction to its severely handicapped students, some of the rudiments of the service delivery model utilized by the Madison Metropolitan School District will be delineated. Before proceeding, the following should be noted:

• Some teachers, therapists, and others in the school district actually utilize the model as described and some others do not;
• The model is designed so that teachers in concert with related service personnel, individual students, and their parents can adapt to constantly changing circumstances; and
• Some related service personnel such as physical, occupational, and instructional aides, and communication therapists provide direct and consulting services in actual vocational environments.

Perhaps the most parsimonious strategy for communicating some of the more important components of the model would be to present operational information about the vocational-community teachers in the middle and high schools, the school to postschool transition teacher, and the instructional personnel inventory strategy.

Vocational-Community Teachers

Vocational-community teachers in the Madison Metropolitan School District provide little if any direct instruction on school grounds. Rather, almost all of their instruction takes place in a work setting and within the community. For example, if three severely handicapped students are to be taught by a vocational-community teacher on Monday morning, she might meet them at school, then teach them to take a public bus to a hospital where she would provide instruction on vocational skills in the pharmacy until approximately 11:00 A.M. At 11:00 A.M., they might take another public bus to a shopping center where she would teach the skills needed to have lunch in a restaurant before returning to school at 12:30 P.M. In order that students receive appropriately comprehensive amounts of nonschool instruction, many classroom teachers, in addition to vocational-community teachers, provide direct instruction in nonschool environments.

During the 1983–1984 school year, the school district employed 6.2 vocational-community teachers, who were administratively assigned to a special education coordinator at the central administration building. They were then allocated to instructional teams at different middle and high schools.

Vocational-Community Teachers in Middle Schools

Middle schools serve severely handicapped students who are 11–15 years old. At the middle school level, direct nonschool instruction in nonsheltered vocational environments is provided at least a half day per week, starting at age 11 or 12. As a student progresses to ages 13 and 14, the instruction expands to at least 2 half-days per week.

Figure 5.2 shows how vocational-community teachers were distributed among three middle schools during the 1983–1984 school year. At Schenk Middle School, there were two classes of 8 and 6 severely handicapped students, respectively, taught by a .7 time vocational-community teacher; a similar situation existed at Jefferson Middle School. At Gompers Middle School, an .8 time vocational-community teacher taught 19 severely handicapped students in three classes.

Vocational-Community Teachers in High Schools

High schools serve severely handicapped students who are 15–21 years old. At the high school level, an increase is provided in the amount of direct vocational instruction in nonsheltered environments per student. In fact, as

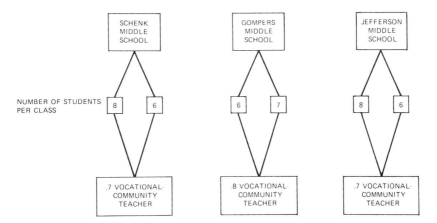

Figure 5.2. Vocational–Community teachers in middle schools in the Madison Metropolitan School District during the 1983–1984 school year.

chronological age increases, up to 100% of a student's school schedule may be devoted to direct nonsheltered vocational and community related instruction. Obviously, it is crucial to have the resources needed to provide increasing amounts of instruction.

Figure 5.3 shows how vocational-community teachers were allocated among three high schools during the 1983–1984 school year. Three high schools had enrollments of 38, 38, and 37 severely handicapped students, and one full-time vocational-community teacher was assigned to each school. Twenty-two of the 38 students at East High School, 19 of the 38 students at LaFollette High School, and 17 of the 37 students at Memorial High School were residents of the Central Wisconsin Center for the Developmentally Disabled. These were 58 of the approximately 100 nonresidents of Madison or Dane County who lived at the institution and attended school in Madison under a federal court order during the 1983–1984 school year.

The School to Postschool Transition Teacher

The city of Madison in Dane County, Wisconsin, claims a total population of approximately 170,000 and a gradually declining school age population of approximately 23,000. Of the Dane County residents who graduate from the Madison Metropolitan School District,

approximately 10–12 each year are severely handicapped.

In the past, there was very little meaningful communication between public school and adult service personnel. In fact, when parents asked school personnel what would happen to their children after graduation from public school, they were usually referred to other agencies. Such a situation worked quite well for some parents because they had the time, tenacity, skills, and the kinds of children for whom extant adult service systems were designed. However, most parents could not arrange for individually habilitative adult vocational services. Consequently, their children stayed at home or spent their days underachieving in sheltered workshops and activity centers. Spending 21 years of public education attempting to prepare a severely handicapped student to function in heterogeneous vocational, domestic, recreation/leisure, and general community environments is untenable, unless systematic arrangements are made to maximize the probability of actual functioning in those environments upon graduation.

In an attempt to enhance the probability of using the skills and attitudes developed during years of public instruction for severely handicapped students, the transition plan was developed, using a school to postschool transition teacher. The transition plan is described more precisely elsewhere (Brown et al., 1981; Nisbet et al., 1983). In brief, such a plan has six

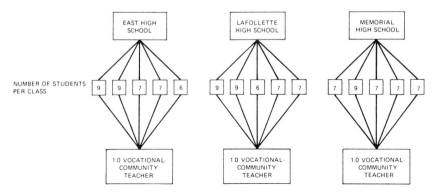

Figure 5.3. Vocational–Community teachers in high schools in the Madison Metropolitan School District during the 1983–1984 school year.

major characteristics: it must be *individualized; longitudinal; comprehensive; sending and receiving agencies and personnel must be involved; parents and guardians must be active participants;* and *related service personnel should offer functional expertise.*

It is the responsibility of the school to post-school transition teacher to coordinate the design and implementation of school to post-school transition plans for each severely handicapped Dane County resident graduating from the Madison Metropolitan School District. In addition to providing direct instruction in conjunction with a variety of other school personnel in nonschool environments, the transition teacher coordinates monthly meetings with all middle and high school vocational-community teachers and coordinates many of the efforts of teachers, parents, therapists, and the adult service agencies that will receive the student in the near future. One full time school to postschool transition teacher is assigned to the three to five annual graduates of each of three high schools. As nonsheltered environments are those that do not violate the natural proportion, the number of new nonsheltered vocational environments that need to be developed each year ranges from approximately six to ten. Undoubtedly, the activities of the transition teacher in conjunction with parents/guardians, the Dane County Unified Services Board, and local adult vocational agencies that offer nonsheltered services have resulted in the dramatic and durable increases in the nonsheltered vocational placement, training, and maintenance of severely handicapped graduates.

Instructional Personnel Inventory Strategy

Obviously, the traditional instructional model of a classroom teacher and an aide assigned to 8–10 severely handicapped students is insufficient to provide the critically needed low ratio, direct, and individualized instruction in nonsheltered settings. It is equally obvious that there may not be large infusions of new funds for such programs in most school districts. Thus, school districts will have to redirect

	\multicolumn{5}{c}{Days}				
	M	T	W	Th	F
A.M.	T ST A	T A PT ST	T ST A	T ST A SL	T ST VC A
P.M.	T A	T A VC SL	T A	T A	T A PT	T A VC

Figure 5.4. Instructional personnel assigned to a class of 10 severely handicapped students. (Code: T = Teacher; A = Aide; VC = Vocational–Community teacher; SL = Speech and language therapist; PT = Physical therapist; ST = Student teacher.)

resources and existing personnel to provide modified services in different places. Figure 5.4 suggests one strategy that can be used to organize instructional personnel for reasonable amounts of nonschool instruction. As can be discerned from Figure 5.4, on Monday afternoon only a teacher and an instructional aide are assigned to the class of 10 severely handicapped students. It is probably inappropriate to attempt to provide nonschool vocational instruction during this time for a variety of obvious reasons. On Tuesday afternoon, however, a teacher, an instructional aide, a vocational-community teacher, and a speech and language therapist are assigned to the 10 students. Obviously, this is a time when nonschool instruction could be provided quite efficiently.

Nonschool and Nonsheltered Vocational Training Environments

During and prior to the 1974–1975 school year, the Madison Metropolitan School District operated a public school program for severely handicapped students that was clearly designed to prepare for functioning only in sheltered environments. The only vocational training experiences provided were offered in simulated sheltered workshops on the grounds of segregated schools. During the 1975–1976 school year, it was decided by some that nonsheltered environments should be utilized for at least the highest functioning students. Thus, one responsibility of school personnel became locating and developing nonschool, nonsheltered vocational environments that could be used for training purposes (Sweet et al., 1982). During 1975–1976, of course, there were few such environments. However, because of the success of this change in direction and the corresponding strong support from parents, school personnel, and the Madison business community, the number of nonsheltered environments and the number of severely handicapped students who received training in these environments increased substantially over time. More specifically, during the 1975–1976 school year, 17 severely handicapped students received instruction in 4 nonsheltered environments (Pumpian et al., 1980). During the 1982–1983 school year, 143 severely handicapped students received instruction in 58 nonsheltered environments. Table 5.5 presents basic information about the actual places used for training during the 1982–1983 school year.

CHARACTERISTICS AND EXAMPLES OF NONSHELTERED VOCATIONAL SERVICE DELIVERY MODELS FOR SEVERELY HANDICAPPED ADULTS

Of the many reasons for severely handicapped adults to work in sheltered environments, three seem particularly relevant here. First, the necessary attitudes and skills for nonsheltered functioning may not have been developed during their first 21 years because of less than acceptable preparatory experiences. Second, service delivery systems are not ideologically, conceptually, financially, or technologically engineered to foster nonsheltered functioning over long periods of time. Indeed, when one communicates with a typical vocational rehabilitation counselor about arranging for a severely handicapped adult to work in a non-

sheltered environment, one is almost always informed of a caseload so large that all that can be offered is extended sheltered maintenance and supervision. Third, most service delivery models that arrange for disabled adults to work in nonsheltered environments utilize the four step strategy of assessment, episodic training, placement, and closure. That is, the general functioning of the client is assessed. As a result of the assessment, the client is provided with short term training. At the completion of training, the client is placed in a nonsheltered work environment, followed for a brief period of time, and then the case is closed (Horner & Bellamy, 1979). This is a particularly inappropriate strategy for use with severely handicapped adults because, throughout their lives, they will need training and supervision in order to function efficiently in nonsheltered environments. Closure is rarely, if ever, appropriate.

If the severely handicapped adults of the future are to work productively in nonsheltered environments, an overwhelming majority of the service delivery systems currently operative will have to be modified substantially or discarded. Vocational service delivery models will need to feature the following characteristics, at least.

They Must Be Instructional in Nature

There can be no doubt that severely handicapped adults need direct and continuous instruction by skilled and inclined personnel throughout their working lives. Service delivery models that offer individually meaningful assessment, placement, and continuous training and monitoring are mandatory.

They Must Have a Low Ratio of Handicapped Persons to Instructors

Those responsible for the direct training and supervision of individual severely handicapped adults in nonsheltered environments should

TABLE 5.5 NONSCHOOL AND NONSHELTERED VOCATIONAL TRAINING ENVIRONMENTS UTILIZED BY SEVERELY HANDICAPPED STUDENTS IN THE MADISON METROPOLITAN SCHOOL DISTRICT DURING THE 1982–1983 SCHOOL YEAR

Environment	Type of Work	Days and Times	Approximate # of Nonhandicapped Persons	# of Students	Chronological Age
Bittersweet Restaurant	Janitorial	Wed. 9:00–10:30	9	2	14,15
Chez Michal Restaurant	Food preparation	Wed. 8:15–10:45	11	3	13,13,13
Ivy Inn Hotel	Housekeeping	Thurs. 9:30–11:00	35	2	13,15
Ovens of Brittany Restaurant	Food preparation	Thurs. 9:00–10:45	45	2	11,13
Concordance Natural Food Store	Packaging, weighing, pricing, and stocking grocery items	Thurs. 9:00–10:45	45	2	12,15
L'Escargot Restaurant Office	Clerical	Wed. 1:00–2:30	10	2	14,15
University of Wis. Student Union	Clerical	Thurs. 1:00–2:30	115	2	15,15
University of Wis. Student Union	Busing and setting tables, and re-filling condiment containers	Tues. 9:30–11:00	120	3	11,13,14
Hill Farms State Office Building	Clerical	Fri. 1:00–2:30	35	3	13,13,13
Madison Public Library Meadowridge Branch	Stamping and repairing books and straightening shelves	Fri. 1:00–2:30	30	3	12,13,13
Wilson State Office Building	Clerical	Fri. 1:00–2:30	32	3	13,14,15
Moravian Church	Janitorial	Mon. 9:00–10:30	3	2	13,13
Mother's Pub Restaurant	Janitorial	Fri. 9:30–11:00	6	2	14,14
Washington Hotel	Janitorial	Tues. 12:15–2:15	9	2	13,13
The Headstart Center	Clerical and food preparation	Weds. 12:30–2:00	10	2	13,15
Madison Public Library Lakeview Branch	Clerical	Tues. 9:00–10:30	15	2	14,14
Chet's Standard Station	Janitorial	Tues. 8:30–11:30	30	2	13,15
Wis. School of Electronics	Clerical and assembly	Mon. 12:15–2:15	85	4	14,14,15,15
The Moose Lodge	Janitorial and dishwashing	Mon. 8:30–11:30	9	3	11,13,15
The Moose Lodge	Janitorial and dishwashing	Thurs. 8:30–11:30	9	3	11,13,14
The Family Practice Clinic	Clerical and janitorial	Mon., Thurs. 12:45–3:15	55	2	15,15
St. Mary's Hospital	Clerical	Tues., Thurs. 9:15–11:30	75	3	15,16,19
American Red Cross	Clerical	Mon., Weds. 12:30–2:15	14	3	15,16,17
Lake Edge Lutheran Church	Clerical	Fri. 9:45–11:30	15	3	17,18,18
Madison Public Library Downtown Branch	Clerical and book repair	Mon. 12:45–2:00	45	4	15,16,17,20

continued

TABLE 5.5. continued

Environment	Type of Work	Days and Times	Approximate # of Nonhandicapped Persons	# of Students	Chronological Age
The Jackson Medical Clinic	Operating photocopy machinery	Tues. 12:45–2:00	15	2	17,19
Dane County Social Services Administration Building	Clerical	Tues. 12:45–2:00	24	2	17,20
Wis. Woman's Network	Clerical	Fri. 12:45–2:00	12	4	16,18,18,20
St. Mathew's Daycare Center	Janitorial	Tues., Thurs. 12:45–3:00	6	2	16,20
Dane County Parks Department	Janitorial and grounds maintenance	Weds., Fri.	12	3	15,16,19
University of Wis. Physics Department	Disassembling and salvaging of computer hardware	Mon., Weds. 8:30–11:00	10	4	18,18,20,20
Special Olympics Office	Clerical and assembly	Weds. 12:45–2:00	12	2	17,18
Special Olympics Office	Clerical and assembly	Thurs. 12:45–2:00	12	3	17,18,19
Blied Plumbing Co.	Janitorial, sorting plumbing supplies and salvaging parts for recycling	Mon., Tues. 9:30–11:15	4	3	18,18,20
East Side Businessman's Association Social Club	Janitorial and grounds maintenance	Mon., Weds. 9:45–11:00	1	4	18,18,18,20
Rocky Rococo's Pizza Restaurant	Janitorial	Mon. through Fri. 8:30–10:30	10	1	21
Madison Public Library Finney Branch	Clerical	Weds. 9:30–11:00	12	3	17,19,19
Immaculate Heart Church	Janitorial	Weds. 9:30–11:00	1	4	17,17,19,19
Immaculate Heart Church	Janitorial	Thurs. 9:30–11:00	1	3	17,17,17
March of Dimes	Clerical	Weds., Thurs. 9:30–11:00	6	3	17,18,19
American Family Insurance	Clerical	Weds., Thurs. 9:30–11:00	55	3	19,20,20
Howard Johnson's Hotel Housekeeping Department	Housekeeping	Mon., Weds. 8:45–11:00	25	3	18,19,20
Howard Johnson's Hotel Laundry	Sorting, folding and storing linen	Mon., Weds. 8:45–11:00	15	2	16,17
Calvary Lutheran Church	Janitorial and clerical	Mon., Weds. 9:45–11:15	10	2	16,16
University of Wis. Student Union (South)	Janitorial	Tues., Fri. 9:00–11:30	110	3	17,17,20
Church of the Living Christ	Janitorial	Fri. 11:30–2:30	3	3	17,20,20

Organization	Task	Schedule			
University of Wis. Hospital and Clinics-Central Service Department	Labeling hospital supplies	Tues., Thurs. 12:00–3:30	200	2	14,20
University of Wis. Hospital and Clinics-Central Service Department	Labeling hospital supplies	Mon., Weds. 9:45–11:00	200	3	17,18,19
University of Wis. Hospital and Clinics-Materials Redistribution Department	Packaging surgical instruments	Tues., Thurs. 12:00–3:30	200	2	19,20
University of Wis. Hospital and Clinics-Pharmacy	Unpacking pharmacy supplies, sorting pills and labeling supplies	Tues., Thurs. 12:00–3:30	200	2	16,16
Methodist Hospital	Housekeeping, clerical and packaging and labeling hospital supplies	Weds., Thurs. 12:00–2:00 12:45–2:00	35	2	17,18
Veteran's Administration Hospital-Outpatient Pharmacy	Packaging, labeling, filling and opening pharmacy supplies, and clerical	Tues., Thurs. 8:30–11:30	175	3	18,18,19
Veteran's Administration Hospital-Inpatient Pharmacy	Packaging, labeling, filling, opening and washing pharmacy supplies	Mon. through Fri. 8:30–11:30	175	1	21
Veteran's Administration Hospital-Special Products Distribution Department	Packaging, wrapping, and labeling surgical supplies	Tues., Thurs. 8:30–11:30	175	2	17,19
Veteran's Administration Hospital-Ambulatory Care	Clerical	Tues., Thurs. 8:30–11:30	175	1	19
McArdle Cancer Research Laboratory	Washing and storing laboratory equipment	Mon. through Fri. 1:00–3:00	20	1	21
Langdon Street Grocery Cooperative	Stocking shelves	Tues., Thurs., Fri. 1:00–3:00	35	2	21,22
American Automobile Association	Clerical	Mon., Weds., and Fri. 9:00–12:00	85	3	21,21,21
WHA Radio Station	Clerical	Tues., Weds., and Thurs. 12:30–3:00	55	1	21
Madison Fire Station #1	Janitorial and washing vehicles	Mon., Weds., and Fri. 1:00–3:00	45	3	21,21,21
Wisconsin State Capitol	Clerical	Tues. 1:00–3:30	50	2	21,21
Rocky Rococo's Pizza Restaurant (West Towne)	Janitorial	Mon. through Fri. 9:00–10:30	40	1	21
Capitol Center Foods	Janitorial and stocking shelves	Tues., Thurs. 1:00–3:30	110	1	21

not be expected to work with more than approximately 12 persons. Further, this group of 12 persons should be heterogeneous (i.e., have a variety of handicapping conditions) to allow reasonable compromises in the allocation of time and resources. It is not advisable for someone to assume responsibility for 12 persons with autism or 12 persons confined to wheelchairs, or 12 persons with relatively severe behavior problems. Responsible balances between those with behavior problems, mobility difficulties, functioning levels, and supervision needs must be arranged.

Coordination Between Those Responsible for Vocational Functioning and Those Responsible for Domestic and Recreation/Leisure Functioning Must Be the Rule

The more severely handicapped persons work in nonsheltered environments that are in accordance with the natural proportion, the more obvious is the need for active and continuous coordination between those who play significant roles in the total life space of an individual. For example, many nonsheltered environments require specific grooming and dressing standards that are not needed in many sheltered environments. Thus, it must be arranged that severely handicapped persons adhere to these standards. This adherence requires frequent and effective communication and cooperation between those responsible both at work and at home.

Relevant Related Services Must Be Incorporated

Adequately meeting the vocational training needs of many severely handicapped adults often requires the expertise of a variety of competent related service personnel such as physical, occupational, and communication therapists. Consider the disastrous long range effects that might be incurred if a severely physically handicapped person was taught to package surgical instruments in a hospital in such a way that the required movements decreased this worker's range of motion, impeded blood circulation, and placed unnecessary and painful strain on certain muscles. Clearly, the expertise of a competent physical therapist would have been in order, both prior to and during training.

Communication and Coordination Between School and Postschool Agencies Must Be Meaningful

Vocational success in adulthood often emanates from complementary and cooperative relationships between school and postschool agency personnel. With professionally responsible cooperation comes effective long range planning, efficient problem solving, smooth transitions, comprehensive rather than segmented orientations, and the inevitable compromises so critical to success.

At this time, three examples of service delivery models offer reasonable potential for providing the services needed to maintain severely handicapped adults in nonsheltered vocational environments: the technical school–community college model; the nonsheltered environment only model; and the sheltered and nonsheltered environment model. However, before each of these models is discussed, it seems appropriate to present some of the reasons why the ubiquitous sheltered to nonsheltered environment model is not afforded credence.

Those who operate sheltered vocational environments often attest to a "continuum of services" designed to move disabled adults from sheltered to nonsheltered environments. To some, this model seems quite reasonable; however, when the history and production records of severely handicapped adults in sheltered models is examined, severe reservations are in order (Greenleigh Associates, Inc., 1975; U.S. Department of Labor, 1977, 1979; Whitehead, 1979). If severely handicapped adults leave one sheltered environment, it is almost always because they are being rejected for behavioral, medical, or productivity reasons. That is, they are almost always ejected to less demanding and more sheltered environments, including their homes (VanDeventer et al., 1981). The utilization of a sheltered to nonsheltered model is particularly dangerous for severely handicapped adults because when large groups of handicapped people are considered for possible movement from sheltered to nonsheltered environments, the higher functioning almost always receive priority; i.e., the necessary training and related resources (Bellamy et al., 1983). The three models to be described are endorsed because they offer *immediate access* to training and support in nonsheltered environments.

The Technical School–Community College Model

Technical schools and community colleges offer training programs designed to teach nondisabled and mildly disabled persons many of the specific vocational skills needed to succeed in a wide variety of nonsheltered vocations and have been remarkably effective in many situations. Keypunch operators, automobile service persons, and electronic circuit board assemblers are but a few examples. The technical school–community college model can be adapted quite easily to the needs of severely disabled adults. Ideologically, conceptually, and technologically appropriate professionals could be hired and assigned the responsibility of teaching approximately 12 severely handicapped adults the attitudes and skills necessary to function in nonsheltered work environments. While these professionals would be based at the school, most, if not all, of the actual training and supervision could be provided in actual nonsheltered environments (Goetz, Lindsay, Rosenberg, & Sailor, 1983).

The Nonsheltered Environment Only Model

Nonsheltered environment only models are founded on the premise that disabled adults should be prepared to function in the same environments as their nondisabled peers. Vocational Education Alternatives, Inc. of Madison, Wisconsin, is an example of a private corporation that exists solely to assist a wide variety of disabled adults, approximately 20% of whom are severely handicapped, to function in nonsheltered vocational environments. Over the past three years, this adult service agency, with funds provided by the Dane County Unified Services Board, hired professionals skilled in the instruction of severely handicapped persons to successfully maintain 36 severely handicapped graduates of the Madison Metropolitan School District in nonsheltered work environments (Shiraga, 1983). Because of this success, the Dane County Unified Services Board has arranged for the establishment of an additional nonsheltered only model, work opportunity in rural communities, to serve severely handicapped adults in two of the smaller towns in the county.

The Sheltered and Nonsheltered Environment Model

Sheltered and nonsheltered environment models are those that have added to an already existing sheltered environment model the option of providing severely handicapped adults with long term training and maintenance in nonsheltered environments. The critical difference between the sheltered *and* nonsheltered environment model and the sheltered *to* nonsheltered environment model is reflected in criteria for access to nonsheltered environments. Sheltered *to* nonsheltered models almost always require that an individual "prove" that he or she is "ready" to learn to function in a nonsheltered environment. Sheltered *and* nonsheltered models offer immediate training and supervision in actual nonsheltered environments when requested to do so by the severely handicapped adult or the significant others in his or her life.

Goodwill Industries of Madison, Wisconsin, is one example. Many of the staff members at Goodwill provide services within a sheltered workshop. However, with funds provided by the Dane County Unified Services Board, additional personnel have been hired, whose sole responsibility is to provide training and supervision to those individuals who prefer a nonsheltered option. As of August 1983, these personnel were supervising five severely handicapped graduates of the Madison Metropolitan School District in nonsheltered environments. In addition, at this writing, the Dane County Unified Services Board is in the process of arranging for Pathways, Inc., an agency in Madison, Wisconsin, that offers sheltered services to developmentally disabled adults, to add a nonsheltered option to its program.

CONCLUSION

This chapter is a mixture of philosophy, ideology, empiricism, pragmatism, frustration, and hope. In affirmation, several important phenomena have been demonstrated: severely handicapped persons can be taught to perform meaningful work in nonsheltered environments; public school programs can be engineered to provide rational and functional preparatory experiences for many of their lowest intellectually functioning students; adult service systems can be engendered to arrange for a reasonable number of severely handicapped persons to function in nonsheltered vocational environments over long periods of time; and nonsheltered functioning is clearly more cost-efficient than sheltered functioning.

On the other hand, the data, concepts, and related information presented force the professional community to address a series of critical ideological, conceptual, and empirical issues. Some of these include

- Can severely handicapped persons be maintained in nonsheltered environments over a lifetime?
- Of the national population of severely handicapped persons, how many in fact can function best in nonsheltered vocational environments, how many can function best elsewhere, and how do we decide who goes where?
- Can the outcomes secured in one community be realized in different communities, of different sizes, ethnic and racial mixtures, etc.?
- How can generations of attitudes, expectations, values, funding patterns, legislation, and administrative codes be modified to allow severely disabled adults to participate in competitive enterprise?
- Can we, as a nation, develop the comprehensive service delivery models and technical expertise that would allow a wide variety of severely handicapped adults to function in large numbers of nonsheltered environments?
- How can we adapt, modify, change, or otherwise engineer public school systems so that functioning in nonsheltered environments becomes the standard, not the exception?

In the past, we assumed that severely handicapped persons could not perform meaningful work. We were wrong. We then assumed that although they could perform some meaningful work, they could only function in sheltered environments. Again, we were wrong. Now, there are those who say that handicapped people can perform meaningful work in nonsheltered environments, but assume nonhandicapped employers and workers do not want them around. Wrong again.

The dream expressed here is that in the near future severely handicapped persons will not live in institutions, will not attend segregated schools, and will not be confined to handicapped only environments of any kind. To the contrary, as adults they will live, work, and play in a wide variety of environments with nondisabled people and experience the rich variety of stimuli so critical to a decent, humane, and productive life. As such a dream is a fact for only a few, the task is to make it a national objective and, shortly, a national reality.

Acknowledgment — The preparation of this manuscript was supported by Grant No. G008102099 to the University of Wisconsin from the Department of Education, Special Education Programs, Division of Personnel Preparation; and by Grant No. 6008302977 to the University of Wisconsin and to the Madison Metropolitan School District from the Department of Education, Special Education Programs, Division for Innovation and Development.

REFERENCES

Baumgart, D. (1981). *Activities and interactions of severely handicapped and nonhandicapped students during recess at two integrated elementary schools.* Unpublished doctoral dissertation, University of Wisconsin, Madison.

Bellamy, T., Horner, R., & Inman, D. (1979). *Vocational habilitation of severely retarded adults: A direct service technology.* Baltimore: University Park Press.

Bellamy, T., Peterson, L., & Close, D. (1975). Habilitation of the severely and profoundly retarded: Illustrations of competence. *Education and Training of the Mentally Retarded, 10,* 174–186.

Bellamy, T., Sheehan, M., Horner, R., & Boles, S. (1980). Community programs for severely handicapped adults: An analysis. *AAESPH Review, 5,* 307–324.

Bellamy, T., Sowers, J., & Bourbeau, P. (1983). Work and work-related services: Postschool options. In M. Snell (Ed.), *Systematic instruction of the moderately and severely handicapped* (2nd ed., pp. 490–502). Columbus, OH: Charles E. Merrill.

Bijou, S. (1966). Functional analysis of retarded development. In N. R. Ellis (Ed.), *International review of research in mental retardation* (Vol. 1, pp. 1–19). New York: Academic Press.

Brolin, D. (1982). *Vocational preparation of persons with handicaps,* (2nd ed.). Columbus, OH: Charles E. Merrill.

Brown, L., Ford, A., Nisbet, J., Sweet, M., Donnellan, A., & Gruenewald, L. (1983). Opportunities available when severely handicapped students attend chronological age appropriate regular schools. *Journal of the Association for the Severely Handicapped, 8*(1), 16–24.

Brown, L., Nisbet, J., Ford, A., Sweet, M., Shiraga, B., York, J., & Loomis, R. The critical need for nonschool instruction in educational programs for severely handicapped students. *Journal of the Association for the Severely Handicapped, 8*(3), 71–77.

Brown, L., Pumpian, I., Baumgart, D., VanDeventer, P., Ford, A., Nisbet, J., Schroeder, J., & Gruenewald, L. (1981). Longitudinal transition plans in programs for severely handicapped students. *Exceptional Children, 47,* 624–631.

Crosson, J. (1969). A technique for programming sheltered workshop environments for training severely retarded workers. *American Journal of Mental Deficiency, 73,* 814–818.

Donnellan, A. M. (1984). The criterion of the least dangerous assumption. *Behavior Disorders, 9,* 141–150.

Egel, A., Richman, G., & Koegel, R. (1981). Normal peer models and autistic children's learning. *Journal of Applied Behavior Analysis, 14,* 3–12.

Falvey, M., Brown, L., Lyon, S., Baumgart, D., & Schroeder, J. (1980). Strategies for using cues and correction procedures. In W. Sailor, B. Wilcox, & L. Brown (Eds.), *Methods of instruction for severely handicapped students* (pp. 109–133). Baltimore: Paul H. Brookes.

Goetz, L., Lindsay, W., Rosenberg, W., & Sailor, W. (1983). *Over 21: A program for severely disabled adults* (Contract No. 81-68120). San Francisco: State of California, Health and Welfare Agency, Department of Developmental Services.

Gold, M. (1972). Stimulus factors in skill training of the retarded on a complex assembly task: Acquisition, transfer and retention. *American Journal of Mental Deficiency, 76,* 517–526.

Gold, M. (1973). Research on the vocational habilitation of the retarded: The present, the future. In N. R. Ellis (Ed.), *International review of research in mental retardation* (Vol. 6, pp. 97–147). New York: Academic Press.

Gold, M. (1974). Redundant cue removal in skill training for the retarded. *Education and Training of the Mentally Retarded, 9,* 5–8.

Gold, M., & Pomerantz, D. (1978). Issues in prevocational training. In M. Snell (Ed.), *Systematic instruction of the moderately and severely handicapped* (pp. 431–440). Columbus, OH: Charles E. Merrill.

Greenleigh Associates, Inc. (1975). *The role of the sheltered workshop in the rehabilitation of the severely handicapped.* New York: Report to the Department of Health, Education, and Welfare, Rehabilitation Services Administration.

Greenspan, S., & Shoultz, B. (1981). Why mentally retarded adults lose their jobs: Social competence as a factor in work adjustment. *Applied Research in Mental Retardation, 2,* 23–38.

Guralnick, M. (1981). The social behavior of preschool children at different developmental levels: Effects of group composition. *Journal of Experimental Child Psychology, 31,* 115–130.

Hill, M., & Wehman, P. (1983). Cost benefit analysis of placing moderately and severely handicapped individuals in competitive employment. *Journal of the Association for the Severely Handicapped, 8*(1), 30–38.

Horner, R., & Bellamy, T. (1979). Structured employment: Productivity and productive capacity. In T. Bellamy, G. O'Connor, & O. Karan (Eds.), *Vocational rehabilitation of severely handicapped persons: Contemporary service strategies* (pp. 85–101). Baltimore: University Park Press.

Huddle, D. (1967). Work performance of trainable

adults as influenced by competition, cooperation, and monetary reward. *American Journal of Mental Deficiency, 72,* 198–211.

Lynch, K. (1979). Toward a skill-oriented prevocational program for trainable and severely mentally impaired students. In T. Bellamy, G. O'Connor, & O. Karan (Eds.), *Vocational rehabilitation of severely handicapped persons: Contemporary service strategies* (pp. 253–265). Baltimore: University Park Press.

Lynch, K., & Gerber, P. (1977). *A survey of adult services to the developmentally disabled in Michigan.* Ann Arbor: University of Michigan Press.

Madison Opportunity Center, Inc. (1981). *When opportunity knocks.* Madison, WI: Madison Opportunity Center, Inc.

Martin, A., Flexer, R., & Newbery, J. (1979). The development of a work ethic in the severely retarded. In T. Bellamy, G. O'Connor, & O. Karan (Eds.), *Vocational rehabilitation of severely handicapped persons: Contemporary service strategies* (pp. 137–159). Baltimore: University Park Press.

Moss, J. (1979). *Employment training of mentally retarded individuals: A proposed plan for rational action.* Seattle: University of Washington.

Nisbet, J. (1983). *The differences in interactions and behavior in sheltered and nonsheltered work environments.* Unpublished doctoral dissertation, University of Wisconsin, Madison.

Pomeranz, D., & Marholin, D. (1977). Vocational habilitation: A time for change. In E. Sontag, J. Smith, & N. Certo (Eds.), *Educational programming for the severely and profoundly handicapped* (pp. 129–141). Reston, VA: Council for Exceptional Children.

Pumpian, I. (1981). *Variables effecting attitudes toward the employability of severely handicapped adults.* Unpublished doctoral dissertation, University of Wisconsin, Madison.

Pumpian, I., Baumgart, D., Shiraga, B., Ford, A., Nisbet, J., Loomis, R., & Brown, L. (1980). Vocational training programs for severely handicapped students in the Madison Metropolitan School District. In L. Brown, M. Falvey, I. Pumpian, D. Baumgart, J. Nisbet, A. Ford, J. Schroeder, & R. Loomis (Eds.), *Curricular strategies for teaching severely handicapped students functional skills in school and nonschool environments* (Vol. 10, pp. 273–310). Madison, WI: Madison Metropolitan School District.

Redkey, H. (1979). A different kind of workshop. *Amicus, 4,* 270–272.

Rusch, F., & Menchetti, B. (1981). Increasing compliant work behaviors in a nonsheltered work setting. *Mental Retardation, 19,* 107–112.

Rusch, F., Weithers, J., Menchetti, B., & Schutz, R. (1980). Social validation of a program to reduce topic repetition in a nonsheltered setting.

Education and Training of the Mentally Retarded, 15, 208–215.

Schneider, K., Rusch, F., Henderson, R., & Geske, D. (1981). *Competitive employment for mentally retarded persons: Costs vs. benefits.* Urbana: University of Illinois at Urbana-Champaign.

Shiraga, B. (1983). *A follow-up examination of severely handicapped graduates of the Madison Metropolitan School District from 1979–1983.* Unpublished masters thesis, University of Wisconsin, Madison.

Sowers, J., Thompson, L., & Connis, R. (1979). The food service vocational training program: A model for training and placement of the mentally retarded. In T. Bellamy, G. O'Connor, & O. Karan (Eds.), *Vocational rehabilitation of severely handicapped persons: Contemporary service strategies* (pp. 181–205). Baltimore: University Park Press.

Stodden, R., Casale, J., & Schwartz, S. (1977). Work evaluation and the mentally retarded: Review and recommendations. *Mental Retardation, 15,* 24–27.

Sweet, M., Shiraga, B., Ford, A., Nisbet, J., Graff, S., & Loomis, R. (1982). Vocational training: Are ecological strategies applicable for severely multihandicapped students? In L. Brown, J. Nisbet, A. Ford, M. Sweet, B. Shiraga, & L. Gruenewald (Eds.), *Educational programs for severely handicapped students, Vol. XII.* Madison, WI: Madison Metropolitan School District.

U.S. Department of Labor (1977). *Sheltered workshop study: Vol. I. Workshop survey.* Washington, DC: U.S. Department of Labor.

U.S. Department of Labor (1979). *Sheltered workshop study: Vol. II. Study of handicapped clients in sheltered workshops and recommendations of the secretary.* Washington, DC: U.S. Department of Labor.

VanDeventer, P., Yelinek, N., Brown, L., Schroeder, J., Loomis, R., & Gruenewald, L. (1981). A follow-up examination of severely handicapped graduates of the Madison Metropolitan School District from 1971–1978. In L. Brown, D. Baumgart, I. Pumpian, J. Nisbet, A. Ford, A. Donnellan, M. Sweet, R. Loomis, & J. Schroeder (Eds.), *Educational programs for severely handicapped students* (Vol. 11, pp. 1–177). Madison, WI: Madison Metropolitan School District.

Voeltz, L. (1980a). Children's attitudes toward handicapped peers. *American Journal of Mental Deficiency, 84,* 455–464.

Voeltz, L. (1980b). Effects of structured interactions with severely handicapped peers on children's attitudes. *American Journal of Mental Deficiency, 86,* 380–390.

Wehman, P. (1981). *Competitive employment: New horizons for severely disabled individuals.* Baltimore: Paul H. Brookes.

Wehman, P., & Hill, J. (1982). Preparing severely handicapped youth for less restrictive environments. *Journal of the Association for the Severely Handicapped*, *7*(1), 33–39.

Wehman, P., Hill, M., Goodall, P., Cleveland, P., Brooke, V., & Pentecost, J. (1982). Job placement and follow-up of moderately and severely handicapped individuals after three years. *Journal of the Association for the Severely Handicapped*, *7*(2), 5–16.

Wehman, P., Hill, J., & Koehler, F. (1979). Helping severely handicapped persons enter competitive employment. *AAESPH Review*, *4*, 274–290.

Wehman, P., & McLaughlin, P. (1980). *Vocational curriculum for developmentally disabled persons*. Baltimore: University Park Press.

Whitehead, C. (1979a). Sheltered workshops — effective accommodation or exploitation? *Amicus*, *4*, 273–276.

Whitehead, C. (1979b). Sheltered workshops in the decade ahead: Work and wages, or welfare. In T. Bellamy, G. O'Connor, & O. Karan (Eds.), *Vocational rehabilitation of severely handicapped persons: Contemporary service strategies* (pp. 71–84). Baltimore: University Park Press.

Wolfensberger, W. (1980). A brief overview of the principle of normalization. In R. Flynn & K. Nitsch (Eds.), *Normalization, social integration and community services* (pp. 7–30). Baltimore: University Park Press.

6 EDUCATION OF THE GIFTED: SIGNIFICANT TRENDS

C. June Maker

During the past 15 to 20 years, many changes have occurred in the education of gifted children, a category of special education. Several of the major, and perhaps most significant, changes took place very recently. The focus of this chapter will be on the research and writing which has caused, changed, perpetuated, or accelerated these trends in four major areas of program development for the gifted: definition, identification, curriculum and teaching strategies, and emphasis on special populations. Each of these four areas will be examined separately. Before examining these issues, however, a few general trends and issues must be noted.

A HISTORICAL PERSPECTIVE

Cycles of Interest

An examination of the research and writing on the subject of education for gifted children shows that interest in and attention to the needs of this group have not been continuous or consistent over time. Although the first identifiable provisions for the gifted were established in 1866 (Witty, 1951), growth in programs has not been continuous (Tannenbaum, 1972; Silverman, in press). From these beginnings until the 1920s, interest and research grew steadily, stimulated by a number of fac-

tors including the development of the Binet Intelligence test in 1905 (Terman, 1916), the publication of the Stanford-Binet Intelligence Scale in 1916 (Terman, 1916), and the political attitudes and writings of such individuals as Thomas Jefferson (Gardner, 1961). Acceleration and flexible promotion were the major program models.

In the 1930s, enrichment in the regular classroom became the preferred method for educating gifted children, and special classes or provisions were discontinued. Along with this change came lowered interest and fewer research projects. Albert (1969), in reviewing the number of articles from *Psychological Abstracts* on the subjects of giftedness, creativity, genius, and related topics, found that the fewest were reported from 1948–1950. A few studies on genius (5) and creativity (18) were included, but giftedness was not a major subject of research efforts until the 1960s. Several factors could have contributed to this decrease in interest: the Great Depression caused cuts in many special programs, educators became concerned about the social and emotional growth of students who were accelerated, and our concentration on World War II took emphasis away from classes or programs for gifted students.

The launching of Sputnik in 1957 caused a sudden interest in the gifted and a flurry of activity. French (1959) notes that there were more articles published on the gifted in the three-year period, 1956–1959, than in the previous 30 years. As Gallagher (1982) reminded us, in times of trouble and fear or in crisis situations, as a country, we tend to look to the gifted for help. Most people perceived this event as demonstrating that the U.S.S.R. had moved ahead of us in the development of technology in all areas—weapons for defense as well as vehicles for space exploration. The perceived threat of Russian superiority caused educators, politicians, and the general public to become concerned about the development of talent, especially in the areas of science and technology. Funding was made available for the establishment of special programs and for research on the best ways to find and develop academic talent. General reform was concentrated on the development of conceptually based curricula that focused on abstract concepts and the key ideas basic to understanding the underlying structure of a discipline. This kind of curriculum is highly appropriate for gifted students capable of understanding the key ideas and needing a grasp of underlying structure to facilitate further study. Nationwide talent searches were conducted and numerous special programs were developed for children gifted in science and mathematics.

Unfortunately, this revived interest did not continue into the late 1960s and early 1970s. Tannenbaum (1972) reports that in the 1970 volume of the *Education Index* there were only half as many entries under Gifted Children as in the 1960 volume. Attention then turned to the civil rights movement and the plight of the disadvantaged and "culturally different." Since minorities and the disadvantaged were underrepresented in most gifted programs and ability grouping or teaching was considered a form of segregation by many, the emphasis on civil rights was incompatible with an interest in programs for the gifted. Although the country was again involved in a crisis, it could not be solved by turning to the gifted; at least, not to those considered gifted by traditional standards. Generally, those who would be included in such programs were from white, middle- and upper-class homes and represented the majority culture. As Silverman (in press) notes, "Gifted education meant one more advantage for the already advantaged group" (p. 35). By this time, we had forgotten our earlier fears that the Russians would get ahead, and were willing to allow those gifted students who had earlier seemed so important to our survival to "make it on their own."

Interestingly enough, however, concern for the gifted was again evidenced in the mid 1970s, and has continued to escalate since that time. At first, the interest was seen largely at the federal level, but concern had shifted to the states by the end of the 1970s. In 1980, 45 states had programs for gifted children and a person in the state department of education who coordinated and supervised these programs, and 39 states required that local districts provide programs for the gifted (Mitchell, 1980; Roberts, 1981). In at least three states, teachers of gifted children were required to have special certification or endorsement; 52 institutions of higher education offered master's degree programs, and 28 universities offered doctoral programs in the field. Silverman (in press) credits the steady increase in interest and development of programs largely to legislation, beginning at the federal level and continuing until most states had established their own.

Trends and Issues

A number of significant trends and issues can be noted in the "cycles" of interest in the gifted. First, in a democracy, there is the recurring dilemma over the question of excellence versus equality. Secretary of Health, Education, and Welfare, John Gardner (1961) reminded us that with too much emphasis on excellence, the country is in danger of creating an elitist society; but, on the other hand, with too great an emphasis on equality, the democracy loses sight of real human differences and ignores outstanding potential. Democratic society seems to waiver between equality and excellence, reluctant to neglect either ideal for very long. Gardner further suggested that the future of democracy depends on holding these competing philosophies in balance.

One can also note a significant trend in the stated purposes for programs for the gifted. During the early 1900s and in the revival of interest after Sputnik, special provisions were justified because these talented individuals would serve society. In other words, we were willing to provide special advantages to those who would be able to help us the most. The gifted would not be allowed to do their own thing or do nothing. They must fulfill their potential for the good of society. During the most recent growth of interest, however, emphasis has been on the fulfillment of individual potential for the good of the individual. I suspect that this change in emphasis resulted from the civil rights movement with its focus on the injustices faced by many members of our society, protests against the handling of authority by those in power, and the writing of individuals such as Maslow (1970) and those involved in the Human Potential movement. Ideally, those individuals who are "self-actualized" will be making positive contributions to society in their own way without feeling pressured into "service." Thus, by fulfilling their potential for their own good, the gifted will benefit society.

A final, and perhaps most significant trend has been toward the "institutionalization" of programs for the gifted. A major factor contributing to the demise of programs in the past has been the perception of such programs as extras or frills rather than necessary, integral parts of the total school program. Programs were started by enthusiastic leaders and teachers but abandoned when these individuals left or when extra funding was not available. In fact, programs for the gifted were not in place long enough to become a recognized, continuous part of the total school curriculum. Only in the last decade have schools concentrated on establishing programs for the gifted on a more permanent basis. Taking a cue from education for the handicapped, and even taking advantage of their lobbying efforts and political knowledge, educators of the gifted began to push for mandatory rather than permissive legislation at the state level; regulations requiring local districts to establish comprehensive,

well-planned, well-articulated provisions rather than hit-or-miss programs; and other requirements designed to institutionalize programs, such as mandatory certification for teachers of the gifted.

What will happen in the 1980s? Have these efforts succeeded in permanently altering the cycles of interest in giftedness and its development? Obviously, one can only speculate. Perhaps programs will remain because they are now a permanent part of many school curriculums. Since most states now have mandatory programs, many universities concentrate on the education of specialists, administrators, and scholars; and since most local school districts make some kind of provisions for their gifted students, there is now a large number of interested and involved people. Parents who have watched their gifted children change from bored, disinterested students to excited, challenged, motivated learners are not willing to allow such programs to die. In effect, the advocacy group or power base seems to be large enough and strong enough to keep programs from dying if federal or state funding ceases to be available. Funding may shift more to the local level.

It is entirely possible, however, that changes will occur in trend toward viewing the purpose of these programs as providing a setting in which the gifted can develop their potential for their own good rather than for the good of society. Because of the critical economic, environmental, and social conditions, the public may demand a shift in viewpoint back to service to society, as a way to justify the costs of programs for the gifted. Perhaps this time, they will be remembered after the crisis is over.

DEFINITIONS OF GIFTEDNESS

The first question to be asked when one considers the education of the gifted is, What is giftedness? or, Who should be considered gifted? Definitions have undergone significant changes over the past several years, generally in the direction of more broadly based, inclusive conceptions. These changes have occurred for a variety of reasons, but seem to be mainly due to two basic factors: social climate and values; and research on intelligence, creativity, and the measurement of these abilities.

Flanagan and his colleagues (Flanagan et al., 1962) remind us that, to a great extent, definitions of giftedness are determined by the needs of a culture. The definition of talent in a primitive tribe may be very simple: tribes whose survival depends on hunting wild game will define giftedness as the ability to hunt, while those who are continually at war will value the ability to fight. Further, even nations such as the Greeks and Romans, which produced brilliant men, had a limited view of giftedness. The Greeks valued the orator and artist but not the inventor, while the Romans prized the soldier and administrator but did not recognize many other talents.

From the early 1900s to the beginning of the 1960s, the major (or only) component of giftedness was a high score on an intelligence test. Leading researchers and practitioners alike (Binet, 1916; Goddard, 1928; Hildreth, 1952; Hollingworth, 1926; Martinson, 1961; Terman, 1925) defined giftedness in terms of IQ scores. Since IQ tests were designed to predict success in school or other academic pursuits, and the validity of IQ tests was measured by their congruence with a child's achievement test scores or a teacher's judgment of academic ability, the definition of giftedness was necessarily limited to the potential for success in an academic setting.

According to Tannenbaum (1972), the perception of giftedness as a high score on an IQ test could be in large part attributed to the fact that for many years, "consuming or producing knowledge was regarded as a human virtue, particularly if it helped conquer nature in order to make man's life more comfortable" (p. 26). Schools were the places where knowledge was consumed and academic institutions, such as colleges and universities, were the places where knowledge was produced. Thus, the perception of giftedness as potential for success in academics was very much in line with the societal values of the time.

As noted earlier, the civil rights movement with its emphasis on the diversity of cultures and values, and on the considerable loss of potential in disadvantaged or culturally different groups, caused a change of focus. In fact, IQ tests were attacked by many as being biased against minorities and those from disadvantaged homes, and their use was discontinued by many school systems. If the major criterion in definitions was no longer acceptable, new definitions had to be developed.

Along with these changes in social climate, perhaps resulting from it, came attention to research on intelligence testing, and the perception of IQ scores began to change. Gallagher (1966) notes that the view of IQ scores has changed in the following ways: (a) from a representation of genetic potential to resulting from a combination of innate characteristics and experiences; (b) from an unchanging index to the possibility of variance caused by development and experience; (c) from a unitary, general factor to a multidimensional construct that consists of many different cognitive abilities; and (d) from an index that measures almost all important aspects of cognitive ability to an index that represents good measures of some cognitive abilities, but misses other important ones.

Most early research on intelligence focused on the identification of general factors, mainly analytical reasoning ability (Binet, 1916; Boring, 1950; Burt, 1949; Chronbach, 1970; Spearman, 1927; Vernon, 1951). Later research concentrated more on the specific factors involved in intelligent behavior (Cattell, 1957; Guilford, 1959, 1967; Horn, 1967; Thurstone, 1938; Wechsler, 1941). While earlier investigators seemed to assume that intelligence was stable and that it was largely a product of heredity, later research indicated that these earlier conceptions were inaccurate. Scores on intelligence tests could be modified by a number of factors, especially by providing a stimulating environment (Gallagher, 1966).

The single, most important influence on definitions of giftedness was the research of J. P. Guilford (1959, 1967). Guilford constructed a model of intelligence that predicted

150 separate abilities and conducted extensive research to identify these abilities. Through this research, Guilford called attention to the fact that most of the widely accepted measures of intelligence assessed no more than half of these abilities. This research emphasized the fact that there was no way that a single IQ score could be an accurate index of an individual's intelligence because there were, in fact, a number of "intelligences." He defined intellect as a "system of thinking and memory factors, functions and processes" (Guilford, 1959, p. 290).

In Guilford's model, intelligence is perceived as having three dimensions: content or information, mental operations, and products. Every ability has these three dimensions, and every ability is related but distinct. According to Guilford, the best model that can be constructed to explain the structure and relationships among these abilities is a morphological one, a three-dimensional cube. Within the content dimension, there are four types: figural, symbolic, semantic, and behavioral. Operations include cognition, memory, divergent production, convergent production, and evaluation. Products can be of six types: units, classes, relations, systems, and transformations. Each human ability is an intersection of three dimensions, and can be identified by tests chosen or constructed by Guilford and his associates. For example, an item included on some intelligence tests requires an individual to put a series of pictures into correct order. This item tests convergent production (an operation) of semantic (a content) systems (a product).

In addition to calling attention to the many factors in intelligence, Guilford's work provided a stimulus for research on creativity, which has also had a significant impact on our conceptions of giftedness. Although many individuals prior to Guilford had shown an interest in creativity, few had included or considered including it as an actual component of intelligence. In Guilford's theory, creativity consists mainly of the divergent thinking abilities from the operations segment of the model and the transformations and implications segments of the product dimension. Guilford constructed tests to measure these abilities and developed criteria for evaluating performance.

Guilford's theory and research provided the stimulus for landmark studies by Getzels and Jackson (1962) and Wallach and Kogan (1965), as well as a lifetime of research by E. Paul Torrance (1966, 1974, 1981). Because of the work of these individuals and the social climate of the times, creativity began to be included as a recognized component of intelligence or as a separate type or category of giftedness, assuming almost equal importance with traditional conceptions of giftedness. The research of these individuals presented convincing evidence that the abilities included under the rubric of creativity were just as important or perhaps more important to academic and/or career success than those abilities classified under the label of intelligence.

Present definitions of giftedness rely heavily on the theory that

> gifted individuals are defined in the context in which they function; [and] that giftedness is relative and dependent on geographical, temporal, and cultural variables that change and shift from time to time. (Williams, 1981, p. 19)

Current definitions also encompass a much larger percentage of the population, with estimates ranging from 5% (Marland, 1971) to 33% (Renzulli, 1981) of the school population.

The change from a restricted definition of giftedness as an IQ score to this all-encompassing, rather theoretical view has been a gradual one. Witty (1940) was perhaps the first to propose such a definition when he suggested that we define as gifted those whose performance is "consistently remarkable" in any "potentially valuable" area of human endeavor. Although this definition did not seem to have a significant widespread impact on practices at the time, it was a precursor to current conceptions of giftedness. Implicit in this definition are two key concepts: (a) intellectual competence of the type revealed by IQ scores is insufficient, thus performance of a consistent and unusual nature is required if one is to be labeled gifted;

and (b) demonstrated precocity is also not sufficient, but the abilities must be focused in a direction valued by society.

The most popular definition of the 1970s was that endorsed by the U.S. Office of Education (Marland, 1971), which included those who possessed demonstrated or potential abilities in areas such as intellectual, creative, specific academic, or leadership ability, or in the performing or visual arts. A clause was added, too, that reflects the influence of special education philosophy: these students, because of their ability, require services or activities not ordinarily provided by the school. This definition reflected an attempt to specify types of giftedness and to define it in terms of educational need.

Currently, one of the most popular definitions is that proposed by Renzulli (1978). He criticized the USOE definition because of the nonparallel nature of the categories, the lack of attention to motivational factors, the lack of guidelines for implementation, and the overemphasis on extremely high scores on intelligence tests. Based on his analysis of research on the qualities of eminent, productive adults, Renzulli proposed a three-ring conception of giftedness that includes above average ability, creativity, and task commitment. He contends that these three clusters of ability interact as they are applied to any performance area, and that evidence of them emerges early in life. Simply having these traits is not enough. They must be applied to some useful field of endeavor, and one is only gifted when actively engaged in high level productive work.

A new definition has been proposed by Silverman (in press), and it will be interesting to note the degree of acceptance of this new idea. Silverman criticizes the popular current definitions because of their apparent concern with finding children of high potential who can make significant contributions to society. Identification then becomes a guessing game to predict who has the most potential for later success. This practice, according to Silverman, could easily appear undemocratic to the general public because of its relationship to the European system of examining young people to determine which should occupy the positions of highest status in the country. Since chance plays such an important part in determining success or eminence, and we cannot predict chance, potential for achievement should not be used as the basis for selecting children for a program. She reminds us that "potential" is never a consideration in other branches of special education and urges us to take another cue from education of the handicapped: focus on the learning needs of these children that "prevent them from functioning optimally in a regular instructional program" (p. 100). Her definition places giftedness within a developmental framework:

> The gifted child is defined as one who is developmentally advanced in one or more areas, and is therefore in need of differentiated programming in order to develop at his or her own accelerated pace. (p. 101)

This definition has a number of advantages reflecting its relationship to the prevailing social attitudes and values as well as its potential for generating useful practices.

1. Advancement can occur in many different areas.
2. Evidence of advancement can be obtained through developmental assessment.
3. Since giftedness occurs on a continuum, the amount of program modification can depend on the extent of advancement.
4. The definition focuses on the developmental needs of a child rather than potential for achievement, thus the child's abilities signal unique needs.
5. Competence is not equated with performance as it is in other definitions. Since the essence of giftedness in her definition is a high level of competence, it recognizes that there may be discrepancies between ability and performance. Such is the case with gifted underachievers.
6. This definition is consistent with accepted definitions of other areas of exceptionality.

Comparison of Silverman's ideas with the approach taken by Renzulli raises some interesting issues regarding both research and practice. With regard to practice, it is clear that Renzulli (1977) believes the best justification for programs for the gifted is the potential value to society. We must, therefore, select those who have the most potential to make the best contribution to society. In fact, the information he uses to justify both his definition and his program model is research on eminent, productive individuals. As he points out, the creativity and motivation clusters have been added to ability because ability alone does not predict success.

Both Renzulli's and Witty's definitions parallel the focus on the purpose of education for the gifted that was popular throughout the 1950s and 1960s and continues today: to justify an expenditure of public monies on special provisions for the gifted, we expect them to return the favor by providing service to the society. Thus, we would not include in the definition those whose abilities are in areas not perceived as necessary or valuable to our survival.

Silverman's approach, however, focuses entirely on the educational needs of the individual students and reflects the trend in program purposes toward emphasis on fulfillment of individual potential for the good of the individual. There is, according to Silverman, no need to justify providing for the gifted for any other reason than educational need. Thus, the definition should be placed in the same context.

With regard to research on the appropriateness of various definitions and the effectiveness of their corresponding identification procedures, it is informative to compare the methods needed to validate the specific procedures used with the two opposing viewpoints. Since Renzulli's and Witty's definitions focus on the potential of an individual to make a positive contribution to society, to determine whether a definition or an identification procedure does this, one must conduct longitudinal studies of individuals identified to see whether they actually make a contribution. In other words, one must answer a crucial question, Are those identified as gifted using a particular definition and certain methods more likely to make a valuable contribution than (a) those identified

by different procedures or (b) those not identified at all? Such validation has not occurred in the field. Only the research of Terman and Torrance has even touched on the issue, and these individuals were only addressing the predictive validity of particular tests, not the validity of a whole identification system or the differential validity of several procedures.

To assess the validity of a definition such as that proposed by Silverman and its corresponding identification procedures, one only needs to assess whether those identified are functioning better in the special program established for them (based on their differing educational needs) than they were in the regular instructional program. Thus, validation can be assessed almost immediately rather than after 20 or 30 years! Obviously, such validation is not easy, since it is difficult to determine whether the educational program or the identification procedure is at fault when a child is not progressing well in the special program. However, this validation can and should occur. At this point, very little, if any, is being done.

Even though a definition such as Silverman's has definite advantages, one must recognize the social and potential issues involved in providing programs for the gifted. The political reality is that it is not easy to justify programs for the gifted (since they are seen as giving more to those who already "have") unless we emphasize the loss to society if their potential goes undeveloped. Given our current economic and political situation, justification for programs on any other basis may be even more difficult than in the past. Which definition of giftedness will gain widespread acceptance remains to be seen. Acceptance will no doubt depend upon many social, political, and economic factors in addition to research on usefulness.

DEFINITIONS AND THE DEVELOPMENT OF THE FIELD

The field of education for the gifted has received widespread criticism for its lack of sophistication, especially in research. Gowan

(1979) stated that "the gifted child movement is not really a discipline at all but merely an applied area of the measurement of individual differences" (p. 9). A former student of mine (Williams, 1981) became concerned with this issue and was convinced that the most important first step in the development of a paradigm to guide research in the field is to establish a better definition. Such a definition must be designed and stated in terms that will hasten the development of a rigorous paradigm. It must (a) provide negative examples, (b) highlight redundant features, (c) focus on essential attributes, and (d) distinguish the rules for combining the stated attributes.

Although the definitions reviewed in the previous section fulfill a definite, pressing need, none of them have been developed through rigorous research, and none meets the requirements necessary for development of a useful paradigm. All definitions have been created by one individual or a group of individuals who applied their own logic and perceptions to the problem. The student and her committee designed a study and a process for determining a core of words that adequately express the culturally determined concept of giftedness.

The study has not yet been completed, but the design is important to consider. First, an instrument was developed to generate a list of words that were potential synonyms for polar factors included in a definition: social vs. self (audience), intangible vs. tangible (product), exploratory vs. traditional (attitude), physical vs. cognitive, psychosocial vs. physical, cognitive vs. psychosocial (modes), and internal vs. external (motivation). These synonyms were then to be sorted by the subjects according to their similarity and difference on a seven-point scale. The two instruments together form a semantic differential. The words from the sorted list would express the attributes of giftedness in such a way that they could be directly translated into a form that relates them to educational practice. The definition derived from such a process could meet the requirements necessary for development of a rigorous paradigm to guide research and move this "applied area of measurement" to the status of a real discipline. However, such research is only a preliminary step in this direction.

IDENTIFICATION

Trends in the procedures used to select children for programs for the gifted have, to a great extent, paralleled the changes in definitions. When a score on an IQ test was perceived as the major element in defining giftedness, these scores were used as the sole criterion determining admission into programs. As definitions began to change, other methods of identification were added. In addition to the expanding definition of giftedness, another factor contributing to the use of multiple measures was the time and expense involved in administering individual tests of intelligence. Other procedures were measured against the individual IQ test and considered useful to the extent that they identified the same children as instruments such as the Stanford Binet. Unfortunately, actual identification practices did not keep pace with accepted theory, and many who purported to have multidimensional definitions of giftedness continued to use an IQ score as their only identification procedure. Even worse, because of the expense involved in administering individual tests, many programs used only a group administered test. Group tests are much less valid than individual ones, especially at the extremes of performance (Pegnato and Birch, 1959; Silverman, in press).

As early as Terman's first study (Terman, 1925), methods other than intelligence tests were used in the selection of gifted students. However, these methods were usually considered supplementary and often employed as screening or referral techniques, with the final decision depending on an IQ score. The most frequently employed methods were teacher ratings, achievement tests, and grades, with other procedures, such as age-grade status, interviews, and performance evaluations (either auditions or assessments of products), used occasionally.

In a landmark study, Pegnato and Birch (1959) tested the effectiveness and efficiency of various methods of identification. Using teacher rating, group IQ tests, group achievement tests, honor roll placement, and artistic creativity measures, five different lists of referrals were obtained. Out of a total of 1400 children, 781 different students were suggested, and they were given the Stanford-Binet. A criterion score of 136 or over was accepted as confirmation of giftedness. In evaluating the procedures, Pegnato and Birch (1959) used two indices: *effectiveness* and *efficiency*. *Effectiveness* was defined as the ratio of the number of gifted found through a particular screening method to the "true" number of gifted (determined by an IQ score on the Binet). *Efficiency* was defined as the ratio of the number of gifted found using a particular method to the total number screened as gifted. Gallagher (1966) presented a summary of the results of this study.

An examination of Table 6.1 reveals that teachers had a surprisingly low level of effectiveness and efficiency, while group IQ tests, group achievement tests, and honor roll placement were much better methods. Only teacher judgment of creativity in art was less effective and efficient than teacher judgment in general! The authors concluded that by combining group intelligence scores and group achievement scores, 88 of the 91 gifted children were found, resulting in an effectiveness index of 97%.

The results of the Pegnato and Birch study were confirmed by other investigations (Baldwin, 1962; Martinson, 1961), so the prevailing belief among educators was that teachers are poor identifiers of the gifted, until a second significant study was conducted. Gear (1975) investigated the effect of inservice training on the ability of teachers to correctly identify gifted students. She found that with only a short training period and the use of a behavior rating scale listing specific characteristics of giftedness, teachers improved in both their effectiveness and efficiency by approximately 50%. Many coordinators of programs for the gifted have reported that each year, the teachers improve greatly in their identification of students, and often nominate students who would otherwise be missed.

Even though, in the past, a variety of methods were used in the identification process, the way these methods were used is significant. In most cases, grades, teacher recommendations, and achievement tests were used as screening or referral techniques, and an IQ test, either individual or group, was used as the final confirmation of giftedness. If the IQ criterion was not met, students were not placed in the program regardless of the strength of teacher recommendation or the quality of other performance. A second type of procedure involved

TABLE 6.1. IDENTIFICATION OF GIFTED CHILDREN
IN JUNIOR HIGH SCHOOLS

Method	Criterion	Number Identified	Correctly Identified	Misidentified	Overlooked	Effectiveness	Efficiency
Teacher Judgment	Mentally gifted	154	41	113	50	45%	27%
Group Achievement Tests	3 grades over grade placement	335	72	268	19	79%	21%
Honor Roll	B average or better	371	67	304	24	74%	18%
Creativity in Art	Teacher judgment on creative ability	66	6	60	85	7%	9%
Group Intelligence	Otis B−IQ:						
	115	450	84	366	7	92%	19%
	120	240	65	175	26	71%	27%
	130	36	20	16	71	22%	56%

Source: Reprinted from Department of Program Development for Gifted Children, Office of the Superintendent of Public Instruction, State of Illinois, 1966. *Research Summary on Gifted Child Education.*

establishing three to five measures, with specific criterion scores, and admitting to the program those who met the criterion scores on two out of three or three out of five of the measures. For example, in the Edwardsville, Illinois Demonstration Center, three measures and criteria were used:

1. IQ scores of 110 or more as measured by the Lorge Thorndike Intelligence Tests;
2. Teacher identification on at least 7 of the 11 identifying characteristics of the intellectually gifted given in Kough and DeHaan (1955);
3. Achievement as shown by the Iowa Test of Basic Skills administered in the spring of each year—a composite score ranking in the 85th percentile or better.

To be included in the program, students had to meet two out of the three criteria.

Recently (in the late 1970s and 1980s), movement has been toward the use of multiple measures in a matrix format or a case study approach. The most common instruments or procedures used in the identification process are the following (Richert, 1982): individual or group intelligence tests, individual or group achievement tests, personal interviews, assessment of student products, auditions or performances, interest inventories, creativity tests, *SOI Learning Abilities Test*, developmental histories, biographies or autobiographies, parent interview, Piagetian Conservation tasks, and structured problem-solving tasks. According to Gillespie (1982), the most widely used is an individual intelligence test.

In the methods using a matrix (Baldwin & Wooster, 1977), a variety of procedures are used with a weighting system, so that higher weights are given to higher scores and lower weights are given to lower scores. These weighted scores are tallied, and admission to the program is based on the total of weighted scores rather than on any individual score. Some matrices are inappropriate because scores from all types of instruments are considered in

the scores for all children even though the instruments are designed to measure very different types of ability or talent.

The matrix has become popular because it offers a method for roughly equating the scores from a variety of methods. It also provides a systematic procedure for examining all the information available on a particular child. With a standardized format such as this, a variety of information about many children can be examined in a similar manner. A very clear problem, however, is that the child's performance on all these measures is reduced to one number, and in selecting students for a program, educators have a tendency to consider only the composite score in placement decisions. There is no way this one score can provide an appropriate basis for decisions about whether or not an individual is gifted or will benefit from a special program. In an experimental project to identify and plan programs for minority and disadvantaged children who showed high potential and might be considered gifted, my colleagues and I (Maker, Morris, & James, 1981) designed a modified matrix. The purpose of this matrix was not to reduce a great deal of information to one score, but to put this information in a format that could be used to examine the strengths and weaknesses of children in three areas of talent: general intellectual ability, creativity, and leadership. Scores on instruments measuring each of these abilities were grouped together, and the matrix was used by a committee in making decisions about placement of each child. All the information was considered when making decisions, not just the final matrix score.

A second trend, closely related to the first, is a case study approach. This method differs from the first mainly in the use of a matrix or method for equating scores. In a case study approach, a variety of procedures are used and the results are considered, but no numerical quantification is included. All test scores, rating scales, and subjective information are considered in decisions about the most appropriate placement of the student. In many instances, a case study approach also includes a selection committee as the decision-making body rather than one individual because the approach is seen as somewhat subjective. The use of a committee makes the decision-making process more defensible.

The overall trend illustrated by these recent developments is toward a process that recognizes the validity of professional judgments in the assessment of giftedness or the potential to benefit from a special program. Educators are becoming less willing to allow psychological test scores to completely determine their decisions about the educational needs of their students. As this represents a definite trend occurring for the past 4 or 5 years, it is predicted to continue.

Even though there is a definite trend toward recognition of the value of professional judgment and other methods as a supplement to IQ test scores, there continues to be an overreliance on the test scores. In the use of a matrix or case study approach, for example, an IQ score of 130 or above often automatically qualified a child for placement in a program for gifted children—regardless of the other available information. Other methods are considered supplementary and valid mainly as ways to judge ability in the absence of a high test score. As noted earlier, in evaluations of the validity or usefulness of identification procedures, a score on an individual intelligence test is often used as the sole criterion for confirmation of giftedness. In other words, it is the standard by which other methods are judged. As more emphasis is placed on definitions such as Renzulli's and Silverman's, with their parallel identification methods, I would suspect that additional standards will be employed.

PROGRAMS AND CURRICULA

The development of programs and curricula has been influenced largely by social and political events and has paralleled many of the philosophical trends discussed in the beginning section of this chapter. The results of research have had an impact but not to the same degree

as the social and political climate. Because education of the gifted involves so many value-laden issues, it is impossible to separate these programs from the prevailing attitudes.

Program Types

The first program provisions for the gifted were forms of acceleration, recognizing generally that some students learn more rapidly than others. Students participated in multiple tracking and flexible promotion, allowing them to advance more rapidly through the educational program (Bentley, 1937). Individual students were accelerated or promoted, and groups of students were tracked. Tracking systems created somewhat homogeneous groups, starting another program type called *ability grouping.* Special classes for the gifted appeared in the early 1900s (Tannenbaum, 1958) and continued to be, along with acceleration, the most popular method of program delivery until resource rooms or pullout programs began to be popular in the 1970s. One exception to this trend was the concern of educators in the 1930s and 1940s about the well-roundedness and social adjustment of the gifted. To these attitudes and concerns were added funding difficulties caused by the Great Depression. Educating gifted students in the regular classroom was less expensive than creating special classes for them. For this period of time, enrichment in the regular classroom was the preferred method.

As a result of his research, Terman (Seagoe, 1975) recommended that gifted children associate with older children, adults, and children with similar ability. This could occur in special classes that emphasized creativity, critical thinking, initiative, social adjustment, and leadership. Terman also felt that the needs of the gifted could be met through acceleration. Other well-known leaders such as Hollingworth (1931a, 1931b) and Witty (1930) encouraged the use of special classes.

With the civil rights movement in the 1960s and the concern with desegregation, special classes and ability grouping were attacked as forms of segregation because they were made up mainly of white, middle-class students. Educators, parents, and the general public began to be concerned about elitist notions in their children and to suggest that gifted students spend a significant amount of their time with a cross-section of students — those from a variety of ability levels, economic levels, and cultural groups.

Despite the criticisms of special classes and ability grouping and the concern with social adjustment if children are accelerated, special classes, acceleration, and enrichment emerged as the major forms of program provisions for the gifted in the late 1960s and 1970s. Research was designed to compare these major program types, and much debate surrounded the question of which program type was the best. Generally, studies showed enrichment programs to have positive effects (Clendening & Davis, 1980; Daurio, 1979; Gallagher, Greenman, Karnes, & King, 1960; Martinson, 1961; Passow, Goldberg, & Link, 1961). However, in most cases, the success of the program varied depending on the interest and motivation of classroom teachers.

Evaluations of special classes or ability grouping have yielded mixed results, with some showing that the students in special classes had more positive attitudes and motivation for learning (Drewes, 1963, Hollingworth, 1931b, Sumption, 1941), others showing that students in special classes had a wider variety of interests (Borg, 1964; Sumption, 1941), and still others showing those in special groups were superior in achievement or skill development (Justman, 1954; Schwartz, 1942). Still others found no consistent differences favoring those in special classes or those in regular classroom settings (Borg, 1964; Goldberg, Passow, Justman, & Hage, 1965). What can be learned from this research, however, is that changing the grouping of students without changing the curriculum or methods used does not produce changes. As one researcher concluded, "ability grouping is by no means a sufficient condition insuring greater academic achievement at any ability level.

At best, it provides a framework within which enhanced learning may be more effectively planned and executed" (Goldberg, 1965, p. 41).

It should be noted, however, that the greatest fears of parents and others regarding the social and emotional development of their children in special classes are generally not well-founded. In a review of such studies, Byers (1961) and Hollingworth (1930) concluded that gifted students did not suffer as a result of ability grouping. Others (Bell, 1958; Grupe, 1961; Passow & Goldberg, 1962) have also found that gifted students do not become snobbish or develop inflated egos as a result of participating in a special program. Generally, their self-estimates tend to go down rather than up, probably because of the continued contact with others of similar or greater ability.

After a review of research prior to 1966, Gallagher (1966) concluded that research on acceleration is generally positive, and that "The advantage of saving a year or two from a long investment in educational time does not seem to be diluted by social or emotional difficulties" (p. 100). Generally, if students are selected carefully, and acceleration includes attention to gaps in knowledge or assistance in adjustment through counseling, students experience no adverse effects (Daurio, 1979; Marland, 1971; Reynolds, 1962; Stanley, 1976; Terman & Oden, 1947; VanTassel-Baska, 1981; Whitlock, 1978).

As a result of several decades of research, there is still no answer to the question of which program type is best: acceleration, enrichment, or special classes. In fact, the one conclusion that seems to emerge most clearly from this research is that what makes a difference is not the administrative arrangement or program type, but the teacher, the curriculum, and the teaching methods used. This conclusion should come as no surprise to anyone, and it is difficult to understand why so much time and effort has been expended in comparisons of program types with no attempts to control for the effects of teacher style, curriculum, and methods. The results of this and other research on program

types is generally reflected in the fact that educators of the gifted are becoming concerned
with the provision of a variety of options for
students with varying characteristics and needs.

Gallagher and his colleagues (Gallagher,
Weiss, Oglesby, & Thomas, 1982) identified
seven major administrative strategies currently
in use in programs for the gifted:

1. *Enrichment in the classroom.* Provision of a
   differentiated program of study for the
   gifted by the classroom teacher within the
   regular classroom without assistance from
   an outside resource or consultant teacher.
2. *Consultant teacher program.* Differentiated instruction provided within the regular classroom by the classroom teacher with the
   assistance of a specially trained consultant
   teacher.
3. *Resource room/pullout program.* Gifted students
   leave the classroom on a regular basis for
   differentiated instruction provided by a specially trained teacher.
4. *Community mentor program.* Gifted students
   interact on an individual basis with selected
   members of the community for an extended
   time period on a topic of special interest to
   the child.
5. *Independent study program.* Differentiated instruction consists of independent study projects supervised by a qualified adult.
6. *Special class.* Gifted students are grouped
   together and receive instruction from a specially trained teacher.
7. *Special school.* Gifted students receive differentiated instruction in a specialized school
   established for that purpose.

Of these program types, the most popular
among local program directors, state directors of programs for gifted children, parents,
teachers, and others is the resource room model at the elementary level and advanced classes
at the secondary level. Consulting teachers and
enrichment are also popular in elementary
schools, while independent study and special
schools are frequently used at the secondary
level. Absent from the list of possible provisions, however, is acceleration. Thus, it is not

known how this method compares in popularity with the others listed above.

Research on the relative effectiveness of
these newer approaches is notably lacking. For
example, in their review of studies of program
effectiveness since 1966, Weiss and Gallagher
(1982) found no studies of the effects of many
of these approaches. They reported that evaluation data regarding resource rooms were usually subjective and based on the perceived
value of the skills learned, and that there was
no documentation of the effectiveness of the
use of enrichment in the regular classroom
either with or without the aid of a consulting
teacher. Data regarding the use of independent study and the use of community mentors
tended to be subjective and consisted of simply reporting that projects were completed.
With regard to advanced classes, evaluation
results consisted of objective achievement or
aptitude test results showing that gifted students can learn advanced material in less time
than is usually required. Special schools and
classes seem to be able to demonstrate that they
can select gifted students and provide a total
curriculum for them.

In a review of research on enrichment and
acceleration, Daurio (1979) concluded that
enrichment may be worthwhile for all students,
but no studies show enrichment to be superior
to acceleration; there are minimal, short lived
social and emotional adjustment problems in
children who have been accelerated; and accelerated students perform at least as well as
controls on both academic and nonacademic
measures.

The most important concept highlighted by
this lack of research on program types is that
such research is futile anyway. It is time that
educators and researchers in the field of education of the gifted abandon their attempt to
determine which type, per se, is the most effective. Most likely, previous results will be
predictive of future results: effectiveness depends on the characteristics and needs of the
students, the teacher, the desired outcomes,
and the methods and strategies used. Essentially, we need to be designing sophisticated

research that examines a number of variables related to the question of success. Questions such as, What program types are most effective for what types of children under what conditions with what desired outcomes? are more clear than questions such as, What is the most effective program type? Two examples of such attempts are the little-known classic studies of different programs at the junior high school level (Passow et al., 1961; Gallagher, 1975). In the first study (Passow et al., 1961), four groups of talented students were matched on IQ, arithmetic performance, teacher ratings, and sex. One group received acceleration in content material, a second group took a curriculum designed to teach the structure of the subject, a third group took the regular curriculum with six enrichment units added, and the fourth group took the standard eighth grade course. Outcomes measured were achievement, mathematical competence, and attitudes. Generally, the results showed the accelerated group to be most superior and all treatment groups to be superior to the controls. In a later, more extensive study conducted in 1966 with a larger population, Goldberg, Passow, Camm, & Neill (Gallagher, 1975) studied two special curriculums and a regular curriculum in both accelerated and normally paced formats. They found that the programs ranked, from highest to lowest, as follows: School Mathematics Study Group (SMSG)—accelerated; (2) University of Illinois Committee on School Mathematics (UICSM)—normal; UICSM—beginning earlier; SMSG—normal; traditional accelerated; and traditional enriched. The most superior was a curriculum organized around key concepts in mathematics and taught in a more concentrated period of time. The least effective were traditional curriculums taught in an accelerated or enriched manner. This study suggests what the results of such research might reveal and indeed common sense might suggest: the most effective approaches are those combining acceleration, special grouping, and different teaching methods with a specially trained teacher.

Another area needing examination philo-sophically, practically, and through systematic research is the current most popular approach to service delivery: the resource room, or pull-out program. This approach has gained popularity because it meets the dual concerns of parents and teachers regarding the social-emotional needs and cognitive needs of gifted students. According to supporters of the idea, by remaining in the regular classroom for a portion of the day, gifted students will have contact with those from a variety of ability levels, will gain valuable social skills, and will not develop elitist attitudes. Since gifted students are taken out of the regular classroom for a portion of their time, they also have a chance to interact with their intellectual peers and experience a curriculum designed to challenge them and develop their intellectual, academic, or creative abilities. Another reason for the popularity of the resource room model is the emphasis in special education on mainstreaming children with handicaps. A resource room provides handicapped children with "normal" models along with remedial assistance with their problems.

On the surface, the reasons for establishing resource rooms for both gifted and handicapped children seem identical: a "normal" environment is provided along with special assistance to meet special needs. However, the underlying philosophy is quite different. In special education, a classroom with only handicapped children was seen as a restrictive environment that did not allow for or encourage the growth of the child because expectations were lowered, there were not enough positive models, and the level of instruction was often lower than in the regular classroom. On the other hand, for the gifted, the regular classroom is a restrictive environment because the nature of the instruction and the lock-step progression of the usual curriculum does not allow them to move ahead at their own pace or provide challenges at a high intellectual level.

When making decisions about whether to set up a resource room program or special classes, educators generally focus on the resource room as offering the best of both worlds. They cite the possible social and emotional problems that gifted students may develop because of being in a classroom with only gifted students as the major reasons for avoiding this as a program model. They often fail to consider (a) that their fears about social and emotional problems or the development of elitist attitudes are not supported by the research, and (b) the many problems associated with a pullout program. As a matter of fact, I suspect that the elitist attitudes that concern educators are a result of the label *gifted* with its perceived status by both the students and parents rather than the result of being in a classroom with only gifted students. Thus, these attitudes will develop regardless of the type of program established, and it is only through counseling and other similar intervention that we can prevent these attitudes from forming or reduce their potential harmful effects.

One of the major problems associated with any pullout program is the regular classroom teacher's perception of his or her role in the child's education. Even though, theoretically, the regular classroom teacher is ultimately responsible for all children, including those who receive support services, the perception of limits of responsibility often changes. In other words, regular classroom teachers see themselves as being responsible for the development of basic skills or the core curriculum, but not responsible for the development of the child's giftedness or remediation of the problems for which they are getting help in the resource room. A usual response of teachers to the question, What are you doing for your gifted students? is, We have a pullout program for them; I don't know exactly what is going on in there. My usual response to such comments is that the child is gifted all day, not just for an hour or two, and that gifted children's needs dictate that changes be made in the regular program to supplement what is happening in the resource room.

A second major problem in development of a resource room program is the potential negative attitudes of both teachers and students toward those who leave the classroom for special services. Teachers often develop negative

attitudes toward those who leave because it causes necessary changes in their routine. It often means more work on the part of the teacher because children who are out of the room miss important instructions or cause disruption of the class when they leave or return. Taking gifted students out of the regular classroom may also cause negative reactions from teachers because these are some of their "best" students: highly motivated, achievement oriented, and intelligent. Even though teachers may be happy for the highly verbal, disruptive, creative, active, gifted student to leave, generally they do not wish to lose their gifted students for a portion of the day.

Teachers who dislike the pullout program and the resulting disruption or additional work may consciously or unconsciously punish students for leaving the room. Gifted students often report examples of this punishment, which may be in the form of (a) planning exciting activities such as a party or guest speaker at times when the students are out of the room, (b) requiring that students make up all the work missed while they were out of the room (regardless of whether or not they need to do the work), and (c) placing contingencies on participation in the program (e.g., you cannot go to the resource room until you finish this paper, or unless you turn in all your homework on time). Such actions can adversely affect the program in many ways, not the least of which by creating competition between the regular classroom teacher and the resource room teacher.

Other students often develop negative attitudes toward children who leave. Those who need remedial help often face the stigma of a label as *handicapped*, while the gifted often encounter the belief that they think they are better than everyone else because they go to the special program and get to do exciting things. Of course, the gifted students themselves or their parents are sometimes responsible for these negative perceptions because they adopt a "better than you" attitude.

A third major problem with the resource room model is the usual lack of continuity between the regular and special programs.

Communication between regular and special teachers is difficult to arrange since both teachers are involved with their classrooms all day. Because the resource room teacher usually pulls students from several very different classrooms, continuity is difficult to establish with all of them. One result of the difficulty in developing resource room programs that provide a coordinated curriculum for gifted students has been the establishment of a resource room program that is totally separate from the regular one. Some of the more common of these "separate" programs are those concentrating on thinking skill development outside the context of a subject area, those in which thinking games are played, and those whose focus is interesting content not covered in the regular curriculum (e.g., arts and crafts, oceanography) regardless of the appropriateness of this content for gifted students.

So, how does one decide on a program model? When asked this question, my usual response is that ideally a school system needs to provide a continuum of services for its children with special needs. Decisions about the type of placement should be made in individual cases. To make these decisions, I would suggest that degree of educational need, or a parallel concept "need for intensity or duration of the program" be the major consideration. For example, students who have strengths in only one academic area or who are achieving slightly above grade level might be best served in the regular classroom with support services provided by a consulting teacher. Those whose strengths are in a few academic areas, those who are achieving 1 or 2 years above grade level, or those who are in the lower ranges of giftedness could be served in a resource room program. Further, those who are very superior in most academic areas, those who are achieving far above their grade level, or those who are highly gifted might need special classes or even special schools. In other words, a higher degree of giftedness suggests a need for greater intensity or duration in a special program. Philosophically and practically, this approach is also satisfying as it takes into account the further the child's abilities and needs are from the

average, the less need the child has for the climate of the regular classroom. Further, the greater the child's abilities, the greater is the probability that the regular classroom will be a restrictive environment.

In addition to degree and extent of giftedness as a consideration in decisions about need for intensity or duration of programs, it is necessary to look at special problems or characteristics such as a disadvantaged background or bilingualism. Generally, children from low income homes lack many experiences and skills, and may be achieving at a much lower level than advantaged children of the same intellectual capacity. Similarly, children who are bilingual or who have English as a second language are often behind in the acquisition of academic skills because they spent the first part of their school experience learning English. When provided with an intensive, accelerated, enriched educational program for 1–2 years, these children can catch up and then be placed in a regular gifted program. The justification for the approach of using a transition class comes from two sources. First, one of the distinguishing characteristics of gifted students is how rapidly they can learn when given an accelerated program, and this characteristic is present regardless of the economic or language background of the child. When provided with an intensive program, these children can progress rapidly and close the gap between their achievement and potential (Maker et al., 1981). A second justification is closely related to the first. When gifted students who have low achievement levels, lack certain basic skills, and are insecure with their language are placed in a regular gifted program with high achieving, highly verbal, gifted students, they are intimidated, lack self-confidence, and find it difficult to compete. They may drop out of the program or participate at a lower level.

Other children who may need an intensive program as a transition are those who are underachieving for other reasons such as perceptual, emotional, sensory, neurological, behavioral, or motivational problems or handicaps. An intensive program can be designed to provide remedial help in an accelerated fashion that will help such children develop skills to compensate for their handicaps. For those who are underachieving due to motivational problems, an intensive program can provide a setting for working out these problems on a daily basis, in cooperation with counselors, parents, and other support personnel. This sort of intensive program could not be provided in a resource room setting (Whitmore, 1980).

In summary, it seems that the best question to ask about program types both when designing programs and when designing research is *not*, What kind of program should we have for our gifted students? but, What kinds of options should be provided for which children? When designing research and programs, in addition to the characteristics of the students, also consider the school setting and climate, the skills and attitudes of the other members of the school staff, the values of the community, and the outcomes desired for the children. Then, an answer can be found for the most important question: What program types are most effective for what types of children, under what conditions, with what desired outcomes? Research has not addressed this question!

Curriculum and Teaching Strategies

The earliest mention of teaching strategies or curriculum for the gifted, during Plato's time, is the provision of "intensive" training in religion, war, art, and science (Sumption & Luecking, 1960). Generally, the earliest provisions emphasized acceleration of content (Bentley, 1937; Hildreth, 1966; Witty, 1951). It was only after the work of Hollingworth (1931a) and Terman (Terman & Oden, 1947) that differentiated teaching strategies were advocated. Terman (Seagoe, 1975) recommended systematic differentiated instruction emphasizing inductive rather than deductive reasoning, self-direction, logic and reason, a maximum of new ideas with a minimum of drill and repetition, and concepts or principles rather than facts.

In the 1950s, the work of several psychologists produced concepts that would greatly influence education for the gifted. Osborn (1963) wrote about applied imagination, developing the rudiments of a creative problem-solving approach that would later be used extensively in the education of the gifted. Maslow (1962) developed a theory of self-actualization based on the study of lives of gifted individuals, and Bloom (1956) produced the taxonomy of educational objectives, which provided educators with specific guidelines for discussing higher level thinking skills. Guilford (1956) constructed his structure of intellect, which suggested that various types of thinking skills (operations) and products be measured and developed as aspects of intelligence and creativity. These works, combined with others of a similar nature, stimulated the research of such individuals as Torrance (1965, 1970), Taylor (1969), Taylor & Ellison (1975), and Parnes (1967), which has had far-reaching impact on methods of teaching the gifted.

Shortly after, in the 1960s, the impact of Sputnik was felt, and many high-level curricula were developed in science and math. Bruner's (1960) classic book, *The Process of Education*, also affected the field, as he emphasized the teaching of the basic structure or most important ideas of a discipline. Many of the new curricula developed in science and math, due to concern about the Russian technological advances, were built upon the philosophy advocated by Bruner. A parallel trend at this time was the realization that society was in the midst of a knowledge explosion and schools could in no way provide breadth of coverage in every content area. Some way of choosing what was to be taught was essential, and Bruner's philosophy of teaching key abstract concepts as early as possible, through a discovery process in which the student acts as a scientist, provided a method of teaching that could develop a deep understanding of the subject matter. Specific facts could be more easily remembered, or even constructed, if the basic structure was understood.

Although ideas such as Bruner's and the development of science and math curricula emphasizing conceptually complex materials had an impact on curricula for the gifted; at the time, this influence was confined to certain areas of the country and was relatively short-lived. The major concern in teaching the gifted was on the development of higher levels of thinking and creativity. As Maker (in press) noted, the most repeated phrase among teachers of the gifted was (and still often is), I teach the children *how* to think, not *what* to think!

Research conducted in the 1960s and early 1970s also had an impact on the development of this emphasis on processes. In a landmark study, Gallagher (1965a, 1965b) found that gifted students generally responded with the level of thinking called for by the teacher. In other words, when teachers asked questions calling for higher levels of thinking, students responded with answers indicating a higher level of thought. Other research (Felker & Dapra, 1975; Taba, 1964, 1966; Watts & Anderson, 1971) has indicated that this phenomenon is true with other groups of students also. In addition, research on the use of certain creativity training programs has shown that changes in divergent thinking can be a result of such programs (Callahan, 1978; Callahan & Renzulli, 1977; Huber, Treffinger, Tracy, & Rand, 1979; Mansfield, Busse, & Krepelka, 1978).

Interestingly enough, at the same time, research was showing the positive effects of the use of more conceptually complex curricula with the gifted. Evaluations of the new curricula, developed particularly in science and math but also in some other areas, showed the effectiveness of these curricula in developing a better understanding of abstract concepts and more positive attitudes toward the subject matter (Gallagher, 1966; Lowman, 1961; Suppes & Binford, 1964; Tatsuoka & Easley, 1963). Others (Begle & Wilson, 1970; Grobman, 1962; Wallace, 1962) found that when progress was measured by traditional tests of achievement, which usually measure factual information, curricula built on Bruner's approach were not as successful as traditional curricula, but these new curricula were more successful when measured by tests constructed to assess conceptual growth. It is also interesting to note that there is evidence suggesting that students at

different levels of ability respond differently to this type of curricula. Generally, students with higher levels of ability profit more from the use of these conceptually complex curriculums than do children with lower ability (Grobman, 1962; Hanley, Whitla, Moo, & Walter, 1970; Lowman, 1961; Wallace, 1962).

As stated earlier, for many years, the major emphasis in teaching strategies for the gifted was on accelerating content. Next came an emphasis on the development of thinking skills and creativity, with some isolated attention to the use of conceptually complex material through the influence of curricula based on Bruner's philosophy. Since the early 1980s, there seems to be a much-needed realization that the use of process strategies designed to develop higher levels of thinking and creativity is certainly important, but that these methods need to be combined with the teaching of conceptually complex content. Indeed, one can argue, as does Renzulli (1977), that the processes advocated for use with gifted students are appropriate and necessary for use with all students. Such methods seem to be equally successful with students at all levels of ability. If we are looking for methods and curricula that are distinctive, or tend to *work better* with those who are gifted, we must look to methods that combine the process strategies with the teaching of abstract, key concepts (Maker, 1982a, 1982b, in press; Gallagher, 1966, 1975). In my first books on the subject (Maker, 1982a, 1982b), I looked at each of the four areas and developed general principles for differentiating the curriculum to meet the needs of gifted students. The underlying assumption for all the principles was that, to be appropriate for the gifted, the curriculum needs to be qualitatively different from that provided for all children. To be qualitatively different, the curriculum needs to be based upon or designed to extend the characteristics that make the children different. One should consider both the present traits and their most likely future characteristics. For example, intellectually gifted students usually have rapid insight into cause–effect relationships. Because of this strength, the content of the curriculum needs to be focused on abstract ideas, complex concepts, and greater depth and breadth of information. This content needs to be organized around general principles and key ideas, and it needs to include the study of gifted people and their work. Because of their rapid insight into cause–effect relationships, gifted students need processes/ methods that are designed to develop further their abstract reasoning skills and their creative thinking. Activities that are open ended, use a discovery process, require explanations of the reasoning used to reach a conclusion, and employ an accelerated pace in the presentation of information. Their products need to address real problems and be directed toward real audiences. To facilitate these content, process, and product modifications of the curriculum, the learning environment needs to be student-centered, encouraging independence, open, accepting, and complex, and must permit high mobility.

With regard to future characteristics, intellectually gifted students will most likely assume certain societal roles (Terman & Oden, 1947; Ward, 1961). They will become the scholars, leaders, and creators of the future. As Ward (1961) noted, the gifted usually become the "reconstructionists" of society, not the "participants." To prepare them for these probable roles, we must provide for the development of problem-solving skills, the study of conceptually complex ideas, the development of relevant products, and the study of methods used in the various disciplines. All the content, process, product, and learning environment modifications listed above as necessary because of their present rapid insight would also be necessary because of their future social roles.

Even though the current trend is toward development of a curriculum that includes modifications in all four areas, most educators of the gifted still continue to focus on processes. These generally include the development of higher levels of thinking, problem-solving skills, and divergent thinking.

Certainly, the process is important, and it is important that children, especially those who are gifted, learn how to think as a result of

their school experience. The development of high levels of reasoning has been neglected in many of our schools. One example of such neglect is the fact that it has been found that only 30% of the freshmen entering one major university in the Southwest could reason at the formal operational level (Lee, 1976). Other studies have consistently shown that 30–50% of late adolescents succeed at formal operational tasks (Kohlberg & Gilligan, 1971). Piaget (1963) suggested that children achieve this level of cognitive development at approximately age 11. Researchers have repeatedly found that even though one cannot teach concepts at a lower stage which children know at a higher stage of development (Kohlberg & Mayer, 1978), educators can arrange an environment that will facilitate cognitive growth so that students achieve the levels they are capable of achieving (Ashton, 1978; Blatt, 1969; Rest, 1974; Taba, 1964, 1966). Positive change, or cognitive growth, occurs through children's *active* interaction with the environment. They need opportunities to construct their own reality, organize the information they encounter, and draw their own conclusions. Gifted students need to use their advanced levels of reasoning, receive feedback and critiques from the teacher, and then improve their reasoning. The teaching techniques that develop thinking skills and move children from one level or stage of cognitive development to the next are generally those labeled *process* or *how to think* activities.

Although the process is important and should continue to be emphasized, educators of the gifted have often placed so much emphasis on process that they neglected the development of ideas/conclusions in the academic disciplines and the teaching of important concepts necessary as a foundation for further learning and creativity.

The teaching of processes, or how to think, must be combined with the teaching of important ideas and information. Even Parnes (1966, 1967), who is known for his creative problem solving process, emphasizes the importance of an information base in the development of creative products. He explains that creative behavior is a function of knowledge, imagination, and evaluation, and that sophisticated, creative products are seldom, if ever, developed by those who have not achieved a high level of understanding of the area in which they are working.

When dealing with the gifted, or when attempting to develop higher levels of thinking, just "any old content" will not do. The content that forms the basis of the teaching process must be as rich and as significant as possible. Taba (1962) suggests that thinking skills can be taught through any subject matter, but that it is impossible to separate content from process. The "richness" and significance of the content with which children work will affect the quality of their thinking as will the processes used. She further suggests that there are certain thought systems in each discipline, and that these systems contain both content and process. The examination of thought systems in the various disciplines would be an important activity both for teachers in the development of teaching strategies and for students as a part of the learning process.

Requirements for Content

In my first book on curriculum, I established certain requirements that must be met by content that becomes a part of the curriculum for gifted students: a focus on abstract ideas and concepts, complexity of ideas and concepts, and an organization of facts and information around key concepts or ideas that facilitates economy in the learning process. With regard to the actual categories of content, I suggest a systematic sampling of major branches of knowledge in addition to the study of creative, productive people and methods of inquiry used in the various branches of knowledge studied.

When developing the content to include in a curriculum for gifted students, it is essential that content experts be involved in reviewing and commenting on the significance, usefulness, and validity of the ideas to be taught. Teachers who must be familiar with many dif-

ferent disciplines cannot be experts in every area they teach, so the advice and assistance of such experts is necessary.

Some examples of key ideas that have been reviewed by experts and included in curriculums for the gifted are the following:

- *Language Arts:* Humans use language for a variety of purposes, including to entertain, to persuade, to inform, to celebrate, to judge, and to solve problems.
- *Science:* Patterns of regularity exist in our physical and living environments. Discovering, measuring, describing, and classifying these patterns is the business of science.
- *Social Studies:* Science and technology are accelerating the rate of change in the world, not only generating data about the earth and human existence, but also providing an expanded range of choices available to human beings in lifestyle, ethics, medicine, environmental modifications, conflict resolution, nutrition, etc. Whether these choices will be made in the best interests of humanity depends upon the ability of individuals and institutions to foresee their ramifications.
- *Mathematics:* The use of mathematics is interrelated with all computation activities. Everyday situations can be translated into mathematical expressions, solved with mathematics, and the results can be interpreted in light of the initial situation.

Requirements for Process

The processes used in programs for the gifted must also meet certain requirements (Maker, 1982a). They must emphasize higher levels of thinking (i.e., the use rather than acquisition of information); must be open-ended, both in the design of the activities and in the attitudes of the teacher implementing them; must develop inductive reasoning processes through discovery whenever possible; should require students to explain their reasoning as well as provide their conclusions; should permit students to choose topics to study and methods to use to the extent that students are self-directed in their learning; should encourage and permit interaction in group situations; and must be paced rapidly so that students do not become bored. To maintain interest and develop a variety of thinking skills, teachers should also employ a variety of methods, including discussions, lectures, learning centers, simulations, field trips, committee work, and projects.

In the development of process plans for a curriculum for gifted students, a variety of models is available. Certain models are more appropriate than others for use in programs for the gifted because they meet many or most of the process requirements just listed (Maker, 1982b), and because they are adaptable to and compatible with each other and with the goals of programs for the gifted.

The use of one particular model as a basis for the development of processes, although common, is not necessary and is usually not desirable, since no one model meets all the process requirements for programs for the gifted. The different approaches have different strengths and weaknesses, which are directly related to their purposes and reasons for development. Thus, the most effective process plans will combine several models to achieve the desired result. However, the use of models is strongly encouraged rather than a hit-or-miss approach, because models have been tested, refined, and constructed as ways to systematically and appropriately develop certain thinking skills in children. An entirely eclectic, or a hit-or-miss, approach does not have the background of research and development that can suggest its potential for success in achieving program goals related to the development of abstract reasoning skills, or how to think, in gifted students (Maker, 1982b).

In addition to the content and process modifications discussed, there must be higher expectations for the products that gifted students will develop (Maker, 1982a). Products, as the ends of instruction, can be tangible or intangible, sophisticated or unsophisticated. Sophisticated products involve detailed, original work, while unsophisticated ones involve paraphrasing or copying. The products expected from gifted students should be sophisticated and should resemble the products developed by professionals in the discipline being studied (Renzulli, 1977). Requirements for products, then, would include the following: address a real problem, directed toward a real (professional) audience, represent transformations or syntheses of existing information rather than being summaries of other people's ideas, and evaluated by the audiences for whom they are intended rather than by only the teacher.

To facilitate the success of the content, process, and product modifications, the learning environment must also meet certain requirements. The learning environment refers to the setting in which learning occurs, both the physical setting of the school and classroom and the psychological climate of the classroom. Many dimensions of learning environments are important, and different individuals have different preferences for certain aspects (for example, amount of noise, light, or presence of color). The learning environments appropriate for gifted students resemble those appropriate for all children but differ in degree. All environment modifications recommended here for the gifted were chosen because they met the following three conditions: (a) they are preferred by the gifted as a group; (b) they are necessary for implementing the content, process, and product modifications advocated; and (c) they build on the characteristics of gifted students.

1. The learning environment should be student-centered rather than teacher-centered. In other words, the focus should be on student ideas and interests with an emphasis on discussions in which students interact with each other.
2. Teachers should encourage independence rather than dependence, with students assuming the responsibility for solving their own problems, even those related to classroom management.
3. The environment needs to be open rather than closed. The physical setting should permit new people, materials, and things to

enter, and the psychological environment should allow new ideas, exploratory discussions, and the freedom to change directions when needed.

4. Teachers' reactions to student ideas and products must be accepting rather than judging. This does not mean that any standards should be lowered, but that the teacher should make certain that ideas are understood before challenging them, should exercise caution in the timing of evaluative comments, and evaluate ideas or products in a way that emphasizes both their good and bad aspects.

5. The physical and psychological environment must be complex rather than simple. This means that there should be a variety of materials, references, and books; and that challenging tasks, complex ideas, and sophisticated methods are also necessary.

6. The learning environment should also permit high mobility rather than restrictive movement. If students are to address real problems in the way that professionals do, the environment must be flexible enough to permit movement in and out of the classroom, different groupings within and outside the classroom, and access to different environments, materials, and equipment.

If all the changes recommended in this section are implemented, a comprehensive, appropriate curriculum would be provided for gifted students, according to most of the writers and leaders in the field. However, it should be noted that although logic and common sense would suggest that the principles recommended in this section are important, there are varying degrees of support of the ideas from research (Maker, 1982a). Many of the principles receive support from one or two studies, and some are validated by many. However, others have not been systematically investigated at all. Studies of the type described earlier (Gallagher, 1966; Passow et al., 1961) would provide a good beginning, but there need to be systematic investigations of each of the principles being advocated for the development of

curricula for the gifted, including comparisons with students who receive different kinds of special programs. To date, this systematic research has not been attempted.

SPECIAL POPULATIONS

For many years, most of those concerned with the education of gifted students focused on mainstream children and youth: those who achieve at a high level, are highly motivated, from families who value education and achievement, and who are from ethnic and cultural groups that share the values of the majority of teachers and administrators in our schools. Relatively speaking, these gifted students are easy to identify and to serve because their scores on standardized tests are high, they perform well in classrooms, they are liked by their peers, their parents support programs established for them, and they are successful in the programs established for them.

Special populations of the gifted are gifted students who are different in some way from these mainstream children. Generally, they have some sort of handicap or barrier to overcome before developing their potential. These barriers may be due to cultural or linguistic differences, geographical isolation, sensory or orthopedic handicaps, behavior or emotional disorders, learning disabilities, economic conditions of the family and home environment, or other school or home-related problems. Girls are often included as a special population because of the unique problems they face. Many of the issues involved in serving these students are similar even though the students are very different. This discussion, however, will be limited to two general groups because of my work: underachievers and the handicapped.

Underachievers

The first work on underachievement was that of Terman and Oden (1947). They selected the

150 most successful and the 150 least success-ful men from Terman's sample and examined their case histories and rating scales completed by those who knew them. They then attempted to determine how the groups were different. The major differences identified were not in IQ but in personality. The underachievers showed a lack of self-confidence, inability to persevere, lack of integration to goals, and feelings of inferiority. After Terman and Oden reported these findings, the majority of research on underachievers was concentrated on compari-sons of personality characteristics between high achievers and low achievers (Haggard, 1957; Morgan, 1952; Pierce, 1959). Following this, a series of studies focused on home and family relationships (McGillivray, 1964; Pierce, 1961; Shaw, 1964). Generally, underachievers were found to be poorly adjusted, have low self-concepts, have poor attitudes toward school, and have less satisfying home and family rela-tionships. Based on reviews of research, both Purkey (1960) and Zilli (1971) confirmed these conclusions, and attributed the problems of underachievement to the individual's person-ality or psychological characteristics. Zilli added the home and school to her list of influential factors.

Program practices that resulted from this view of the underachiever were mainly out-of-class counseling, with the school viewed as a vehicle for treatment. Teachers believed they could do little to change the established pat-terns of underachievement (Whitmore, 1980). Because of this view of underachievement, focus centered on personality characteristics and home and family relationships rather than the school. What the researchers and educators alike did not seem to realize is that it was dif-ficult to tell from the type of research they were doing whether the characteristics they had identified were the *causes* or the *results* of underachievement. For example, lack of self-confidence and feelings of inferiority are quite likely to result if a child is experiencing frus-tration at school and is not performing at the level as his or her capabilities might predict. Often parent interactions with their children

change when they discover that the child they perceived as very bright is not doing well in school. If they view the problem as lack of mo-tivation or, if they cannot figure out what the problem is, the difficulties are compounded.

A major breakthrough in research and prac-tice with underachievers occurred however, with the work of Joanne Whitmore (1980). She established a special program for highly gifted underachievers in a Cupertino, Cali-fornia, School District, and completed a clin-ical study of 27 children in the program for 1–3 years. Based on this work, she identified three categories of causal factors: psychologi-cal or personality characteristics, physical or developmental characteristics, and the social and academic environment of the school. Whitmore concluded that most previous stud-ies had described symptoms not causes of underachievement, and she asserted that the goal of education must be prevention, to seek to understand the causes and design an effec-tive early intervention program that would pre-vent the development of chronic patterns of underachievement.

Even though educators of the gifted seem to be listening to Whitmore, most programs con-tinue to focus on serving those children who are highly motivated, easy to teach, and suc-cessful in the usual type of program.

Handicapped

Recognition of the special needs of gifted chil-dren who are also handicapped has been a more recent phenomenon, even though the idea that people who are disabled can pos-sess special abilities is not a new one (Maker, 1977). In the 1890s, for example, those con-cerned with the education of individuals with sensory impairments were describing the ac-complishments of outstanding handicapped people as a way to inspire others similarly handicapped to overcome their disability and aspire to greater heights of achievement. The first real recognition of the need for special programs came in 1975 when the federal Bureau for Education of the Handicapped (BEH) funded two demonstration projects to establish programs for gifted handicapped preschoolers. In 1976, the Office of the Gifted and Talented (OGT), a division of BEH, commissioned the writing of the first book on the subject, *Providing Programs for the Gifted Handicapped*, (Maker, 1977). Later, model projects were funded by the OGT and a few state departments of education. The Association for the Gifted, a division of the Council for Exceptional Children, also showed interest through its establishment of a standing committee on the gifted handicapped.

In 1978, the first research was reported. My colleagues and I (Maker, Redden, Tonelson, & Howell, 1978) reported on a study of critical events and attributions of success in the lives of successful handicapped scientists, and Karnes (Karnes & Bertschi, 1978) reported the first results of a model project for preschool handicapped children.

I began my research in the area of gifted handicapped with a retrospective study as an attempt to identify factors that might need to be investigated in longitudinal studies. This research was concentrated in the following areas: events perceived by successful handicapped individuals as significant in helping them realize their potential, their perceptions of the causes and effects of these events, and their perceptions of the coping and learning strategies useful in helping them reach their level of success. Most of the events perceived as significant, either in a positive or a negative way, were those involving the attitudes of others: educators, employers, parents, and the general public. These other individuals either demonstrated their confidence or their lack of confidence in the handicapped person's ability. The second most frequent type of event reported involved attitudes about self, while the third involved environmental and programmatic concerns such as attending a special school vs. being in a mainstream setting. With regard to causes of success, the most frequent attributions were to ability, other people, effort, and intent. Strategies they found helpful

in their success could be classified into the same categories as the perceived causes for success. For example, strategies designed to use or develop their ability, strategies involving other people in assisting them, strategies involving extra effort, and strategies for reducing the difficulty of the tasks encountered were among those considered helpful.

One of the most interesting findings of the study was that the effect of the significant events reported was almost always that of increasing the individual's motivation to succeed. Even those events involving severe, pervasive negative attitudes and treatment by others tended to cause these persistent individuals to become even more determined to succeed. The barriers they encountered seemed to cause them to want to "show" others that they were indeed capable, not handicapped, individuals.

Obviously, the self-perceptions of these successful handicapped individuals need to be compared with those of similarly handicapped people who have not achieved the same degree of success. However, attempts to secure funding for such studies have not met with success. Another limitation of this study is inherent in any retrospective research: it is impossible to determine whether the characteristics of those individuals were the causes or the results of their success.

It is interesting, however, to compare the results of this research with Terman and Oden's (1947) study of successful and unsuccessful gifted men. Many parallels exist between the groups that were successful: they are self-confident; they have clearly established goals; and they are persistent. Terman and Oden found that these same characteristics differentiated the two groups when they were 10 years old. Whether or not these characteristics result from or cause success may be unimportant. As with underachievers, the important message for educators may be that they should be designing educational programs that prevent the formation of negative attitudes and self-perceptions and provide an environment where many kinds of abilities are encouraged.

Although Whitmore (1980) places a great

deal of responsibility for intervention and change on schools and teachers, my research also indicates that the handicapped individuals had to and *could* assume a significant part of the responsibility themselves. The context in which this idea needs to be placed is that of expectations and self-fulfilling prophesies. Research in this area has shown that for expectations to become self-fulfilling prophesies, a five-step process must occur:

1. The teacher expects specific behavior and achievement from particular students.
2. Because of these different expectations, the teacher behaves differently toward different students.
3. This teacher treatment tells each student what behavior and achievement the teacher expects from him and affects his self-concept, achievement motivation, and levels of aspiration.
4. If this teacher treatment is consistent over time and if the student does not actively resist or change it in some way, it will tend to shape his achievement and behavior. High-expectation students will be led to achieve at high levels, while the achievement of low-expectation students will decline.
5. With time, the student's achievement and behavior will conform more and more closely to that originally expected of him. (Good and Brophy, 1973, p. 75.)

With the handicapped scientists studied, the process was essentially complete up to step four. Research has documented the fact that teachers have lower expectations for handicapped students than for nonhandicapped, that they behave differently toward handicapped students, and that this behavior communicates their lowered expectations (Maker et al., 1978). However, the lowered expectations of significant individuals in the lives of these handicapped scientists did not result in a self-fulfilling prophecy. The major reason seems to be that these individuals developed elaborate and effective strategies for *actively resisting* and *changing* these negative stereotypes. Thus, educators can assist in the process of change,

but they must also instill a certain responsibility within the individual for his or her own destiny.

Underachievement and Handicaps

One of the first issues I identified when writing about the gifted handicapped, particularly the learning disabled, is the close connection between characteristics of learning disabled students and gifted underachievers (Maker, 1977). A hypothesis I have held for some time is that learning disabled children constitute a subgroup of gifted underachievers. Whitmore's research lends support to this hypothesis, and a recent study by one of my former students (Beckwith, 1983) also supports the idea and further suggests, as does Whitmore (1980), that children with behavior disorders or emotional difficulties could also be perceived as a subgroup of underachievers. Beckwith, in what may become a classic study, examined a wide variety of achievement and intelligence test information and behavior ratings for 137 underachieving gifted students and performed cluster analysis on the data. She identified 11 distinct clusters or types of underachievers that paralleled quite closely the categories identified by Whitmore (1980). The identifying characteristics were: (a) evenness or unevenness of ability (performance vs. verbal), (b) behavioral problems vs. no behavioral problems, (c) learning disabilities vs. no disabilities, and (d) academic difficulties vs. no academic difficulties. Some clusters of children were characterized by behavior and learning disorders as well as academic problems while others only showed problems in one or two areas.

Research on the relationships between handicaps and underachievement needs to be continued since the studies reported here are exploratory and singular. These need to be replicated and others designed to answer crucial questions about the most effective identification methods and the most successful educational programs.

Before this discussion of special populations

is concluded, it is important to call attention to a final parallel between the issues surrounding underachievers and handicapped, and to relate this to the whole field of special education.

EMPHASIZING STRENGTHS AND TALENTS

The field of education of the gifted has been greatly influenced by the larger field of special education. Educators have borrowed the idea of a continuum of services, the justification of special provisions on the basis of educational need, and many techniques for individualizing instruction. The field of special education has not been influenced greatly by those working with the "gifted." They tend to be perceived as the sore thumb that sticks out or the renegade child who tends to go his/her own way.

Perhaps, now is the time for educators of the handicapped to borrow at least one idea from educators of the gifted: *recognition of and development of strengths and talents.* In the past, educators of the handicapped have been so concerned about what these children *cannot* do that they have failed to recognize what the children *can* do. Chesler (1974), in a discussion of the need to recognize abilities and talents of learning disabled students, provides two examples of children whose talents were not recognized. One had the ability to portray the third dimension in his drawings when only 4 years old. In his free time during his first years of school, he drew many of these pictures. His parents and the teachers saw this as a curiosity at first, and later as an annoyance. A second boy developed an intense interest in growing things. He caught butterflies and moths, identified them, and learned about their life cycles. He would also go around the neighborhood gathering up discarded plants and trees, plant them, and try to make them come to life again. Others saw these interests as frivolous and beside the point, and encouraged him to turn his attention back to phonics. One special education teacher said recently, "I am in the business of finding out what children cannot do and

teaching them how to do it. I don't care about what they can do!" How sad for the children she teaches! But also, how sad for many handicapped children that their teachers do not pay any attention at all to their abilities because of such an overriding concern about their disabilities.

In both the cases described above, the talents of these children could have been developed in school. Who knows, perhaps these interests could have developed into a career! If not a career, perhaps they could be an area of strength and interest that would give these individuals much-needed confidence in themselves.

Some researchers have been concerned about the abilities of handicapped children, particularly the learning disabled (Argulewicz, Mealor, & Richmond, 1979; Ellis-Schwabe & Conroy, 1983; Sigg & Garguilo, 1980; Tarver, Buss, & Maggiore, 1979) and found these children to be equal to or superior to nondisabled children in certain areas of creativity. Others (Vautour, 1976) have found artistic talents in learning disabled children.

With regard to teaching, Maker (1979) reviews studies that indicate that it is possible to develop a child's weaknesses through his or her strengths without even concentrating on the weaknesses. For example, Carlson (1974) reported the use of a multiple baseline-successive treatments model in which she used a child's creative strengths in fluency and elaboration to increase academic achievement and efforts in self-evaluation. The child showed substantial improvements in goal-directedness, ability to assess her own progress, and several areas of academic achievement. Torrance (1977) reviewed studies in which children's creative strengths were used in an attempt to develop their creative weaknesses. The children's creative weaknesses improved and, to everyone's surprise, so did their achievement in math, spelling, and reading! When one considers the pervasive influence self-concept can have on learning and motivation, it seems only reasonable that learning will occur at a faster rate in all areas if the learner is concentrating on some tasks that he or she can do well. School is not such an alien place if the child can do some things well while there.

SUMMARY/CONCLUSION

In this chapter, a number of trends have been noted in the development and refinement of programs for the gifted. These trends have been linked to developments in research as well as to the social and political climate of the times. Although it is impossible to predict whether interest in the gifted will continue at its present high level, we can predict that at some point in the future, interest will be renewed.

In each of the four areas discussed in this paper, significant trends have been noted. Generally, research and practice have contributed to positive growth, including greater clarity, more valid practices, and better information for decision making. However, before the field can move ahead as a true scientific area, some very basic issues must be resolved, particularly those surrounding the definition of giftedness. Greater efforts need to be concentrated in this direction. Identification practices have improved and have been expanded. The view of issues surrounding and practices in curriculum and teaching strategies have become more realistic, recognizing the need to differentiate programs based on the differing characteristics of students instead of providing one program for all of them. Finally, educators have begun to recognize, identify, and provide programs for special subgroups of gifted students who were not served in the past.

Generally, it seems that educators have moved forward in an attempt to resolve the competing philosophies of equality and excellence. They have come a long way toward an interpretation of equality as equal opportunity to reach one's potential rather than equal treatment. They have also seen a reinterpretation of the term *excellence*, so that it does not imply elitism to the same extent it did in the past. By including minorities, disadvantaged children, underachievers, and handicapped children in programs for the gifted, schools can change much of their elitist perception. Due to the recent report of the National Commission on Excellence in Education (1983), *A Nation at Risk*, many individuals in all walks of life have begun to consider the question of excellence with regard to education. In this report, the commission emphasizes that our nation is in danger of losing its place as a major world power and strongly recommends looking to children as the strongest national resource. To prepare them adequately, the nation must improve their education — must raise its standards and expectations, must challenge and provide programs for its gifted and talented students, and must provide the resources needed by schools to do their task.

It is difficult to predict what will happen in the future. Will the recommendations of this group be heeded? Will they be listened to, but no changes take place? Will the nation unite as a people, and plan ahead rather than wait for a crisis? As a positivist, I believe we will make some changes in our schools. As a realist, I do not believe these will be the sweeping changes needed to make our public schools the best they can be in preparing gifted children for the world of the future. I do believe that programs for the gifted will increase and improve.

REFERENCES

Albert, R. S. (1969). Genius: Present-day status of the concept and its implications for the study of creativity and giftedness. *American Psychologist, 24,* 743–752.

Argulewicz, E. N., Mealor, D., & Richmond, B. (1979). Creative abilities of learning disabled children. *Journal of Learning Disabilities, 12*(1), 30–33.

Ashton, P. T. (1978). Cross-cultural Piagetian research: An experimental perspective. *Stage theories of cognitive and moral development: Criticism and applications.* Reprint No. 14. Harvard Educational Review.

Baldwin, A., & Wooster, J. (1977). *Baldwin identification matrix inservice kit for the identification of gifted and talented students.* Buffalo, NY: D.O.K. Publishers.

Baldwin, J. W. (1962). The relationship between teacher-judged giftedness, a group intelligence test, and kindergarten pupils. *Gifted Child Quarterly, 6,* 153–156.

Beckwith, A. (1983). *Patterns of underachievement in gifted students.* Unpublished doctoral dissertation, University of New Mexico, Albuquerque.

Begle, E., & Wilson, J. (1970). Evaluation of mathematics program. In the National Society for the Study of Education (Eds.), *Sixty-ninth yearbook* (Part I), Chicago: University of Chicago Press.

Bell, M. E. (1958). *A comparative study of mentally gifted children heterogeneously and homogeneously grouped.* Unpublished doctoral dissertation, Indiana University.

Bentley, J. E. (1937). *Superior children.* New York: W. W. Norton.

Binet, A., & Simon, T. (1916). L'intelligence des imbeciles. *L'Annee Psychologique,* 1909, 1–147. Cited in L.M. Terman, *The measurement of intelligence.* New York: Houghton Mifflin.

Blatt, M. (1969). *Studies of the effects of classroom discussion upon children's moral development.* Unpublished doctoral dissertation, University of Chicago.

Bloom, B. S. (1956). *Taxonomy of educational objectives: The classification of educational goals. Handbook I: Cognitive domain.* New York: Longmans, Green & Co.

Borg, W. R. (1964). *An evaluation of ability grouping.* U.S. Office of Education Cooperative Research Project No. 577. Logan: Utah State University.

Boring, E. G. (1950). *A history of experimental psychology* (2nd ed.). Englewood Cliffs, NJ: Prentice-Hall.

Bruner, J. S. (1960). *The process of education.* Cambridge, MA: Harvard University Press.

Burt, C. (1949). The structure of the mind: A review of the results of factor analysis. *British Journal of Educational Psychology, 19,* 100–111, 176–199.

Byers, L. (1961). Ability grouping: Help or hindrance to social and emotional growth? *School Review, 69,* 449–456.

Callahan, C. M., & Renzulli, J. S. (1977). The effectiveness of a creativity training program in the language arts. *The Gifted Child Quarterly, 11,* 538–545.

Carlson, N. A. (1974). *Using the creative strengths of a learning disabled child to increase evaluative effort and academic achievement.* Unpublished doctoral dissertation, Michigan State University.

Cattell, R. B. (1957). *Personality and motivation structure and measurement.* New York: World Book.

Chesler, B. M. (1974). Who wants to wash the dishes? *Exceptional Parent, 43,* 47–51.

Chronbach, L. J. (1970). *Essentials of psychological testing* (3rd ed.). New York: Harper & Row.

Clendening, C. P., & Davies, R. A. (1980). *Creating programs for the gifted.* New York: R. R. Bowker.

Daurio, S. P. (1979). Educational enrichment versus acceleration: A review of the literature. In W. C. George, S. J. Cohn, & J. C. Stanley (Eds.), *Educating the gifted: Acceleration and enrichment.* Baltimore: Johns Hopkins University Press.

Drewes, E. (1963). *Student abilities, grouping patterns, and classroom interaction.* U.S. Office of Education Cooperative Research Project No. 608. East Lansing: Michigan State University.

Ellis-Schwabe, M. A., & Conroy, D. (1983). A discussion of the creative abilities of learning disabled, gifted, and learning disabled/gifted children. *Journal for the Education of the Gifted, 6,* 213–221.

Feldhusen, J. F., Treffinger, D. J., & Bablke, S. J. (1970). Developing creative thinking. *The Journal of Creative Behavior, 4,* 85–90.

Felker, D. P., & Dapra, R. A. (1975). Effects of question type and question placement on problem-solving ability from prose material. *Journal of Educational Psychology, 67,* 380–384.

Flanagan, J. C., Dailey, J. T., Shaycoft, M. F., Gorham, W. A., Orr, D. B., & Goldberg, I. (1962). *Design for a study of American youth.* Boston: Houghton Mifflin Co.

French, J. L. (Ed.). (1959). *Educating the gifted.* New York: Henry Holt & Company.

Gallagher, J. J. (1964). *Teaching the gifted child.* Boston: Allyn & Bacon.

Gallagher, J. J. (1965a). Expressive thought by gifted children in the classroom. *Elementary English, 42,* 559–568.

Gallagher, J. J. (1965b). Productive thinking of gifted children. U.S. Office of Education Cooperative Research Project No. 965. Urbana: University of Illinois.

Gallagher, J. J. (1966). *Research summary on gifted child education.* Springfield, IL: Office of the Superintendent of Public Instruction.

Gallagher, J. J. (1975). *Teaching the gifted child* (2nd ed.). Boston: Allyn & Bacon.

Gallagher, J. J. (1982, October). Seminar presented to the Special Education Department, University of Arizona, Tucson.

Gallagher, J. J., Aschner, M. J., & Jenné, W. (1967). *Productive thinking in classroom interaction.* Reston, VA: Council for Exceptional Children.

Gallagher, J. J., Greenman, M., Karnes, M., & King, A. (1960). Individual classroom adjustments for gifted children in elementary schools. *Exceptional Children, 26,* 409–422, 432.

Gallagher, J., Weiss, P., Oglesby, K., & Thomas, T. (1982). *Report on education of gifted* (Vol. 1). Unpublished manuscript. (Available from Frank Porter Graham Child Development Center, University of North Carolina at Chapel Hill, Chapel Hill, NC 27514.)

Gardner, J. W. (1961). *Excellence: Can we be equal and excellent too?* New York: Harper & Row.

Gear, G. H. (1975). Effects of the training program, *Identification of the potentially gifted*, on teachers' accuracy in the identification of intellectually gifted children. Unpublished doctoral dissertation, University of Connecticut.

Getzels, J. W., & Jackson, P. W. (1962). *Creativity and intelligence.* New York: Wiley.

Gillespie, W. J. (1982). *A national survey of urban gifted educational programs.* Unpublished doctoral dissertation, University of Denver.

Goddard, H. H. (1928). *School training of gifted children.* Yonkers, NY: World Books.

Goldberg, M. (1965). *Research on the talented.* New York: Bureau of Publications, Teachers College, Columbia University.

Goldberg, M., Passow, A. H., Justman, J., & Hage, G. (1965). *The effects of ability grouping.* New York: Bureau of Publications, Columbia University.

Good, T. L. & Brophy, J. E. (1973). *Looking in classrooms.* New York: Harper & Row.

Gowan, J. C. (1979). Creativity and the gifted child movement. In J. C. Gowan, J. Khatena, & E. P. Torrance (Eds.), *Educating the ablest: A book of readings*, pp. 4–17. Itaska, IL: F. E. Peacock.

Grobman, H. (1962). Some comments on the evaluation program findings and their implications. *Biological Sciences Curriculum Study Newsletter, 19,* 5–29.

Grupe, A. J. (1961). *Adjustment and acceptance of mentally superior children in regular and special fifth grade classes in a public school system.* Unpublished doctoral dissertation, University of Illinois.

Guilford, J. P. (1959). Three faces of intellect. *American Psychologist, 14,* 469–479.

Guilford, J. P. (1967). *The nature of human intelligence.* New York: McGraw-Hill.

Haggard, E. A. (1957). Socialization, personality, and academic achievement in gifted children. *School Review, 55,* 388–414.

Hanley, J. P., Whitla, D. K., Moo, E.W., & Walter, A. S. (1970). *Man: A course of study: An evaluation.* Cambridge, MA: Education Development Center.

Hildreth, G. (1952). *Educating gifted children at Hunter College Elementary School.* New York: Harper.

Hildreth, G. H. (1966). *Introduction to the gifted.* New York: McGraw-Hill.

Hollingworth, L. S. (1926). *Gifted children: Their nature and nurture.* New York: Macmillan.

Hollingworth, L. S. (1931a). How should gifted children be educated? *Baltimore Bulletin of Education, 2,* 195–197.

Hollingworth, L. S. (1931b, June 20). Personality development of special class children. *University of Pennsylvania Bulletin, Eighteenth Annual Schoolmen's Week Proceedings, 31,* 442–446.

Horn, J. L. (1967). Intelligence—Why it grows, why it declines. *Trans-Action, 5,* 23–31.

Huber, J., Treffinger, D., Tracy, D., & Rand, D. (1979). Self-instructional use of programmed creativity—training materials with gifted and regular students. *Journal of Educational Psychology, 71*(3), 303–309.

Justman, J. (1954). Academic achievement of intellectually gifted accelerants and non-accelerants in junior high school. *School Review, 62,* 142–150.

Karnes, M. B., & Bertschi, J. D. (1978). Identifying and educating gifted/talented nonhandicapped and handicapped preschoolers. *Teaching Exceptional Children, 10,* 114–119.

Kohlberg, L., & Gilligan, C. (1971). The adolescent as a philosopher: The discovery of the self in a postconventional world. *Daedalus, 100,* 1051–1086.

Kohlberg, L., & Mayer, R. (1978). Development as the aim of education. *Stage theories of cognitive and moral development: Criticisms and applications.* Reprint No. 13. Harvard Educational Review. Montpelier, VT: Capital City Press.

Kough, J., & DeHaan, R. (1955). *Teacher's Guidance Handbook.* Chicago: Science Research Associates.

Lee, N. (1976). *Formal operational thought: Component skills and observational learning.* Unpublished doctoral dissertation, University of New Mexico.

Lessinger, L. M. (1963). Test building and test banks through the use of the Taxonomy of Educational Objectives. *California Journal of Educational Research, 14,* 195–201.

Lowery, J. (1982). Developing creativity in gifted children. *The Gifted Child Quarterly, 26,* 133–139.

Lowman, L. M. (1961). An experimental evaluation of two curriculum designs for teaching first year algebra in a ninth grade class. Doctoral dissertation, University of Oklahoma, 1961. *Dissertation Abstracts, 22,* 502. (University Microfilms No. 61-2864.)

Maker, C. J. (1976). Searching for giftedness and talent in children with handicaps. *The School Psychology Digest, 5,* 24–36.

Maker, C. J. (1977). *Providing programs for the gifted handicapped.* Reston, VA: The Council for Exceptional Children.

Maker, C. J. (1979). Developing multiple talents in exceptional children. *Teaching Exceptional Children, 11,* 120–124.

Maker, C. J. (1982a). *Curriculum development for the gifted.* Rockville, MD: Aspen Systems Corporation.

Maker, C. J. (1982b). *Teaching models in education of the gifted.* Rockville, MD: Aspen Systems Corporation.

Maker, C. J. (in press). Integrating content and

processes in the teaching of gifted students. In C. J. Maker (Ed.), *Critical issues in gifted education. Vol. 1: Defensible programs for the gifted.* Rockville, MD: Aspen Systems Corporation.

Maker, C. J., Morris, E., & James, J. (1981). The Eugene Field project: A program for potentially gifted young children. In *Balancing the scale for the disadvantaged gifted.* Los Angeles: National/State Leadership Training Institute on the Gifted and Talented.

Maker, C. J., Redden, M. R., Tonelson, S., & Howell, R. M. (1978). *The self-perceptions of successful handicapped scientists.* BEH Grant No. G00-7701-905. Albuquerque: University of New Mexico.

Mansfield, R. S., Busse, F. V., & Krepelka, E. J. (1978). The effectiveness of creativity training. *Review of Educational Research, 48,* 517–536.

Marland, S., Jr. (1971). *Education of the gifted and talented.* Report to the Congress of the United States by the U.S. Commissioner of Education. Washington, D.C.: U.S. Government Printing Office.

Martinson, R. (1961). *Educational programs for gifted pupils.* Sacramento: California State Department of Education. (Final report of the California Pilot Project.)

Maslow, A. H. (1962). *Toward a psychology of being.* Princeton, NJ: Van Nostrand.

Maslow, A. (1970). *Motivation and personality* (2nd ed.). New York: Harper & Row.

McGillivray, R. H. (1964). Differences in home background between high-achieving and low-achieving gifted children: A study of one hundred grade eight pupils in the city of Toronto public schools. *Ontario Journal of Educational Research, 6,* 99–106.

Mitchell, B. M. (1980). What's happening to gifted education in the United States today. *Phi Delta Kappan, 61,* 563–564.

Morgan, H. H. (1952). A psychometric comparison of achieving and nonachieving college students of high ability. *Journal of Consulting Psychology, 16,* 292–298.

National Commission on Excellence in Education. (1983, April). *A nation at risk: The imperative for educational reform.* Washington, DC: U.S. Government Printing Office.

Osborn, A. (1963). *Applied imagination.* New York: Scribners.

Parnes, S. J. (1966). *Programming creative behavior.* Buffalo: State University of New York at Buffalo.

Parnes, S. J. (1967). *Creative potential and the education experience* (Occasional Paper No. 2). Buffalo, NY: Creative Education Foundation.

Parnes, S. J., Noller, R., & Biondi, A. (1967). *Guide to creative action.* New York: Scribners.

Passow, A. H., & Goldberg, M. L. (1962). The talented youth project: A progress report, 1962. *Exceptional Children, 28,* 223–231.

Passow, A. H., Goldberg, M. L., & Link, F. (1961). Enriched mathematics for gifted junior high school students. *Education Leadership, 18,* 442–448.

Pegnato, C. W., & Birch, J. W. (1959). Locating gifted children in junior high schools: A comparison of methods. *Exceptional Children, 25,* 300–304.

Piaget, J. (1963). *The origins of intelligence in children.* New York: Norton.

Pierce, J. V. (1959). *The educational motivation patterns of superior students who do and do not achieve in high school.* Mimeograph report, University of Chicago.

Pierce, J. V. (1961). Personality and achievement among able high school boys. *Journal of Individual Psychology, 17,* 101–102.

Purkey, W. W. (1969). Project self discovery: Its effect on bright but underachieving high school students. *Gifted Child Quarterly, 13,* 242–246.

Renzulli, J. S. (1977). *The enrichment triad model: A guide for developing defensible programs for the gifted and talented.* Wethersfield, CT: Creative Learning Press.

Renzulli, J. S. (1978). What makes giftedness? Reexamining a definition. *Phi Delta Kappan, 60,* 180–184.

Renzulli, J. S. et al. (1981, November 12). The great debate: Panel discussion presented at the National Association for Gifted Children Conference.

Rest, J. (1974). Developmental psychology as a guide to value education: A review of "Kohlbergian" programs. *Review of Educational Research, 44,* 241–257.

Reynolds, M. C. (Ed.). (1962). *Early school admission for mentally advanced children.* Reston, VA: Council for Exceptional Children.

Richert, E. S. (1982). *National report on identification.* Sewell, NJ: Educational Improvement Center-South.

Roberts, J. L. (1981, December 16). More gifted children get classes that match their own fast pace. *Wall Street Journal,* pp. 1, 17.

Schwartz, W. P. (1942). *The effect of homogeneous classification on the scholastic achievement and personality development of gifted pupils in elementary and junior high schools.* Unpublished doctoral dissertation, New York University.

Seagoe, M. V. (1975). *Terman and the gifted.* Los Altos, CA: William Kaufmann.

Shaw, M. C. (1964). Note on parent attitudes toward independence training and the academic achievement of their children. *Journal of Educational Psychology, 55,* 371–374.

Sigg, J., & Garguilo, R. (1980). Creativity and cognitive style in learning disabled and nondisabled school age children. *Psychology Reports*, *46*, 299–305.

Silverman, L. (In press). *Gifted education: Providing for gifted and talented learners.* St. Louis, MO: C.V. Mosby.

Spearman, C. (1927). *The abilities of man.* New York: Macmillan.

Stanley, J. C. (1976). The case for extreme educational acceleration of intellectually brilliant youths. *The Gifted Child Quarterly*, *20*, 66–75.

Stoker, H. W., & Kropp, R. P. (1964). Measurement of cognitive processes. *Journal of Educational Measurement*, *1*, 39–42.

Sumption, M. R. (1941). *Three hundred gifted children.* Yonkers, NY: World Books.

Sumption, M. R., & Luecking, E. M. (1960). *Education of the gifted.* New York: The Ronald Press.

Suppes, P., & Binford, T. (1964). *Experimental teaching of mathematical logic in the elementary school.* U.S. Office of Education Cooperative Research Project D-005. Stanford, CA: Stanford University.

Taba, H. (1962). *Curriculum development: Theory and practice.* New York: Harcourt, Brace, & World.

Taba, H. (1964). *Thinking in elementary school children* (U.S.O.E. Cooperative Research Project, No. 1574). San Francisco: San Francisco State College. (ERIC Document Reproduction Service No. ED003 285.)

Taba, H. (1966). *Teaching strategies and cognitive functioning in elementary school children.* (U.S.O.E. Cooperative Research Project No. 2404). San Francisco: San Francisco State College.

Tannenbaum, A. J. (1958). History of interest in the gifted. In N. B. Henry (Ed.), *Education for the gifted.* The fifty-seventh yearbook of the National Society for the Study of Education. Chicago: University of Chicago Press.

Tannenbaum, A. J. (1972). A backward and forward glance at the gifted. *National Elementary Principal*, *51*(5), 14–23.

Tarver, S., Buss, B., & Maggiore, R. (1979). The relationship between creativity and selective attention in learning disabled boys. *Learning Disabled Quarterly*, *2*, 53–59.

Tatsuoka, M. M., & Easley, J. A., Jr. (1963). *Comparison of UICSM vs traditional algebra classes on COOP algebra test scores* (Research Report No. 1). Urbana: University of Illinois Committee on School Mathematics.

Taylor, C. W. (1969). The highest talent potentials of man. *The Gifted Child Quarterly*, *13*, 9–30.

Taylor, C. W., & Ellison, R. L. (1975). Moving toward working models in creativity: Utah creativity experiences and insights. In I.A. Taylor & J.W. Getzels (Eds.), *Perspectives in creativity.* Chicago: Aldine.

Terman, L. M. (1916). *The Stanford revision of the Binet-Simon tests.* Boston: Houghton-Mifflin.

Terman, L. M. (Ed.). (1925). *Mental and physical traits of a thousand gifted children. Genetic studies of genius* (Vol. 1). Stanford: Stanford University Press.

Terman, L. M., & Oden, M. H. (1947). *The gifted child grows up. Genetic studies of genius* (Vol. 4). Stanford: Stanford University Press.

Thurstone, L. L. (1938). *Primary mental abilities.* Psychometric Monographs, No. 1.

Torrance, E. P. (1965). *Rewarding creative behavior.* Englewood Cliffs, NJ: Prentice-Hall.

Torrance, E. P. (1966). *Torrance tests of creative thinking: Norms-technical manual.* Princeton, NJ: Personnel Press.

Torrance, E. P. (1970). *Encouraging creativity in the classroom.* Dubuque, IA: William C. Brown.

Torrance, E. P. (1974). *Torrance tests of creative thinking: Norms-technical manual.* Lexington, MA: Ginn.

Torrance, E. P. (1977, June 20). *Perspectives on the status of the gifted: Current Perspectives.* Presentation to the 1977 Summer Institute on the Education of the Gifted/Talented Teachers College, Columbia University.

Torrance, E. P. (1981). Predicting the creativity of elementary school children (1958–80) — and the teacher who "made a difference." *Gifted Child Quarterly*, *25*, 55–62.

Tyler, L. L. (1966). The taxonomy of educational objectives: Cognitive domain — Its use in evaluating programmed instruction. *California Journal of Educational Research*, *17*, 26–32.

VanTassel-Baska, J. (1980). *The Illinois replication effort of the Johns Hopkins study for precocious youth.* Paper presented at the SMPY Symposium, John Hopkins University.

VanTassel-Baska, J. (1981, December 3). *The case for acceleration.* Paper presented at the CEC-TAG Topical Conference on the Gifted and Talented, Orlando, Florida.

VanTassel-Baska, J., Schuler, A., & Lipschutz, J. (1982). An experimental program for gifted four-year-olds. *Journal for the Education of the Gifted*, *5*(1), 44–45.

Vautour, J. A. C. (1976). Discovering and motivating the artistically gifted LD child. *Teaching Exceptional Children*, *9*, 92–96.

Vernon, P. E. (1951). *The structure of human abilities.* New York: Wiley.

Wallace, W. L. (1962). The BSCS 1961–62 evaluation program — A statistical report. *Biological Sciences Curriculum Study Newsletter*, *19*, 22–24.

Wallach, M. A., & Kogan, N. (1965). *Modes of thinking in young children: A study of the creativity-intelligence distinction.* New York: Holt, Rinehart & Winston.

Walter, A. S. (1970). *Man: A course of study: An evaluation.* Cambridge, MA: Education Development Center.

Ward, V. S. (1961). *Educating the gifted: An axiomatic approach.* Columbus, OH: Charles E. Merrill.

Watts, G. H., & Anderson, R. C. (1971). Effects of three types of inserted questions on learning from prose. *Journal of Educational Psychology, 62*, 387–394.

Wechsler, D. (1941). *The measurement of adult intelligence* (2nd ed.). Baltimore: Williams & Wilkins.

Weiss, P., & Gallagher, J. J. (1982). Report on education of gifted (Vol. 2). Unpublished manuscript. (Available from Frank Porter Graham Child Development Center, University of North Carolina at Chapel Hill, NC 27514.)

Whitlock, B. W. (1978). *Don't hold them back.* New York: College Entrance Examination Board.

Whitmore, J. R. (1980). *Giftedness, conflict, and underachievement.* Boston: Allyn & Bacon.

Williams, P. (1981). *Deriving potential lexical elements of a definition of giftedness.* Thesis proposal submitted to the Department of Special Education, University of New Mexico, Albuquerque.

Witty, P. A. (1930). *A study of one hundred gifted children.* Bulletin of the University of Kansas, Vol. 2.

Witty, P. A. (1940). Some considerations in the education of gifted children. *Educational Administration and Supervision, 26*, 512–521.

Witty, P. (Ed.). (1951). *The gifted child.* Boston: D. C. Heath.

Zilli, M. G. (1971). Reasons why the gifted adolescent underachieves and some of the implications of guidance and counseling to this problem. *Gifted Child Quarterly, 15*, 279–292.

7 EDUCATING THE LEARNING DISABLED

Deborah Deutsch Smith
Suzanne Robinson

Setting forth to write about the education of those with learning disabilities caused us to analyze our own work and that of our colleagues who concentrate their efforts in similar and related areas. Through this self-study, it became increasingly apparent that our interests rest almost exclusively with the learning disabled (LD) student in the classroom. The study of learning disabilities extends far beyond the education of these youngsters. Despite the interesting and important work conducted in areas such as causality, identification of psychosocial characteristics, diagnosis, and family life, we are basically teacher-researchers. Our work and interests center on those youngsters, already identified as LD, who are attending classes where teachers specialize in these students' education. It became clearer to us that our primary focus is the discovery and development of better instructional methods and materials. We are interested particularly in those that teach LD students academic and social skills. Therefore, the thrust of this chapter (and its delimiting features) is how to best educate these students. We have summarized how the field has viewed the education of LD students. We suggest, using the knowledge and research currently available, what we think are some good instructional approaches and strategies for LD teachers to adopt. We identify

exciting areas of current research that will influence educational programs during the remainder of this decade. Also, we discuss those areas where today's researchers must begin to focus their efforts, so programs in the next decade will have far greater impact than those today.

Work with children now referred to as LD began long before the Association for Children with Learning Disabilities was formed, in 1963, or public school classes emerged in the middle of the 1960s. Although many excellent and comprehensive histories are available (Hallahan & Cruickshank, 1973; Kirk & Chalfant, 1984; Myers & Hammill, 1976, 1982; Weiderholt, 1974), a very brief tracing will review where the field came from and why these youngsters have been taught using various methods. It is important to note the field's origins in the work of early neurologists, who studied the brain and how it functioned (e.g., Gall, Broca, Wernicke, Head, and Jackson). Their theories influenced those therapists who worked with young men returning from World War I who, because of head injuries, lost their functional abilities to speak, read, or write. Although Hinshelwood did distinguish between children who never possessed reading abilities from adults who due to cerebral accidents or injury had lost that function, many professionals in the field did not distinguish between these two very different groups. Are the procedures used to retrain skills lost due to injury viable to teach similar skills to a child who never possessed them? Can correlations be drawn between head injury and deficits due to stroke with youngsters trying to learn to read? Regardless of the answer, the field of learning disabilities came from those who assumed that these two groups were related. Youngsters who did not learn basic academic skills must be brain damaged.

Due in part to the support of Weiner, Strauss and Lehtinen (1947), one of the earliest documentations of a comprehensive education program was designed to remediate what we have come to refer to as learning disabilities, and it fully documented past practices and thoughts. It is interesting that many of the teaching tactics they used are similar to those used in LD classes today: number wheels, color cuing, counting blocks, reducing distractions. The field, however, did not pay as much attention to their significant documentation of successful remediation procedures as it did to their clear inference that these students were brain injured. This legacy—implied brain injury, or minimal brain dysfunction (MBD)—remains with us today. Although it is part of most definitions of learning disabilities, it is not particularly helpful to the present field of learning disabilities. In our view, the assumption of MBD has clouded the educational arena for these youngsters since classes were first opened.

Today, researchers (Hallahan & Bryan, 1981; Kauffman & Hallahan, 1979) and practitioners question both the utility and accuracy of the MBD premise. They came to this position because the evidence linking behavioral characteristics to brain dysfunction is circumstantial, speculative, and in most cases clearly not documentable. Identifying brain damage does not lead to sets of instructional or remediation strategies that produce guaranteed or uniform results. The notion of brain damage often leads practitioners to misattribute a behavioral pattern to some innate characteristic of the pupil. Environmental factors, which can be modified with some rather simple reinforce-

ment or instructional procedures, are overlooked. In addition to the reasons Hallahan and his colleagues provide, we feel that this orientation has left some teachers with a defeatist attitude about planning instructional programs for LD youngsters. After all, regardless of what is done, how can a teacher repair brain damage? This is a particularly unfortunate position since the documentation of brain damage is very difficult and only applicable with a very small number of youngsters we serve. Even as neuropsychological assessment procedures advance rapidly with the increasing sophistication of medical, computerized technology, remediation techniques that match these diagnostic abilities remain decades from development and verification.

The assumption of brain damage in those with LD has left another, possibly negative, legacy. Because of the roots in neurology and the medical profession, various medical practices and philosophies have permeated the field. One of those is the diagnostic–prescriptive model. The continuing theme was that if the exact brain damage could be identified, even through a behavioral manifestation, a method could be prescribed, much as a doctor prescribes a medicine to a patient, and the illness (or academic deficit) would be cured. Unfortunately, education does not correlate with medicine. Treatment strategies do not work with all LD youngsters or even those with similar behavioral patterns. Possibly, future neurological research will determine a relationship between physiological structures and educational practices or even find a medical cure for various learning problems. The medical profession, however, is far from providing advances that will benefit the education of youngsters presently enrolled in LD classes. We cannot wait for current neurological research to manifest itself in treatment procedures that will enhance learning. Today's teachers of LD students must possess knowledge of a wide variety of instructional procedures appropriate for each curriculum area. They must be flexible enough to change from one method to another as student performance indicates a need for change. Because of the heterogeneity of the LD population, teachers must be sensitive to the individual learning patterns of their students. Discussion of such approaches and teaching strategies are presented in the next sections of this chapter.

Another past practice, which did not benefit LD students, might have its roots in the field's origins. Possibly, because the work of educational pioneers (e.g., Strauss, Lehtinen, Kephart, and Frostig) appeared so impressive, it was thought that learning disabilities were remediable in the early years of school. It is only recently that classes at the middle and high school levels have been available. Possibly, because of the research of Deshler and his colleagues (Alley, Deshler, Clark, Schumaker, & Warner, 1983; Deshler, Schumaker, Alley, Warner, & Clark, 1982) and particularly because practical evidence indicates that learning disabilities are pervasive problems that do not disappear at the advanced levels of school or in adulthood, a growing concern about LD adolescents and young adults is emerging. Unfortunately, because this finding is fairly recent, many LD persons were denied the continued educational support they needed to maintain the growth they experienced in elementary school. Although programs are now available in middle schools, high schools, and colleges, professionals are still uncertain about what they should emphasize: vocational, life skills, tutorial, college preparatory, or compensatory skills. The reasons for these confusions result from the dearth of information about LD adults and what they become.

With such a negative view of the field's history, its philosophical and theoretical inheritances, one might wonder whether we found anything beneficial from the past practices. We most certainly did. First, there are classes for LD students throughout public schools. In many districts, there are different kinds and types of services for these students ranging from itinerant services, resource rooms, to fully self-contained classrooms. Just as a range of youngsters is served, in many instances a variety of educational options is available. This is good. Second, there is a primarily optimistic

attitude about the education of these students. This feeling surrounds the field. Possibly stemming from the stated clinical success of the early work of Strauss and Lehtinen (1947), Kephart (1971), Frostig (Frostig & Horn, 1967), and Kirk (Hegge, Kirk, & Kirk, 1936; Kirk & Johnson, 1951), the overwhelming belief is that such students can learn and profit from the educational system. It should be noted that much of this early work was conducted before the LD category of exceptionality was developed. Kephart's work, for example, was conducted with youngsters he referred to as slow learners; Kirk's early work at the Wayne County Training School was with mildly retarded pupils. It is quite probable, however, that many of their subjects would, today, be assessed as LD. Most certainly, their work laid the foundation for that conducted later with youngsters labeled *LD*. It definitely influenced the positive attitude that keeps current teachers and researchers alike continually looking for more effective methods, more precise delineations of strategies, and more responsive instructional materials.

EDUCATIONAL APPROACHES

From the middle of the 1960s, researchers have worked to identify overall educational approaches and specific instructional strategies that are effective with LD students. Unlike the work of earlier pioneers, these professionals carefully and methodically researched the efficacy of the specific procedures they came to advocate. Through their amassed work, statements can be made about general approaches and specific procedures proven efficacious with many of the youngsters who comprise the LD population. This section, and the next (Instructional Interventions), suggest educational methods that we feel are most appropriate for application with LD students. In this first section about educational approaches, we have selected several that are somewhat general in nature, such as direct and daily measurement, stages of learning, and information processing.

In the next section, some teaching tactics of particular interest to us and verified through substantial research activities are discussed.

Direct and Daily Measurement

The efficacy of the direct and daily measurement approach to instruction is well established and documented (Haring, Lovitt, Eaton, & Hansen, 1978; Lovitt, 1981; Rhine, 1981; Smith, 1981). Its roots come directly from the applied behavior analysis research methodology, and the features of its clinical application are well founded in both research and practice.

Lovitt (1970, 1975a, 1975b, 1977, 1981, 1982) delineates the major elements of this instructional approach quite clearly. He characterizes it as having five elements: direct measurement, daily measurement, replicable teaching procedures, individual analysis, and experimental control. Those who adopt this approach typically include all of these elements in their classroom routines.

Here, the word *direct* simply means that the behavior of concern is taught specifically and precisely. If Travis needs to learn addition facts from 1 to 9, his performance on those problems is measured or evaluated. The teacher keeps a record of his performance on those problems each time he is assigned them. This measurement might take a variety of forms: number of problems correct and incorrect, percentage correct, or correct rate and incorrect rate. Regardless of the measurement system employed, the student is evaluated directly on classroom assignments.

Both instruction and evaluation occur daily, if possible. For Travis, those arithmetic facts would be given to him to solve each school day, and a record of his performance kept for each time he computed those problems. This consistent evaluation provides an accurate picture of his entry level and progress across time. This approach differs from the traditional pre-post evaluation method, where student progress is checked only periodically, possibly once or twice a year. The benefits of these frequent evaluations are obvious. The teacher has a record of student progress on each target of instruction for each student across time. This allows him or her the opportunity of judging the success of the teaching tactics employed and provides information valuable for further instructional planning. If, for example, a teaching tactic is not helping a student learn a specific academic task, the teacher knows that within a short period of time. The teacher does not have to wait for a year-end report to discover that a student did not profit from certain instructional activities. Because the information is collected on a daily or very frequent basis, the teacher has sufficient information to judge what kinds of techniques should be tried next. In addition to letting the teacher know when to change interventions, because they are not sufficiently successful, frequent evaluation lets the teacher know when the student has mastered the instructional target. Once a predetermined criterion is met, he or she can move the student to other academic tasks that must be learned. This readily available information saves days of instructional time, for students can be moved exactly when their performance indicates they are ready to advance to more challenging tasks.

The teaching procedures used by those who adhere to this educational approach are replicable. Researchers using the related research methodology — applied behavior analysis — are careful to detail the specific procedures they employed to achieve the results they reported. Also, teachers using the direct and daily approach usually are very careful to document their teaching procedures. When sharing those with others the exact behaviors pinpointed for instruction, procedures employed, and scores and progress made by individual students are reported. This is quite beneficial to those youngsters taught with this approach. Present benefits rest with teacher accountability, already discussed. Future benefits result from the information available. Teachers that specific LD youngsters will have in ensuing school years will know which instructional procedures were effective and exactly what were the past targets of instruction.

One key component of this approach is that youngsters are treated as individuals. Even when group instructional methods are used, evaluation of individual performances are kept. This is particularly important for students with LD, for they are a very heterogeneous group of learners (Kirk & Chalfant, 1984; Lyon, 1982; Lyon & Watson, 1981). No one instructional technique produces effective and efficient learning for all LD students. Therefore, particularly for these students, individually based instructional planning, implementation, and evaluation are necessary if maximal learning is to occur for every student.

The notion of experimental control is of utmost concern for the researcher using the applied behavior analysis research methodology. The key here is that changes noted in the dependent variable are attributable to the scheduling of the independent variable. It is through the achievement of experimental control that researchers have the confidence to communicate the effectiveness of one reading approach or another. Teachers, many times, are not particularly concerned with why youngsters learned but rather that they mastered an academic skill. However, when teachers want to use a procedure with confidence with other students, it is valuable to know whether a particular instructional strategy can be attributed to past successful programming. It is through replications that confidence and experimental control are gained.

To us, the direct and daily approach should be advocated as the educational approach to use in programs designed for LD students. First, research data support its effectiveness (Jenkins, Mayhall, Peschka, & Townsend, 1974; Lovitt & Fantasia, 1983; Mirkin & Deno, 1979). Second, the built-in accountability system inherent in the measurement and evaluation of student performance provides teachers with information critical and sensitive to instructional planning. Third, daily instruction, an integral component of this approach, produces improved performance (Mayhall & Jenkins, 1977). Fourth, the approach is uniquely flexible. Almost any instructional technique can be used with this system. The approach does not dictate what is taught or the procedures used; however, it does mandate that evaluation be conducted.

Stages of Learning

The notion that a learner's level of entry influences efficiency of learning (the amount of time required to master a skill) and the selection of instructional methods is not a new premise. One does not expect a youngster just learning the names of the letters to be able to read passages fluently within a short period of time. Neither does a parent teach a young child to eat with utensils by delivering a lecture but demonstrates and guides that child's practice. For many, the consideration of the learner's entry level as instructional procedures and expectations are planned is instinctive. Unfortunately, a match between a stage of learning and the selection of instructional procedures has not been obvious to many educators.

Not so long ago, many researchers (Kazdin, 1973; O'Leary & Becker, 1967; Packard, 1970) doubted the power of instructions. The discrediting of instructions and the support of reinforcement as an educational panacea was widespread. Several studies in the 1960s, however, indicated that reinforcement procedures are not always effective. The research of Ayllon and Azrin (1964) and Hopkins (1968) showed that reinforcement is ineffective when the targeted behavior is not in the learner's repertoire and, therefore, cannot be reinforced. Much to the surprise of those researchers, in both studies, instructions had to be used initially to bring the desired behaviors to a level where reinforcement could become influential. These studies led Smith and Lovitt (1976) to design a study which looked specifically at the relationship between student entry level and the success of reinforcement. The results of their research indicated a definite relationship between students' entry levels and the influence of specific interventions. In that study, reinforcement did not help students learn how to solve computational arithmetic problems but did successfully bring them to fluency. Since that research, others (Affleck, Lowenbraun, &

Archer, 1980; Buckley & Walker, 1978; Haring, et al., 1978; SCAT, 1977; White & Haring, 1976) have all found that the influence of specific intervention procedures is related to the entry level of the student. The basic premise is that certain tactics are more effective when a person is first learning how to perform a specific skill; others are more effective when the skill needs to be refined or more thoroughly incorporated into the learner's repertoire.

Educators have sought to delineate these entry levels of stages of learning to guide both researchers and practitioners. Possibly, past equivocal findings can be accounted for by reexamining the entry levels of each subject. By considering subjects' entry levels, researchers might be able to cumulatively determine which tactics have a higher probability of successful application for given learning situations. The results of such research should help teachers select those procedures that have the highest chance for success with their individual pupils. This approach has not yet led to perfect educational plans for all LD youngsters. It has, however, reduced instructional time, because teachers do not select tactics that

research has indicated are not scheduled appropriately in particular learning stages.

So far, researchers have identified five broad stages of learning applicable for instruction on academic tasks: acquisition, proficiency, maintenance, generalization, and adaption. Most likely, future research will define these stages more precisely and the interventions that best match each stage. Research currently available offers teachers some general guidelines about the effects of specific procedures for many of these stages. Those are summarized in the following discussion. To help the reader understand the conceptual scheme for this approach, Figure 7.1 illustrates a linear display of the stages of learning and students' learning levels.

During the first stage of learning, *acquisition*, the learner needs to learn how to execute the task. The person needs to learn how to borrow, how to write cursively, how to use a microcomputer, how to play tennis. Here the entry level of the learner is very low, possibly 0%. Our experience with LD youngsters has indicated that many times after some period of instruction the skill is almost mastered, but has not reached a predetermined mastery criterion

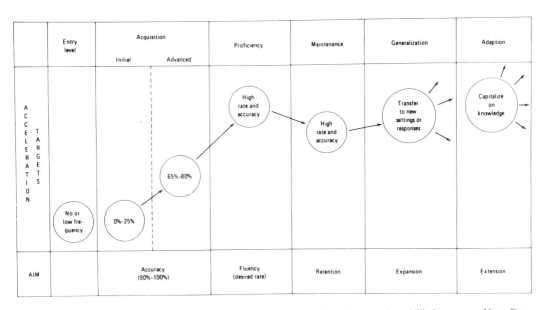

Figure 7.1. Stages of learning that led to ultimate mastery through continual increase in a skill's frequency. (Note. From *Teaching the Learning Disabled* [p. 68] by D. D. Smith, 1981, Englewood Cliffs, NJ: Prentice-Hall. Copyright 1981 by Prentice-Hall. Used with permission.)

(e.g., three days at 100%, two out of three days at 95%). To reach this aim, another intervention must be scheduled. Because of our experience, we have divided the acquisition stage into two levels: *initial* and *advanced*. It should be noted that many youngsters learn how to perform the target skill and achieve criterion with the first intervention applied and, therefore, pass from acquisition to the next stage without need of further instruction; many, however, do not. The interventions appropriate at the initial acquisition stage (e.g., modeling, shaping, match-to-sample) are not always appropriate at the advanced acquisition stage (e.g., error drill, feedback, reward for accuracy). For example, Jason needed to learn how to solve long division problems. The teacher scheduled a demonstration, where she solved the first problem on Jason's worksheet and described the process she used as she solved the problem. She also had Jason solve the next problem for her. He then computed the remaining problems independently. Clearly, the tactic worked, for Jason's scores rose from 0% to 70% within a few days. However, no additional progress was noted over the next three days. On close examination of Jason's worksheets, the teacher noted that his errors were now due to careless subtraction within the long division problems. Now, she added specific instructions about his careless subtraction, and Jason's scores rose to 100%. This student needed instruction at both the initial and advanced acquisition levels to achieve criterion completely.

Once learners have acquired a skill—they know how to do the task—it still should not be considered mastered. They need to execute that task with some fluency. The target is now no longer mere accuracy but accuracy and speed of performance. Simply being able to recall words read orally is not sufficient. The learner must be able to read with enough speed so the passage is fluent and comprehensible. At the *proficiency* stage, the instructor's role is to help the learner become fluent or proficient at performing the skill. It is here that drill, practice, and reinforcement are powerful interventions. And, the target is to retain accuracy achieved during the acquisition stage and add speed of performance. The criterion for mastery could be the amount of words read, math facts solved, or words written within a specific time limit. Often, teachers use rate (correct and incorrect rates)* to judge the learners' progress.

The next stages are often problematic for exceptional learners. Teachers bemoan the fact that although a considerable amount of instructional time was spent on a skill, and the youngster had attained scores that indicated mastery, the skill was not retained. With the passage of summer or a long school break, the student returns to school and has forgotten what was learned. For this reason, the *maintenance* stage should be an important part of the instructional sequence. For many, after mastery in both the acquisition and proficiency stages is noted, continued practice (overlearning) with the skill is sufficient. Some teachers set criterion levels for the two previous stages much higher than necessary so some loss in performance level still leaves the behavior at an acceptable level. For others, additional instructional time with the application of specific interventions, such as self-management (discussed in a later section) are necessary to ensure that the targeted skill remains in the youngster's repertoire in a useful form. Because of the problems centering around retention of learning, it is recommended to have students continue to work on the now "mastered" tasks on a periodic basis (possibly once a week for several months). This allows for a monitoring of the recently learned skill. If performance levels begin to drop, interventions can be scheduled to avoid further deterioration of the skill.

After maintenance comes a period of *generalization*, where the learned behavior should

---

*Correct rate is the number of accurate response units divided by the time it took to complete the task; and, incorrect rate is the number of incorrect response units divided by the time it took to complete the task.

occur in all appropriate situations, regardless of the setting or other environmental differences. Many LD students do not generalize (Lovitt, 1977). For these students, direct instruction specifically aimed at generalizing learned skills is necessary. For example, Heather had learned and become proficient at computing subtraction problems that required borrowing or regrouping. She was given worksheets that contained such problems for several months after achieving mastery and meeting the criterion scores the teacher had set. However, when asked to balance a checkbook, she was unable to generalize or transfer the skill of subtraction. For Heather, the teacher had to create a variety of situations where the skill of subtraction was required and provide instruction to program for generalization of borrowing.

The last stage of learning, *adaption*, has not been the target of much research, but clearly needs to become the focus of future work. In this stage, learners must use learned skills, extend on previous learning, and apply them in novel situations. It is important for LD persons to be able to apply previous learning, so they may be more flexible in life situations. Perhaps using the discovery approach and problem solving techniques (discussed in a later section of this chapter) will lead to a better understanding of what skills are required to adapt knowledge to novel situations. Most definitely, those researchers and practitioners beginning to work with LD persons in transition from school to adulthood will have to turn their attention to this important, but frequently neglected, stage of learning.

The stages of learning are important for all educators to keep in mind. Not all students require direct and specific instruction at all stages. Some students, once taught a skill, are proficient at its execution, remember it, apply it in all appropriate situations, and build on that information in new and novel situations. Unfortunately, this is not the case for most LD persons. It is the educators' task to program and check for each stage as part of their instructional sequences. By using the

stage of learning approach, researchers can better identify which intervention procedures are most efficient at each stage for specific instructional areas. Teachers could use this information by matching the learner's entry level with those procedures that have the highest probability of success at that stage of learning. This should avoid wasting precious instructional time because tactics with a higher probability of success will be selected first. Also, by remembering that a number of stages must be considered, curricula can be planned that are more complete and lead to more thorough usefulness by their students throughout their lives.

Information Processing

Information processing is a term used to describe the way in which individuals acquire, retain, and transform knowledge. This orientation toward the study of thinking has garnered growing attention over the last decade. Research findings are encouraging and provide an explanation of how LD persons might differ from nondisabled learners. To some, however, focusing on inferred, cognitive activity as an explanation of learning disabilities comes perilously close to endorsing a resurgence of the perceptual process training orientation (Attribute Treatment Interaction) to learning disabilities; a perspective that has not proved efficacious (Hallahan & Cruickshank, 1973; Hamill & Wiederholt, 1973).

Hallahan and Bryan (1981) addressed this concern, identifying three major ways in which the information processing and perceptual motor processing literature differ. First, information processing research reflects far better research practice using adults, normal children, and most recently, LD subjects in the evolution of its conclusions. Second, the information processing perspective has a more solid theoretical base than did the perceptual motor processing literature. Third, information processing researchers have been cautious in advocating educational activities to teach LD students. Perceptual motor advocates, on the other hand, were quick to encourage educational practice before research verified these procedures. Furthermore, we find researchers who explore this explanation of individual differences cautious; they attempt to identify disconfirming as well as positive evidence of information processing differences in LD subjects when compared to normal subjects (Bauer, 1982; Swanson, 1982; Torgesen & Greenstein, 1982; Torgesen & Houck, 1980). There are thorough reviews of information processing research elsewhere (see Hall, 1982, and Hallahan & Bryan, 1981). In this section we will only synopsize predominant research findings so the educational implications that evolve from information processing research can be put in context.

Researchers (Bauer, 1977; Hallahan & Bryan, 1981; Torgesen, 1977; Wong, 1980) reported that many LD students do not approach learning situations strategically. Instead, they are passive; unaware that they must interact with information in order to organize, store, or retrieve it. However, when LD students are taught an appropriate learning strategy (for example, cumulative rehearsal or clustering), they perform at levels comparable to their nondisabled peers. Therefore, their initial inability to do the task cannot be attributed to a capacity deficit (i.e., *less* capacity). Instead, their inability to do the task is attributed to a strategy deficit.

LD students are deficient not only in learning strategies; preliminary investigations also lead us to believe they lack metacognitive skills (Kotsonis & Patterson, 1980; Wong, 1980). Metacognition refers both to knowledge about cognition and also regulation of one's own cognition. Flavell and Wellman (1977), in their example about memory, delineated knowledge one must have about cognition. They identified three classes of variables: (a) memory-relevant characteristics of the person, (b) memory-relevant characteristics of the task, and (c) potential employable strategies. Cavanaugh and Perlmutter (1982) attempted to define more clearly the regulation component of metamemory. *How* knowledge about memory (or cognition) is used comes under the

domain of executive processes. Executive processes include *if* and *how* one monitors and evaluates any ongoing memory activity. This would include

> generating and inventing memory strategies (most often by combining aspects of several strategies to fit the task better), selecting the most appropriate strategy, testing and evaluating strategies (does the strategy now in use help one advance to goal), changing strategies if necessary and sequencing multiple strategies. (p. 15)

The two facets of metacognition (or metamemory) interact in a symbiotic relationship (Brown & Palincsar, 1982).

Researchers are only beginning to investigate metacognitive characteristics of LD students. However, the study of metacognition promises insights into self-regulatory learning behaviors that characterize successful independent learning. Furthermore, if LD students lack metacognitive skills, it may prove necessary to train these skills directly. A precursor to strategy usage may be knowledge about the utility of such strategies. It is assumed that "in strategy transfer contexts, decisions (or metacognition) are required about whether to use a previously learned rule or strategy and how to adapt it to new task demands" (Cavanaugh & Borkowski, 1980, p. 452). Researchers using nondisabled subjects (Borkowski, Levers, & Gruenenfelder, 1976; Kennedy & Miller, 1976) and LD subjects (Brown & Palincsar, 1982; Wong & Jones, 1982) found that information about strategy usefulness determined the extent of strategy transfer.

However, other researchers found it difficult to demonstrate the relationship between cognition and metacognition. Cavanaugh and Borkowski (1980) attempted to test whether children's verbalized metamemory related to how they performed on various memory tasks. They did not find correlations between metamemory and performance. Children who demonstrated broad metamemory knowledge did not necessarily do well on the memory tasks, and children who performed well on the memory activities did not necessarily exhibit broad metamemory knowledge. These results indicate our limited knowledge about the relationships between metacognition, executive processes, and strategic behavior. While it appears efficacious to train LD students in strategy usage, metacognitive knowledge, and executive processes, further research must describe the relationships among these three factors before optimum training sequences can be devised.

Some educational practices have been developed that incorporate principles drawn from information processing research. Cognitive behavior modification is one. Cognitive behavior modification incorporates the use of systematic instruction. It adheres to behavioral principles while focusing on modifying inner speech with the intent of encouraging the student to adopt a more reflective or thoughtful cognitive style (Keogh & Glover, 1980; Meichenbaum, 1980). Learning, or cognitive strategy instruction (reviewed in a later section of this chapter) is a related educational procedure that utilizes cognitive behavior modification principles and is receiving extensive examination with LD students (see, for example, Hallahan, Lloyd, Kauffman, & Loper, 1983). While promising, it is apparent from current information processing research that the complex interactions between developmental, individual person, task, and strategy factors must be unraveled before conclusive answers about the appropriateness of this approach can be provided.

INSTRUCTIONAL INTERVENTIONS

In this section, we review some intervention strategies, or teaching tactics, that have particular interest to us. It was a difficult task to select which interventions we would summarize, for comprehensive texts and reviews have been written about interventions appropriate for classroom use. Clearly, a comprehensive review of all of the teaching procedures available is beyond the scope of this chapter, but a select sampling was necessary, we felt. Those interested in more detailed reports should refer to the many excellent documents available. For social behavior the reader may review the following: Axelrod (1983), Kerr and Nelson (1983), Smith (1984), and Stephens (1977). For academic remediation, these sources might be of interest: Alley and Deshler (1979), Haring et al. (1978), Lovitt (1984), and Smith (1981).

Modeling

Modeling, showing someone how to execute a skill, probably has been a part of human repertoires from time immemorial. It is a natural human response. Parents use it rather instinctively to teach their children skills; athletic instructors show their pupils how to perform the right movements to play the game correctly. The influence of modeling has been studied in a variety of classroom related tasks: disruption (Csapo, 1972), imitation (Baer, Peterson, & Sherman, 1967; Brigham & Sherman, 1968), and children's phobias (Bandura, Grusec, & Menlove, 1967). Its influence on academic skills has been a continuing interest of ours. Its influence is powerful and quick and has produced similar results with a substantial number of research subjects and students in LD classrooms in a variety of academic areas.

The clear power of this intervention to teach LD pupils in the acquisition stage of learning how to compute computational arithmetic problems has been demonstrated many times. In our first studies (Smith, 1973; Smith & Lovitt, 1975), 17 individual experiments using seven subjects indicated that modeling produced remarkable effects. The subjects' scores rose from 0–100% within a matter of several days. The technique used was very simple, requiring a mere 45 seconds of teacher time, daily. We called the procedure the *demonstration plus permanent model*. The teacher came to each student's desk during the intervention condition and solved the first problem on the worksheet. As she did, she verbalized the steps she used to solve the problem. This problem remained with the child as he or she independently solved the rest of the problems on the worksheet. Another study (Fleming, 1977;

Smith, 1976) replicated and extended the first to group situations as well. As before, the students learned how to solve the computational problems quickly when the procedure was individually applied. The results, although still quite good, were not as effective in the group situation. Each group was comprised of four students. Although they all learned how to solve the problems, the number of days needed to reach criterion (3 consecutive days of 100%) was longer. This was due to several children's inability to obtain criterion as quickly as the others. Since the whole group was scheduled to remain together, this caused some youngsters to stay with the task longer than necessary.

Blankenship (1978) also demonstrated the power of modeling on the acquisition of computational skills. The procedure she used added a feature to the one we had used earlier. In her study, after the teacher solved the first problem on the worksheet, the student computed one for the teacher. She did this to ensure that the student understood the steps to follow when solving the problem. Since her study, we have used this additional feature in our studies and practice with LD students.

Since the publication of the Computational Arithmetic Program (CAP) (Smith & Lovitt, 1982), which advocates the use of this demonstration technique when youngsters need to

acquire computational skills, hundreds of case studies have come to our attention that verify this technique again. Also, in some recent research (Rivera & Smith, 1984) investigating LD youngsters' generalization abilities, the tactic has served to promote both acquisition and transfer of various computational abilities. Table 7.1 summarizes the research we have identified that verifies using demonstration technique in the acquisition of computational arithmetic. Most definitely, we advocate its use and further replication with LD students.

Modeling has also been researched in the proficiency stage of learning. In several reading studies (Smith, 1978, 1979), the teacher read at a rate of 100 words per minute before the students read their succeeding passages orally. With that intervention alone, their correct rates indicated substantially more fluency (one boy's scores improved from 12.4 to 29.8) in a very short period of time. These data suggest the power of modeling across several stages of learning for at least two very important curriculum areas: arithmetic and reading.

Self-management

Since Lovitt's (Lovitt, 1973; Lovitt & Curtiss, 1969) demonstration of the power of self-management procedures on students' academic

TABLE 7.1. SUMMARY OF DEMONSTRATION PLUS PERMANENT MODEL RESEARCH

Study	No. of Experiments	Baseline $\overline{X}$	Intervention $\overline{X}$	Days to Criterion	Criterion Scores
Smith (1973); Smith & Lovitt (1976)	17	0%	99%	8.6	Condition length: minimum 7 days; 3 consecutive 100% scores
Fleming (1977); Smith (1976) Study I	6	0%	100%	5	Condition length: minimum 5 days; 3 consecutive 100% scores
Study II	2* groups	0%	83%	14	
Rivera & Smith (1984)	3	22%	96%	9	Condition length: minimum 3 days; 3 consecutive 90% scores
Blankenship (1978)	9	0%	93%	—	Unstated

*8 subjects.

performance, interest from both researchers and teachers has grown. Self-management procedures have great appeal for many reasons. First, research has indicated that they produce excellent changes in student performance. As interventions used alone in both the advanced acquisition and proficiency stages of learning, they produce outstanding improvement in student learning. Second, they seem to be one of few demonstrated sets of procedures that enhance maintenance of learning. Third, they provide, in their very nature, instruction in an important life skill. In this section, a short review of the self-management literature is presented (for more thorough reviews please refer to these sources: Hallahan et al., 1983, O'Leary & Dubey, 1979; Rosenbaum & Drabman, 1979; Smith, 1984; and Workman, 1982). Much exciting work is being conducted in this area, and initial results hold great promise. The application of these procedures will result in substantial changes in the way LD students are taught.

Self-management requires students to become actively involved in their own educational programs. Several researchers have characterized LD students as passive learners (Torgesen, 1977; Wong, 1980). When the instructional methods employed require active participation by the learners, many students seem to change their motivational levels, thereby learning more. Self-management often is used as a treatment package that includes three different elements: self-regulation, self-evaluation, and self-reinforcement. However, each element has been studied separately and has produced positive results.

Self-regulation is most often used when the youngster does not possess the necessary self-control to be a nondisruptive member of the class. It can, however, have application to academic situations, as well. By allowing a student to schedule the individualized segments of the academic day (self-scheduling), the youngster learns an important survival skill (time-management) and might improve task performance (Lovitt, 1973).

Self-evaluation, sometimes referred to as *self-*

recording, requires the students to evaluate their performances. This can be in either the social or academic area. In either case, it has proven to be quite effective in producing desired behavioral changes (Broden, Hall, & Mitts, 1971; Hallahan, Marshall, & Lloyd, 1981; Kneedler & Hallahan, 1981; Lloyd, Hallahan, Kosiewicz, & Kneedler, 1982). An interesting result of the Kneedler and Hallahan (1981) study was that students did not have to record their performances accurately for positive changes to occur.

Self-reinforcement, where the person determines how much and what should be the reward for improved performance, has proven to be quite successful for both the proficiency and maintenance stages of learning. In one of the first demonstrations of this procedure, Lovitt and Curtiss (1969) showed that when pupils rewarded themselves they achieved better changes in performance than when teachers imposed the reinforcement procedures on the students' classroom work. After this initial study, researchers (Billingsley, 1977; Felixbrod & O'Leary, 1973; Glynn, 1970) debated and further studied the relative merits of having the teacher or the student arrange the reinforcement. The debate was put to rest with the results of an exceptionally well controlled study conducted by Dickerson and Creedon (1981). That research showed that the earlier results of Lovitt and Curtiss were correct: self-reinforcement is superior to teacher-reinforcement. Dickerson and Creedon found self-management to be extremely beneficial in three ways: (a) it produced substantial improvement in behavior; (b) it encouraged active involvement by the students in their educational programs; and (c) it served to teach an important skill beneficial to independent adult living. It is interesting to note that in many of these self-reinforcement studies, the students established more stringent standards for themselves than their teachers did in the teacher-imposed reinforcement conditions.

Many researchers (Nelson & Hayes, 1981) suggest that all three elements of self-management be used concurrently. They believe that the by-products of the entire treatment package teaches youngsters to observe, monitor, and reward their own performances. This, they maintain, is a valuable life skill and also produces enhanced learning of the skills targeted for instruction.

Learning Strategies

Many researchers currently are directing their energy toward the evaluation of teaching LD students to be active, strategic learners. This avenue of research hints at a new conceptualization of learning disabilities while providing validation of teaching procedures that promote not only skill acquisition but also skill generalization. If one accepts that LD students are "passive" learners (Torgesen, 1977; Wong, 1979), then teaching LD students to use learning (or cognitive) strategies appears to be a means of encouraging them to be active, effective learners.

Learning strategies are defined by Alley and Deshler (1979) "as techniques, principles, or rules that will facilitate the acquisition, manipulation, integration, storage, and retrieval of information across situations and settings" (p. 13). Learning strategies focus on enhancing the learner's self-control, self-awareness, and conscious participation in organized learning (Meichenbaum, 1980). Thus, instructional thrust is directed toward teaching students "how to learn" rather than toward instruction of specific content. For example, the focus in strategy instruction would be teaching a student *how* to identify important information in a biology text rather than drilling the student on a list of biology facts. A learning strategy typically is a content-free rule that a student can use not only to meet immediate task requirements, but also to generalize to other, novel situations (Schumaker, Deshler, Alley, & Warner, 1982). So, while aiding students in the immediate acquisition of needed information, it also addresses directly the need to teach with skill generalization in mind.

Researchers have demonstrated the effectiveness of instruction in the use of learning strategies to remediate many learning deficits of both adolescent and elementary aged students. Deshler and his associates (Alley, Schumaker, Denton, Warner, & Deshler, in press; Schumaker, Deshler, Alley, & Warner, 1982; Schumaker, Deshler, Alley, Warner, & Denton, 1982) found that knowledge of a variety of learning strategies enabled adolescent LD students to increase their reading comprehension, writing proficiency, listening and notetaking, and test taking skills to a level which enabled them to succeed in the regular high school curriculum. Other researchers (Brown & Palinscar, 1982; Cappelli & Markman, 1982; Wong, 1980; Wong & Jones, 1982) taught elementary and junior high aged LD students' comprehension monitoring strategies, which increased the students' recall and comprehension of written materials. We (Robinson, 1983) found that instruction in various memory and comprehension strategies increased elementary aged LD students' ability to listen and comprehend oral directions or nonfiction material. Others (Camp, Blom, & van Doorninck, 1977; Douglas, Parry, Martin, & Garson, 1976; Kneedler, 1980; Schumaker & Ellis, 1982) attempted to increase social skills through cognitive training and achieved moderate success.

Researchers not only have concerned themselves with *what* to teach, but also have addressed the important question of *how* to teach learning strategies to maximize instructional success. Deshler, Alley, Warner, & Schumaker (1981) developed a sequence of instructional steps that they found successful in promoting the acquisition of learning strategies. Their instructional procedures include evaluation of a student's current, inefficient learning style; teacher modeling; verbal rehearsal; practice in materials of sequenced difficulty; and corrective feedback. Meichenbaum (1982) suggested a similar instructional approach, which emphasizes student collaboration in the development of the training components.

Others advocate instructional procedures that directly teach skills required for generalization. Brown and Palinscar (1982) included self-regulation training in a strategy acquisition sequence. Their intent was to increase the individual's ability to orchestrate the use of a strategy in a variety of settings and increase knowledge about the range of the strategy's utility. Schumaker, Deshler, Alley, and Warner (1982) also noted that LD students must be taught how to generalize. They included generalization instruction in their strategy acquisition steps. Clearly, researchers found that maintenance and generalization of trained strategies in children's performances is more likely to occur when instruction includes systematic and direct instruction of strategies, information about the utility of any given strategy, and instruction in self-regulatory behaviors to monitor strategy usage.

We also must acknowledge that research results are not totally convincing in their demonstration of maintenance and generalization of learning. Flavell and Wellman (1977) describe the complexity of strategic learning:

> Suppose a person judges that categorized stimuli are easier to recall than noncategorized ones. Would he inevitably use categorization as a storage strategy, given obviously categorizable stimuli? Not at all. He may know about categorization but think that something else might be better yet in this situation. He may think the list easy enough so that he can use simple inspection for storage. He may have enough knowledge to judge that categorization would be a good strategy, if asked about it, but not enough to think to utilize such a strategy on his own. Lastly, there are undoubtedly gaps between metamemory and memory behavior that have to be chalked up to Original Sin. Moral action does not always accord with moral beliefs, and similarly, we do not always try to retrieve information or prepare for future retrieval in what we believe to be the most effective ways. (pp. 27–28)

Surely, many LD students' learning styles will amplify the normal variability just described. Are these procedures powerful and sensitive enough to identify and overcome this variability?

Finally, we do not know if all LD students will profit from instruction in learning strategies. Cognitive psychologists suggest developmental trends are seen in the evolution of strategic learning in the normal child. Are some strategic behaviors beyond the cognitive maturity of some students? Furthermore, how much of LD students' academic problems can be attributed to lack of learning strategies?

While this relatively new intervention holds promise, many questions remain to be answered before concluding success. For example, the effectiveness (ease of use and power) of each strategy measured against its potential generalized use must be considered. Newell (1979) described various cognitive strategies as existing on an inverted cone. At the base of the cone are powerful but task-specific strategies. When known and employed correctly, their use ensures successful task completion. However, these strategies are specific to a limited domain. At the tip of the cone are highly general, but weak strategies. If this analogy is accurate, researchers need to identify where strategies fall along this continuum. In addition, a full array of such strategies must be identified and then validated through research before they can be suggested for wide use in applied settings.

CURRENT ISSUES

We feel a number of current issues will affect the field of learning disabilities. These issues have implications for how students who are identified and placed in LD classes will be taught. Although many important issues currently draw attention from the leaders in this field, we identified several that we believe have significant bearing on classroom procedures.

Who We Serve

Certainly, one predominant issue in the field of learning disabilities is deciding who and how many students we will serve. At the heart of this issue is the multitude of "professional opinions" on the most appropriate definition of learning disabilities paired with an incomplete picture of the causes of the condition. In addition, financial realities now influence the issues, as government cannot afford to serve all who are displaying academic deficits. When services were provided initially to LD students, numbers were small, involving less than 1% of the school population. As years have passed and services expanded, estimates reveal that as high as 20% of the school population has been labeled and served as LD. This posed a financial burden on the limited resources available to educate the handicapped. In part, it is this reality that has caused state education agencies and the professional community to question the LD identification criterion. It is evident that existing definitions are neither totally convincing nor satisfactory in summarizing what educators believe comprises learning disabilities; hence, disagreement about who will be served. We do not attempt to resolve this continuing debate here. (Those interested in an indepth treatment of that issue should refer to the January 1983 issue of *Journal of Learning Disabilities* or Hallahan & Bryan, 1981). Instead, we would like to examine the issue from a different perspective: separating who is LD from who will we serve.

Currently, many states serve a higher number of LD students than is expected. Whether all these students are truly LD is questionable. However, it does reflect teachers' beliefs that a greater than expected percentage of students need and benefit from the instructional procedures and structure utilized by special educators. (It also might reflect a preference of diagnosticians to use the LD label.) A cynic might suggest that a high number of LD referrals demonstrates a pervasive desire by regular educators to rid themselves of unsuccessful students. An alternative explanation would perpetuate the myth that "learning disabilities specialists cure kids who are not learning." We propose a more acceptable explanation: most teachers are concerned about students who, for whatever reasons, are not learning and recognize that procedures used by special educators enhance learning for many students.

Being served in a special education class for LD students is expensive. To receive direct services from a learning disabilities specialist, a student must be referred, assessed, diagnosed, and then served in a class with fewer students.

Costs restrict the number of students states can serve in this manner. While this delimiting factor might be irrelevant to the issue of who is truly LD, it is, nonetheless, relevant to the issue of who will we serve.

Given these realities, how might we address the provision of services? Assuming the status quo (many youngsters are not succeeding in regular education) remains, it might be advisable to modify or reemphasize the *possible* roles of the learning disabilities specialist. As Ysseldyke and Algozzine (1983) so aptly point out, "Serving all children failing in school is impossible, serving those meeting arbitrary criteria is impractical, and serving only the severely handicapped is unacceptable" (p. 30). We suggest, as have others (Christie, McKenzie, & Burdett, 1972; Reid & Hresko, 1982; Wiederholt, Hammill, & Brown, 1983), that learning disabilities teachers must provide educational services not only to students identified as LD, by whatever criteria, but also to regular education teachers and parents so that they may utilize the teaching technology special educators have refined over the last 20 years. Much work has been done to transform procedures developed and validated with exceptional students in individual interactions to formats applicable to the regular classroom. Classroom and discipline management (Smith, 1984), direct and daily measurement procedures (Blankenship & Lilly, 1981), parent training (Kroth, 1975), as well as academic interventions (Idol-Maestas, 1983), are only a few examples of the many efforts in this area.

Advocating that learning disabilities teachers provide consultative services to regular educators is not new (Christie et al., 1972; Deno, 1970; Lilly, 1971). In fact, it is integral to all descriptions of a continuum of services. Yet, minimal attention is directed toward consultative skills in most learning disabilities preparation programs. For example, there are few courses on consultation in the classroom. This is unfortunate. However, even if training in consulting skills were available, special education must be perceived in a changed light, resulting in changes in administrative structure. Without administrative changes, cooperation among teachers will be hampered by lack of time and opportunity to work together.

It could be that regular educators, because of a degree of naivete in regard to learning disabilities, have overreferred students who might be helped by instructional procedures historically used by special educators. Hallahan and Kauffman (1976) assert that the most fruitful use of the term *learning disabilities* might be as a *concept* rather than as a specific category, which segregates who gets what kind of instruction. It seems appropriate to quote from these authors' discussion of this issue as it relates to the division of services for children labeled *ED, LD,* and *EMR*.

> "learning disabilities" can provide a much needed unifying theme whose emphasis is upon specific behavior, abilities, and disabilities of the child. Overworked verbally, though underworked in practice, is the established maxim that it behooves the teacher to be aware of "*individual differences*." Children have different abilities and disabilities, and patterns of these abilities and disabilities. Not really until the advent of the "learning disabilities specialist" was anything but lip service paid to the concept of individual differences. What must be achieved is the application of this concept in its purest form to all children with learning problems, regardless of the diagnostic classification of those children. (p. 41)

We *do not* believe that classes for LD students be discontinued. We firmly feel that many LD pupils must be served in special classes where highly trained teachers can fully address their unique educational needs. We do believe that there are many benefits of expanding the role of the LD specialist.

The *concept* of individualized instruction determined by individual differences is applicable also to those who are not diagnosed. We believe learning disabilities teachers are educators foremost and as such should be encouraged, through a variety of administrative alternatives, to serve students without the label of *learning disabilities*. Responsible consultation with regular education teachers and parents, might reduce the referral rate and

effectively maintain many youngsters in regular classrooms.

More Research Precision

Recently, a number of researchers have expressed concern about the subjects used and the way they are described in learning disabilities research reports (Harber, 1981a, 1981b; Kavale & Dye, 1981; Keogh, Major-Kingsley, Omori-Gordon, & Reid, 1982; Lovitt & Jenkins, 1979). Any review of LD subject description sections reveals that many researchers are somewhat cavalier about the information they provide regarding the subjects who participated in their studies. A common description of subjects merely indicates that the subjects were "school identified learning disabled." Some subject descriptions indicate that the students were enrolled in LD classrooms on the basis of state and local education agency guidelines, without specifying what those were. If, as in the field of mental retardation, the criterion of identification and placement were consistent across the United States (or even within specific states), such a casual method of describing subjects might be acceptable. Even under those conditions, however, more details should be included because the LD population is comprised of such different members.

Lack of specificity in descriptions of the LD subjects used in research is a critical problem for the field in general. First, it makes research replications and extensions impossible. This factor alone might explain contradictory and equivocal findings because different researchers studying the influence of the same technique might not have used the same or similar populations. Second, teachers or practitioners cannot be certain that the subjects who made substantial progress in a research study are like any of their students or clients. Third, it does not allow for careful post hoc analyses of research already conducted. If, for example, future research identifies subgroups within the LD population, insufficient or incomplete demographic data will render all previous research useless.

Reflecting professional concern and acknowledging the seriousness of this situation for the field, the Council for Learning Disabilities charged its research committee with the task of studying the issue. It encouraged the committee to establish guidelines for researchers to use as they develop subject description sections in their research reports. The product of their work (Smith et al., 1984) is a set of minimum standards to be used for the description of subjects in LD research reports. Included are guidelines for the demographic information that should be included and what to do when it is not available. Ideally, these minimum standards will become adopted by the entire field and all journals that publish research about learning disabilities. If these standards become practice, research findings should be more meaningful to current and future researchers and practitioners.

FUTURE DIRECTIONS

From our review, we believe that many educational approaches and interventions have proven highly effective and have broad applicability in educating LD students. However, there remain important areas of skill development in which we are devoid of guidelines about what and how to teach, in spite of demonstrated deficits among LD students. Possibly, research on subgroups within the LD population will assist in matching interventions to present problems.Current intervention approaches must be extended to incorporate the areas of listening and problem solving, both prominent examples of important areas not addressed regularly by learning disabilities specialists. Further research also is needed to direct programs for LD students as they move through high school and into adulthood. We must begin to address the demonstrated need for a longitudinal continuum of services: LD students grow and change; how can they be helped in this process? What follows, then, are some observations about future directions we hope to see researchers pursue.

Subgroups Within the LD Population

The Attribute Treatment Interaction (ATI) approach to learning disabilities remediation has not proven fruitful (Cronbach & Snow, 1977; Hammill & Larsen, 1974; Kavale, 1982). Because of these findings, we did not advocate this approach in earlier sections of this chapter. However, Watson (1983) maintains that the lack of success with the ATI approach is due to inadequate identification of subjects.

Watson and his colleagues (Lyon, 1978; Lyon, Steward, & Freedman, 1982; Lyon & Watson, 1981) determined that the LD population is comprised of definite subgroups. It appears that there are six subgroups at the older ages (11 and 12 years old) and five subgroups, which have their counterparts in the data with the older children, at the younger ages (6–9 year olds). The evidence of subgroups within the LD population is not useful to teachers unless these groups of youngsters respond differently to teaching techniques. If a subgroup, for example, responds uniformly and positively to one type of remediation strategy, instructional planning and implementation would be both more efficient and effective for those students. Beyond the fascination of researchers, who focus their attention on determining these subgroups of youngsters, research efforts could be directed towards the identification of those instructional procedures that work best with particular groupings of LD students.

In an initial study, Lyon (1983) found that the effects of one reading approach, phonics instruction, did have differential effects with youngsters in different subgroups. Lyon's work is the first in this regard. Because his sample size was small, only one intervention tactic was studied for one curriculum area (reading), and no preintervention regression between achievement and aptitude was computed; therefore, no broad conclusions can be drawn. Also, the diagnostic battery presently necessary to sort youngsters into various subgroups is both cumbersome and complicated. Clearly, these researchers are not ready to propose this newly developing model to the field. However, the results from their future research could have a significant impact, if their current theories about relationships between specific subgroups members' performances and intervention procedures are supported in their continued study.

Listening as a Component of Information Reception and Communication

Students are required to listen to varied messages in many different settings within school. Indeed, school success is dependent, in part, on students' ability to follow oral directions accurately, comprehend lectures or extended discourses, and respond appropriately in conversations and group discussions. Moreover, as children grow older, teachers require them to listen more during instructional time. Moran (1980) found that junior and senior high school teachers talked for 80% of the time spent in verbal interactions in the classroom and that this discourse consisted of 75% lecturing and 25% questioning about subject matter content. Furthermore, teachers seldom presented advance organizers to help students listen more effectively and their rate of speech was not modified for ease in note taking. Children with adequate listening skills must find this environment demanding; for those with listening deficiencies, it invariably becomes overwhelming.

Teachers of LD students often modify their presentations to facilitate listener comprehension. However, it is an undesirable and impossible proposition to insist that teachers assume all responsibility for communicative success. Listening is a critical act for most LD students. This is because LD students often are expected to compensate for poor reading and writing through listening. The listening demands of school are great (Moran, 1980). Because LD students' ability to develop compensatory skills in deficit areas without direct instruction is minimal, they must have instruction in listening as an integral part of the curriculum if they are to develop these skills.

We have proposed elsewhere (Robinson & Smith, 1981) a model of listening, which is useful in providing a broad framework to examine the different component skills of listening for the purpose of assessment or instruction. This model included three major parts: the message, listening (the cognitive process), and the listener's response. We suggest there is a reciprocal interaction between the major parts, and a careful analysis of the components in realistic classroom situations is necessary before appropriate instruction can be designed. Effective listening requires accommodating to variations in messages (including clarity, vocabulary level, conceptual complexity, duration, level of informativeness or ambiguity, and nonverbal information) with one's own varied cognitive skills (including attention, hearing acuity, language level, memory, and comprehension). Motivation, interest, prior knowledge of the topic, age, organizational ability are other individual characteristics that affect how well one listens, and these must be considered before adequate instruction is developed (Alley & Deshler, 1979). In a teaching-learning exchange, a verbal, written, or physical response by the listener enables the teacher to judge the success of the communication. This model underlines the complexity one must grapple with in developing effective, yet *efficient* instructional procedures.

In light of the listening demands of the school and the listening deficiencies of many LD students (Bauer, 1977; Bryan, Donahue, & Pearl, 1981; Kotsonis & Patterson, 1980; Spekman, 1981), we recommend including instruction in listening as a regular component of the special education curriculum. However, when advocating the inclusion of new instructional areas into existing programs, one becomes sensitive to the constructs of effective *and* efficient instruction. With those constructs in mind, a learning strategies approach (as discussed earlier) appears to be a viable instructional approach to the teaching of listening skills. Teaching students how to use strategic, cognitive behavior to listen more effectively has intuitive appeal. Because of the inherent diversity of listening demands, teaching task specific behaviors would become unwieldy as an instructional approach. Instead, teaching students how to utilize strategies that can be generalized to many tasks and settings should be more beneficial.

Preliminary research findings lend support to the use of a learning strategies approach in listening instruction. LD students have used memory strategies that increased listening proficiency in both experimental listening tasks (Bauer, 1977; Dawson, Hallahan, Reeve, & Ball, 1980) and classroom listening tasks (Robinson, 1983). Comprehension monitoring strategies also have been taught to LD students and improved their comprehension of prose material (Robinson, 1983). Lenz (1982) found teaching both teachers and students about advance organizers effective in increasing LD students' comprehension of lectures.

However, substantial research is needed to extend and substantiate these initial findings. Until this occurs, teachers of students with listening deficiencies have modest and yet incomplete guidelines to follow in the development of appropriate assessment procedures or effective interventions. Be this as it may, it is important for teachers to address this component of the information reception process in a direct and comprehensive manner. Until this occurs, many LD students will demonstrate difficulty listening, not only because of individual deficiencies but also because of lack of instruction. Most certainly, researchers need to direct their efforts towards this important and relatively neglected instructional area.

Problem Solving

The final stage of learning, *adaptation*, requires one to extend the use of learned skills to novel situations (i.e., to solve problems). While the relationship of effective problem solving to a student's successful transition to independent living seems apparent, little research has addressed how one teaches effective problem solving to LD students. Reviewed here, then, are some disparate threads of research that, when

woven together, advance some of our ideas on how this important area of instruction might be viewed.

Problem solving can be defined as a multiple-step process including identification of the problem, understanding the problem by reviewing information pertinent to it, identifying a solution, and implementing the solution (Maker, 1981; Newell & Simon, 1972; Resnick & Glaser, 1976). Newell and Simon conceptualized problem solving in a manner that clearly communicates how one might have difficulty solving a problem. During the initial step the problem solver develops a representation of the problem. How it is represented may render problem solutions obvious, vague, or unattainable; however, problem solving will proceed according to that representation. Then one selects a method of searching for a solution, gathering information to help understand and solve the problem. Depending upon the perceived success of the solution finding process, the problem solver may decide to change that method at any time. If this occurs, three options are open to the problem solver: (a) select another search method, (b) redefine the problem, or (c) abandon the attempt to solve the problem. During this process, subgoals may be formed, and the problem solver has the option of attempting to solve those subgoals. LD students might have difficulty at any step of the problem solving process or be unaware that they must move through certain steps to increase their chances of successful solution finding.

In fact, research has demonstrated the LD students have significantly greater difficulty at each step of the problem solving process than nondisabled students. For example, Havertape and Kass (1978) analyzed adolescent LD students' self-reports on solving of novel problems. They found that LD students either did not develop problem attack strategies or use strategies already within their repertoire. Instead, they were much more willing to pull solutions out of thin air than average students and did not evaluate their solutions' adequacy. This nonstrategic behavior of LD students of all ages has been empirically validated in numerous domains and was discussed in prior sections on information processing and learning strategies. This research lends support to our premise that LD students are poor problem solvers.

What constitutes relevant problems must be a consideration in the study and development of instructional procedures to teach problem solving. Academic problem solving often can be described as a set of "best moves" or a sequence of steps that is accepted as the most efficient way to reach the solution. Many math problems are an example of such problems. This class of problems has fixed goals, fixed structures, and known variables (Brown & French, 1979).

Many problems that one encounters in life, however, are not structured like academic problems. Instead, they may have many variables that can be considered and many methods of reaching a solution, as well as more than one acceptable solution. Furthermore, as Flavell (1976) and Brown and French (1979) note, speed is often unimportant in real life problem solving, therefore, the problem solver should not select necessarily the most efficient strategy. Instead, an *effective* but not the most *efficient* strategy often is selected to relieve cognitive strain. For example, rather than using memory strategies to remember a phone number, one might write down the number. One might rely on a past successful experience to guide current problem solving.

There are other characteristics that differentiate real life problems from academic ones. A component of real life problems is deciding initially that a problem does in fact exist and then describing it in a manner that allows it to be solved. Often, some relevant information is missing and must be collected or invented; conversely, careful selection of a manageable number of facts from a profuse amount of relevant information may be necessary (Lesh, 1980).

Teaching LD students to be adaptive (i.e., good problem solvers) is problematic. When teaching them to acquire and maintain specific skills, teachers can focus on a discrete and identifiable sequence of behaviors. However, by definition, to problem solve in real life situations means to move away from the discrete and specific (Haring & Eaton, 1978).

The question then arises of how to use what we know about instruction for the LD student to teach the less defined skills of problem solving. We have substantial evidence that LD students profit from direct and systematic instruction. Also, through research in information processing and strategy training, we now know more about how LD students think. It seems appropriate to combine and extend these findings in the development of problem solving instruction.

In an earlier section, we discussed that strategic behavior must fall along a continuum from specific and powerful (ensuring task completion in a narrow set of circumstances) to general but weak (applicable in a broad array of situations, but not ensuring solutions). It could be argued that problem solving behavior encompasses the range of strategic behavior; yet, in an adaptive sense, problem solving must focus on the orchestration of strategies. Research in training LD students to use general cognitive strategies to increase independent task completion and problem solving has been positive *if* the prerequisite skills necessary for task completion were also in the student's repertoire (Camp et al., 1977; Lloyd, 1980; McKinney & Haskins, 1980; Meichenbaum, 1980, 1982; Torgesen, 1982). An example of a general cognitive strategy might include instruction in directing oneself through a task with self-talk: What is it I have to do? What is my plan? I'll do . . . ; Be careful, this is a tricky part; and so forth. Ellis (1983) took this research one step further in his investigation of the efficacy of teaching adolescents a general cognitive strategy that could be used to orchestrate other, more specific strategies in novel situations. In this situation, the student had to be proficient in a number of task specific strategies before success was seen in the use of the problem solving strategy. This type of instruction, the teaching of metacognitive strategies, seems to be a step in the right direction, if encouraging adaptive behavior in LD students is a goal. His successful results are exciting; further replications, refinement, and extension of these findings are warranted.

In developing problem solving instruction, it is important to remember that students must possess the skills we wish them to orchestrate. Therefore, problem solving training could be an extension of a learning strategies approach. However, it also must include direct instruction in defining problems, collecting relevant information, setting goals, processes of finding solutions, and solution evaluation. Currently, several programs purport to develop this type of behavior. The goals of these programs are to increase creativity, fluency, and divergent thinking. According to a review by Mansfield, Busse, and Krepelka (1978), the most effective of such programs seems to be the Parnes Creative Problem Solving Program (Parnes, 1967). Meichenbaum (1982) reviewed a variety of such programs and reports that in no case was generalization positive. Research on such "thinking" programs has not included LD students as subjects. There is, however, evidence that divergent, creative thinking abilities can be developed through the use of applied behavior analysis techniques. Maker (1981), in reviewing this research, found applications of these combined teaching technologies successful in increasing various problem solving abilities in average learners. There is need to extend and expand this work for the LD learner.

The time has come for LD researchers to address the area of problem solving. Some preliminary research needed as a base for the development of problem solving instruction exists. If we hold as an ultimate goal in instruction the successful transition to independent learning, problem solving instruction must deserve more of our attention.

Adolescence to Adulthood: The Transition

Taking on the responsibilities of adulthood is difficult for many adolescents. One might question, however, whether teachers of LD students adequately address this transition. Undoubtedly, much progress has been made during the last decade in recognizing that LD children grow into LD adolescents and LD adults. Deshler and his colleagues (Alley et al., 1983; Deshler, Schumaker et al., 1982) as well as others (Blalock & Dixon, 1982; Cronin & Gerber, 1982) have provided substantial data about the setting demands, characteristics, needs, and possible intervention approaches for the LD adolescent. We applaud their diligence and encourage it to continue, for a long road of needed research lies ahead.

Programs at the secondary level can be characterized by their purported purposes: college preparatory, vocational, life-centered skills, tutorial, basic skills, compensatory. It could be argued that this is representative of the confusion about the needs of LD adolescents. It could also demonstrate the diversity of needs of students by this age. Regardless of how one interprets the existing situation, it is apparent that few teachers are trained or competent in providing all models. In an attempt to do everything, it becomes difficult to do anything well.

Professionals concerned with programming for the secondary LD student must determine the composition of special education services. However, rather than making that decision reactively, professionals must take a proactive stance. To make such a decision, information must be collected about the adequacy of existing services in preparing students for the life they lead after graduation or termination of formal schooling. The field does not know what becomes of the LD students served in secondary schools: what percentage attend college, find successful employment, enter job training programs, or are unsuccessful in making the transition to adulthood? Once available, these data must be compared to that collected on the nondisabled person's transition from high school to independent living. Until these longitudinal data are collected, it will be difficult to determine accurately what should be the goals of special education for the LD adolescent.

In conjunction with setting goals for LD service, it becomes necessary to think about the provision of services longitudinally. For those students who receive special education services throughout their education, a nongoal directed approach is inappropriate. Instead, LD educators must think of providing a longitudinal continuum of services so that they culminate in a logical and appropriate whole. For these students it might be necessary to move away from a remedial orientation to the development of an entirely new curricula.

These concerns exemplify many of the critical issues that must be addressed. What is the purpose of a high school education, direct training of life skills or the presentation of information? If we provide options (basic skills, remedial, vocational) in the type of services we offer secondary LD students, who will make the decision about what type of education is most appropriate for any given student? Is there a need for a new philosophy of special education for LD students at the secondary level? Should the current eclectic approach be abandoned? It is time to reconsider the content of our instruction for the LD adolescent. Perhaps educators need to develop multi-option programs, each with distinct goals and curricula. Currently, no deliberate educational options are available. LD students are a heterogeneous population, should not the educational programs truly reflect that heterogeneity? Most clearly, what and how LD adolescents are taught will be influenced by those who conduct long term follow-up studies and the curriculum planners who interpret those results.

CONCLUSION

The education of LD youngsters has changed drastically since the emergence of public school classes in the middle of the 1960s. Twenty years of research, centering on how these students learn best, provides professionals with an excellent foundation and information regarding important future directions. We have attempted to summarize these educational foundations by advocating several general approaches and specific instructional procedures in which we feel confident. We believe these encourage efficient and effective learning for those who comprise the LD population. Since this group of learners, at present, must be viewed as a heterogeneous population; the approaches and procedures we selected are both flexible and sensitive. Their applications have proven successful with a large portion of this population. When used in conjunction with the direct and daily instructional approach we described, they are evaluated on an individual basis so their effectiveness can be judged quickly and efficiently.

We sought to provide a picture of those procedures that might become commonplace practices in educational programs for LD youngsters in the future. We selected those that indicate the most promise for application and utility, although much research needs to be conducted before they are advocated on a wide scale. We hope we have stimulated thought about what LD programs should be like today and what they might be like in the future.

REFERENCES

Affleck, J. Q., Lowenbraun, S., & Archer, A. (1980). *Teaching the mildly handicapped in the regular classroom* (2nd ed.) Columbus, OH: Charles E. Merrill.

Alley, G., & Deshler, D. D. (1979). *Teaching the learning disabled adolescent: Strategies and methods.* Denver: Love Publishing.

Alley, G. R., Deshler, D. D., Clark, F. L., Schumaker, J. B., & Warner, M. W. (1983). Learning disabilities in adolescent and adult populations: Research implications (Part II). *Focus on Exceptional Children, 15*(9), 1–14.

Alley, G. R., Schumaker, J. B., Denton, P., Warner, M. M., & Deshler, D. D. (in press). *Paraphrasing: A learning strategy for understanding written material* (Research report). Lawrence: The University of Kansas Institute for Research in Learning Disabilities.

Axelrod, S. (1983). *Behavior modification for the classroom teacher.* (2nd ed.). New York: McGraw-Hill.

Ayllon, T., & Azrin, N. H. (1964). Reinforcement and instructions with mental patients. *Journal of Experimental Analysis of Behavior, 7*, 327–331.

Baer, E. M., Peterson, R. F., & Sherman, J. A. (1967). The development of imitation by reinforcing behavioral similarity to a model. *Journal of Experimental Analysis of Behavior, 10,* 405–416.

Bandura, A., Grusec, J. E., & Menlove, F. L. (1967). Vicarious extinction of avoidance behavior. *Journal of Personality and Social Psychology, 5,* 16–23.

Bauer, R. H. (1977). Memory processes in children with learning disabilities, evidence for deficient rehearsal. *Journal of Experimental Child Psychology, 24,* 415–430.

Bauer, R. H., (1982). Information processing as a way of understanding and diagnosing learning disabilities. *Topics in Learning and Learning Disabilities, 2,* 33–45.

Billingsley, F. F. (1977). The effects of self- and externally-imposed schedules of reinforcement on oral reading performance. *Journal of Learning Disabilities, 10,* 549–559.

Blalock, G., & Dixon, N. (1982). Improving prospects for the college-bound learning disabled. *Topics in Learning and Learning Disabilities, 2,* 69–78.

Blankenship, C. S. (1978). Remediating systematic inversion errors in subtraction through the use of demonstration and feedback. *Learning Disability Quarterly, 1,* 12–22.

Blankenship, C., & Lilly, M. S. (1981). *Mainstreaming students with learning and behavior problems and techniques for the classroom teacher.* New York: Holt Rinehart Winston.

Borkowski, J. G., Levers, S., & Gruenfelder, T. M. (1976). Transfer of mediational strategies in children: The role of activity and awareness during strategy acquisition. *Child Development, 47,* 779–787.

Brigham, R. M., & Sherman, J. A. (1968). An experimental analysis of verbal imitation in preschool children. *Journal of Applied Behavior Analysis, 1,* 151–158.

Broden, M., Hall, R. V., & Mitts, B. (1971). The effect of self-recording on the classroom behavior of two eighth-grade students. *Journal of Applied Behavior Analysis, 4,* 191–199.

Brown, A. L., & French, L. A. (1979). The zone of potential development: Implications for intelligence testing in the year 2000. *Intelligence, 3,* 255–273.

Brown, A. L., & Palincsar, A. S. (1982). Inducing strategic learning from texts by means of informed, self-control training. *Topics in Learning and Learning Disabilities, 2,* 1–17.

Bryan, T., Donahue, M., & Pearl, R. (1981). Learning disabled children's peer interactions during a small-group problem-solving task. *Learning Disability Quarterly, 4,* 13–22.

Buckley, N. K., & Walker, H. M. (1978). *Modifying classroom behavior: A manual of procedure for classroom teachers* (rev. ed.). Champaign, IL: Research Press.

Camp, B. W., Blom, G. E., Herbert, F., & van Doorninck, W. J. (1977). "Think aloud": A program for developing self-control in young aggressive boys. *Journal of Abnormal Child Psychology, 5,* 157–169.

Capelli, C. A., & Markman, E. M. (1982). Suggestions for training comprehension monitoring. *Topics in Learning and Learning Disabilities, 2,* 87–96.

Cavanaugh, J. C., & Borkowski, J. G. (1980). Searching for metamemory-memory connections: A developmental study. *Developmental Psychology, 16,* 441–453.

Cavanaugh, J. C., & Perlmutter, M. (1982). Metamemory: A critical examination. *Child Development, 53,* 11–28.

Christie, L. S., McKenzie, H. S., & Burdett, C. S. (1972). The consulting teacher approach to special education: Inservice training for regular classroom teachers. *Focus on Exceptional Children, 4,* 1–10.

Cronbach, L. J., & Snow, R. E. (1977). *Aptitudes and instructional methods.* New York: Irvington.

Cronin, M. E., & Gerber, P. J. (1982). Preparing the learning disabled adolescent for adulthood. *Topics in Learning and Learning Disabilities, 2,* 55–68.

Csapo, M. (1972). Peer models reverse the "one bad apple spoils the barrel" theory. *Teaching Exceptional Children, 5,* 20–24.

Dawson, M. H., Hallahan, D. P., Reeve, R. E., & Ball, D. W. (19180). The effect of reinforcement and verbal-rehearsal on selective attention in learning disabled children. *Journal of Abnormal Psychology, 8,* 133–144.

Deno, E. (1970). Special education as developmental capital. *Exceptional Children. 37,* 229–237.

Deshler, D. D., Alley, G. R., Warner, M. M., & Schumaker, J. B. (1981). Instructional practices for promoting skill acquisition in generalization in severely learning disabled adolescents. *Learning Disability Quarterly, 4,* 415–421.

Deshler, D. D., Schumaker, J. B., Alley, G. R., Warner, M. M., & Clark, F. L. (1982). Learning disabilities in adolescent and adult populations: Research implications. *Focus on Exceptional Children, 15*(1), 1–12.

Dickerson, E. A., & Creedon, C. F. (1981). Self-selection of standards by children: The relative effectiveness of pupil-selected and teacher-selected standards of performance. *Journal of Applied Behavior Analysis, 14,* 425–433.

Douglas, V. L., Parry, P., Marton, P., & Garson, C. (1976). Assessment of a cognitive training program for hyperactive children. *Journal of Abnormal Child Psychology, 4,* 389–410.

Ellis, E. (1983). *The effects of teaching learning disabled adolescents an executive strategy to facilitate self generation of task specific strategies.* Unpublished doctoral dissertation. The University of Kansas, Lawrence.

Felixbrod, J. J., & O'Leary, K. D. (1973). Effects of reinforcement on children's academic behavior as a function of self-determined and externally imposed contingencies. *Journal of Applied Behavior Analysis, 6,* 241–250.

Flavell, J. H. (1976). Metacognitive aspects of problem-solving. In L. B. Resnick (Ed.), *The nature of intelligence.* Hillsdale, NJ: Erlbaum.

Flavell, J. H., & Wellman, H. M. (1977). Metamemory. In R. V. Kail & J. W. Hagen (Eds.), *Perspectives on the development of memory and cognition.* Hillsdale, NJ: Erlbaum.

Fleming, L. (1977). *The application of modeling in group and individual situations to help learning disabled students acquire computational skills.* Unpublished thesis, George Peabody College for Teachers.

Frostig, M., & Horne, D. (1967). *The Frostig program for the development of visual perception.* Chicago: Follett.

Glynn, E. L. (1970). Classroom applications of self-determined reinforcement. *Journal of Applied Behavior Analysis, 3,* 123–132.

Hall, R. J. (1982). An information processing approach to the study of exceptional children. In B. K. Keogh (Ed.), *Advances in special education* (vol. II). Greenwich, CT: JAI Press.

Hallahan, D. P., & Bryan, T. H. (1981). Learning disabilities. In J. M. Kauffman & D. P. Hallahan (Eds.), *Handbook of special education.* Englewood Cliffs, NJ: Prentice-Hall.

Hallahan, D. P., & Cruickshank, W. M. (1973). *Psycho-educational foundations of learning disabilities.* Englewood Cliffs, NJ: Prentice-Hall.

Hallahan, D. P., & Kauffman, J. M. (1976). *Introduction to learning disabilities: A psycho-behavioral approach.* Englewood Cliffs, NJ: Prentice-Hall.

Hallahan, D. P., Lloyd, J. W., Kauffman, J. M., & Loper, A. B. (1983). Academic problems. In R. Morris, & T. Kratochwill (Eds.), *The practice of child therapy.* New York: Pergamon.

Hallahan, D. P., Marshall, K. J., & Lloyd, J. W. (1981). Self-recording during group instruction: Effects on attention to task. *Learning Disability Quarterly, 4,* 407–413.

Hammill, D. D., & Larsen, S. C. (1974). The effectiveness of psycholinguistic training. *Exceptional Children, 41,* 5–14.

Hammill, D. D., & Wiederholt, J. L. (1973). Review of the Frostig Visual Perception Test and the related training program. In L. Mann, & D. Sabatino (Eds.), *The first review of special education* (Vol. 1). New York: Grune & Stratton.

Harber, J. R. (1981a). Critical evaluation of published research: Some guidelines. *Learning Disability Quarterly, 4,* 260–270.

Harber, J. R. (1981b). Learning disabilities research: How far have we progressed? *Learning Disability Quarterly, 4,* 372–381.

Haring, N. G., & Eaton, M. D. (1978). Systematic instructional procedures: An instructional hierarchy. In N. G. Haring, T. C. Lovitt, M. D. Eaton, & C. L. Hanson (Eds.), *The fourth R: Research in the classroom.* Columbus, OH: Charles E. Merrill.

Haring, N. G., Lovitt, T. C., Eaton, M. D., & Hansen, C. L. (1978). *The fourth R: Research in the classroom.* Columbus, OH: Charles E. Merrill.

Havertape, J. T., & Kass, C. E. (1978). Examination of problem solving in learning disabled adolescents through verbalized self-instructions. *Learning Disability Quarterly, 1*(4), 94–100.

Hegge, T. G., Kirk, S. A., & Kirk, W. D. (1936). *Remedial reading drills.* Ann Arbor, MI: George Wahr.

Hopkins, B. L. (1968). Effects of candy and social reinforcement instructions and reinforcement schedule leaning on the modification and maintenance of smiling. *Journal of Applied Behavior Analysis, 1,* 121–129.

Idol-Maestas, L. (1983). *Special educator's consultation handbook.* Rockville, MD: Aspen.

Jenkins, J. R., Mayhall, W. F., Peschka, C., & Townsend, V. (1974). Using direct and daily measures to increase learning. *Journal of Learning Disabilities, 7*(1), 14–17.

Journal of Learning Disabilities. (1983, January), [Special issue],· *16,* 6–31.

Kavale, K. (1982). Meta-analysis of the relationship between visual perceptual skills and reading achievement. *Journal of Learning Disabilities, 15,* 42–51.

Kavale, K., & Dye, D. (1981). Identification criteria for learning disabilities: A survey of research literature. *Learning Disability Quarterly, 4,* 383–388.

Kauffman, J. M., & Hallahan, D. P. (1979). Learning disabilities and hyperactivity. In B. B. Lahey & A. E. Kazdin (Eds.), *Advances in clinical child psychology* (Vol. 2). New York: Plenum Press.

Kazdin, A. E. (1973). Role of instructions and reinforcement in behavioral changes in token reinforcement programs. *Journal of Educational Psychology, 64,* 63–71.

Kennedy, B. A., & Miller, D. J. (1976). Persistent use of verbal rehearsal as a function of information about its value. *Child Development, 47,* 566–569.

Keogh, B. K., & Glover, A. T. (1980). The generality and durability of cognitive training effects. *Exceptional Education Quarterly, 1,* 75–82.

Keogh, B. K., Major-Kingsley, S., Omori-Gordon,

H., & Reid, H. P. (1982). *UCLA marker variable project*. Syracuse, NY: Syracuse University Press.

Kephart, N. C. (1971). *The slow learner in the classroom*. Columbus, OH: Charles E. Merrill.

Kerr, M. M., & Nelson, C. M. (1983). *Strategies for managing behavior problems in the classroom*. Columbus, OH: Charles E. Merrill.

Kirk, S. A., & Chalfant, J. C. (1984). *Academic and developmental learning disabilities*. Denver: Love Publishing.

Kirk, S. A., & Johnson, G. O. (1951). *Educating the retarded child*. Boston: Houghton-Mifflin Co.

Kneedler, R. P. (1980). The use of cognitive training to change social behaviors. *Exceptional Education Quarterly, 1*, 65–74.

Kneedler, R. D., & Hallahan, D. P. (1981). Self-monitoring of on-task behavior with learning disabled children: Current studies and directions. *Exceptional Education Quarterly, 2*, 73–82.

Kotsonis, M. R., & Patterson, C. J. (1980). Comprehension-monitoring skills in learning disabled children. *Developmental Psychology, 16*, 541–542.

Kroth, R. L. (1975). *Communicating with parents of exceptional children*. Denver: Love Publishing.

Lenz, B. K. (1982). *The effect of advance organizers on the learning and retention of learning disabled adolescents within the context of a cooperative planning model*. Unpublished doctoral dissertation, The University of Kansas, Lawrence, KS.

Lesh, R. (1980). *Applied mathematical problem solving*. Unpublished paper. Northwestern University, Evanston, IL.

Lilly, M. S. (1971). A training based model for special education. *Exceptional Children, 37*, 754–759.

Lloyd, J. (1980). Academic instruction and cognitive behavior modification: The need for attack strategy training. *Exceptional Education Quarterly, 1*, 53–64.

Lloyd, J. W., Hallahan, D. P., Kosiewicz, M. M., & Kneedler, R. D. (1982). Reactive effects of self-assessment and self-recording on attention to task and academic productivity. *Learning Disability Quarterly, 5*, 216–227.

Lovitt, T. C. (1970). Behavior modification: The current scene. *Exceptional Children*, 85–91.

Lovitt, T. C. (1973). Self-management projects with children with behavioral disabilities. *Journal of Learning Disabilities, 6*, 138–150.

Lovitt, T. C. (1975a). Part I: Characteristics of ABA, general recommendations, and methodological limitations. *Journal of Learning Disabilities, 8*, 432–443.

Lovitt, T. C. (1975b). Part II: Specific research recommendations and suggestions for practitioners. *Journal of Learning Disabilities, 8*, 504–518.

Lovitt, T. C. (1977). *In spite of my resistance . . . I've learned from children*. Columbus, OH: Charles E. Merrill.

Lovitt, T. C. (1981). Charting academic perfor-

mance of mildly handicapped youngsters. In J. M. Kauffman & D. P. Hallahan (Eds.), *Handbook of Special Education*. Englewood Cliffs, NJ: Prentice-Hall.

Lovitt, T. C. (1982). *Because of my persistence, I've learned from children*. Columbus, OH: Charles E. Merrill.

Lovitt, T. C. (1984). *Tactics for teaching*. Columbus, OH: Charles E. Merrill.

Lovitt, T. C., & Curtiss, K. A. (1969). Academic response rate as a function of teacher- and self-imposed contingencies. *Journal of Applied Behavior Analysis, 2*, 49–53.

Lovitt, T. C., & Fantasia, K. (1983). A precision teaching project with learning disabled children. *Journal of Precision Teaching, III* (4), 85–91.

Lovitt, T. C., & Jenkins, J. R. (1979). Learning disabilities research: Defining populations. *Learning Disability Quarterly, 2*, 46–50.

Lyon, R. (1978). *The neuropsychological characteristics of subgroups of learning disabled readers*. Unpublished doctoral dissertation. University of New Mexico.

Lyon, R. (1982). Subgroups of learning disabled readers: Clinical and empirical identification. In H. Myklebust (Ed.), *Progress in learning disabilities* (Vol. 5). New York: Grune & Stratton.

Lyon, R. (1983). Differential subgroups responses to a phonics teaching approach. University of Vermont.

Lyon, R., Steward, N., & Freedman, D. (1982). Neuropsychological characteristics of learning disabled readers. *Journal of Clinical Neurology, 4*, 343–365.

Lyon R., & Watson, B. (1981). Empirically derived subgroups of learning disabled readers: Diagnostic Characteristics. *Journal of Learning Disabilities, 14*, 256–261.

Maker, J. C. (1981). Problem solving: A general approach to remediation. In D. D. Smith, *Teaching the learning disabled*. Englewood Cliffs, NJ: Prentice-Hall.

Mansfield, R. S., Busse, T. V. & Krepelka, E. J. (1978). The effectiveness of creativity training. *Review of Educational Research, 48*, 517–536.

Mayhall, W. F., & Jenkins, J. (1977). The effects of scheduling daily or less-than-daily instruction: Implication for resource programs. *Journal of Learning Disabilities, 10*, 159–163.

McKinney, J. D., & Haskins, R. (1980). Cognitive training and the development of problem-solving strategies. *Exceptional Educational Quarterly, 1*, 41–52.

Meichenbaum, D. (1980). Cognitive behavior modification with exceptional children: A promise yet unfulfilled. *Exceptional Education Quarterly, 1*, 83–88.

Meichenbaum, D. (1982). Teaching thinking: A cognitive behavioral approach. *Interdisciplinary Voices in Learning Disabilities*. Austin, TX: Pro-Ed.

Mirkin, P. K., & Deno, S. L. (1979). *Formative evaluation in the classroom: An approach to improving instruction*. (Research report no. 10). Institute for Research on Learning Disabilities.

Moran, M. R. (1980). *An investigation of the demands on oral language skills of learning disabled students in secondary classrooms* (Research report no. 1). Lawrence, KS: The University of Kansas.

Myers, P. I., & Hammill, D. D. (1976). *Methods for learning disorders* (2nd ed.). New York: Wiley.

Myers, P. I., & Hammill, D. D. (1982). *Learning disabilities: Basic concepts, assessment practices, and instructional strategies*. Austin, TX: Pro-Ed.

Nelson, R. O., & Hayes, S. C. (1981). Theoretical explanations for reactivity in self-monitoring. *Behavior Modification, 5*(1), 3–14.

Newell, A. (1979). One final word. In D. T. Turna, & F. Reif (Eds.), *Problem solving and education: Issues in teaching and research*. Hillsdale, NJ: Erlbaum.

Newell, A., & Simon, H. A. (1972). *Human problem solving*. Englewood Cliffs, NJ: Prentice-Hall.

O'Leary, K. D., & Becker, W. C. (1967). Behavior modification of an adjustment class: A token reinforcement program. *Exceptional Children, 33*, 637–642.

O'Leary, K. D., & Dubey, D. R. (1979). Applications of self-control procedures by children: A review. *Journal of Applied Behavior Analysis, 12*, 449–465.

Packard, J. A. (1970). The control of "classroom attention": A group contingency for complex behavior. *Journal of Applied Behavior Analysis, 3*, 13–28.

Parnes, S. J. (1967). *Creative behavior guidebook*. New York: Scribner's.

Reid, D. K., & Hresko, W. P. (1982). *A cognitive approach to learning disabilities*. New York: McGraw-Hill.

Resnick, L. B., & Glaser, R. (1976). Problem-solving and intelligence. In L. B. Resnick (Ed.), *The nature of intelligence*. Hillsdale, NJ: Erlbaum.

Rhine, W. R. (1981). *Making schools more effective: New directions from follow through*. New York: Academic Press.

Rivera, D., & Smith, D. D. (1984). *The influence of the demonstration plus permanent model technique to enhance learning disabled students' computational skills: A working paper*. The University of New Mexico, Special Education Department, Albuquerque, NM.

Robinson, S. M. (1983). *A study of the efficacy of instruction in two strategies, rehearsal and self-questioning, to increase listening skills of learning disabled students*. Unpublished doctoral dissertation, University of New Mexico, Albuquerque, NM.

Robinson, S. M., & Smith, D. D. (1981). Listening skills: Teaching learning disabled students to be better listeners. *Focus on Exceptional Children, 13*(8), 1–15.

Rosenbaum, M. S., & Drabman, R. S. (1979). Self-control training in the classroom: A review and critique. *Journal of Applied Behavior Analysis, 12*, 467–485.

SCAT (Support, Competency-Assistance & Training Project) (1977). *Systematic instruction*. Document from Title VI-G Child Service Demonstration Project, State of Idaho.

Schumaker, J., Deshler, D. D., Alley, G. R., & Warner, M. (1982). *The evaluation of a learning strategies intervention model for LD adolescents* (Research Report No. 67). Lawrence, KS: The University of Kansas Institute for Research in Learning Disabilities.

Schumaker, J. B., Deshler, D. D., Alley, G. R., Warner, M. M., & Denton, P. H. (1982). Multipass: A learning strategy for improving reading comprehension. *Learning Disability Quarterly, 5*, 295–304.

Schumaker, J. B., & Ellis, E. S. (1982). Social skills training with LD adolescents: A generalization study. *Learning Disabilities Quarterly, 5*, 388–397.

Smith, D. D. (1973). *The influence of instructions, feedback, and reinforcement contingencies on children's abilities to acquire and become proficient at computational arithmetic skills*. Doctoral dissertation, University of Washington.

Smith, D. D. (1976). *A comparison of group versus individual application of a modeling technique on children's abilities to acquire new arithmetic skills*. Presentation to the National Council for Exceptional Children Convention, Chicago.

Smith, D. D. (1978). The influence of modeling on children's oral reading performance. In A. Sink (Ed.), *International perspectives on future special education*. Reston, VA: Council for Exceptional Children.

Smith, D. D. (1979). Modeling effects on reading. *Journal of Learning Disabilities, 12*, 172–175.

Smith, D. D. (1981). *Teaching the learning disabled*. Englewood Cliffs, NJ: Prentice-Hall.

Smith, D. D. (1984). *Effective discipline*. Austin, TX: Pro-Ed.

Smith, D. D., Deshler, D., Hallahan, D. P., Lovitt, T. C., Robinson, S., Ysseldyke, J., & Voress, J. (1984). *Minimum standards for the description of subjects used in learning disabilities research reports*. Council for Learning Disabilities.

Smith, D. D., & Lovitt, T. C. (1975). The use of modeling techniques to influence the acquisition of computational arithmetic skills. In E. Ranup & G. Semb (Eds.), *Behavior analysis: Areas of research and application*. Englewood Cliffs, NJ: Prentice-Hall.

Smith, D. D., & Lovitt, T. C. (1976). The differential effects of reinforcement contingencies on arithmetic performance. *Journal of Learning Disabilities, 9*, 21–29.

Smith, D. D., & Lovitt, T. C. (1982). *The com-

putational arithmetic program (CAP). Austin, TX: Pro-Ed.

Spekman, N. (1981). Dyadic verbal communication abilities of learning disabled and normally achieving fourth- and fifth-grade boys. *Learning Disability Quarterly, 4*, 139–151.

Stephens, T. M. (1978). *Social skills in the classroom*. Columbus, OH: Cedar Press.

Strauss, A. A., & Lehtinen, L. E. (1947). *Psychopathology and education of the brain-injured child*. New York: Grune & Stratton.

Swanson, H. L. (1982). Strategies and constraints — A commentary. *Topics in Learning and Learning Disabilities, 2*, 79–81.

Torgesen, J. K. (1977). The role of nonspecific factors in the task performance of learning disabled children: A theoretical assessment. *Journal of Learning Disabilities, 10*, 27–34.

Torgesen, J. (1982). Comments to D. Meichenbaum: Teaching thinking: A cognitive behavioral approach. In *Interdisciplinary voices in learning disabilities and remedial education*. Austin, TX: Pro-Ed.

Torgesen, J. K., & Greenstein, J. J. (1982). Why do some learning disabled children have problems remembering? Does it make a difference? *Topics in Learning and Learning Disabilities, 2*(2), 54–61.

Torgesen, J. K., & Houck, D. G. (1980). Processing deficiencies of LD children who perform poorly on the digit span test. *Journal of Educational Psychology, 12*, 141–160.

Watson, B. (1983). *Analysis of the responses of em-pirically derived subgroups of learning disabled readers to different methods of reading instruction*. Research grant application submitted to Special Education Programs.

White, O. R., & Haring, N. G. (1976). *Exceptional teaching for exceptional children*. Columbus, OH: Charles E. Merrill.

Wiederholt, J. L. (1974). Historical perspectives on the education of the learning disabled. In L. Mann, & D. Sabatino (Eds.), *The second review of special education*. Philadelphia: JSE Press.

Wiederholt, J. L., Hammill, D. D., & Brown, V. L. (1983). *The resource teacher: A guide to effective practice*. Boston: Allyn & Bacon.

Wong, B. L. (1979). Increasing retention of main ideas through questioning strategies. *Learning Disability Quarterly, 2*, 42–47.

Wong, B. L. (1980). Activating the inactive listener: Use of questions/prompts to enhance comprehension and retention of implied information in learning disabled children. *Learning Disability Quarterly, 1*.

Wong, B. L., and Jones, W. (1982). Increasing metacomprehension in learning disabled and normally achieving students through self-questioning training. *Learning Disability Quarterly, 5*, 228–240.

Workman, E. A. (1982). *Teaching behavioral control to children*. Austin, TX: Pro-Ed.

Ysseldyke, J. E., & Algozzine, B. (1983). LD or not LD: That's not the question. *Journal of Learning Disabilities, 16*, 29–31.

8 EDUCATING CHILDREN WITH BEHAVIOR DISORDERS

James M. Kauffman

The foremost characteristic of children with behavior disorders is confusion. These children are confused about who they are, what is expected of them, where they belong in the social milieu of school, and how they can obtain the gratification that most children seem to earn so easily. Their confusion is evident in their spoiled personal identities, which make them unwelcome members of their classes and burdens on their families. And their confusion is typically heightened by their caretakers and teachers, who purposely or unwittingly toy with their emotions by providing ambiguous feedback and inconsistent consequences for their behavior. Ultimately, their behavior marks them as children who have lost their way, who must be helped to find direction, meaning, and satisfaction in interpersonal relations.

Current issues in behavior disorders are nearly as confused as the children the field is intended to serve. Emotional disturbance (ED) and behavior disorder (BD) defy crisp definition. The origins of the field are uncertain, and its terminology is a thicket. Leaders in special education have reached no consensus about who should be served under the current federal categorical label *seriously emotionally disturbed* or about how special educators can serve them best. Professionals engaged in educating such

children are often unsure of their proper role in the schools. Education of children with behavior disorders is identified by some taxpayers as a budgetary burden and as a factor contributing to the malaise that afflicts American public education. Some ostensible advocates for behavior disordered children work to establish policies that appear to be ineffective or even counterproductive. Government agencies send ambiguous and inconsistent messages to educational practitioners regarding what constitutes behavior disorder in the context of school.

In a field so permeated by confusion, one cannot expect to find great clarity in the research literature. The state of the art in educating children with behavior disorders is advancing slowly, and it remains primitive by comparison to some fields of special education. Very basic issues remain unresolved and must be addressed before the field can be advanced rapidly. Some of these are philosophical or social policy issues that cannot be answered directly by research; others are open to direct empirical analysis.

BASIC ISSUES

Aging researchers and neophytes in children's behavior disorders alike are confronted by

several unsettling realities. Among these realities, which are the basis for current issues in
the field, are the following:

- Children's behavior disorders have no commonly accepted definition, and similar disorders are called by a bewildering array of
terms.
- Estimates of the prevalence of behavior disorders among school age children and youth
are markedly different from statistics indicating the number of BD children served by
special education under federal laws.
- Classification within the general category of
behavior disorders is unreliable and often
meaningless for educational intervention.
- Distinctions between the appropriate role
of special educators and the roles of other
professionals serving behavior disordered
children are not clear, and the special methods of education for BD children have not
been clearly delineated.
- Few data are available to indicate the success
of special education for BD children in general, although many studies support the
argument that effective short term intervention in specific problem behavior is readily
available.
- Most programs for BD children lack a clear
statement of their theoretical or philosophical base and do not include clear guidelines
for evaluation.

HISTORICAL OVERVIEW

Where did special education for behavior disordered children begin? One could argue that
in a sense the field is as old as the problem of
child discipline, at least the problem of child
discipline in organized educational settings.
To the extent that a teacher used special methods for dealing with behavior that today is
recognized as indicative of psychological or
emotional disorder (e.g., frequent aggression,
disruption, daydreaming, social withdrawal, or
failure to learn), special education of sorts was
being practiced. A reasonable history of special
education for BD children could, however,

begin with the first systematic attempts to educate deviant children.

The work of Itard and Seguin in the 19th
century often has been identified as the beginning of special education for the mentally
retarded. Their work also represents the beginning of special education for the children
known today as emotionally disturbed or behavior disordered (Kauffman, 1976, 1985;
Lane, 1976). Nevertheless, several important
histories of the treatment of emotionally disturbed children have dismissed the 19th century as a period of ignorance and neglect or
have failed to make the necessary connection
between emotional disturbance and mental
retardation (e.g., Despert, 1965; Kanner, 1962;
Rubenstein, 1948). These histories have tended
to focus on the emergence of the medical specialty of child psychiatry in the 1930s as the
origin of enlightened treatment of behaviorally
deviant children. However, 19th century literature in both psychiatry and special education
is richer and more enlightened regarding children's behavior disorders than many writers
have suggested (Kauffman, 1976; Lane, 1976).

History of the recognition and treatment of
children's behavior disorders illustrates the
contemporary issue of professional "ownership"
of the problem. Those written by child psy-
chiatrists tend to focus on the emergence of
psychiatric treatment, particularly treatment
guided by the insights of Sigmund Freud (e.g.,
Kanner, 1962; Rubenstein, 1948). Histories
written by psychologists tend to concentrate on
broader concepts of psychopathology but give
short shrift to special education (e.g., Achenbach, 1982; Ollendick & Hersen, 1983). Sociological histories emphasize the social forces
at work in determining who should deal with
deviants (e.g., Rhodes & Paul, 1978; Scull,
1975). Special educators attempt to trace the
development of tactics used by teachers and
school administrators in dealing with troublesome behavior (e.g., Hoffman, 1975; Kauffman, 1985; Lewis, 1974). In reality, the histories of all the professions dealing with BD
children are intertwined to such a degree that
they cannot be understood independently

(Kauffman, 1981). Moreover, the concepts and methods of these professions are not clearly separable today.

In the profession of special education, the histories of educational intervention in behavior disorders, mental retardation, and learning disabilities are more overlapping than separate (Hallahan & Kauffman, 1976, 1977). The characteristics of the children carrying these labels and the methods used in teaching and managing their behavior are more alike than different (Hallahan & Kauffman, 1976). One is hard pressed to explain how the preparation of teachers for any one of these three categories should be different from the others. Thus the histories of these fields of specialization bear directly on the current issue of noncategorical special education. Special education's history of behavior disorders is the history of managing problem behavior in the classroom, regardless of the categorical designation of the handicapped children involved.

An overview of the history of research in special education for children with behavior disorders, then, is necessarily cross-disciplinary and cross-categorical. In this chapter, however, the focus is on studies of disordered child behavior in the context of education and attendance at school. Due to space limitations, the research reviewed is necessarily representative rather than comprehensive.

Early Studies of Definition and Prevalence

One of the earliest studies of disordered behavior in the context of school was an investigation by Wickman (1929). He asked approximately 500 teachers and 30 mental hygienists to rate the seriousness of 50 behavioral characteristics of children. The teachers rated disruptive, aggressive behaviors as most serious, whereas the mental hygienists saw withdrawn, neurotic characteristics as most indicative of serious problems. The Wickman study has frequently been misinterpreted as indicating that mental health professionals are better judges of children's emotional disturbance than are teachers. After all, teachers and mental health professionals disagreed regarding the significance of children's behavior, and the common assumption was that the mental health professionals were right and the teachers wrong in their judgments (Bower, 1981).

The Wickman study was misinterpreted because many readers failed to observe that teachers and mental hygienists were given very different instructions. Teachers were told to rate as most serious the behaviors that produced the greatest difficulty in the classroom; mental hygienists were told to rate behavioral characteristics according to their seriousness in reflecting the child's mental health. Naturally, as Wickman himself noted, each group rated the characteristics most relevant to their everyday work with children, and it was both reasonable and predictable that teachers and mental hygienists would be concerned with different types of problems. Notwithstanding Wickman's own explanation of the meaning of his results, his study contributed to the mistaken notion that teachers are poor judges of children's social–emotional adjustment, while mental health experts can more accurately appraise the significance of children's behavior.

Bower (1981), Walker (1982), and others have concluded, based on their own studies, that teachers are in a particularly good position to make judgments about the significance of children's behavior because they can observe behavior directly and daily in its social context. But, as Bower (1981) has pointed out,

> The myth still exists that someone, somewhere, somehow, knows how to assess behavior and/or mental health as positive or negative, good or bad, healthy or nonhealthy, independently of the social context in which the individual is living and functioning. (p. 130)

As discussed later, the current problems of definition and terminology in behavior disorders are related to this persistent myth, which attributes to some professionals the ability to discriminate the difference between behavior problems caused by deeply hidden, internal, intrapsychic conflicts and those that are purely external and superficial in origin.

During the late 1950s, Bower began a study in the California public schools that was designed to delineate the characteristics of emotionally disturbed children in the school setting (1981 [first edition published in 1960]; see also Bower, 1982). Children in elementary grades through high school in 200 classrooms located in about 75 different school districts were rated by their teachers. Approximately 6000 children were rated in all, about 200 of whom had been designated as emotionally disturbed by mental health practitioners, who were seeing them as clients. In addition to the teacher ratings, the researchers obtained a variety of information related to academic aptitude and achievement, peer ratings, and self-perception ratings. Based on these data, Bower (1960) suggested a definition of the emotionally disturbed child, one setting forth five behavioral characteristics that nearly all (even nondisturbed) children were found to exhibit to some degree at some time but that disturbed children exhibited *to a marked degree and over a prolonged period of time.* These characteristics are

1. An inability to learn that cannot be explained by intellectual, sensory, or health factors.
2. An inability to build and maintain satisfactory interpersonal relationships with peers and teachers.
3. Inappropriate types of behavior or feelings under normal conditions.
4. A general, pervasive mood of unhappiness or depression.
5. A tendency to develop physical symptoms, pains, or fears associated with personal or school problems.

Bower (1982) stated the characteristics more succinctly: The disturbed children were poor learners (although they were capable of learning), had few if any satisfying interpersonal relationships, behaved oddly or inappropriately, were depressed or unhappy, and developed illnesses or phobias. Bower's study is a particularly important one from a historical perspective because the behavioral character-

istics derived from it later became the basis for the federal definition of emotional disturbance. Noteworthy, too, is the fact that no subsequent study has refuted his major findings or questioned the basic accuracy of his description of the disturbed child.

Among Bower's findings was the estimate that at least three children in the average class (i.e., about 10% of the school population) had problems of such seriousness and duration that they could reasonably be considered emotionally handicapped. Bower's figure of 10% is in the high range of other prevalence estimates when the criterion is that special education and related services are needed to deal with the behavior problem. However, it is a comparatively conservative estimate of the number of children who, in studies during the 1960s and 1970s, have been found to exhibit "noticeable" behavior problems in school (cf., Cullinan, Epstein, & Lloyd, 1983).

Federal agencies began using a prevalence estimate of 2.0% in the 1950s. The federal estimate, which was used for about 25 years, was actually a "guesstimate" based on a survey of principals, who were asked their opinions about what percentage of children in their schools were emotionally disturbed (Wood & Zabel, 1978). A national survey of programs for disturbed children conducted about 1970 revealed that the prevalence estimates used by the states ranged from 0.5–15%. Many state education agencies followed the federal lead, basing their estimates on the 2.0% figure derived from the survey of principals (Schultz, Hirshoren, Manton, & Henderson, 1971). Although the federal estimate of prevalence has not changed (except to include a lower figure as an interval or range, as discussed further under current issues), several significant studies have indicated that it is an underestimate by a factor of 2 or 3 (cf., Cullinan et al., 1983; Graham, 1979; Kauffman, 1985).

Rubin and Balow (1978) reported a particularly significant longitudinal project in which teachers were asked each year during the course of the study to report whether or not children in the study sample ($n = 1586$) had shown behavior problems. In any given year,

20–30% of the children were considered by at least one of their teachers to be a problem, and over half the children in the sample were, at some time during a 3-year period, considered by at least one of their teachers to show a behavior problem. Thus, problem behavior per se is widespread among school-age children and is not indicative of a handicapping condition, as indicated also by the early research of Griffiths (1952) and Macfarlane, Allen, and Honzik (1955). However, Rubin and Balow also found that *nearly 7.5% of the children in their sample were considered a behavior problem by every teacher who rated them over a period of 3 years.* Most of these children, one might surmise, would fit the definition proposed by Bower.

Early Studies of Classification

Classification in psychiatry has a long and desultory history (Menninger, 1963). The history of *child* psychiatry and psychology particularly has been marked by the lack of reliable and valid classification (cf., Achenbach, 1982; Achenbach & Edelbrock, 1983; Phillips, Draguns, & Bartlett, 1975). Psychiatric classification has had almost no relevance for special education, as the categories included in the various nosological systems have been organized around psychodynamic concepts rather than observable child behavior.

An alternative to the psychiatric-dynamic approach is classification based on clusters of overt behaviors or behavior ratings. These clusters or factors describe behavioral dimensions constituted by highly intercorrelated behaviors. Ackerson (1942) and Hewitt and Jenkins (1946) listed behavioral descriptions taken from children's case histories and grouped similar characteristics together simply by visual inspection of their lists. Later studies were based on factor analysis techniques.

Perhaps the most important early line of research in behavioral classification was begun by the study of Peterson (1961). He began by examining the referral problems listed in over 400 case histories on file in a child guidance clinic. Based on the frequency with which these problems were noted, he constructed 58 items describing behavioral difficulties and compiled them in a checklist that can be completed by parents, teachers, or other adults who observe the child's behavior frequently. Peterson asked 28 teachers (involving over 800 children in kindergarten through sixth grade) to complete the checklist. Two major factors or dimensions emerged from his factor analysis of the ratings: conduct problem (connoting acting out, disruptive behavior) and personality problem (indicating social withdrawal and neuroticism).

Since Peterson's original study, numerous factor analyses have been made using the *Behavior Problem Checklist* developed by Quay and Peterson (1967). The results have been remarkably consistent in demonstrating the factor structure of disordered child behavior (Cullinan et al., 1983; Quay, 1979).

Early Descriptions of the Role of Education

In the late 19 century, following enactment of compulsory school attendance laws, disordered child behavior in the classroom was recognized as a problem requiring action on the part of school administrators and teachers (Hoffman, 1974, 1975). Children about whom educators became concerned were described by various labels, including *truant, incorrigible, vagabond, antisocial, wayward,* and *behavior problem.* The typical response of school officials was to establish special classes for disruptive students or simply exclude the children from school.

By the 1920s, however, the child study movement had resulted in greater sensitivity on the part of school personnel to the characteristics and needs of children who do not behave as expected or demanded in the classroom. In 1928, the National Education Association published a report on the preparation of teachers for dealing with children with behavior problems. The report began with the following commentary by Howard W. Nudd, chairman of the National Committee of Visiting Teachers:

> Every teacher, every social worker, and many a parent is familiar with the problem child —

the boy or girl whose school progress or whose reactions to normal requirements point toward later inefficiency, delinquency, or some other failure in personal or social adjustment.

What is the trouble with such children, and what can be done for them? How can the school obtain and utilize a knowledge of the forces that are affecting their success, and give them in fullest measure the benefits of their educational experience? Puzzles or pests at home, in school, or elsewhere, their personal welfare and the welfare of society require painstaking effort on their behalf. They cannot wisely be regarded as temporary nuisances, whose present weaknesses a kindly fate will in some way heal with the balm of time, nor can they wisely be ignored without serious study and effort, as inevitable liabilities which society must expect along with its blessings. Tomorrow they will be citizens, for weal or for woe, and their shortcomings today, if left uncorrected, may have dire effects upon the character of their citizenship tomorrow. They present the most baffling, the most urgent, and the most interesting problems in the field of education. (National Education Association, 1929, p. 3)

Thus the child who exhibits disordered behavior has long been seen as a problem to be dealt with, at least in part, by regular educators.

Special educators expressed concern in the 1920s that the public school might be a significant factor in causing behavior problems. For example, Elizabeth Woods, a clinical psychologist in the Wisconsin Department of Public Instruction, made the following comments at the first meeting of the International Council for Exceptional Children in 1923:

It would be very easy to show how bad school conditions, ranging from unsanitary and unwholesome physical conditions in the school plant, to the curriculum itself, operate in case after case to produce restlessness, discontent, irritation, insubordination, truancy, and all the youthful misdemeanors so often attendant thereon. It would be especially easy to show how teachers, ignorant of and unsympathetic with children's instincts and emotions, not infrequently fail ever to reach their minds, and so instead of being priestesses daily at

the sacred ceremony of a child's mental unfoldment they are rather the pallbearers at a ghastly sort of living death. (International Council for Exceptional Children, 1923, p. 28)

Thus the possible role of the school in contributing to disordered behavior has been recognized for well over half a century. Moreover, the observation that children may exhibit conduct problems or personality problems (i.e., aggression or withdrawal) in the context of school and the idea that child behavior and the social environment affect each other reciprocally—both notions that were later to be confirmed by empirical research—may be found in the descriptive literature of the 1930s (e.g., Baker & Stullken, 1938; Wallin, 1938).

Assuming that behavior disorders are a problem to be recognized and dealt with in some manner by regular educators and that the experiences of children in public schools may contribute to their disordered behavior, what role do regular and special education play in rectifying the problem? More specifically, what role does the regular classroom teacher play, what is the role of the special educator, and what is the role of other professionals in dealing with the BD child? The literature prior to the early 1960s was dominated by a psychoanalytic orientation, concern for severely disturbed children or delinquent youth, education and social services for children placed in institutional settings, and a primary focus on the work of mental health personnel (see, for example, Berkowitz & Rothman, 1960; Bettelheim, 1950; Bettelheim & Sylvester, 1948; Kornberg, 1955; Krugman, 1953; Redl & Wineman, 1951, 1952; Stullken, 1950).

Kornberg (1955), who wrote the first book describing classroom teaching of disturbed children, recounted his experiences in teaching 15 disturbed boys at Hawthorn-Cedar Knolls, a residential school. His teaching approach was based primarily on psychoanalytic ideas and drew heavily on the interpersonal therapeutic process—"dialogue" and responding to "I" and "otherness." In his words, "The essential classroom event is the transaction of meaning among more than two persons, as contrasted with the two-person contact of a therapy situation" (Kornberg, 1955, p. 132).

Beginning in the late 1950s, however, the role of education and the role of the teacher began to take on greater significance in the thinking of many professionals, and the influence of psychoanalytic theory waned. Fenichel and his colleagues, who founded the first day school for severely disturbed children in the United States in 1953, highlighted the central role of education and teachers in the lives of BD children (Fenichel, 1974; Fenichel, Freedman, & Klapper, 1960). Hobbs and others, who initiated an ecological approach to the problem of emotional disturbance called Project Re-ED, saw the school and teachers as invaluable tools in working with children (Hobbs, 1965, 1974). Morse and his colleagues developed the crisis teacher concept, a plan to help teachers manage serious behavior problems in the context of the regular public school (Morse, 1965, 1974). Whelan, who directed education at the children's division of the Menninger psychiatric clinic, and Berkowitz and Rothman, who worked with disturbed children in institutions and public schools in New York City, found that education could be the mainstay of intervention in BD children's lives (Berkowitz, 1974; Berkowitz & Rothman, 1967; Rothman, 1974; Whelan, 1963, 1966, 1974). In short, education and teachers came to be viewed by professionals with divergent theoretical orientations as central to the work of helping BD children (see Knoblock, 1964, 1966; Knoblock & Johnson, 1967; Long, Morse, & Newman, 1965).

Clear distinctions have not always been drawn between education and therapy, nor have clear differences always been made among the roles of teachers, psychologists, social workers, and other professionals (Hewett & Taylor, 1980; Kerr & Nelson, 1983). One early design for intervention and personnel preparation, which remains a viable model today, makes use of the overlapping roles of professionals — the *educateur* or teacher-counselor training program associated with Project Re-ED. An educateur or teacher-counselor is a professional trained to adopt various aspects of the roles of teacher, social worker, advocate, recreation specialist, surrogate parent, counselor, and so on (Hobbs, 1965, 1974).

Traditional university training programs and certifying agencies may make the differing routes to employment clear, but the actual functions and roles of professionals who serve BD children often become indistinct in practice (Kerr & Nelson, 1983). Part of the reason for the frequent lack of clear differentiation among professional roles is the fact that much of the conceptual base for understanding and intervening in disordered child behavior is derived from the literatures of child development and child psychology. Particularly since the rise of applied behavioral psychology in the 1960s, the lines separating the interests and methods of psychologists and educators have become blurred and complementary (cf., Bijou, 1970).

Early Studies of Special Instruction and Management

Early reports of the education of BD children were psychoanalytically oriented — descriptive case studies rather than controlled empirical tests of methodologies or techniques (e.g., Berkowitz & Rothman, 1960; Kornberg, 1955). During the 1960s, however, behaviorally oriented teaching and management strategies were pioneered with a variety of handicapped individuals, including BD children. Zimmerman and Zimmerman (1962) published one of the earliest case studies describing specific behavior modification techniques with disturbed children. Subsequently, special educators and psychologists interested in the education and management of BD children published a veritable flood of reports illustrating specific behaviorally oriented teaching and management techniques. Particularly noteworthy among these were the work of Haring and Phillips (1962), Hewett (1968), and Lovaas (1966, 1967). (Note that the publications of these individuals cited here are only representative of their work.)

Haring and Phillips (1962) devised a structured, directive, behaviorally oriented approach to teaching and managing disturbed children that was a marked departure from the highly permissive, psychoanalytically oriented methods that had dominated the field. Their emphasis was on clear directions, firm expectations, and consistent consequences for children's behavior in the classroom and at home. Hewett (1968) designed what he called an "engineered classroom," one in which children could earn rewards for academic performance and desirable behavior throughout the school day. He emphasized the selection of tasks appropriate for the child's level of performance, meaningful and frequent rewards for improvement, and clearly stated contingencies for reward in a highly organized classroom environment. Lovaas, whose work has been with psychotic (autistic and schizophrenic) children, pioneered methods of teaching functional language and affective responses, as well as controlling or eliminating such severe maladaptive behavior as excessive self-stimulation and self-injury.

Many psychologists and special educators contributed to the burgeoning literature of behavior management in the 1960s and 1970s. The body of literature variously termed *behavior modification* and *applied behavior analysis*, now a vast and varied literature covering nearly every conceivable behavior problem, became the foundation for much of special education's practice.

Early Program Descriptions and Studies of Outcome

In 1962, the Council for Exceptional Children published a 30 page pamphlet entitled *Considerations for Planning Classes for the Emotionally Handicapped* (Hollister & Goldston, 1962). The authors noted that they provided merely an outline, or taxonomy, of considerations, not recommendations for practice, based on their study of 68 classroom programs for emotionally disturbed children. Two years later, CEC published a research analysis of practices in nearly 300 special public school classes for the emotionally handicapped, drawn from a national sample (Morse, Cutler, & Fink, 1964). The Morse et al. study provides in many ways

a reference point for judging change and progress in the field, as it includes rich information regarding program initiation and operation, pupil and teacher characteristics, and program philosophy — or lack of it.

In their preface, Hollister and Goldston (1962) observed that

> School administrators, special education supervisors, teachers, teacher-trainers and others are asking: 'What are we trying to do with these emotionally handicapped students? What procedures are being used? What are the essential component parts of such a program? and What is happening to these children as a result of these programs?'

The current literature in the field suggests, unfortunately, that the professionals involved are still asking the same questions (Grosenick & Huntze, 1983; Noel, 1982).

Some early programs for BD children were both clearly described and evaluated in terms of their effects on children. Although one might hope for more dramatic results and tighter or more sophisticated research designs, the program evaluations of Haring and Phillips (1962) and Hewett (1968) indicated the beneficial effects of behavioral methods, including a highly structured, directive atmosphere in the classroom. Moreover, the behavioral interventions of Lovaas (e.g., 1966, 1967) and his colleagues, as well as many other behavioral psychologists, have repeatedly and rigorously been evaluated in terms of their immediate effects on children's behavior. Unfortunately, too few *programs* (as distinct from specific methods or techniques) have been evaluated, and too few studies of the long-term effects of interventions have been reported, a matter to be discussed further.

CURRENT ISSUES

The current issues in the field are remarkably similar to those of 20 years ago, an indication of how frustratingly slow progress has been. Noel and Haring (1982) noted

> The past 25 years of research and development have resulted in a large body of

literature as well as the establishment of a separate, albeit not necessarily distinct, field within special education. For, despite the amount of work that has been done, special education for the emotionally disturbed has consistently been plagued with certain problems. Chief among these is the very definition of "emotional disturbance." Clearly apparent throughout . . . the professional literature is the uncertainty and outright confusion over what constitutes emotional disturbance and which students can be classified as such. This confusion is evident in the terms used to describe these students—terms such as "seriously emotionally disturbed," "behavior disordered," and "emotionally impaired." These definitional problems, with the attendant difficulties in identification, clearly seem to be the greatest impediment to full educational programming for these students. (p. viii)

Current Issues in Definition

The problem of definition has been highlighted since the enactment, in 1975, of PL 94-142, which mandates the identification of all "seriously emotionally disturbed" children. Implementation of PL 94-142 required a working definition, and one was therefore promulgated in the rules and regulations accompanying the law. The issue today is the adequacy of the definition for facilitating the delivery of special education services to handicapped children, as the law mandates.

Before considering the problems presented by the definition itself, one should observe that the terminology of this category is significantly different from others included under the law and its rules and regulations. "Seriously emotionally disturbed" seems to imply that some children are emotionally disturbed but not seriously so. While it is true that emotional disturbance or behavior disorder may range from minor to profound, the same can be said for mental retardation, physical disability, visual impairment, and so on. Yet the law and its rules and regulations do not refer to the seriously mentally retarded, the obviously physically disabled, or the significantly visually impaired. The qualifier attached to the emo-

tionally disturbed categorical label seems to indicate concern for *disqualification* of children for special education and related services, perhaps under the assumption that too many children would be identified were the terminology more straightforward (see Bower, 1982).

The definition that was adopted for federal purposes was, in the main, the one proposed by Bower (1960). However, Bower's definition was not taken simply as he proposed it. Rather, it was altered by two significant addenda—without consultation with Bower about the implications (Bower, personal communication, 1984). The first addendum follows Bower's introductory statement that a child may be considered emotionally handicapped (or, in the federal language, seriously emotionally disturbed) if he or she exhibits one or more of the five characteristics over a long period of time and to a marked degree. The wording of the addendum is "which adversely affects educational performance." The second addendum, which follows the list of five characteristics, is "The term includes children who are schizophrenic" [or autistic, a category later deleted from the definition]. "The term does not include children who are socially maladjusted, unless it is determined that they are seriously emotionally disturbed" *(Federal Register, 42*(163), August 23, 1977, p. 42478).

These addenda may at first seem to be minor and insignificant changes. Careful reflection, however, leads one to conclude that a definition based on study of disordered behavior in the context of school, and one admirably suited for use in educational settings, has been made contradictory and nonsensical (Bower, 1982; Kauffman, 1980, 1982, 1985). Apparently, the changes in Bower's definition were made to satisfy political concerns regarding the number of children to be served. The addenda can not be justified by research or logic (see Bower, 1982).

"Which adversely affects educational performance" is a particularly puzzling and illogical addition. Perhaps it is a pro forma statement that PL 94-142 is concerned with *educationally relevant* handicaps. Nevertheless, it is both obfuscatory and redundant as part of Bower's definition. A child who could exhibit one or more of the five characteristics described in the definition over a long period of time and to a marked degree, yet *not* suffer adverse effects on educational performance, would be a peculiar individual, indeed. One notes that "adversely affects educational performance" is obviously redundant with the first characteristic listed in Bower's definition ("an inability to learn") if educational performance is equated with academic achievement. But does "educational performance" mean something more than *academic* progress? What of the child who exhibits, for example, Bower's fourth characteristic ("a general, pervasive mood of unhappiness or depression") to an extreme degree and over a period of a year but is academically advanced for his or her age and grade? The "which adversely affects educational performance" addendum could be used to exclude such a child from special education by the argument that this sort of emotional or behavioral problem is not *educationally* relevant! One should also note that if "educational performance" is interpreted to include personal satisfaction and social-interpersonal relations — the affective aspects of school life — then "which adversely affects educational performance" is superfluous. Very clearly, this phrase was added to the definition without adequate consideration of its logic and purpose — unless the purpose was to give school personnel an out, a hedge against the expectation that certain handicapped children will be served under the law (see Wood, 1985).

The first addendum to Bower's definition may be puzzling, but the second is indecipherable. Why, one might ask, are schizophrenic children specifically included? Could a schizophrenic child possibly be excluded by the definition as written by Bower? Any schizophrenic child will most certainly exhibit one or more of the five characteristics to a marked degree and over a long period of time. Childhood psychoses in general, and childhood schizophrenia in particular, are defined primarily by persistent and extreme "inability to build or maintain satisfactory relationships with peers and teachers" (and others) and "inappropriate types

of behavior or feelings under normal circumstances." Hence, the specific inclusion of schizophrenic children is meaningless on logical grounds. A child who is labeled *schizophrenic* but who would not otherwise be included under the definition obviously carries an inappropriate label. Were such a child to be referred for special education, the referral would be simply on the basis of a meaningless label rather than because of handicapping behavioral characteristics. Thus, the addendum seems only to cloud the issue of definition and allow misplacement of children by virtue of a diagnostic label, the opposite effect one would hope for.

The fact that autistic children have been specifically excluded by a recent change in the rules and regulations is most curious. Bower (1982) notes that, in January 1981, the U. S. Department of Education deleted childhood autism from the classification of "seriously emotionally disturbed" and included it in the category of "other health impaired." The education department could make this change in the rules in regulations without public participation because the Secretary of Education determined that the change was not substantive. The explanation given in the *Federal Register* for the change in the regulations included the argument, said to be based on research, that not all autistic children are seriously emotionally disturbed. Such children are now considered to be members of the category of handicapped children exhibiting severe communication and other developmental and educational problems or having limited strength, vitality, or alertness due to chronic or acute health problems such as heart condition, tuberculosis, rheumatic fever, nephritis, asthma, sickle cell anemia, hemophilia, and so on. Bower (1982) comments:

> There is, however, no significant research that would suggest that childhood autism is a product of other childhood diseases or a communicative disorder as the term is understood. Definitions do not change reality: at best they assist in human and scientific communication about an agreed upon and pre-

scribed condition. Communication between the behavioral scientist and the policy maker is difficult at best. If now each adopts different definitions and categories to fit their different epistemologies, the Tower of Babel may need a high rise extension. (p. 60)

Finally, the addendum excluding "children who are socially maladjusted, unless it is determined that they are seriously emotionally disturbed" is logically nonsensical. Furthermore, it suggests that discriminations must be made between children's social and emotional problems when, in fact, such distinctions are both infeasible and undesirable. What is social maladjustment if it is not the behavioral characteristics listed in Bower's definition? Only by appealing to unobservable, hypothetical constructs related to intrapsychic phenomena can one propose a distinction between emotional disturbance and social maladjustment; and a definition that appeals to such constructs is not defensible on the basis of the research leading to Bower's definition (Bower, 1981, 1982) or recent research on the nature of children's behavior disorders (Kauffman, 1985; Kauffman & Kneedler, 1981; Kerr & Nelson, 1983; Walker, 1982). Bower (1982) states bluntly, "The [current federal] definition is contradictory in intent and content with the intent and content of the research from which it came" (p. 60). One can only hope that the current definition will be studied with an eye toward repairing the wreckage of its internal logic and reconstructing it in the light of research on the nature of behavior disorders in the context of school.

Bower's original research (1960) still provides a sound beginning point for a definition of behavior disorders, and his original definition still is admirably suited for identification of BD children in school. Today, the primary problem of definition is not the limitations of Bower's research, nor is it his criteria for determining that a child is handicapped behaviorally in school. The primary problem is the law's requirement that children be identified for special education services *as if their handicaps were a disease or an objectively definable and isolatable*

entity. This requirement of the law, a requirement based on the assumption that children can be reliably identified in isolation from the school environment as having or not having a handicapping condition, is simply not consistent with reality.

The identification of children with behavioral disorders is necessarily a subjective process, even when identification is based on objective observation of the child's behavior. Part of the reason for this is that the child's behavior per se does not define disorder. Rather, the setting in which the behavior occurs and the expectations and tolerance of peers and adults must be taken into account. Recent research indicates the necessity of a truly ecological approach to defining disordered behavior, one that considers the interactive effects of the child's behavior and others' reactions to it (e.g., Emery, Binkoff, Houts, & Carr, 1983; Hersh & Walker, 1983; McConnell et al., 1984; Walker, 1982; Walker & Rankin, 1983).

One frequently hears the call to distinguish between child behavior that is disturbed and behavior that is simply disturbing. The assumption that some children possess (internally) a disturbance while other children are merely nuisances to peers and adults accounts, perhaps, for the exclusion by the federal definition of socially maladjusted children who are not emotionally disturbed. However, from an ecological perspective, the disturbed–disturbing or emotionally disturbed–socially maladjusted distinction is counterproductive, if the objective of identification is to provide effective intervention for handicapped children. Walker (1982) suggests that it may be impossible to make reliable distinctions between disturbed and disturbing behavior.

> Further, we may not want to. If a given child's behavior is viewed by a teacher as problematic and disturbing, is that child at any less risk than one whose behavior is viewed as disordered but not disturbing? One could make a convincing argument that the educational adjustment and/or social development of both children may be equally impaired.

The response of educators should be identical in both situations. (Walker, 1982, pp. 24–25)

Bower (1960) and his colleagues, as well as many other researchers, have studied emotionally handicapped and normal children and delineated the characteristics that distinguish those children who are disabled by their behavior—or adults' perceptions of it (e.g., Achenbach & Edelbrock, 1981; Cullinan, Epstein, & Kauffman, 1984; Rubin & Balow, 1978; see Kauffman, 1985, for a review). Some writers suggest that defining BD in terms of the perceived behavioral characteristics of children already identified as BD is illogical (cf., Algozzine, 1982). Others, however, argue that actual referral for mental health services or special education is the best criterion against which to validate identification procedures (Achenbach & Edelbrock, 1981; Cullinan et al., 1984). That is, the most reasonable way to validate a set of behavioral characteristics or behavioral ratings that distinguish BD from non-BD children is to delineate the characteristics or ratings of children known to be BD. The more recent studies of Achenbach and Edelbrock (1981) and Cullinan et al. (1984) tend to confirm the earlier studies of Bower (1960) that led to his definition. In short, one is drawn to the conclusion that Bower's definition, unencumbered by the confusing and irrelevant addenda in the federal version, is very much "on target" in describing the characteristics of children who are handicapped by their disordered behavior in the context of school.

The adequacy of Bower's definition for describing the general category of BD children and guiding the delivery of special education services does not mean that his definition is adequate for all purposes. Wood and Lakin (1979) have reviewed the problem of definition for research purposes and concluded that most research studies contain inadequate descriptions of subjects. Defining populations for research demands a much more fine-grained analysis behavior. Wood and Lakin suggest this problem be addressed by making better

use of the behavior rating scales that are readily available to psychologists and educators. More specifically, researchers are encouraged to describe their subjects in terms of scores on one or more widely used behavior checklists (see Achenbach & Edelbrock, 1981; Epstein, Kauffman, & Cullinan, 1985; Walker, 1982). Clearer inferences could then be drawn for interventions with children who have particular types of problems, and replication of their studies would be facilitated.

Current Issues in Terminology

Psychiatry and clinical psychology are fields in which terminology has traditionally been a controversial topic. Professionals in these fields have long traded in the subtle, hidden meanings and magic of words. The penchant of professionals in these influential fields of practice for professional argot, in addition to the fondness of special educators for jargon and the lead pipe stiffness with which government bureaucracies respond to research, have produced terminological confusion both in the literature and in laws guiding the delivery of services.

The confusion is not limited to terms applied to subclassifications or specific disorders; it begins with the label applied to the category. The various states have chosen to use a hodgepodge of categorical labels. In 1983, one could find at least the following official terms (and variations on them) used in states' special education legislation: behavior impairments; behaviorally disordered; emotional/behavioral disorder; emotionally conflicted; emotionally disturbed; emotionally handicapped; emotionally impaired; educationally handicapped; personal and social adjustment problem; seriously emotionally disturbed; socially and emotionally disturbed; and socially and emotionally maladjusted.

Whether the first part of the term is *emotionally*, *behaviorally*, or *socially*, it indicates concern about the way the child acts. And whether the second part of the term is *disturbed*, *disordered*, *impaired*, *maladjusted*, or *handicapped*, the essential meaning is the same: the child falls far short of meeting significant adults' expectations.

On purely logical grounds, one could advance the argument that *behavior disorder* is a more accurate and appropriate categorical label than *emotional disturbance*, because the focus of special education for the children in question is their observable behavior (Walker, 1982). More important, perhaps, is the question of the effects of various labels on children and teachers, the extent to which they carry significantly different connotations. Feldman, Kinnison, Jay, and Harth (1983) studied the meanings that teachers and teacher trainees attach to the terms *seriously emotionally disturbed* and *behavior disordered. Behavior disordered* was significantly less negative in its connotations than *emotionally disturbed*: children labeled *behavior disordered* were seen as more teachable, more likely to be successful in a mainstream classroom, and more likely to have a good future.

Logic and research weigh on the side of replacing *emotionally disturbed* and similar labels with *behaviorally disordered. Emotionally disturbed* connotes intrapsychic problems that are relatively immutable and inaccessible to the teacher. On the other hand, *behaviorally disordered* connotes observable behavior problems with which teachers can work directly. Huntze (1985) outlined the logical and empirical arguments for change in terminology. Unfortunately, however, the conclusion of a special study on terminology, mandated by Congress in 1983, was that "there is no compelling reason to change the current Federal terminology or definition" (Tallmadge, Gamel, Munson, & Hanley, 1985, p. vii). States, however, are free under current regulations to adopt their own terminology. The authors of the special study report concluded on the basis of their review of literature, indeed, "that parents and education professionals tend to have a more negative response to the SED [*seriously emotionally disturbed*] label than the BD [*behaviorally disordered*] label" (Tallmadge et al., 1985, p. xi). Primary arguments against changing the *SED* label to *BD* were that (a) the change would entail much unproductive work and confusion in states now using the Federal terminology, (b) the BD label would eventually carry as many negative connotations as are now carried by SED, (c) the change from SED to BD may result in special education services to a different and less deserving population than is now receiving services or "open the flood gates" of services to an unmanageable number of students, and (d) fashions in labeling are changeable, and one cannot predict what additional labels may be proposed in the future.

Terminological confusion is most evident in classification systems applied to children's behavior disorders. Classification has been a problem in every area of special education, but it remains today what Hobbs (1975) described as "a thicket of thorny problems" (p. 57).

Current Issues in Estimating Prevalence

As noted in the previous discussion of early prevalence studies, the federal education bureaucracy began using a prevalence estimate of 2.0% of the school-age population in the 1950s. In recent years, however, the Department of Education began publishing an estimated prevalence *interval* of 1.2–2.0%. The most recent report to Congress by the Department of Education (1984), however, contains no estimates of prevalence of handicapping conditions. The report indicates that in the school year 1982–1983, approximately 0.89% of the in-school population between the ages of 3 and 21 (i.e., about 353 thousand out of 40 million children and youth) were identified as seriously emotionally disturbed under federal laws.

The number of children now served is still clearly below the most conservative research-based prevalence estimates. Moreover, one is struck by the fact that, while census statistics included in the *Sixth Annual Report to Congress on the Implementation of Public Law 94-142* (U.S. Department of Education, 1984) show that the U.S. population between the ages of 3 and 21 years is approximately 70 million, the percentage of children and youth served (0.89%) is

based on a school-enrolled population of approximately 40 million. One notes, then, that
about 40% of those who are ostensibly eligible
for special education and related services are
excluded from consideration. Granted that
some children and youth between the ages of
3 and 21 are not enrolled in a public school for
legitimate reasons (being younger or older than
the ages for which attendance is required or
being enrolled in a private school, for example), it is a safe assumption that a significant
proportion of the 30 million not enrolled are
handicapped and in need of special education.

Prevalence is a current issue of critical importance because pressure seems to be building to use lower estimates or evade the issue
entirely in the face of evidence that hundreds
of thousands of BD children and youth have
not been identified and are not receiving special education and related services (Kauffman,
1984; Paul, 1985a). The federal bureaucracy
appears to be whittling away at prevalence estimates or simply ignoring them, focusing attention on the number of children served without
reference to prevalence estimates based on the
best available research. The possible political
motivation for doing this is obvious. Special
education budgets have grown large, and local,
state, and federal resources for education are
already perceived as severely strained. If the
federal government were to persist in estimat-
ing that several times more children are behavior disordered than have been identified, then
the failure of PL 94-142 for many children
would be obvious. Neither the fiscal resources
nor the trained personnel are readily available
to serve several-times more children than are
presently identified. On the other hand, if the
prevalence estimate can be trimmed to corre-
spond roughly to the number of children now
identified, then the law can be lauded as a
success.

Some federal officials have suggested that
nearly all handicapped children in the United
States are now appropriately identified and are
receiving special education (*Report on Education
Research*, 1983; *The Washington Post*, 1982). This
suggestion is clearly contrary to the 1981 report of the General Accounting Office (GAO,

1981), the call by the National Institute for
Handicapped Research for improved services
to disturbed children and youth (*Federal Register, 49*(49), March 12, 1984, p. 9330), information from the Children's Defense Fund
(Knitzer, 1982), and prevalence research as
well (Achenbach & Edelbrock, 1981; Cullinan,
et al., 1984). Nevertheless, the "official" suggestion that not many handicapped children
remain unserved is likely to foster misinterpretation of prevalence research and make advocacy for unserved or underserved children
extremely difficult, if not impossible.

Consider the statement, attributed to an official of the Office of Special Education Programs, that "just about all handicapped school-
age children who need special education have
been identified. . . . As you look at this [child
count data], you also accept that there are not
hundreds of thousands of children out there in
need of services" (*Report on Education Research*,
1983, p. 5). Using simple arithmetic, and
being severely conservative in choosing the
numbers used in estimation, one easily arrives
at the conclusion that this statement is almost
certainly false. As stated previously, the number of children and youth enrolled in public
schools in the United States today is approximately 40 million, but let us use the conservative figure of 30 million for our estimate to
allow for these facts: (a) about 4 million are
identified as handicapped already and (b) the
school-age population has been declining. Most
major prevalence studies suggest that at least
6.0% of the school-age population are BD
(Achenbach & Edelbrock, 1981; Cullinan et
al., 1984; see Graham, 1979, and Kauffman,
1985, for reviews), but let us use the conservative estimate of 2.0%. Using a 2.0% prevalence estimate for a population of 30 million
children, one arrives at an estimate of 600,000
BD children. According to the most recent
government figures, about 353,000 children
are now being served under the category "seriously emotionally disturbed" (U.S. Department of Education, 1984). Again, being always
conservative, let us suppose that the number
has grown to 400,000. Still, one must conclude
that 200,000 children who are BD and could

profit from special education have not been identified.

The current political and professional contexts in which identification of BD children takes place are working against the growth of services to this subpopulation of the handicapped (Kauffman, 1984). As Bower (1982) notes, current federal policy makes a zero-sum game of services to BD children, limits services to only the most severely handicapped, and negates the potential role of the school in primary prevention of disordered behavior.

Current Issues in Classification

Classroom teachers of BD children have little reason to concern themselves with issues in classification. "Although [these] issues may seem remote from everyday work with disturbed children, they lurk about in many guises" (Achenbach & Edelbrock, 1983, p. 65). As Achenbach and Edelbrock suggest, the issues are implicit in much of what mental health workers and special educators do, including their professional communication, treatment and administrative decisions, diagnoses and prognostications, and research. The issues are also relevant to matters of public policy.

Much current opinion and research can be summarized in two statements: (a) psychiatric systems of classification for children, including the most recent version of the American Psychiatric Association's *Diagnostic and Statistical Manual* (DSM-III, APA, 1980), are unreliable and of little value to special educators and child psychologists and (b) multivariate analyses of behavior ratings have yielded more reliable and useful classifications than have clinical psychiatric systems, although the dimensions or syndromes derived from such analyses are now of much greater value to researchers than to teachers and policy makers (Achenbach & Edelbrock, 1983; Cullinan et al., 1983; Kauffman, 1985; see also Phillips et al., 1975; Prugh, Engel, & Morse, 1975; Quay, 1979). Considerably more research, involving large sam-

ples and extensive statistical analyses, will be necessary to bring significant advances in the everyday usefulness of any system of classification for educators.

Research to date has repeatedly demonstrated the existence of two primary broadband behavioral dimensions or syndromes. Across all age groups, the behavior problems exhibited by both normal and BD children can be characterized by two broad dimensions, which Quay (1979) has labeled *conduct disorder* and *personality problem* and Achenbach and Edelbrock (1983) have called *externalizing* and *internalizing* disorders. Disorders of the *conduct* or *externalizing* variety are characterized by aggression, hyperactivity, cruelty, delinquency, destructiveness, disruptiveness, and similar problems that involve acting out against the environment. *Personality* or *internalizing* disorders are characterized by anxiety, depression, shyness, social withdrawal, somatic complaints, self-consciousness, and so on, that are typical of neurotic self-absorption.

Other somewhat less reliable and pervasive behavioral dimensions also have been found frequently in factor analyses of behavioral ratings. These narrower, more specific behavioral dimensions (e.g., socialized delinquency, sex problems, anxious-obsessive, depression, attention deficit) tend to vary with age and sex (Achenbach & Edelbrock, 1983; Epstein, Kauffman, & Cullinan, 1984). The extent to which these dimensions or syndromes can be reliably demonstrated statistically in different samples of children, the reliability with which individual children can be assigned to the categories, and the implications of children's assignment to a given category for the selection and evaluation of intervention techniques are matters for future research.

Current Issues in Educational Programming and Programs

Confusion, disorder, diversity, inadequacy — these are the disquieting terms that best describe educational provisions for behavior disordered children. One is hard pressed, especially given the confused definition of behavior disorders, to summarize the literature in any coherent way, except to say that it is incoherent. Consider the fact that in addition to the problem of definition one is faced with a wide age range (neonate through young adult under PL 94-142), problems ranging from profound psychotic withdrawal to relatively minor problems of personal adjustment, and diverse theoretical models. Consider also the difference between *programming* — strategies and techniques for managing specific problems—and a *program* involving the application of programming in a comprehensive, coherent service delivery system. Programming has been extensively researched, and well-organized compendia of programming approaches are available (e.g., Kerr & Nelson, 1983). Few programs, on the other hand, have been adequately described; and surveys of the literature lead one to the suspicion that many apparent programs for BD children cannot be described as coherent service delivery systems (Noel, 1982; Grosenick & Huntze, 1983).

Of all the alternative approaches to programming, behavioral methods have the surest foundation in empirical research (Kauffman & Kneedler, 1981; Kerr & Nelson, 1983; Morris & Kratochwill, 1983). Behavioral methods, once assumed to exclude consideration of affective concerns and to focus exclusively on manipulating the child's behavior by controlling external contingencies, have been broadened in recent years. Today, the behavioral approach encompasses the interactionist theory of ecological psychologists, which includes recognition of the mutual influences of children and adults on each others' behavior (Emery et al., 1983). It encompasses also a concern for children's cognitions and affect, which radical behaviorists dismissed as irrelevant (Kauffman & Kneedler, 1981; Mahoney, 1974; Meichenbaum, 1977, 1980).

Current issues in behavioral programming for BD children do not involve the question of strategies or techniques peculiar to the categorical label, that is, to children whose primary problem or handicapping condition is maladaptive behavior. The issues cut across categorical lines and are applicable, in fact, to *all*

children, handicapped and normal alike. As Bower (1981, 1982) and others have stated, the problem of disordered behavior is common to children with all manner of handicapping conditions and to children not identified as handicapped. The relevant questions today have to do with making behavioral programming more efficient, humane, and conducive to generalized, long-term behavioral change. Thus research studies involving self-management and involvement of the peer group, as well as longitudinal studies, are among the most important current work in the field. Several exemplary research programs related to these issues are briefly noted here. These research programs are merely illustrative of the work that is advancing the field most rapidly, and the citations should not be interpreted as exhaustive or exclusive.

At the University of Virginia's Learning Disabilities Research Institute, Hallahan and his colleagues have evaluated self-monitoring procedures for children with severe attention problems (labeled for special education purposes as *learning disabled*) (Hallahan, Hall, Ianna, Kneedler, Lloyd, Loper, & Reeve, 1983; Hallahan, Lloyd, Kauffman, & Loper, 1983). They have shown that typically inattentive, disruptive children can be trained to become aware of their own on-task and off-task behavior and record their behavior when prompted by tones presented at random intervals by a tape recorder. The effects of the self-monitoring procedure have been improved attention to task and academic performance for most of the children studied. The procedure is low cost (in terms of teacher time and effort, materials, and equipment) and encourages children's self-control.

At the University of Pittsburgh, Strain and his colleagues have researched the use of peer confederates in modifying children's social withdrawal (Strain, 1981a, 1981b; Strain, Odom, & McConnell, 1984). Their work has demonstrated the feasibility of using even very young (preschool) peers as intervention agents to increase the social interaction of severely withdrawn children. It has also led to the conclusion that mainstreaming will not succeed in the long run unless the programming includes "the entire social ecology and friendship network within a particular setting" (Strain, 1981a, p. 102).

Strain and his colleagues also have studied the long-term effects of behavioral programming with oppositional children, whose characteristics included prolonged temper tantrums, continual opposition to adults' requests and commands, and physical aggression toward their parents (Strain, Steele, Ellis, & Timm, 1982). These researchers made follow-up observations of 40 oppositional children who were 3-, 4-, and 5-year-olds when behavioral intervention was begun in their homes, with the mothers serving as the primary agents of intervention. Three to nine years after intervention, observation in the homes and classrooms of the children showed that (a) the children were likely to comply with their parents' requests and commands, (b) the children's social interactions at home were overwhelmingly positive and their nonsocial behavior was predominantly appropriate, (c) the parents continued to use the child management techniques they had been taught during intervention, (d) in school, the children behaved like randomly selected peers, and teachers responded to them as they did to other children, and (e) the outcome of intervention was best for the children who were youngest at the time intervention was begun and for those families that had remained intact. The work of Strain et al. (1982) is particularly important, given the poor prognosis for aggressive children whose behavior is not brought under control at an early age (cf., Loeber, 1982; Patterson, 1982).

Lovaas and his colleagues and students at the University of California at Los Angeles recently reported the long-term effects of behavior therapy with autistic children (Lovaas, 1982). The basic behavior therapy program was begun in 1963, but a research project involving early, intensive intervention (the Young Autism Project) was begun in 1970. The major and remarkable finding of the project was that when intensive intervention (i.e., 40 or more hours of one-to-one treatment per week) was begun early (i.e., before the child was 42 months old), about 50% of the children recovered completely and another 40% made substantial improvement. Complete recovery meant that the child, though diagnosed as autistic before the age of $3\frac{1}{2}$ years, was advanced from first to second grade in a normal class of first graders in a normal public school, achieved a normal IQ, and was considered by the teacher to be well adjusted socially and emotionally. These results are in stark contrast to those in which less intensive behavior therapy was offered or the child was over $3\frac{1}{2}$ years old when treatment was begun. The results are also in stark contrast to the outcome of nonbehavioral treatment. Lovaas' research offers hope that even the most intransigent behavior disorders may yield to intensive, systematic behavioral programming when early intervention is possible.

Unfortunately, the majority of programming for BD children is not done in the context of a coherent program of research or practice. In fact, two recent reviews of program description and development have led to very discouraging conclusions (Grosenick & Huntze, 1983; Noel, 1982).

Noel (1982) summarized the conceptual models that may guide service delivery in a program (psychodynamic, psychoeducational, behavioral, ecological, and psychoneurological; see also McDowell, Adamson, & Wood, 1982). She also provided capsule descriptions of the types of programs currently offered BD children and youth: basic instructional, instructional and adjunct (e.g., counseling, psychotherapy, or vocational), supplemental (e.g., social skills training), special school, and preschool. Although she found evidence of program development in her informal survey of the field, she concluded that the development is frenetic and that one cannot determine how programs fit into a comprehensive service continuum. The disarray of programs is in her opinion so great, in fact, that "If one overall recommendation can be made, it is to stop scattered, episodic program implementation and to begin to develop system-wide service plans based both on empirical evidence of what works and the precise student needs that are being addressed" (Noel, 1982, p. 24). Additional analysis of program descriptions culled from the literature during the past 2 years indicates that no apparent progress has been made, that program development is, if anything, more haphazard than one might at first conclude (Noel, personal communication, 1984).

Grosenick and Huntze (1983) conducted an extensive computer aided search of the literature on BD programs published since 1960. To qualify as a *program*, a literature source had to include description of six of the following eight elements: (a) philosophy or ideational context, (b) program goals, (c) population definition, (d) criteria or procedures for child entry into the program, (e) methods, curriculum, and materials, (f) criteria or procedures for child exit from the program, (g) evaluation, (h) program operation. Only 81 different program descriptions could be found in the literature when these elements were applied.

For the 81 programs, Grosenick and Huntze (1983) judged descriptions of the eight program elements to be weak or not present for the following percentages:

philosophy	54%
goals	63%
population	46%
entry	59%
methods	31%
exit	80%
evaluation	43%
operation	26%

Additionally, the 81 programs represented a disproportionate emphasis (given the number of children and youth served) on mental health services and services for adolescents.

These results are quite disheartening in the light of the legal mandates for comprehensive services and progress on many fronts in special education. One might hope that the professional literature is not reflective of actual practices in the field in this case, that many coherent programs are in operation but are simply not described in a coherent way in the literature. Even with this hope, however, one is forced to the dreary conclusion that the current literature of the field does not provide adequate guidance for program development or improvement.

CONCLUSIONS AND FUTURE DIRECTIONS

In many ways, special education for BD children and youth is at a crossroads. In fundamental matters of definition and terminology, prevalence estimates, and program development and description the next few years will be a critical period (Paul, 1985b).

Chief among the problems needing early resolution is the matter of definition. The Department of Education must decide whether it will respect the intent and content of Bower's work and remove the garble it has added to his definition or add confusion to the matter by suggesting yet another statement of what a BD child is for purposes of special education. One might hope that respect for logical thinking, relevant research, and intent to serve children in need of special education will prevail in the coming decisions. If they do, then Bower's definition may be used in its original wording, as it remains today the clearest description of disordered child behavior in the context of school. Political and fiscal pressures may, however, force the Education Department to adopt a definition that is no improvement over the one currently in the rules and regulations, perhaps even one that is more restrictive or excludes greater numbers of troubled and troubling students.

Current federal policy, particularly as embodied in the definition and terminology of *seriously emotionally disturbed*, channels intervention primarily to severely handicapped and older students. Yet, the importance of early intervention — early in the child's life and early in the emergence of disordered behavior — is clearly indicated by research (cf. Lovaas, 1982; Strain et al., 1982). The focus of federal policy is, as Bower (1982) has noted, the antithesis of prevention. Federal policy makers will have to decide whether special or regular education has primary responsibility for primary prevention and determine the extent to which a child must have a history of social difficulty and failure in school before special education is legitimate. The current demand that the full force of PL 94-142 be brought to bear on every child identified as in need of special education artificially hardens the lines that separate handicapped from normal children and regular from special teachers, and the result is reluctance to recognize children's needs until they are extreme (Kauffman, 1982, 1984).

Federal policy now results in the neglect of delinquent and incarcerated youth (Rutherford, Wolford, & Nelson, 1983; Wolford, 1983). Future attention must be given to the education of children and youth who tend to be dismissed as the problem of some professional group other than special educators because they are "socially maladjusted" but not "seriously emotionally disturbed." The terminology of the field, including that used in federal documents, should be adjusted to reflect the legitimate concern of special educators for children and youth who are in difficulty with the law and/or the social demands of the school, although no one is willing to legitimize the label *seriously emotionally disturbed* by hypothesizing or "diagnosing" intrapsychic conflicts. Moreover, the terminology should communicate the concern of teachers for disordered behavior as clearly as possible and with as few negative connotations as possible. *Behavior disorder* would be a desirable substitute for *serious emotional disturbance* in federal rules and regulations; and a desirable future development would be states' adoption of uniform terminology matching that of the federal government.

The immediate future holds little hope that special education and related services will be extended to the number of children and youth who, according to prevalence research, need them. Federal and state authorities have at least three options in this matter: (a) adopt lower prevalence estimates that match or approximate the current number of children served, (b) base prevalence estimates on the best available research without regard to the number currently served and take legal action against thousands of public education agencies, or (c) give up the notion (because of the unthinkable litigation implied by the second option) that services can quickly be made to

match or approximate needs and offer every possible incentive to local schools to increase the level of service to BD students. The evidence and history of education legislation suggest that the future will bring the first option.

If substantial progress is to be made in services for BD children and youth, then future efforts will have to be concentrated on personnel preparation and program description and evaluation. Teachers of BD children are not being prepared in adequate numbers to meet present needs. If school systems were to attempt rapid expansion of their special education for BD students, then the number of personnel prepared would be even more inadequate (Smith-Davis, Burke, & Noel, 1984). Future personnel preparation efforts must train larger numbers of teachers to deal with BD pupils; they also must consider more carefully the roles such teachers are required to play in schools and other institutions. Program descriptions in the professional literature must become more complete and detailed in the aspects judged by Grosenick and Huntze (1983). Rigorous evaluation of programs is a critical need for the future (Grosenick & Huntze, 1983; Noel, 1982).

REFERENCES

Achenbach, T. M. (1982). *Developmental psychopathology* (2nd ed.). New York: Wiley.

Achenbach, T. M., & Edelbrock, C. S. (1981). Behavior problems and competencies reported by parents of normal and disturbed children aged four through sixteen. *Monographs of the Society for Research in Child Development*, *46*, whole No. 1, serial No. 188.

Achenbach, T. M., & Edelbrock, C. S. (1983). Taxonomic issues in child psychopathology. In T. H. Ollendick & M. Hersen (Eds.), *Handbook of child psychopathology* (pp. 65–93). New York: Plenum Press.

Ackerson, L. (1942). *Children's behavior problems*. Chicago: University of Chicago Press.

Algozzine, B. (1982). Assessment of severe behavior disorders. In M. M. Noel & N. G. Haring (Eds.), *Progress or change: Issues in educating the emotionally disturbed. Vol. 1: Identification and program planning* (pp. 43–60). Seattle: Program Development Assistance System, University of Washington.

American Psychiatric Association. (1980). *Diagnostic and statistical manual of mental disorders* (3rd ed.). Washington, DC: Author.

Baker, E. M., & Stullken, E. H. (1938). American research studies concerning the "behavior" type of exceptional child. *Journal of Exceptional Children*, *4*, 36–45.

Bell withdraws six proposals for educating handicapped. (1982, September 30). *Washington Post*. A1, A5.

Berkowitz, P. H. (1974). Pearl H. Berkowitz. In J. M. Kauffman & C. D. Lewis (Eds.), *Teaching children with behavior disorders: Personal perspectives* (pp. 24–49). Columbus, OH: Charles E. Merrill.

Berkowitz, P. H., & Rothman, E. P. (1960). *The disturbed child*. New York: New York University Press.

Berkowitz, P. H., & Rothman, E. P. (Eds.). (1967). *Public education for disturbed children in New York City*. Springfield, IL: Charles C Thomas.

Bettelheim, B. (1950). *Love is not enough*. New York: Macmillan.

Bettelheim, B., & Sylvester, E. (1948). A therapeutic milieu. *American Journal of Orthopsychiatry*, *18*, 191–206.

Bijou, S. W. (1970). What psychology has to offer education — now. *Journal of Applied Behavior Analysis*, *3*, 65–71.

Bower, E. M. (1960). *Early identification of emotionally handicapped children in school*. Springfield, IL: Charles C Thomas.

Bower, E. M. (1981). *Early identification of emotionally handicapped children in school* (3rd ed.). Springfield, IL: Charles C Thomas.

Bower, E. M. (1982). Defining emotional disturbance: Public policy and research. *Psychology in the Schools*, *19*, 55–60.

Cullinan, D., Epstein, M. H., & Kauffman, J. M. (1984). Teachers' ratings of children's behaviors: What constitutes behavior disorder in school? *Behavioral Disorders*, *10*, 9–19.

Cullinan, D., Epstein, M. H., & Lloyd, J. W. (1983). *Behavior disorders of children and adolescents*. Englewood Cliffs, NJ: Prentice-Hall.

Despert, J. L. (1965). *The emotionally disturbed child — then and now*. New York: Brunner.

Emery, R. E., Binkoff, J. A., Houts, A. C., & Carr, E. G. (1983). Children as independent variables: Some clinical implications of child effects. *Behavior Therapy*, *14*, 398–412.

Epstein, M. H., Kauffman, J. M., & Cullinan, D. (1985). Patterns of maladjustment among the behaviorally disordered: II. Boys aged 6–11, boys aged 12–18, girls aged 6–11, and girls aged 12–18. *Behavioral Disorders*, *10*, 125–135.

Feldman, D., Kinnison, L., Jay, R., & Harth, R. (1983). The effects of differential labeling on professional concepts and attitudes toward the emotionally disturbed/behaviorally disordered. *Behavioral Disorders*, *8*, 191–198.

Fenichel, C. (1974). Carl Fenichel. In J. M. Kauffman, & C. D. Lewis (Eds.), *Teaching children with behavior disorders: Personal perspectives* (pp. 50–75). Columbus, OH: Charles E. Merrill.

Fenichel, C., Freedman, A. M., & Klapper, Z. (1960). A day school for schizophrenic children. *American Journal of Orthopsychiatry*, *30*, 130–143.

General Accounting Office. (1981, September). *Disparities still exist in who gets special education*. Gaithersburg, MD: Author.

Graham, P. J. (1979). Epidemiological studies. In H. C. Quay & J. S. Werry (Eds.), *Psychopathological disorders of childhood* (2nd ed., pp. 185–209). New York: Wiley.

Griffiths, W. (1952). *Behavior difficulties of children as perceived and judged by parents, teachers, and children themselves*. Minneapolis: University of Minnesota Press.

Grosenick, J. K., & Huntze, S. L. (1983). *More questions than answers: Review and analysis of programs for behaviorally disordered children and youth*. Columbia, MO: Department of Special Education, University of Missouri.

Hallahan, D. P., Hall, R. J., Ianna, S. O., Kneedler, R. D., Lloyd, J. W., Loper, A. B., & Reeve, R. E. (1983). Summary of findings at the University of Virginia Learning Disabilities Research Institute. *Exceptional Education Quarterly*, *4*(1), 95–114.

Hallahan, D. P., & Kauffman, J. M. (1976). *Introduction to learning disabilities: A psycho-behavioral approach*. Englewood Cliffs, NJ: Prentice-Hall.

Hallahan, D. P., & Kauffman, J. M. (1977). Categories, labels, behavioral characteristics: ED, LD, and EMR reconsidered. *Journal of Special Education*, *11*, 139–149.

Hallahan, D. P., Lloyd, J. W., Kauffman, J. M., & Loper, A. B. (1983). Academic problems. In R. J. Morris & T. R. Kratochwill (Eds.), *The practice of child therapy* (pp. 113–141). New York: Pergamon.

Haring, N. G., & Phillips, E. L. (1962). *Educating emotionally disturbed children*. New York: McGraw-Hill.

Hersh, R. H., & Walker, H. M. (1983). Great expectations: Making schools effective for all students. *Policy Studies*, *2*(1), 147–188.

Hewett, F. M. (1968). *The emotionally disturbed child in the classroom*. Boston: Allyn & Bacon.

Hewett, F. M., & Taylor, F. D. (1980). *The emotionally disturbed child in the classroom: The orchestration of success* (2nd ed.). Boston: Allyn & Bacon.

Hewitt, L. E., & Jenkins, R. L. (1946). *Fundamental patterns of maladjustment: The dynamics of their origin*. Springfield, IL: State of Illinois.

Hobbs, N. (1965). How the Re-ED plan developed. In N. J. Long, W. C. Morse, & R. G. Newman (Eds.), *Conflict in the classroom* (pp. 286–294). Belmont, CA: Wadsworth.

Hobbs, N. (1974). Nicholas Hobbs. In J. M. Kauffman & C. D. Lewis (Eds.), *Teaching children with behavior disorders: Personal perspectives* (pp. 142–167). Columbus, OH: Charles E. Merrill.

Hobbs, N. (1975). *The futures of children*. San Francisco: Jossey-Bass.

Hoffman, E. (1974). The treatment of deviance by the educational system: History. In W. C. Rhodes & S. Head (Eds.), *A study of child variance. Vol. 3: Service delivery systems* (41–79). Ann Arbor: University of Michigan.

Hoffman, E. (1975). The American public school and the deviant child: The origins of their involvement. *Journal of Special Education, 9,* 415–423.

Hollister, W. G., & Goldston, S. E. (1962). *Considerations for planning classes for the emotionally handicapped*. Reston, VA: Council for Exceptional Children.

Huntze, S. L. (1985). A position paper of the Council for Children with Behavioral Disorders. *Behavioral Disorders, 10,* 167–174.

International Council for Exceptional Children. (1923). *Proceedings of the first annual meeting of the International Council for Exceptional Children*. Washington, DC: Author.

Kanner, L. (1962). Emotionally disturbed children: A historical review. *Child Development, 33,* 97–102.

Kauffman, J. M. (1976). Nineteenth century views of children's behavior disorders: Historical contributions and continuing issues. *Journal of Special Education, 10,* 335–349.

Kauffman, J. M. (1980). Where special education for emotionally disturbed children is going: A personal view. *Exceptional Children, 48,* 522–527.

Kauffman, J. M. (1981). Introduction: Historical trends and contemporary issues in special education in the United States. In J. M. Kauffman & D. P. Hallahan (Eds.), *Handbook of special education* (pp. 3–23). Englewood Cliffs, NJ: Prentice-Hall.

Kauffman, J. M. (1982). Social policy issues in special education and related services for emotionally disturbed children and youth. In M. M. Noel & N. G. Haring (Eds.), *Progress or change: Issues in educating the emotionally disturbed. Vol. 1: Identification and program planning* (pp. 1–10). Seattle: Program Development Assistance System, University of Washington.

Kauffman, J. M. (1984). Saving children in the age of Big Brother: Moral and ethical issues in the identification of deviance. *Behavioral Disorders, 10,* 60–70.

Kauffman, J. M. (1985). *Characteristics of children's behavior disorders* (3rd ed.). Columbus, OH: Charles E. Merrill.

Kauffman, J. M., & Kneedler, R. D. (1981). Behavior disorders. In J. M. Kauffman & D. P. Hallahan (Eds.), *Handbook of special education* (pp. 165–194). Englewood Cliffs, NJ: Prentice-Hall.

Kerr, M. M., & Nelson, C. M. (1983). *Strategies for managing behavior problems in the classroom*. Columbus, OH: Charles E. Merrill.

Knitzer, J. (1982). *Unclaimed children: The failure of public responsibility to children and adolescents in need of mental health services*. Washington, DC: Children's Defense Fund.

Knoblock, P. (Ed.). (1964). *Educational programming for emotionally disturbed children: The decade ahead*. Syracuse, NY: Syracuse University Press.

Knoblock, P. (Ed.). (1966). *Intervention approaches in educating emotionally disturbed children*. Syracuse, NY: Syracuse University Press.

Knoblock, P., & Johnson, J. L. (Eds.). (1967). *The teaching-learning process in educating emotionally disturbed children*. Syracuse, NY: Syracuse University Press.

Kornberg, L. (1955). *A class for disturbed children: A case study and its meaning for education*. New York: Teachers College Press.

Krugman, M. (Chairman). (1953). Symposium, 1953: The education of emotionally disturbed children. *American Journal of Orthopsychiatry, 23,* 667–731.

Lane, H. (1976). *The wild boy of Aveyron*. Cambridge, MA: Harvard University Press.

Lewis, C. D. (1974). Introduction: Landmarks. In J. M. Kauffman & C. D. Lewis (Eds.), *Teaching children with behavior disorders: Personal perspectives* (pp. 2–23). Columbus, OH: Charles E. Merrill.

Loeber, R. (1982). The stability of antisocial and delinquent behavior: A review. *Child Development, 53,* 1431–1446.

Long, N. J., Morse, W. C., & Newman, R. G. (Eds.). (1965). *Conflict in the classroom*. Belmont, CA: Wadsworth.

Lovaas, O. I. (1966). A program for the establishment of speech in psychotic children. In J. K. Wing (Ed.), *Early childhood autism: Clinical, educational, and social aspects* (pp. 115–144). New York: Pergamon.

Lovaas, O. I. (1967). A behavior therapy approach to the treatment of childhood schizophrenia. In J. P. Hill (Ed.), *Minnesota symposia on child psychology (Vol. 1,* pp. 108–159). Minneapolis: University of Minnesota Press.

Lovaas, O. I. (1982, September). *An overview of the Young Autism Project*. Paper presented at the annual convention of the American Psychological Association, Washington, DC.

Macfarlane, J., Allen, L., & Honzik, M. (1955). *A developmental study of the behavior problems of normal children between 21 months and 14 years*. Berkeley: University of California Press.

Mahoney, M. J. (1974). *Cognition and behavior modification*. Cambridge, MA: Ballinger.

McConnell, S. R., Strain, P. S., Kerr, M. M., Stagg, V., Lenkner, D. A., & Lambert, D. L. (1984). An empirical definition of elementary school adjustment: Selection of target behaviors for a comprehensive treatment program. *Behavior Modification, 8*, 451–473.

McDowell, R. L., Adamson, G. W., & Wood, F. H. (Eds.). (1982). *Teaching emotionally disturbed children.* Boston: Little, Brown & Co.

Meichenbaum, D. (1977). *Cognitive-behavior modification: An integrative approach.* New York: Plenum Press.

Meichenbaum, D. (1980). Cognitive-behavior modification: A promise yet unfulfilled. *Exceptional Education Quarterly, 1*(1), 83–88.

Menninger, K. (1963). *The vital balance.* New York: Viking.

Morris, R. J., & Kratochwill, T. R. (Eds.). (1983). *The practice of child therapy.* New York: Pergamon.

Morse, W. C. (1965). The crisis teacher. In N. J. Long, W. C. Morse, & R. G. Newman (Eds.), *Conflict in the classroom* (pp. 251–254). Belmont, CA: Wadsworth.

Morse, W. C. (1974). William C. Morse. In J. M. Kauffman & C. D. Lewis (Eds.), *Teaching children with behavior disorders: Personal perspectives* (pp. 198–217). Columbus, OH: Charles E. Merrill.

Morse, W. C., Cutler, R. L., & Fink, A. H. (1964). *Public school classes for the emotionally handicapped: A research analysis.* Reston, VA: Council for Exceptional Children.

National Education Association. (1929). *The preparation of teachers for dealing with behavior problem children: A report of the committee on behavior problems of the NEA.* Washington, DC: Author.

Noel, M. M. (1982). Public school programs for the emotionally disturbed: An overview. In M. M. Noel & N. G. Haring (Eds.), *Progress or change: Issues in educating the emotionally disturbed. Vol. 2: Service delivery* (pp. 1–28). Seattle: Program Development Assistance System, University of Washington.

Noel, M. M., & Haring, N. G. (1982). Preface. In M. M. Noel & N. G. Haring (Eds.), *Progress or change: Issues in educating the emotionally disturbed. Vol. 1: Identification and program planning* (pp. vii–ix). Seattle: Program Development Assistance System, University of Washington.

Number of handicapped students leveling off, ED official says. *Report on Education Research.* (1983). *15*(14), 5–6.

Ollendick, T. H., & Hersen, M. (1983). A historical overview of child psychopathology. In T. H. Ollendick & M. Hersen (Eds.), *Handbook of child psychopathology* (pp. 3–11). New York: Plenum Press.

Patterson, G. R. (1982). *Coercive family process.* Eugene, OR: Castalia.

Paul, J. L. (1985a). Behavioral disorders in the 1980s: Ethical and ideological issues. *Behavioral Disorders, 11*, 66–72.

Paul, J. L. (1985b). Where are we in the education

of emotionally disturbed children? *Behavioral Disorders, 10*, 145–151.

Peterson, D. R. (1961). Behavior problems of middle childhood. *Journal of Consulting and Clinical Psychology, 25*, 205–209.

Phillips, L., Draguns, J. G., & Bartlett, D. P. (1975). Classification of behavior disorders. In N. Hobbs (Ed.), *Issues in the classification of children* (Vol. 1, pp. 26–55). San Francisco: Jossey-Bass.

Prugh, D. C., Engel, M., & Morse, W. C. (1975). Emotional disturbance in children. In N. Hobbs (Ed.), *Issues in the classification of children* (Vol. 1) San Francisco: Jossey-Bass.

Quay, H. C. (1979). Classification. In H. C. Quay & J. S. Werry (Eds.), *Psychopathological disorders of childhood* (2nd ed., pp. 1–42). New York: Wiley.

Quay, H. C., & Peterson, D. R. (1967). *Manual for the behavior problem checklist.* Urbana: University of Illinois, mimeographed.

Redl, F., & Wineman, D. (1951). *Children who hate.* New York: Free Press.

Redl, F., & Wineman, D. (1952). *Controls from within.* New York: Free Press.

Rhodes, W. C., & Paul, J. L. (1978). *Emotionally disturbed and deviant children: New views and approaches.* Englewood Cliffs, NJ: Prentice-Hall.

Rothman, E. P. (1974). Esther P. Rothman. In J. M. Kauffman & C. D. Lewis (Eds.), *Teaching children with behavior disorders: Personal perspectives* (pp. 218–239). Columbus, OH: Charles E. Merrill.

Rubenstein, E. A. (1948). Childhood mental disease in America: A review of literature before 1900. *American Journal of Orthopsychiatry, 18*, 314–321.

Rubin, R. A., & Balow, B. (1978). Prevalence of teacher identified behavior problems: A longitudinal study. *Exceptional Children, 45*, 102–111.

Rutherford, R., Wolford, B., & Nelson, C. M. (1983). *CSET: Correctional/special education training project.* Grant proposal funded by Special Education Programs, U.S. Department of Education.

Schultz, E. W., Hirshoren, A., Manton, A. B., & Henderson, R. A. (1971). Special education for the emotionally disturbed. *Exceptional Children, 38*, 313–319.

Scull, A. T. (1975). From madness to mental illness: Medical men as moral entrepreneurs. *Archives of European Sociology, 16*, 218–251.

Smith-Davis, J., Burke, P. J., & Noel, M. M. (1984). *Personnel to educate the handicapped in America: Supply and demand from a programmatic viewpoint.* College Park: Department of Special Education, University of Maryland.

Strain, P. S. (1981a). Peer-mediated treatment of exceptional children's social withdrawal. *Exceptional Education Quarterly, 1*(4), 93–106.

Strain, P. S. (Ed.). (1981b). *The utilization of class-*

room peers as behavior change agents. New York: Plenum Press.

Strain, P. S., Odom, S. L., & McConnell, S. (1984). Promoting social reciprocity of exceptional children: Identification, target behavior selection, and intervention. *Remedial and Special Education, 5*(1), 21–28.

Strain, P. S., Steele, P., Ellis, T., & Timm, M. (1982). Long-term effects of oppositional child treatment with mothers as therapists and therapist trainers. *Journal of Applied Behavior Analysis, 15*, 163–169.

Stullken, E. H. (1950). Special schools and classes for the socially maladjusted. In N. B. Henry (Ed.), *The education of exceptional children* (pp. 281–301). Forty-ninth yearbook of the National Society for the Study of Education, Part II. Chicago: University of Chicago Press.

Tallmadge, G. K., Gamel, N. N., Munson, R. G., & Hanley, T. V. (1985). *Special study on terminology.* Mountain View, CA: SRA Technologies.

U. S. Department of Education (1984). *Sixth annual report to Congress on the implementation of Public Law 94-142.* Washington, DC: Author.

Walker, H. M. (1982). Assessment of behavior disorders in the school setting: Issues, problems, and strategies. In M. M. Noel & N. G. Haring (Eds.), *Progress or change: Issues in educating the emotionally disturbed. Vol. 1: Identification and program planning* (pp.11–42). Seattle: Program Development Assistance System, University of Washington.

Walker, H. M., & Rankin, R. (1983). Assessing the behavioral expectations and demands of less restrictive settings. *School Psychology Review, 12*, 274–284.

Wallin, J. E. W. (1938). The nature and implications of truancy from the standpoint of the schools. *Journal of Exceptional Children, 5*, 1–6.

Whelan, R. J. (1963). Educating emotionally disturbed children: Reflections upon educational methods and therapeutic processes. *Forum for Residential Therapy, 1*, 9–14.

Whelan, R. J. (1966). The relevance of behavior modification procedures for teachers of emotionally disturbed children. In P. Knoblock (Ed.), *Intervention approaches in educating emotionally disturbed children* (pp. 35–78). Syracuse, NY: Syracuse University Press.

Whelan, R. J. (1974). Richard J. Whelan. In J. M. Kauffman & C. D. Lewis (Eds.), *Teaching children with behavior disorders: Personal perspectives* (pp. 240–271). Columbus, OH: Charles E. Merrill.

Wickman, E. K. (1929). *Children's behavior and teachers' attitudes.* New York: The Commonwealth Fund.

Wolford, B. I. (1983). Correctional education and special education — An emerging partnership; or "born to lose." In R. B. Rutherford (Ed.), *Monograph in behavioral disorders* (pp. 13–19). Reston, VA: Council for Exceptional Children.

Wood, F. H., & Lakin, K. C. (1979). Defining emotionally disturbed/behaviorally disordered populations for research purposes. In F. H. Wood & K. C. Lakin (Eds.), *Disturbed or disturbing? Perspectives on the definition of problem behavior in educational settings* (pp.49–70). Minneapolis: Department of Psychoeducational Studies, University of Minnesota.

Wood, F. H., & Zabel, R. H. (1978). Making sense of reports on the incidence of behavior disorders/emotional disturbance in school-aged populations. *Psychology in the Schools, 15*, 45–51.

Wood, F. H. (1985). Issues in the identification and placement of behaviorally disordered students. *Behavioral Disorders, 10*, 219–228.

Zimmerman, J., & Zimmerman, E. (1962). The alteration of behavior in a special classroom situation. *Journal of the Experimental Analysis of Behavior, 5*, 59–60.

9 LANGUAGE RESEARCH AND PRACTICE: A MAJOR CONTRIBUTION TO SPECIAL EDUCATION

Katharine G. Butler

To speak about language is to speak about the human race (Butler, in press). As Laird (1953) many years ago noted, "there must have been a time when there was no language, and then there was a time when there was a language, but we do not know how, when, where or by whom language came into being" (p. 23). Whether or not the birthplace of language can be identified, societies throughout the world have come to depend upon it, first in its oral form, and then, in its written form. Language, whether received by ear or by eye, is central to learning. Speaking (or a substitute symbol system) is central to human interaction in all societies, while reading and writing are important aspects of living in literate societies.

Today, the critics of public education have made clear their concern regarding the level of literacy achieved by students in the public education system in America. However, little public attention has been drawn to how the quest for literacy has affected not only children with special needs, but also those economically disadvantaged or culturally/linguistically different children who are frequently placed in special education. Those who seek to focus upon academic excellence for all children make little, if any, differentiation between those for whom language skills come easily and those for whom language poses difficulties.

Mainstreamed handicapped children are encountering greater demands by the schools for academic success, with much of that success being dependent upon linguistic competence. Those who seek "excellence in education" frequently translate that to mean improved scores in reading, writing, mathematical skills and problem-solving. The demand for excellence has been transmuted into more rigorous requirements for secondary school graduation, and in a number of states, competency requirements for graduating high school have begun to be seen as major barriers for the handicapped. It may yet come to pass that the social and psychological values inherent in the notion of mainstreaming are outweighed by the increased stringency of requirements for all children. It should be remembered that at the core of such requirements is the need for children to understand the "language of instruction," for therein lies success.

Since the comprehension and production of language (listening, speaking, reading and writing) are so intimately tied with not only academic success but human communication as well, the existence of language disorders among large numbers of handicapped individuals is of major concern to all who touch their lives. Fortunately, the study of language acquisition and language disorders has been underway since the 1700s.

It is frequently reported that the true study of children's disordered language development attained recognition through the work of Itard, a physician, with the "wild boy of Aveyron" whose history has been frequently traced by those whose major interest is mental retardation. The boy was found roaming nude in a French forest when he was approximately 12 years of age, and taken to a school for the deaf in Paris (Lebrun, 1980). Itard named him Victor and undertook the task of educating him. He was able to make many changes in the boy's performance throughout long years of effort, and reported that the child was able to understand "everyday language." However, Victor was never able to produce intelligible speech. Victor died at about 40 years of age in 1828, never having acquired expressive language. The child language researchers of today would undoubtedly note that Victor lacked the early social and linguistic environment necessary for normal comprehension and production of speech and language.

Only a few years ago, another case of a child isolated from society was reported by Curtiss (1977). This child, a girl identified as Genie, is reported to have spent her first 13 years in a closet. Genie has been the subject of intensive investigation by psycholinguists and has received extensive language instruction. It is reported that her understanding of informal language, that is, the language of the home, rather than the more formal language of the school, has developed to some degree. However, at last report a number of deficits remain.

There have been a number of cases like Victor and Genie reported. It has been the general consensus of opinion that the acquisition of language in such cases is retarded by the lack of contact with other human beings, the absence of linguistic and sensory stimulation, and insufficient nutrition (Lebrun, 1980). In the past few years, psycholinguists and child language experts have made us aware once more of the importance of very early caregiver–child interaction and the role of the social context. As Snow (1984) states, a child's experience with "effective communication is the source of knowledge about the form and content [of language]. A child who could not already interact could never learn to communicate; a child who cannot communicate would never learn language" (p. v).

But what about the vast number of children and adults who exhibit speech and language disorders, but have never run wild in the forest or jungles, have never been locked away or deprived of human communication for years on end? There are literally millions of such individuals in the United States; individuals with speech, language and hearing handicaps severe enough to require identification, assessment, and intervention. While language disorders may have existed from the time that humankind developed language, it has only been in the last few hundred years that certain groups of individuals have come to be identified as communicatively disordered: the deaf, the mentally retarded, the aphasic, the cerebral palsied, the severely emotionally disturbed, to mention but a few. During the 19th and 20th centuries, the quest for appropriate treatment of such individuals began.

As the decades move swiftly by and as we approach the 21st century, there has been increasing emphasis on the importance of language skills, not only for human communication, but for the acquisition of knowledge as well. While the acquisition of language in the child's early years has long been of interest to linguists, the 1970s and 1980s have brought into focus the role of education in the child's language development. Recent research has made prominent the differences between the language of the home and the language of the school. The language of the home reflects a social, interactive level of discourse, while the language of the teacher and the text reflects the more formal instructional purposes of the school. We have begun to examine more closely whether the nexus of language disorders lies within the child *or* within the environment (including the schools). What seems likely at this point in time is that the answer may lie at the intersection of the child's internal and external worlds. It also seems likely that the life experiences of handicapped children may well differ, from the earliest months of their lives, from those of non-handicapped children. The result, then, is that language form, content and use may be at variance with the "norm," just as the internal and external world of language handicapped children is at variance with their nonhandicapped peers.

WHERE HAVE WE BEEN?

As indicated earlier, we can easily document the existence of speech and language disorders throughout recorded history. One of the founders of speech–language pathology, Dr. Charles Van Riper, reported in 1947 that the remnants of the primitive attitudes of rejection, humor, and pity towards these disorders remain alive today. He cites the casting of cripples into the Ganges in ancient India, the belief in the Middle Ages that the physically disable were possessed of evil spirits, the role of the fool and the buffoon at Attila the Hun's banquets, where he displayed those individuals who were deformed and of "ridiculous dress, antic gestures and absurd speech" (p. 6). As Van Riper wryly comments, "Now you may find them used to provide laughter only in the circus side shows, in the movies, on the radio and in every school yard" (1947, p. 8). To this array, we must add television and advertising, at least during the period from the 1950s to the 1980s.

As research and practice in speech–language pathology gained a greater understanding of the origins of communicative disorders and their subsequent treatment, an interesting series of events occurred. Speech–language pathology emerged as a distinct profession in the 1930s and 1940s, growing out of a number of related disciplines, including medicine, education, psychology, and speech communication. While early research borrowed heavily from those disciplines, the focus was upon the defectiveness of speech disorders, and the correction of those disorders. As a clinical profession, the emphasis was on speech disabilities. These were thought to include (Van Riper, 1947):

- *Articulation disorders:* i.e., difficulty with spoken speech sounds; and focusing upon the abnormal substitution, distortion, insertion, or omission of sounds.
- *Delayed speech:* i.e., difficulties in speaking that ranged from baby talk to "speech retardation" to mutism; noted to be caused by "low intelligence," hearing defects, poor coordination, illness, lack of motivation, poor speech standards, shift of handedness, bilingual conflicts, emotional shocks, accidents and/or conflicts, poor auditory memory span, and aphasia.
- *Voice disorders:* i.e., disorders of vocal intensity, pitch or quality, either organic or functional in nature.
- *Stuttering:* i.e., disruption of the rhythmic flow of speech; characterized by blockings, prolongations or repetitions of words, syllables, sounds, or mouth postures.
- *Cleft palate speech:* i.e., a disorder of voice and articulation typically related to cleft and/or "harelip," whether surgically repaired or not.
- *Bilingualism and foreign dialect:* i.e., often referred to as foreign accent difficulty; thought to be both a speech difference and a handicap, although perhaps not a disorder, as such.
- *Cerebral palsied speech:* i.e., defective articulation, voice, and fluency resulting from spastic contractions or athetoid tremors of the individual with specific types of brain injury.
- *Deaf and hard-of-hearing speech:* i.e., difficulty with voice quality, articulation, and speech intelligibility, vocabulary, and language as the result of peripheral hearing loss.

This, then, was the "turf" of the speech correctionist. Serving in public schools as the speech teacher and in some agencies and hospitals as the speech therapist or clinician, the speech correctionist dealt with children and adults whose speech was "defective." The definition of who was speech defective was tripartite, and included individuals whose speech (a) deviated so far from the speech of other people that it called attention to itself, (b) interfered with communication, or (c) rendered its possessor maladjusted (Van Riper, 1947).

As is readily apparent, the focus in those years was on specific speech disorders, and language impairments were subsumed under delayed speech. But, despite the nomenclature, clinicians dealt with children and adults who clearly demonstrated language disorders, that is, what are now referred to as disorders of phonology, syntax, semantics, and pragmatics. Little was it recognized in the 1940s and 1950s that research in communicative disorders would restructure not only the nosology of the profession but its basic assumptions.

Another area of research and practice in the early decades of the profession was drawn from early studies that dealt with the psychological aspects of speech and language disorders. Early textbooks were weighted with references to the presumed functional nature of many of the disorders, and in particular, to the overt symptoms of stuttering and voice disorders. Indeed, in the 1930s and early 1940s, Western European clinicians were reporting the results of their work to American audiences in the area of stuttering, or as it was known on the continent, stammering (Bleumel, 1932, Froschels, 1942). Stuttering held center stage in terms of research interests in communicative disorders, followed by interests in articulation and delayed speech, an ordering that has been reversed over the last 20 years. Early on, however, the primary interest of a good number of clinical researchers was to solve the "riddle of stuttering." Their search for clinical and theoretical constructs led to the utilization of psychological literature, for example, Brown's work (1933) and that of Bryngelson (1937) could be found in *Mental Hygiene*, while that of Despert (1943) appeared in *The Nervous Child.* Travis, whose work at the University of Iowa focused on the psychological aspects of stuttering (see, for example, "The Need for Stuttering," 1940), established a framework for research that was prominent for three decades. There was, of course, early interest in the physiological aspects of stuttering (Fletcher, 1928), including cerebral dominance theories. Much of that interest dissipated over time

when research efforts could not provide the needed pieces of the puzzle. However, speech scientists have revived their interest in the physiological aspects as vastly more sophisticated instrumentation permits researchers to not only reinterpret older findings, but to address much more directly the laryngeal activity that occurs during stuttered and non-stuttered speech (Conture, 1982, 1984).

Some time has been spent discussing disfluent speech, since, as will be seen later in this chapter, a somewhat different group of researchers are now focusing upon children's disfluencies within the instructional context (Silliman, 1984). It is now hypothesized that such disfluencies may reflect difficulties in narrative discourse, which surface primarily within the formal academic setting. Later in the chapter this possibility will be considered in greater detail, when some notions about the future direction of language research and practice are expressed.

In retrospect, my own research in language acquisition and its disorders stemmed from an intense interest in both stuttering (Butler, 1953, 1960a, 1960b, 1961, 1962, 1963, 1964, 1965; Butler & Holland, 1968; Butler & Naliboff, 1967) *and* in children's communicative performance in the classroom (Butler, 1956, 1960c; Butler & Poon, 1972; Butler & Pratt, 1968, 1969, 1972). Since the early 1970s, however, my research has focused primarily upon children's comprehension and production of language, first in dyadic and then in interactive settings, with particular emphases on language disorders and differences among special populations.

The conduct of language research over the past few decades moved from a focus on empirically conducted research in schools (Butler, 1960a, 1960c) to more carefully controlled laboratories and more rigorous procedures in clinical settings. Looking back, it is easy to see where and why the pendulum has now returned to the more "naturalistic" setting of the home and the school. While research conducted in these settings carries with it major problems, and does not lend itself to easy replication, it does provide an opportunity to explore a number of the more important parameters of child language. Researchers in communicative disorders have been aware of the progress psycholinguists have made in the understanding of normal child language through the recording and analyzing of children's naturally occurring utterances (Wellman & Somerville, 1980), and have shown an increasing use of naturalistic contexts in which to obtain a representative sample of children's language performance in a communicative context (Miller, 1981).

Not all research is thus conducted, obviously. As the field of speech correction grew to become the field of communicative sciences and disorders, researchers and practitioners in two subspecialties, speech-language pathology and audiology, continue to reveal the typical dichotomies that exist in other professions. Basic researchers remain in their laboratories and practitioners find it difficult to apply their results to problems of the moment. There are applied researchers who attempt to bridge the gap between the laboratory, the clinic and the schools. The concept of the clinician-researcher (or researcher-clinician, depending on one's priorities) is frequently applauded as the desirable blend of science and service. Too few exist, but that is undoubtedly symptomatic of most disciplines where there are clinical/educational, as well as research, components. The so-called "great clinicians" of an earlier era represented this ideal, combining ongoing research and clinical activity. This is how research in communicative disorders began. Perhaps, research will return to this in the future, albeit in a modified and more sophisticated manner.

WHERE ARE WE NOW?

It would be impossible to encapsulate the many strands of language research within the confines of a single chapter. While many fields have witnessed an explosion of knowledge, the explosion in language acquisition and its disorders is almost nuclear in nature. Conceptualizing the breadth of research adequately requires that one be aware of ongoing research

in a variety of disciplines. Many disciplines have something to offer the practitioner who is interested in dealing with language in (and of) the schools (Butler, 1984a).

One must know something about language from the perspective of developmental psycholinguists, who are addressing issues in communicative competence in the post-Chomsky era (Schiefelbusch & Pickar, 1984). One must also know something about language from the perspective of cultural anthropologists and sociolinguists, who may hold opposing viewpoints in reference to children's language use in a variety of cultural settings. The importance of cultural variation in adult-child communication, both verbal and nonverbal, is increasingly relevant in today's pluralistic schools (Gumperz & Cook-Gumperz, 1981; Gumperz & Hymes, 1964; Gumperz & Tannen, 1972; Schieffelin & Eisenberg, 1984; Slobin, 1967).

Further, one must know something about very early language development and disorders, since children begin school with a substantial history of language interaction with parents and caretakers in the preschool years (Heath, 1982; Lieven, 1984; Snow, 1982; Sugarman, 1984). In addition, one must have more than a nodding acquaintance with neurological and physiological development (Daniloff, Schuckers, & Feth, 1980) and its disorders (Kertesz, 1983; Maxwell, 1984) and brain function (Bryden, 1983; Butler, 1984b; Hart, 1983; Segalowitz, 1983). And since auditory information is thought to be processed in quite complex ways within the brain, a grasp of information-processing and cognition is essential (Anderson, 1980; Arbib, Caplan, & Marshall, 1982; Bertenthal, 1981; Butler, 1984c; Fischer & Bullock, 1981; Nelson, 1984).

As if the above were not sufficient, there are a number of other disciplines and subdisciplines to be considered. While all cannot be addressed within the confines of this chapter, the importance of memory cannot be ignored. To what purpose would one deal with "language," if it were impossible to code, store, and recall it from memory? Surely, then, in order to serve any useful purpose, it is necessary to consider how language, as presented orally or as read in its orthographic form, comes to be perceptually recognized and to take on meaning? Indeed, just how is it that a child is (or is not) able to comprehend and integrate incoming new information with old information and to form new mental representations? Memory processing (Kail & Hagen, 1977; Ornstein, 1978; Perlmutter, 1980) must be high on any language list. While efficient episodic and semantic memory is critical for all children, it is essential to the survival of language-learning disordered children in the less-than-ideal, less-than-real context of our nation's classrooms (Israel, 1984; Klein-Konigsberg, 1984; Miller, 1984).

Within each of the major areas just listed, there are particular theories and/or research topics that lend themselves to enhanced understanding of children with language disorders, suspected or demonstrated. For example, Piaget's (1970) theory "has been the preeminent theoretical framework for studying the development of communication skills in children" (Dickson, 1983, p. 29). Psychologists (Brainerd, 1983), speech-language pathologists (Johnston, 1981; Miller, 1984), and child language researchers (Shantz, 1981) have all attempted to utilize the Piagetian framework to assess language skills and to devise remediation strategies. However, as Dickson notes, "Piaget's pessimistic view of children's communication skills was brought forward into research in the United States. From the mid-1960s to the mid-1970s research on the development of communication skills followed Piaget's view" (Dickson, 1983, p. 30). More recently, Piaget's view of young children's communication competence is thought to be unnecessarily limited. Perhaps it was the eagerness of language researchers to adopt, rather than adapt, Piaget's constructs that resulted in over-application of Piagetian stages to language-disordered children. Piaget's colleague, B. Inholder, focused on this point at the Congrès Internationale Psychologie de L'Enfant, held at the University of Rene-Descartes, Paris, France, in July, 1979, when she protested that it had not been Piaget's intent to address the development of

language. (There were, however, later exchanges between Piaget and Chomsky on the topic of language.)

Whatever Piaget may have believed and whatever the outcomes of later interactions with Chomsky, Piagetian constructs were warmly greeted by a large number of researchers in language learning and language disorders. Disenchantment has come slowly — and not to all. However, early on, Menyuk (1975) noted that there were inherent difficulties in "forcing" linguistic and nonlinguistic formulations into congruency. She pointed out that there were a number of cognitive theories of language development and that diverging paths of inquiry were providing variable data. While many theorists viewed early language acquisition as primarily dependent on nonlinguistic cognitive development (as represented by Piaget's developmental stages of sensorimotor, preoperational, concrete operational, and formal thought), Menyuk reported that there was little reason to assume that linguistic performance was entirely dependent on the appearance of specific nonlinguistic operations.

In a 1980 summary of language research related to cognitive prerequisites, Miller, Chapman, Branston, & Riechele reported that the "results offer little direct evidence of a relation between sensorimotor performance and language comprehension. . . . [Such] findings make clear that different sensorimotor scales and items are differentially predictive of language comprehension" (pp. 285–286). Nevertheless, these authors continue to support the notion that evaluation of a young child's cognitive status is important, since there are statistically significant correlations between cognitive and language measures. However, they caution against making particular cognitive achievements a prerequisite to language comprehension intervention.

Despite these concerns and others (Bowerman, 1978; Schlesinger, 1977), it is evident that the Piagetian-based procedures have remained popular, not only for assessment but language intervention. Clinician-researchers are still searching for appropriate strategies for assessing at-risk infants and for evaluation and intervention with a large number of children with special needs, including cognitive procedures to aid the severely mentally retarded and multihandicapped (Finch-Williams, 1984; Kahn, 1984; Rieke & Lewis, 1984).

Notwithstanding the strong interest in the Piagetian framework for research and practice, during the late 1970s other research paths emerged. They provide information for both psychologists and language specialists leading to increased understanding and approval of cognitive strategies for training oral communication that are not anchored to Piagetian concepts. It has been demonstrated that testing children on such tasks as conversation, classification, seriation, perspective taking, and so forth, can overlook skills that young children possess (Gelman, 1978; Hand, 1981).

Today, there is a growing consensus that Piagetian tasks do not reflect preschool children's abilities. In fact, it may be that their skills have been generally underestimated. Brainerd (1983) has suggested that not all roads lead to Rome and that a variety of cognitive strategy training approaches are successful.

Some of these approaches include the use of modern working memory models. Although Piagetian tasks may be used, it is now felt that successful performance results from the activation of a system dependent upon the encoding of some crucial background facts; i.e., what past experience and knowledge provides the child, as well as the ability to hold such information in short-term memory until the task has been completed successfully (Brainerd, 1981).

Brainerd (1983) hypothesizes that children's ability to succeed following cognitive strategy training may be due to "working-analysis" in memory and is not necessarily attributable to Piagetian stages of development, in and of themselves. Brainerd points out that effective training (even in Piagetian tasks) may result from working-memory analysis since the child's working memory system has several components, "all of which are necessary to correct performance" (p. 22). For example, even simple *feedback* (e.g., "David, keeping your columns straight helped you to add correctly, didn't it?") may increase the chances that David will respond accurately the next day on another mathematics assignment. Feedback has provided the necessary cues that will assist David in retrieving processing operations from long-term memory. Second, *attentional training* is thought to encourage children to encode certain facts that strengthen their ability to respond appropriately to both short and long term memory demands.

Since the late 1970s, a distinction has been made between listening (comprehending) and speaking (production) by researchers dealing with referential communication. As Dickson (1983) notes, such communication tasks are useful in research since there can be adequate experimental control over *communicative intent*; i.e., the experiment defines for the speaker his communicative intent (what the speaker wants to say) and specifies the target referent. In addition, the listener is required to make a response so that there can be no question about listener understanding. While this approach is admittedly artificial, any practicing educator or clinician can identify numerous school-related instances that specify for the child either his intent or response:

> TEACHER: John, tell me exactly what you read just now. What does that last sentence mean?
> PRINCIPAL: Mary, I can see the dime in your hand. Tell me where you got it.
> PRESCHOOL TEACHER: David, do you remember the two things you did when you mixed the paints yesterday? (*David smiles and nods.*) Good. Now, tell Joan how she can mix the paints.

These excerpts provide everyday exemplars of referential communication tasks wherein the listener listens to a message, holds it in short-term memory, compares it with the available alternatives, and selects the appropriate alternative. If the message refers to more than one alternative, the listener must ask for more information in order to determine the appropriateness of the selection. Skilled listeners have little difficulty in asking questions to assist in the selection of an appropriate alternative; e.g., an adult asked to provide a sweater from the closet responds, "Do you want the beige or the blue?" Children, however, particularly young children, frequently fail to ask questions. Thus, the question arises, Can children benefit from training in question asking behavior as a strategy for learning?

The answer appears to be yes. There have been a number of successful applications of cognitive strategy training whereby children are assisted in asking questions when they are in need of more information. Cosgrove and Patterson (1977) provided such strategy training, for example. They instructed children, whose ages ranged from preschool through the elementary years, to ask questions by telling them, "Whenever you are not sure what the right answer is, you can ask questions to help yourself to figure it out" (p. 559). Even such brief strategy training was dramatically successful with all age groups *except* the preschool group (Dickson, 1983).

The failure of the preschool group in the above study brings up some interesting questions about the development of metacognitive strategies for normal youngsters, particularly at the school-entry age of 5. Flavell, Speer, Green, & August (1981) asked both kindergarten and second grade children to build a tower of blocks but gave them incomplete information. The children's responses to these inadequate messages meant they must engage in the metacognitive task of deciding whether or not they had received sufficient information to build the tower. Analysis revealed that while awareness of verbal ambiguities increased across the age span, "even second graders were far from perfect in their detection and criticism of inadequate messages" (Dickson, 1983, p. 38).

Metacognitive growth may not be the only factor influencing young children's performance. The specificity of parental or teacher commentary may also be relevant. For example, 5 year olds were found to provide much better answers when asked a specific question; that is, "Tell me how this [referent] looks different from the other [referent]" than when they were given general instructions, such as "Tell me about it so that I will know which one you are talking about" (Whitehurst & Sonnenschein, 1981).

Successful cognitive strategy training within an educational context has been reported by Meichenbaum and Goodman (1971) as well as by Flavell et al. (1981) and others. Indeed, there is growing evidence that a number of communication skills can be increased (Dickson, 1983), although such training has not proved particularly effective in training role taking skills (Asher, 1979; Shantz, 1981) or in simple practice paradigms (Dickson, 1974). Readers familiar with learning disabled children will recognize that role-taking skills are particularly difficult for even adolescent LD children (Donahue & Bryan, 1984). In contrast, training has been successful (at least with normal children and some groups of exceptional children) in the area of question-asking. Children have been able to greatly increase the number of questions they ask when they are uncertain about the speaker's intent simply by being instructed to do so as a comprehension strategy. Consequently, they have been able to gain more information, understand the adult's meaning more readily, and respond more accurately. Even early elementary school-age children increased not only the number of their questions but asked more specific questions under this "listening and questioning" training (Dickson, 1984). In addition, adults can change the kinds of questions children ask from global (Which one is it?) to specific (Is it red or blue?) by modeling such behavior.

As noted earlier, preschoolers frequently do not respond to listening strategy training. However, child language researchers have been analyzing the communication skills of children in their homes and at play and found that normal preschoolers reveal sophisticated communication strategies. For example, Shatz and Gelman (1973) found that even 4 year olds adapt the form of their messages to the age of their listeners, although this may not be the case with language-disordered preschoolers. Foster (1985) provides evidence from infant and toddler research that preverbal infants, well before their first birthday are able to "communicate" through the use of gestures, vocalization, and eye gaze, thus gaining their mothers' attention and directing it to specific objects in the environment. By the second year of life, normal children are able to use language and to direct their hearers' attention to objects not in the immediate environment and to speak about past events. However, these sophisticated strategies are frequently not available to language disordered children, whether retarded, autistic, aphasic, and so forth.

Speech and language disorders are frequently an important first sign or signal to parents and professionals of a handicapping condition. When such disorders occur in the preschool years, it may be the first symptom noted, particularly if there are no other deviations in the developmental milestones. Research in the early 1970s found that there are special features of parent-to-child language, and child language researchers (Cross, 1984) surmised that it was the caretaker's "input" that explained "the ease with which normal children master the complex task of language acquisition" (p. 1). Such studies were followed by another wave of studies that looked at parent's language to linguistically and communicatively disordered preschoolers. In general, this latter group of students involved the mothers of children with specific impairments (hearing loss, dysphasia, Down syndrome, autism) and found that there were a number of differences in the language parents direct toward language impaired children than to normal children. The first, and perhaps naive interpretation, was that these differences contributed to the child's delay in language (Cross, 1984).

In the late 1970s, the focus shifted to considering whether the parental differences noted were, in reality, a reaction to, and not the cause of, the child's impaired communication skills. Cross (1984) maintains that by the time a child's language impairment has been identified, the problem of parent-to-child input has become interactive. The parental differences noted are now thought to be a reflection of trying to meet their language-impaired child's special language needs and, as such, reflect the effect of the child's language impairment on the parent.

In the 1980s, the evidence suggests that the differences in parental language to language disordered children result from the child's language impairment. What are these differences in parental language? A number of studies have suggested that:

- Parents of language disordered children do not respond in the same way to their children's nonverbal behavior (gestures, gaze); i.e., the parents fail to comment on the meaning of that nonverbal behavior to the same degree that parents of normal children model such "conversational interactions" (Lasky & Klopp, 1982).
- Parents of language disordered children are less positive and accepting of their children's attempts at communication, quite possibly because such attempts may be unintelligible. Nevertheless, language impaired children, as a group, receive less reinforcement for their attempts to communicate (Cross, 1984).
- Maternal self-repetition, e.g., imperatives or directives (No. No.; Stop that. Stop that.), have a strong relationship with impaired language (Newport, Gleitman, & Gleitman, 1977).
- Mothers' conversations to their developmentally delayed children are more directive and controlling than mothers' conversations to normally speaking children; i.e., they give more commands and directives, they may ask fewer questions, and make fewer statements (Cross, 1984).
- Some studies indicate that the mothers of language-impaired children speak to them significantly less often, again perhaps because the children themselves are less responsive (Cross, 1984).

We have only recently begun to think of the importance of "conversation" and interactive communication skills as very important in language acquisition and language intervention. Snow (1984) highlights that when she states, "A child who could not already interact could never learn to communicate; a child who cannot communicate would never learn language" (p. v). What, then, of children who have difficulty with interaction in its broadest sense? Let us look briefly at three types of language impaired children.

Autistic Children

Duchan (1984) maintains that the remediation of the primary deficits of autistic children (social withdrawal and language difficulties) are likely to be treated based upon the clinician's or teacher's theory of autism. She nominates three theories or approaches to intervention: behaviorism, psycholinguistic, and social-interaction. In the behavioristic approach, language is viewed as a response (Skinner, 1957); the unusual language of the autistic child is viewed as inappropriate and their lack of social interaction is viewed as being off-task or inattentive. A clinician or teacher trained as a behaviorist would then attempt to extinguish inappropriate behaviors, while reinforcing appropriate behaviors through a systematic sequence of instruction that concentrates on observable responses. On the other hand, the psycholinguistic approach requires the clinician to look at the cognitive or linguistic processes or knowledge that underlie autistic children's behavior. A review of the literature indicates that autistic children suffer most from disorders of language meaning (semantics) and of responding to context (pragmatics) and less from syntax (the ordering of sentences) and phonology (articulation) problems. In addition, echolalia and pronominal reversal (you/I) are viewed as linguistic events (Tager-Flusberg, 1981). Social withdrawal is thought to occur as a result of language problems that prevent the children from understanding their environment (Duchan & Palermo, 1982). Finally, the social-interaction theory examines how well others respond to autistic children's communication attempts; how parents, teachers, and others interact with these children. Social withdrawal is viewed as an interactional breakdown and that both the child and the adult are responsible for keeping the interaction going,

even when the child's language is inappropriate (Duchan, 1984).

As can be easily surmised, clinical interactions are largely structured by the theory the clinician espouses. Behaviorism would lead to highly structured lessons; psycholinguistic theory to structured or naturalistic lessons, and the social-interactional theory would replace lessons with high quality interactions within everyday contexts (Duchan, 1984). Indeed, there is an emerging consensus that the social-interactional approach may be the most useful (Duchan, 1984).

Hearing Impaired Children

It is obvious that the degree of hearing loss and the age at which the hearing is lost have profound implications for language learning. Very early language intervention is strongly recommended where necessary. As Spear and Gerber (1982) state, "There is no age that is too young for diagnosis and no time that is too soon to begin habilitation" (p. 2). Habilitation of the young hearing impaired child shares some characteristics with children who are mentally retarded or even mothers of premature and physically handicapped youngsters. In all these cases, it has been found (Cunningham, Reuler, Blackwell, & Deck, 1981; Meadow, 1980; Wasserman, Allen and Solomon, 1982) that parental language carries a heightened use of directives. White and White (1982) note that the increased use of directives (imperatives) may reflect the social interaction strategy adopted by many individuals when speaking with someone whose conversational responses appear limited. They point out that the tendency to be directive as the parent of a handicapped child may be an adaptive response, as is the tendency to simplify language. However, an overuse of imperatives (e.g., Put that over there! Sit down!) does not assist the child in building language skills, since they typically require no response and are frequently accompanied by gestures. The same may well apply to teachers and clinicians. Research with normal children suggests that the effects of motherchild interactions are bidirectional and can be positive, or as in this case, negative. Certainly, we know that children whose hearing impairment keeps them from understanding spoken language must respond to other stimuli, such as the nonverbal information that surrounds spoken language, including the affective behavior of the speaker. The *quality* of the language, spoken and unspoken, to hearing impaired children is highly significant, whether in the home or in the school.

Visually Handicapped Children

The acquisition of language by visually handicapped children, including the blind, can be troublesome. For young children, the parents must build a shared world of sound, particularly when sight is severely impaired. Visually handicapped children are literally cut off from the seeing world and are denied access to such things as eye contact, gestures, gaze behavior, etc., all of which serve to enhance language acquisition in normal children.

There is a relatively small number of studies conducted with blind and visually impaired children. The studies available indicate that the visually impaired child is likely to be relatively passive (Urwin, 1984), thus parents and teachers may read that passivity as disinterest in language and learning. Urwin concludes that many visually handicapped children's language acquisition is limited by cognitive delay, restrictions in social interactions, or both. Very early intervention is suggested, since alternative communication strategies and the development of other sensory systems must be instituted during infancy, if possible. Language retardation is not a necessary outcome of a visual handicap, although it is a common one. Some children do develop communicative competence through the use of alternative strategies, as fostered by parents, caretakers, and teachers.

In even this cursory review of the research on autistic, hearing, and visually impaired children, one is struck by the need for intensive instruction during the very earliest years by parents and teachers alike. The same is true for many other handicapping conditions, such as multihandicaps, mental retardation, learning disabilities, and so forth.

No figures are currently available for the number of children, ages 0–3, who have handicapping conditions and are being served, since P.L. 94-142 did not mandate service for children under age 3. Figures from the U.S. Department of Education (1984) indicate that there are over 4 million handicapped children currently being served under P.L. 94-142, and another approximately 250,000 being served under Chapter 1 State Programs for the Handicapped (P.L. 899-313). When special education services under both P.L. 94-142 and P.L. 899-313, are totalled by handicapping condition for ages 3–21, for the year 1983–1984, the data reveal the following:

Handicapping Condition	Children Served
Mentally Retarded	750,534
Hard of Hearing	41,023
Deaf	41,190
Speech Impaired	1,130,569
Visually Handicapped	31,576
Emotionally Disturbed	362,073
Orthopedically Impaired	56,209
Other Health Impaired	54,660
Learning Disabled	1,811,451
Deaf-Blind	2,531
Multihandicapped	67,514
TOTAL	4,341,399

Viewing the data for one year alone does not provide sufficient background for analysis. Over time, the handicapping conditions to which children are assigned have shifted, with a decrease in both the mentally retarded and speech impaired, concurrently with an increase in the learning disabled category. A possible explanation may be that mildly mentally retarded and speech impaired children are now being identified as learning disabled.

Undoubtedly, there are a host of reasons for the shifting labels applied to children with special needs: fiscal, political, professional, and parental, to name a few. There is little doubt that funding patterns to state and local education agencies from the federal government may influence how children are classified. There is also little doubt that parents have become much more active in advocating for their children. Parents and professionals may seek a change of categorical label to reflect more accurately the level of service the child may need. It has even been suggested that some children's learning problems are embedded in the classroom, that is, the teaching style does not match the child's learning style. In these cases, it may be that modifying the regular education instruction will be sufficient to meet the child's needs, since the instructional program is the "handicap." This possibility will be explored further somewhat later.

An additional point must be made regarding handicapping conditions. As noted earlier, language disorders are a frequent concomitant or characteristic of the mentally retarded, the hearing impaired, the speech impaired, the visually handicapped, and the emotionally disturbed. It is also a co-occurring condition of almost every other category but is particularly prominent among the learning disabled and the multihandicapped, as shall be seen.

Learning Disabilities

It is interesting to note that no single category is labeled *language impairment* or *language disorders*. For many years, the category speech impaired included the language impaired. With the advent in the 1960s of the *learning disabilities* label and subsequent legislation to include this rather diverse population as a single handicapping condition, language disorders (i.e., disorders of listening, speaking, reading, and writing) were stressed as relevant dimensions. Wiig and Semel (1980) note the importance of language when they state: "The characteristic processing and production deficits of the learning disabled are not the primary effect of mental retardation, severe emotional disturbance, sensory impairments of hearing or vision, social maladjustment, cultural deprivation, or poor instruction" (p. 11).

Many definitions of learning disabilities attempt to differentiate learning disabilities

(including the language components) from other handicapping conditions and to exclude the effects of social class or poor classroom instruction. Implicit in the original designation of learning disabilities was the assumption that the child exhibited average or perhaps better than average skills in some areas, resulting in a severe discrepancy between ability and achievement.

As history now attests, there has been difficulty in clearly delineating handicapping conditions, not only from each other but from the effects of socioeconomic status and/or poor instruction. However, it is clearly the case that language disorders play a major role across almost all major handicapping conditions. Thus, special education and special educators have a central role to play in language instruction and intervention, since language disorders may be found in children ranging across the severity continuum, from the mildest of handicapping conditions to the most severe.

Severely and Multiple Handicapped

In the 1970s and 1980s, there has been a tremendous growth of interest in the most severely handicapped children, many of whom are either nonspeaking or have limited communication skills and are severely physically handicapped. The importance of communication to this population has been stressed by Yoder when he said:

> The ability to interact effectively is essential to life. . . . For many multiply handicapped persons, the ability to effectively interact will have important consequences on the personal, social, and educational processes, as well as future vocational considerations. . . . Above all, a person must be able to verbally or nonverbally communicate an intentional message in such a way that there is an exchange of meaning and a maintenance of conversation. (Yoder, 1982, p. ix)

Again, we see the importance of language comprehension and use among the most severely handicapped. Fortunately, there is a rapidly increasing armamentarium of electronic communication aids to assist the nonspeaking or those with unintelligible speech. It is no longer necessary to rely on sign language or other manual communication systems. Speech–language pathologists, psychologists, special educators, and rehabilitation engineers have teamed up to provide support systems that will greatly expand the lives of the severely handicapped. (For a current review of communication aids, and an analysis of the cognitive, motoric, communicative and technological considerations required for assessment and intervention, see Romski, Sevcik, & Joiner, 1984).

Culturally Different and Second Language Populations

Children who arrive upon the American educational scene from other cultures and who speak English as a second language may experience difficulty in learning, although they are not, in the traditional sense, handicapped. These children, and those who come from the homes of the economically disadvantaged, frequently exhibit learning and language problems. Indeed, they may be classified as handicapped when they fail to benefit from regular classroom instructional strategies. Where does the problem lie? Is it within the child? The teacher? The text? Are these children handicapped? How can the schools, under a basic skills mandate by the American public, assist? The answers to such questions are being sought, but once again, the intermeshing of social, cultural, and educational expectations and issues makes progress difficult.

The Language of the Schools

Over the past few years, researchers have begun a careful analysis of the more formal language of the schools in contrast to the less formal language of the home. Such research is seen as applicable to all children, including those with language differences or disorders, at least to some degree. Not unexpectedly, the information beginning to emerge reflects the importance of language skills to school success and leads us to further analyses of the triad of teacher talk, child talk, and test talk (Butler, 1981d, 1984a; Michaels, 1981; Morine-Dershimer, 1981; Olson, 1982; Silliman, 1984; Wiig & Semel, 1980).

For centuries, teaching has centered on teacher-to-student instruction, delivered primarily in the oral tradition. In today's schools, much of the interaction remains at the verbal level, although the role of text comprehension has increased mightily and the literate learner must now read and write as well as listen and speak. In classroom discourse, as in other communicative attempts, the structure of the language used is determined by the needs and constraints of speakers and listeners. Slobin (1977) specified four "rules" of language: "(1) Be clear. (2) Be humanly processible in ongoing time. (3) Be quick and easy. (4) Be expressive." (p. 186). That is all well and good, until one realizes that handicapped children, and particularly those with concomitant language disorders, *may* have particular difficulty in processing incoming language, and *frequently* have difficulty in being clear, being quick and easy, and being expressive, when required to respond. To illustrate, excerpts from children's responses during a language evaluation are provided below:

1. *Student, age 17:1, in a transitional classroom, resource room and speech therapy provided.*

EXAMINER: How would you change a tire?
STUDENT: . . . Well . . . um . . . I change a wheel Saturday night coz when I went outside, the wheel was flat. An' me an' my frien', we hadda change it.
EXAMINER: Can you tell me exactly what you did?
STUDENT: Well . . . um . . . first my frien', he got the . . . um . . . thing that you use . . . un the thing for puttin' under the um . . . (*20 second pause*) . . .
EXAMINER: (*Prompting*) Jack?
STUDENT: Yeah, that's it. I knowed what it was but I just couldn't think of it.

2. Student, age: 4:3, in an early childhood program, enrolled at age 2:6 in speech therapy.

EXAMINER: What is a bicycle?
STUDENT: Ride it.
EXAMINER: What's a chair?
STUDENT: I donno.
EXAMINER: What's a stove?
STUDENT: I have to go potty. It's a cooking.

3. Student, age 10:7, in a self-contained special education class, enrolled following a sledding accident and temporal-parietal damage of the brain; speech therapy, occupational therapy, physical therapy.

EXAMINER: Say these sentences after me: The girl likes walking by herself.
STUDENT: Girl walk herself.
EXAMINER: Mommy is playing because it is fun.
STUDENT: Mommy play.
EXAMINER: (*Shows picture of fireman putting out a fire*) What is the fireman doing?
STUDENT: Fire . . . fire-place . . . hose . . . puttin' on hose . . . drink'n beer.

4. Student, age 7:11, in a pre-first grade special classroom, English is the child's second language.

EXAMINER: Tell me a story . . . anything you like . . . take your time.
STUDENT: Richard's goin' on the hill. And he's goin' to jump on the snow with his friend, C. P. And he do somethin' with him and Richard. They have fun with the snow and they make a big hill with lots of snow so they won't get kill. We have to go under the snow, Richard me and Charlie. Mens doesn't get us. They got a gun on their hand so they won't shoot us cause we go under there, under the snow. 'Cause they won't know where we are. (*The narrative continues but with diverse elements embedded.*) Then Richard and me and Charlie went and get my new sneakers . . . and I don't have tie them 'cause they got blue on the bottom with three things. (*Topic returns to playing in the snow, followed by a series of new topics, including walking the dog, skiing, going to McDonald's, and the presence of "company."*) . . . We ate dinner for 'sert. And it's jello. And we dinner for 'sert 'cause we have to stay

outside so we won't get bother them. . . . We go under the snow. . . . Than means we won't get hurt and we, we, we won't get kill.

It can be easily seen that each of the four student's attempts to respond to the examiner epitomizes the inability of the language disordered individual to be clear and expressive. It is also clear that language does not come either quickly or easily. The impact of their language difficulties is further exemplified when one considers their current or future problems:

- Student 1, already the father of two children, has been unable to benefit thus far from the vocational training or to find work. Past employers have complained that he cannot follow directions.
- Student 2, born at risk and developmentally delayed, exhibits semantic and processing difficulties. Fortunately, early language intervention may ameliorate some of those difficulties.
- Student 3 is 18 months post-trauma. In those months, speech and language have returned, although the structure of the language remains telegraphic in nature. It is not possible at this point to predict the degree of recovery from aphasia, but it is likely that there will be some residual deficits.
- Student 4 has been retained twice in school. His language problems, noted on school entry, appear to be above and beyond that which might be anticipated from a bilingual child. He has had little or no success in mastering the decoding skills required for reading.

It is clear that children such as these will have difficulty in processing the language of instruction. Their failure to do so indicates that they have not yet been able to employ the cognitive or linguistic strategies necessary for success in school.

As Olson (1982) notes, "the central problem in reading and writing, as for speaking and listening, is linguistic—learning how to map the surface structures of language onto meaning" (p. 1). It may well be that the central problem facing speech-language pathologists and special educators in working with handicapped children is to determine how best to assess, intervene, and instruct in the area of language, with particular attention to semantic processing (i.e., meaning).

I have proposed a model of assessment and intervention (Butler, 1984d) that is conceptually anchored in Sajavaaro's (1981) work in message processing and integrates his constructs related to the acquisition of a second language to the acquisition of the first language. The model includes the analysis of comprehension and production tasks in terms of the individual's discourse history, lexical and semantic information, grammar and syntax, prior knowledge stored in long-term memory, short-term memory constraints, social and emotional variables, motivation, and performance potential or capacity. This model takes into account Wiig and Semel's (1984) contention that it is essential to consider the matters of race and ethnicity, social class, educational level and first and second language comprehension and performance. It also takes into account the current movement away from attempting to measure comprehension or retrieval or isolated language rules, since for successful functioning in the classroom, children must use a variety of language rules in an integrated manner (Butler, 1984d; Cullata et al., 1983).

Westby (1984b) pointed out some of the differences between learning to talk and talking to learn:

> When children learn to talk, they are learning the phonology, syntax and semantics necessary to communicate their basic desires and needs. When they talk to learn, children use language to monitor and reflect on experience, to reason about, plan and predict experiences.

Viewing language and learning in this way leads to a very different kind of analysis, including a much more careful measurement of language comprehension skills (Butler, 1981a, 1981b, 1981c) and of retrieval and

recall of previously presented information (Butler, 1981d, 1983b).

Three patterns of difficulty have been found among children with true language learning difficulties (Westby, 1984a). These include (a) inefficient processing—often exemplified by response delays, difficulty in modifying or changing tasks, and the need for repetition of clues; (b) difficulty in organizing a narrative, or even in utilizing adult cues, (c) limited semantic knowledge, e.g., the disordered child has difficulty recognizing narrative schemas, even when explicitly presented. Westby (1984b) also points out from her extensive work with American Indian and Spanish children that "many children, especially culturally different children or learning disabled children, experience difficulty when confronted with the increasing decontextualization of literature language and the use of language for thinking, reason, and planning."

How can we, then, best look at language? As Lund and Duchan (1983) noted, new approaches now emerging in assessment focus on both the semantic content of language and its cognitive base. They also point out that meanings shift across the contexts in which they are used. Both meaning and the functions of language are modified by place, time, and the roles of the speaker and listener. The contextual influence noted here now is subsumed under the area of pragmatics. Children's performance in conversations are now examined rather than utterances (Gallagher, 1983), as a reflection of the pragmatic perspective.

As a consequence, assessment and intervention of language disorders is gradually moving out of the clinic and into the classroom and away from a one-to-one relationship between the clinician and the client toward a collaborative arrangement with teachers and parents (Hedrick & Kemp, 1984; Spinelli & Terrell, 1984). However, many procedures remain to be developed to assess children's performance within this broader concept of language. Norm-based, formal tests will no longer suffice, since most of them reflect the use of controlled stimuli and a very limited permissible range of responses. Such tests do not reflect the diversity of the child's language environments, and therefore measure only a portion of his language skills or deficits. Ironically, this realization that "language in context" is a highly important variable comes at a time when many state departments of education are requiring educators and related service personnel to be ever more specific in the use of formal testing instruments, while, at the same time, requiring that testing be nonbiased.

An additional problem for those professionals attempting to adapt formal language tests and/or present a variety of language tasks in a number of contexts (i.e., during reading class; during interactive discussion groups; while telling or retelling a story; with peers, with teachers, with parents; in clinical settings; in the classroom; at play; and so forth) is the need to be "quick and easy" when it comes to evaluation. There is the perception abroad in the land that time spent on language assessment is not as valuable as time spent in remediation, and that one must move as quickly as possible from screening through diagnostics to intervention in order to be efficient and effective (the terrible two Es of the educational system). Efficient, it may be. Effective? For the more severely (or the more subtly) disordered, time spent in careful assessment may yield information regarding the child's cognitive strategies, attentional and perceptual behavior, semantic and linguistic knowledge, form and use, motivation and learning potential and capacity that will far outweigh the time invested. Language and learning do not come easily to handicapped children. They will be spending years of their lives in that endeavor. Professionals have the responsibility to do more than as one psychologist put it: "WISC them and WRAT them and send 'em on their way." Language specialists, too, have the responsibility to do far more than to "ITPA, CELF, and MLU them and put 'em into therapy."

Ineffective intervention frequently follows insufficient and inappropriate evaluation. The time gained in the initial weeks of the school year by moving rapidly from cursory screening or assessment is lost over the intervention period; be that a month, a year, or 10 years.

Those administrators responsible for the activities of language specialists, whatever the work setting might be, need to recognize that principle. While the advent of IEPs should have contributed to the specification of appropriate assessment and intervention goals, many specialists report the continuing need to move rapidly to intervention. As noted earlier in this chapter, the concept of language and its disorders has broadened and deepened over time. If one's view of language encompasses listening, speaking, reading, and writing, and if that view acknowledges the complex interrelationships between language, cognition, perception, and attention, then it is apparent that a language disorder seriously interferes with all aspects of learning. As such, it deserves a full analysis of its parameters. It also requires the interaction of reading specialists, special education and regular education teachers, and speech-language pathologists in evaluation, remediation, and instruction.

As noted in the opening pages of this chapter, the schools of America are focusing more heavily on literacy in their search for academic excellence. In so doing, the relationships between oral language and literacy must be considered. Those relationships have been nicely documented in the book intriguingly entitled *Language by Ear and by Eye* (Kavanaugh & Mattingly, 1972). Well before the current concern about America's education of its young, Kavanaugh and Mattingly noted that, while many normal children learn spoken language with ease, reading problems abound. They also suggest that the relationship between language received by the eye, rather than the ear, should actually be easier but, for a variety of reasons, is not. In this postindustrial society, wherein the growth of knowledge industries and informational systems plays a central role, the need to be literate is of increasing, rather than decreasing importance for normal and handicapped alike. Reading involves more than a decoding process. It involves the comprehension of the message in print, just as listening requires the comprehension of the spoken message. Both require an understanding of the world and the ability to interpret that understanding into spoken or written language (Westby, 1984c).

A vehicle for evaluation of this understanding is the narrative form of discourse. Narratives (stories) have been of importance in oral societies (i.e., those without written forms of expression) for centuries. Narratives remain, even today, a viable source of information. The telling of a story requires that the narrator reflect on other than the immediate present (Sachs, 1980). Narratives provide some sense of whether or not the storyteller can provide a temporal sequence of events that are related in some way to each other. Cause and effect relationships are also clearly demonstrated in the stories of most competent language users. (The reader may wish to return to the story told by the language disordered child on page 285, and note that the student's narrative holds some promise, in that cause-and-effect statements are made and that temporal relationships in the past are addressed. However, it also reveals considerable difficulty with interrelating the events reported, and discloses the depth of the language disorder.)

How early may narratives be used to analyze language comprehension and production? Formal story beginnings ("Once upon a time," or "Yesterday, I," or "Listen, Daddy said") and the use of past tense appear early in the preschool years and may even be found in the narratives of 2-year-olds (Applebee, 1978). While the range of normal narrative development is currently thought to be quite broad, research now indicates that language-disordered children, including those with reading problems, produce less complex stories, use simpler words in the telling of the story, and have difficulty in describing the motivational relationships between the story characters (Westby, 1984c).

The following selected excerpts from children's stories provide a framework for considering the range of narratives among the language disordered:

> 1. *Christine, age 10:00, is language/learning disabled; she has been placed in a special class. She had a serious illness, with resultant brain injury during her preschool years.*

EXAMINER: Tell me the story of Little Red Riding Hood.
CHRISTINE: Once upon the time, pretend like once upon a time, a little squirrel talked to Cinderella. Cinderella? Okay, pretend like right here, a sheep, and right here, a duck. And pretend like right here a wolf and that a man working that cuts trees. Pretend like right here a bad wolf (*remainder of sentence is unintelligible*). Mom want me to catch Cinderella and Grandma.
EXAMINER: Is she going to Grandma's house?
CHRISTINE: Yes. Where Grandma's house? Thataway, bye-bye, okay? Knock, knock, who's there? What have, what big eyes she got, the better to eat she. Okay. What okay? Pretend like. . . . Okay, pretend like right here that bad wolf . . . no, pretend like here that bad wolf and Cinderella, Cinderella meet the man, take Cinderella out and put rock in it, and (*remainder is unintelligible*). Okay, right here that other one she want me tell one more Cinderella?
EXAMINER: I want to know what the Wolf said to Little Red Riding Hood.
CHRISTINE: Okay. That Cinderella how big, how big, she nose is. I get scared. Okay. Another one . . . that one right here she know it right. Okay. Pretend like that Cinderella, pretend like right here the bad wolf and pretend like right here the her house, a sheep. Okay? Shhhh. Hi, little duck. Hi, little man, want be friends with me? Yeah, bye-bye. What way, that knock, knock? Who there? What big nose she got to smell and eat she. (*Christine screams.*)
EXAMINER: Where did Grandma go?
CHRISTINE: Okay, okay. Pretend like right here that man, pretend like right here grandma, and pretend right here Grandma the man and right here Cinderella. Oh, honey, I love she. Let's get married. No, No. She see that wolf, run and come back here. Okay, okay. she had tea and tea forever and ever.

Christine's performance during this story-telling reveals that she has understood the broad outline of story structure. She has the appropriate opening (i.e., once upon [the] time) and closing (forever and ever). However, she has difficulty in keeping her story in the past, frequently reverting to a very concrete present (i.e., right here). Included in her narrative are attempts to give the story a sequence, although the order is disturbed by the conflation of two stories, that of Little Red Riding Hood and Cinderella. Despite the difficulties noted, Christine's interest in stories and in symbolic play is reported to be high, although her decoding skills in reading are very limited.

2. *Mark, age 12:11, is language/learning disabled; he has resource room assistance, but remains in a 5th grade regular classroom.*

EXAMINER: Tell me a story.
MARK: I don't know any.
EXAMINER: Well, here's a picture of a dog. Can you tell me a story about this picture?
MARK: One day, on July 4, 1983, my dog, Snoopy, was left alone in the house. We had the lamp plugged in and the light on 'cause we weren't gonna be home later at dark. When we came, before we came home, my dog bit the cord out and busted the lamp. And he got a shock, and when we came home, he was layin' on the ground scared and hot. The end.

Upon completion of the story, Mark confessed that it was a "true story," that is, a report of an episodic memory. The incident had happened to his dog, Bozo, at the date and time specified in the story.

Mark was then given a paragraph to read, and asked to choose something in the paragraph that would help him understand the word *survive*, which appeared in the following target sentence: "If you settle your differences and stick together, our family will be stronger and we will be able to survive any problem which comes up." Mark looked puzzled, and responded to the question, "What can you find in this paragraph that helps you understand *survive*?" by stating, "You could look in the dictionary."

It is apparent that Mark's language disorder is less obvious than Christine's. Mark's teacher reports great difficulty with both spoken and read language. She notes that he has been retained twice, and that he has great difficulty in organizing language concepts. The psychologist reports that while Mark's performance is within the normal range on most verbal tasks, Mark displays word omissions, substitutions, grammatical errors, and so forth, well below his age level. The speech–language pathologist reports that Mark's performance on standardized language measures ranges from the first to the eighth percentile with an age equivalency of 7–9 years.

To clarify Mark's language and learning problem, one needs to look beyond the narrative provided. Recall that Mark could not "tell a story" upon first request. Recall as well that the use of a picture elicited an episodic memory (an experience from his past), rather than a creative use of language, such as might be anticipated from a child who is almost 13 and whose performance on standardized psychological instruments reflects verbal skills within the normal range, but whose performance on language tasks falls considerably below the normal range.

Mark is one of 10 children, whose family includes a mother, stepfather, and assorted uncles and aunts. The family has continuous financial difficulties and moves frequently, perhaps accounting for Mark's need to repeat the second and fifth grades. However, school records indicate otherwise. A language problem was identified when Mark entered school and continued to be evident in first grade. "Mark needs to improve listening, reading, and following directions," are comments that appear in the first grade report card, and over the years that follow. In the "second time around" fifth grade, teacher comments again include the well worn phrases, "Mark lacks study skills; written expression is poor; following directions and listening are also poor." It may be conjectured that as Mark approaches the more difficult tasks inherent in the increasing demands for literacy in the classroom, many of which require sophisticated metalinguistic and metacognitive skills, his performance will fall further behind. Perhaps, Mark is one of the "puzzle children" for whom the term *learning disabled* was originally coined, that is, a child with normal intellectual skills who experiences considerable difficulty in learning within the academic environment. To sort out the environmental from the cognitive aspects of Mark's performance, the pragmatic from the semantic/linguistic considerations, and the multiple roles played by the varying instructional contexts over the last 9 years, will require considerable effort. How much of the language disorder is attributable to internal factors and how much to external factors is a tantalizing question. Mark's future depends upon the answer to such questions.

As Silliman (1984, p. 288) points out, the language of teachers is meant to assist children in the attainment of general cognitive and social goals. We now know that many language and learning disabled (LLD) children manifest difficulties in using higher order problem-solving strategies (Meichenbaum, 1980). The language of the schools, as reflected in the language demands of the curriculum and of teacher-directed instruction may be responsible for exacerbating the difficulties not only of language and learning disordered children but of some normal children as well (Butler, 1984a). That there is frequently a mismatch between children's language, the teacher's instructional language, and the language of textbooks and workbooks has been acknowledged (Gerber & Bryen, 1981). Nelson (1984) has expressed the prevailing attitude that culturally different children, for example, may have had experiences that do not lend themselves easily to the cognitive and social expectations of the classroom. The more remote a child's life experiences are from the conventional and conceptual demands of the classroom, the more difficult it may be to benefit from the academic setting (Cazden, 1979).

Upon school entry, the child must shift from the home, with its familiar linguistic and non-linguistic contexts, to an increasingly lexically bound language of instruction. These language demands continue and, indeed, expand as the child moves through the elementary and secondary school. Illustrative of this sequence of events are some examples provided by Nelson (1984):

1. The language of the schools is frequently used to give directions and to control behavior, e.g. a first grade teacher begins the day:
   > All right, let's get back to your seats.
   > Let's have our flag salute.
   > Dedra, we're waiting on you, honey.
   > Drew, forget how it starts?
   > It starts with "I".
   > Remember, you're standing up/tall and straight/and you look like a letter. (p. 163)

2. Teacher talk is frequently directed to attentional strategies, as this second grade teacher illustrates:
   > Now, before you start I want to check to see about my listeners.
   > OK, Lisa was a good listener.
   > Randy was fairly good.
   > Aaaaa, and this Randy was fairly good.
   > Eric, you were not good, you got almost all your work filled in/you weren't listening.
   > Now boys and girls/listening/is important/for one reason/you'll need it later on.
   > Now/some of you know your number words just as well as you/you know your name and you know your color words.
   > If you get in the habit of listening/then/no matter what job you have to do/then we'll have, we'll have that to do it with. (p. 163)

3. Teacher talk, although designed to enhance understanding, is not always clear. In this example, the teacher's discourse is designed to link past classroom experiences with a current science project. The reader may judge if this third grade teacher has accomplished that objective:
   > OK, everybody sit down now.
   > What you're gonna be doing today/is/you're gonna grow/you're gonna grown your own crystals.
   > If you remember last week/we grew some crystals back there but I kinda put it together didn't I?
   > Well this week you're gonna grow your own.
   > How many people in here/know what a tea bag is?

Right, only these tea bags are a different kind of tea bag.

These things/they look about the same on both ends but if you're really careful you can open the top part up. (p. 168)

4. In the following example, metalinguistic skills are being tapped. Using language to think about language requires a level of abstraction that may not be present in some children. This sixth grade teacher is providing instructions for a group reading task:

OK/uh/now we're working with the/ base form and the /s/form of verbs.

The first part/you're supposed to/uh/ complete the sentence with/uh/with what/either one, either the "s" form or the base form.

Will you please read the sentence?

No you're on the wrong sentence. (p. 171)

Thus, we see that the spoken language in the classroom is subject to the "faults" of most conversations. There are revisions, repetitions, false starts, and references to immediate and past contexts that do not always amplify the intended meaning of the discourse. And yet, there is the possibility for replacing the errors inherent in spoken discourse. Teachers are able to respond to the verbal and nonverbal behavior of the children, thus rectifying some of the confusion inherent in the slippery stream of speech. In addition, the redundancy of spoken language also provides an advantage in classroom discourse, when appropriately used. However, for children with language disorders who have difficulty processing the incoming verbal messages, confusion may replace comprehension. Indeed, if care is not taken by the teacher in terms of instructional discourse, the processing load may be too heavy even for normal listeners.

As we have seen, reading is a more difficult skill, one which eludes not only the language and learning disordered but a good number of normal children as well. Language by eye requires linguistic awareness and the processing of text at a number of levels (Roth & Perfetti, 1980). For example, the reader must hold the most salient parts of a sentence or a paragraph in short-term memory, in order to match incoming new information with old information present in the text. Thus, not only are memory and past experience involved, but the selection of salient information also requires a certain level of "world knowledge," which is enhanced by a knowledge of certain scripts or schemas. For example, it is much easier to read about John's birthday party, if one has some general concept of what happens at birthday parties in general. A birthday party script is built upon former personal (episodic) memories of birthday parties attended, which then blend into a notion of a prototypical party (a semantic memory).

While many children with subtle language or learning problems begin to flounder in second or third grades as the semantic load of reading increases, others experience great difficulty from the time the reading task is introduced. Blachman (1984) notes that it is critical that children who are beginning to read succeed in the task of segmenting sentences into words and words into phonemes. Sentence segmentation can be accomplished by children as young as 4 (Fox & Routh, 1975), but segmenting into the syllables and phonemes that represent the alphabetic orthography is a more difficult task. Blachman (1984) points out that the level of linguistic awareness (i.e., metalinguistic skill) required to segment language into phonemes may be a skill that requires instruction, rather than reflecting a developmental process. She acknowledges that precocious children may learn to read simply through exposure to print and may even develop metalinguistic awareness without formal instruction, although this may be a relatively rare event. Finally, she reports that many children with learning disabilities experience considerable difficulty in "constructing the link between the sounds of speech and the signs of print—the first step in learning to read the alphabetic writing system" (p. 285).

Norman (1972) provides an interesting insight into the speed at which memory processing occurs in reading. He notes that the capacity of the sensory store for incoming information may be in the range of 1,000–60,000 bits per second. He adds, "Even 60,000 bits is not very much, for each of the 25,000 neurons in the basilar membrane need only have a memory store for a few bits" (p. 286).

This brief look at the connecting link between speech, language, memory processing and instructional discourse requirements highlights the fact that research and practice in the area of language disorders can provide information that is useful in determining the needs of children, whether they be "special" or "ordinary," whether the instructional setting be special, or regular education. In addition, there are implications for classroom management through teacher discourse, as well.

IF WE'RE HERE, WHAT'S THE PROBLEM?

Thus far we've looked at where we have been and where we are. What now are the issues to be confronted in the mid-1980s? Those involved in research in language acquisition and language disorders face a certain set of issues, frequently of a rather esoteric nature. Those involved in practice face another set of issues. Let us examine a few concerns of each set.

Research Issues

As intimated earlier, researchers in language acquisition currently are exploring the best methods for obtaining information on early language acquisition on the one hand, while attempting to identify the parameters of such language skills as metaphor development and figurative language in older children. Although a large group of child language researchers still view syntactical and phonological acquisition as central, many others favor moving on to pragmatic and processing issues. As Becker (1984) suggests

> It is time for those of us studying language development, particularly pragmatics, to take a look at the ethology literature. . . . Unfortunately, ethologists do not usually concern themselves with language. . . . Conversely, psycholinguists usually do not concern themselves with ethology. (p. 2)

Since ethologists concern themselves with the origins of nonhuman animal behavior, it is the application of ethology principles, rather than content, that may be of assistance to those studying language acquisition. These principles involve a thorough description of the behaviors prototypical of a species in its natural habitat, followed by, perhaps, more controlled experiments, and finally by organizing their findings in specific ways that attempt to address the ontogeny, phylogeny, and function of the behaviors (Becker, 1984, p. 3). Here one sees the suggestion that the current interest in natural settings, as previously identified as the language of the home or the language of the school, be expanded even further.

Second, there is a need to define more clearly the role of semantics and lexical access and retrieval. Jackendoff (1983) attempted to view the cognitive foundations of semantics and the problems related to lexical analysis (word meanings) from two perspectives: one, linguistic philosophy; the other, the grammatical structure of "natural" language. Again, we see the emphasis on the natural occurrence of language, rather than language observed under the experimental conditions of the psychology laboratory.

Third, as a review of atypical language learners and their language usage will suggest, there has been a lag in research efforts regarding this group in contrast to normal language development. As Friel-Patti and Conti-Ramsden (1984) suggest, research has frequently been fragmentary in regard to atypical learners (p. 179). Again, the comment is made that investigators have tended to look at particular tasks at a particular moment in time, and that studies of the development of atypical language learners over time are almost nonexistent. They hypothesize that some children may fail to acquire syntax and phonology appropriately, while others may fail to acquire pragmatics and discourse, that is, the communicative aspects of language. They point out that there may be subsystems of language yet to be explored and that both qualitative and quantitative data may yield disparate findings.

Fourth, researchers have utilized both a

Chomskian framework and a Piagetian frame-work to analyze language comprehension and production over the past two decades. Both are now in question as appropriate frameworks for analyzing atypical language learners. While certain trends are evident, there is yet no clear direction for language research, except as certain subsets of researchers wend their way through the poppy-fields of cognitive psychology, information processing, anthropology, ethology, and so forth. Borrowers we have always been. It would seem that we will continue to look to other disciplines to set the stage for research directions.

Fifth, language acquisition and language disorders researchers currently represent a blending of psycholinguistic, developmental, and language pathology perspectives. Increasingly, the lines between the disciplines are becoming blurred. However, the imprint of the discipline remains. That imprint is most frequently reflected in the narrowness of the research each discipline undertakes. While bemoaning the narrowness of these endeavors, one is forced to acknowledge that both the study of language acquisition and the study of communicative disorders is immense. The old question remains, How does one eat an elephant? And the answer remains as well, One bite at a time. In this case, it is not only the composition of the elephant, but the collaborative gustatory initiatives that must be considered.

Sixth, the last decade brought particular problems to both research and practice in that the researchers within each discipline tend to write in the vocabulary associated with their field, thus lessening accessibility to important information. Too, federal legislation has identified labels and categories at variance with theoretical models. To be understood by others in and out of special education, it is thought necessary to use federally defined categories, knowing full well that the current and past definitions of, say, learning disabilities, lend themselves poorly to the identification of this heterogenous group, many of whom are language impaired. Should, then, one speak of the language impairment for all language based

disorders? Even if this were theoretically sound, it would be difficult, since language impairment is not a federally funded or recognized category. Yet, many children placed in other categories (mental retardation, autism, hearing impairment, etc.) reveal significant difficulties in comprehending and producing language.

In the main, child language researchers, dealing with normal language acquisition and development, have not been troubled by the distinctions required of those who must either provide assessment and intervention services or even those who wish to make their research in language disorders relevant to the concerns of the field. Nor have those interested in research in applied psycholinguistics (i.e., second language teaching) been impressed with the need to make their results known to any but those teachers who deal with second language acquisition, some of which is equally important to first language learners.

While conversation between researchers and practitioners has been historically difficult, the descriptive properties of Public Law 94-142 have contributed to the current uncertainties of both groups. The consequences fall most heavily upon the practitioner, the schools, and those children with special needs.

Practitioner Issues

In reflecting upon the impact of P.L. 94-142, most practitioners would assert that they are now able to work with fewer children (i.e., the more severely handicapped) in a more intensive manner. This has been a mixed blessing, since "success rates" with the more severely handicapped are not likely to be as significant as those with the mildly or moderately handicapped. In many ways, the tradition of services in the schools has remained much the same, having been modified only in terms of the number of times and the number of hours a child is to be seen. Meanwhile, researchers have been suggesting that practitioners should involve themselves and their students in the following areas.

First is the development of pragmatic skills. Research has now sufficiently identified the structure and content of pragmatic skills to permit the practitioner to develop strategies for measurement and intervention. Whether one deals with preschool, school age, or adult language disordered individuals, the importance of communication and speech to communicative competence has been established. The question now is, How can the practitioner put this knowledge into practice within the perceived confines of the work setting?

Second is the language of the schools. Research in instructional discourse has disclosed the tremendous influence of the formal language of the classroom on children's learning. How can the language specialist best utilize this knowledge to enhance the language disordered child's success within the school? We now know that teacher's discourse strategies may or may not be effective; texts may or may not permit the child to derive full benefit from text-based information; children may or may not comprehend how the language of the schools is at variance with the language of the home. How best may the language specialist intervene in the cycle of the language of the child, the language of the teacher, and the language of the text? The broader implications would portend a new view of oral and written language.

Third, if the practitioner, no matter what his/her persuasion, accepts the concept that language is reflected in oral, written, and read forms of communication, there must be a greater alliance between the intersecting disciplines of speech–language pathology, reading, and learning disabilities and/or resource room specialist, and regular educator. To stand alone means to fail alone. To stand together may mean renewed hope for the language and learning disabled child. Turf issues notwithstanding, the focus must be on the child and his or her special needs. It is within the school environment that such transdisciplinary activities may truly occur. However, this will take more than a multidisciplinary effort. Special education and related services are servants to funding formulas. This will require the intercession of administrators who recognize the contributions that may be derived from true transdisciplinary efforts. A recognition that intensive analysis of the child's language functioning may result in a real pay-off for the child and for the school is also required, since administrators hold the key to the delivery of services within that environment.

Third, closer links between practitioners and researchers are dependent not only on researchers making their results more understandable to practitioners, but also on the practitioners utilizing the results of research, even when that research is not easily translated. Practitioners must demand, if not of basic researchers then of those who are researcher/clinicians, that research be translated into some useful medium. This need not be an antagonistic relationship. The field of speech correction grew out of a dual concern for research and clinical practice, as its history has indicated. There has always been an untapped wealth of information within the confines of practice, typically unmined. The inherent gold of school-based practice has never been well considered. Perhaps it is now time that the needs of the researcher for subjects in a natural setting, and the needs of the practitioner for improved services, be addressed. This will only happen if researchers and practitioners can communicate. As has been wryly noted on a number of occasions, how is it that we in communication have so much difficulty communicating?

This list of issues and concerns is not meant to be all inclusive. Certainly, there are many more, both for the practitioner and the researcher. These serve only as illustrations. The question remains, How do we address the larger questions facing basic and applied language researchers, while providing practitioners with sorely needed information, so that they in turn may meet the needs of individuals with language (and language-based) disorders?

How do societal changes affect the language handicapped? On the one hand, we have seen a new awareness and advocacy on behalf of the handicapped permeate our culture over the past 15 years. There is no doubt that services to and for the handicapped have increased dramatically. On the other hand, the contemporary search for excellence in education fails to include the handicapped and the renewed emphasis on the acquisition of literacy places a premium on language. When a language disorder is integral to a handicapping condition, as it is to so many, society's explicit requirement for literacy and its implicit requirement for academic and economic success provide a challenge of considerable proportions. The challenge is reflected in our continuing search for further knowledge not only of the structure, form, and use of language, but for those variables that underpin communicative competence as well.

The major task of the practitioner is to unravel the multiple skeins of inquiry and to weave more sophisticated garments with which to clothe the language impaired. This is no simple task. While the looms of theory are taking shape, the warp and woof remain tantalizingly incomplete. As McCormick and Schiefelbusch (1984) point out, there is no simple solution or formula for translating research information into such real world questions as how best to conduct language intervention. In all likelihood, there is no one best way. Rather, program strategies for language intervention are multiple, each reflecting prevailing research and theory, and each following one of the current research directions. "[T]hey include early intervention, . . . non-speech intervention, . . . milieu or incidental teaching, . . . developmental intervention, . . . and remedial intervention" (McCormick & Schiefelbusch, 1984, p. 390). Each of these program strategies requires a different and unique pattern of intervention, and each must be woven by the practitioner.

WHERE DO WE GO FROM HERE?

What are the next steps? Where does the future lie? Our past is a predictor of our future. The field of communicative disorders originated from a number of other disciplines: psychology, education, and medicine, to name but three. Since that time, the field has continued its practice of borrowing research methodology and theory from those disciplines, while adding others. For example, developmental psycholinguistics recently emerged as a subdiscipline of linguistics and has much of value to offer those whose primary interest is in language disorders. Not only will researchers and practitioners continue to rely on the broad field of linguistics and its subfields, such as psycholinguistics and sociolinguistics, they will increase their involvement with, and use of, the outcomes of semantic research. Such research has dealt with language meaning and thus assists in understanding how ideas about the real world of objects, events, and relationships emerges in normal children. Practitioners will return to the teaching of vocabulary, that outward manifestation of semantic relationships, but within a much more sophisticated paradigm. Intervention strategies will be developed that take into consideration how verbal and nonverbal comprehension develops.

As interest in semantics waxes (Butler, 1983b, 1984d), interest in syntax will wane at the level of intervention, although there will be continuing interest at the research level, with particular emphasis on later developing syntactical forms. Concurrently, the present interest in pragmatics (Snyder, 1983) will continue to grow among researchers for at least the next decade. The study of acts of speech and the contexts in which they are performed is of interest to sociologists, psychologists, speech-language pathologists, and linguists, particularly sociolinguists and applied linguists. It is a particularly fertile area of cross-disciplinary research. Practitioners, however, may discover that implementing pragmatic intervention strategies is a task fraught with difficulties. It requires much greater interaction and cooperative planning with teachers and parents than has been the norm in the past. The constraints of time and place will emerge anew. Providing language intervention concurrently across settings is accomplished with greater ease with very young children, whose world is bound more closely to the home and perhaps a preschool. Older children, particularly language-disordered adolescents, need to develop and test their pragmatic skills in a much larger variety of settings, including transitional and work environments.

The past few years have brought amazing changes in the practitioner's ability to assist the most severely handicapped individuals and to provide means of communication to non-speaking individuals. There is no reason to believe that such changes will continue, perhaps at a less accelerated pace. Instrumentation and computer technology research have had a profound impact on the delivery of services. And it is not only the most severely language impaired who will benefit from technological advances, although they may be the chief beneficiaries of the growing role of robotics to assist the severely handicapped in everyday living. Mild and moderately language handicapped people will have access to computer-assisted instruction, which will be based upon ongoing research in cognition. Practitioners now have at their disposal considerable software that makes the lengthy task of language assessment and analysis a more manageable task. The future promises even more capabilities in that regard and provides an answer to some of the current concerns regarding efficient use of professional energy and time. In addition, software programs that go well beyond a worksheet on a screen will be available. Interactive systems are now being developed that will permit a more finely grained approach to language intervention.

As our knowledge of higher order cognitive strategies, including metacognitive and metalinguistic skills, increases, intervention will address these areas in a more systematic way. Research in cognition will provide an increasing number of answers to questions regarding how children move from being naive learners to experts and how problem solving interacts with language.

Research in brain organization will provide further glimpses into the processing of language in the right and left hemispheres and there may well be a return to a more holistic view of brain function and language learning and relearning, in contrast with today's attempts to "train" the right brain, for example.

Some language research being conducted today is attempting to view "language" in its totality, rather than considering, for example, reading as distinct from oral language, or written expression as distinct from listening and speaking. There is a growing acknowledgment that language must be defined across disciplines rather than within a discipline. The dream of transdisciplinary research and practice is still to come, although there are encouraging signs that it may some day become a reality. Surely, if that should not occur, language disordered individuals will be ill-served in the decades to come.

Finally, it may be that we will come to realize that the acquisition of literacy is no mean feat, and that it is not a simple process that requires the efforts of a few to allay the concerns of the many. Technology will not decrease the need for literacy; in fact, the reverse may well be true. To that end, schools will increase their efforts to focus upon all parts of educational enterprise, but will also consider more carefully the many facets of spoken language in the search for student literacy and will take into account the disparate cultures from which America's children are drawn.

SUMMARY AND CONCLUSIONS

The origins of language precede recorded history. Over the centuries, humankind has traversed a path leading from the oral societies of yesteryear to the largely literate societies of today's developed countries. The handicapped, including the language impaired, have only recently been considered as capable of contributing to society and, thus, worthy of the investment that society, vis à vis the schools, may offer.

Language disorders are of central importance to many handicapping conditions: autism, retardation, hearing and visual impairments, learning disabilities, the multihandicapped, among others. The past 50 years have witnessed a dramatic increase in our understanding of how and when language is acquired normally and how and when it may become impaired. Research drawn from psycholinguistics, cognitive psychology, sociology, philosophy, and medicine has amplified the scope of our endeavors.

The field of communicative disorders evolved at a time when intensive study of child development had begun. In addition, public schools were acknowledging the needs of exceptional children, particularly the mentally retarded, the deaf, and the orthopedically handicapped, by devising special curricula and by instituting special classes. The growth of special education services included the expansion of speech correction services, the forerunner of today's speech–language pathology services, and those of remedial reading teachers and other language specialists, although the major task of such professionals was to deal with children who exhibited difficulties in speech, language, or reading, but who were not in special education classrooms. Such services were provided in the mainstream, long before that concept emerged.

Research in language acquisition has been largely conducted by psycholinguists, while research in language disorders has been largely conducted by speech-language pathologists. However, the distinction is now less clear, with researchers from both disciplines looking at typical and atypical language development. The work of Piaget and Chomsky had tremendous impact on both fields: their views contributed substantially to research and practice not only in communicative disorders, but in much of special education. At least some of today's researchers are now focusing upon models of information processing and cognition, based upon advances in artificial intelligence.

Language has come to be viewed very differently from the past, when those involved in intervention spoke of articulation disorders, delayed speech, voice disorders, and stuttering. Now language (a derivative of delayed speech) is viewed as knowledge of a code that represents ideas about the world, while speech is considered to be only one avenue for expressing such ideas; others would include gestures, sign language, and so forth. In addition, communication and the concept of communicative concept have come into being. Communication is interactive, involving an exchange of information between two or more individuals. It requires a knowledge of one's societal and cultural norms to communicate effectively.

Language is thought to involve, at a minimum, phonology, syntax, semantics, and pragmatics, and those categories have become the target for many of today's language intervention strategies. At the same time, it has come to be recognized that language exists within a number of communicative contexts, thus broadening both research and clinical concerns and interests. Indeed, it is now realized that the language of the schools (i.e., instructional discourse by teachers and texts) interacts with the language of children. This interaction can be helpful in the learning process but, for many children with language disorders or language differences, the formal language typical of the classroom is problematic. We have yet to solve how teacher talk, child talk, and text talk may be most advantageously intertwined, particularly for children with special needs.

Much of this chapter has been devoted to identifying specific strands of language research, relating that research to the practicalities of special education services in the schools. When practitioners understand how children acquire language in the real world of home and school and how they use language to learn and to solve problems, that knowledge will eventually provide us with better templates for language intervention and instruction.

Finally, there has been an attempt to summarize the issues and concerns of researchers and practitioners across disciplines. The centrality of language to the human condition underlies much of what has been said. Above and beyond the use of language for communication is the use of language in developing literacy, a prerequisite for much of life in today's society. Indeed, there is some resemblance between today's need for comprehending written discourse and Washington Irving's comments in 1824:

> The land of literature is a fairy land to those who view it from a distance, but, like all other landscapes, the charm fades on a nearer approach, and the thorns and briars become visible. The republic of letters is the most factious and discordant of all republics, ancient or modern.

Truly, the landscape of language is filled with thorns and briars for those individuals whose skills are insufficient to the task. The role of education is to make language accessible to those who need it most, the language and learning handicapped.

REFERENCES

Anderson, J. R. (1980). *Cognitive psychology and its implications.* San Francisco: W. H. Freeman & Co.

Applebee, A. (1978). *The child's concept of story.* Chicago: University of Chicago Press.

Arbib, M. A., Caplan, D., & Marshall, J. C. (1982). *Neural models of language processing.* Orlando, FL: Academic Press.

Asher, S. R. (1979). Referential communication. In G. J. Whitehurst & B. J. Zimmerman (Eds.), *The functions of language and cognition.* New York: Academic Press.

Becker, J. A. (1984). Implications of ethology for the study of pragmatic development. In S. A. Kuczaj, II (Ed.), *Discourse development, progress in cognitive development research.* New York: Springer-Verlag.

Bertenthal, B. I. (1981). The significance of developmental sequences for investigating the what and how of development. In K. W. Fischer (Ed.), *Cognitive development* (pp. 43–55). San Francisco: Jossey-Bass.

Blachman, B. (1984). Language analysis skills and early reading acquisition. In G. P. Wallach & K. G. Butler (Eds.), *Language learning disabilities in school-age children.* Baltimore: Williams and Wilkins.

Bleumel, C. S. (1932). Primary and secondary stammering, *Proceedings of the American Speech Correction Association, 2,* 91–102.

Bowerman, M. (1978). Words and senteces: Uniformity, individual variation and shifts over time in patterns of acquisition. In F. D. Minifie & L. L. Lloyd (Eds.), *Communicative and cognitive abilities — Early behavioral assessment.* Baltimore: University Park Press.

Boyd, W. R., & Butler, K. G. (1971). Response

patterns of five, six and seven year olds to the intraverbal gesture subtest of the Parsons language sample, *Journal of Speech and Hearing Research, 15,* 303–307.

Brainerd, C. J. (1981). Working memory and the developmental analysis of probability judgment, *Psychological Review, 88,* 463–502.

Brainerd, C. J. (1983). Varieties of strategy training in Piagetian concept formation. In M. Pressley & J. R. Levin (Eds.), *Cognitive strategy research: Educational applications.* New York: Springer-Verlag.

Brown, F. W. (1933). The permanent cure of stuttering, *Mental Hygiene, 18,* 266–277.

Bryden, M. P. (1983). *Laterality: Functional asymmetry in the intact brain.* Orlando, FL: Academic Press.

Bryngelson, B. (1937). Psychological problems in stuttering, *Mental Hygiene, 21,* 162–197.

Butler, K. B. (1953). *Parental comprehension of the adolescent stutterer's attitude toward his stuttering,* pp. iii–62. Unpublished master's thesis, Western Michigan University.

Butler, K. G. (1956). Even the stalwart stumble. *Education, 77*(2), 108–112.

Butler, K. G. (1960a). *Problems in public school therapy for stutterers.* Paper presented to the American Speech and Hearing Association, Los Angeles.

Butler, K. G. (1960b). *Maternal insight into the adolescent stutterer's attitude toward his stuttering.* Paper presented to the American Speech and Hearing Association, Los Angeles.

Butler, K. G. (1960c). *An empirical investigation of speech improvement in the public schools.* Paper presented to the American Speech and Hearing Association, Los Angeles.

Butler, K. G. (1961). *A child who stutters: A longitudinal study of a therapeutic failure.* Paper presented to the American Speech and Hearing Association, Chicago.

Butler, K. G. (1962). *Prognosis in speech therapy and the use of projective techniques.* Paper presented to the American Speech and Hearing Association, New York.

Butler, K. G. (1963). *Diagnosis of speech disorders in hospitalized emotionally disturbed children.* Paper presented to the American Speech and Hearing Association, Chicago.

Butler, K. G. (1964). *Self-concept of emotionally disturbed children as reflected in human figure drawings and speech patterning.* Paper presented to the American Speech and Hearing Association, San Francisco.

Butler, K. G. (1965). *Psychological manifestations of speech defects as revealed through projective techniques.* Paper presented to the American Speech and Hearing Association, Chicago.

Butler, K. G. (1967). *Perceptual-motor problems of young stutterers.* Paper presented to the American Speech and Hearing Association, Chicago.

Butler, K. G. (1981a). Language disorders: Assessment of certain comprehension factors. In B. Sigurd & J. Svartvik (Eds.), *Proceedings of the international association of applied linguistics, Lund, Sweden* (pp. 371–374). Lund: University of Lund.

Butler, K. G. (1981b). Language processing disorders: Factors in diagnosis and remediation. In R. W. Keith (Ed.), *Central auditory and language disorders in children.* San Diego: College Hill Press.

Butler, K. G. (1981c). Language processing and its disorders. In P. S. Dale & D. Ingram (Eds.), *Child language: An international perspective.* Baltimore: University Park Press.

Butler, K. G. (1981d). Language processing and disorders of retrieval. In B. J. Urban (Ed.), *Proceedings of the 18th congress of the international association of logopedics and phoniatrics, Washington, D.C., 1980, Vol. II,* 403–406.

Butler, K. G. (1983a). Language processing: Selective attention and mnemonic strategies. In E. Lasky & J. Katz (Eds.), *Central auditory processing disorders: Problems of speech, language and learning.* Baltimore: University Park Press.

Butler, K. G. (1983b). *Language disorders in children: Comprehension and retrieval difficulties.* Paper presented before the International Association of Logopedics and Phoniatrics, Edinburgh, Scotland.

Butler, K. G. (1984a). The language of the schools. *Asha, 26*(5), 31–35.

Butler, K. G. (1984b). *What's right about the left brain? Brain organization and language research: Implications for treatment of aphasic children.* A paper presented before the International Association of Logopedics and Phonatics, Zurich, Switzerland.

Butler, K. G. (1984c). Language processing: Halfway up the down staircase. In G. P. Wallach & K. G. Butler (Eds.), *Language learning disabilities in school-age children.* Baltimore: Williams and Wilkins.

Butler, K. G. (1984d). *Semantic processing and the language disordered child.* A paper presented before the third International Congress for the Study of Child Language, Austin.

Butler, K. G., & Holland, J. (1968). *The modification of stuttering behavior: A pilot study.* A paper presented to the American Speech and Hearing Association, Denver.

Butler, K. G., & Naliboff, E. (1967). *Ego strength as a function of the personality dynamics of stutterers.* Paper presented to the American Speech and Hearing Association, Chicago.

Butler, K. G., & Poon, W. R. (1972). Response patterns of five, six and seven year olds to the intraverbal gesture subtest of the Parsons language sample. *Journal of Speech and Hearing Research, 15,* 303–307.

Butler, K. G., & Pratt, J. (1968). *A normative study of auditory closure skills in school age children.* Paper presented at the American Speech and Hearing Association, Denver, CO.

Butler, K. G., & Pratt, J. (1969). Relative performance of auditory closure skills among speech defective children. A paper presented to the American Speech and Hearing Association, Chicago.

Butler, K. G., & Pratt, J. (1972). The S. I. E. V. E. Approach. In M. Val Jones (Ed.), *Language development* (pp. 49–62). Springfield, IL: Charles C Thomas.

Butler, K. G., & Smith, D. E. (1967, Winter). The self-concept and its relation to speech and reading (pp. 59–64). *Reading Horizons.*

Cazden, C. B. (1979). Peekabo as an instructional model: Discourse development at home and at school. *Papers Reporting Child Language Development, 17,* 1–29.

Conture, E. (1982). *Stuttering.* Englewood Cliffs, NJ: Prentice-Hall.

Conture, E. (1984). Observing laryngeal movements of stuttering. In R. Curlee & W. Perkins (Eds.), *Nature and treatment of stuttering: New Directions*(pp. 116–129). San Diego, CA: College Hill Press.

Cosgrove, J. M., & Patterson, C. J. (1977). Plans and the development of listener skills. *Developmental Psychology, 13,* 557–564.

Cross, T. J. (1984). Habilitating the language impaired child: Ideas from studies of parent–child interaction. *Topics in Language Disorders, 4*(4), 1–14.

Culatta, B., Page, J. L., & Ellis, J. (1983). Story retelling as a communicative performance screening tool. *Language, Speech, and Hearing Services in the Schools, 14:2,* 66–74.

Cunningham, C. E., Reuler, E., Blackwell, J., & Deck, J. (1981). Behavioral and linguistic developments in the interactions of normal and retarded children with their mothers. *Child Development, 52,* 62–70.

Curtiss, S. (1977). *Genie.* New York: Academic Press.

Daniloff, R., Schuckers, G., & Feth, L. (1980). *The physiology of speech and hearing.* Englewood Cliffs, NJ: Prentice-Hall.

Despert, J. L. (1943). A therapeutic approach to the problem of stuttering in children. *The Nervous Child, 2,* 34–147.

Dickson, W. P. (1974). The development of interpersonal referential communication skills in young children using an interactional game device. Doctoral dissertation, Stanford University. *Dissertation Abstracts International, 35,* 3511A. University Microfilms, No. 74-27,008.

Dickson, W. P. (1983). Training cognitive strategies for oral communication. In M. Pressley &

J. R. Levin (Eds.), *Cognitive strategy research: Educational applications.* New York: Springer-Verlag.

Donahue, M., & Bryan, T. (1984). Communicative skills and peer relations of learning disabled adolescents. *Topics in Language Disorders, 4*(2), 10–21.

Duchan, J. (1984). Clinical interaction with autistic children: The role of theory. *Topics in Language Disorders, 4*(4), 62–71.

Duchan, J., & Palermo, J. (1982). How autistic children view the world. *Topics in Language Disorders, 3*(1), 10–15.

Finch-Williams, A. (1984). The developmental relationship between cognition and communication: Implications for assessment. *Topics in Language Disorders, 5*(1), 1–13.

Fischer, K. W., & Bullock, D. (1981). Patterns of data: Sequence, synchrony, and constraint in cognitive development. In K. W. Fischer (Ed.), *Cognitive development.* San Francisco: Jossey-Bass.

Fitzgerald, E. (1937). *Rubaiyat of Omar Khayyam,* (translated into English verse). Garden City, NY: Garden City Publishing.

Flavell, J. H. (1981). Cognitive monitoring. In W. P. Dickson (Ed.), *Children's oral communication skills.* New York: Academic Press.

Flavell, J. H., Speer, J. R., Green, F. L., & August, D. L. (1981). The development of comprehension monitoring and knowledge about communication. *Monographs of the Society for Research in Child Development, 46*(5, Serial No. 192).

Fletcher, J. M. (1928). *The problem of stuttering.* New York: Longmans-Green.

Foster, S. (1985). The development of discourse topic skills by infants and young children. *Topics in Language Disorders, 5*(2), 31–45.

Fox, B., & Routh, D. K. (1975). Analyzing spoken language into words, syllables, and phonemes: A developmental study, *Journal of Psycholinguistic Research, 4,* 331–342.

Friel-Patti, S., & Conti-Ramsden, G. (1984). Discourse development in atypical language learners. In S. A. Kuczaj, II (Ed.), *Discourse development, progress in cognitive development research.* New York: Springer-Verlag.

Froschels, E. (1942). Pathology and therapy of stuttering. *The Nervous Child, 2,* 146–161.

Gallagher, T. (1983). Revision behaviors in the speech of normal children developing language. *Journal of Speech and Hearing Research, 20,* 303–318.

Gelman, R. (1978). Cognitive development. *Annual Review of Psychology, 29,* 297–332.

Gerber, A., & Bryen, D. N. (1981). *Language and Learning Disabilities.* Baltimore: University Park Press.

Gumperz, J. J., & Cook-Gumperz, J. (1981). Ethnic differences in communicative style. In C. A. Ferguson & S. B. Heath (Eds.), *Language in the USA.* New York: Cambridge University Press.

Gumperz, J. J., & Hymes, D. (Eds.). (1964). The ethnography of communication, part II. *American Anthropologist, 66*(6).

Gumperz, J. J., & Tannen, D. (1972). *Directions in Sociolinguistics.* New York: Holt, Rinehart and Co.

Hand, H. H. (1981). The relation between developmental level and spontaneous behavior: The importance of sampling contexts. In K. W. Fischer (Ed.), *Cognitive development.* San Francisco: Jossey-Bass.

Hart, L. A. (1983). *Human brain and human learning.* New York: Longmans.

Heath, S. B. (1982). What no bedtime story means: Narrative skills at home and at school. *Language in Society, 11*(1), 49–77.

Hedrick, D. L., & Kemp, J. C. (1984). Guidelines for communicative intervention with younger retarded children. *Topics in Language Disorders, 5,* 1.

Irving, W. (1824). Tales of a traveller. Quoted in J. Bartlett (Ed.), *Familiar quotations,* p. 446. Boston: Little, Brown and Co.

Israel, L. (1984). Word knowledge and word retrieval: Phonological and semantic strategies. In G. Wallach & K. G. Butler (Eds.), *Language learning disabilities in school-age children.* Baltimore: Williams and Wilkins.

Jackendoff, R. (1983). *Semantics and cognition.* Cambridge, MA: MIT Press.

Johnston, J. (1981). Thinking and talking about space. *Topics in Language Disorders, 2*(1), 17–32.

Kahn, J. V. (1984). Cognitive training and initial use of referential speech. *Topics in Language Disorders, 5,* 1, 14–28.

Kail, R. V., & Hagen, J. W. (1977). *Perspectives on the development of memory and cognition.* Hillsdale, NJ: Erlbaum.

Kavanaugh, J. F., & Mattingly, I. G. (Eds.). (1972). *Language by ear and by eye, The relationship between speech and reading.* Cambridge, MA: The MIT Press.

Kertesz, A. (1983). *Localization in neuropsychology.* Orlando, FL: Academic Press.

Klein-Konigsberg, E. (1984). Semantic integration and language learning disabilities: From research to assessment and intervention. In G. Wallach and K. G. Butler (Eds.), *Language learning disabilities in school-age children.* Baltimore: Williams and Wilkins.

Laird, C. (1953). *The miracle of language.* New York: Fawcett.

Lasky, E. Z., & Klopp, K. (1982). Parent-child interactions in normal and language disordered children. *Journal of Speech and Hearing Research, 47,* 7–18.

Lebrun, Y. (1980). Victor of Aveyron: A reappraisal in light of more recent cases of feral speech. *Language Sciences*, *2*(1), 32–43.

Lieven, E. V. M. (1984). Interaction style and children's language learning. *Topics in Language Disorders*, *4*(4), 15–23.

Lund, N. J., & Duchan, J. E. (1983). *Assessing children's language in naturalistic contexts*. Englewood Cliffs, NJ: Prentice-Hall.

Maxwell, D. (1984). The neurology of learning and language disabilities: Developmental considerations. In G. Wallach & K. G. Butler (Eds.), *Language learning disabilities in school-age children*. Baltimore: Williams & Wilkins.

McCormick, L., & Schiefelbusch, R. L. (1984). *Early language intervention*. Columbus, OH: Charles E. Merrill.

Meadow, K. (1980). *Deafness and child development*. Berkeley: University of California Press.

Meichenbaum, D. (1980). Cognitive behavior modification with exceptional children. *Exceptional Education Quarterly*, *1*(1), 83–88.

Meichenbaum, M. H., & Goodman, J. (1971). Training impulsive children to talk to themselves: A means of developing self control. *Journal of Abnormal Psychology*, *77*, 115–126.

Menyuk, P. (1975). Children with language problems: What's the problem? *Proceedings of the Twenty-sixth Annual Georgetown Linguistics Roundtable*, pp. 129–144. Washington, DC: Georgetown University.

Michaels, S. (1981). "Sharing time": Children's narrative styles and differential access to literacy. *Language in Society*, *10*, 423–442.

Miller, J. F. (1981). *Assessing language production in children, experimental procedures*. Baltimore: University Park Press.

Miller, J. F., Chapman, R. S., Branston, M. B., & Riechle, J. (1980). Language comprehension in sensorimotor stages V and VI. *Journal of Speech and Hearing Research*, *23*, 284–311.

Miller, L. (1984). Problem solving and language disorders. In G. Wallach & K. G. Butler (Eds.), *Language learning disabilities in school-age children*. Baltimore: Williams & Wilkins.

Morine-Dershimer, G. (1981). *The literate pupil*. Syracuse, NY: Syracuse University.

Nelson, N. W. (1984). Beyond information processing: The language of teachers and textbooks. In G. Wallach & K. G. Butler (Eds.), *Language learning disabilities in school-age children*. Baltimore: Williams and Wilkins.

Newport, E. L., Gleitman, H., & Gleitman, L. R. (1977). Mother, I'd rather do it myself: Some effects and non-effects of maternal speech style. In C. E. Snow & C. A. Ferguson (Eds.), *Talking to children: Language input and acquisition*. Cambridge, England: Cambridge University Press.

Norman, D. (1972). The role of memory in the understanding of language. In J. F. Kavanaugh & I. G. Mattingly (Eds.), *Language by ear and by eye, The relationship between speech and reading*. Cambridge, MA: MIT Press.

Olson, D. (1982). The language of schooling. *Topics in Language Disorders*, *2*(4), 1–12.

Ornstein, P. A. (Ed.). (1978). *Memory development in children*. Hillsdale, NJ: Erlbaum.

Paivio, A. (1983). Strategies in language learning. In M. Pressley & J. R. Levin (Eds.), *Cognitive strategy research: Educational applications*. New York: Springer-Verlag.

Perlmutter, M. (Ed.). (1980). *Children's memory*. San Francisco: Jossey-Bass.

Piaget, J. (1970). Piaget's theory. In P. H. Mussen (Ed.), *Carmichael's Manual of Child Psychology* (Vol. 1). New York: Wiley.

Potter, D. (1954). *Language in the modern world*. Baltimore: Penguin Books.

Rieke, J. A., & Lewis, J. (1984). Preschool intervention strategies: The communication base, *Topics in Language Disorders*, *5*(1), 41–57.

Romski, M. A., Sevcik, R. A., & Joyner, S. E. (1984). Nonspeech communication systems: Implications for language intervention with mentally retarded children. *Topics in Language Disorders*, *5*(1), 66–81.

Roth, S. F., & Perfetti, C. A. (1980). A framework for reading, language comprehension, and language disability. *Topics in Language Disorders*, *1*, 15–28.

Sachs, J. (1980). The role of adult-child play in language development. *New Directions in Child Development*, *9*, 33–48.

Sajavaaro, K. (1981). *Message processing and language acquisition in the foreign language teaching context*. A paper read at the BAAL Seminar on Interactive Strategies in Language Learning, University of Lancaster, England, September 24–25.

Schiefelbusch, R. L., & Pickar, J. (1984). *The acquisition of communicative competence*. Baltimore: University Park Press.

Schieffelin, B. B., & Eisenberg, A. R. (1984). Cultural variation in children's conversation. In R. L. Schiefelbusch & J. Pickar (Eds.), *The acquisition of communicative competence*. Baltimore: University Park Press.

Schlesinger, I. M. (1977). The role of cognitive development and linguistic input in language acquisition. *Journal of Child Language*, *4*, 153–169.

Segalowitz, S. J. (1983). *Language functions and brain organization*. Orlando, FL: Academic Press.

Shantz, C. U. (1981). The role of role-taking in children's referential communication. In W. P. Dickson (Ed.), *Children's oral communication skills*. New York: Academic Press.

Shatz, M., & Gelman, R. (1973). The development

of communication skills: Modifications in the speech of young children as a function of the listener. *Monographs of the Society for Research in Child Development*, 38(5, Serial No. 152).

Silliman, E. (1984). Interactional competencies in the instructional context: The role of teaching discourse in learning. In G. P. Wallach & K. G. Butler (Eds.), *Language learning disabilities in school-age children*. Baltimore: Williams and Wilkins.

Skinner, B. G. (1957). *Verbal behavior.* New York: Appleton-Century-Crofts.

Slobin, D. I. (Ed.). (1967). *A field manual for the cross-cultural study of the acquisition of communicative competence.* Berkeley: University of California, Language Behavior Research Lab.

Slobin, D. I. (1977). Language change in childhood and in history. In J. McNamara (Ed.), *Language learning and thought.* New York: Academic Press.

Snow, C. E. (1982). Are parents language teachers? In K. Borman (Ed.), *Social life of children in a changing society.* Hillsdale, NJ: Erlbaum.

Snow, C. E. (1984). Foreword. Language development and disorders in the social context. *Topics in Language Disorders*, 4(4), v.

Snyder, L. (1983). Pragmatics and information processing. *Topics in Language Disorders*, 4(1), 75–86.

Spear, J. M., & Gerber, S. F. (1982). After early identification: Next steps for very young severely hearing impaired children, *Topics in Language Disorders*, 2(3), 1–7.

Spinelli, F. M., & Terrell, B. Y. (1984). Remediation in context. *Topics in Language Disorders*, 5(1).

Sugarman, S. (1984). The development of preverbal communication: Its contribution and limits in promoting the development of language. In R. L. Schiefelbusch & J. Pickar (Eds.), *The acquisition of communicative competence.* Baltimore: University Park Press.

Tager-Flusberg, H. (1981). Linguistic functioning in autism. *Journal of Autism and Developmental Disabilities*, 11, 45–56.

Travis, L. E. (1940). The need for stuttering. *Journal of Speech Disorders*, 5, 193–202.

Urwin, E. V. M. (1984). Language for absent things: Learning from visually handicapped children, *Topics in Language Disorders*, 4:(4), 24–37.

U.S. Department of Education (1984). Children receiving special education, by disability. *Education of the Handicapped*, 10(15), 6.

Van Riper, C. (1947). *Speech correction: Principles and methods* (2nd ed.) New York: Prentice-Hall.

Wasserman, G. A., Allen, R., & Solomon, R. C. (1982). *At-risk toddlers and their mothers: The special case of physical handicap.* Unpublished manuscript available from Department of Child Psychiatry, New York State Psychiatric Institute, West 168th St., New York, NY.

Wellman, H. H., & Somerville, S. C. (1980). Quasi-naturalistic tasks in the study of cognition: The memory-related skills of toddlers. In M. Perlmutter (Ed.), *Children's memory*, pp. 33–48. San Francisco: Jossey-Bass.

Westby, C. (1984a). Development of narrative language abilities. In G. P. Wallach & K. G. Butler (Eds.), *Language learning disabilities in school-age children.* Baltimore: Williams and Wilkins.

Westby, C. (1984b). Learning to talk — talking to learn: Oral/literate language differences. In C. Simon (Ed.), *Communication and classroom skills in school-aged children: Assessment and programming methodologies.* San Diego, CA: College-Hill Press.

Westby, C. (1984c, July). Language prerequisites for literacy. A paper presented before the International Child Language Congress.

White, S. J., & White, R. E. C. (1982). The deaf imperative: Characteristics of maternal input to hearing-impaired children. *Topics in Language Disorders*, 4(4), 38–49.

Whitehurst, G. J., & Sonnenschien, S. (1981). The development of information messages in referential communication: Knowing when vs. knowing how. In S. P. Dickson (Ed.), *Children's oral communication skills.* New York: Academic Press.

Wiig, E. H., & Semel, E. M. (1980). *Language assessment and intervention for the learning disabled.* Columbus, OH: Charles E. Merrill.

Wiig, E. H., & Semel, E. (1984). *Language assessment and intervention for the learning disabled.* Columbus, OH: Charles E. Merrill.

Yoder, D. E. (1982). Foreword, Communication strategies for the severely communicatively impaired. *Topics in Language Disorders*, 2(2), ix.

10 CHILDREN WITH SENSORY IMPAIRMENTS: PERSPECTIVES ON DEVELOPMENT

Ivan S. Terzieff
Shirin D. Antia

This chapter will explore the research on the effects of sensory deficits of hearing and vision on linguistic, cognitive, and psychosocial development. Since these senses are the major avenues for interaction with the social and physical environment, the loss of either sense is likely to have major repercussions on development. Three major areas of development will be examined: communication development, cognitive development, and psychosocial development. A final section will deal with technological aids that are expected to assist the functioning of these children.

The term *sensory impairment* refers to a loss of either hearing or of vision. *Hearing impairment* is a generic term indicating a hearing disability that may range from a mild to a profound loss. In general, children with mild to moderate hearing losses are referred to as *hard of hearing*, while children with severe or profound losses are referred to as *deaf*. Researchers differ regarding the level of loss considered moderate, severe, or profound. Most research has examined the behavior of children with severe to profound hearing losses sustained before the age of three years.

Visual impairment indicates a loss of vision that may range from total blindness to partial vision. Most research has examined the behavior of congenitally totally blind children.

COMMUNICATION DEVELOPMENT

Hearing Impaired

A considerable body of research is concerned in some way with the effects of hearing impairment on communication. In general, this research can be divided into two major categories: research describing the communication development and communication behavior of hearing impaired children as compared to hearing children; and research comparing the effects of different communicative environments on communication behavior. Early research on the effect of hearing impairment on communication has centered mainly on describing the written language of hearing impaired children through classification of errors in language structure and vocabulary (Heider & Heider, 1940; Myklebust, 1960; Simmons, 1962). The procedures in these studies involved obtaining and analyzing written language samples from prelingual severe-profound hearing impaired children. Findings from these early studies indicated that hearing impaired children had less flexible use of language than hearing children (Simmons, 1962), used shorter and simpler sentences (Heider & Heider, 1940), and used a higher proportion of nouns and tended to omit function words (Myklebust, 1960). One of the problems with such research was that, although it provided a description of the problems of hearing impaired children in producing correct English structure, the researchers were not able to determine whether specific errors of hearing impaired children were rule generated or random errors; that is, although these studies indicated major differences between the language structures of hearing and hearing impaired children, they were not able to determine whether hearing impaired children were delayed or deviant in their language production.

A few studies attempted to discover whether hearing impaired children had internalized a knowledge of English structure. Odom and Blanton (1967) presented hearing impaired children with the task of imitating structurally sound English phrases and phrases in which the word order had been scrambled. They hypothesized that children who had internalized the structural rules of English would perform better on the structurally sound phrases than on the scrambled phrases. The hearing impaired children performed similarly on both tasks, which led researchers to conclude that these children attempted to remember single words rather than "chunk" words into phrases according to their knowledge of language structure. A similar procedure was used by Tomblin (1977) with hearing and hearing impaired adolescents, aged 14–17. He found that both groups of children made fewer errors on the scrambled phrases than the structurally sound phrases, though the hearing impaired children were less accurate than the hearing on both tasks. These results indicated that the hearing impaired children had, by adolescence, acquired sufficient knowledge of English structural rules to enable them to process language at a level higher than single words, although they were still considerably delayed when compared to their hearing peers.

During the last 15–20 years, the knowledge and techniques of transformational generative grammar have enabled researchers to use more sophisticated methods to examine the language of hearing impaired individuals. Quigley and his associates at the University of Illinois spent the last 10 years examining the acquisition of a variety of syntactic structures by hearing impaired individuals, 11–18 years of age (Quigley & King, 1980; Quigley, Montanelli, & Wilbur, 1976; Quigley, Wilbur, & Montanelli, 1974, 1976; Wilbur, Quigley, & Montanelli, 1975). The purpose of the research was to identify how well established English transformational rules were in the language of hearing impaired individuals and to determine whether hearing impaired individuals followed the same sequence of rule-learning for English structures as did hearing individuals. The research also examined whether hearing impaired individuals acquired and used rules that were not acquired by hearing individuals. An extensive testing program was carried out between 1969 and 1976 using as subjects over 400 severe-profound hearing impaired students, 10–18 years of age, from residential schools and day schools for the hearing impaired throughout the country. All the subjects in the research had normal intelligence and no disability apart from hearing impairment. A group of 60 hearing children between the ages of 8–10 provided a comparison group. It is not possible to compare hearing and hearing impaired children of similar chronological ages on a language assessment measure because any measure that provides information on the language structures of hearing impaired children is too simple for hearing children, while language measures that discriminate among hearing children are generally inappropriate for the hearing impaired due to the severe language delay.

An assessment tool was developed that examined major areas of English syntactic structure: negativization, question formation, conjunction, pronominalization, relativization, and the verb system. A variety of formats were used to assess these structures including judgments of grammatical correctness, rewriting incorrect sentences, and comprehension of grammatical structures. Results showed that, in general, both hearing and hearing impaired students had difficulty with the same kinds of structures. However, no conclusions can be made about similarity in order of acquisition of language structures. For several of the structures studied, it was found that hearing students did not show improvement with increasing age, but performed at high levels across ages. Thus, no conclusions can be made about the order of acquisition in hearing children. An order of acquisition was established for the hearing impaired children who showed marked delays in all structures. At 18 years of age, the hearing impaired children did not reach the level of competence of hearing children on any structure studied.

Within each structure, hearing impaired children were found to follow sequences of development similar to those described for hearing children in the literature on development. However, several errors made by the hearing impaired students appeared to be generated by rules that were not learned by hearing children. Thus, although a large number of errors in the language of adolescent hearing impaired children were due to developmental delays, several were due to deviant language rules. It is important to note that Quigley et al. found these errors to be rule generated and not random, indicating that the hearing impaired children were not processing language at the single word level.

The research by Quigley et al. has provided the field of hearing impairment with a major portion of the knowledge base on the acquisition of English structure by hearing impaired children and a detailed analysis of the errors produced by these children. The research, however, concentrated on children 11–18 years of age and examined fairly complex language structures. There is a major gap in our knowledge of hearing impaired children's language at younger ages and their acquisition of basic sentence structure.

Research in the language development of young hearing impaired children is complicated by several factors. Unlike older hear-

ing impaired children, a stable sample of language, such as a written sample, is not readily available. Interpretation of oral language behavior is complicated by unintelligible speech, and interpretation of sign language may be confounded by the presence of idiosyncratic sign systems and gestures that developed between mother and child in the absence of an accepted communication system. Nevertheless, it is of utmost importance to study the early language acquisition of hearing impaired children, since research with hearing children suggests that there is a critical language learning period from age 0–5 years, when the foundation is laid for all language learning.

Recent research in communication development in hearing children has emphasized the importance of function and content in children's language. Thus, hearing children have been found to use gestures and one word utterances to code communicative acts such as requesting, responding, labeling, and so on (Dore, 1975; Halliday, 1979). In addition, longitudinal studies of hearing children's early utterances have generated semantic grammars, which are composed of such "meaning" categories as agents, actions, patients, instruments, and so forth, in contrast to syntax grammar categories of nouns, verbs, adjectives, and so forth. Early utterances of hearing children have been found to code several different semantic relationships, even though their language syntax is incomplete and lacks many features of the adult language.

Research on the development of language function and content in hearing impaired children is just beginning. Typically, these studies have recorded the communication attempts of hearing impaired children both verbal (oral and sign language) and nonverbal (gestures and pantomime) and attempted to classify these by the semantic and functional categories used to classify communicative attempts of hearing children. Due to the restricted number of studies and the small numbers and variability of the children studied, conclusions from this research are necessarily tentative. However, they do provide a new direction for future research with hearing impaired children and have some major implications for language intervention.

An early study by Scroggs (1977) indicated that semantic categories and semantic relationships generated by researchers studying the language of hearing children could be used to describe the language of hearing impaired children. Since then, several researchers have analyzed the verbal and nonverbal communication of hearing impaired children in an attempt to determine whether they use the same communicative functions and semantic relations as hearing children acquiring language. Curtiss, Prutting, and Lowell (1979) studied communicative and semantic functions of 12 hearing impaired children exposed only to an oral language system. The children ranged in age from 22 months to 60 months and had severe to profound hearing losses. Videotapes were made of their communicative behaviors in five different settings. The tapes were then analyzed for the number of communicative acts, verbal and gestural. Each communicative act was classified for its communicative function as well as its semantic intent, using taxonomies developed by Dore (1975), and Greenfield and Smith (1976) to categorize early one and two word utterances of hearing children. Results indicated that the number of communicative acts of the hearing impaired subjects increased with age, and that the entire range of communicative functions found in hearing children was present in each age group. The number of semantic categories used also increased with age, with the youngest group (2 year olds) expressing only two categories and the oldest group (4 year olds) expressing nine categories. Unlike hearing children, the hearing impaired children were reported to use gestures to communicate both communicative functions and semantic relations. Thus, most of the semantic relations (conjoining of two semantic functions to express a relationship) expressed by the 4 year old hearing impaired children consisted of a word plus a gesture. Despite the use of gesture, increased semantic complexity was accompanied by an increase in mean length of utterance (MLU), which is an index of lan-

guage complexity in hearing children. The authors concluded that hearing impaired children were, for the most part, developing language along lines essentially similar to hearing children. Since the researchers did not intend to compare the language development of hearing and hearing impaired children, they did not include any hearing children as controls in the study. It would be valuable for future researchers to determine whether MLU is as appropriate an index for language growth in young hearing impaired children as it is in young hearing children by comparing the semantic complexity in the language of hearing and hearing impaired children with similar MLU. It is possible that hearing impaired children will continue to use gesture-word combinations rather than multiword utterances to communicate semantic relations, which may result in an increase in the number of semantic categories and relations being communicated without a corresponding growth in MLU. In hearing children, semantic and syntactic complexity proceed on parallel lines; that is, complex semantic relations are expressed using increasingly complex syntactic structures. Some authors have speculated that the reverse might be true for hearing impaired children; that is, they may learn increasingly complex semantic relations without the corresponding learning of language structures (Miller, 1980).

A logical extension of the work of Curtiss et al. would be to examine the language growth of hearing impaired children using a longitudinal design. A cross-sectional approach, which involves inferring developmental patterns by comparing children of different ages at the same time, tends to obscure individual developmental patterns and the factors that influence them. Curtiss et al. found, for example, that individual differences within age groups were, at time, larger than differences between age groups. In order to draw conclusions and to generalize the findings of such cross-sectional research, a large number of subjects is needed and factors that may lead to intragroup variation need to be controlled. This may not be feasible, since the population of prelingually hearing impaired children is small, and there is wide variation in degree of hearing loss and communicative environment, both of which contribute substantially to language acquisition. Longitudinal designs may be able to pinpoint more realistically the patterns of language development, their comparability to normal language development, and the factors that influence language development in young hearing impaired children.

One of the factors that influences communication development in hearing impaired children is the communication environment. Most research in the field of hearing impairment has looked at oral vs. total communication environments in an effort to determine which mode is most beneficial for communication development. Oral communication involves the use of speech, speech reading, and audition, while total communication adds to these the use of a sign system and fingerspelling. Some of these studies have taken the form of comparing the communication and academic abilities of hearing impaired children of hearing impaired parents, who use sign in the home, with hearing impaired children of hearing parents, who use oral language (Meadow, 1968; Stuckless & Birch, 1966; Vernon & Koh, 1970). Generally, these studies have found children with hearing impaired parents to be superior to children of hearing parents in the area of written language and reading, although no differences were found in speech or speech reading abilities. However, since these were ex post facto studies, the differences could be due to factors other than communication environment; for example, parental acceptance of the hearing impaired child. In addition, differences found between the two groups, although statistically significant, were not necessarily educationally significant.

Other studies have attempted to demonstrate the superiority of one communication mode over another by testing comprehension of language presented through several different modes of communication. Klopping (1972) presented 30 students at a residential school

with stories under three different conditions: speech reading and voice, fingerspelling, and total communication. He found that comprehension scores were highest for the stories presented through total communication and lowest for those presented through speech reading and voice. White and Stevenson (1975) also compared comprehension of factual passages presented through oral, total, and manual (sign only) modes and reading. Students gained the least information from oral communication. There are several major problems in these studies that prevent any conclusions being drawn from them. No information was provided on the mode of communication with which the subjects were most familiar. It would be unusual for students exposed only to manual communication to obtain much information through an oral mode. In addition, language comprehension is dependent on the child's knowledge of the language code as well as the mode of communication used. No information was available on the language level of the subjects, a crucial omission, since language knowledge rather than mode of communication may have been responsible for the results reported. In short, such studies provide the field with little understanding of communication development in hearing impaired children.

Brasel and Quigley (1977) compared the language ability of hearing impaired children from four different communicative environments. One group had hearing impaired parents who used American Sign Language, a second group had hearing impaired parents who used Manual English (English representation in sign), a third group had hearing parents who provided an intense oral language environment, while the fourth group had hearing parents who, though their children were enrolled in oral programs, made no undue effort to provide a good language environment in the home. Results showed that children with Manual English environments performed significantly better than the other groups on communication ability, while the groups from average oral environments (the fourth group) performed significantly poorer than the other three groups. Though this research used an ex post facto design, the presence of two groups of children with hearing impaired parents enabled the researchers to separate the effects of communication environment from parental acceptance of deafness. It also demonstrated that researchers comparing communication environments need to look not only at the mode of communication but also at the kind of language used in the home.

The communication environment extends to the classroom, which is where many hearing impaired children are expected to acquire their communication skills. Early research on classroom communicative environments concentrated mainly on the ratio of student talk to teacher talk (Craig & Collins, 1970). Recently researchers have turned their attention to the grammaticality of signed English representation within the classroom. Marmor and Petitto (1979) examined the signed English used by two teachers of the hearing impaired and found that only 5–8% of their declarative sign sentences were exact representations of spoken English. Deletions of main subject and verb of the sentence occurred, as well as deletions of bound morphemes such as verb tense markers and plural markers, and functions such as articles and prepositions. This research should be considered preliminary research, for no attempt was made to objectively determine the signing competence of the teachers, the sign policy of the school, or the training the teachers had received in signed English. Nevertheless, it leads to the speculation that one reason for the delayed English structure acquisition in hearing impaired children may be due to the incomplete models of English provided in instructional environments. Such an incomplete language model has been often cited as a reason for the poor performance of hearing impaired children in oral environments and has been used as a rationale for the move towards total communication. Unfortunately, it appears that a total communication environment need not necessarily provide a suitable language model either.

A final area of language research that holds great promise is research on sustained dialogue between children. McKirdy and Blank (1982) studied the dialogue between dyads of hearing and hearing impaired preschoolers. They found that the hearing impaired dyads engaged in language behavior quite different, both in its cognitive complexity and its social interactive quality, from the hearing dyads. Hearing impaired children initiated significantly less communication than the hearing children and commented less on the speaker's utterances; for example, they tended not to sustain dialogue. The content of hearing impaired children's utterances tended to center almost exclusively around simple labeling of objects and events and requesting attention and objects. Hearing children, on the other hand, commented on attributes, possession, location, and function of objects, and on conditional relationships. They also formulated solutions to problems, identified causes, and explained inferences of an event. This is one of the few studies to examine hearing impaired children's communication in an interactive situation. With the exception of one dyad, the hearing impaired children were drawn from oral environments. It is possible that quite different results would be obtained from children in total communication environments. It would also be interesting to note whether linguistic competence measured by MLU or some other index is related to hearing impaired children's ability to sustain continued dialogue and use cognitively complex language. Another profitable area for research would be to examine the transfer of linguistic principles learned in the classroom to communication situations which require connected discourse.

A review of research on the communication development of deaf children indicates that although there is a considerable body of information on school age children, there is comparatively little information on communication development in young deaf children. Researchers need to take a critical look at the communicative environment and its effect on language acquisition. There is also a need to examine the ability of hearing impaired children to transfer language knowledge from a classroom to other communication situations.

Visually Impaired

A cursory look at the literature indicates that it is primarily an accumulation of observations. Although these observations have raised many questions, few of those have been thoroughly researched. Visually impaired children, with no other handicapping conditions, presumably acquire language successfully and have no difficulty in verbal communication. Traditionally, however, visual impairment has been regarded as having an inhibiting effect in most areas of development. It would follow that visual impairment may have a debilitating effect on language development and communication efficiency.

Burlingham (1961) and Haspiel (1965) indicated that there are no basic differences in babbling between visually impaired and sighted infants. This view supports the findings of Wilson and Halverson (1947) in a study of a single blind child. Wilson and Halverson reported developmental lags in all areas but in babbling. However, Maxfield and Fjeld (1942) in a study involving a group of visually impaired preschool children reported that this sample showed a developmental lag in babbling when compared to sighted children. That conclusion was based on responses to a single item from the Vineland Social Maturity Scale. The later stages of babbling, when sound sets are being refined, have not been investigated. Although several investigations dealing with speech and voice production have been conducted, there appears to be no agreement among researchers on the prevalence of speech defects or voice disorders in visually impaired children. Brieland (1950), in a study involving congenitally blind youths aged 12–18 from several residential schools and a matching sighted control group from a public high school, concluded that both groups performed equally well. Each subject recited a previously memorized story and each recitation was filmed and tape recorded. The performance was

rated by speech teachers on degrees of lip movement, pitch modulation, vocal variety, use of loudness, and rate of speaking. The results indicated that the visually impaired scored significantly better on pitch modulation and spoke at a slower rate, while the control group scored significantly better on lip movement with no difference in sound production. The judges were unable to distinguish between visually impaired and sighted subjects on the basis of vocal performance alone.

Entirely different results were reported by Miner (1963). In a study of 293 visually impaired elementary schoolchildren from residential schools (no control group was reported), Miner concluded that the overall incidence of speech deviations was four to five times that of sighted children. In a conversation with a speech therapist, each child was judged on articulation defects, 3.4% had voice disorders, and one child was found to stutter. These conclusions are strikingly different from those of Brieland (1950) but support the findings of an earlier study by Stinchfield (1933), who reported that 49% of the subjects she studied exhibited speech defects. Although the results reported that 49% of the subjects she studied exhibited speech defects. Although the results of these studies may be interpreted with caution, the possible relationship between sound production and restricted motor behavior (Sibinga & Friedman, 1971) warrants detailed investigation.

The area of word meaning is perhaps the one most thoroughly investigated, because of the concern that use of words out of the realm of tangible sensory experiences for the visually impaired may restrict their cognitive capacities to some unknown extent (Warren, 1977). Cutsforth (1932) coined the term *verbalism* to define the use of such words. In a study with congenitally blind children employing a word association test, each subject was asked to respond to words representing objects varying in their degree of sensory availability. Cutsforth found that 48% of the responses contained descriptions of visual qualities. He concluded that congenitally visually impaired children tend to employ more visual concepts than other sensory concepts that were just as available and perhaps more meaningful to them.

In a subsequent discussion of verbalism, Cutsforth (1951) argued that use of verbalism leads to "incoherent and loose thought." This conclusion had an effect on educational programming to the extent that use of concepts that did not have direct sensory referents were avoided.

In a review of the literature on verbalism, Dokecki (1966) argued that sighted people, like their visually impaired counterparts, also use many words that can not have sensory referents. These words obviously have specific meaning and do not lead to "loose thinking."

Burlingham (1961) pointed out that visually impaired children are encouraged to use words from the vocabulary of the sighted through reinforcement for imitation of parental speech. Thus, they develop vocabulary that in part is related to their sensory experiences and in part is not. This distinction, however, tends to diminish with development (Burlingham, 1955).

Nolan (1960) replicated Cutsforth's study of the frequency of visual responses in word association. He concluded that blind subjects "closely resembled" sighted children in their responses.

Harley (1963) investigated the relationship of verbalism to age, intelligence, experience, and personal adjustment. Forty congenitally totally blind subjects (7–14 years old) with a mean IQ of 100.12 from two residential schools were asked to provide definitions of 39 words and identify the objects corresponding to those words. The verbalism score was derived by subtracting the number of correctly identified objects from the number of "appropriate" definitions. Personal adjustment was measured by the Tuddenham Reputation Test, while experience was determined by counting the number of objects with which the subject had previous contact. Harley concluded that the younger, lower IQ, and lower experienced children showed higher incidence of verbalism, while personal adjustment was not affected by verbalism. In addition to supporting Burling-

ham's (1965) arguments, Harley attributed verbalism to the lack of sensory experiences and suggested that the "key to the reduction of verbalism among blind children is the increasing of interaction with their environments" (Harley, 1963 p. 32).

DeMott (1972) investigated the relationship between verbalism and affective meaning. Two groups of visually impaired children (7–20 years old) and a matching sighted control group were asked to define 30 words and identify the physical objects corresponding to those words (measure of verbalism). To measure affective meaning, DeMott presented his subjects with 15 words, representing concepts, as stimuli for the semantic differential measured on a 5 point scale. A factor analysis indicated that there were no significant differences between groups in the affective meaning of concepts. This finding supports Dokecki's (1966) argument that "it still remains to be demonstrated that associative and word-thing meanings are functionally different for the blind or for any other group" (p. 528).

Anderson and Olson (1981) investigated object-concepts and verbal descriptions of objects. Ten congenitally visually impaired children (ages 3–9) of normal intelligence and a matching sighted control group were interviewed individually to obtain definitions and descriptions of 10 tangible and 10 intangible items. All responses were tape recorded and evaluated on the basis of egocentric (relating to personal experience), functional (function and action), and perceptual (color, etc.) attributes given in the definitions and description of each item. The results indicated that younger visually impaired children made a larger number of incorrect responses in regard to intangible items. The older visually impaired children, however, used more egocentric, functional, and perceptual attributes on both types of items than the younger visually impaired subjects, while no significant differences were found between age groups in the sighted controls. Data suggest that the language of visually impaired children represents a mental conceptualization of objects developed through experiences. Presumably, the older visually impaired subjects have had greater and more varied experiences than did the younger ones. These findings support Harley's (1963) argument that use of word-meaning is based on experience and that use of attributes is related to age.

McGinnis (1981) investigated the functional linguistic strategies of visually impaired children. Six visually impaired (ages 4.2–5.0) and six sighted (ages 3.5–5.0) children were engaged in formal conversations and tape recorded. The author examined the children's "management of specific linguistic task-visual reference" (p. 212); more specifically, reference to items only visually perceivable and "see" verbs. The results indicated that sighted children used more color words than did the blind. The author suggests that use of color words for the visually impaired is "only a linguistic description while for the sighted it is a linguistic representation of a visual distinction" (p. 212). In total use of "see" verbs, the sighted children exceeded the visually impaired by almost three times. A further investigation revealed that both groups used "see" verbs unrelated to vision with comparable frequency. This result may be due to the fact that such verbs as "think" and "understand" are equally nonsensory concepts for both groups. However, the sighted used "see" verbs directly related to vision more frequently than visually impaired children. McGinnis suggests that presence or absence of vision has an effect on the linguistic strategies used by children in managing visual references.

The research to date suggests that the language of visually impaired children, which to some extent and in some categories differs from that of the sighted, can not be considered as deviant as suggested by Cutsforth (1932, 1951). Verbalism appears to be developmental and based on the sensory experiences of the child.

A closely related issue, but less researched, is the development of early vocabulary and use of personal references by visually impaired children. Some investigators (Haspiel, 1965; Maxfield & Fjeld, 1942; Wilson & Halverson 1947) suggest that vocabulary development in visually impaired children is equally comparable to that of sighted children. Others (Burlingham, 1961, 1965; Keeler, 1958) suggested that in the early stages of vocabulary development the visually impaired lag behind their sighted counterparts. Thus, the question of an early vocabulary developmental lag can not be satisfactorily resolved at this time.

McGuire and Meyers (1971) in a longitudinal study of 27 totally blind children of mixed ages reported that 46% of the children referred to themselves in the third person. This report concurs with the findings by Fraiberg and Adelson (1973) who distinguished between the use of "'I' with verb forms" and that "used inventively in new combinations." Fraiberg and Adelson found that the use of "I" with verb forms did not differ from that of the sighted, while the use of inventive "I" did not appear in some visually impaired children until age 4.8. The investigators attributed the delay to the difficulties of visually impaired children with conceptual relationships between object and the word used to denote it, as suggested by Burlingham (1965). Similar findings were reported by McGinnis (1981), who found that visually impaired children "exceeded the sighted children in "I" confusion" (p. 213). Warren (1977) suggests that such delay may be due to the greater difficulties of visually impaired children to develop a cognitive self-image.

Research on syntactic development is almost nonexistent, but the studies conducted thus far (Maxfield, 1963; Maxfield & Fjeld, 1942; McGinnis, 1981; Tilman & Williams, 1968; Wilson & Halverson, 1947) suggest that the syntax of visually impaired children is similar to that of the sighted and that the mean length of utterances matched and in some cases exceeded those of the sighted children. It is interesting to note, however, that visually impaired children used fewer declarative and negative statements but asked more questions about themselves (Maxfield, 1936; McGinnis, 1981) and changed the topic of conversation more often (McGinnis, 1981).

Although communicative efficiency is enhanced by nonverbal communications, little research has been conducted in that area with visually impaired children. Obviously, a totally blind individual will not be able to interpret unseen nonverbal messages; however, effective use of such messages will enhance his or her ability in communication with the sighted. In a review of selected literature on nonverbal communication, Apple (1972) concluded that to a large extent nonverbal expressiveness is learned.

In a study involving blind adults, Dumas (1932) found that they had difficulties in production of appropriate facial expressions upon request. Freedman (1964), studying the early smiling behavior of blind and sighted infants, concluded that there is no significant difference in the course of its development. The discrepancy in findings between Dumas (adults) and Freedman (infants) suggests that the refinement and/or the maintenance of appropriate facial expressions may be dependent upon visually mediated imitation. Fulcher (1942), in a study involving visually impaired subjects (ages 6–21) and sighted controls (ages 4–16), requested the production of facial expressions representing happiness, fear, sadness, and anger. All subjects were photographed and the facial expressions were rated according to adequacy, amount of facial activity, and movement of specific facial parts. The results of the rating indicated that the sighted subjects exhibited age-related improvement in all three categories while the visually impaired did not.

In a more recent study, Parke, Shallcross, and Anderson (1980) investigated the coverbal behavior (nonverbal behavior that accompanies verbal interpersonal communication) of blind and sighted children. The study involved 30 braille reading and 30 sighted students (ages 5 years 8 months to 15 years 10 months). Subjects were matched according to race, sex, and intelligence. Four topical prerecorded questions were posed to each subject to initiate the interviews conducted by two of the authors. The interviews were videotaped for later evaluation of facial expressions. The investigators measured the duration and frequency of head nod, smile, and raised eyebrows. The results showed that blind subjects spent fewer percent of total interaction time nodding and their nods

were of shorter duration than the control subjects. Similar results were reported for duration of raised eyebrows, while no significant differences were found in percent of interaction time spent in raising eyebrows, smiling, and duration of smiles. In closer investigation of the results, it was found that 12 of the blind subjects did not nod their heads at all and 7 of the blind subjects "spent an extremely large amount of time smiling " (ranging from 30 to 91% of interaction time). The investigators concluded that the coverbal behaviors among blind and sighted persons are different.

The evidence suggests that the lack of vision may play a role in use of facial expression by visually impaired individuals. However, whether such expressiveness is trainable or, more important, whether the lack of expressiveness has a negative effect on the communicative efficiency of visually impaired individuals still remains to be determined.

The research on language development and language use indicates that, overall, there is little, if any, difference between visually impaired and sighted children, with notable exceptions in the area of verbalism and nonverbal communication. The review of the research reveals that almost all of the visually impaired subjects have been drawn from residential schools and the questions studied dealt with developmental lags between visually impaired and sighted individuals.

More reasonable questions, although more difficult to research, would be whether such lags are functionally involved in other abilities that depend on language, such as interpersonal communication, cognitive development, etc. In addition, the diversity among the visually impaired and diversity of educational placements demand that the degree of visual impairment and environmental influences on language development be investigated.

Discussion

It is clear that, while communication development has received a great deal of attention in the area of hearing impairment, comparatively little research is available on the communication development of visually impaired children. Research with hearing impaired children indicates major delays in syntactic development and reveals certain differences between hearing and hearing impaired children in the areas of semantic and pragmatic development as well. Conclusions from the research with visually impaired children are more difficult to make. It appears that no two investigators can fully agree to the effect of visual impairment on communication. Some researchers suggest that there is considerable delay in all stages of language development, while others indicate that there is little, if any, difference between visually impaired and sighted children.

Both fields have spent a considerable amount of time in what might be considered dead-end research. In the field of hearing impairment, large amounts of time and energy have gone into attempting to show the superiority of one mode of communication over another. It is becoming increasingly obvious that mode of communication is only one of many factors that affect the communicative competence of the child. Unfortunately, the emphasis on mode of communication has deflected attention from research on intervention techniques that would enable hearing impaired children to communicate to their maximum capacity. Techniques such as imitation, modeling, expansion, and various linguistically based approaches have been used in classrooms, but little systematic inquiry has been made of their effectiveness in developing language.

Researchers in the field of visual impairments have studied word meaning because of Cutsforth's notion of "verbalisms" and his argument that verbalism leads to "incoherent and loose thinking." Obviously, this argument cannot be substantiated and has deflected researchers from such issues as the relationship between early linguistic development and concept development in visually impaired children. Current information and research techniques in child language development, specifically the area of semantic development, can probably be applied profitably to the study of language development in visually impaired children.

Research techniques to study semantic and pragmatic language development in normal children can also be applied to the study of language development in hearing impaired children. A considerable amount of knowledge has been accumulated on the syntactic development of school-age children, but little information is available on the other aspects of language development. Information on the child's ability to control, or fail to control, his environment through intentional communication, gestural or verbal, is the base for further language development and the starting point for language intervention programs. Research in this area may correct the tendency of educators to emphasize the development of surface structure rules and ignore other aspects of communication.

An area of investigation that seems promising for both fields is the development of conversational skills that are essential for integration into the larger society. The research suggests that visually impaired children may change topics frequently, a behavior that may be negatively perceived by their conversational partner. Communication between two individuals is generally thought to be facilitated by facial expressions and body movements. Such coverbal behaviors are visually mediated and learned, yet the relationship between these behaviors and the onset of visual impairment has not been investigated. Another question to be investigated might be the extent to which conversation is affected by the lack of, or improper use of, coverbal behaviors.

Hearing impaired children have been found to have difficulty maintaining conversational topics and initiating and ending conversations (Geoffrion, 1982a, 1982b; McKirdy & Blank, 1982). Again, little is known about the development of these skills, and intervention techniques to develop these skills. In fact, conversation skills are often neglected when an emphasis is laid on syntax development.

An area of concern specific to the hearing impaired concerns the ability of teachers to provide a visible English model to their students (Marmor & Petitto, 1979). It raises the questions of whether it is possible to represent

English through a manual model and under what circumstances such a representation is possible. A corresponding question is the effect of an incomplete language model on the language acquisition of the hearing impaired child. Brasel and Quigley (1977) indicate that language models affect the learning of syntactic structures. However, it would be interesting to investigate whether syntax errors made by models (either parents or teachers) are reflected in syntax errors made by the child.

Speech development in visually impaired children is an area of concern, since some investigators (Miner, 1963; Stinchfield, 1933) found that the incidence of voice quality and sound production problems is greater among visually impaired than sighted children, although early sound production (i.e., babbling) does not seem to be affected. This raises the questions of whether later sound production is visually mediated and whether there is a relationship between sound production and restricted motor behavior.

Finally, it should be noted that there are few indepth longitudinal studies on the communication development of either visually or hearing impaired children. This is surprising when one considers that longitudinal research has provided the richest body of knowledge on normal language development and can be expected to provide both fields with similar knowledge. It is hoped that such research will be given priority for sensory impaired children.

COGNITIVE DEVELOPMENT

Hearing Impaired

The area of cognitive development has received considerable attention in the literature on deafness because of the link between linguistic and cognitive development. The hearing impaired population has often served as a "laboratory" group to test the dependence or independence of cognition and language. Much of the research on cognitive development has followed a Piagetian model. Researchers have

compared the performance of hearing and hearing impaired children on several Piagetian tasks, mainly conservation tasks, and drawn conclusions about the relationship between language and cognition.

Early researchers such as Olerón and Herren (reported in Furth, 1966a) examined the performance of hearing impaired children on Piagetian conservation tasks to determine whether cognitive growth could take place in the "absence" of language. They found that hearing impaired individuals reached the level of concrete operations 6 years later than the hearing children and concluded that language was not a necessary condition for cognitive development. However, linguistic deficiency could retard cognitive development.

Much of the interest in cognitive development in hearing impaired children stems from the work of Hans Furth who hypothesized that any delay in cognitive development was due to experiential deprivation. Furth conducted a series of research studies examining the performance of hearing impaired children on various Piagetian tasks (Furth, 1964, 1966a). He realized that one of the formidable barriers to assessing cognitive development in hearing impaired children was the ability of the examiner to communicate the critical dimensions of the task and to provide the hearing impaired child with a means of responding that did not penalize him for his language or speech ability. Furth (1964), therefore, developed some nonverbal techniques for testing conservation of weight in hearing impaired children. His subjects consisted of 8 year old hearing impaired children and two groups of hearing controls aged 6 years and 8 years. He reported that 90% of the 8 year old hearing children and 41% of the 6 year old hearing children could conserve weight, while only 45% of the hearing impaired children were conservers. He concluded that hearing impaired children were 2 years behind hearing children, a considerable improvement over the 6 year year delay found by Olerón and Herren. Another study by Furth (1966b) examined the performances of hearing and hearing impaired adults on a color-form discovery task. He found no differences between the two groups on application of the concept; however, the hearing impaired adults had more difficulty than the hearing adults in initial attainment of the concept. In yet another study, Furth and Youniss (1969) found that hearing impaired adolescents were able to complete successfully at least one of six tasks designed to tap cognitive skills at the formal operational level. The results of these studies led Furth to conclude that language was not a necessary prerequisite to cognitive development and that the gap between cognitive development in hearing impaired and hearing children was considerably narrowed, if not erased, by adulthood. In order to explain this phenomenon, Furth reasoned that the delay in cognitive development of deaf children was due to a restricted environment rather than intellectual or linguistic deficiency. The hypothesis of experiential deficiency was supported by Darbyshire and Reeves (1969), who found no significant differences between hearing and hearing impaired children on the attainment of concepts at the preoperational and concrete operational levels. In this study, socioeconomic background rather than hearing loss proved to be the variable that contributed significantly to differences in performance.

Since Furth's early research, several attempts have been made to test the experiential vs. linguistic deprivation hypotheses. It has been assumed that a residential school generally provides a less stimulating environment than the home and, therefore, differences in the cognitive development of hearing impaired children in day and residential schools might reflect the relative influence of environment. Rittenhouse and Spiro (1979) compared the performance of 36 hearing children, 16 hearing impaired children in residential schools, and 24 hearing impaired children in day schools on conservation of number, liquid, volume, and weight. The hearing impaired subjects ranged between 7–19 years of age, while the hearing subjects ranged between 4–16 years of age. The conservation tasks were performed under two conditions: in one, the directions were given and questions were asked in the conventional Piagetian manner, using relational terms such as *more* and *less;* in the other, the directions and questions used attribute specific terms, which were expected to be less ambiguous. When directions were given using the Piagetian terms, significantly fewer residential students conserved than hearing students. There were no differences in the proportion of day or hearing students who conserved using conventional directions. When directions were given using the attribute specific terms, all the subjects improved their performance. However, there remained a significant difference between the number of residential and hearing students who were able to conserve. Under both conditions, the day school students' performance fell between that of the residential and hearing students but was not significantly different from either.

The results of the study indicate that the language used by the examiner affects conservation performance in all children, thus demonstrating one possible reason for the significant gap between the hearing impaired and hearing students in previous studies. However, the results are ambiguous regarding the effect of environment on cognitive development, since the difference between hearing impaired subjects in different educational environments did not reach significance. There is, most likely, an interaction between linguistic development and environment that this study was not able to examine.

Watts (1979) attempted to determine the effect of linguistic deficiency on cognitive development by comparing groups of hearing impaired children differing in degree of hearing loss. He compared the performance of deaf, hard of hearing, and hearing children on conservation tasks, spatial thinking, and social thinking. Hard of hearing children have less severe hearing loss than deaf children and generally reach higher levels of achievement and communication ability (Jensema, 1975). Thus, superiority of hard of hearing children over deaf children might reflect the contribution of language to cognitive development. Unfortunately, Watts reported neither the level of hearing loss nor the educational placement of the subjects in his study. He reported that some subjects were given reading and vocabulary tests that could provide an index of linguistic proficiency but did not report the results of these tests either.

Watts' subjects consisted of 70 deaf, 70 hard of hearing, and 70 hearing children ranging in age from 10–16 years. The conservation tasks involved conservation of cardinal numbers, quantity, length, weight, and area; the spatial thinking task involved predicting the water level in a bottle tilted at various angles; the social thinking task consisted of sequencing a series of pictures depicting a short story or a social situation. Results on the conservation tasks showed that at the younger ages (10–14), the hard of hearing children performed better than the deaf children; while at the older ages (15–16), the deaf children performed better than the hard of hearing children. A two-way analysis of variance yielded significant main effects for age and group (hearing, hard of hearing, and deaf) variables. There appears to be no satisfactory explanation for the group differences between the deaf and hard of hearing children. Watts reported that there was no improvement in reading scores between the deaf 10–14 year olds and 15–16 year olds. Therefore, the older deaf group's superiority could not be explained by a sudden spurt in linguistic growth. No significant differences were found between groups in spatial thinking or social thinking. A further examination of the results showed no increase with age in spatial thinking scores for the hearing or hard of hearing groups. There did, however, appear to be an age effect for the deaf students. This may indicate that the concept of space was attained earlier by the hearing and hard of hearing children than the deaf children.

Rittenhouse, Morreau, and Iran-Nejad (1981) also compared the performance of deaf and hard of hearing children on conservation of weight and liquid and found no difference between the groups. In fact, a multiple regression analysis to determine the influence of degree of hearing loss on conservation perfor-

mance yielded no significant results. Thus, the supposedly superior linguistic ability of hard of hearing children does not necessarily result in superior cognitive development.

It seems clear that attempts to examine the effect of linguistic deficiency or environmental impoverishment by comparing children with differing degrees of hearing loss or in different educational environments has yielded ambiguous results. However, the consistent delay in attainment of cognitive concepts by hearing impaired children (both deaf and hard of hearing) needs to be examined further, since it is probable that it exerts some influence on academic achievement. It should be possible to compare the cognitive development of hearing impaired children with poor linguistic skills and those with good linguistic skills to determine the effect of linguistic ability on cognitive development. Very few researchers have attempted to measure the linguistic ability of the subjects in these studies. Instead, it has been assumed that the presence of a hearing loss necessarily implies the presence of a linguistic deficiency. Since this is not necessarily true and since the degree of linguistic deficiency, when present, varies, it is essential that linguistic ability be directly measured. It may be that a certain minimum level of linguistic ability must be attained in order to function at the concrete and/or formal operational level. Oleron (1953) has theorized that language calls attention away from the perceptual aspect of the task and may help facilitate the acquisition of certain logico-mathematical concepts. This would explain the similarity of performance between hearing and hearing impaired adults, even though differences exist between hearing and hearing impaired children. The slower rate of linguistic development would account for the gap present in young children but overcome by adults, who have presumably developed the minimum linguistic abilities necessary for the attainment of cognitive concepts.

Furth's hypothesis of an impoverished environment contributing to the cognitive gap between hearing and hearing impaired individuals also needs further exploration. According to Piaget, the foundations of cognitive development are laid during the sensori-motor stage, in which the child is able to explore and act upon his physical environment. Several authors (Schlesinger & Meadow, 1972) have commented on the physical curtailment of the hearing impaired child due to safety considerations or overprotection. Early preschool environments for young hearing impaired children tend to stress formal language training over sensori-motor exploration. Thus, the hearing impaired child may in fact be deprived of physical experiences that lay the base for later development of logical concepts. However, it should not be assumed that attendance in a day program rather than a residential program automatically provides a wider base of experience for the hearing impaired child. It is intuitively thought that the home allows more opportunities for various kinds of experience than a residential school, which is considered a more regulated environment. However, homes where parents restrict the child's freedom of movement may not be conducive to later cognitive development. In addition, it should be noted that even residential school children spend the first 2–3 years at home. It may be that constraints placed on their environmental exploration in the home during the early years contributes to later cognitive delays. It is also not clear what kinds of experiences are conducive to cognitive development in hearing impaired children. Inhelder, Sinclair, and Bovet (1974) conducted a series of experiments in which hearing children were provided opportunities to physically manipulate materials to arrive at solutions to problems posed by the experimenters. Such semistructured manipulation may be part of the physical experience base that the young hearing impaired child lacks. Another fruitful area for research is the problem solving strategies used by hearing impaired children. Pendergrass and Hodges (1976), for example, found that hearing impaired children were not able to request appropriate information for solving a problem. Becker (1974), however, found that hearing impaired children were able to use several different strategies to reach a solution. Research on techniques of developing problem solving strategies and the linguistic skills accompanying these strategies would probably be of great use to the field.

Visually Impaired

Lowenfeld (1948) delineated three general limitations imposed by visual impairment: range and variety of experiences, ability to move about, and control of the environment. Such limitations restrict the total experience of the visually impaired child and decrease the range of available learning experiences. Foulke (1962) pointed out that visually impaired children must depend on verbally transmitted information from other people in order to experience the environment rather than through direct interaction with it. Thus, the totally blind child builds up concepts of the environment "on the basis of other than visual information" (Warren, 1977, p. 83). The restrictions pointed out by Lowenfeld and Foulke may have an effect on the cognitive development of the child. Wolff (1966) posited some relevant questions along which the research on cognitive development in visually impaired children has evolved: Is there a lag in cognitive development in visually impaired as compared to sighted children? To what extent can such lag (if any) be attributed to the effects of visual impairment?

Research in this area has been spurred by Piaget's theory of cognitive development. Piaget provided the framework for the understanding of object constancy, classification, and conservation, and so forth, as they evolve through the developmental stages. Studying the child's development through those stages facilitates the isolation of areas of possible developmental differences between visually impaired and sighted children. In the early stages of development, Piaget emphasized the importance of the child's interaction with his or her environment. Although both visually impaired and sighted infants are equally restricted in their physical interaction with the environment during the first two stages of sensori-motor development, the presence of vision affords the sighted infant some internal organization of his or her environment. This internal element is manifested in the third stage, where the infant directs his or her actions to the external world. Since these actions are visually controlled, it might be expected that a divergence in development would begin here. This divergence might be due to what Sandler (1963) called lack of "sensory continuity" afforded by vision and/or the failure of the visually impaired infant to begin reaching towards objects during this stage (Fraiber, Siegel, & Gibson, 1966). Because of the lack of vision, the visually impaired infant is not attracted to objects outside of the "immediate" environment and, therefore, does not reach out to retrieve a desired object. This restriction leads to a slowdown in the development of manipulative and exploratory behaviors, the formation of object concept, and the establishment of object permanence. Although auditory cues facilitate the attainment of spatial relationships to some degree, their inconsistency make the process extremely difficult, and do not serve as stimuli for tactile exploration until the last trimester of the first year (Fraiberg et al., 1966).

Thus, the child needs to develop the tools for exploratory behavior in order to abstract the attributes of the objects, to organize the information, and develop the concepts of causality and means to an end. Delays in motor development, primarily in self-initiated mobility (Adelson & Fraiberg, 1974; Norris, Spaulding, & Brodie, 1957) may further restrict the infant's experimentation with the environment. Fraiberg (1968) pointed out that the visually impaired infant fails to engage in any sustained searching, which leaves him or her "with a temporary handicap in cognitive development" (p. 287)

Two areas in which the "handicap in cognitive development" is most evident are classification and conservation. Hence, most of the research with visually impaired children has emphasized these two areas. A major assumption of all investigations has been that visually impaired children develop classification and conservation abilities in a manner similar to sighted children as they pass through the stages described by Piaget and Inhelder.

Foulke (1964), in an initial trial of his Multi-

Sensory Test of Conceptual Ability, noted that the procedures followed by visually impaired children of various ages were similar to the procedures followed by sighted children. This view was supported by Rich and Anderson (1965) in their standardization study of a tactile form of the Raven Progressive Matrices Test. They found that 6 and 7 year old children had difficulty comprehending the task and approached it in a very unsystematic manner, while most 8 year olds seemed to understand the relations easily and searched systematically for the correct response. These studies suggest the existence of developmental stages in classification tasks, compatible with the findings of Piaget and Inhelder, without indicating the relationships of those stages.

Higgins (1973) investigated the sequence of classification stages in visually impaired children, testing the hypothesis that visually impaired children's classification performance "is inferior to that of sighted children" and that they "are less successful in applying the scheme of class inclusion to abstract content than in applying it to concrete content" (p. 4). Thirty-nine congenitally totally blind children (ages 5–11) drawn from three residential schools for the blind in Australia served as the experimental group. The age group of 7–9 ($N = 19$) was studied most intensively, since it corresponds to Piaget's transitional period from preoperational to operational thought. This group was matched with three sighted control groups on the basis of age, sex, socioeconomic status, and number of years in school. Higgins employed the Modified Kofsky Battery (MKB), the Tactual Test of Class Multiplication, and the Verbal Test of Class Inclusion. He concluded that mastery of classification skills "increases more or less uniformly from one age group to the next" (p. 28). These findings suggest a similar developmental sequence of classification skill in both sighted and blind children.

Performance on the Verbal Test of Class Inclusion showed that the visually impaired subjects responded correctly to more class inclusion questions relating to concrete content than to comparable questions involving abstract content, while the performance patterns of the controls did not vary from one question category to the other. Higgins concluded that the visually impaired subjects exhibited developmental asynchrony. He attributed his findings to the problem of verbalism or the rote use of vocabulary that depends for its meaning on visual experience.

To test the hypothesis of developmental lag, Higgins compared the MKB mean scores of the experimental group and the control groups (under tactual and visual conditions). An analysis of variance disclosed that the mean scores of the visually impaired and the sighted under the tactual condition did not differ significantly. Similar results were found when the mean scores of the experimental and two of the control groups under the visual condition were analyzed. Thus, Higgins (1973) concluded that the evidence agrees "against the developmental lag hypothesis" (p. 27), based on sensory and experiential deprivation. The fact that the mean scores of the control groups (visual condition) were somewhat higher than those of the experimental group may be explained as a deficiency of perceptual input and absence of visual imagery.

Higgins' findings suggest that congenitally visually impaired children do not show deficits in intellectual processes involved with classification, but that they might be handicapped in utilizing their capabilities because of the inability to obtain the "prerequisite data" from their environment. The educational implications of these findings suggest that the educator should be concerned with helping the blind child "derive maximum benefit from his available senses so that information flow is sufficient to support the thought of which the child is capable" (p. 37).

Friedman and Pasnak (1973) studied the feasibility of accelerating the acquisition of classification skills in visually impaired children. Sixteen totally blind children (ages 6–12) served as subjects. The subjects were paired on the basis of various characteristics. One member of each pair received specific training in classification skills, while the other member received an "enrichment" program that was not directed toward classification skills. The train-

ing consisted of various classification tasks, including verbal and tactual discovery of class problems, and form, texture, size, and orientation classification problems. The training consisted of 26 sessions (30 minutes each) over a period of 13 weeks. The training model was similar to that suggested by Higgins (1973); that is, "children who were chronologically mature were aided in acquiring a concept that they had failed to master because of a sensory handicap" (p. 337). Comparisons of pre-post test mean scores for the two groups showed significant improvement for the experimental group.

The studies on classification show that there are selective developmental lags among visually impaired children, that these lags can be attributed to the effects of blindness, and more important, that training can ameliorate classification skills and bring blind children to the level demonstrated by sighted children. These findings, however, raise more questions than they provide answers (Warren, 1977). First, what specific abilities show lags? Second, how are specific cognitive abilities related to specific effects of blindness? Third, how do those selective lags in classification skills affect other areas of cognitive development dependent on classification? These questions must be addressed in future research. Perhaps the findings of this research may lead to more efficient training programs.

The literature on the development of conservation skills in sighted children is abundant. Simplistically, conservation may be explained as maintaining a state of equilibrium between the child's schemas and his or her perceptual information about the world. Since the lack of vision limits the perceptual information for the visually impaired child, it would be reasonable to investigate whether conservation in blind children develops in different time sequences or, more important, in different ways than in sighted children. The research with visually impaired children has concentrated primarily on the first point.

Hatwell (1966) reported a 3-year lag with conservation of substance and a 4-year lag with conservation of weight in visually impaired children as compared to sighted children. Further investigations on conservation of substance by Miller (1969), Tobin (1972), Gottesman (1973), and others support the general findings of Hatwell.

Miller (1969), using 17 totally blind and 9 partially sighted children (ages 6–10), tested conservation ability by presenting a pair of clay objects (one deformed) and asking the subjects for judgements of equality. To control for the degree of visual impairment, Miller blindfolded every subject. Miller found that only the partially sighted group showed evidence of conservation ability. His findings suggest that vision may be an important determinant to the development of conservation. Tobin (1972) investigated the conservation of substance with 189 totally blind and partially sighted subjects (5–16) and compared his results to those of Elkind's (1961) study of sighted subjects. The comparison suggested a considerable lag in the visually impaired children. Unfortunately, no comparison was made between the totally blind and partially sighted subjects. Gottesman (1973) investigated conservation of substance, weight, and volume with three groups of children (ages 4–11): blind (45), sighted blindfolded (45), and sighted (45). He further subdivided the subjects into three subgroups according to age (4–5, 6–7, and 8-11). The sighted group was allowed the full use of vision throughout the study, while the blindfolded and the blind groups used only their tactile sense. The tasks for conservation were presented in the same order for all subjects. Each subject was asked a prediction, a judgement, and an explanation question. A three-way analysis of variance was followed by contrast analysis in order to isolate the performance of each group and contrast it with that of the other groups. The results of the study showed that the totally blind children followed the same developmental stages as the sighted. For conservation of substance, blind children showed a slower rate in the younger age group (6–7). In the youngest group (4–5), very few subjects showed conservation; while in the oldest group (8–11), almost all showed conser-

vation. Thus, the developmental lag exhibited by the blind subjects in the 6–7 age level was apparently eliminated by the age 8–11. The study also showed that conservation of substance (mass) was the easiest, followed by conservation of weight and volume.

Stephens and Simpkins (1974) investigated conservation tasks with three age groups (25 subjects in each: 6–10, 10–14, and 14–18) of randomly selected visually impaired subjects matched with similar age groups of sighted subjects. The conservation tasks included substance, weight, volume, length, and liquid. Comparison of the performance of sighted and visually impaired subjects was performed by using measures of central tendency and dispersion on all variables. To determine differences among the three age groups, the investigators employed analysis of variance. On the measures of conservation of substance (mass) and length, the performance of the visually impaired subjects approximated that of the sighted. However, comparison of the visually impaired and sighted groups at the three age levels showed significant differences at each level. A comparison of the performance of the three age levels of visually impaired subjects only indicated a growth of conservation abilities over time. These data support earlier findings that visually impaired children develop conservation skills along similar patterns but at a slower rate than sighted children.

Discussion

The research on cognitive development with hearing impaired and visually impaired children has progressed on somewhat parallel lines. It was spurred by and followed Piaget's theory of cognitive development. Generally, it has investigated abilities and skills acquired during the various stages of development. A general conclusion that can be drawn from the research is that both hearing and visually impaired children are severely delayed when compared to sighted and hearing children. The research further suggests that in the final stage of development, hearing impaired and visually impaired individuals somehow catch up with their nonhandicapped peers.

The notion of developmental lag addresses the first question raised by Wolff (1966). The second question, the factors contributing to such delay, is riddled with controversy in both fields. Early research suggests that the developmental lag in hearing impaired children is primarily due to their delayed language development, while severely reduced vision is the major contributing factor in visually impaired children. Currently, most researchers attribute the cognitive delays to environmental and experiential deprivation.

Unfortunately, the link (if any) between cognitive and linguistic competence in hearing impaired children has not been extensively explored. Frequently, an assumption has been made that a child with hearing impairment is delayed in language development. This assumption, although likely, may not necessarily be true, given the various degrees of hearing loss and variety of environmental conditions. Further, children with the same degree of hearing loss may vary widely in their linguistic ability. Controlling for hearing loss does not necessarily allow the investigator to draw conclusions regarding the effect of language delay on cognitive development.

This same argument may be advanced in the area of the visually impaired. The heterogeniety of the population precludes any sweeping generalization. No two children with the same visual loss (measured visual acuity) function visually in the same manner. Furthermore, the etiology of the visual loss may contribute to the degree of functional visual efficiency under identical or different environmental conditions. Controlling for visual loss does not allow the researcher to conclude that the lack of vision or reduced vision is the major contributor to cognitive delay.

The term *experiential deprivation* has been used extensively in the literature, unfortunately, thus far it has not been well defined. Hearing impaired and visually impaired children may be restricted in both their physical and social experiences, due to imposed immobility for

safety or education. Restricted exploration of the environment in infancy may, in fact, lead to a delay in development of prerequisites for later cognitive tasks. Some educators (Schlesinger & Meadow, 1972) have criticized the practice of placing hearing impaired preschool children in programs that emphasize the mastery of the linquistic code through formal instructional programming, limit mobility, and therefore the opportunity to learn through motor experiences. Additionally, the inability of the hearing impaired child to communicate easily and proficiently with a variety of different people may restrict the acquisition of social information and certain abstract concepts.

Similarly, a visually impaired preschooler placed in a program that deemphasizes motor development limits the child's ability to exercise control over the environment, thus restricting his or her learning through motor experiences. The restricted mobility, in turn, limits social interaction and the opportunity to acquire additional information.

Both kinds of deprivation may be contributing factors to cognitive delays. Neither can be associated definitively with a particular type of educational setting, nor can they be considered the sole variables. Other contributing factors such as intelligence, early intellectual and sensory stimulation, opportunity for interaction, and family environment have been largely neglected. In addition, individual characteristics associated with the handicapping condition, such as functional use of hearing or vision, etiology, onset and duration of the handicapping condition, although not under control of the investigator, must be more completely reported.

To date, research in both areas has centered on classification and conservation tasks. Researchers have generally concluded that the hearing impaired child does not exhibit any delays during the sensori-motor stage. Conversely, the developmental delay in visually impaired children becomes apparent during the third substage of the sensori-motor period, yet there is a major gap in the research during this period.

The literature has provided abundant data comparing hearing impaired and hearing children, visually impaired and sighted children, but has entirely neglected the effects of cognitive delays on academic achievement. Furthermore, little research is available on the effects of intervention on cognitive development. If experiential deprivation limits the opportunities to develop certain cognitive abilities, major questions then must be posed; What exactly is this deprivation? and How can it be eliminated? On the other hand, if we are to agree that by early adulthood both hearing impaired and visually impaired individuals catch up with their hearing and sighted peers, one may ask, What are the factors that facilitate such rapid cognitive development during this time? The answer to this question may provide extensive information for intervention programs during the early stages of cognitive development.

PSYCHOSOCIAL DEVELOPMENT

Hearing Impaired

The communication barrier imposed by a hearing impairment can be a major factor affecting the child's ability to interact with family and peers, thus affecting both his or her social and emotional growth. The mother–child relationship may be disrupted in the presence of a hearing impairment due to the mother's reaction to the diagnosis and also due to the constraints on communication. Hearing impaired children who are educated in residential schools from a very early age may be deprived of both adult and peer models, necessary for social development. Residential schools have also been criticized for creating a segregated, overprotective environment with little opportunity for the growth of independence.

Most of the information on the psychosocial growth of hearing impaired children is anecdotal. Research is scanty and addresses only a few of the areas mentioned earlier. One reason for the paucity of research is the same communicative barrier that is hypothesized to

cause the problems in the first place. It is difficult, when administering a self-concept scale or other measure of personality development to a hearing impaired child, to be certain that the child in fact understands the vocabulary and sentence structure used in the questions or statements. The language difficulty leads to the necessity of explaining complex concepts in simple language or through pictorial displays. Both of these techniques may lead to oversimplification and possible misinterpretation of the concepts by the child. Similarly, an evaluative tool that requires a language response from the child may be invalid because of the difficulty the child may have in expressing himself and the consequent difficulty the examiner may have in comprehending the child.

An alternate technique for examining social behavior or emotional adjustment is to ask a teacher or a parent to rate the child on certain aspects of behavior. Most of the research with hearing impaired children has used this technique. The ratings can be considered valid only if completed by individuals who are familiar with the child's behavior in several different environments. This can pose a problem for hearing impaired children, since parents are not familiar with the behaviors of children in residential schools, dormitory counselors may rotate and therefore may not be accurately considered surrogate parents, while teachers have knowledge of the child's behavior only in the classroom.

The incidence of emotional and behavior problems among hearing impaired children has been studied by several researchers. Schlesinger and Meadow (1972) asked teachers and dormitory counselors to identify emotionally disturbed children in a state residential school. The results of the survey were compared with a similar survey of hearing students conducted by the county school system. Schlesinger and Meadow found that 11.6% of hearing impaired children were reported to exhibit severe emotional problems, while only 2.4% of hearing students were so reported. The survey also found that an additional 19.6% of the hearing impaired students were reported to display disruptive behaviors but were not considered disturbed enough to be referred for psychiatric help. Only 7.3% of hearing children were reported to display such disruptive behavior.

Jensema and Trybus (1975) present a picture of emotional disturbance much different from that presented by Schlesinger and Meadow. Their data on incidence of emotional disturbance was taken from the 1972–1973 Annual Survey of Hearing Impaired Children and Youth conducted by the Office of Demographic Studies. The survey obtained demographic information from 68% of the educational programs serving hearing impaired children in the United States. These data showed that 7.9% of hearing impaired children were reported by teachers to be emotionally disturbed. The difference in the incidence figures may be due to sampling errors in the Schlesinger and Meadow study or to differing definitions of emotional disturbance used by the researchers. In general then, the Jensema and Trybus data do not confirm a major difference in the incidence of emotional disturbance between the hearing and hearing impaired population.

A detailed examination of the data presented by Jensema and Trybus (1975) reveals some interesting patterns and suggests areas for future research. A higher percentage of children with moderate and severe losses were reported as being emotionally disturbed compared to children with mild or profound losses (although the data were not tested for statistical significance). Several researchers have suggested that adjustment and peer acceptance are poorer in children with less severe handicaps because they are expected to behave more "normally" than more severely handicapped children (Elser, 1959; Havill, 1970). It may be that children with moderate to severe hearing loss are rejected by both the "deaf" society and the "hearing" society, a situation that may lead to problems in social and emotional adjustment. An alternative explanation may be that moderately hearing impaired children are likely to be educated in resource rooms in public schools, where their behavior is more likely to be rated in comparison with hearing than hearing impaired children. In fact, Jensema and Trybus report a higher rate of emotional

disturbance in resource room children as compared to children in day school, residential school, or full-time special education classes.

The lowest incidence of emotional disturbance was reported among hearing impaired children receiving itinerant services only. These results agree with findings by Reich, Hambleton, and Houldin (1977) showing that fully integrated children were significantly better adjusted than partially integrated children.

Goulder and Trybus (1977) compared the classroom behavior of children reported as being emotionally disturbed with other hearing impaired children. A checklist inventory of social and emotional behaviors was completed by teachers. The researchers found that the children reported as being emotionally disturbed displayed a significantly lower need for achievement, more aggressiveness, more anxiety, and a greater degree of hostile isolation. The researchers concluded that the incidence of emotional disturbance reported by the schools was accurate since children labeled emotionally disturbed did in fact display behaviors different from other children.

Both educational placement and degree of hearing loss are factors that may affect the social and emotional development of the child. Unfortunately, it is not always possible to separate the two since children with profound hearing losses are most likely to be in residential schools while those with mild and moderate losses are more likely to be in resource rooms in the public schools. Research by Quigley and Frisina (1961) and Schlesinger and Meadow (1972) attempted to evaluate the effect of educational environment on psychosocial adjustment. Quigley and Frisina (1961) compared the adjustment of students living at the residential school with students attending the same school but living at home. They found no differences between the two groups on a behavior rating scale completed by teachers, and concluded that the residential living environment had no detrimental impact on psychosocial adjustment.

Schlesinger and Meadow examined the self-image and psychosocial adjustment of three groups of hearing impaired children: residential school children with hearing impaired parents, residential school children with hearing parents, and day schoolchildren. They found that the hearing impaired children with hearing impaired parents had the highest self-image scores and also that proportionately more of these children had a positive self-image. There were no significant differences between the other two groups. Hearing impaired children with hearing impaired parents scored highest on psychosocial adjustment behavior, on social maturity, independence, sociability, popularity with peers and adults, and positive adjustment to deafness. The lowest scores were obtained by deaf children of hearing parents in residential schools, while the day students scored in between the two groups of residential students.

It would appear that the residential environment in and of itself may not create problems in psychosocial development and adjustment. Unfortunately, comparisons between self-selected populations, such as residential and day schools, do not necessarily allow the researcher to infer cause-effect relationships. It would probably be more profitable to examine possible changes in psychosocial adjustment due to therapy or specific changes in environments in which the hearing impaired children are placed.

Schlesinger and Meadow identified another factor that appears to contribute to psychosocial adjustment of hearing impaired children; the ability to communicate with their parents. Hearing impaired children with hearing impaired parents share a communication system and are therefore raised in a communication environment similar to that of hearing children. Hearing parents, on the other hand, have to either learn a new system (total communication) to interact with their children or communicate through oral language, a system which may be difficult for their child.

An area of interest to researchers has been the relationship of hearing impaired children to their families, a relationship that lays the foundation for later social development. The discovery of hearing impairment causes major emotional stresses in parents, which may affect

the relationship between them and their child. Most of the research available has examined the interaction between mothers (hearing and hearing impaired) and their preschool hearing impaired children. Very little is known about the relationships of hearing impaired children with their fathers or their siblings.

One of the landmark studies on the relationship between preschool hearing impaired children and their mothers was done by Schlesinger and Meadow in 1972. They compared the interaction of mothers with their hearing and hearing impaired children. Forty mother–hearing impaired child dyads and 20 mother–hearing child dyads were observed and rated on several attributes. Mothers with hearing impaired children were found to be significantly less permissive, more intrusive, more didactic, and less flexible than mothers of hearing children. There were no differences between mothers in enjoyment of the child or ability to achieve the child's cooperation. Mothers were also interviewed on child rearing practices. It was found that mothers of hearing impaired children had less reservations than mothers of hearing children about corporal punishment and reported greater frustration due to communication difficulties.

Greenberg (1980) compared the attitudes of mothers using oral communication and total communication with their hearing impaired preschoolers. He found no differences between the two groups on parental attitudes or in parental stress as reported by the mothers. He did find, however, that children using total communication were rated significantly higher in social age by their mothers than children using oral communication. Meadow, Greenberg, Erting, and Carmichael (1981) compared the interaction of four groups of mother–child dyads. The four groups consisted of dyads of hearing mothers with hearing impaired children using total communication; hearing mothers with hearing impaired children using oral communication; hearing impaired mothers with hearing impaired children; and hearing children and hearing mothers. They found that the quality of interaction differed significantly in these groups. In general, the mother–hearing impaired child dyads using oral communication spent less time in interaction and had shorter interactions with fewer conversational turns. The communication between hearing impaired mothers and their hearing impaired children was similar to hearing mothers with hearing children. Hearing mothers with hearing impaired children using total communication usually communicated better than the oral dyads but worse than the hearing impaired dyads.

Since 91% of hearing impaired children are reported to have hearing parents, it is likely that the interaction patterns of hearing mothers with hearing impaired children is more typical of the hearing impaired population than the interaction patterns between hearing impaired mothers and hearing impaired children. Disruption of interaction patterns between mothers and their children may be a factor contributing to later emotional disturbance.

Yet another area of research in social development is the relationship of hearing impaired children with their peers. Most research has examined the social acceptance of hearing impaired children by their hearing peers, or the frequency and quality of the interaction of hearing impaired children with their peers. Elser (1959) found hearing impaired children to be significantly less accepted than their hearing peers, while Kennedy and Bruininks (1974) found hearing impaired children to be well accepted by hearing peers, a finding that they attributed to the good communication skills of the hearing impaired children being studied. Brackett and Henniges (1976) found that children with good oral communication skills interacted more frequently with hearing children than did hearing impaired children with poor oral skills. Antia (1982) found that hearing impaired children interacted significantly less with peers than did hearing children.

The results of this admittedly scanty research paints a general picture of the hearing impaired child as possibly being socially isolated. This isolation may, of course, be more apparent than real due to restricted sample size and the restricted number of situations in which peer relationships have been examined. Most of the research has examined the interaction between hearing impaired children and hearing peers, a situation in which communication difficulties rather than abnormal social behavior may result in social isolation. Antia (1982), however, compared the interaction of hearing impaired children with hearing impaired and hearing peers and found no significant differences in interaction, indicating that hearing impaired children, in general, interacted infrequently with peers, both hearing and hearing impaired. Higginbotham and Baker (1981) examined the play interactions of preschool hearing impaired children and found that they indulged in significantly more solitary play and significantly less cooperative play than did hearing children.

Several studies (Antia, 1982; Kennedy, Northcott, McCauley, & Williams, 1976; McCauley & Bruininks, 1976) also reported that hearing impaired children interacted more frequently with teachers than with peers, an interaction pattern opposite to that of hearing children, who interacted more frequently with peers than with teachers. These researchers reported that such an interaction pattern may indicate a dependence on adults and an inability to maintain peer relationships, although much additional research in the area is needed to substantiate this hypothesis.

Visually Impaired

Socialization is an interactive process that involves other people. Thus, the psychosocial development of the visually impaired child may be affected by the attitudes of the community toward the handicapping condition. In addition, the disruption of the mother–child relationship, imposed by the lack of vision and the residential placement of visually impaired children at an early age, provides limited opportunity for independent growth. Research in this area is extremely limited. Despite the great abundance of case histories, no conclusions or generalizations can be made.

Sommers (1944), on the basis of structured interviews with parents of visually impaired children, distinguished four types of parental attitudes toward blindness: (a) punishment of the parents, (b) fear of community's belief that blindness was caused by a social disease (c) feelings of guilt for having violated some moral or social code, and (d) feelings of personal disgrace. Along with these attitudes, Sommers also identified the modes of parental adjustment as acceptance, denial, overprotection, disguised rejection, and overt rejection. Tait (1972) pointed out that parental feelings toward the child are to a great extent dependent upon the parent's own psychological well-being. Using an Eriksonian model of stage development of socialization, Tait suggested that during the first stage the visually impaired child may be on an equal basis with the sighted child. However, during the second stage the visually impaired child, being less efficient in acquiring information from the environment, remains more self-oriented than the sighted child. Tait indicated that this may result in the parents ignoring the visually impaired child. One consequence of this behavior "for the blind child may be a feeling that he is unable to control his/her environment" (Warren, 1977, p. 182).

Fraiberg (1968), describing two cases of very young visually impaired infants, pointed out that separation, both physical and mental, of parent from child had a retarding effect on all areas of development and an increase in self-stimulating behaviors. McKay (1936), using the Vineland Social Maturity Scale with blind subjects drawn from institutions concluded that there was a definite lag in social maturity for his subjects as compared to the sighted norm. It is not clear, however, whether the reported lag was attributable to institutionalization or lack of vision. One might suspect that both factors played a role in the psychosocial development. McGuinness (1970) compared the social maturity of visually impaired children enrolled in residential school, integrated school, and those receiving the services of an itinerant teacher. The subjects (fourth through sixth grade), congenitally totally blind, were individually evaluated with the Vineland Scale. McGuinness reported that the scores for all these groups were lower than the sighted

norms. Children from the residential school showed lower social maturity scores than those taught by itinerant teachers and in integrated schools. McGuinness attributed the low scores of residential children to the lack of contact with age appropriate social behavior and the greater availability of special help.

These results are supported by the findings of Schindele (1974), who compared the social adjustment of blind children from residential and public schools to that of sighted children. Schindele found no differences in adjustment among the groups. However, closer analysis revealed that the older children from the residential school were less well adjusted than the children of the same age in the public school. Schindele suggested that this finding may be the result of the sheltered and unrealistic environment provided by the residential school.

In view of the studies reported, two explanations have been advanced for the discrepancies in social maturity and adjustment. Hallenbeck (1954) noted that a significant factor of normal social development is the establishment of a good relationship between the blind child and a significant other before entering school. Tait (1972) added that the adequacy of exploratory behavior seems to be related to the degree of social adjustment. Exploratory behavior appears to be a step toward the establishment of relationships and social independence.

Scott (1968) advances the hypothesis that development of positive self-concent is the basis for social adjustment. Self-concept, according to Scott, is acquired in large part through interactions with other people. Thus, the expectations that other people hold may have a large effect on the development of self-concept. The implications of Scott's hypothesis are quite apparent. The psychosocial development of the blind child is influenced by the expectations that other people hold for him or her. It would seem that it is a case of self-fulfilling prophecy. If they expect the child to behave in a certain manner, the child will respond correspondingly. Thus, the social competency of the blind child need not be different from that of the sighted child. Scott's hypothesis was to some extent confirmed by McGuinness (1970). McGuinness pointed out that children in the public school "have less opportunity to receive special help," and this "may force them to learn how to work out problems for themselves. The significantly lower scores of children from the residential school setting may perhaps reflect the lowered expectations resulting from lack of competition with sighted children their own age" (p. 40).

Mayadas (1972) investigated the relationships between the role expectations held by significant others and the behaviors exhibited by blind adolescents from a residential school. The results indicated that there is a positive relationship between these two factors. Caution must be taken, however, in further interpreting these results. It is not clear whether the subjects' behavior was influenced by the expectations of the significant others or whether these expectations were shaped by the pattern of the subject's behavior. Perhaps longitudinal studies with young visually impaired children following them through both settings and carefully monitoring the attitudes and expectations of significant others as well as the children's self-expectations may more precisely isolate the variables that influence the psychosocial development of the visually impaired child.

Discussion

Research on psychosocial development with sensory impaired children has taken two general directions. One body of research examined the effect of the impairment on psychosocial adjustment and tried to determine certain factors that might contribute to adjustment. The other body of research attempted to describe the relationship of the child to his or her parents and peers.

Some research on the incidence of emotional disturbance in hearing impaired children (Jensema & Trybus, 1975) indicate that no differences exist between hearing and hearing impaired children, whereas other research (Schlesinger & Meadow, 1972) seems to indicate that the incidence of emotional disturbance is higher among hearing impaired than

hearing children. No data on incidence of emotional disturbance in visually impaired children are available, but researchers (McKay, 1936; McGuinness, 1970) have found that these children are less socially mature than their sighted peers. Several reasons can be given for differences in adjustment between hearing and visually impaired children and their nonhandicapped peers. The argument most commonly put forth is that educational placement affects the self-perfection and self-concept of the child, as well as his or her social interactions with others, hence his or her overall social adjustment. Unfortunately, studies examining the effect of placement on psychosocial adjustment have produced contradictory results. Some have shown differences favoring students in public schools (McGuinness, 1970; Reich et al., 1977; Schindele, 1970), while others have found no differences between students in the two settings (Quigley & Frisina, 1961). Since degree of loss is closely related to educational placement for both visually and hearing impaired children, it is possible that some observed differences can be associated with severity of loss rather than educational placement.

In the area of family relationships, mother–child bonding has received the most attention in both fields. An examination of parent attitudes (Schlesinger & Meadow, 1972; Scott, 1968) shows that mothers of sensory impaired children may view their child differently than mothers of nonhandicapped children. However, there are few data relating parental attitudes to children's behavior adjustment. Few studies have examined the relationship between the sensory impaired child and other family members, such as fathers or siblings. An interesting area of study would be the relationship between the child's interaction with family members and social interaction with peers and others outside of the family circle.

Another area for research is the effect of age of onset of hearing or vision loss on psychological adjustment. Can family bonds, once established, be drastically affected by the onset or diagnosis of a sensory impairment? Parents have been noted to pass through several stages of grief and to resolve their feelings toward the child in different ways. It would be of interest to clinicians to know how parents behave toward their children during different cycles of grief and how their behavior affects the child.

Sibling attitudes may affect the sensory impaired child as well. It is open to question whether siblings share the grief of parents (particularly older siblings) and whether they also share their parents' attitudes toward their sensory impaired brother or sister. The absence of the child for prolonged periods, either due to hospital stays or residential school placement, may adversely affect the relationship with the family and deserves systematic inquiry.

Some researchers (Mayadas, 1972) have studied the relationship between role expectation and certain behaviors exhibited by visually impaired adolescents. This may be true also of hearing impaired individuals, who may learn certain dependent behaviors due to expectations placed on them by parents, siblings, and peers.

Another promising area of study is the development of peer relationships. To date, research has focused on the relationship of the sensory impaired child with his nonhandicapped peers (Antia, 1982; Kennedy et al., 1976). Little is available on the development of friendships with other sensory impaired peers, particularly within residential schools. The development of peer relationships is a function of social maturity and allows the child to expand his social experiences. It thus deserves some attention by researchers.

The bulk of this discussion has centered around factors that might cause maladjustment in sensory impaired individuals. This is not surprising, since it is the business of researchers to search for differences. However, constant comparison between sensory impaired and nonhandicapped children may lead to several faulty conclusions. Such research does not allow one to account for the necessary adaptations that are made due to the sensory impairment itself. All attitudinal and behavior differences between sensory impaired and nonhandicapped individuals need not be negative but may instead be signs of the person's ability to cope with a strange environment.

Although the behavior may be somewhat different, the adaptation itself may be healthy.

Also, it is necessary to keep in mind that measures used to assess adjustment and maturity were developed for nonhandicapped individuals and, as such, contain certain items that may not be appropriate for sensory impaired children. For example, the Vineland Social Maturity Scale, a rating scale commonly used with the sensory impaired, includes items on vocal behavior, which may penalize the hearing impaired child, and on motor behavior, which may penalize the visually impaired child. Rating scales may be biased not only because of the items themselves but because of the different reference groups used by raters when rating the child. The teacher whose reference group is other sensory impaired children may rate a child quite differently than a teacher or parent whose reference group is nonhandicapped children. Thus, it is necessary to know something about the kinds of instruments used and the raters before definite conclusions about social adjustment can be made.

The search for differences has also obscured the fact that there are many well adjusted and socially mature invididuals in both populations. Attention should be given to the social environment that produces these individuals. A thorough investigation of the variables within such environments may be of considerable value to professionals serving sensory impaired children.

A final note on this section is a comment on research techniques used to study family relationships. It may be that research methods in the fields of psychology and education are inadequate and that methods that have evolved to study cultures and relationships of individuals within cultures may be more suitable. Thus, research methods drawn from anthropology and related fields may be profitably used and should be considered.

TECHNOLOGY

Hearing Impaired

The technological advancements of the last 20 years have had a major impact on the development of communicative devices for the hearing impaired. Sophisticated amplification equipment, the use of captioning for films and television, and the development of telecommunications devices have allowed the hearing impaired to join the information processing society. This section will review some of the research involving the use of new technological devices. The reader is reminded that the growth in the development of new technology is so rapid that only a few aspects can be discussed.

Since the major limitation of a hearing impairment is the ability to perceive the speech of others, it is not surprising that speech amplification aids are the most widely used technological devices in educational programs serving hearing impaired children. The earliest hearing aid used by hearing impaired individuals was the ear trumpet. This was followed by cumbersome electric hearing aids (Berger, 1976), which have evolved into today's miniature aids which can be worn behind or in the ear. Major changes have enhanced the ability of the hearing aid to amplify sound without undue distortion. Parallel advances have been made in group amplification systems with hard-wire systems giving way to FM radio frequency systems that do not limit the mobility of teachers or children and that provide a high quality of sound amplification. Thus, technological advances have made amplification available to the majority of hearing impaired individuals in the United States. This section will deal with research in the use of amplification in the education of the hearing impaired.

Amplification devices, such as individual or group aids, are only of use to the hearing impaired child if they function correctly and are used consistently. Hearing impaired children need to learn to interpret and comprehend incoming auditory information. Such learning involves having consistent access to an auditory signal. Unfortunately, the research on the use of amplification by hearing impaired children indicates that access to auditory information has not been consistent. Bess (1977) examined the condition of hearing aids worn by children in a public school and found that 27% were physically faulty, 15% had weak batteries, and 25–30% failed the electro-acoustical analysis. Forty percent of the children set controls to lower than the maximum gain needed. One would have to conclude from these results that very few children received clear and consistent auditory information.

Karchmer and Kirwin (1977) conducted a nationwide survey of hearing aid usage. They mailed questionnaires to teachers and parents of 1362 hearing impaired children, asking about consistency of hearing aid use, environments in which aids were used, and factors associated with hearing aid use. They found that 82% of students used amplification for at least part of the day. Only 63.7% reported always using an aid in the classroom, while a mere 32% reported always using an aid in the home. The highest percentage of consistent hearing aid use was found for students with moderate to severe losses, which is the group most likely to benefit from such use. Younger children were more likely to use amplification than older children. Residential students were least likely to use consistent amplification (47.5%), while students in full-time special education classes in the public schools were the most likely to use consistent amplification (83.5%).

It appears that amplification is not being used as consistently as is necessary for maximum benefit to the student. The problem appears not to be in the amplification equipment but in its use by children. Certainly, invervention and future research needs to focus on the consistency with which amplification is used.

Another aspect, besides hearing aid use, that affects the child's access to auditory information is the acoustic environment. Background noise is amplified along with the speech signal and affects the hearing impaired child's ability to comprehend the speech message. Finitzo-Hieber and Tilman (1978) found that hearing impaired children's speech discrimination scores showed a consistent decline as the signal to noise ratio decreased. Blair (1977) examined the speech perception of 18 moderately hearing impaired children ages 7–14 years under actual classroom listening conditions. He found that even classrooms treated to minimize background noise through use of carpeting, drapes, and acoustic tile generated an unacceptable amount of background noise. He also found that the children obtained considerably lower speech perception scores in classrooms with the higher background noise. Apparently, additional work needs to be done in creating better listening conditions for hearing impaired children, as well as in training for speech perception in noise. In addition, teachers and hearing impaired children need to learn techniques for increasing signal to noise ratio through microphone placement and use of the appropriate amplification equipment under different acoustic conditions.

For profoundly hearing impaired children, amplification may provide comprehension of environmental sounds, not speech sounds. In order for speech information to be available to these children, another modality must be used. Attempts have been made to translate speech sounds into vibratory patterns using tactile devices. Simple tactile vibrators have been used as adjuncts to hearing aids with some children, but these can convey only limited speech information. A 23 channel tactual vocoder was devised by Engelmann and Rosov (1975) and used to train four hearing impaired children, 8–14 years of age, in recognition of words and sentences. Subjects were trained for 1 hour per day, 5–6 days per week. At the end of the training sessions, three subjects could recognize words with about 84% accuracy, though the size of each subject's vocabulary varied considerably. The researchers also found that while initial learning was slow, the acquisition rate for new words increased with time.

Oller, Payne, and Gavin (1980) trained eight profoundly hearing impaired adolescents to discriminate between six pairs of words on a tactual vocoder. They found that subjects could, after about 2 hours of training, distinguish between pairs of words with long vowel sounds, at a level greater than chance performance. Discrimination of word pairs with short vowel sounds remained at chance levels.

Tactual vocoders appear as yet to be of limited ability to aid in speech perception, partly because of the complexity of the speech and the corresponding complexity of the tactual information received. Speech perception training on tactual vocoders has consisted of single words or sentences. It remains to be seen whether conversational speech messages can be decoded through vibrotactile patterns. It is possible that tactile devices can be profitably used in conjunction with auditory and visual input—an area that awaits further research.

A consistent trend in communications technology for the hearing impaired is the effort to make audiovisual media such as film and television accessible to this population by providing captions to accompany the spoken presentation. Captioned films are a valuable educational tool and are widely used in educational programs. A major concern of researchers has been the ability of the hearing impaired child to comprehend the captions.

Caldwel (1973) examined the effect of reading level of the captions on the acquisition of subject matter. The subjects were two groups of adolescents at a school for the deaf between 13–15 years of age. The experimental group had a 2.9 grade reading level and was exposed to science education films captioned at a reading grade level ranging 2.8–5.2. The control group had a reading grade level of 4.0 and was exposed to captions at 1.0–3.5 grade reading level. No significant differences were found between the two groups on acquisition of subject matter and vocabulary. Either the reading level of the captions had no effect on subject matter acquisition or the captions themselves had no effect.

Shroyer and Birch (1980) questioned the ability of the average deaf reader to read captions at the rate at which they are presented on the screen. They examined the reading rates of 185 students, ranging in age from 8 years 9 months to 21 years 8 months, at a residential school for the deaf. They found that the majority (156) of the students had reading rates averaging 116–142 words per minute. Caption rates are generally dependent on the amount and rate of verbal information presented in the film. Shroyer and Birch state that normal extempore speech is presented at about 159 words per minute. Captions presented to match the speaking rate would be too rapid for many hearing impaired readers. They suggest that additional research on reading rates is needed to identify optimum rates for captioning.

Braverman and Hertzog (1980) examined the effect of both caption rate and the language level of the captions on comprehension of video presentations. Their subjects were 187 residential school elementary and secondary students ranging in age from 8–20 years, with reading grade levels ranging 1.9–12.4. Captions were presented at 60, 90, and 120 words per minute and were written at two linguistic levels. They found that comprehension was not affected by caption rate but was significantly affected by the linguistic level of the captions. There was no interaction between rate and linguistic level. It thus appears that if the linguistic level of the caption is within the reading ability of the students, caption rates may not affect comprehension.

Murphy-Berman and Jorgensen (1980) examined the effect of both the linguistic complexity of captions and the kind of programs being viewed on program comprehension. They captioned three commercial children's programs at three different linguistic levels. Each program was shown to 148–252 hearing impaired children aged 11–18 years at residential schools for the deaf. They found that children shown captioned presentations received higher comprehension scores than children shown noncaptioned presentations. The linguistic level of the captions affected comprehension scores on only one program. Thus, there appeared to be an interaction between the kind of material presented and the linguistic level of the captions.

It can be concluded that captioning is an effective way to increase the hearing impaired individual's comprehension of film or video presentation and that the linguistic level of the captions appears to be a major factor affecting comprehension. It is possible that the cognitive demands of the presentation, the amount of visual display, and the amount of auditory verbal explanation may be factors that interact with the captions to affect comprehension.

The advent of telecommunications systems has allowed hearing impaired individuals to communicate effectively over distances. Keyboard telecommunication devices for the deaf (TDD) allow print messages to be transmitted and received over telephone lines. Geoffrion (1982a, 1982b) studied teletype conversations of hearing impaired teenagers, focusing on the opening, the main body, and closing sequences. Students were divided into groups according to their English language ability as judged by their teachers. He found that students in the high English language groups were more likely to identify themselves spontaneously, while the low English language groups exhibited an impoverished greeting chain. The low English language groups were less likely to set the topic of the conversation or to request information. They were also more likely than the high English language groups to terminate the conversation without any leave taking behavior. Geoffrion concluded that hearing impaired students may need specific instruction in learning to make effective use of a TDD.

Using a TDD effectively is likely to take on additional importance as the telecommunication network widens. At present, TDD messages can only be sent if both parties have the equipment for reception and transmission of messages. Glaser (1982) described a message converter that can be used with an ordinary push button telephone. The converter will provide a graphic display of the letters and numbers depressed on the push button telephone. Further advances may allow the message to be converted into artificial speech (Stoker, 1982). Such advances will increase the number of people with whom hearing impaired individuals can communicate on a regular basis.

Additional engineering research will no doubt increase the hardware available to assist hearing impaired individuals. The educator's role will be to ensure that the hearing impaired individual can make maximum use of the technology that is available.

Visually Impaired

The lack of direct access to printed material of the severely visually impaired individual has been a primary problem in all areas of vocation, education, and recreation. Communication between employer, employee, and consumer is generally in print. The inability of the blind to read print presents an inherent difficulty in partaking in that communication, thus limiting the possibilities of obtaining and/or maintaining employment. The introduction of the "discovery" methods of instruction and learning through the investigation of a variety of publications places the blind student at a great disadvantage. The inability to have direct access to the complex information storage and retrieval system, designed for the sighted, further restricts the educational process.

In common with the sighted, severely visually impaired people have enjoyed a continuous increase in benefits from the rapid, indeed bewildering, advances in scientific knowledge and technological development. The increasing volume and variety of braille literature, available through the development of automated methods of production, appears to be insufficient to keep pace with the production of print materials. It is obvious then, that the most efficient resolution will be technology designed for the blind that can utilize the existing delivery system developed for the sighted reader. Numerous efforts have been made over the years to develop reading aids for the blind based on conversion of visual information for detection by hearing or touch.

The intent of this discussion is not to provide an exhaustive list of all technical devices available to the visually impaired. Indeed, with the rapid production rate of such devices, a new device could be on the market by the time this chapter is in print. The intent, however, is to provide a historical development and brief description of research in the area of technology directly applicable to the visually impaired.

The development of reading aids for the blind has been in progress for several decades. In fact, the first reading aid was developed in 1912 by Barr and Straud Engineering Company of England. That device was known as the British Fournier d'Albe Optaphone. The electric capabilities at that time were very limited and the machine produced numerous extraneous signals, thus seriously interfering with the interpretation of the tones representing the printed letter. Reading with the d'Albe Optaphone was, of course, an impossible task and the device was soon abandoned.

It was not until late in World War II that efforts to produce reading devices were renewed. This renewal came as a result of the newly formed Committee on Sensory Devices of the National Research Council. After several committee meetings, a general consensus emerged based on a broad analysis of the problem of independent reading of print. It appeared that reading devices for the blind with either audible or tactile outputs needed to be developed, if a resolution to the common problem of access to print were to be found. Because of the then current status of the technology, efforts were placed on developing a device which would translate the shape of the printed character into an auditory pattern (Murphy, 1972). The first of these devices was developed by Radio Corporation of America (RCA). The RCA A-2 reading device, commonly known as the reading pencil, was based on direct translation of the shape of the letter into sound patterns by mean of a scanning mirror and an oscillating circuit wire at approximately 60 cycles per minute. As the reading pencil was moved across the printed line, a chirping or canarylike sound characteristic of each letter was produced. The user was expected, through the interpretation of these sounds, to read printed material.

In 1957, under sponsorship of the Veterans Administration, the Battelle Memorial Institute of Columbus, Ohio, had primary responsibility for the development and evaluation of a reading machine for the blind known as the Optaphone. The Optaphone translates the shapes or printed symbols, such as letters and numbers, into tone patterns. The tonal representation for a particular symbol is directly related to its shape. For example, a straight horizontal bar, such as a dash (−) is represented by a single tone as the device slides over the dash.

The Visotoner, like its predecessors the RCA A-2 and the Optaphone, translates the printed character into audible tones. It is through the accurate interpretation of these tones that print is read. The Visotoner consists of three components: an optical system, a vertical column of nine photocells, and an electronic circuit that generates an audible tone for each photocell. It also includes control mechanisms for magnification and contrast of the print. Each printed symbol has its own characteristic tone pattern. The user must learn to interpret these tone patterns as letters and synthesize the letters into words. It must be stated at this point that there has been no rigorous evaluation procedure involving any of these reading devices. What information is available comes from personal experiences and studies that offer no empirical data other than achieved reading rates.

The primary concern throughout the years appears to have been the possibility of developing a personal reading device that would enable the totally blind person to participate in and share the information available to sighted people. It appears that, with the advancement of technology in general, the development of such devices becomes a reality. However, it should also be noted that development and evaluation of the devices must occur concurrently.

In the mid 1960s a new reading device (Optacon), based on translation of the printed letter into vibrating tactile patterns, was developed by the Stanford Research Institute. The development of the Optacon followed closely the results obtained from its evaluation both in laboratory setting and in the field. By 1970, the Optacon was already used by several blind individuals (Bliss, 1972). Perhaps an important element of the evaluation procedure was the distribution of Optacons to those individuals able to use them. Beginning with 1972, a worldwide evaluation of the Optacon and development of instructional materials were initiated. A number of studies explored its potential use (Bliss, 1972; Bertora, 1974; Marmolin & Nilsson, 1973; Nelton, 1972; Tobin, 1973; Weisgerber, 1974). The primary objectives of these studies were to isolate factors that contribute to successful Optacon reading and development of instructional material.

Zierer (1972) concluded that the most important factors are age, intelligence, motivation, and actual time spent in preparation and independent reading. Tobin (1973), in a 1 year study involving 30 teenagers and adults, examined the relationship between successful Optacon reading and sex, age, degree of vision, previous visual experience, speed of reading braille, short-term memory, and personality factors. He concluded that only age, short-term memory, and speed of reading braille were contributing factors.

Weisgerber (1974), in a 2 year study involving a stratified sample of students, grades 4–12, reported that a significant relationship exists between accuracy of reading with the Optacon and intelligence, tactile ability, accuracy in braille reading, age, sex, spelling ability, and attitude toward education. Schoof (1975) analyzed the relationship between the combined score of speed and accuracy of Optacon reading and age, sex, age of onset of blindness, and braille reading speed. The study involved 58 subjects, age 10 and over, trained at Telesensory Systems Incorporated (TSI). He concluded that only age at time of training was positively related to speed and accuracy of reading with the Optacon with the younger students developing higher speeds at the completion of a 50-hour training course.

Nelton (1972), in a 10 day, concentrated instructional program (50 hours total), reported an average reading rate of 7 words per minute with subjects ranging 24–41 years old. Zierer (1972), with subjects ranging 19–31 years old and with 29 instructional hours spread over a period of 2 months, reported an average of 8 words per minute with the words being isolated rather than incorporated within a text. Tobin (1973) was able to achieve an average of 11.2 words per minute with one group of subjects (ages 16–18) with a maximum of 30 hours of instruction over a 12 day period. Marmolin and Nilsson (1973) used two groups of subjects and provided 60 hours of instruction over 15 days for the first group, and 6–7 months for the second group. They reported no significant difference in reading rates between the two groups (7.1 and 7.4 words per minute). Bertora (1974) demonstrated that the use of the pacing device (which regulates scanning with the camera at a preset uniform rate) produced a relatively higher rate of reading (average of 27.4 words per minute) ranging from 10–42 words per minute. Although the number of instructional hours was not reported, the individual who achieved 42 words per minute had participated in the study for more than 2 years. Schoof (1975) found the average reading rate for 41 adult Optacon trainees after 50 hours of training was 9.61 words per minute, while Weisgerber (1974) reported 12.3 words per minute after 58 hours of training with school age children.

From the studies conducted thus far it is apparent that one of the disadvantages of the Optacon is the slow reading rate. Terzieff, Stagg, and Ashcroft (1982) investigated the possibility of increasing the reading rates through systematic language instruction and prediction employing language redundancy. All subjects ($N = 9$) had previous Optacon training and an average reading rate of 15–16 words per minute. After 24 hour long sessions of training, the average reading rate increased to 41.72 words per minute. The investigators concluded that through systematic instruction, reading rates with the Optacon can be increased, and suggested that a strong language based reading instruction be employed for teaching reading with the Optacon.

The origins of the Kurzweil Reading Machine (KRM) stem from the interest in artificial intelligence, mainly print recognition, decision making, and speech output. It uses a small computer-controlled camera that automatically scans lines of print on a page. The image in the camera is processed by the computer that can recognize strings of letters as separate words. The computer determines the pronunciation of the word through programmed rules of English grammar and activates a speaker to produce synthetic speech. The KRM has now been placed in over 300 agencies, libraries, universities, and schools. Perhaps the most interesting fact is that many of its functions are controlled by programs. Thus, existing machines can easily be upgraded by means of new program tapes, making it very versatile.

Unfortunately, to date, no formal investigations have involved the KRM and its usefulness in school or on the job. Most of the literature consists of personal reports by users and those who promote the device.

Following in the footsteps of the KRM, a number of computer companies began the production of braille and voice output devices. Perhaps the latest and most versatile representations are the Braille-Edit system and the Cybertalker.

The Braille-Edit is a program that allows the user to write, edit, correct, and print written work in braille and/or print. It contains two translators that convert print into grade two braille and/or grade two braille into print. Thus, a sighted and a visually impaired individual can share information with each other. A visually impaired individual can obtain braille transcriptions of any information available to the computer. Obviously, the system enables a visually impaired person to work side by side with his or her sighted peers.

The Cybertalker is a synthetic speech adapter designed to add full verbal output to most computers and computer-based systems (word processors, electronic typewriters, computer terminals, and microcomputers). The device has its own command system, making it totally independent from the host device. As such, the Cybertalker is perhaps the most versatile voice output device.

The second area that has profited from the advancement of technology is orientation and mobility. Since the lack of vision precludes the safe and efficient negotiation through the environment, the blind individual is severely restricted. Although many blind persons travel with a long cane or guide dog, a number of electronic devices can enable them to interact with the environment in a way similar to sighted persons. Recently, some of these devices have been successfully used with young visually impaired children in developing spatial concepts.

The least complicated travel device is the Pathsounder. The device is a small rectangular box that hangs on the user's chest by a neck strap. It scans the environment directly in front of the user by emitting an ultrasound beam and converting the reflected beam into audible tones. The pitch of the tone determines the distance of the object from the individual, thus providing ample time and opportunity for the user to avoid the obstacle in his path, or locate openings, such as doors. However, since the device emits a single unidirectional beam, its usefulness is limited and must be used in conjunction with a long cane or a guide dog.

The Mowat Sensor is a device similar in function to the Pathsounder. It is handheld and designed to be used with a long cane or a guide dog. The Pathsounder and the Mowat Sensor are equipped with electronic converters, which convert the beams into vibratory impulses, thus enabling a deaf-blind individual to travel within the environment with safety.

The Laser cane is a device that offers its user more information than the long cane and the above-mentioned devices combined. It operates on the same principle. However, it emits three infrared light beams. The *straight ahead* beam can detect objects up to 12 feet, the *upward looking* beam can detect objects at head height at a distance of 5 feet, and the *downward looking* beam detects drop-offs deeper than 5 inches (such as curbs, stairs, etc.) up to 5 feet from the user. The reflected light beams are converted into auditory or vibration signals to warn the user of potential obstacles along his path of travel. Information on actual use of the laser cane is still scant. Personal reports of users have praised its usefulness. However, no detailed investigations have been undertaken to date.

The electronic mobility aid that provides most information about the environment is the Sonicguide™. It operates on the same principle as the other devices; however, the information provided about the object is more complete. Its user will know the direction of, distance from, and surface characteristics of the object. A light transmitter and two receivers are mounted on a lightweight eyeglass frame. The transmitter sends out pulses of high frequency sound waves. Reflected sound waves are converted into audible sound and transmitted to the ears by small tubes. Thus, the device is stereophonic and allows the user to detect an object's direction. Effective range of the aid is

6–15 feet, 30 degrees each side of center, and up to head height. This range provides the user with sufficient warning time and enables him or her to navigate around objects without making physical contact. It is, however, recommended that the device be used in conjunction with a long cane or guide dog.

Baird (1977) compared the potential use of the Pathsounder, the laser cane, and the Sonicguide™ for spatial concept development in young visually impaired children. By carefully reviewing the functional use of the devices, Baird suggested "that the usual approach of progressive introduction of electronic devices as supplementary aids to the dog guide or long cane might be reversed" (p. 101). Thus, she indicated and strongly recommended that the use of electronic devices begin at an early age to bridge the developmental gaps and provide a conceptual framework from which the blind child can build orientation and mobility skills. Kay (1980) investigated the possibility of developing an acoustic schema in blind children through the use of sensory devices. Five visually impaired children (ages 9–16) were trained to use the Sonicguide™. Subjects were presented with blocks and asked to build a tower by taking turns. The location of the tower was changed with each turn, thus forcing the child to locate it and reach for it in order to place his or her block on the tower. Kay reported that four of the five subjects quickly attained accuracy in reaching. The author suggested that electronic devices may be used in the development of acoustic schema and the position of objects in space can be built into the cognitive development of a blind child. Aitken and Bower (1982) investigated the potential use of the Sonicguide™ with visually impaired infants. They suggested that early intervention with the device is a definite possibility. However, they cautioned that the advantages to be gained depend upon the way in which the aid is used by the infant.

Ferrell (1980), using four infants aged 6–30 months, investigated developmental changes during a 2 year study. The Sonicguide™ was adapted so that it was mounted on the child's forehead. All training occurred in the children's homes to provide a consistent and familiar environment. All lessons were videotaped and evaluated on a monthly basis. The investigation concluded that the device provided sensory information that could be assimilated and accommodated internally. Thus, it can be expected that with the introduction to the Sonicguide™ at the "optimum" age of 4–6 months, a visually impaired infant will develop at a rate comparable to that of sighted infants. From the studies conducted thus far, it is difficult to draw any definite conclusions. However, it appears that the potential of the Sonicguide™ as a device to facilitate the development of visually impaired children needs to be investigated in more detail.

Technology and its application with visually impaired children is a relatively new area, and there is an apparent need for further investigation. The potential use of reading devices as tools for teaching print reading (along with braille) to young visually impaired children may prove to increase the reading ability of the children. Since totally blind children begin to fall behind the sighted at about age 4 months in all developmental areas (due to restricted experiences with the environment), it would seem that use of devices that can enhance the spatial awareness of the infant will increase the rate of their development. Further, the use of sensory devices as employment tools needs to be investigated. It would seem that the effect of technology on the visually impaired population may prove to be a positive one. However, that effect may be seen only through well designed longitudinal studies.

Perhaps the ultimate technological device is one that addresses visual loss itself rather than its effects on the daily functioning of visually impaired persons. This device will attempt to provide a substitute for vision; that is, a visual prosthesis. The ultimate goal of this type of research is to place a miniature camera in the eye socket that would provide "visual" information to the visual cortex through numerous electrodes stimulating the brain to "see" an orderly pattern of phosphemes yielding an image of the outside world. Obviously, such a device is a long way in the future. However, advances in technology and neuroscience have made it possible thus far for several totally blind individuals to "visually" differentiate between horizontal and vertical lines.

This preliminary exploration, and its success, clearly map the way for future collaboration between technological and neuroscientific research. Such research may lead to the production of the ultimate sensory aid: visual prosthesis.

Discussion

The development of technological devices has contributed greatly to the integration of the sensory impaired into society. It is not surprising that the focus of technological development has been in the area of assistive communication devices because of the difficulties encountered by hearing impaired individuals with oral communication and visually impaired individuals with print communication. Although the research to date indicates that these devices have a potential for effective information gathering and processing, it still remains to be seen whether continued use and engineering improvements would effectively integrate the sensory impaired population into the mainstream of society both educationally and vocationally.

While sophisticated technological devices are available, it must also be remembered that it is not the device itself but its effective use by the sensory impaired individual that is of major importance. Research in the application of technology lies within the domain of the educator. It is necessary to determine the skills that the individual needs, both to use and to maintain the device. Educators need to develop effective techniques to train sensory impaired individuals to use the device. Frequently, training in the use of the device involves instruction only in its mechanical use. Such instruction, while necessary, may be insufficient to enable the individual to use the device to its maximum potential. Experience with the Optacon, for example, indicates that training in tracking and letter recognition are not sufficient for its optimum use, and that training in a linguistically based reading program may also be necessary. Hearing aid technology is of little use to the hearing impaired individual who is not taught to interpret the auditory signal that is detected.

There is also a need to examine the effects of the use of technological aids on several areas of development. Thus, one would want to examine the effect of early training with orientation and mobility aids on the development of spatial concepts in visually impaired children, or the effects of captions on the linguistic development and reading achievement of hearing impaired children. The environment in which the technological aid can best be used is also a factor that needs to be considered. A high level of background noise, for example, diminishes the potential use of a hearing aid.

It is clear that systematic inquiry into the application and effective use of technological devices is as important as the development of the hardware. Cooperation between educators, engineers, and sensory impaired individuals can result in major advances in the development and efficient use of technology that truly serves the individual for whom it is meant.

CRITICAL PERSPECTIVES

A considerable amount of research has been conducted in the developmental areas for sensory impaired children. Unfortunately, few conclusions can be made. A careful study of the literature reveals some of the major reasons. This section will explore the reasons and suggest some directions for future research.

A review of the literature reveals a preponderance of research on children with severe sensory losses, while research with children who have mild to moderate losses is extremely scarce. Yet low vision and hard of hearing children are more numerous than blind and deaf children and deserve some attention from researchers. Little information is currently available on the effect of a mild or moderate sensory loss on development. Still less is known about the kinds of intervention techniques that work well with these children and in which areas of development intervention would yield the best results. Educational environments for these children vary widely, ranging from regular

public school classrooms to self-contained special classrooms. We need to examine the interaction between educational setting and degree of sensory loss to try to determine which educational environments are best for these children. In short, research information on children with mild to moderate sensory impairments is sorely needed.

The development of technology has helped many sensory impaired individuals to become part of the larger society. Future research should concentrate not only on developing new technology, but on application of this technology to best serve the sensory impaired user. Research is necessary to determine how sensory impaired individuals can make maximum use of available technology and how teachers can educate sensory impaired learners using such technology. Research indicates that the existence of a technological tool does not necessarily result in its appropriate or maximal use. It is to be hoped that researchers will expend some energy examining the techniques by which present and future technological aids can be used to their full potential.

The research models used with children with sensory impairments have been borrowed, with practically no modifications, from research with nonhandicapped children and are not ideally suited for research with such a heterogeneous and low incidence group. These models lead to methodological weaknesses that affect the quality of the research. Perhaps the first and most common weakness is the lack of adequate specification and analysis of subject characteristics. These characteristics are "status" or "self-selected"; that is, they are brought by the subject to the research and are not under the control of the investigator (Warren, 1977). Because of the relatively small and diverse population, status characteristics, such as chronological age, mental age, functional sense utilization, etiology age at onset, and duration of the handicapping condition, must be recorded and considered in the selection of subjects and the analysis of the results. The sample for any research study contains individuals who differ with respect to these variables. The options available to the investigator are (a) to select a homogeneous sample; (b) to integrate these variables into the research design and statistical analysis; and (c) to employ carefully designed single subject research models.

Selection of homogeneous sample will eliminate possible influences of status variables on the question under investigation. In research with nonhandicapped children, the sample is selected at random from a given pool of subjects. This procedure ensures that the sample will be representative of the population with respect to the characteristics that might influence the outcome of the investigation. Obviously, random selection of the sample is desirable but, unfortunately, not practical with sensory impaired children. Given the small number of sensory impaired in any geographical area, the investigator is not likely to obtain an adequate sample for statistical analysis and generalize his or her findings to the rest of the population.

The integration of status variables into the research design and statistical analysis could be a better research model, since statistical procedures for treatment of heterogeneous samples are available. The utilization of such procedures would allow the investigator to evaluate the results with respect to those variables in much the same way as he or she would evaluate the effect of a treatment variable, thus making it possible statistically to control for these variables. There appear to be several advantages to such models. Obviously, the issue of heterogeneity becomes an asset in subject selection rather than a liability, particularly with a limited number of subjects available. The utilization of an integrated model provides for the evaluation rather than the elimination of possible effects, thus allowing for comparative conclusions about various subgroups. In addition, if it is found that any of these variables have no significant effect on the question studied, then more generalized conclusions may be drawn.

Research models with sensory impaired children seem to combine both of these approaches. Unfortunately, complete description of subject characteristics is not often included. In many instances, the results of apparently similar studies are in direct contradiction to each other because of unequivalent samples resulting from immense heterogeneity of the population. The reader can at least attempt to resolve such contradictions if provided with complete descriptions of subject selection procedures and subject characteristics. In the case of comparative studies, where visually impaired are compared to sighted children or hearing impaired to hearing children, the issue of representation must indeed be questioned due to the heterogeneity and low incidence of the population.

Several issues regarding research methodology need to be addressed. These issues are indeed common to all research, but take on a great significance in the area of sensory impairments. Several studies provide vague definitions of the variables being examined. It is of utmost importance to operationalize and provide within each study the variables that may affect the outcome of the investigation, as well as the independent variable studied. Providing such information will enable the reader and other investigators to draw identical conclusions to those of the researcher, and to build future research on more solid bases.

Selection of appropriate evaluation tools is of particular importance in research that compares sensory impaired to normal individuals. The evaluation measures must be sensitive to differences between subjects. Many tools developed primarily for use with normal children are not able to measure the small gains achieved by some sensory impaired children. At the same time, tools developed primarily for use with sensory impaired children may result in a ceiling effect because the items are too simple for normal children at similar chronological ages.

Another significant issue, particularly in research on cognitive development, is the thorough understanding of the task by the subjects. In many studies where significant lags in cognitive development are reported, it may be entirely due to the subject's failure to understand the nature of the task for a variety of reasons. It is the researcher's responsibility to provide time, effort, and perhaps a different approach to ensure that all subjects involved in the study equally understand the task under investigation. Failure to do so inevitably leads to greater score variability. This issue is closely connected to the statistical treatment of the data. Researchers generally report and employ the mean scores in their statistical analyses in comparative studies. Mean scores are indeed very important but, without some information about the variability of the scores around the mean, may lead to false conclusions.

Thus far we have examined some of the drawbacks in research involving sensory impaired children. It appears that group models borrowed from research with nonhandicapped children without specific modifications, for extremely heterogeneous and small groups of children do not provide the necessary results to derive accurate conclusions from which to build a solid body of knowledge on the development of sensory impaired children.

Warren (1977) proposed a hierarchical model that will involve not only evaluation of the characteristic to be studied but also its etiology and expression in real life behavior. The key to Warren's model in measuring developmental abilities is to evaluate the "present and past factors that might produce variations in that ability" (p. 283) and the ways in which it is expressed in the child's behavior in everyday life. A hierarchical model is indeed a promising one. However, at the present time, there is no methodology for studying etiology factors, and to omit such factors will result in violating the basic tenets of the model.

Research, as it can be seen in this chapter, has generally concentrated on a single developmental area with little consideration of how each area affects the others. Thus, a new approach to study developmental abilities is needed. Such an approach should address the issues just discussed, including the sensory, learning, language, and social aspects of the child's environment. Greater attention to these issues and to current environmental conditions as well as major environmental changes from the past will provide necessary information on experiential background and its effect on the child's ability. One way of implementing this approach is through carefully designed longitudinal research involving small but homogeneous groups of children. Thus, the research will look at the development of the total child rather than single abilities. The major advantage of such research would be a comparison of the various abilities within the subjects rather than comparing them with sighted and/ or hearing children. A series of studies of this type will certainly enable us to look at the influences of the different variables as well as provide information toward a theory of different developmental patterns in sensory impaired children.

Finally, research is needed in determining the effects of intervention on development. Currently, the effects of global interventions, such as placement at a residential school, have been examined; however, very few specific intervention strategies have been validated by research. If sensory impaired children are to be effectively educated to function independently in the larger society, intervention strategies need to be based not only on tradition and historical precedent but also on a scientific research base.

REFERENCES

Adelson, E., & Fraiberg, S. (1974). Gross motor development in infants blind from birth. *Child Development*, *45*, 114–126.

Aitkin, S., & Bower, T. (1982). The use of the sonicguide in infancy. *Journal of Visual Impairment and Blindness*, *76*, 91–100.

Anderson, D. W., & Olson, M. (1981). Word meaning among congenitally blind children. *Journal of Visual Impairment and Blindness*, *75*, 165–168.

Antia, S. (1982). Social interaction of partially mainstreamed hearing impaired children. *American Annals of the Deaf*, *127*, 18–25.

Apple, M. M. (1972). Kinesic training for blind persons: A vital means of communication. *New Outlook for the Blind*, *66*, 201–208.

Baird, A. (1977). Electronic aids: Can they help blind children? *Journal of Visual Impairment and Blindness*, *71*, 97–101.

Becker, S. (1974). The performance of deaf and hearing children on a logical discovery task. *Volta Review*, *77*, 537–544.

Berger, K. W. (1976). From telephone to electric hearing aid. *Volta Review*, *78*, 83–89.

Bertora, de F. (1974). New method of tactile reading. *The Sciences*, *6*, 34–41.

Bess, F. H. (1977). Conditions of hearing aids worn by children in a public school setting. Washington, DC: U.S. Office of Education, Pub. No. 77-05002.

Blair, J. C. (1977). Effects of amplification, speech reading, and classroom environments on reception of speech. *Volta Review, 79,* 443-449.

Bliss, J. C. (1972). Optacon evaluation considerations. In *Evaluation of sensory aids for the visually impaired,* pp. 51-54. Washington, DC: National Academy of Sciences.

Brackett D., & Henniges, M. (1976). Communicative interaction of preschool hearing impaired children in an integrated setting. *Volta Review, 78,* 276-285.

Brasel, E. E., & Quigley, S. P. (1977). Influence of certain language and communication environments in early childhood on the development of language in deaf individuals. *Journal of Speech and Hearing Research, 20,* 95-107.

Braverman, B. B., & Hertzog, M. (1980). The effects of the caption rate and language level on comprehension of a captioned video presentation. *American Annals of the Deaf, 125,* 943-948.

Brieland, D. M. (1950). A comparative study of the speech of blind and sighted children. *Speech Monographs, 17,* 99-103.

Burlingham, D. (1961). Some notes on the development of the blind. *Psychoanalytic Study of the Child, 16,* 121-145.

Burlingham, D. (1965). Some problems of ego development in blind children. *Psychoanalytic Study of the Child, 20,* 194-208.

Caldwel, D. C. (1973). Use of graded captions with instructional television for deaf learners. *American Annals of the Deaf, 118,* 500-507.

Craig, W., & Collins, J. (1970). Analysis of communicative interaction in classes for deaf children. *American Annals of the Deaf, 115,* 79-85.

Curtiss, S., Prutting, C. A., & Lowell, E. L. (1979). Pragmatic and semantic development in young children with impaired hearing. *Journal of Speech and Hearing Research, 22,* 534-552.

Cutsforth, T. D. (1932). The unreality of words to the blind. *Teachers Forum, 4,* 86-89.

Cutsforth, T. D. (1951). *The blind in school and society.* New York: American Foundation for the Blind.

Darbyshire, J. O., & Reeves, V. R. (1969). The use of adaptations of some of Piaget's tests with groups of children with normal and impaired hearing. *British Journal of Disorders in Communication,* 197-203.

DeMott, R. M. (1972). Verbalism and affective meaning for blind, severely visually impaired, and normally sighted children. *New Outlook for the Blind, 66,* 1-8.

Dokecki, P. C. (1966). Verbalism and the blind: A critical review of the concept and the literature. *Exceptional Children, 32,* 525-530.

Dore, J. (1975). Holophrases, speech acts and language universals. *Child Language, 2,* 21-40.

Dumas, M. G. (1932). Mimicry of the blind. *And There Was Light, 2,* 30-33.

Elkind, D. (1961). Children's discovery of the conservation of mass, weight and volume: Piaget replication, study II. *Journal of Genetic Psychology, 98,* 219-227.

Elser, R. P. (1959). The social position of hearing impaired children in the regular grades. *Exceptional Children, 25,* 305-309.

Engelmann, S., & Rosov, R. J. (1975). Tactual hearing experiment with deaf and hearing subjects. *Exceptional Children, 41,* 243-253.

Ferrell, K. (1980). Can infants use the Sonicguide? Two years experience of Project View. *Journal of Visual Impairment and Blindness, 74,* 209-220.

Finitzo-Hieber, T., & Tilman, T. W. (1978). Room acoustic effects on monosyllabic word discrimination ability for normal and hearing impaired children. *Journal of Speech and Hearing Research, 21,* 440-458.

Foulke, E. (1962). The role of experience in the formation of concepts. *International Journal for the Education of the Blind, 12,* 1-6.

Foulke, E. (1964). A multi-sensory test of conceptual ability. *New Outlook for the Blind, 58,* 75-77.

Fraiberg, S. (1968). Parallel and divergent patterns in blind and sighted infants. *Psychological Study of the Child, 23,* 264-300.

Fraiberg, S., & Adelson, E. (1973). Self-representation in language and play: Observations of blind children. *Psychoanalytic Quarterly, 42,* 539-562.

Fraiberg, S., Siegel, B., & Gibson, R. (1966). The role of sound in the search behavior of a blind infant. *Psychoanalytic Study of the Child, 21,* 327-357.

Freedman, D. G. (1964). Smiling in blind infants and the issue of innate vs. acquired. *Journal of Child Psychology and Psychiatry, 5,* 171-184.

Friedman, J., & Pasnak, R. (1973). Accelerated acquisition of classification skills by blind children. *Developmental Psychology 9,* 333-337.

Fulcher, J. S. (1942). "Voluntary" facial expression in blind and seeing children. *Archives of Psychology,* No. 272.

Furth, H. G. (1964). Conservation of weight in deaf and hearing children. *Child Development, 35,* 143-150.

Furth, H. G. (1966a). Research with the deaf. Implications for language and cognition. *Volta Review,* Reprint No. 852, 22-44.

Furth, H. G. (1966b). *Thinking without language.* New York: Macmillan.

Furth, H. G., & Youniss, J. (1969). Thinking in deaf adolescents. Language and formal operations. *Journal of Communication Disorders, 2,* 195-202.

Geoffrion, L. (1982a). An analysis of teletype conversations. *American Annals of the Deaf, 127,* 747-752.

Geoffrion, L. (1982b). The ability of hearing impaired students to communicate using a teletype system. *Volta Review, 127*, 96–108.

Glaser, R. E. (1982). Telephone communication for the deaf. *American Annals of the Deaf, 127*, 550–555.

Gottesman, M. (1973). Conservation development in blind children. *Child Development, 44*, 824–827.

Goulder, T. J., & Trybus, R. J. (1977). *The classroom behavior of emotionally disturbed hearing impaired children.* Washington, DC: Office of Demographic Studies.

Greenberg, M. T. (1980). Mode use in deaf children. The effects of communication method and communication competence. *Applied Psycholinguistics, 1*, 65–79.

Greenfield, P., & Smith, J. (1976). *The structure of communication in early language development.* New York: Academic Press.

Hallenbeck, J. (1954). Two essential factors in the development of young blind children. *New Outlook for the Blind, 48*, 308–315.

Halliday, M.A.K. (1979). One child's proto-language. In M. Bullowa (Ed.), *Before speech.* New York: Cambridge University Press.

Harley, R. K. (1963). *Verbalism among blind children.* Research Series No. 10. New York: American Foundation for the Blind.

Haspiel, G. S. (1965). Communication breakdown in the blind emotionally disturbed child. *New Outlook for the Blind, 59*, 98–99.

Hatwell, Y. (1966). *Privation sensorielle et intelligence.* Paris: Presses Universitaires de France.

Havill, S. J. (1970). The sociometric status of visually handicapped children in public school classes. *American Foundation for the Blind Research Bulletin, 20*, 57–81.

Heider, F. K., & Heider, G. M. (1940). A comparison of sentence structure of deaf and hearing children. *Psychological Monograph, 52*, 42–103.

Higginbotham, D. J., & Baker, B. M. (1981). Social participation and cognitive play differences in hearing impaired and normally hearing preschoolers. *Volta Review, 83*, 135–149.

Higgins, L. C. (1973). Classification in congenitally blind children. Research Series No. 25. New York: American Foundation for the Blind.

Inhelder, B., Sinclair, H., & Bovet, M. (1974). *Language and the development of cognition.* Cambridge, MA: Harvard University Press.

Jensema, C. (1975). *The relationship between academic achievement and the demographic characteristics of hearing impaired children and youth.* Washington, DC: Office of Demographic Studies.

Jensema, C., & Trybus, R. J. (1975). *Reported emotional/behavioral problems among hearing impaired children in special education programs: United States 1972–73.* Washington, DC: Office of Demographic Studies.

Karchmer, M. A., & Kirwin, L. A. (1977). *The use of hearing aids by hearing impaired students in the United States.* Washington, DC: Office of Demographic Studies.

Kay, N. (1980). Reaching to sound. *Journal of Visual Impairment and Blindness, 74*, 163, 165–166.

Keeler, W. R. (1958). Autistic patterns and defective communication in blind children with retrolental fibroplasia. In P. H. Hoch & J. Zubin (Eds.), *Psychopathology of communication.* New York: Grune and Stratton.

Kennedy, P., & Bruininks, R. H. (1974). Social status of hearing impaired children in regular classrooms. *Exceptional Children, 40*, 336–342.

Kennedy, P., Northcott, W., McCauley, R., & Williams, S. N. (1976). Longitudinal sociometric and cross sectional data on mainstreamed hearing impaired children. Implications for preschool planning. *Volta Review, 78*, 71–81.

Klopping, H. W. E. (1972). Language understanding of deaf students under three auditory visual stimulus conditions. *American Annals of the Deaf, 117*, 389–396.

Lowenfeld, B. (1948). Effects of blindness on the cognitive functions of children. *Nervous Child, 7*, 45–54.

Marmolin, H., & Nilsson, L. (1973). *Optacon reading aid: An evaluation of instructional methods and applicability.* Report No. 43. Pedagogial Institute, Uppsala, Sweden: Uppsala Normal School.

Marmor, G. S., & Petitto, L. (1979). Simultaneous communication in the classroom: How well is English grammar represented? *Sign Language Studies, 23*, 99–136.

Maxfield, K. E. (1936). The spoken language of the blind preschool child. *Archives of Psychology,* (201).

Maxfield, K. E., & Fjeld, H. A. (1942). The social maturity of the visually handicapped preschool child. *Child Development, 13*, 1–27.

Mayadas, N. S. (1972). Role expectations and performance of blind children: Practice and implications. *Education of the Visually Handicapped, 4*, 45–52.

McCauley, R. W., & Bruininks, R. H. (1976). Behavioral interactions of hearing impaired children in regular classrooms. *Journal of Special Education, 10*, 277–284.

McGinnis, A. R. (1981). Functional linguistic strategies of blind children. *Journal of Visual Impairment and Blindness, 75*, 210–214.

McGuinness, R. M. (1970). A descriptive study of blind children educated in the itinerant teacher, resource room, and special school setting. *American Foundation for the Blind Research Bulletin, 20*, 1–56.

McGuire, L. L., & Meyers, C. E. (1971). Early personality in the congenitally blind child. *New Outlook for the Blind, 65*, 137–143.

McKay, B. E. (1936). Social maturity of the preschool blind child. *Training School Bulletin, 33*, 146–155.

McKirdy, L. S., & Blank, M. (1982). Dialogue in deaf and hearing preschoolers. *Journal of Speech and Hearing Research*, *25*, 487–499.

Meadow, K. (1968). Early manual communication in relation to the deaf child's intellectual, social, and communicative functioning. *American Annals of the Deaf*, *113*, 29–41.

Meadow, K. P., Greenburg, M. T., Erting, C., & Carmichael, M. (1981). Interactions of deaf mothers and deaf preschool children compared with three other groups of deaf and hearing dyads. *American Annals of the Deaf*, *126*, 454–467.

Miller, C. K. (1969). Conservation in blind children. *Education of the Visually Handicapped*, *1*, 101–105.

Miller, J. F. (1980). *Assessimg language production in children*. Baltimore: University Park Press.

Miner, L. E. (1963). A study of the incidence of speech deviations among visually handicapped children. *New Outlook for the Blind*, *57*, 10–14.

Murphy, E. F. (1972). Evaluation of certain reading aids for the blind. In *Evaluation of Sensory Aids for the Visually Handicapped*, pp. 37–45. Washington, DC: National Academy of Sciences.

Murphy-Berman, V., & Jorgensen, J. (1980). Evaluation of a multilevel linguistic approach to captioning television for hearing impaired children. *American Annals of the Deaf*, *125*, 1072–1081.

Myklebust, H. (1960). *The psychology of deafness*. New York: Grune and Stratton.

Nelton, A. (1972). *Optacon technique: An evaluation of reading training with serious visually handicapped with optacon*. Furulund, AMU Center.

Nolan, C. Y. (1960). On the unreality of words to the blind. *New Outlook for the Blind*, *54*, 100–102.

Norris, M., Spaulding, P. J., & Brodie, F. H. (1957). *Blindness in children*. Chicago: University of Chicago Press.

Odom, P. B., & Blanton, R. L. (1967). Phrase learning in deaf and hearing subjects. *Journal of Speech and Hearing Research*, *10*, 600–605.

Olerón, P. (1953). Conceptual thinking of the deaf. *American Annals of the Deaf*, *98*, 304–310.

Oller, D. K., Payne, S. L., & Gavin, W. J. (1980). Tactual speech perception by minimally trained deaf subjects. *Journal of Speech and Hearing Research*, *23*, 769–778.

Parke, K. L., Shallcross, R., & Anderson, R. J. (1980). Differences in coverbal behavior between blind and sighted persons during dyadic communication. *Journal of Visual Impairment and Blindness*, *74*, 142–146.

Pendergrass, R. A., & Hodges, M. (1976). Deaf students in group problem solving situations: A study of the interactive process. *American Annals of the Deaf*, *121*, 327–330.

Quigley, S., & Frisina, D. (1961). *Institutionalization and psychoeducational development of deaf children*.

Washington, DC: Council for Exceptional Children.

Quigley, S. P., & King, C. M. (1980). Syntactic performance of hearing impaired and normal hearing individuals. *Applied Psycholinguistics*, *1*, 329–356.

Quigley, S. P., Montanelli, D. S., & Wilbur, R. B. (1976). Some aspects of the verb system in the language of deaf students. *Journal of Speech and Hearing Research*, *19*, 536–550.

Quigley, S., Wilbur, R., & Montanelli, D. (1974). Question formation in the language of deaf students. *Journal of Speech and Hearing Research*, *17*, 699–713.

Quigley, S., Wilbur, R., & Montanelli, D. (1976). Complement structures in the language of deaf students. *Journal of Speech and Hearing Research*, *19*, 448–457.

Reich, C., Hambleton, D., & Houldin, B. K. (1977). Integration of hearing impaired children in a regular classroom. *American Annals of the Deaf*, *122*, 534–543.

Rich, C. C., & Anderson, R. P. (1965). A tactual form of the progressive matrices for use with blind children. *Personnel and Guidance Journal*, *43*, 912–919.

Rittenhouse, R. K., Morreau, L. E., & Iran-Nejad, A. (1981). Metaphor and conservation in deaf and hard of hearing children. *American Annals of the Deaf*, *126*, 450–453.

Rittenhouse, R. K., & Spiro, R. J. (1979). Conservation performance in day and residential school deaf children. *Volta Review*, *81*, 501–509.

Sandler, A. M. (1963). Aspects of passivity and ego development in the blind infant. *Psychoanalytic Study of the Child*, *18*, 343–361.

Schindele, R. (1974). The social adjustment of visually handicapped children in different educational settings. *American Foundation for the Blind Research Bulletin*, *28*, 125–144.

Schlesinger, H. S., & Meadow, K. P. (1972). *Sound and sign: Childhood deafness and mental health*. Berkeley: University of California Press.

Schoof, L. T. (1975). An analysis of optacon usage. *American Foundation for the Blind Research Bulletin*.

Scott, R. A. (1968). *The making of blind men*. New York: Russell Sage Foundation.

Scroggs, C. L. (1977). Analyzing the language of hearing impaired children with severe language acquisition problems. *American Annals of the Deaf*, *122*, 403–406.

Shroyer, E. H., & Birch, J. (1980). Captions and reading rate of hearing impaired students. *American Annals of the Deaf*, *125*, 916–922.

Sibinga, M. S., & Friedman, C. J. (1971). Restraint and speech. *Pediatrics*, *48*, 116–122.

Simmons, A. (1962). A comparison of the type token ratio of spoken and written language of deaf children. *Volta Review*, *64*, 417–421.

Sommers, V. S. (1944). *The influence of parental attitudes and social environment on the personality development of the adolescent blind.* New York: American Foundation for the Blind.

Stephens, B., & Simpkins, K. (1974). The reasoning, moral judgement, and moral conduct of the congenitally blind. Final Project Report, H23-3197. Office of Education, Bureau of Education for the Handicapped.

Stinchfield, S. M. (1933). *Speech disorders.* New York: Harcourt, Brace and Co.

Stoker, R. G. (1982). Telecommunications technology and the hearing impaired: Recent research trends and a look into the future. *Volta Review,* *84,* 147–155.

Stuckless, E. R., & Birch, J. W. (1966). The influence of early manual communication on the linguistic development of deaf children. *American Annals of the Deaf,* *111,* 452–462.

Tait, P. (1972). The effect of circumstantial rejection on infant behavior. *New Outlook for the Blind,* *66,* 139–151.

Terzieff, I., Stagg, V., & Ashcroft, S. C. (1982). Increasing reading rates with the optacon: A pilot study. *Journal of Visual Impairment and Blindness,* *76,* 17–22.

Tilman, M. H., & Williams, C. (1968). Associative characteristics of blind and sighted children to selected form classes. *International Journal for the Education of the Blind,* *18,* 33–40.

Tobin, M. J. (1972). Conservation of substance in the blind and partially sighted. *British Journal of Educational Psychology,* *42,* 192–197.

Tobin, M. J. (1973). *Print reading by the blind: An evaluation of the optacon and an investigation of some learner variables and teaching methods.* Birmingham, England: University of Birmingham.

Tomblin, J. B. (1977). Effect of syntactic order on serial recall performance of hearing impaired and normal hearing subjects. *Journal of Speech and Hearing Research,* *20,* 421–429.

Vernon, M., & Koh, S. D. (1970). Effects of early manual communication on achievement of deaf children. *American Annals of the Deaf,* *115,* 527–536.

Warren, D. (1977). *Blindness and early childhood development.* New York: American Foundation for the Blind.

Watts, W. J. (1979). The influence of language on the development of quantitative, spatial and social thinking in deaf children. *American Annals of the Deaf,* *124,* 46–56.

Weisgerber, R. A. (1974). *Educational evaluation of the optacon (optical-to-tactile converter) as a reading aid to blind elementary and secondary students.* Palo Alto, CA: American Institute for Research.

White, A. H., & Stevenson, V. M. (1975). The effects of total communication, manual communication, oral communication and reading on the learning of factual information in residential school deaf children. *American Annals of the Deaf,* *120,* 48–57.

Wilbur, R., Quigley, S., & Montanelli, D. (1975). Conjoined structures in the language of deaf students. *Journal of Speech and Hearing Research,* *18,* 319–335.

Wilson, J., & Halverson, H. M. (1947). Development of a young blind child. *Journal of Genetic Psychology,* *71,* 155–175.

Wolff, P. (1966). Developmental studies of blind children: II. *New Outlook for the Blind,* *60,* 179–182.

Zierer, I. (1972). *Study in optacon reading in blind rehabilitation subjects.* Heidelberg, Germany: Institute for Teaching of the Deaf and those with Speech and Visual Handicaps.

11 THE SOCIOLOGY OF SPECIAL EDUCATION

Robert Bogdan

A few sociologists have had formal affiliation with university departments of special education but, for the most part, they have been marginal to that field. In spite of this, the contribution of sociology to special education has been substantial. A growing number of sociologists are taking special education and disability issues as a research focus and special educators continue to develop and incorporate sociological concepts in their work.

Sociologists and special educators who approach special education from a sociological perspective can be divided into two groups. The first operates within the assumptions of the field's practitioners. These assumptions include (a) disability is a condition that individuals have, (b) disability/typical distinction is useful and objective; (c) special education is a rationally conceived and coordinated system of service that helps disabled children; (d) progress in the field comes from improving diagnosis, intervention, and technology (Bogdan and Kugelmauss, in press). Those embracing these assumptions practice what could be called *special education sociology*. The other group looks critically at the underlying logic of special education and practices the *sociology of special education* (Freidson, 1970).

Some people in the field of special education, as well as in sociology (Dexter, 1956; Faber, 1968), have questioned the basic premises of special education and related disciplines and have thereby made a lasting contribution to the field. Blatt (1970), Braginsky and Braginsky (1971), Goffman (1961, 1963), Sarason and Doris, (1979), Scheff (1966), Scott (1969), and Szasz (1961) pointed out that "client" categories are metaphors and have laid the groundwork for thinking about so-called handicaps as social constructions rather than as objective conditions. These same authors and their associates in the interactionist, or labeling, school of sociology pointed to the importance of examining how labelers interact with those labeled as a prerequisite for understanding clients (see Goffman, 1961; Lemert, 1951; Wiseman, 1970). The interface of human service agencies, including schools, with clients became an area in which social researchers could develop theoretical perspectives on how labels and definitions were applied. There are a number of empirical studies that look at special education clients and practitioners from alternative perspectives (Conrad, 1976; Higgins, 1980). While the ideas that developed in sociology and related fields have been incorporated into and, in some cases, developed within the field of special education—note the use of the word *labeling* and the development of the so-called ecological approach—for the most part, special educators are not aware of the theoretical underpinnings of such an approach. The purpose of this paper is to provide the theoretical background to show the connections between a particular sociological theory and special education and to point to some research implications. The goal is to more systematically develop a particular kind of a *sociology of special education*.

WHAT'S THEORY?

Special education has been more closely aligned with psychology than with sociology. When psychologists say *theory* they mean something different than when sociologists say it. For sociologists, *theory* is interchangeable with the word *paradigm*, referring to a general approach to the world rather than a limited set of testable propositions that explain a discrete set of behaviors; that is, learning theory. An example of a sociological theory is conflict theory (Karl Marx is associated with this approach). It is an approach to understanding human behavior that emphasizes the distribution of power and resources in society and how the differential distribution structures relationships. Conflict theory is a loose collection of logically held together assumptions, concepts, and propositions that orient thinking in research. Whether stated or not, all research is guided by some theoretical orientation. Symbolic interaction is another approach to the world, a theory in the loose sense, that provides the basic background assumptions of the labeling approach to disability and underlies the critical work mentioned earlier.

SYMBOLIC INTERACTIONAL THEORY

Symbolic interaction developed as the conceptual underpinning of research strategy at the University of Chicago's Sociology Department in the 1920s. Chicago sociologists such as Robert Park, W. I. Thomas, and Florian Zaniecki were concerned with understanding the range of human behavior as it occurred in the real world and from the point of view of the subjects. Thus, they told their students to follow their example and do research among the immigrants, hobos, juvenile delinquents, and other people of Chicago. One of their students, Everett Hughs, continued the tradition by training his students—who included Howard S. Becker, Blanche Geer, Anselm Strauss, and Erving Goffman—to do field work in ordinary places in a manner like that of anthropologists in strange lands. Herbert Blumer (1969) played an important role in carrying on the early Chicago tradition by systematically writing about the theory that underlies the approach. He was the person who coined the word *symbolic interaction*. His translation of George Herbert Mead's (1934) ideas (Blumer, 1969) provided the conceptual base for the research done in the labeling school tradition.

The cliche beauty is in the eye of the beholder embodies the emphasis of the symbolic interactionist approach. We all know, but seldom take seriously when conducting research, that objects, people, situations, life, and the world do not carry their own meaning, rather meaning is conferred upon them. To put it another way, meaning does not lie in things; the interpretation or definition that the viewer imputes is paramount. For symbolic interactionists, the subjects of investigation are how people define the world and the process by which that understanding is constructed. Human beings are foremost interpreting, defining, symbolic creatures, whose behavior can only be understood by entering the defining process.

Conferring meaning is not an autonomous act; human beings are social and meaning develops through interaction with others. People who are in contact with each other, who share the same situation, are influenced by each other in how they come to define the situation. They may see things in a similar way. A person who enters a new situation may, in the process of defining the setting, use the definitions and interpretations others have, or they may try to apply meanings they encountered in other settings. The individual, through the process of feeling out the situation, attempts to make it meaningful. It is from the complex interaction among the setting and with others in it, the past, and the larger social present that meaning emerges for the person. Groups in a particular situation and/or in similar positions — students in a particular school, for example — often develop common definitions and see these as the truth or as the only meaning of what they are defining. Their constructions of "reality" are seen as reality, and the commonality of definitions help to confirm this truth. People living their lives see objects or acts as having an inherent meaning, or an essence. This, rather than the similarity of the defining process, is taken as the explanation for consensus.

To use this symbolic interactionist perspective in understanding the meaning of the situation, one has to look at the group that defines the object and the history and the nature of the defining and sharing process rather than the object itself. The theory shys away from terms like *truth* in that it emphasizes human experience as subjective not absolute. You can be empirical because it is possible to systematically study the subjective states of others, but the goal is to piece together and analyze the world from the subject's point of view and to understand the process whereby meaning develops. In certain historical periods, among certain groups, a specific definition or set of definitions of the world or objects may dominate: again, its domination has more to do with the politics of perspective than its congruence with the world in which it is applied.

The terms *perspective, definition, meaning,* and *interaction* are the key tools in understanding behavior. We act toward objects on the basis of the meaning they construe rather than on the basis of internal drives, personalities, attitudes, and conscious motives, role obligations, social control mechanisms, or structural, cultural, or demographic variables. These concepts, which other social scientists use to discuss, understand, and predict behavior, place meaning and interaction in the background. Other theoretical constructs might be useful in understanding special aspects of behavior but, from the symbolic interactionist perspective, they miss the central element of human behavior — meaning. For example, a proponent

of symbolic interaction would not deny that there is a drive to eat and that there are certain norms as to how, what, and when one should eat. But eating cannot be understood adequately in terms of drives and norms. Eating must be studied in terms of how people come to define eating in specific situations in which they find themselves (Bogdan, 1972). Eating is experienced differently, and people exhibit different behaviors while eating in different situations. Employees in one school come to define the proper time to eat lunch, what to eat, and how to eat in a way significantly different from people in a school in a similar location. Eating lunch can be a break from work, an annoying intrusion, a chance to do some low keyed business, or a time to diet. (I do not suggest that these are mutually exclusive.) Eating meals has a very involved meaning, with which concepts like drive and norm cannot deal. For some people, meals provide a benchmark for specific developments in their day. Here, eating takes on significance of time spacing, providing an orderly set of events by which one can measure what has or hasn't been accomplished, how much of the day must still be endured, or how soon an exciting day will end. For some, lunch is the central event of the day, for others it is hardly noticed.

Symbolic interactionists do not deny that there are rules, regulations, norms and belief systems that people can recite, but they do suggest that these are important in understanding behavior only as they are taken into account by people. It is not the general rules and regulations and norms that cause behavior but how these may be defined and used in interpreting specific situations. People define objects, and it is these definitions and the process of defining them that is important in understanding human behavior.

An important part of the perspective, and compatible with everything said thus far, is how the theory presents the "self." The self is not seen as lying inside the individual like an ego or organized body of needs, motives, internalized norms, or values. The self lies outside the individual and is a product of the person's self-definition. People become objects to themselves and the definition they construct of that object is the self. In defining self, people attempt to see themselves as others see them. By interpreting gestures and actions directed toward them and by placing themselves in the role of observer, they come to construct their own definition. They see themselves, in part, as others see them. The self is, thus, a social construction, the result of perceiving oneself as an object, then developing self-definition through interaction. People use feedback as a source of discovering who they are. This interaction enables them to grow as they learn more about themselves in relation to others.

THE IMPLICATIONS OF SYMBOLIC INTERACTIONIST THEORY FOR SPECIAL EDUCATION

From a symbolic interactionist perspective, "disabled students" do not exist in any absolute sense (Bogdan & Kugelmauss, in press). The generic term *disabled* and specific disability categories are ways of thinking about and categorizing others. Whether people are thought of as disabled and the criteria used to determine whether someone is disabled has to do with how the definers think about these things. The mentally retarded, emotionally disturbed, learning disabled, and even the blind only appear after development of a way of thinking toward them that acknowledges them as existing and important to take note of.

There are no "true" counts of the number of people with disability or "correct" definitions of mental retardation, blindness and other disability categories (Bogdan & Ksander, 1980). Counts and definitions are reifications of customs and practices. Standardized diagnostic measures and procedures make conventionalized judgments appear to be truths, but they should not be confused with truth in any absolute sense. As concepts like mentally retarded and learning disabled become reified, so do the criteria and conceptual base developed for placement of individuals take on a reality that belies their existence as social creations. For example, people actually come to believe that

people really have IQs and that grade levels exist.

Professionals and researchers dealing with disability have continuously debated the definitions of diagnostic terms and the incidence and prevalence of various clinical categories. While, at any given time, a definition may be said to be official (the one accepted by the most influential professional organizations), there is never a clear consensus as to the meaning of such terms as *disability*, or the specific diagnostic categories falling under the heading. A number of social scientists have pointed to the ambiguity of such terminology and a differential application of the terms in different contexts.

Mercer (1973) demonstrated that the reported number of mentally retarded persons in the population is more a function of age than any "mental" condition, because the overwhelming majority of persons diagnosed as mentally retarded are not identified until school entrance and later "disappear" when the labeled group reaches adulthood. Dexter (1964) presents similar arguments. Braginsky and Braginsky (1971), in their study of institutionalized children, present evidence that even such relatively "hard" and "official" measures of mental capacity as IQ scores are effectively manipulated by the allegedly incompetent children in order to make themselves "bright" or "dull," given different consequences. Scott (1969), in his analysis of the seemingly objective area of blindness, demonstrates that stereotypic preconceptions and arbitrary operational measures result not only in a widely varying count of the "officially" blind, but also in a situation in which the overwhelming majority of people thus classified are able, in fact, to see. Szasz (1961) and a host of others have noted the ambiguity and metaphorical terminology in the area of mental illness and emotional disturbance.

Symbolic interactionist theory suggests that rather than concentrating on arriving at accurate definitions and true counts, official definitions and counts should be understood as the products of the people, processes, organizations, and societies that compile them. To the symbolic interactionist, definitions and counts are artifacts of the process of their production rather than reliable or unreliable information. While other theoretical approaches assume definitions and counts are ways of measuring reality, symbolic interactionists suggest that they should be approached as methods of constructing reality.

Counts and definitions of concepts such as mental retardation are temporal and represent larger political and social forces. Professionals in special education, as well as government officials and organization leaders, choose one dimension of meaning or develop one set of conventions to arrive at a method of constructing a definition and a real rate of disability; but what is arrived at is the product of the assumptions used, the concepts employed, and the processes as they evolve. To claim to have a true measure or an accurate definition is to claim the supremacy of one definition and method over another and should not be confused with "truth" in any strict sense.

Symbolic interactionists are not radical idealists. They emphasize the subjective, but they do not deny a reality "out there" that stands over and against human beings, capable of resisting action towards it (Blumer, 1980). The physical, behavioral, social, and mental characteristics of children enter into the process through which the meaning of the child emerges but not in the deterministic way that is commonly believed. The external reality of what is being defined or counted influences the emerging definitions and counts, but there is always a social process of discerning and procedures that lie between the phenomena and its results. Such things as not being able to read, not being able to pass a test, not being able to walk, or having organic brain damage set parameters in which definitions develop, but they do not determine how people with these characteristics will be defined or even if special note will be taken of them. To repeat, to say that disability is a social construct is not to deny physiological, behavior, or other differences among people, it is to point out the importance of meaning (*if* they are perceived and

how they are thought of) of these differences in constructing our actions towards those with specific designations.

Some children have difficulty accomplishing the tasks required of them in school and, in other ways, act different. *Retarded* tells us what being perceived as slow and different means. How *retarded* is manifested in the treatment and reactions to children is what symbolic interactionists dwell on. While not denying physical and behavioral realities, symbolic interactionists emphasize that human beings treat others on the basis of the meaning they have with them and that such treatment can result in a self-fulfilling prophesy. Not being able to perform up to level in school and acting funny need not mean that a child will be socially isolated and reacted to a specific way by others. The slow child's functioning may be as dependent upon the definition given to his condition by those in positions to influence the circumstances of his life as the "reality" of his "slowness."

Be it mental retardation, cerebral palsy, deafness, blindness, emotional disturbance, or learning disability, disability is only in a particular and most narrow sense something that someone has. Disability is always interactional. It does not simply symbolize a condition that is there in advance; it makes possible the existence or the appearance of the conditions, for it is part of the mechanism whereby the condition is created (Rose, 1962). Disability is a designation and, therefore, imbedded in social relations. Disability is a particular way of thinking about and a way of acting and reacting. The creation of concepts of disability and their application as specific settings, the effect it provokes, is derived and sustained in interaction. In one sense, disability changes by changing how we think about it.

The meaning of disability varies at different levels of our society. Disability can only be understood by understanding as a tiered situational occurrence. Official definitions are produced high in bureaucracies, yet they are applied by practitioners. Clients think about disabilities differently than officers in professional organizations. Often those collecting the data about disability operate on different assumptions than those who receive the data. Those who issue data requests are often not intimately familiar with the nature of the phenomena to be counted or with the dilemmas and concerns of the counters.

A 1976 study (Bogdan, 1976) of the 1973 congressional mandate to include 10% handicapped children in Project Headstart indicated that, when a directive came out of Washington to report the number of handicapped children, there were repercussions up and down the bureaucracy. People in the programs did not think in terms of the disability categories those in Washington were proposing. Data collection at the program level came to be defined very differently when it reached Washington. The meaning and purpose of definitions and counting were viewed differently in Washington, in regional offices, in state run programs, in local administrative centers, and in Headstart classes. To understand what occurs as the result of such a directive and to understand the meaning of the figures created about who is served, all these levels have to be studied.

Data produced at one level are often aggregated at another level and released through the mass media. The difference between the understanding of what is produced from the counter's perspective and what is understood when received by the general public can be pronounced. The general public is bombarded with reports of incidents and prevalence that paint a picture that leads to misunderstandings and a mentality that certain disability categories are growing at epidemic proportions.

The assumption that disability definitions are tiered phenomena is not meant to suggest that people at particular levels all share common understandings concerning disability. Those at similar levels but at different geographic locations, as well as people in the same setting in the same level can have different understandings of disability. In September 1978, as the result of Public Law 94-142, school officers were asked to turn in figures reporting the number of handicapped children

served in the schools. Rates of handicapped children varied widely, so widely, in fact, that there was some real question as to the differential meaning of disability in various geographic locations. In Utah, for example, the rate of emotionally disturbed children reported was 3.1% of the school population, while in Mississippi it was .01 (McDaniels, 1979). Bogdan's (1976) research on the mandate to integrate handicapped children into Project Headstart indicated that staff members of the same level responded to the mandate quite differently. Some saw it as a more bureaucratic exercise in form filling, while others took it more seriously and drastically altered their way of thinking about children as a result.

The reason for defining disabilities and the source of disability designations affect the meaning the process and the understandings generated. When federal funding is tied to having certain rates of particular categories of people served, there may be a tendency for that number to be designated to reach the required level independent of what actually changes, who is served, and what is done.

Bogdan studied a congressional mandate that required Headstart programs to, through affirmative action, increase the number of "handicapped" children to 10% of those served. He found that programs reported doubling the number of handicapped children and reaching 10.1% handicapped without appreciably altering the characteristics of those served (Bogdan, 1976). In the 1979 letter to the chief school officers, U.S Commissioner of Education Boyer stated his concern with the statistics that were being reported as a result of Public Law 94-142, which requires all handicapped children to be served by local schools. He indicated that "professional experts" estimated that they should be finding approximately 12% of the school age population handicapped, yet the data turned in gave the percentage as only 7. The letter suggested his concern with handicapped children who were not counted (Boyer, 1979). Scott's study of the services to the blind reveals the influence professionals have on the defining process. The definition of legal blindness, which is the basis of producing counts of blind people and which was developed by professionals, is such that the overwhelming majority of people who are counted as blind can see (Scott, 1969).

The recently created diagnostic category of learning disability again illustrates the importance of studying professionals and definitions. Some learning disabilities specialists report that up to 40% of all children are afflicted, while other professionals not associated with this growing specialty claim that "learning disability" is a contrived diagnosis (Schrag & Divosky, 1975). Professional specialists grow by enlarging their definition of who they are trained to serve.

Disability, as special education constructs it, is a particular frame of mind by which to organize the world. The salience of special education's way of seeing human differences, and influencing how others see them, needs to be understood as an issue of the politics of competing perspectives. For example, whether a child is conceptualized as learning disabled, mentally retarded, or illiterate is an issue that can only be understood in a political frame of mind. The development and politics of special education, and how they came to construct disability as they have, who they fought within the process, and what are their common sense unnoticed assumptions, is an important part of understanding special education (Conrad & Schneider, 1980). Histories in special education written by special educators should be taken as the data of a symbolic interactionist's history of special education, not the conclusion.

People who develop and apply definitions of disability in schools are subject to social processes and societal forces similar to those touching other work groups. Studies of factory workers and other workers have provided useful concepts such as quota restriction, gold bricking, self-aggrandizement, cooptation, and goal displacement to describe the effect of group process on structural forces on work production. It is important to understand the effect of social processes and structural forces on how people come to define and use the con-

cept of disability in their particular situations. Disability is situational. Alleged differences — be they physical, behavioral, or psychological — have particular meanings in particular settings. Not knowing how to read has a different meaning from one school to another. Its meaning in one class may be different from its meaning in another. The concept of the 6 hour retarded student points out that a student defined as retarded in the context of the school may not be thought "slow" in his family or his neighborhood. Questions about the efficacy of various special education programs have to be approached in terms of the meaning of special education and various disability categories in a wide range of contexts. The culture of the professional work group and the structural constraints that teachers and specialists operate under have to be understood in coming to an understanding of the situational meaning of disability designations.

While many research approaches try to control for political and social contexts, all special education programs exist in a larger context. They are part of schools, social systems, states, and nations. Definitions, ways of thinking, do not get formed in a vacuum nor are they formed at random. They reflect the environment of which they are a part. They will reflect the values, the problems, and the concerns of people who operate in those settings. They will also reflect economic conditions. Meaning does not occur in isolated bits; it is part of larger complex clusters. To isolate education and the disabled from the context of the systems of which they are a part is to distort them, leaving significant aspects unexamined. In order to understand the meaning of being "behind in school" we have to go beyond isolated pieces.

Symbolic interactionists can help us understand that when we apply the concept of disability, or any specific designation falling under this generic term, we cast the situation in a particular way. Disability can change the meaning of behavior. The word *disability* or, more specifically, its many subcategories, such as mental retardation, emotional disturbance, and deafness, makes it selectively sensitive to certain behaviors and actions. Things that might not have been noticed before jump out and take on meaning within the framework of such ideas. Behavioral and physical characteristics that were made note of and interpreted in one way get interpreted in another way through the ideas of special education.

Disability categories give those who use them a sense of knowing and, therefore, a way of relating and programming for those who fall under their headings. Labeling a child suggests that he or she is understood as being like those in the category. A whole set of expectations and assumptions is applied. Thus, the child is subject to a set of behaviors, ways of thinking, and settings that alter his or her circumstances. These alterations may have negative as well as positive consequences for the child.

How an individual defines himself or herself in regard to an alleged disability is a function of and constructed through interaction. People come to see themselves as blind, mentally retarded, or by other epithets, or they reject such concepts. Whether they are ashamed or proud of their condition or they feel neutral about it is mediated by significant others—parents, teachers, peers, attendants—who enter their lives in social interaction. People interpret others' gestures and actions in attempting to see themselves as others see them and, thereby, constructing a self-concept. In fact, in rehabilitation, it has been found that an individual's prognosis for recovery may be strongly associated to his self-concept. People with particular disabilities do not have particular personalities or ways of thinking about themselves. For some, disability dominates how they see themselves; for others, it is an insignificant part of how and what they think.

Behind much of what I have said thus far is the understanding that disability has moral meaning. The way we think about people with alleged disabilities is filled with judgments about good or bad, normal and abnormal (Bogdan & Biklen, 1977). The meaning of disability in special education goes far beyond the alleged physical, behavioral, and psychological differences. Disability has symbolic meaning that must be looked at in terms of what society honors and what it degrades.

Society's thoughts about intelligence, confidence, beauty, and winning must be understood in order to understand what we mean when we mockingly call someone *retarded* or *blind as a bat*. Our society has traditionally been structured to bring shame to people with alleged disabilities. Symbolic interactionists understand that only a small part of problems of discrimination are technical—providing physical access to wheelchairs, building communication systems for nonverbal people. The problems of disability are much more social; they are located much deeper in the seams of our society than professionals in the field of special education acknowledge.

THE IMPLICATIONS OF SYMBOLIC INTERACTION FOR RESEARCH IN SPECIAL EDUCATION

Closely aligned with symbolic interaction is a particular approach to research. It is an approach that turns its back on isolating variables, carefully controlled laboratory experiments, and getting quantitative measures and counts of people in categories. The approach is referred to as *qualitative research*. The term refers to several research strategies that share certain characteristics. The data collected has been termed *soft*; that is, rich in description of people, places, and conversations but not easily handled by statistical procedures. Research questions are not framed by operationalizing variables; rather, they are formulated to investigate in all the complexity, in context. While people conducting qualitative research may develop a focus as they collect data, they do not approach the research with specific questions to answer or hypotheses to test. They are equally concerned with understanding behavior from the subject's frame of reference; external causes are of secondary importance. They tend to collect their data through sustained contact with people in settings where subjects normally spend their time. The best known representatives of qualitative research and those that most embody the characteristics just touched upon are participant observation and indepth interviewing. There are a number of qualitative researchers studying special education settings. For the most part these researchers are trained as sociologists or anthropologists. Training in qualitative research has not yet been incorporated into the special education advanced degree curriculum. For those interested in pursuing this research approach some of the following studies should be helpful.

THE LIFE HISTORY

Rather than review the variety of qualitative research techniques, I want to discuss an approach to research that I have become associated with but that has not been popular in special education. This method is the use of first person life histories. By *first person life histories*, I mean those materials through which clients, in their own words, reveal their view of personal experiences, organizations, and other aspects of the world in which they live. Such materials reflect and describe a certain period or a whole life rather than recounting an isolated incident. They are either spontaneously produced and intended for confidential use only, as in the case of personal diaries, or they can be elicited, as in the case of someone asked to write or tell his or her own story. The approach I discuss here has been advocated by researchers throughout the history of the social sciences (Bogdan & Taylor, 1975; Dollard, 1935). It was most popular in the studies of the Chicago school of American sociology after the turn of the century (Shaw, 1966; Sutherland, 1937; Thomas & Znaniecki, 1927). In the period 1920–1940, people who called themselves *students of human behavior* were familiar with personal documents (Allport, 1942; Angell, 1945). As important as these early studies were, interest in first person accounts waned with the growth of the prominence of positivist theories and quantitative procedures. The pursuit of "facts" and statistical relationships relegated interests and subjective states, "meaning," to a minor place in the social sciences.

The first person story or autobiography can

be valuable, because it makes available the client's own view of the situation, unaltered by the interpretations of professionals. It offers a reality generated from a different place in the service delivery system. The political, moral, and research implications of using this approach and its connections with symbolic interactionist theory will become clearer as I discuss the insights gained from first person documents.

In a discussion that follows, I draw upon excerpts from transcripts of tape recordings of long, unstructured life history interviews a colleague and I conducted with two clients: a man, Ed Murphy (Bogdan & Taylor, 1976) and a woman, Patty Burt (Bogdan & Taylor, 1983). Both are now in their 20s, have been labeled *retarded*, have spent years of their lives in large residential state schools for the mentally retarded, and at the time of the interviews were clients of a number of service organizations. I have been involved in this type of interviewing for 8 years and have spent hundreds of hours with various people who were processed through the human service system. Although I say "retarded," much of what I have to say is directly relevant to all categories of special education human service clients. The "retarded" are clients we listen to the least. By advocating including their voices in our research, I am saying that all categories of clients need to be heard.

DISTRUST OF THE CLIENT'S PERSPECTIVE

In 1966, Burton Blatt and Fred Kaplan published their now famous photographic essay on "mental retardation." *Christmas in Purgatory* (Blatt & Kaplan, 1966) depicts the atrocious conditions at state facilities. The pictures on which the essay was based were taken with a camera secured to Kaplan's belt and hidden from view by his sports jacket. On one occasion, an inmate of one of the institutions discovered Kaplan's camera and reported it to an administrator, whose attention Blatt had monopolized up to that time. The administrator laughed and casually dismissed the report with the remark, "Boy, these retardates have imaginations!"

Ironic, but not surprising or unusual. Those who are labeled *retarded* have a wide range of imperfections imputed to them in addition to their alleged low intelligence (Lorber, 1974). According to the stereotype, they are incompetent, irrational, undependable, dangerous, and unable to analyze their lives and current situations. The mass media are filled with derogatory references to people with low intelligence: at prime time, our living rooms resonate with such phrases as "You imbecile," or "Don't be stupid." The Sunday cartoons depict characters who use *idiot* as a generic curse word. And, in everyday conversations, at all age levels, the indictment rings: "Hey dumbbell," or "Did you hear about the moron who threw the clock out the window?" It is no wonder that when studying organizations, what the retarded have to say is devalued. As Ed told me, "Once you have been labeled *retarded*, you can't convince them how smart you are." Similarly, when discussing a friend of his who had Down syndrome, Ed related that the major problem his friend had was that people didn't take him seriously. In Ed's words, "He was a mongoloid — people couldn't see beyond that — he was locked into what other people thought he was."

These stereotypes and beliefs do not tell the whole story. *Mental retardation* is an administrative category, a metaphor, and a reification that often lends little insight into the nature of people so labeled (Braginsky & Braginsky, 1971; Dexter, 1964; Mercer, 1973). In point of fact, many of the so-called retarded do not possess the imperfections and characteristics imputed to them (Sarason & Doris, 1969). Many can express themselves and analyze their lives, if we care to listen (Lorber, 1974). As a society and as researchers, we have chosen not to listen but rather devalue their perspectives and understandings. Seldom are those labeled *retarded* approached with the idea that they have important insights to offer researchers. Their views are almost completely neglected in the professional and organizational literature (see Lorber, 1974). What we know about how these people evaluate the services they receive is next

to nothing (Edgerton & Bercovici, 1976; see also Edgerton, 1967).

In addition to stereotypes, there are other factors that get in the way of hearing those labeled *retarded*. In most encounters with such people, it is common for the "client" to speak in a manner less than candid and straightforward when describing his or her life and feelings. Similarly, nonretarded people talking to those so labeled tend to selectively skew the content of the interaction (Goffman, 1959, 1963). This is in part true because each party is acting according to social roles and expectations of how others want them to behave (see Mercer, 1973). In certain relationships, such as that between the professional and the retarded client, the distortion is complicated further by the fact that the professional has certain rewards and punishments at his or her disposal and definite ideas about what he or she will sanction (Braginsky & Braginsky, 1971). The clients, realizing this, are pressured to give impressions that are in their best interests. For example, in one discussion with Pat, she told of the sex lives of the residents of the institution in which she was a resident and how information about such activities was systematically kept from the professional and ward staff. In a good first-person account, the person tells his or her story anonymously, no holds barred, because the sanctions have been minimized.

INSIDERS' VIEWS OF MENTAL RETARDATION

The first-person account of a "retarded" person is valuable because it brings us together in a different kind of relationship with a person we might casually dismiss as dumb or incoherent or "not all there." In reading and collecting such accounts the goal is to understand the narrator's point of view; the assumption is that the person has something to say. The responsibility of the listener is to abandon his/her biases and work at comprehending the subjective reality of that person's life.

Reading and collecting first-person life histories of people labeled *retarded* in the manner I suggested can put a distance between the research and preconceived notions and prejudices that would be difficult to obtain in other forms of research (Becker, 1966). This distance can lead to the development of empathy to see the world from the subjects' point of view. This freedom from predispositions, personal concerns, and organizational roles lends an insight through which to examine commonsense assumptions about the "kind" of person sharing his or her life. For example, when I first began studying organizations in which retarded people were clients I assumed that they would not be articulate, that they would not have the ability to think abstractly, and that they didn't have all that much to say worth listening to. Clearly, the people I talked to did not match my preconceived notions. They were anomalies to my commonsense understanding. At first, I dealt with this dissonance by thinking of the people I talked to as exceptions; that is, I assumed that they were misdiagnosed and not really "retarded." But, while I knew that the people I talked to were not necessarily typical of that category of people labeled *retarded*, they were clearly legitimate members of that classification—they had been officially diagnosed and were being treated and related to by professionals as being retarded. A colleague and I met and talked to other ex-state school residents and people in state schools. We found many who were articulate and as "intelligent" as the people whose stories we collected (for others see Dybwad, 1974; Edgerton, 1967; Lorber, 1974). I came to resolve the dissonance these anomalies created, not by treating them as inauthentic cases but rather by questioning the value of this system that classified people as either "retarded" or "normal" (see Kuhn, 1962). It was through the collection of first-person accounts that we began to understand how metaphors are reified.

The person labeled *mentally retarded* has participated in various groups and organization subcultures that those of us who are not so labeled have not. These groups, like all groups, have their own norms, values, social structure, system of classifying people, and vocabulary. The first-person account can provide a rich understanding of these segments of society and how they affect the "retarded" by giving us a description of their day-to-day activities and their view of the world. Through the personal document, one can begin to understand the problems of the interaction of these groups with others and the mechanisms and definitions developed to deal with such difficulties. For example, exresidents of state institutions, I discovered in my interviews, have a particularly difficult problem, upon leaving, in managing the stigma associated with having been a ward of the state. As Pat told me,

> When I was working at these places [various community based businesses], I usually made a big mistake. You can make friends by telling people a little about your life. Well, I made enemies by telling them about mine. Right away I would start telling them about the state schools I had been in and the life I had had. They started burning me so I just don't talk about it to anybody now.

Exresidents will share their secret with each other but not with people who are not alumni. Exresidents who share experiences by telling people of their past find out

> You would think it would make them sympathetic but it makes them worse. . . . They say that is the reason that you get upset because you was in a school with retarded and crazy people. . . . That really hurts. I tell them that there are people there that need more help than others but it doesn't sink in.

From statements like these, one can begin to understand the criteria the "retarded" develop to evaluate themselves and others. One can see how they define their participation in their subgroup and in the larger society. While the life histories cannot provide a complete ethnography of this culture, it can be the first foot in the door to understanding that world.

The autobiography of the person labeled *retarded* provides us with a view of organizations from the point of view of those who participated in them at levels beyond those generally heard from (Becker, 1966). By traveling with a "retarded" person through his or her encounters with schools, clinics, institutions, and professionals, a new perspective can be viewed on these facilities. Through their stories, it becomes plain that client-professional relationships in facilities have very different meanings to the resident than to the professionals in charge. Very often cure and treatment dominate the official view, while boredom, manipulation, and coercion constitute the client's perspective. From the perspective of the staff, behavior modification, seclusion, and tranquilizing medication serve therapeutic ends. From the point of view of the "retarded," however, they are often methods of punishment and behavior control. Some routine practices used in admission to retardation facilities are humiliating when viewed from the point of view of the client. Pat tells of her admittance to a state school.

> They took me out of the examination room and took me and put me on a table like a little baby and showered me. I was 10 years old and they showered me. I wanted to bathe myself. I felt they were treating me like a baby and they were. . . .
> They left me in this room waiting to be examined. I was still screaming, "I want to go home. I don't want to stay here. . . . " The first thing that they did was stick a thermometer in my cula [rectum]. I hated that because I was used to having it done by my mother. . . . It was a frightening feeling. I thought they were trying to hurt me.

Statements like these and others allow us to see the contradiction between the vocabulary of therapy and the view of the patient and bring into bold relief the fact that a facility is a far different place for the client than it is for the staff.

The life histories of people labeled *retarded* also allow researchers to understand facilities from the perspective of those who use them. In order to develop programs that have the desired effect, one has to realize that people participating in programs define their own involvement. It is these definitions, rather than the ideas and wishes of program planners, that determine how participants act toward a program and its effect on them. The young resi-

dent who is seeing a counselor, for whom he feels contempt because the counselor represents a facility he hates, knows that he has to "lay a good story on him" in order to get certain privileges in the institution. This is a very different picture from that of professionals toward counseling relationships. Devaluing the client's perspective by viewing it as naive, unsophisticated, immature, or a symptom of pathology or ignoring that perspective makes many of the organizations that serve people with special needs indulge in one-sided rituals in the name of science. The life history can help us deal with this problem by educating us with the words of those who know the most about their difficulties and about what is on their minds.

To change the thrust of our discussion but to recall a point made earlier, the autobiographical account provides us with a holistic view of people in organizations (Allport, 1942). Case record material found in official folders shows only very selected aspects of a person's life and character. People are much more complicated than a profile constructed from a series of IQ tests or a few pages of selected "facts" and anecdotes. Similarly, there is a lot more to understanding a family than knowing that its members are on welfare and lack education, which all too often is all that is said. The records emphasize the person as a client, obscuring the importance of understanding him as a member of a family, a peer group, a neighborhood, a church, and so on. The file often emphasizes the person's "pathological" behavior and the strikes against him or her, and therefore serves more as an indictment of the client than a balanced picture of the client's condition and nature. The life history allows us to see through these biases; it offsets the often one-sided nature of records by presenting the other side.

As I have already suggested, the life history allows us to view the person in the context of his or her present relationships as well as in a historical sense. It presents a person from birth to the time of writing. It can lead to a fuller understanding of stages and critical periods of development and the role of organizations in those transitions. It can also lead to understanding the effect of factors that, seen in the context of a small time segment, may seem unimportant. For example, knowing that a child is occasionally teased in class for being odd looking or dumb may not seem important unless put in the context of a life of teasing and ways the person has tested to combating it. The following statement from Pat demonstrates the importance of understanding how the sadness that she feels is related to her past.

> At Empire State School, they put me in strait-jackets, in dark closets, and made me scrub stairs and the bathroom. Those kinds of things, even now, are built up inside. All this anger going through my mind. Why me? Why me locked up in a stupid place like that? I look back into my past and say, "Pat, look at those things you went through and now look at all you can do. Why did you have to go through what you went through? Why did you have to go to Empire and Central?" Why did I have to go through that cruelty? It really disturbs me. Here I am 20 years old. It makes me upset in my mind, in my body, everywhere. It is an awful feeling. I remember one day I came home from work and sat down on the couch, right there and I just burst out crying. I didn't have anything to cry about. But the tears just came. Nobody was here. I just closed the curtains and shut everything up and cried. I just felt that I wanted to be in the dark all closed in. I can't give an explanation why I felt like that—and that wasn't the first time. Just everything goes through my mind. I remember about Empire and Central. Why did Mom ever say Pat needs professional help, she is retarded, she does things a normal girl wouldn't do? This is what goes through my mind. Mom didn't have that much love she had to call me retarded. I am saying that I am normal. Just because I did those things doesn't mean I am retarded. It's the things that happen in life that I did it—like I told you back in the foster home, and things that they did to me when I was a baby.

In short, the autobiography can sensitize professionals to the importance of knowing the client's past, to better comprehend how he or she sees the present and the future.

Clients are subjects for therapeutic practices, which are extensions of theories created by researchers. By experiencing the service delivery world with the client through his or her life history, one can become keenly aware of how discrepancies in interpretation and application of these theories of causation and cure can affect treatment. For example, it has become current practice to move state school residents out of institutions into halfway houses. Residents are placed in menial jobs, and people with similar institutional backgrounds live together. While the clients I talked to favor these placements over institutions, living in close proximity to other similarly employed residents creates a great strain on them. The sense of this can be obtained from Ed's discussion of a meal at the group living facility where he resides. Some of the men at the house are late night pot washers at a local steak house. Others are janitors at nursing homes.

> We all eat in one place—about eight to a table. If he [the person in charge] points out something about their dress or manners or something, they get mad. The others will come over and start a conversation and then it gets bigger and louder. The other night I got mad. I said "Just quiet down. You've said your piece."—But how would you like to be sitting at the breakfast table or the dinner table and hear bark bark, quack quack. You can get used to some things. The landlord always yells at this one guy. He must be about 40 years old. They yell at him. But this guy really gets bugged—annoying—quack, quack. He does it just to charge the other guys up.

Through the life history, others can experience and begin to understand the web of life with which the client has to deal. This should make professionals more sensitive in designing our service systems.

Standard methodological procedure is to isolate variables so as to show relationships among them. Even the new statistical procedures are unable to deal with a complexity of variables and the ways they related to each other in the reality of people's lives. It is the purpose of the life history to deal with life in all its complexity. It therefore provides the interrelationships of all the variables to be sorted out. While the autobiography does not bring forth exact statements of relationships, it does provide the opportunity to wrestle with this complexity in context and in the system of the client's logic, rather than in a mathematical logic (Becker, 1966). It helps one be careful about believing simple explanations to complex problems and points up the fact that there are many unknowns in human behavior.

The personal document makes it possible to deal with concepts that do not lend themselves to discussion or study in other forms of research. Such subjective phenomena as beauty, faith, pain, suffering, frustration, hope, and love can be dealt with as they are experienced by real people in the real world. The value of the first-person account in this regard can be seen in part of Ed's description of a girlfriend he had:

> It took a while for her to understand how she felt. She didn't want to be too friendly. She didn't like me putting my arm around her. We went for walks during lunch and she got pretty fond of me and I got pretty fond of her. One day I asked her, "Well, how about a movie?" She said, "All right, " but she had to get her mother's permission. Then one day she said she could go. It was a Saturday matinee gangster movie. We arranged to meet at the bus stop downtown. I remember that I got down there early and bought the tickets before she came. I met her at the stop and then I went up to the ticket office with the tickets in my hand. I was a little fuzzy, nervous you might say. Of course, you were supposed to give the tickets to the man inside. The ticket woman looked at me — sort of stared and motioned with her finger. It was kind of funny considering our ages. I was 22 and she was 48. It was like teenagers going on our first date. Being at the State School and all you never have the chances romantically like you might living on the outside. I guess I was always shy with the opposite sex even at Empire. We did have dances and I felt that I was good looking but I was bashful and mostly sat. I was bashful with Joan at the movie. In my mind I felt funny, awkward — I didn't know how to approach her. Should I hug her? You can't hug the hell out of her because you don't know how she would take it. You have all the feeling there but you don't know what direction to go in. If you put your arm around her, she might scream and you're finished. If she doesn't scream you are still finished. I wish I was more of a ladies' man. (Bogdan & Taylor, 1975)

Narratives such as this can bring a better understanding of human phenomena, not as operationally defined by the researcher but as defined by the subject in the context of his or her life.

The life history of a person labeled *retarded* is a political document: it provides a platform from which a different conception of human behavior can be given force in the research as well as the larger community. Professional groups have certainly had more access to print than those they call their clients. Seldom is a forum provided for a confrontation between the client and the professional. The autobiography throws into the struggle of diagnosis and theory another voice, which allows examination of the possibility that professionals misrepresent those they say they represent. The confrontation in reality is important for the good of research as well as for the liberation of clients.

Often, the retarded are studied as a separate category of human beings, as "deviants," using the common definitions of society. It is assumed that people labeled *retarded* are basically different from others and have to be understood using special theories. Studying this subject in this way has reified the commonplace categorizing of people as either "normal" or "retarded" and legitimized service organizations as rational instruments to attain goals. The autobiography allows intimate knowledge of the client as a person. It is through this intimacy that what the subject is to himself or herself and all he or she has in common with others becomes clear, while what is different takes on less importance. Through the autobiography, professionals are forced to think of clients as people. Concepts of pathology become less relevant and in many cases even harmful.

The collection and use of first-person life histories is only one approach to research that is theoretically compatible with symbolic interaction and the sociology of special education. I have discussed the uses of this approach for special educators because I have been identified with it, it has been neglected in the literature, and it embodies so many of the strengths of the qualitative approach, an approach that has and in the future will make an important contribution to special education.

REFERENCES

Allport, G. (1942). *The use of personal documents in psychological science.* New York: Social Science Research Council.

Angell, R. (1945). A critical review of the development of the personal document method in sociology, 1920–1940. In L. Gottschalk, C. Kluckhohn, and R. Angell, *The use of personal documents in history, anthropology, and sociology.* New York: Social Science Research Council.

Becker, H. S. (1966). Introduction. In C. Shaw, *The jack roller.* Chicago: University of Chicago Press.

Blatt, B. (1970). *Exodus from pandemonium.* Boston: Allyn and Bacon.

Blatt, B., & Kaplan, F. (1966). *Christmas in purgatory.* Boston: Allyn and Bacon.

Blumer, H. (1969). *Symbolic interactionism.* Englewood Cliffs, NJ: Prentice-Hall.

Blumer, H. (1980). Comment, Mead and Blumer. *American Sociological Review, 45.*

Bogdan, R. (1972). *Participant observation in organizational setting.* Syracuse, NY: Syracuse University Press.

Bogdan, R. (1976). National policy and situated meaning: The case of Head Start and the handicapped. *American Journal of Orthopsychiatry, 46,* 229–235.

Bogdan, R., & Biklen, D. (1977, March–April). Handicapism. *Social Policy.*

Bogdan, R., & Ksander, M. (1980). Policy data as a social process: A qualitative approach to quantitative data. *Human Organization. 39,* no. 4.

Bogdan, R., & Kugelmauss, J. (In press). Case studies of mainstreaming. In L. Barton & S. Tomlinson (Eds.), *Special education: Policy practices and social issues.* New York: Harper & Row.

Bogdan, R., & Taylor, S. (1975). *Introduction to qualitative research methods.* New York: Wiley.

Bogdan, R., & Taylor, S. (1983). *Inside out: The social meaning of mental retardation.* Toronto: University of Toronto Press.

Boyer, E. (1979, 29 January). Letter to chief school officers.

Braginsky, D., & Braginsky, B. (1971). *Hansels and Gretels.* New York: Holt, Rinehart and Winston.

Conrad, P. (1976). *Identifying hyperactive children: The medicalization of deviant behavior.* Lexington, MA: D.C. Heath & Co.

Conrad, P., & Schneider, J. (1980). *Deviance and medicalization.* St. Louis: Mosby.

Dexter, L. (1964). *The tyranny of schooling: An inquiry into the problem of "stupidity."* New York: Basic Books.

Dexter, L. A. (1956). Towards a sociology of the mentally defective. *American Journal of Mental Deficiency, 61,* 10–16.

Dollard, J. (1935). *Criteria for the life history.* New Haven, CT: Yale University Press.

Dybwad, G. (1974). *New Neighbors.* Washington, DC: President's Committee on Mental Retardation.

Edgerton, R. (1967). *The cloak of competence.* Berkeley: University of California Press.

Edgerton, R., & Bercovici, S. (1976). The cloak of competence: Years later. *American Journal of Mental Deficiency, 80*(5), 485–497.

Faber, B. (1968). *Mental retardation: Its social context and social consequences.* Boston: Houghton Mifflin.

Freidson, E. (1970). *Professional dominance: The social structure of medical care.* New York: Atherton Press.

Goffman, E. (1959). *The presentation of self in everyday life.* Garden City, NY: Doubleday.

Goffman, E. (1961). *Asylums.* Garden City, NY: Anchor Books.

Goffman, E. (1963). *Stigma: Notes on the management of spoiled identity.* Englewood Cliffs, NJ: Prentice-Hall.

Higgins, P. (1980). *Outsiders in a hearing world: A sociology of deafness.* Beverly Hills, CA: Sage Publications.

Kuhn, T. (1962). *The structure of scientific revolutions.* Chicago: University of Chicago Press.

Lemert, E. (1951). *Social Pathology.* New York: McGraw Hill.

Lorber, M. (1974). *Consulting the mentally retarded: An approach to the definition of mental retardation by experts.* Ph.D. dissertation, University of Michigan, Ann Arbor Microfilms.

McDaniels, G. (1979, 29 January). Memo to grantees of Programs in Division of Innovation and Development, U.S. Department of Health, Education and Welfare, Bureau of Education for the Handicapped.

Mead, G. H. (1934). *Mind, self, and society.* Chicago: University of Chicago Press.

Mercer, J. (1973). *Labeling the mentally retarded.* Berkeley, CA: University of California Press.

Rose, A. (1962). A systematic summary of symbolic

interaction theory. In A. Rose (Ed.), *Human behavior and social processes*. Boston: Houghton, Mifflin Company.

Sarason, S., & Doris, J. (1969). *Psychological problems in mental deficiency*. New York: Harper and Row.

Sarason, S. B., & Doris, J. (1979). *Educational handicap, public policy and social history*. New York: The Free Press.

Scheff, T. J. (1966). *Being mentally ill: A sociological theory*. Chicago: Aldine Publishing Co.

Schrag, P., & Divosky, D. (1975). *The myth of the hyperactive child*. New York: Pantheon Books.

Scott, R. (1969). *The making of blind men*. New York: Russell Sage Foundation.

Shaw, C. (1966). *The jack roller* (2nd ed). Chicago: University of Chicago Press.

Sutherland, E. (1937). *The professional thief*. Chicago: University of Chicago Press.

Szasz, T. S. (1961). *The myth of mental illness*. New York: Harper and Row.

Thomas, W. I., & Znaniecki, F. (1927). *The Polish peasant in Europe and America*. New York: Knopf.

Wiseman, J. (1970). *Stations of the lost*. Englewood Cliffs, NJ: Prentice-Hall.

12 SPECIAL EDUCATION RESEARCH IN PERSPECTIVE

Kathryn A. Blake
Charlotte L. Williams

This book is devoted to perspectives in special education research with emphasis on the current state of the art. Given that mission, one of the first perspectives that must be considered is the context of research in special education; that is, the role it plays and where it fits into the practice of special education.

THE CONTEXT OF RESEARCH IN SPECIAL EDUCATION

In an applied discipline like this, the major raison d'etre for research is ultimately to help in decision making—to supply the motivation, the understanding, and the information needed to select among options for delivering special education services to exceptional persons. And so, to put special education research in context, we first examine major bases for making decisions in special education and the foci of decision making. Then, we move to the current status of research work, to future needs and possibilities for research in the field, and in a final wrap-up, to look at the state of the art in special education research.

Before we begin, however, we need to stress the delimitation of the problem for this chapter. It is a truism, but well to emphasize, that special educators' decisions do not stand in iso-

lation. Quite so, concurrently, crucial decisions are being made by the exceptional persons when they are able, by their families, and by professionals in the related professions; for example, speech/language pathologists, psychologists, social workers, physical therapists, occupational therapists, recreational therapists, nutritionists, and physicians. This state of affairs not only affects the outcomes of special education decisions, it also affects the reliability and validity of research results in this area, as well as the social validation of these results. Consequently, educators need to be aware of these other influences and the interactions they have with decisions.

Bases for Decision Making in Special Education

Special educators, like many other educators, primarily base their decisions on normative or societal standards, on the people's will as it is expressed through public policy, and on research results (e.g., Ballard-Campbell & Semmel, 1981; Haskins & Stifle, 1979; Holland, 1980; Knoff, 1983).

Normative Standards

Normative standards are a crucial basis for special education decision-making. A normative standard is a given, a self-evident truth, an imperative for conduct that requires no proof or rationale. It mandates that actions must conform to that standard because they are right and prevents actions not conforming to that standard because they are wrong. These standards have been a foundation for the judicial decisions, legislative laws, and administrative rules that are having so much impact on current decision making in special education.

The People's Will Expressed Through Public Policy

The people's will is another crucial base for special education decision making. Ours is a system of government of the people, by the people, and for the people. This principle of self-determination is implemented at every level from the smallest local political unit through the federal government. As a result, exceptional persons, their families, and friends, as well as those professionals who serve them, have taken political action to get executive orders issued and laws passed that have mandated *specific* activities — like admission of all persons to school no matter how severe their handicaps. Individuals also have access to the courts at all levels to ensure that the mandates in the constitution, executive orders, and legislative acts are enforced. Examples of these two types of activities include, respectively, the mobilization of people who took part in stimulating the passage of such legislation as P.L. 94-142 and its amendments and the conduct of such litigation as Mills vs. Board of Education of the District of Columbia (1972). These events show that political organization for exercising the will of the people in making decisions about exceptional persons is still an extremely strong and important force.

Scholarly Inquiry

Scholary inquiry is another crucial basis for special education decision making. In special education, primarily five scholarly approaches are used: philosophical inquiry and argumentation, historical and retrospective analyses,

legal analyses, qualitative examinations, and studies following the scientific method. We examine these approaches briefly.

Philosophical inquiry and argumentation are related approaches. Philosophical inquiry uses logical reasoning, rather than an empirical collection of facts, to find truth. Argumentation is a presentation of ideas and information designed to convince someone to accept a point of view on a question; essentially, it is a debate on the issues. Dunn's (1968) *Special education for the mildly retarded: Is much of it justifiable?* is an example of scholarly inquiry using this approach.

Historical and retrospective analyses are procedures by which to locate original, primary sources of information, evaluate their authenticity, and synthesize them. The purposes are to identify facts and conclusions about the past and to relate them to the present and future. A good example of this form of research can be found in *Perspectives in special education: Personal orientations* (Blatt and Morris, 1984), where contributors were asked to take a critical look at the field, from their unique perspectives, and address where the field is going.

Legal analyses include identifying constitutional mandates and rules of law pertinent to questions at issue, locating previously adjudicated cases and legislative enactments that bear on the questions, and collecting evidence about the need for a particular legal outcome to assure justice for the people affected. As examples consider Mercer's (1979) analysis of the judicial law pertaining to the constitutional guarantees for gifted public school students and Ballard, Ramirez and Weintraub's (1982) revision of their earlier overview of special education's legal and governmental foundations.

Qualitative examinations — primary research approaches in sociology, anthropology, and some fields of business — have always been a part of education. Today, the qualitative approach is seeing a resurgence as a recognized, valued, and accepted research approach. Bogdan and Biklen (1982) prepared one of the few modern texts showing qualitative research applied to educational concerns. In brief, qualitative research aims to capture the diversity of the human condition, be this diversity reflected in the experiences of persons labeled mentally retarded, of those who are desperately poor, or of those new parents who are experiencing the trauma that comes with learning that their child has been born with severe physical handicaps. That is, we seek to "gain insights into the human condition. . . ." [realizing that the] description of social reality is the description of a mosaic. (Rist in Bogdan & Biklin, 1982, pp. ix–x)

To obtain data, qualitative researchers use such methods as case studies of individuals and groups, indepth interviews, participant observation, field notes at single or multiple sites, content analyses of documents, and process analyses of complex activities. Bodgan's chapter in this volume summarizes research in this area. Other examples of this research are the works of Blatt and his associates portraying the dynamics of institutionalization; for example, *Christmas in purgatory* (Blatt & Kaplan, 1967); and *The family papers: A return to purgatory* (Blatt, Ozolins, & McNally, 1979).

The *Scientific method* refers to a set of rules that pertain to the following essential components of scientific study: (a) posing the question for investigation and, when possible, formulating hypotheses; (b) in case of group research, selecting unbiased samples from those populations for which generalization is to be ultimately made; (c) delimiting the independent and dependent variables and how they shall be manipulated and measured; (d) in the case of group research, specifying the procedures to use in making probability estimates about the consistency of the effects noted; (e) deriving both generalizations about and limitations of these effects, (f) reducing or eliminating the contribution of either systematic or random error to the results of the study, (g) specifying, as much as possible, the conditions under which the study was conducted, as well as the operations associated with the procedure, so that the study may be replicated by other researchers, and (h) in the case of single subject studies, making sure that experimental control has been demonstrated by the inde-

pendent variable over the dependent variable. This entire process, and each component separately, is undergirded by strict assumptions and complex technologies. Meeting the assumptions and correctly using the technologies are the sine qua non for valid and reliable results obtained through the scientific method. Special education uses descriptive scientific research and experimental/quasiexperimental scientific research.

Descriptive scientific research is a process of uncovering the status quo pertaining to a phenomenon. Stated another way, descriptive research aims at identifying such things as frequency or incidence, distribution, component parts, activities, and attitudes/options. Survey research, bivariate and multivariate correlational procedures (regression analyses), and psychometric studies are frequently used types of descriptive research. Varied examples of descriptive research in special education are Alley's (1979) work studying the use of a Bayesian procedure for identifying learning disabled students, Gully and Hosch's (1979) work on the use of discriminant analysis in identifying mentally retarded youngsters, and Macmillan's (1980) work applying the Delphi technique in futures forecasting.

Experimental and quasiexperimental scientific research is a process of manipulating independent variables to assess their impacts on dependent variables. Stated more simply, experimental and quasiexperimental research encompasses cause and effect studies that are rigorously objective and controlled. Many experimental and quasiexperimental research designs are available. No one has improved on Campbell and Stanley's (1963) classic description of the nature of those designs, the potential sources of their invalidity, and possible controls (solutions) for some of these potential problems with invalidity. Works by Gerber and Zinkgraf (1982), Johnson and Johnson (1983), and Swanson (1982) are varied examples of experimental and quasiexperimental research in special education. Gerber and Zinkgraf studied the effects and interaction effects of two subject variables; Johnson and

Johnson, the effects of a treatment variable; and Swanson, the effects and interaction effects of a subject variable and a treatment variable.

Foci of Decision-Making in Special Education

As noted earlier, a major reason for research in special education is to supply the motivation, understanding, and information needed to select among options for delivering special education services to exceptional persons. To use research terminology then, in decision making and consequently in research, special educators work with populations (the exceptional persons and their families) and treatments (the tools of special education).

The Populations: Exceptional Persons and Their Families

Special educators are concerned with subject variables when they focus on the populations. These subject variables may be identified, defined, and given dimension in various ways; for example, by degree, by type, or by combinations, as in the multiple exceptional. The most common set used is hearing acuity, visual acuity, speech adequacy, language adequacy, physical (structural and physiological) adequacy, emotional-social status, intelligence level, and intellectual abilities.

Sometimes, these subject variables are used as independent variables; that is, they are manipulated and their effects on dependent variables, such as the rate of and level of learning, are examined. Other times, they are used as dependent variables; that is, they are examined to see how they are affected by such independent variables as timing of and type of language instruction.

The Treatments: The Tools of Special Education

The treatments are the independent variables used to deliver and manage educational and treatment programs for exceptional persons. These treatment variables may be very simple, as in studying the effects of amount of material or number of spelling words learned in a given time. Or, they may be very complex, as in studying the effects of due process procedures on parents' perceptions of the adequacy of school programs.

A large number and variety of treatment variables are studied in special education research. One useful way to categorize these treatment variables is by the tools used to conduct special education programs in today's world; that is, the tools for serving exceptional persons directly (identification, nondiscriminatory testing, individualized instruction, placement in the least restrictive environment, and arranging activities within the individual education program) and the tools for organizing and coordinating the five direct-service tools (personnel training, program administration, program evaluation, and program monitoring/compliance) (Blake, 1981). These categories are useful for categorizing independent variables because they subsume most treatment variables pertinent to special education and because they serve as a clear framework for generalizing from research results to decisions about special education practices.

CURRENT RESEARCH IN SPECIAL EDUCATION

Today, special educators do not have all of the research needed in some areas of decision making, and they do not use all of the research available in other areas (e.g., Drew, Preator, & Buchanan, 1982). Nevertheless, an extensive range of special education research is presently available and some of it is used in decision making, to aid in selecting among options for delivering special education to exceptional persons. It would require many volumes to fully portray research designs in the five major methods of scholarly inquiry used in special education, as well as the research results and their applications to decision making. However, it is appropriate to call attention to the broad domain. Consequently, in this section, we give important samples of some special education research design considerations and some aspects of the present special education research situation.

Some Research Design Considerations

Research in special education has its light side. It can supply so much information from which to derive concepts and principles and then concomitant promising practices. Yet, as is fairly universal in most of life, research has its dark side as well. It has so many possibilities for the intrusion of error and harm. Consequently, while considering the questions studied by research, special educators must be aware of the tremendous difficulties surrounding the use of research with exceptional persons and their families — difficulties that must be dealt with in order to conduct research and apply the results as a basis for decision making.

Questions for Study

As in all problem solving, research starts with an issue and a question. Table 12.1 has a sample of some of the issues and questions pertaining to special educators' decision making and, thus, the focus of their research. Additional issues are presented in such sources as Ballard-Campbell and Semmel (1981), Curlette and Stallings (1979), Hessler and Sosnowsky (1979), Higgins (1979); McLoughlin and Kelly (1982); McMahan (1983); Mollica (1983); Orlansky (1982); Palmer (1983); Phipps (1982); Polsgrove (1983); and Schmid and Negata (1983).

Difficulties to Deal With

Inquiry in any discipline and through any research approach is fraught with difficulties that threaten or attenuate the internal validity, external validity, and reliability of the work. The discrepancy between the research philosopher's ideals and the research practitioner's realities certainly is extreme and is a difficult problem in research in special education; e.g., Curo (1979); Drew et al. (1982); Milne and

Mountain (1980); and Sandow (1979). This is so because of the range, extent, and variation in individual differences among subjects; the emotional, social, and values pressures surrounding their well-being, and similar problems.

We briefly described five methods of scholarly inquiry in the discussion regarding the basis for decision making. Each approach has its procedures, and these procedures have their own limitations, assumptions, sources of error, and methods for identifying those errors and appropriately limiting generalizations. Again, it's beyond the mission and possibilities of this chapter to consider all of these aspects; nevertheless, it is our responsibility to call attention to and illustrate the incredible difficulties that must be faced in doing research with exceptional persons and their families. Therefore, consider two sources of illustration. One source is the specific difficulties in conducting research that are pinpointed in other chapters of this book. The other source of illustrations is the general difficulties that cut across particular content areas. Briefly, consider samples of three representative sets of difficulties: (a) difficulties surrounding the use of human subjects in research, (b) difficulties in performing research, and (c) difficulties in processing research for decision making.

Consider first the set of *difficulties surrounding the use of human subjects in research.* Throughout the research community, there is great sensitivity about using human beings in research. For example, the federal government provides strict mandates about the problem. Generally, funding proposals require policy assurances about safeguarding human subjects, universities and other organizations where research is done require strict review of proposed research procedures, and most researchers and their respective professional organizations (e.g., American Medical Association, American Psychological Association) are very concerned with the care of their subjects.

The whole complex of issues surrounding the use of human subjects in research yields a formidable set of difficulties. These difficulties

TABLE 12.1 SOME ISSUES AND QUESTIONS IN SPECIAL EDUCATION
RESEARCH AND RESEARCH SYNTHESES*

Exceptional Persons and Their Families

Decision: To decide what personal characteristics have implications for delivering special education to exceptional persons.

At Issue: Answers to questions about definitional characteristics and about related characteristics of exceptional persons and about characteristics of their families.

Definitional Characteristics of Exceptional Persons
1. What characteristic or characteristics are used to identify the person as exceptional?
2. What implications do the definitional characteristic or characteristics have for the exceptional person's ability to learn and perform, with reasonable adequacy, important developmental tasks in such areas as ambulation, self-care, communication, social-emotional relations, academic achievement, occupational attainment, and so on?
3. What do these implications mean for decisions among options for delivering special education to the exceptional person?

Related Characteristics of Exceptional Persons
1. What characteristics are usually associated with the characteristic or characteristics employed in identifying the person as exceptional?
2. What implications do these related characteristics have for the exceptional person's ability to learn and perform, with reasonable adequacy, important developmental tasks?
3. What do these implications mean for our decisions among options for delivering special education to the exceptional person?

Characteristics of Families of Exceptional Persons
1. Who are the immediate and extended families of the exceptional person?
2. What is the impact of exceptionality on the family, individuals and the family constellation, in such areas as emotional-social reactions, financial well-being, general management, and so on?
3. What implications do these family characteristics have for the exceptional person's ability to learn and perform, with reasonable adequacy, important developmental tasks?

Identification

Decision: To decide how best to locate and describe exceptional persons who need special education.

At Issue: Answers to questions about child-find procedures, categorization, labeling, and definitions.

Child-Find Procedures
1. What information needs to be transmitted in, and what media are most effective for, *awareness campaigns*, designed to help the public realize the kinds of problems exceptional persons have, the services available to them, and the need to get the exceptional persons and/or their families in touch with helping programs?
2. What characteristics need to be examined in *screening programs*? What procedures should be used to sample these characteristics?
3. What evidence from the screening programs indicate a need for *referral* of the person for further study to identify possible exceptionalities?

Categorization
1. Should exceptional persons be assigned to categories; e.g., mentally retarded or emotionally disturbed?
2. Or, should a noncategorical approach be taken and education based on each person's strengths and weaknesses as they are found?

*Material in this table is based on Blake (1981, pp. 39–43). Questions were also contributed by Dr. Sara Real, Cobb County Public Schools, Georgia; Dr. Acquilla Mims, University of Georgia; and Dr. Jane Lee, Georgia Department of Education.

continued

TABLE 12.1 continued

Labeling
1. If exceptional persons are placed in categories, should those categories be named; e.g., emotionally disturbed or blind?
2. Or should the labeling of exceptional persons be avoided, especially the use of negative labels?
3. What options exist for grouping without labels?

Definitions
1. If exceptional persons are categorized, what characteristics shall be used in defining the categories? What cutting points shall be used in deciding whether a person belongs in a category?
2. When definitions conflict, what definition shall be used? Are some definitions more functional than others? Does the value of a definition depend on the purpose for which it is used?

Nondiscriminatory Testing

Decision: To decide what information is needed and how to get that information without mistakes that harm exceptional persons.

At Issue: Answers to questions about validity, reliability, and standards for comparisons.

Validity
1. What information is really needed to identify and plan for exceptional persons? What behavior should be measured?
2. What tests or other procedures provide true measures of that behavior? What tests should be discarded as useless?

Reliability
1. What are the sources of error when testing exceptional persons?
2. What tests or other procedures can be used to keep such mistakes at a minimum?

Standards for Comparison
1. What standards should be used in judging exceptional persons? Should they be compared to the requirements of the task to be accomplished? To nonexceptional persons? To other persons who have the same gifts/talents or handicaps?
2. What conditions cause discrimination against exceptional persons when compared to nonexceptional persons? That is, what are the sources of test biases?
3. What procedures can be used to deal with these discriminatory conditions? To what extent might such procedures vitiate norms and, thus, lead to misrepresentation?

Individualizing Instruction

Decision: To decide what should be the nature of the education delivered to exceptional persons.

At Issue: Answers to questions about objectives, schedules, procedures, settings, and minimum competency requirements.

Objectives
1. What should be taught exceptional persons: Academic content? Reading and other literacy skills? Survival skills? Perceptual processes? Linguistic processes? Daily living skills? Social skills? Emotional responses? Other material?
2. Should everything to be taught be reduced to behavioral objectives specified ahead of time?

Schedules
1. Should an exceptional person be allowed to progress at his or her own rate? Or, should he or she be kept on the group's schedule?

TABLE 12.1 continued

2. Should objectives be eliminated if an exceptional person does not have time to accomplish what others do because he or she requires more time to learn? Or, should he or she be kept in a grade longer or in school longer?
3. Should objectives be added if an exceptional person learns faster than others do? Or, should he or she be allowed to move through school in a shorter time?

Procedures
1. What methods should be used with exceptional persons? How should tutoring or solitary activity be used? On what should decisions be based as to which methods are effective for instruction and yet not harmful, emotionally or socially, to persons?
2. Should behavior modification be used? For what purposes? What role do more humanistic procedures have?
3. What media and devices should be used with exceptional persons? On what should decisions be based as to which media and devices are effective for instruction and yet not harmful, emotionally or socially, to persons?
4. Is there an Aptitude × Treatment Interaction? That is, do persons who vary on important characteristics differ in the *way* they learn? Or, do they differ only in *how fast* they learn and *how far* they can go? What does this mean for teaching?

Settings
1. What effect does the environment have? How can personnel and space be best arranged to be effective and helpful to exceptional persons?
2. Should the environment be carefully structured and controlled? Should it be more fluid and flexible?

Minimum Competency Requirements
1. To what extent should exceptional persons be expected to meet minimum competency requirements?
2. Should special adjustments for handicaps be made during testing if the handicap interferes with the exceptional person's ability to demonstrate his or her true level of competency?
3. If the minimum competency level is beyond the exceptional person's capacity, what should be done about certificates of graduation or completion? What should be done about graduation or completion ceremonies?

Placement in the Least Restrictive Environment

Decision: To find the best balance in decisions about where to use scarce resources; what is best for exceptional persons, and what is best for other people?

At Issue: Answers to questions about right to education, early childhood special education, institutionalization, school location, transportation, facilities, extracurricular activities, safety, postsecondary education, and continuing education.

Right to Education
1. Who is eligible for education at public expense? Should anyone have priority when resources become scarce?
2. Should education of severely/profoundly handicapped persons be continued if they do not show some learning after a reasonable period?

Early Childhood Special Education
1. What are the aims of infant stimulation and preschool education programs? That is, what are the instructional objectives for young exceptional children?
2. Do infant stimulation and preschool education programs really give exceptional youngsters a head start? Would as much be accomplished if education were delayed until pupils were more mature?
3. Is it possible to really influence characteristics such as intelligence? Or, are they fixed by inheritance?

continued

TABLE 12.1 continued

4. What instructional procedures and settings are most beneficial and comfortable for young exceptional pupils?

Institutionalization
1. Should placement of an exceptional person in an institution be prohibited?
2. Or should decisions about institutionalization be based on the ecology of the situation — the whole set of interacting forces around the exceptional person?
3. If residential schools are to remain, how would it be possible to ensure that they are helpful to exceptional persons?

School Location
1. What should determine which is the least restrictive environment that will enable the exceptional person to function with comfort and benefit?
2. Should ability grouping (special classes) or special schools ever be used with exceptional persons? Full time? Part time? Under what conditions?

Transportation
1. On what should decisions as to a handicapped person's special transportation needs be based? A gifted/talented person's? Is there a point of diminishing returns at which the time a person spends to get to special centers for special education or related services outweighs the value of services received?
2. How much should special transportation be a public responsibility? How much a family responsibility?

Facilities
1. When do inappropriate facilities become barriers to handicapped persons' access to education and other public programs?
2. What is the public responsibility to provide equal access? Is it justifiable to send a person to a more distant facility with no barriers instead of modifying a nearby structure that has barriers?

Extracurricular Activities
1. Should handicapped persons participate in extracurricular activities with other persons? How much should the activities be adapted to the handicapped persons' limitations and safety needs?
2. Should there be special extracurricular activities restricted to handicapped persons? To gifted/talented persons?

Safety
1. Who is responsible for assuring a handicapped person's safety during delivery of special education?
2. Is it ever justifiable to rule a program off limits to a person, if it is extremely hazardous to him or her as, for example, using power machinery in industrial arts for a person who has hemophilia? If not, how can the person's safety be guaranteed?

Postsecondary Education
1. Can admission requirements and retention requirements be modified in areas where the exceptional person might be unnecessarily penalized; e.g., foreign language requirements or mathematics requirements for some learning disabled students? If so, how?
2. On admission and retention examinations, can the methods of assessment be altered so that exceptional persons will not be unnecessarily handicapped in demonstrating their knowledge because of the impact of their disability on responding to a test? If so, how?
3. Can/should some major fields in postsecondary education be ruled out because of the nature of the handicapped vis à vis the job requirements? For example, should a blind student prepare to be an industrial arts teacher?
4. Can methods of student classroom activity be adjusted to the students' exceptionality, for example, can a blind student take notes on a tape recorder and have term papers taped? Can we vary time by allowing exceptional students longer to complete requirements? If so, to what extent?

TABLE 12.1 continued

---

5. To what extent should postsecondary institutions supply assistance to handicapped persons, for example, notetakers for blind, deaf, or quadriplegic students?

Continuing Education
1. What instructional programs should be provided to enable the exceptional person to keep job skills current with changing occupational requirements? To upgrade job skills?
2. What instructional programs should be provided to enable the exceptional person to continue to acquire knowledge to enhance the quality of life?
3. In programs for keeping current or upgrading job skills and/or in programs for enhancing the quality of life, to what extent can the admission/retention requirements and procedures be altered and delivery systems be modified?
4. To what extent should special education deliver instruction on such issues of the aging as management, the hospice movement, and so on?

Management Through the IEP

Decision: To decide about the most appropriate options for delivering services to exceptional persons and how best to organize these options and monitor their effectiveness.

At Issue: Answers to questions about programming, accountability, and cooperative decision making.

Programming
1. For an exceptional person with a given set of identifying characteristics, what are the most appropriate options for nondiscriminatory testing, individualized instruction, and placement in the least restrictive environment? (See the respective areas above for the decisions and issues about these special education tools.)
2. Given the options selected, what is the best schedule for determining the appropriateness of the options chosen; i.e., checking how the person is responding to the selected options?

Accountability
1. Given the options selected, what are objective criteria and evaluation procedures for determining appropriateness of the options chosen for the exceptional person's education?
2. If revisions (i.e., changes in options) are indicated by the evaluation, what should the new options be? How should their implementation be scheduled and, in turn, evaluated?
3. What are the best practices for ensuring that equal protection and due process are extended to each exceptional person?
4. What personnel training is needed to ensure that the exceptional person, if appropriate, the parents, and the professionals involved understand these constitutional safeguards and ways to implement them effectively? How can this training be delivered?

Cooperative Decision Making
1. Within a group consisting of the exceptional person (if he or she can participate), the parents, and the diverse professionals, what procedures can facilitate each participant's understanding of the options open to choice, their potential effectiveness, and their possible interaction with other options?
2. What ways would facilitate communication among those engaged in cooperative planning with different training and interests? What ways could resolve differences in judgements, preferences, and wishes?

Personnel Training

Decision: To decide how to best train personnel to deliver special education to exceptional persons.

At Issue: Answers to questions about characteristics, competencies, specialization, practical experiences, continuing education, certification, and burnout. These questions pertain respectively to teachers, administrators, supervisors, and paraprofessionals.

Characteristics
1. What should be the intellectual, emotional/social, and physical characteristics of personnel who work with exceptional persons?

continued

TABLE 12.1 continued

2. What procedures can be used to assess these characteristics?
3. How would this information be relevant to decisions about admission to, retention in, and completion of training programs? What legal requirements are involved? How should the legal requirements be managed?

Competencies
1. What competencies are appropriate for personnel to acquire vis à vis such areas as the knowledge base, instruction, management, the related services, the law?
2. What procedures can be used to assess these competencies?
3. How would this information be relevant to decisions about retention in, and completion of, training programs? What legal requirements are involved? How should the legal requirements be managed?

Specialization
1. How much specialization should there be vis à vis categories, extent of exceptionality, and ages of the exceptional persons being served?
2. Should personnel have training and experience in working with nonexceptional persons? If so, what is the minimum level? At what part in the training sequence should this experience come?

Practical Experiences
1. What practical experiences are appropriate?
2. To what extent should the experiences in practice occur during the course-work period? Following the course-work period?
3. What types, and timing, of supervisory experiences make practical experiences most effective?
4. How can performance of a trainee during the practicum period be used in decisions about retention in and completion of the practicum?

Continuing Education
1. What are the criteria for choosing among such continuing education systems: full-time instruction, single courses, short-courses, conferences, and consultation media like telecommunications?
2. To what extent should content of continuing education programs be tied to the general knowledge base and state of the art? To individual needs and particular problems?
3. What are the relative merits of academic credit approaches and noncredit continuing education approaches?
4. How should performance in the various types of continuing education programs be evaluated? How should this information be used?

Certification
1. How should information about characteristics, competencies, specialization, practical experiences, and continuing education be tied to certification?
2. How should certification be tied to hiring, retention, advancement, and rewards for personnel in service?

Burnout
1. How do characteristics of the person and the work situation contribute to burnout? Singly? In interaction?
2. What early signs indicate that burn-out has begun? Later signs?
3. What procedures can be used to prevent burnout? To reduce burnout? To cure burnout?

Program Administration

Decision: To decide what policies and procedures should be used for organizing and coordinating programs for exceptional persons.

At Issue: Answers to questions about legality, program development, and finance.

Legality

1. What laws (federal or state) affect programs for exceptional persons?
2. What LEA Board policies affect programs for exceptional persons? IEA Board policies? State board policies?
3. What must be done to implement the laws and identify board policies? For example, what training will be needed? What communication systems will be required?
4. At what phases of the admissions review and dismissal process or case flow should such requirements as due process be implemented?
5. What procedures can be used to identify and serve exceptional persons more expeditiously?

Program Development

1. To what extent should existing school programs be modified to meet the needs of an exceptional person's Individual Education Program (IEP)?
2. Given the people required by law to participate in the IEP committee, what additional persons should be involved; e.g., vocational education instructors?
3. How does the administrator prepare a needs assessment based on all the IEPs of exceptional persons in that jurisdiction?
4. In preparing the needs assessment, how does the administrator obtain the resources required?
5. In preparing the needs assessment, how does the administrator go about getting the special education and related services required?

Finance

1. Given the requirements of the law (e.g., an equal educational opportunity, a free appropriate public education, and a barrier-free environment) and the reality of limited resources, how can decisions be made to meet legitimate needs of all exceptional and nonexceptional persons?
2. What procedures can be used to help people understand that regardless of the potential for attainment, funds must be expended to ensure that each exceptional person receives a free appropriate public education, an equal educational opportunity, and a barrier-free environment?
3. What are the most cost effective arrangements for providing services across school district lines and what procedures should be used to implement these arrangements?

Program Evaluation

Decision: To determine the most appropriate procedures for assessing the effectiveness and efficiency of programs for exceptional persons.

At Issue: Answers to questions about evaluation, accountability, and appropriateness.

Evaluation

1. How should the personnel involved be informed about the reasons for program evaluation?
2. What are the relative roles of the following in program evaluation: (a) the administrators, (b) the principal, (c) the teacher, (d) the parents, (e) the exceptional person, if able?
3. How much emphasis should be put on products/outcomes? How much emphasis should be put on processes/procedures?
4. What system or approach should be used to organize the program evaluation?
5. What procedures should be used to implement the continuation or changes indicated by the evaluation?

Accountability

1. In delivering special education to each exceptional person, what are the specific areas of responsibility for the following: (a) the administrators, (b) the principal, (c) the teacher, (d) the parents, and (e) the exceptional person?
2. How should work be organized and coordinated to facilitate carrying out of each person's responsibilities as efficiently and effectively as possible?

continued

TABLE 12.1 continued

Appropriateness
1. Given the requirements for a free appropriate public education, an equal educational opportunity, and a barrier-free environment for handicapped persons, what indices and procedures can be used to ensure that these requirements are being met for each individual?
2. What can be done to observe the spirit of these requirements for gifted/talented individuals?

Program Monitoring/Compliance

Decision: To decide how to ensure effectiveness of procedures for equal protection, due process, and confidentiality in classification, testing, instruction, and placement.

At Issue: Answers to questions about implementing identification, nondiscriminatory testing, individualized instruction, placement in the least restrictive environment, and the individual education program; more specifically, questions about people's understanding the law, monitoring procedures, sanctions, and equity across units in enforcement and funding.

Understanding the Law
1. What program contents should be used for teaching people the legal requirements for confidentiality, an equal educational opportunity, a free appropriate public education, and a barrier-free environment?
2. What procedures should be used in teaching this content?
3. How should this content and these procedures be differentiated for the various audiences: Exceptional persons? Their families? Regular teachers? Special teachers? General administrators and supervisors? Paraprofessionals? School boards? The general public?

Monitoring Procedures
1. Given each requirement, what criteria and procedures should be used to monitor compliance?
2. How can the reliability, validity, and appropriateness of these criteria and procedures be demonstrated?
3. How should monitors and people being monitored be trained about the nature of these criteria and procedures and their use? Hearing officers and other appropriate personnel?

Sanctions
1. What levels of compliance across requirements are reasonable and appropriate? When do legal sanctions become necessary?
2. To what extent are reasonableness and appropriateness dependent on a program's stage of development?
3. Are some profiles of level of appropriateness across requirements better than others?
4. What inducements, short of organizational and individual/legal sanctions, can be used to motivate compliance?

Equity Across Units
1. To what extent can there be equity in compliance across LEAs and other units required to be in compliance? Across states?
2. To what extent are inequities attributable to differences in availability of funds? In information about requirements? In other factors?
3. What financial, informational, and other procedures can be used to reduce inequities?

---

are especially marked in special education research because of the ethical, humanitarian, and legal concerns of working with exceptional persons and their families. Some examples follow.

One concern is with *hurtful intrusion*. Some studies could hardly be hurtfully intrusive; for example, a case study of the processes used in a group of volunteers organizing and implementing a Special Olympics. On the other hand, some studies could be crude and harmful invasions of privacy, for example, a case study of the reactions of a group of adolescents dealing with diagnoses of life-threatening chronic illnesses, with the unpleasant side-effects accompanying treatments of those illnesses, and with the implications of those illnesses and side-effects for their getting on with the developmental tasks of our culture. Consider John Gunther's *Death be not proud* (1958, 1975), Barbara Gordon's *I'm dancing as fast as I can* (1979), or Larry Pringle's *This is the child* (1983) to see the pain people experience. These authors chose to share their pain; many exceptional persons and their families do not so choose. To approach these people with requests to participate in research or to interview them without notification and consent in such approaches as field studies would be unconscionably intrusive.

Another concern is the *confidentiality*. In research, as in special education programs, many data are collected about the participants. Some of these data may be erroneous; all are personal. Some people encountering such data will not know how to evaluate their accuracy or meaning. There are endless possibilities for mishandled confidential data leading to prejudice against a research participant in his or her success in personal and social relations, admission to some schools and training programs, and access to some employment opportunities. As an illustration, refer to *Flowers for Algernon*, in which Keyes (1959) wrote a discerning account of how people react differently to positive and negative information about an exceptional person.

Still another concern is with the *effects of some negative treatments*. There are many examples. But, to pick one, consider an experiment to test the relative effects of several types of aversive treatments to prevent or reduce unproductive or hurtful behavior. Some of these aversive variants could harm a subject physically, or socially/emotionally, or both, or they could be degrading. Anthony Burgess (1963) wrote a powerful illustration of such harm in *Clockwork Orange*.

Complementary to the concern about nega-tive treatments is the concern about *withholding a believed-to-be positive treatment* in order to have an experimental control. If the positive treatment has a powerful effect or a crucial effect, or if it involves long-term testing, then control subjects could be harmed, sometimes strongly, by being denied its benefits. Sinclair Lewis (1925) wrote a moving illustration of this dilemma in *Arrowsmith*.

There are other concerns with using exceptional persons and their families as subjects in research. However, these examples using intrusion, confidentiality, negative treatments, and controls for positive treatments give the flavor. In sum, such difficulties preclude asking some questions and using some research approaches and they put tight constrictions on involvement in other questions and research approaches — again, for ethical, humanitarian, and legal reasons.

Now turn to a second set of difficulties in doing research with exceptional persons and their families: *difficulties in performing research*. Again, the topic is extensive. As a very small illustration, sample some technical difficulties in using the scientific method to assess change and look at ways researchers seek to deal with these technical difficulties.

Assessment of change — the *description* of change and the *ascription* of causes of that change — is one of the most important and intractable of the research interests. Van Dalen's early comments still get to the heart of the matter.

> To teach effectively, one must have a knowledge of the nature and rate of changes that take place in human organisms. One must know what interrelated factors affect growth at various stages of development; when various aspects of growth are first observable, spurt forward, remain rather stationary, reach optimal development, and decline; and how the duration, intensity, and timing of an experience in the developmental period affect growth. (1973, p. 41)

Researchers have long recognized the problems in describing how people's characteristics and behavior change and in ascribing that change to the independent variables identified for study. Harris (1963) and his coworkers, Campbell and Stanley (1963) and Bracht and Glass (1968), wrote the definitive works on this difficult topic. They described how extraneous variables, singly and in combination, interfere with meeting the requirements and assumptions of psychometric, statistical, and research design procedures often confounding, and sometimes vitiating, the time series studies required to assess changes and the causes of these changes. They clearly delineated threats to the internal and external validity of studies seeking to identify subject and treatment variables causing change; that is, threats, including variables related to history, maturation, testing, instrumentation, statistical regression, selection, experimental mortality, selection-maturation interaction, reactive or interactive effects of testing, interactive effects between selection bias and the experimental variable, reactive effects of experimental arrangements, and multiple treatment interference.

The problems in describing change and determining its causes are magnified in special education research due to the wide, multiple variations within and among exceptional persons. Since the publication of the previously mentioned seminal works on measuring change, people have grappled with these problems. Blake and Allen (1976) did a detailed analysis of problems in measuring change in special education research and ways to deal with these problems. Others also have worked with these problems and their solutions; Fortune, Hutson, and Endahl (1983) is one example.

Going beyond the scientific research discussed as an illustration, technical difficulties abound in all research approaches, and these technical difficulties make some special education research less sound and useful than it could be. Yet, research cannot, and should not, be eliminated as a basis for decision-making in special education. Rather, research should be carried out as rigorously as possible — with extreme vigilance about error — and then researchers should be very conscientious in pointing out the values and limitations of their information. At the same time, the research consumer and decision-maker should never forget the age-old caveat emptor and act accordingly.

Finally, a third set of difficulties must be faced in research with exceptional persons and their families: *difficulties in processing research for decision-making*. Two subsets of difficulties are especially formidable: one is processing so many bits of, sometimes conflicting, information; the other is cross-connecting the variables studied in research with the conditions and behavior involved in decision making. This chapter confines the examples to the first subset: difficulties in processing large amounts of information.

A major historical trend since the 1950s has been the flood of funds and other stimulation to support research, to train leadership personnel to open new frontiers, and to training specialists to do the research needed to help decision making on those frontiers. A happy effect of all this activity has been a large outpouring of research. An unhappy effect is the inundation of diverse bits of information. This inundation comes through print and electronic media and through personal contacts in informal sessions and formal professional meetings.

Given a plethora of information, the task is to process it, to organize and synthesize it, into a form possible to grasp and apply to decision making in particular cases. This information-processing task is a very hard one. Glass, McGaw, and Smith (1981) portray the situation well for education in general. They maintain that, by necessity, professionals are developing better ways to extract knowledge from research and communicate it. This search for coherence is required because research results on most problems have, in the last generation, grown beyond the ability of the unaided human mind to comprehend patterns in the wealth of separate studies. For example, on some problems, there are hundreds of studies, and these studies quite often vary partly or completely in methodology. Therefore, new ways are needed to process and synthesize research. No longer can chronological narratives and crude classifications be used in the search for relationships. But, there is still a long way to go before techniques are found for dealing with this information explosion. Glass and his associates made a beginning. They call their technique *meta-analysis*, "the analysis of analyses (i.e., the statistical analysis of the findings of many individual analyses)" (Glass et al., 1981, p. 12).

Meta-analysis is beginning to be used in studies pertaining to special education and the related services. The following examples are excerpted from a list of studies from throughout education that Glass et al. (1981) presented: the effects of special classes, resource rooms, and other treatments on exceptional children (Carlberg, 1979); the treatment of stuttering (Andrews, 1979); neuropsychological assessment of children (Davidson, 1978); individualized mathematics instruction (Hartley, 1977); psycholinguistic training (Kavale, 1979); treatment of hyperactivity (Kavale, 1980a); correlation of auditory perceptual skill and reading (Kavale, 1980b); drug therapy and psychological disorders (T. I. Miller, 1977, 1980); patient education programs in medicine (Posavac, 1980); psychological intervention and recovery from medical crisis (Schlesinger, Mumford, & Glass, 1980); and diagnostic/remedial instruction and science learning (Yeany & Miller, 1980).

Meta-analysis has been criticized rather roundly; for example, Bandura (1978), Eysenck (1978), and Simpson (1980), among others. Glass et al. (1981) summarize, and respond to, these criticisms. Generally, as with most phenomena, meta-analysis has its values and its limitations.

In sum, we presented some examples of difficulties in processing research in decision making to illustrate an important set of difficulties. For special educators, as for others, it is possible only to deal with a limited few separate bits of information before some form of organization must be imposed on the body of work to make it useful in decision-making. As in many areas of general education research, special education researchers have accumulated a vast amount of data. Whatever the outcome of meta-analysis and other attempts to deal with the problems and pitfalls of analyzing and synthesizing voluminous amounts of information,

special educators and their coworkers in the related services must recognize the issues and choose how to deal with the matter. The time is fast approaching, or has already arrived, when selective sampling and simple box-score counting will not do to determine the best variable. Again, inadequate information can be harmful to exceptional persons and nonproductive in using precious resources and limited time and energies. However, it is certain that the future will bring a great deal more attention to procedures and problems of processing research data for use in decisionmaking.

Special Note. In closing this section on examples of difficulties in doing research with exceptional persons and their families, we wish to point out that we have been fairly heavy-handed in stressing difficulties. We intended to be. During over 2 decades as producers and consumers of research in special education and general education, we have looked grim reality in the face and struggled with it long enough to recognize that, by the nature of things, most research is flawed and special educators must act accordingly. We partly agree with the old crackerbarrel philosopher who Gallagher (1979, p. 100) quoted as saying, "It ain't what we know that causes us so much trouble, it's what we know that ain't so." Special educators certainly need more research results. But, just as important is the need to separate the wheat from the chaff: the sound and useful from the flawed and useless or harmful. We intend our samples of difficulties to point the way to the great deal of attention and precaution that must be learned about and observed.

Aspects of the Present Special Education Research Situation

Research Available

A graph of indices showing concern for the handicapped and the gifted/talented would be jagged; however, the overall pattern would be a positively accelerating curve with major inflections coming with the end of World War II and the upsurge of civil libertarian and humanitarian activism in the 1960s and 1970s. One part of this expansion in special education, and the related services, has been a vast increase in research and development activities.

Granted, there are impediments to doing research (see, for example, Ballard-Campbell & Semmel, 1981; Drew & Buchanan, 1979; Lovitt & Jenkins, 1979; and Strain & Shores, 1979). Nevertheless, there is available a great deal of research that is sound and useful in decision making. For example, consider the research syntheses in the rest of this volume; that is, research on sociology of the handicapped, assessment of the handicapped, early childhood services for the handicapped, severe and multiple handicaps, communication disorders (including learning and language disabilities), behavioral disorders, learning disabilities, sensory impairments, and gifted talented. Consider also research syntheses available from other sources like Achenbach (1982); M. Ellis (1979); N. Ellis (1966, 1978); Foa and Emmelkamp (1983), Kozloff (1979); Mann and Sabatino (1973, 1974, 1976, 1980); Ross and Ross (1982); Tannenbaum (1983); and Toro (1982).

And a lot of research has been applied to decision-making. For example, in terms of some of the current research in the field, the reader is referred to the research investigations and programs described by Bricker (1982), Carlson and Keimig (1983), Chaffin (1982; 1983), Edgar, Haring, Jenkins, & Pious (1982), Karnes (1983), and Wood (1979, 1980, 1981). There are also, of course, many earlier examples; e.g., Cawley (1979); Goldstein (1980a,b); and Wehman and McLaughlin (1981).

Limits in time, space, and content in this chapter preclude being too extensive in generalizing about special educators' accomplishments in performing research and applying it to decisions. However, special educators can certainly point with pride in many directions. Take three major directions as examples. Research has been useful in applying electronic technology to assessing hearing and facilitating communication and self-help activities for the severely disabled. Research has been useful in demonstrating the abuses and needs that led to the tremendous changes in the legal status of handicapped people. Research has been useful in formulating individual procedures and total programs for teaching academic content and social-emotional patterns and skills to exceptional persons. Across special education, the list of such accomplishments is long and growing. Readers can add their own examples from the viewpoint of the field as they experience it.

Research Needed

Accepting that there is a fine domain of research and it is useful in decision making, what research is still needed?

Consider first the research needed in specific areas, such as communication disorders or early childhood special education. One mandate that Morris and Blatt gave to authors participating in this volume was that they "describe overlooked research topics, mis-starts/mis-directions in the research area being addressed, and further directions—Where should the field be going? What is/are the next steps?" Consequently, the chapters preceding this one have information about research needed to help in decision making in particular areas of special education. In addition, research needed in particular areas has been pinpointed by writers publishing elsewhere; for example, Ballard-Campbell and Semmel (1981), Drew and Buchanan (1979), Hessler and Sosnowsky (1979), and Reed (1980).

Let's consider now research needs in a more general context. As noted in our discussion of difficulties in processing research for decision making, there is a plethora of special education research. We are somewhat like groups of settlers in a vast wilderness who have organized and managed a clear view of small discrete areas but do not have a picture of the status quo in the entire territory. To be less metaphorical, special educators do not have a clear, comprehensive picture of the present special education research domain in its entirety— where are the appropriate emphases, where are overemphasized areas, where are underemphasized areas. For example, in 1979, Lee reported a pertinent, interesting study. He did a content analysis of the *Journal of Special Education* for the 13-year period 1966–1978. He concluded that the material published did not reflect contemporary and current changes in the special education discipline. Lee's observation is an important one, even though his conclusion is necessarily restricted by limiting his study to one journal.

Stated in the positive, special educators need an inventory of the extant research in the field. Within the framework used in this chapter, the overarching questions would be

- Very generally, what foci are emphasized appropriately in special education research? Overemphasized? Underemphasized?
- Very generally, what research approaches do special educators employ appropriately often for getting information to use in making their decisions? Underemploy? Overemploy?

Answering these broader questions would require collecting information pertaining to more specific questions, such as those directed to four important dimensions — type of exceptionality, age, population characteristics and special education tool, research approach — and their interactions; namely

- What types of exceptional persons are most frequently studied in special education research? How frequently are some types disregarded to study uncategorized exceptional persons?
- What age levels are most frequently addressed in special education research?
- What population characteristics and special education tools are most frequently considered in special education research?
- What research approaches are most frequently used in special education research?
- Within each type of exceptionality, what age levels are most frequently considered in special education research?
- Within each type of exceptionality, what population characteristics and special educa-

tion tools are most frequently studied in special education research?
- Within each type of exceptionality, what research approaches are most frequently used in our special education research?
- Within each age level, what population characteristics and special education tools are most frequently studied in special education research?
- Within each age level, what research approaches are most frequently used in special education research?
- For each special education tool, what research approaches are most frequently used in our special education research?

Given answers to such questions, it would be possible to appraise the appropriateness of research emphases and the adequacy of the knowledge-base in order to approach the vast changes affecting the discipline, and those served by it, now and in the near future, in the coming new era — the Information Age. In turn, this appraisal could identify directions for conducting research and for training personnel, both researchers and practitioners.

In general, as we consider in the section on Future Research in Special Education, this is a period of transition, not only in special education but in all of society. On the one hand, there is still the need to grapple with yesterday's problems, such as the continuing issues surrounding the definition and diagnosis of learning disabilities. On the other hand, tomorrow's problems are beginning to emerge, such as translating new knowledge from psychoneuroimmunology into educational procedures useful in making decisions about those classified as exceptional due to illnesses or dysfunctions of their immune systems (e.g., multiple sclerosis, rheumatic disorders, and neoplastic diseases) and testing the effectiveness of those procedures with people at various ages; i.e., developmental levels across the life span.

The point is that another big positive inflection in that positively accelerating curve is coming, or perhaps is already started, describing research and other activities in special education. And so, what does all of this mean to our description of needed research? In short, it means that though much is given, still more is needed. Stated another way, although much research has been done and is being used well, a great deal of research is still needed, and this research must be well charted.

FUTURE RESEARCH IN SPECIAL EDUCATION

So far we examined the context of research in special education and current research in special education. Our concern now becomes, What next? What research is needed for decision making in today's world — and tomorrow's? Answering these questions requires considering the projected trends in society and the implications of these trends for research in special education.

Projected Societal Trends

Toffler and other futurists work diligently to discern what is presently being done and where the future is headed. For example, Naisbitt (1982–1983) reports his group's qualitative research on deeply rooted social, economic, political, and technological movements in society. Work in special education is, of course, part of the warp and woof of this broader societal movement. It is a truism that as we go forward, we need a clear view, first, of this complex fabric of trends and, second, where we are and where we are going within this complex fabric. In the concluding statement of *Megatrends*, Naisbitt trenchantly stated this need for grasping and capitalizing on trends in social change.

> We are living in the *time of the parenthesis*, the time between the eras. It is as though we have bracketed off the present from both the past and the future, for we are neither here nor there.
>
> We have not quite left behind the either-or America of the past — centralized, industrialized, and economically self-contained. With one foot in the old world where we lived mostly in the Northeast, relied on institutional help, built hierarchies and elected represen-

tatives, we have approached problems with an eye toward the high-tech, short-term solutions.

> But we have not embraced the future either. We have done the human thing. We are clinging to the known past in fear of the unknown future. . . .
>
> [Yet, we] must study trends and interpret that future in order to make it more real and knowable. Those who are willing to handle the ambiguity of this in-between period and to anticipate the next era will be a quantum leap ahead of those who hold on to the past. The *time of the parenthesis* is a time of change and questioning. (Naisbitt, 1982, pp. 249–250)

The responsibility of special educators is to prepare exceptional persons and the personnel who serve them to live in the Information Age, the world to come as well as the current transitional society.

Naisbitt (1982) and his group identified 10 new directions transforming our lives; they labeled these megatrends. In sum, they conclude from their research that we are moving from an industrial society to an information society; from forced technology to high tech/high touch (i.e., a combination of high automatization accompanied by increased human concerns); from a national economy to a world economy; from short-term planning and activities to long-term approaches and projects; from centralization to decentralization; from getting institutionalized help to relying on self-help; from representative democracy to participatory democracy; from conforming to hierarchies to operating through networking; from living and working in the North to locating in the South; and from being constrained to either-or choices to being free to choose among multiple options.

In addition, other broad social trends affect the work in special education. Important examples are from a larger birth rate to a smaller population growth; from a shorter life expectancy to increased longevity; from a more passive acceptance to increased consumer expectations and demands; from an immersion in the work-ethic to greater attention to the quality of life; from high incidence of fatality with some illnesses and dysfunctions to an increased survival rate; from ample funds for social programs to reduced economic resources; from an inattention to individuals' personal/social needs to an increased humanism; from a settling for palliation to emphasis on amelioration; from an unawareness of conditions for human efficiency to a greater participation in practices conducive to physical, emotional, and social well-being; and from acceptance of lower amounts of formal education to recognition of needs for higher levels of education.

Implications of the Societal Trends for Research in Special Education

Special education and the related services for handicapped persons and their families made a great leap forward in the 1960s and 1970s and now is somewhat in a period of consolidation and regrouping, especially in this politically conservative, economically difficult time. Yet, the field must stay up with the rapid progress reflected in the trends just specified.

Given the need to increase options available to exceptional persons and given the bases for decision making in special education, three mandates should provide guideline in facing the exciting possibilities and, sometimes, active assaults, passive indifference, and unfortunate ineptitude and incompetence.

1. *Normative standards.* Vigilance is needed to assure that the normative standards of the Constitution and other parts of the cultural heritage be honored with exceptional persons and their families.
2. *Public policy.* Assiduousness is needed to get and keep the public leverage and influence necessary to continue the major positive inflection in special education trends witnessed so far.
3. *Research.* Perspicaciousness is needed to discern a clear vision of the road ahead, to identify the decisions necessary, and to conduct the research that will produce the data required for decision making.

Again, professionals must be committed to increasing the options of exceptional persons in the era that is approaching so rapidly. And so, specifically, Where does that road lead? What decisions will need to be made? What research is needed? Some special educators have been considering these questions in a more general sense; for example, Fendt (1980); Menolascino (1979); Nesbitt (1979); Office of Special Education and Rehabilitation (1983); Safer (1979); and Vernon and Rabush (1981). Others have started working on particular activities like incorporating computers into direct and indirect work with exceptional persons; for example, Bitzer (1979); Goldenberg (1979); Stepp (1979); and Taber (1983). Such beginnings need expanding. In short, in order to continue seeking answers to our questions about the future, special educators need to use the problem-solving method, the method that is the hallmark of research as well as most other activities. That is, the problem must be delimited and then the necessary steps taken to solve it.

How should problems be delimited? There is a need to identify the research required to help make decisions in this new information era. This identification requires pinpointing gaps — what data is needed for decision making — by juxtaposing projections about future societal trends with information about the current knowledge base in particular areas and information about research emphases throughout special education. In other words, the problem is delimited by the discrepancy between the current status in research and the projected future trends, which demonstrate where to go in order to stay in the context of the general society.

Given the delimited problem, then what steps are necessary to solve it? Having identified the problem — the gap between what knowledge is needed in the future and what is already known in the present, three steps follow: breaking the general issues, or broad questions, into discrete research questions; undertaking research on those specific questions for which there is the technology and training to deal; and developing the technology and the training programs to prepare for those questions beyond the present state of the art.

SUMMARY

Context of Research in Special Education

Research results, along with normative standards and the people's will expressed through public policy, serve as major bases for making decisions about delivering special education to exceptional persons. Major approaches used in special education research include philosophical inquiry and argumentation, historical and retrospective analyses, legal analyses, qualitative examinations, and experimental and quasiexperimental research using the scientific method. Decision making is focussed on the groups of exceptional persons and their treatments; that is, the many specific practices subsumed by the nine generic special education tools (identification, nondiscriminatory testing, individualized instruction, the individual education program, placement in the least restrictive environment, personnel training, program administration, program evaluation, and program monitoring and compliance).

Current Research in Special Education

In research design, studies focus on issues and questions pertaining to exceptional persons and their families and specific practices subsumed by the nine broad generic special education tools. At the same time, it is necessary to recognize and try to deal with some tremendous difficulties in conducting special education research; for example, difficulties in using human subjects in research, difficulties in performing research, and difficulties in processing research for decision making. A broad overview of aspects of the present special education research situation shows that one facet of the relatively recent large expansion in special education is a big increase in research and development. A lot of research is available and it has been used well in decision making. However, to stay viable and responsive, additional research is needed to help in our decision making in the new Information Age, which is just beginning. Part of this needed research is a broad assessment of research emphases across the entire special education field.

Future Research in Special Education

Society is in transition into a new era, the Information Age. Major societal trends that are apparent include a move toward an information society, to high tech/high touch procedures, to a world economy, to long-term approaches and projects, to decentralization, to relying on self-help, to a participatory democracy, to operating through networking, to living and working in the South, to being free to choose among multiple options, to a smaller population growth, to increased longevity, to increased consumer expectations and demands, to greater attention to the quality of life, to increased survival rates with some illnesses and dysfunctions, to reduced economic resources for social programs, to increased humanism, to emphasis on amelioration rather than palliation, to greater participation in practices conducive to physical, emotional, and social well-being, and to recognition of needs for higher levels of formal education. These societal trends have major implications for research in special education. As those in special education commit themselves to increasing the options of exceptional persons in the era that is approaching so rapidly, they must identify the research needed to help make decisions in this information era and undertake the steps required to initiate that research. That is, they must identify the gaps between the current knowledge-base and that which will be required to make decisions within the projected societal trends.

The State of the Art in Special Education Research

Given this chapter's brief scan of the context of research in special education, current research in special education, and future research in special education, what can be concluded about the state of the art in special education research?

In general, the field of special education does not bat a thousand, but does fairly well—as well as any other field of clinical-social science. Special education research made valuable contributions to serving exceptional persons in the past, it is currently a useful asset in decision making, and, potentially, can be most helpful in increasing the personal options of exceptional persons within the Information Age, which is upon us.

More specifically, professionals can affirm these generalizations. Special education has met the test as a useful basis for making decisions with exceptional persons, along with normative standards and the people's will expressed through public policy. Quite appropriately, the heavy reliance on experimental and quasiexperimental research approaches is broadening and shifting to include valuable contributions available through qualitative research, legal research, historical and retrospective analyses, and philosophical inquiry and argumentation.

A wide range of variables have been studied. In delineating independent and dependent subject variables, populations have been sampled along such dimensions as age, and type and degree of exceptionality. In delineating independent treatment variables, facets of the special education tools (identification, nondiscriminatory testing, individualized instruction, placement in the least restrictive environment, personnel training, program administration, program evaluation, and program monitoring and compliance) are examined.

Special education research is like research in other clinical-social sciences, which deal with people in all of their infinite variety and complexity. Using research to account for—to identify the sources of—a major portion of the variance in exceptional persons' behavior remains very hard. Among the impediments are those associated with such problems as difficulties in using human subjects in research, difficulties in performing research, and difficulties in processing research for decision making. However, for those in special education research, our reach must continue to stay a lit-

tle bit ahead of our grasp. Or, to adapt an allusion from politics, doing reliable, valid, and appropriate special education research and using it accurately in decision making is the art of deciding what is possible, doing it the best we can, recognizing what we have done with all of its restrictions, and using the results with appropriate caution.

Given our limitations and imperfections, and accepting them, special educators must prepare ourselves for new directions and increased activity. The last 30 years or so has seen changes greater than those in any similar period of history. These changes will continue and the growth curve is positively accelerated and exponential to a factor greater than 1. We are on the front edge of a new era, the Information Age. Certainly, this means great problems, problems as intractable as those that accompanied transitions between eras in ages past. At the same time, this means great opportunities in the favor of increased options for all people, especially exceptional persons. For example, consider the vast impact of developments in such areas as electronics and miniaturization on a large range of activities from saving lives to facilitating communication, to innervating muscles, to using microcomputers in teaching, and to using robotics in performing purposeful and precise physical activities. In short, it is easy to discern very clearly a number of changes, trends in new directions, in the society exceptional persons are preparing to live in.

It's going to be a new ball game. As Casey Stengel, perhaps apocryphally, put it, "It's easier to grow old than to grow up." And so, if special education researchers are going to perform as well as they have in the past or better, they have their work cut out for them. In the future, it will be necessary to identify and address the research questions emerging with the Information Age. This process has already begun. Setting sights and getting a bearing on the future requires assessing where we are now in the context of where we need to be; in short, to identify the gaps between the societal trends that will emerge and the present base of knowledge, a knowledge base resulting from our special education research in the past. And, of course, once the course has been charted, research must begin.

Naisbitt (1982, p. 247) said it well in his exhaltation about this time of parenthesis between eras, "My God, what fantastic time to be alive!" It is. It certainly is. And, we in special education research have a fantastic trust, to continue to produce the research results that will help us and the exceptional persons we serve make the most appropriate decisions. As the authors of the other chapters of this book, as well as other authors, amply demonstrate: we in special education research are ready and able to continue honoring that trust.

REFERENCES

Achenbach, T. M. (1982). *Developmental psychopathology* (2nd ed.). New York: Wiley.

Alley, G. R. (1979). Identification of learning disabled adolescents: A Bayesian approach. *Learning Disability Quarterly*, 2, 76–83.

Andrews, G. (1979). A meta-analysis of the treatment of stuttering. Paper presented at the convention of the American Speech and Hearing Association.

Ballard, J., Ramirez, B., & Weintraub, F. J. (1982). *Special education in America: Its legal and governmental foundations*. Reston, VA.: Council for Exceptional Children.

Ballard-Campbell, M., & Semmel, M. I. (1981). Policy research and special education: Research issues affecting policy formation and implementation. *Exceptional Education Quarterly*, 59–68.

Bandura, A. (1978). On paradigms and recycled idealogies. *Cognitive Therapy and Research*, 2, 79–103.

Bemporad, J. R. (1979). Adult recollections of a formerly autistic child. *Journal of Autism and Developmental Disorders*, 9, 179–197.

Bitzer, D. (1979). Uses of BCE for the handicapped: Educational technology for the '80s. *American Annals of the Deaf*, 124, 553–558.

Blake, K. A. (1981). *Educating exceptional pupils.* Reading, MA: Addison-Wesley.

Blake, K. A., & Allen, J. C. (1976). Conducting longitudinal research in reading. In R. Farr, S. Weintraub, & B. Tone (Eds.), *Improving reading research.* Newark, NJ: International Reading Association.

Blatt, B., & Kaplan, F. (1967). *Christmas in purgatory.* Boston: Allyn and Bacon.

Blatt, B., & Morris, J. R. (1984). *Perspectives in special education: Personal orientations.* Glenview, IL.: Scott, Foresman & Co.

Blatt, B., Ozolins, A., & McNally, J. (1979). *The family papers: A return to purgatory.* New York: Longman.

Bodgan, R. C., & Biklen, S. K. (1982). *Qualitative research for education: An introduction to theory and methods.* Boston: Allyn and Bacon.

Bracht, G. H., & Glass, G. V. (1966). The external validity of experiments. *American Educational Research Journal*, 5, 437–474.

Bricker, D. (1982). *Intervention with at-risk and handicapped infants: From research to application.* Baltimore: University Park Press.

Bronfenbrenner, U. (1976). The experimental ecology of education. *Educational Researcher*, 5.

Burgess, A. (1963). *Clockwork orange.* New York: Norton.

Campbell, D. (1978). Qualitative knowing in action research. In M. Brenner, P. Marsh, & M. Brenner (Eds.), *The social contexts of method.* New York: St. Martins.

Campbell, D. T., & Stanley, J. C. (1963). Experimental and quasiexperimental designs in research on teaching. In N. L. Gage (Ed.), *Handbook of research on teaching* (pp. 171–264). Chicago: Rand McNally.

Carlberg, C. G. (1979). *Meta-analysis of the effects of special classes, resource rooms, and other treatments on exceptional children.* Doctoral dissertation, University of Colorado at Boulder. Ann Arbor, MI: University Microfilms.

Carlson, S., & Keimig, J. (1983). *Learning how to learn teaching strategies.* Allen, TX: DLM.

Carter, S. (1983). *Case management seminars for the developmentally disabled in Georgia.* Unpublished doctoral dissertation, University of Georgia, Athens.

Cawley, J. (1978). *Project math: Levels I–IV.* Tulsa, OK: Educational Progress Corporation.

Chaffin, J. (1982). *Academic skillbuilders in math.* (Computer software). Allen, TX: DLM.

Chaffin, J. (1983). *Academic skillbuilders in reading.* (Computer software). Allen, TX.: DLM.

Cronbach, L. (1975). Beyond the two disciplines of scientific psychology. *American Psychologist*, 38, 116–127.

Curlette, W. L., & Stallings, W. M. (1979). Ten issues in criterion-referenced testing: A response to commonly-heard criticisms. *Clearing House*, 53(3), 145–148.

Curo, A. J. (1979). Multiple-baseline design in instructional research: Pitfalls of measurement and procedural advantages. *American Journal of Mental Deficiency*, 34, 219–228.

Davidson, T. B. (1978). *Meta-analysis of the neuropsychological assessment of children.* Denver, CO: University of Denver.

Department of Health and Human Services. (1983, 7 March). Regulations for nondiscrimination on the basis of handicap: Discriminatory denial of food or other medical care to handicapped infants. Interim Final Rule. *Federal Register, 48*(45).

Drew, C. J., & Buchanan, M. L. (1979). Research on teacher education: Status and need. *Teacher Education and Special Education*, *2*(2), 50–55.

Drew, C. J., Preator, K., & Buchanan, M. L. (1982). Research and researchers in special education. *Exceptional Education Quarterly*, *2*, 47–56.

Dunn, L. M. (1968). Special education for the mildly retarded: Is much of it justifiable? *Exceptional Children*, *35*, 20.

Edgar, E. B., Haring, N. G., Jenkins, J. R., & Pious, C. G. (1982). *Mentally handicapped children: Education and training*. Baltimore: University Park Press.

Eiseley, L. (1978). The star thrower. In L. Eiseley (Ed.), *The star thrower* (pp. 169–185). New York: Quadrangle/The New York Times Book Company.

Ellis, M. (Ed.). (1979). *Handbook of mental deficiency. Psychological theory and research* (2nd ed.). Hillsdale, NJ: Erlbaum.

Ellis, N. (Ed.). (1966, 1978). *International review of research and mental retardation* (vols. 1 & 9). New York: Academic Press.

Eysenck, H. J. (1978). An exercise in mega-silliness. *American Psychologist*, *33*, 517.

Fendt, P. F. (1980). Alternatives in education: A futurist view. *Education Unlimited*, *2*(3), 11–16.

Foa, E. B., & Emmelkamp, P. M. G. (Eds.). (1983). *Failures in behavior therapy*. Somerset, NJ: Wiley.

Fortune, J. C., Hutson, B. A., & Endahl, J. (1983, Summer). A typology of models for measuring change. *Journal of Research and Development in Education*.

Gallagher, J. J. (1979). Rights of the next generation of children. *Exceptional Children*, *45*, 98–105.

Gallagher, J. J., Torrance, P., Passow, A., & Gowan, J. (1979). *Issues in gifted education*. Papers presented at the National/State Leadership Training Institute on the Gifted and Talented, Los Angeles.

George, W. C., Cohn, S. J., & Stanley, J. C. (Eds.). (1980). *Educating the gifted: Acceleration and enrichment*. Baltimore: The Johns Hopkins University Press.

Gerber, P. J., & Zinkgraf, S. A. (1982). A comparative study of social perceptual ability of learning disabled and non-handicapped students. *Learning Disability Quarterly*, *5*, 374–378.

Glass, G. (1975). A paradox about excellence in the schools and the people in them. *Educational Researcher*, *4*.

Glass, G. V., McGaw, B., & Smith, M. L. (1981). *Meta-analysis in social research*. Beverly Hills: Sage.

Goldenberg, E. P. (1979). *Special technology for special children: Computers to serve communication and autonomy in the education of handicapped children*. Baltimore: University Park Press.

Goldstein, H. (1980a). *RADEA: A developmental program for the moderately and severely/profoundly handicapped*. Dallas: Melton Peninsula.

Goldstein, H. (1980b). *SAIL: Skills to achieve independent living*. Dallas: Melton Peninsula.

Gordon, B. (1979). *I'm dancing as fast as I can*. New York: Harper and Row.

Gresham, P. M. (1983). Social skills assessment as a component of mainstreaming placement decisions. *Exceptional Children*, *49*, 331–336.

Guba, E. G. (1978). Toward a methodology of naturalistic inquiry in educational evaluation. *CSE monograph series in evaluation*, 8. Los Angeles: Center for the Study of Evaluation, University of California.

Gully, K. J., & Hosch, H. M. (1979). Adaptive behavior scale: Development as a diagnostic tool via discriminant analysis. *American Journal of Mental Deficiency*, *83*(5), 518–523.

Gunther, J. (1958, 1975). *Death be not proud*. New York: Modern Library Original Edition and Harper Row Memorial Edition, respectively.

Harris, C. W. (Ed.). (1963). *Problems in measuring change*. Madison: University of Wisconsin Press.

Hartley, S. S. (1977). *Meta-analysis of the effects of individually paced instruction in mathematics*. Doctoral dissertation, University of Colorado.

Haskins, J., & Stifle, J. M. (1979). *The quiet revolution: The struggle for the rights of disabled Americans*. New York: Thomas Y. Crowell.

Hessler, G. L., & Sosnowsky, W. P. (1979). A review of aptitude-treatment interaction studies with the handicapped. *Psychology in the Schools*, *16*(3), 388–394.

Higgins, S. (1979). Options and alternatives: Policy decisions yet to be made. *Exceptional Children*, *46*(1), 34–39.

Holland, R. P. (1980). An analysis of the decision-making processes in special education. *Exceptional Children*, *46*(7), 551–554.

Johnson, R. T., & Johnson, D. W. (1983). Effects of cooperative, competitive, and individualistic learning experiences on social development. *Exceptional Children*, *49*, 323–329.

Jones, R. (Ed.). (1983). *Reflections on growing up disabled*. Reston, VA : Council for Exceptional Children.

Karnes, M. B. (1983). *Know me—know you*. (A guide for affective education with emphasis on oral language demonstrated in real life situations.) Allen, TX: DLM.

Kavale, K. (1979). *The effectiveness of psycholinguistic training: A meta-analysis*. Riverside: University of California.

Kavale, K. (1980). *Meta-analysis of experiments on the treatment of hyperactivity in children*. Riverside: University of California.

Kavale, K. (1980b). The relationship between auditory perceptual skills and reading ability: A meta-analysis. *Perceptual and Motor Skills*, *51*, 947–955.

Keyes, D. (1959). *Flowers for Algernon*. New York: Bantam.

Knoff, H. M. (1983). Effect of diagnostic information on special education placement decisions. *Exceptional Children, 49*, 440–444.

Kozloff, M. A. (1979). *A program for families of children with learning and behavior problems.* Somerset, NJ: Wiley.

Lee, R. D. (1979). *Content analysis of the Journal of Special Education, 1966 through 1978.* Doctoral dissertation, University of Oklahoma. Ann Arbor, MI: University Microfilms.

Lewis, S. (1925). *Arrowsmith.* New York: Grosset and Dunlap. Reissued by Bucaneer Books, 1981.

Lovitt, T. C., & Jenkins, J. R. (1979). Learning disabilities research; Defining populations. *Learning Disability Quarterly, 2*(3), 46–50.

Macmillan, R. C. (1980). *Futures forecasting: Special education in 1990.* Doctoral dissertation, University of Alabama. Ann Arbor, MI: University Microfilms.

Mann, L., & Sabatino, D. A. (Eds.). (1973). *First review of special education,* 2 vols. New York: Grune and Stratton.

Mann, L., & Sabatino, D. A. (Eds.). (1974). *Second review of special education.* New York: Grune and Stratton.

Mann, L., & Sabatino, D. A. (Eds.). (1976). *Third review of special education.* New York: Grune and Stratton.

Mann, L., & Sabatino, D. A. (Eds.). (1980). *Fourth review of special education.* New York: Grune and Stratton.

McLoughlin, J. A., & Kelly, D. (1982). Issues facing the resource teacher. *Learning Disability Quarterly, 5*, 58–64.

McMahan, J. (1983). Extended school year programs. *Exceptional Children, 49*, 457–460.

Menolascino, F. J. (1979). Handicapped children and youth: Current-future international perspectives and challenges. *Exceptional Children, 46*, 168–173.

Mercer, J. W. (1979). *The constitutional guarantees of due process and equal protection for gifted public school students.* Doctoral dissertation, University of Minnesota. Ann Arbor, MI: University Microfilms.

Miller, S. R. (1980). Issues in the professional preparation of secondary school special educators. *Exceptional Children, 46*, 344–350.

Miller, T. I. (1977). *The effects of drug therapy on psychological disorders.* Doctoral Dissertation, University of Colorado. Ann Arbor, MI: University Microfilms.

Miller, T. I. (1980). Drug therapy for psychological disorders. In *Evaluation in education: An international review series* (Vol. 4, pp. 96–97). Elmsford, NY: Pergamon Press.

Mills vs. Board of Education of the District of Columbia. (1972). 348 F. Supp. 866, DDC.

Milne, N. M., & Mountain, L. (1980). Publishing policies of special-education-related journals. *Journal of Special Education, 14*, 121–125.

Mollica, R. F. (1983). From asylum to community: The threatened disintegration of public psychiatry. *The New England Journal of Medicine, 308*, 367–373.

Naisbitt, J. (1982). *Megatrends: Ten new directions transforming our lives.* New York: Warner.

Naisbitt, J. (1982, 27 December–1983, 3 January). Restructuring America—When, where, how, and why. *U. S. News and World Report,* 49–55.

Nesbitt, J. A. (1979). The 1980's: Recreation a reality for all. *Education Unlimited, 1*(2), 12–19.

Office of Special Education and Rehabilitaion. (1983). *Conference on future trends and issues.* Washington, DC: Author.

Orlansky, M. D. (1982). Education of visually impaired children in the U. S. A.: Current issues in service delivery. *The Exceptional Child, 29*, 13–20.

Palmer, D. J. (1983). An attributional perspective on labeling. *Exceptional Children, 49*, 423–429.

Patton, M. Q. (1980). *Qualitative evaluation methods.* Beverly Hills, CA: Sage.

Phipps, P. M. (1982). The merging categories: Appropriate education or administrative convenience. *Journal of Learning Disabilities, 15*, 153–154.

Polsgrove, L. (Issue Ed.). (1983). Aversive control in the classroom. *Exceptional Education Quarterly, 3*(4), 1–75.

Posavac, E. J. (1980). Evaluations of patient education programs: A meta-analysis. *Evaluation and the Health Professions, 3*, 47–62.

Pringle, T. (1983). *This is the child.* New York: Knopf.

Reed, C. G. (1980). Voice therapy: A need for research. *Journal of Speech and Hearing Disorders, 45*(2), 157–169.

Reschly, D. J. (1980). *Nonbiased assessment.* Des Moines: Iowa State Dept. of Public Instruction.

Rieth, H. J., & Semmel, M. I. (1979). The use of microcomputer technology to prepare and to enable teachers to meet the educational needs of handicapped children. *Teacher Education and Special Education, 2*(2), 56–60.

Rist, R. (1977). On the relations among educational research paradigms: From disdain to detente. *Anthropology and Education, 8.*

Ross, D. M., & Ross, S. A. (1982). *Hyperactivity: Current issues, research, and theory* (2nd ed.). Somerset NJ: Wiley.

Safer, N. (1979). Exploration 1993: The effects of future trends on services to the handicapped. *Focus on Exceptional Children, 11*(3), 1–24.

Sandow, S. (1979). Action research and evaluation: Can research and practice be successfully combined? *Child: Care, Health, and Development, 5*(3), 211–223.

Schlesinger, H. J. (1981). Psychological treatment of asthma. In G. V. Glass, B. McGaw, & M. L.

Smith (Eds.), *Meta-analysis in social research*. Beverly Hills, CA: Sage.

Schlesinger, H. J., Mumford, E., & Glass, G. V. (1980). Effects of psychological intervention on recovering from surgery. In F. Guerra & J. A. Aldrete (Eds.), *Emotional and psychological responses to anesthesia and surgery*. New York: Grune and Stratton.

Schmid, R. E., & Nagata, L. M. (1983). *Contemporary issues in special education* (2nd ed.). New York: McGraw-Hill.

Scriven, M. (1972). Objectivity and subjectivity in educational research. In L. G. Thomas (Ed.), *Philosophical redirection in educational research*. The 75th NSSE Yearbook. Chicago: University of Chicago Press.

Simpson, S. N. (1980). Comments on meta-analysis of research on class size and achievement. *Educational Evaluation and Policy Analysis*, *2*, 81–83.

Stepp, R. E., Jr. (1979). Educational technology for the 80's: Introduction. *American Annals of the Deaf*, *124*(5), 518–520.

Strain, P. S., & Shores, R. E. (1979). Additional comments on multiple-baseline designs in instructional research. *American Journal of Mental Deficiency*, *84*(3), 229–234.

Swanson, L. (1982). Verbal short-term memory encoding of learning disabled, deaf, and normal readers. *Learning Disability Quarterly*, *5*, 21–28.

Taber, F. M. (1983). *Microcomputers in special education: Selection and decision-making process*. Reston, VA: Council for Exceptional Children.

Tannenbaum, A. J. (1983). *Gifted children: Psychological and educational perspectives*. New York: Macmillan.

Toro, P. A. (1982). Developmental effects of child abuse: A review. *Child Abuse and Neglect*, *6*, 423–431.

van Dalen, D. B. (1973). *Understanding educational research: An introduction* (3rd. ed.). New York: McGraw-Hill.

Vernon, M., & Rabush, D. (1981). Major developments and trends in deafness. *Exceptional Children*, 48, 254–256.

Walker, J. E., & Shea, T. M. (1980). *Behavior modification: A practical approach for educators* (2nd ed.). St. Louis: Mosby.

Weaver, R. A., & Wallace, B. (1980). Technology and the future of gifted child education., *Roeper Review*, *2*(4), 19–21.

Wehman, P., & McLaughlin, P. J. (1981). *Program development in special education: Designing individual education programs*. New York: McGraw-Hill.

Wiig, E. H., & Semmel, E. M. (1980). *Language assessment and intervention for the learning disabled*. Columbus, OH: Charles E. Merrill.

Wood, M. M. (1979). *Developmental therapy objectives* (3rd revised ed.). Baltimore: University Park Press.

Wood, M. M. (1980). Developmental therapy: A model for therapeutic intervention in the schools. In T. B. Gutkin & C. R. Reynold (Eds.), *Handbook for school psychology*. New York: Wiley.

Wood, M. M. (1981). Education's responsibility for seriously disturbed and behaviorally disordered children and youth. In P. Wood (Ed.), *Perspectives for a new decade*. Reston, VA: Council for Exceptional Children.

Yeany, P. H., & Miller, P. A. (1980). *The effects of diagnostic/remedial instruction on science learning: A meta-analysis*. Athens: Department of Science Education, University of Georgia.

AUTHOR INDEX

Abramovitz, A., 113
Abramson, E. E., 82
Achenbach, T. M., 250, 253, 260, 262, 263, 376
Ackerson, L., 253
Adams, M., 44
Adamson, G. W., 265
Adelson, E., 40, 311, 318
Adelstein-Bernstein, N., 82
Adubato, S., 44
Affleck, J. Q., 226
Aguerrevere, L., 107
Ahlster-Taylor, J., 36, 51
Aiken, M. C., 8
Albert, R. S., 190
Albin, J., 107
Alfieri, P. A., 106
Algozzine, B., 10, 11, 12, 14, 15, 16, 17, 18, 22, 236, 260
Allen, D., 17
Allen, J. C., 374
Allen, L., 33, 47, 49, 253
Allen, P., 106
Allen, R., 281
Alley, G. R., 224, 231, 234, 235, 239, 242, 362
Allport, G., 352, 355
Altman, K., 108
Anderson, D. W., 310
Anderson, J. R., 276
Anderson, R. C., 207
Anderson, R. J., 312
Anderson, R. P., 318
Ando, H., 85
Andrasik, F., 66, 115
Andres, J. R., 18
Andrews, G., 375
Angell, R., 352
Anson, J. E., 104
Antia, S., 5, 325, 328
Apolloni, T., 72, 77
Apple, M. M., 312
Applebee, A., 288

Apter, S., 2
Arbib, M. A., 276
Archer, A., 226
Arena, J. J., 19
Argulewicz, E. N., 215
Armstrong, P. M., 80
Arnold, S., 97
Aronson, M., 34
Arter, J. A., 10, 12, 19
Ashcroft, S. C., 334
Ashem, B. A., 66
Asher, S. R., 279
Ashton, P. T., 208
Atuber, J., 207
August, D. L., 279
Axelford, S., 231
Axelrod, S., 99, 109
Ayllon, T., 77, 93, 97, 109, 112, 113, 226
Ayres, A. J., 19
Azrin, N. H., 68, 70, 80, 84, 85, 86, 87, 89, 90, 91, 96, 97, 102, 106, 111, 226

Baer, A. M., 101
Baer, D. M., 57, 68, 69, 70, 101
Baer, E. M., 231
Bailey, E., 30, 53
Bailey, J. S., 109
Baird, A., 335
Bakeman, R., 54
Baker, B., 43, 54
Baker, E. M., 254
Baker, T. G., 109
Baker-Ward, L., 31
Baldwin, A., 199
Baldwin, G., 106
Baldwin, J. W., 198
Baldwin, V., 42
Ball, D. W., 240
Ball, T., 81, 82, 107
Ballard, J., 361
Ballard, K. D., 79

SUBJECT INDEX

verbalism studies, 309–310
vocabulary development, 311
language disorders, 282–283
psychosocial development, 325–327
parental influences, 326
self-concept, 326
social maturity, 326
technology for, 331–336
computer devices, 334

reading aides, 332–334
travel devices, 334–336
Vocational skills
behavior modification, 87–89
direct instruction, age factors, 174–175

Work. *See* Meaningful work

Young Autism Project, 265

ABOUT THE EDITORS
AND CONTRIBUTORS

THE EDITORS

Richard J. Morris (Ph.D., Arizona State University, 1970) is Professor of Educational Psychology, School Psychology Program, Division of Educational Foundations, College of Education, the University of Arizona. Previous to this position, he was Professor of Special Education, the University of Arizona; Assistant to Associate Professor of Psychology, Clinical Psychology Training Program, Syracuse University; and Clinical Assistant Professor of Pediatrics, Upstate Medical Center, State University of New York at Syracuse. In addition, he has been Visiting Professor, Department of Clinical Psychology, Uppsala University (Uppsala, Sweden) and Scientific Consultant, Bavarian State Institute for Early Childhood Education (Munich, West Germany). He has authored or edited several books including *Behavior modification with exceptional children: Principles and practices* and *Perspectives in abnormal behavior*, is co-editor with Burton Blatt of *Perspectives in special education: Personal orientations*, is co-author with Thomas R. Kratochwill of *Treating children's fears and phobias. A behavior approach*, and co-editor with Thomas R. Kratochwill of *The practice of child therapy*. He has published numerous journal articles and chapters on intervention strategies with handicapped children. He is a Fellow of the American Psychological Association and of the American Association on Mental Deficiency and is currently President of the Division of Rehabilitation Psychology of the American Psychological Association. He has

also served on the editorial boards of several journals in special education and school psychology, and has been a consultant to several developmental disabilities programs.

Burton Blatt (Ed.D., Pennsylvania State University, 1956) was at the time of his death Dean of the School of Education at Syracuse University. Previous to this position he was Director of the Division of Special Education and Rehabilitation at Syracuse University and founded the Syracuse University Center on Human Policy in 1971. He was also Professor and Chairman of the Special Education Department, Boston University, and Professor and later Chairman of the Special Education Department, Southern Connecticut State College. He authored or edited numerous books including *The intellectually disfranchised: Impoverished learners and their teachers; Exodus from pandemonium: Human abuse and a reformation of public policy; In and out of mental retardation: Essays and educability, disability, and human policy*; and *The conquest of mental retardation*, and co-authored with S. Sarason and K. Davidson, *The preparation of teachers: An unstudied problem in education*; with F. Kaplan, *Christmas in purgatory: A photographic essay on mental retardation*; with A. Ozolins and J. McNally, *The family papers: A return to purgatory*; and co-edited with R. Morris, *Perspectives in special education: Personal orientations*. He also published almost 200 papers and chapters on topics pertaining to the field of special education. He was past-President and a Fellow of the American Association on Mental Deficiency, past-

417

President of the Teacher Education Division of the Council for Exceptional Children, and named Outstanding Educator in the United States in 1965. He served on the editorial boards or was an associate editor of several journals in special education, and was a consultant to many agencies and organizations.

THE CONTRIBUTORS

Shirin D. Antia received her undergraduate education in India at Calcutta University and her Ph.D. at the University of Pittsburgh in 1979. She is currently Assistant Professor in the College of Education at the University of Arizona. Her research interests are in the area of language development and the development of peer interaction skills of hearing impaired children.

Kathryn A. Blake is a faculty member in the Division for Exceptional Children, College of Education, at the University of Georgia. She has done extensive research and writing on characteristics of exceptional pupils and programs for them.

Robert Bogdan received his Ph.D. in sociology from Syracuse University. He is a Professor of Special Education and Sociology at Syracuse where he teaches courses in qualitative research methods and sociology of disability. He is the author, with Steve Taylor of *Inside Out: The Social Meaning of Mental Retardation*, and with Sari Biklen of *Qualitative Research for Education*.

Diane Bricker received her Ph.D. from Peabody College in Special Education in 1970 and is currently a Professor of Special Education and Director of the Early Intervention Program, Center on Human Development, University of Oregon. Her interests are in early intervention, communication development, and programmatic assessment/evaluation.

Lou Brown received his Ph.D. in Special Education and is currently a Professor in the Department of Studies in Behavioral Disabilities at the University of Wisconsin–Madison. He is author and co-author of numerous chapters and journal articles. His research interests are in the area of serving individuals who are severely intellectually disabled in integrated environments.

Katharine G. Butler has taught and conducted research at Western Michigan University, San Jose State University, and Syracuse University. She currently serves as Director, Center for Research, and Professor, Communication Sciences and Disorders, Syracuse University. The author of more than 65 articles, chapters, and monographs, her work focuses upon communicatively handicapped children in both special education and the mainstream. She earned a Ph.D. at Michigan State University.

Alison Ford is Assistant Professor of Special Education and Rehabilitation at Syracuse University.

James M. Kauffman received his Ed.D. degree in Special Education in the School of Education, University of Virginia. He is editor of *Remedial and Special Education*, and author or co-author of numerous books and journal articles in special education and psychology.

Ruth Loomis is the administrator of programs for students who are severely intellectually disabled in the Madison Metropolitan School District.

C. June Maker is Associate Professor of Special Education at the University of Arizona. She received her Ph.D. from the University of Virginia. She holds national offices in several organizations for the gifted. Her publications are on the subjects of curriculum development for the gifted, teaching models in education of the gifted, the gifted handicapped, teacher training, the development of talents in exceptional children, and teaching learning disabled students.

Rebecca A. McReynolds received her Ph.D. in School Psychology from Syracuse University and is currently in private practice in Tucson, Arizona. Her research interests are in the area of teacher training in classroom behavior management skills.

Jan Nisbet is Assistant Professor of Special Education and Rehabilitation at Syracuse University.

Suzanne Robinson received her Doctorate in Special Education in 1983 from the University of New Mexico. Currently, she is an Assistant Professor in special education at Kansas University.

Betsy Shiraga is the Executive Director of Community Work Services, Inc., a private nonprofit agency that serves adults with intellectual disabilities in integrated vocational environments.

Deborah Deutsch Smith is Professor and Chair at the Department of Special Education at the University of New Mexico. She received a Doctorate in Special Education from the University of Washington in 1973. She has authored several books and numerous chapters and articles about methods to improve student learning and behavior.

Mark Sweet is the Director of Training at the Wisconsin Coalition for Advocacy in Madison, Wisconsin.

Ivan S. Terzieff is currently a member of the faculty at Western Michigan University.

Pat VanDeventer is a Program Support Teacher in the Madison Metropolitan School District.

Charlotte L. Williams is a retired faculty member in the Division for Exceptional Children, College of Education, at the University of Georgia. She has done extensive research and writing on characteristics of exceptional pupils and programs for them.

Jennifer York is a Physical Therapist operating in Minneapolis, Minnesota.

James E. Ysseldyke received his Ph.D. in Educational Psychology from the University of Illinois at Urbana-Champaign in 1971. Currently, he is a Professor of Educational Psychology at the University of Minnesota. His research interests are in assessment and decision making in special education, public policy on education of handicapped students, and instructional effectiveness.